Lenore's Natural Cuisine

your essential guide to wholesome, vegetarian cooking

Lenore Baum, M.A.
author of *Sublime Soups*

 Culinary Publications

For inquiries, address:
Culinary Publications, 132 Rainbow Drive #3205, Livingston, TX 77399-1032
Website www.lenoresnatural.com

Cover art copyright © 1999 by Mary Hickey
Illustrations copyright © 1999 by Barbara Overdier
Author photograph © 1999 by Gail Konz
Graphic artist, Alan Grayson

Library of Congress Catalog Card Number: 99-90885

ISBN 0-9674627-3-8

First Printing, 2000
Revised Edition 2003

dedication

With love and appreciation, I dedicate this book to:

my beloved husband, Joe

my mother, Anna Yalisove

the memory of my father, Dr. Irving Yalisove

my mentor, the late Marcia Halpern,
    who shared her vision with me

and to everyone who chooses to eat wholesome food

contents

acknowledgments

First, I would like to express my deepest appreciation to my husband, Joe. He lovingly and persistently encouraged me to write this cookbook. He devoted countless hours helping me with the innumerable decisions involved in writing a book. Joe was also responsible for the layout of the book and was editor of the revised edition. Lastly, I want to thank him for his clear and gentle feedback as a taster for all my cooking experiments.

My gratitude goes to Anna Yalisove, my mother and teacher. Her successful dinner parties inspired me to cook. By choosing fresh, local produce and simple ingredients, she modeled whole foods cooking at its best. At age 84, she continues to lead a vital, active vegetarian lifestyle.

I am particularly thankful to my teachers: Aveline Kushi, Cornelia Aihara, Wendy Esko, Diane Avoli, Marcia Halpern and Meredith McCarty. To Michio Kushi, Herman Aihara, Ed Esko, Kaare Bursell, Bob Carr, Ronald Kotzch, Charles Millman and Patrick McCarty.

Immeasurable appreciation to my extraordinary editors:
Sian Yardley, for her calm, organized and meticulous efforts to make this book as flawless as any cookbook could be. Also, for the innumerable hours she devoted to developing new recipes with me on Tuesday nights.
Anne Meuchel, for her tireless and relentless efforts to organize and polish my writing, and for the sparkle and spunk she added to each page.
Bonnie Cohn, for transforming my original, unruly recipes into a concise format, always with a sense of humor.
Ron Roush, for his skill at finding the perfect word, great sense of humor, gallant support and advice.
Debbie Walter, for her wonderful laugh, culinary expertise and encouragement.

My special appreciation for the artists:
Mary Hickey, not only for her wisdom, but for her vibrant watercolor painting on the cover of this book.
Barbara Overdier, for all the time she devoted to her accurate illustrations.

Gail Konz, for the years of friendship and my back cover photo.

I also want to thank all the superb cooks who unknowingly inspired me through their wonderful cookbooks: AnneMarie Colbin, Mary Estella, Margaret Lawson, Deborah Madison, Rachel Matez, Vicki Chelf, Lorna Sass, Kristina Turner and Jeff Woodward.

I am grateful to William Dufty, Dennis Fairchild, Molly Runcie, Chris Smith and Beth Newman for their insightful support.

I give my heartfelt gratitude to Rachel Thornberry, who is like a daughter to me. She has been a loyal friend, offering encouragement and the perspective of a beginning cook.

I am grateful to all my students and assistants, from whom I continue to learn.

Working on a project of this scope, so many people are involved that it is impossible to thank each one individually. To all whose names have not been mentioned, I extend my thanks to you.

introduction

My interest in healthful cooking, I must admit, was not for health reasons. When I moved to Boston in 1972, I lived down the street from a small health food store on Commonwealth Avenue. This store was owned by two cute guys who played guitar. I spent a lot of time there under the guise of learning to become vegetarian. Eventually, their good habits wore off on me.

For more than twelve years, I righteously followed a 1970's vegetarian-style diet. Lots of juicing, homemade whole wheat bread, cheddar cheese, baked potatoes, nuts, sweet treats and huge salads loaded with alfalfa sprouts and spirulina. I broadened this lifestyle by owning and managing a vegetarian deli. Nevertheless, I developed many health problems: extreme hypoglycemia, systemic candida yeast infection, arthritis in my toes, fingers, knees and elbows, endometriosis and mood swings.

Simple activities like walking my dog or stirring soup became impossible. Pain and fatigue forced me to lie down for several hours every afternoon. Between meals, I would begin to shake and feel faint. Moreover, I snacked and could not lose unwanted pounds. Extreme mood swings caused me to seek counseling. The candida made my abdomen swell at least two inches by the end of the day. Gynecologists recommended a hysterectomy to relieve the pain from endometriosis. I did not know what to do.

Then, I had the good fortune to meet Marcia Halpern, a macrobiotic counselor, at a lecture. She understood the relationship between food and dis-ease. What I learned from her made all the difference:

- cheese and yogurt are not healthy protein substitutes
- potatoes and tomatoes can contribute to joint pain
- too many sweets and fruits worsen yeast problems
- including ample whole grains helps prevent hypoglycemia and mood swings
- lacking the five tastes in the diet contributes to cravings and snacking

I was skeptical, but after only two weeks of adjusting my diet, all my symptoms began to subside. It took a year to reach full recovery. By that time, my chronic yeast problem and hypoglycemia had magically disappeared. My joints no longer hurt. I finally lost the unwanted pounds and have kept them off for over ten years. My energy soared. I no longer felt the need to see a counselor. I was elated!

After much experimentation with the few cookbooks available at the time, I decided to study with inspirational teachers: Aveline Kushi, Wendy Esko, Diane Avoli, Marcia Halpern, Meredith McCarty, Ann Marie Colbin and other great pioneers in vegetarian and macrobiotic cooking. I attended French Meadows summer camp in California and spent a year at the Kushi Institute in Massachusetts. In addition, I apprenticed with Marcia Halpern in South Carolina and studied at the Vega Institute in California.

I began to relish the challenge and creativity of transforming recipes to my own style of vegan cooking. Countless requests by students for a comprehensive guide to my cooking inspired me to write this book. My goal is to help you incorporate tasty, wholesome and balanced meals into your busy life. My hope is that this book will save you from years of making unsuitable food choices, as I did.

Starting anything new, you might wonder where and how to begin. Start at the beginning. Read the chapters How To Use This Book and What It's All About. Soups are nourishing and easy to prepare, so you might turn to that chapter next. Look up unfamiliar ingredients and tools in the Glossary and buy them at your local natural foods store.

Since your taste buds are accustomed to "heavy hitters" like salt and sugar, give yourself two to three weeks to make the transition to this simpler way of eating. Also remember that you can make healthier choices when eating in restaurants, so read the Travel and Dining Out chapter. I am convinced that you will feel the difference.

making the most of this book

following a recipe
First, skim through the entire recipe and cook's tips before beginning to cook. Then, if you have time, review the general cook's tips in the chapter overview. Lastly, measure all of the ingredients. I like to use stainless steel bowls to hold cut vegetables and measured herbs or spices until it is time to use them.

unfamiliar foods and utensils
Unfamiliar foods are explained in the Glossary. Unfamiliar utensils are described and illustrated in the Appendix. Most items are available at your local natural foods store. If not, refer to the Resources in the Appendix.

fresh produce
Fruits and vegetables should be thoroughly washed before being eaten. If organic, simply scrub off surface dirt with a natural brush. If vegetables are not organic, fill the sink with several inches of water. Add a few drops of mild, natural soap such as Basic H® by Shaklee®. Swish produce in this solution. Scrub until clean. Rinse well. While pesticides can be removed from the surface this way, they will remain under the skin.

Be aware that commercial apples, bell peppers, cucumbers and rutabagas are usually waxed to extend their shelf life. Peel them so that the wax will not clog your small intestines where food absorption is supposed to take place!

seasonings
These recipes are flexible. Adjust seasonings to your taste. Omit ingredients, such as garlic or ginger, if you do not want to use them. Freely use suggested variations or create your own.

beans, grains and herbs
These ingredients are dried, unless otherwise noted.

abbreviations used
TBS. = Tablespoon (3 teaspoons equals 1 tablespoon)
 tsp.   = teaspoon

cutting methods
See Appendix, page 243.

cooking time
Approximate cooking times are given. Check for doneness at the shortest recommended time.

cooking terms
blanch: Briefly boiling, about 1 minute.

boil: Cooking over high heat until bubbles appear or, as my mother would say, until the water "dances."

dry-roast: Cooking food in a hot skillet, without oil, until golden brown in color.

pressure-cook: Cooking in a sealed pot under 15 pounds of pressure per square inch. Pressure-cooking recipes will indicate whether to quick-release or natural-release the pressure-cooker when cooking time is over. To **quick-release**, place the pressure-cooker into the sink with the lid locked on. Run cold water over the top until the pressure valve comes down. You can now safely open the lid. To **natural-release**, remove the pressure cooker from the heat source and allow the pressure to come down on its own, naturally. This takes about thirty minutes.

sauté: Cooking food quickly and lightly in a small amount of oil. Heat the oil to the sizzling point, but not smoking. Sprinkle several drops of water onto the hot oil. When it sizzles, it is ready.

simmer: Cooking gently over low heat, just below the boiling point, with bubbles occasionally breaking the surface.

steam: Cooking in a covered pot in which a steamer basket is placed above boiling water.

storing prepared food
The dishes you prepare will keep refrigerated for about a week, unless otherwise noted. Of course, the fresher the food, the more vitality and nutrition you will gain from it. Realistically, it is more healthful to eat six-day-old homemade soup than soup from most restaurants. I strongly believe in storing food in glass jars. Wide-mouth canning jars are preferable. An entire shelf is dedicated to them in my kitchen. A stainless steel funnel makes them simple to fill.

what it's all about

vegetarian

Why eat vegetarian? People become interested in a vegetarian diet for a variety of reasons ranging from compassion for animals, to religion, to world hunger issues. But the most recent trend in eating this way has to do with health. Research has linked lower rates of heart disease, high blood pressure, cancer, diabetes and obesity with a vegetarian diet.

Simply eliminating meat, however, will not lead to optimum health. A diet based on refined grains, sugar and dairy products is not the basis of a wholesome, vegetarian diet. Rather, it consists of whole grains, beans, vegetables, nuts and seeds.

vegan

Vegans (pronounced vee-gans) choose not to eat any meat or animal products, including dairy (milk, cheese, butter and yogurt), eggs and honey. A vegan lifestyle often excludes using anything leather, wool or silk. Usually this choice is made for ethical reasons.

protein

Eating too much protein can cause kidney stones and contribute to calcium and bone loss. Your body requires less protein than you may think. A regular diet of beans, tofu, nuts, seeds, tempeh, peas and whole grain breads provides sufficient protein. However, if you are body-building, pregnant or doing heavy physical labor, eat more beans and bean products.

calcium and dairy

"Got milk?"™ Milk is advertised as one of the healthiest foods for children and adults alike. Most of us have grown up believing we need it for strong teeth and bones. After all, it is high in calcium and is fortified with vitamin D. However, there are downsides to dairy products which you may want to consider.

Pesticides, industrial wastes, antibiotics and hormones are consumed in vast quantities by most cattle raised in the United States. These toxic substances accumulate in animal fat. We consume these toxins when we eat dairy products. Over 4,000 doctors associated with The

Physicians Committee for Responsible Medicine have concluded that milk, cheese, butter and yogurt contribute to diseases such as cancer, allergies, digestive problems and heart disease.

Without dairy products, how can we include enough calcium in our diets? Eat dark leafy greens like collards, kale, turnip greens, broccoli and bok choy. Other good sources are beans, sesame seeds, sea vegetables, tofu and soy beverages. If you are still skeptical, here are the numbers:

milligrams of calcium per 1/2 cup:

Milk	119
Collard greens	117
Kale	135
Parsley	130
Sea Vegetables	500-1300
Tofu	100

healthful dairy alternatives

Non-hydrogenated canola spread (butter substitute)
Non-dairy frozen dessert
Soy or rice beverage
Non-dairy sour cream
Soy cheese
Soy yogurt

organic

Organic foods are those grown without the use of chemical fertilizers and pesticides. Pesticides are poisons which are designed to kill living organisms. They have been linked to cancer in human beings. Recent surveys show that random samples of fruit from supermarkets are saturated with pesticides. Ironically, it is a good sign when you find bug holes and other imperfections in organic produce. This indicates that the produce was not sprayed!

When organic produce is unavailable, you can remove oily pesticides from the surface of produce by washing with a mild, natural soap. A good products is the liquid soap, Basic H® by Shaklee®. Squirt five drops of soap in a sink filled with three to four inches of water. Clean produce in this soapy solution and rinse well. Realize that while you can remove pesticides from the surface of produce, they will remain under the skin.

Although organic produce, grains, beans, nuts and seeds can be higher in cost, you may find that your good health is well worth it. Buying organic also supports small farmers who care about the quality of the soil and the environment.

Finally, the natural sweetness of fruits and vegetables is masked by the bitter flavor of pesticides. Because of this, organic vegetables taste sweeter than their sprayed counterparts. This is especially noticeable with carrots.

nightshade vegetables

Nightshade vegetables contain glycoalkaloids, which have been found to contribute to joint pain. According to Dr. Norman F. Childer's research, which spans over four decades, consumption of these vegetables causes arthritic-like symptoms in 17% of the population. Nightshade vegetables include: white and red-skinned potatoes, tomatoes, eggplant and all varieties of peppers. Yams, sweet potatoes and black pepper, however, are not nightshades.

Other vegetables that may contribute to joint pain because of their oxalic acid content are Swiss chard, raw spinach and beet greens. If you are willing to experiment by not eating any of these vegetables for two weeks, you might think it is worth giving them up to live pain-free.

pressure-cooking

Pressure cookers are amazing. A bean soup, requiring two hours to cook in a standard stock pot, can be pressure-cooked in 12 minutes. Pressure-cooking quickly tenderizes food, reducing cooking time by up to 80%. Best of all, it makes mouth-watering dishes because the flavors marry in the pot. The new, second generation pressure cookers are completely safe to use. For more information, see Lorna Sass' outstanding book, *Great Vegetarian Cooking Under Pressure*.

microwave cooking

Research confirms that the molecular structure of food is altered during microwave cooking, causing abnormal changes in human blood and immune systems. Not surprisingly, the public has been denied details on these significant health dangers. The following article describes the incident that spurred investigations into the safety of microwaving.

"In early 1991, word leaked out about a lawsuit in Oklahoma. A woman named Norma Levitt had hip surgery, only to be killed by a simple blood transfusion when a nurse 'warmed the blood for the transfusion in a microwave oven'! Logic suggests that if heating or cooking is all there is to it, then it doesn't matter what mode of heating technology one uses. However, it is quite apparent that there is more to 'heating' with microwaves than we've been led to believe. Blood for transfusions is routinely warmed - but not in microwave ovens! In the case of Mrs. Levitt, the microwaving altered the blood and it killed her. It would appear that this form of heating does do 'something different' to the substances being heated." See the full article at www.macrobiotics.org for more details.

fermented foods

Common fermented foods include pickles, sauerkraut, tempeh, miso, tamari and shoyu. There are many reasons these foods have played a key role in traditional diets. Their friendly bacteria help the body to digest food, encourage a sluggish appetite and fight off unfriendly bacteria. In addition, lactic acid helps cleanse the liver and aides in elimination.

Adding pickles to your plate adds zip to any meal. Homemade pickles bear no resemblance to ready-made ones. Pickles from the supermarket are not naturally fermented. Rather, they are steeped in chemicals and vinegar with flavor enhancers and preservatives.

In the traditional process of pickle fermentation, vegetables are submerged in a salt water solution, or brine. This allows them to remain edible for several months. Peoples from around the world continue to use this method to make pickles and prevent food from spoiling.

A tablespoon of naturally-fermented sauerkraut or a pickle for lunch and dinner balances the meal. Soon, you will find that no meal is complete without the pizzazz of pickles.

Soybeans are difficult to digest and have traditionally been fermented to make them more digestible. Popular fermented soy products are tempeh, miso, tamari and shoyu. Hearty tempeh can be steamed, grilled or pan-fried to create dishes that will even please meat-lovers. Miso pastes range from light and sweet, to rich and salty. They add complex flavor to soups, spreads and gravies. Shoyu tastes nothing like chemically-fermented, supermarket soy sauce. Its subtle, savory flavor enhances soups, sauces and stir-fried dishes.

naturally-leavened bread

You may be surprised to learn that conventionally-yeasted breads have been linked to cancer. True sourdough bread is naturally leavened. It is yeast-free and requires several hours to rise before baking. In contrast, conventionally-yeasted bread uses a high concentration of an isolated yeast strain to make bread rise within minutes. In an article, published in 1984 in *East West Journal*, Ronald Kotsch describes why conventionally yeasted bread contributes to disease.

> "In [conventional] yeast fermentation, the starch cells of the bread actually explode. The patterns they form are identical to those of cancer cells. According to French researcher Jean Claude Vincent, the bioelectrical energy of the dough also is identical to that of cancer cells."

German and Swiss researchers concur with Vincent that this fast-acting yeast sends an electrical message to the body for the cells to mimic this exploding replication. This is cancer. Beyond these facts, sourdough bread may win you over by its taste alone. It is wonderful, chewy, old-world bread.

Unfortunately, many so-called healthful whole wheat loaves, pita breads and crackers are yeasted. If you do not have a natural sourdough baker in your area, you can bake this kind of bread yourself. For recipes, see Meredith McCarty's fine cookbook, *Fresh From A Vegetarian Kitchen*. Alternatively, you can request that your local natural foods store stock French Meadows® sourdough breads. Whole Foods Market® is a national chain of natural foods stores which sells several varieties of naturally-leavened breads.

refined sugar

Neither my father, a professor of dentistry, nor my own dental hygiene training could stop me from eating sugar. It was not until I read the enlightening book, *Sugar Blues*, by William Dufty that I went cold turkey. If you are eating sugar, you are probably addicted to it, either physically or emotionally. The November, 1998 issue of the *Nutrition Action Health Letter* states that an American consumes, on average, over 150 pounds of sugar per year. This translates to over one cup of sugar daily!

Sugar is everywhere. A 12-ounce can of non-diet cola contains ten teaspoons of sugar, while one cup of Sunkist® orange soda has 13 teaspoons. Flavored yogurt has five teaspoons of sugar per six-ounce portion and one cup of Haagen-Dazs® Chocolate or Vanilla Ice Cream contains 11 teaspoons.

In her book, *Feeding the Whole Family*, Cynthia Lair clearly explains the drawbacks of eating sugar. White sugar is so refined that the body does not need to digest it. Like a drug, it travels directly into the bloodstream, setting off a chain reaction that makes the body crave more sugar. It is an addictive cycle. In addition, sugar impairs the immune system by reducing white blood cells' ability to destroy bacteria. As Lair notes, it is not surprising that children frequently become sick after birthday parties and holidays.

A weakened immune system not only contributes to colds, cavities and flu, but also to degenerative diseases including arthritis, heart disease and cancer. Moreover, sugar can contribute to mood swings, lethargy, bone loss, obesity and the onset of diabetes.

When reading food labels, you will discover that refined sugar is described by many names: corn syrup, sucrose, fructose, dextrose, maltose, turbinado, brown sugar and molasses. For healthful, delicious alternative sweeteners, see the Desserts chapter. An additional benefit of giving up sugar is that many unhealthy and fattening foods will automatically be eliminated from your diet. Many friends and students have also gone cold turkey after learning about sugar's effects on the body. You can too.

artificial sweeteners

While artificial sweeteners may seem like a good solution for a sweet tooth, they are, in fact, hazardous. Saccharin® has been proven to cause cancer in rats. Aspartame, used in Equal® and Nutrasweet™, has been linked to many health problems. Dr. Richard Wurtman, a professor of neuroendocrinology at MIT, states that "a typical adult who drinks about four or five aspartame-sweetened soft drinks a day might introduce enough pheynlalanine into the brain to affect the synthesis of brain neurotransmitters, possibly leading to mood swings, irritability, anxiety, depression, insomnia, headaches, high blood pressure, increased appetite and even seizures." Aspartame is now reputed to be found in over 1200 products, including everything from baked goods to breakfast cereals, children's vitamins, laxatives and drugs.

For further information on artificial sweeteners, see *Food and Nutrition* by Rudolph Ballentine, M.D. He notes that although the consumption of artificially-sweetened foods and drinks has skyrocketed, Americans are still gaining weight. Artificial sweeteners simply perpetuate your sweet tooth and make you more likely to succumb to highly sugar-sweetened foods. You might want to reevaluate your intake of these harmful chemicals.

fats

Fats lend a creamy, satisfying texture to food. We do not need to give them up to be healthy. In fact, fats are needed by the body to build cell walls, to synthesize hormones and to prevent dryness in skin and hair. The key is to eat the right kinds of fat.

Saturated fats are found mostly in coconut and palm kernel oils, animal fats and dairy products. These hydrogenated fats clog the arteries, contributing to heart disease. Monounsaturated fats are considered the healthiest choice. They are found in vegetable and nut oils like canola, sesame and olive oil. In place of butter or margarine, use Spectrum Naturals® Canola Spread. It is non-hydrogenated and tastes like butter. Also, drizzle extra-virgin olive oil on bread at a restaurant or at home.

Each oil has a unique flavor. Choose an appropriate oil for the dish you are preparing. Use:

    Canola (neutral and light) for baking and everyday use
    Unrefined corn oil (buttery-tasting) for baking
    Extra-virgin olive oil (light and fruity) for bread, salad dressings
        and stir-fries
    Sesame (light and nutty) for stir-fries and sauces
    Toasted sesame (toasted nutty flavor) for stir-fries and sea
        vegetables

water
Most of us know that it is important to drink eight to ten glasses of water a day. This is solid advice, especially if the water is purified. According to Dr. Andrew Weil, recent data shows that over one million Americans drink water that contains significant levels of cancer-causing chemicals: arsenic, radon and chlorine by-products. He recommends a reverse osmosis or carbon-KDF system to purify water. Since impurities from plumbing and hot water tanks can leach into the water, it is equally important not to use hot water for cooking, washing or soaking food. In addition, it has been proven that the chemicals in plastic bottles also leach into bottled water. Carry your filtered water in non-leaching, polycarbonate bottles by Nalgene® and New Wave Environ Products®.

salt
Good quality salt, in moderation, is necessary for digestion, nerve connections and muscle contractions. It assists the immune system by inhibiting the growth of harmful bacteria, viruses, fungi, parasites and by enhancing proper intestinal flora. Recommended high quality sources of salt are unrefined sea salt, miso, shoyu and gomashio.

menu
planning

Menu planning is essential in helping you eat well on a consistent basis. Spending fifteen minutes planning the week's meals will save you time. In addition, you will be eating wholesome food which will contribute to your health, peace of mind and energy level.

I have found that the easiest way to plan a weekly menu is to create theme nights. For example, Tuesday is pasta night, Thursday is soup night, and so on. With a routine like this, menu planning becomes almost automatic. You only need to fill in with your favorite recipes. Use weekends or blocks of time to make pickles and condiments and to cook large pots of beans, grains and soup. Grains, in particular, can be transformed into many new dishes. See *Beyond Brown Rice, page 112.* Bake cookies to have on reserve in the freezer. During the week, fill in the menu with these precooked foods.

Keep a supply of frozen commercial products for particularly hectic days. A popular line of frozen organic entrées, Amy's®, is available at natural foods stores. Try their vegan pizza, grain burgers, vegan pot pies and others. If you are too exhausted to cook by Friday night, pop a frozen pizza into the oven and make a simple salad. You will have a healthy, hassle-free meal in the comfort of your own home. See Last-Minute Meals for additional quick meals.

When planning meals, strive for variety and balance. Preparing boiled beans, boiled grains and boiled vegetables can be, well, boring! Choose different cooking styles. Consider steaming, pressure-cooking, stir-frying and baking. Vary the texture by adding toasted nuts and seeds for crunch, or by making creamy soups or a tofu sauce. Lastly, try using rice molds, available at Asian markets, to turn grain into fun shapes. This is a great way to entice children to eat brown rice!

Plan your menu around the largest meal of the day. For most of us, this is dinner. Simplify this meal into three major components: grain, vegetables and beans. Choose whole grains such as brown rice, millet or barley. If your time is limited, use quicker cooking grains like bulgur, quinoa, couscous or pasta. For optimum health, always include leafy greens plus additional vegetables. With beans, you need to consider your time constraints. Dried beans require soaking in addition to regular cooking time. Organic canned beans and soybean products like tofu and tempeh are quick and delicious alternatives. Remember to include a pickle. See What It's All About for the benefits of fermented foods.

An indispensable tool for my menu planning is a chart I developed called The Buy List. See page 27. This is how it works. On Sunday, plan the week's menu. Write down the menu for each day in the first column and the required ingredients in the second column. Remember to include dishes made from planned leftovers. Keep an ongoing list of needed staples for specific stores to reduce the number of shopping trips. If the store is out of an item on your Buy List, you can substitute. For example, if a pasta dish calls for asparagus, but the market is out of it, you can buy another ingredient, like broccoli. Lastly, it is helpful to jot down ideas for the next week's meals when you think of them. To get started, make copies of The Buy List. Keep this and the staples list in the kitchen for handy reference. Then, clip them to a small clipboard and take them with you to the store.

Do not feel as though you need to cook a new and exciting dish every day. Repeating familiar recipes makes cooking much easier. Many people find that adding one new recipe a week works well. Choose a day that is not too hectic. If you make a commitment to add one new recipe a week, you will have tried 52 recipes in one year. In five years, you will have 260 recipes from which to choose! In time, you will develop your own favorites and specialties.

Lastly, consider the seasons when planning a menu. In warm weather, use lighter cooking methods like boiling, steaming and quick sautéing. Eat fermented foods like tempeh and sauerkraut. Serve cool grain, bean and noodle salads along with leafy green ones. In cool weather, bake grains, vegetables and beans, or sauté rice and noodles. Use more oil than in summer. Cook winter vegetables like squash, onions, carrots and parsnips. Lastly, bean, seitan and vegetable stews are perfect for cold, wintry nights. For those who want a truly balanced meal and are ready for the next level, review the chapter Cravings and The Five Tastes.

breakfast

An easy way to make a satisfying breakfast is to cook a large pot of miso soup once a week and eat it every morning. Add leftover brown rice, other grains or noodles for substance and variety. If soup in the morning is not your preference, try some of the ideas listed in the Breakfast introduction, like *Overnight Oatmeal* or a bowl of natural cereal.

lunch

To simplify lunch, use leftovers from dinner. If something fresh is added to the dish, like scallions or a sprinkle of vinegar, it will liven up the taste. Take leftovers to work with you in a 3- or 4-compartment thermos. You can bring soup, grain, vegetables and a pickle.

theme nights

    Monday- casserole and greens
    Tuesday- pasta and salad
    Wednesday- pressure-cooked rice and beans with vegetables
    Thursday- soup with bread and vegetables
    Friday- stir-fried noodles or rice with vegetables
    Saturday- dining out
    Sunday- new recipe

a typical day's menu

- **breakfast**
  Miso soup
  Muffin, toast, oatmeal or corn grits

- **lunch**
  Reheated rice, pasta, casserole or soup
  Steamed vegetables
  Pickle

- **dinner**
  Bean soup
  Brown rice, pasta or casserole
  Leafy green vegetable
  Pickle
  Homemade cookies

sample menus
- **spring meal**
  Green Split Pea Soup, pages 56 or 180
  Quick and Easy Polenta, page 108
  Ambrosial Asparagus, page 158
  Dill Brine Pickle, page 174
  Walnut-Lemon Shortbread, page 206

- **summer meal**
  Summer Vegetable Chowder, page 64
  Wheatberry Dill Salad, page 93
  Sunomono, page 95
  Leafy Green Salad, page 84
  Terrific Turnip Pickle, page 173
  Fresh fruit or *Strawberry Mousse Delight*, page 214

- **fall meal**
  Red Lentil Soup, page 52
  Pressure-Cooked Brown Rice, page 100
  Steamed Bok Choy, see variation, page 156
  Dill Brine Pickle, page 174
  Indian Pudding, page 217

- **winter meal**
  Creamy Cauliflower and Chickpea Soup, page 58
  Natural sourdough bread
  Boiled Collard Greens, page 151
  Pickled Cabbage, page 94
  Baked Apples, page 203 or *Almond Amazake Pudding*, page 215

- **brunch**
  Maple Pecan Pancakes, page 44 or *Muffins*, pages 74-77
  Scrambled Tofu, page 46 or *Tempeh "Bacon,"* page 143
  "Coffee," page 221
  Fresh fruit

- **summer picnic**
  Tofu Paté, page 139 with crackers
  Macro Baked Beans, page 134 or *Tofu "Egg" Salad*, page 195
  A Grain Salad, pages 91-93
  Leafy Green Salad, page 84
  Dill Brine Pickle, page 174
  Fresh fruit or *Blueberry Couscous Cake*, page 220

- **summer barbecue**
  Grilled veggie hot dogs or burgers
  Grilled Vegetables, page 165
  Steamed Corn On-The-Cob, page 155
  Leafy Green Salad, page 84
  Terrific Turnip Pickle, page 173
  Chocolate Chip Cookies, page 208 or
  Soy Dream® "ice cream"

- **mideastern feast**
  The Ultimate Lentil Soup, page 54
  Tabouli, page 90
  Hummus-in-a-Hurry, page 194
  Romaine lettuce leaves
  Whole wheat pita bread
  Terrific Turnip Pickle, page 173
  Rice Pudding, page 216

- **children's birthday party**
  Veggie hot dogs
  Sesame Rice Patties, page 192
  Carrot sticks
  Crispy Rice Treats, page 212 or *Brownies*, page 210
  Sweet Nothings® "ice cream"

- **children's lunch**
  Chapati roll-ups (Spread peanut butter on whole wheat
     chapati. Roll-up and slice diagonally into small portions.)
  Lenore's Nutty Seed Mix, page 172 or corn tortilla chips
  Fresh or dried fruit, such as organic raisins, all-fruit leather or
     organic applesauce
  Pure, natural juice box

- **italian dinner party**
  Lasagna, page 122
  Italian sourdough bread
  Leafy Green Salad, page 84
  Terrific Turnip Pickle, page 173
  Flan Custard, page 213

- **thanksgiving**
  Adzuki-Chestnut-Rice, page 104
  Steamed Kale with Savory-Sesame Dressing, page 156
  Baked Garnet Yams, page 160
  Dill Brine Pickle, page 174
  Pumpkin Spice Cookies, page 207

- **superbowl party**
  Chili Sans Carne, page 136
  Cornbread, page 78
  Corn tortilla chips
  Leafy Green Salad, page 84
  Terrific Turnip Pickle, page 173
  Double Chocolate Chip Cookies, page 209

buy
list

The Buy List - Week Of _____

	Menus	Ingredients
Mon.		
Tues.		
Wed.		
Thurs.		
Fri.		
Sat.		
Sun.		
Next Week		

sweet

salty

sour

bitter

pungent

cravings
and the five tastes

Often, people cannot stop eating even though they are full. Why is this? According to traditional oriental medicine, the body requires five tastes: sweet, salty, sour, bitter and pungent. These tastes nourish the internal organs and satisfy the taste buds. If any of the tastes are lacking in the diet, your body will be unsatisfied, causing cravings. By understanding how this principle affects you, you can begin to control your appetite.

Sweet is the most sought-after taste. Americans frequently choose candy, soda or commercial pastries to try to meet this craving. However, what the body really needs are naturally-occurring complex carbohydrates like carrots, sweet corn, yams, onions and winter squash. Only then, will the pancreas, which regulates the blood sugar level, be satisfied.

Another favorite taste is salty. Good quality salt, in moderation, is necessary for digestion, nerve connections and muscle contractions. In addition, it assists the immune system by inhibiting the growth of harmful bacteria, viruses, fungi, parasites and by enhancing proper intestinal flora. Recommended high quality sources of salt are unrefined sea salt, miso, shoyu, gomashio and sea vegetables.

Lemon, lime and sauerkraut are commonly known sour foods. But, most people do not eat them on a regular basis. This taste is needed to nourish the liver and gall bladder. Including naturally-fermented pickles is an easy way to add a sour, salty and crunchy texture to any meal. In addition, umeboshi or brown rice vinegar adds a delicious splash of sour when sprinkled on cooked vegetables.

Americans rarely eat bitter-tasting foods. Since bitter nourishes the heart, traditional medicine maintains that a lack of this taste can contribute to heart disease. There are several easy ways to include bitter in the diet. Add endive, chicory or radicchio to salads, or garnish soups with parsley. Eat tabouli, celery sticks and bitter greens such as kale and collards. Or, for a quick fix, drink an instant grain cereal coffee alternative, like Roma® after your meal.

The last taste, pungent, is also described as spicy. It supports the lungs and large intestines. Its properties help the body disperse fat from oily foods. Fresh garlic and ginger, mustard, turnips, scallion, red radish, daikon radish and horseradish are included in this category.

The underlying principle of the five tastes theory is that opposite flavors are complementary. For example, eating sweets causes cravings for salty foods and vice-versa. In contrast, when you eat a meal including all five tastes, you feel completely nourished. You will not snack on additional food later to satisfy out-of-balance cravings.

The recipes in this book take these principles into account. For example, hummus contains pungent garlic and sour lemon. These ingredients help to balance the oil in tahini. Salt brings out sweetness when sautéing onions. With practice and observation, you will learn to create your own balanced recipes and meals.

Please do not let this information overwhelm you. A balanced meal can be as simple as a bean soup, cooked grain, steamed greens and a few pickles. A copy of the table below, posted on your refrigerator, would help you plan balanced meals using the five tastes.

food and the five tastes

sweet	salty	sour	bitter	pungent
cabbage, cooked carrots corn, fresh fruit grains, cooked onions, cooked parsnips winter squash yams, garnet	fermented dishes gomashio miso pickles salt sea vegetables shoyu	fermented dishes lemon lime pickles sauerkraut umeboshi plum	arugula celery collards endive escarole grain cereal beverages kale mustard greens parsley turnip greens	daikon radish, raw garlic ginger onions, raw red radish scallions turnip wasabi

travel
and dining out

Maintaining a healthy diet at restaurants, work, company parties, weddings and on a cruise or an airplane can be challenging. Nevertheless, after much trial and error, I have found the following strategies to be helpful.

breakfast
- Choose oatmeal or corn grits for a high-energy, low-fat start to the day. Take *Gomashio* with you to sprinkle on top.
- Order an English muffin, wheat or rye toast and spread butter on it. Anything is okay in moderation.
- Take a travel packet of instant grain coffee with you. Request a cup of boiling water.
- Order buckwheat or whole wheat pancakes.
- Take along a wide-mouth thermos to make your own oatmeal. See *Overnight Oatmeal*, page 41.

lunch at work
- Pack a hot or cold lunch in an insulated thermos. See page 23.

lunch or dinner at restaurants
- Consider bringing along purified water. Ask for an empty glass and several lemon wedges.
- Order a cup of herbal tea.
- Realize that restaurant portions are extremely large. Consider sharing a meal with a friend or setting aside some for lunch the next day.
- Choose ethnic restaurants for more healthful food choices.

national chain restaurant or american grille
- Order pasta with olive oil and garlic. Request a salad with Italian dressing or olive oil and balsamic vinegar on the side.
- Select a salad and a baked potato. Take *Gomashio* to sprinkle on top.
- A Garden Burger® can be ordered almost everywhere. However, be aware that it contains three different types of cheese. Request a side salad or vegetables in place of the French fries.

chinese restaurant

- Chinese restaurants are not high on my list for dining out. Most places do not follow requests for light oil and no MSG, sugar, eggs or chicken stock.
- Do not order soup. It almost always contains chicken parts, MSG, steroids and hormones.
- Order steamed or Moo Shu Vegetables.

indian restaurant

- Order Vegetable Biryani (stir-fried vegetables with rice). Request no eggs.
- Select Channa Masala (chickpea stew). Be aware that tomatoes are an ingredient.
- Choose Aloo Gobi (cauliflower-potato stew).
- Order an unbuttered, wheat chapati to accompany your meal.

japanese restaurant

- Order Nori Rolls filled with cucumber, nuka pickle or natto (fermented soybeans).
- Select Nabe Mono (a large bowl of soup filled with noodles). Request soba (buckwheat) noodles.
- Order Vegetable Tempura only occasionally, since it is deep-fried. Ask for a large portion of shredded daikon radish to help balance the oil.
- Order Miso Soup, but be aware that it will not be as high quality or delicious as yours.

mexican restaurant

- Ask whether the tortilla chips, rice and refried beans are strictly vegetarian. Many restaurants use beef lard and chicken stock to cook these foods.
- Order Vegetable Fajitas. Substitute extra guacamole for the cheese, sour cream and tomatoes. Request more healthful corn tortillas instead of the white flour tortillas.
- Choose a Bean Burrito. For a more balanced burrito, ask the server to substitute rice and lettuce for half the beans.
- Order a bowl of pinto or black beans. Top with diced onions and cilantro. Request a side of corn tortillas to accompany them.

mideastern restaurant

- For an appetizer, select Hummus, Tabouli, Lentil Soup, a Vegetarian Platter or a Greek Salad. Be aware that restaurants frequently serve feta cheese made from cow's milk. True feta is made from goat or sheep's milk and does not contain harmful chemicals. If this concerns you, inquire.
- Request vegetarian entrées such as Couscous Vegetable Stew or Mjadra (a lentil and bulgur dish).
- Ask if the Falafel Platter or Sandwich can be prepared baked rather than fried. It does not hurt to ask, unless you are a guy...

pizzeria

- Order a Vegetarian Pizza with no cheese. Request grilled or steamed vegetables for the topping. Otherwise, they will be essentially raw and tasteless. Sprinkle a little parmesan cheese on top, if you choose.

thai restaurant

- Order Pad Thai (a thin rice noodle dish). Substitute vegetables or tofu for meat. Request no eggs or MSG.
- Select an entrée-size bowl of Tom Yum Vegetable Soup with or without noodles. Verify with the chef that the broth is vegetarian.
- Choose Drunken Noodles (a wide, flat noodle dish). Note that it is more oily than Pad Thai.
- Order Vegetable Curry only occasionally since it is made with coconut milk, which is high in saturated fat.

movie theater

- Ask the staff what kind of oil is used to pop the corn. If it is canola or corn oil, feel free to indulge. Avoid other oils, such as coconut and cottonseed, which are high in saturated fat.

on-the-road

- Consult a vegetarian restaurant resource book or the internet before your trip. When you get there, ask a deli worker at a local natural foods store for a recommendation. In a pinch, try the following choices at these national chain restaurants:

applebee's
- Order a Vegetable Platter or a Vegetable Fajita.

chili's
- Order a Bean Burger.

olive garden
- Order Pasta Primavera with penne pasta, salad with dressing on-the-side.

sweet tomatoes, souplantation, souper salad, shoney's
- Select Salad Bar and plain pasta.

taco bell
- Order a Seven-Layer Burrito without sour cream or cheese. Rice, beans, lettuce, tomatoes and guacamole remain.
- Choose a Bean Burrito without cheese.

whole foods market
- Choose from their salad bar and deli.

camping
- Camping is an excellent way to eat well while traveling. Pack rolled oats, dry cereal, instant ramen noodles and canned soups from a natural foods store.
- In a cooler, store prewashed fruit and salad fixings, and soy or rice beverage for cereal.
- If a freezer is available, take frozen soups and Amy's® organic frozen food products. Good choices are No-cheese, Roasted Vegetable Pizza, Burritos and Vegan Pot Pies.

airplane
- Take along nori rolls, popcorn, apples or a peanut butter sandwich.
- If you really want airplane food, request a non-dairy vegetarian or meatless Kosher meal at least three days before the flight.
- Take purified water to offset the drying atmosphere of the airplane cabin.

cruise

- It is possible to go on a cruise, enjoy yourself, eat a lot of food and not gain a pound. See the Appendix for a request list to fax to the cruise line several months before your trip. They are usually thoroughly accommodating.
- For breakfast, order oatmeal or corn grits and toast with grain cereal beverage. Occasionally, choose a whole wheat bagel.
- For lunch, request large salads with minimal vinaigrette dressing, with or without a little feta cheese.
- For dinner, skip the appetizers, soups and desserts. Order pasta, stir-fried vegetables with rice or noodles, or couscous dishes.
- Drink purified water, which is for sale by the gallon in the ports.
- Walk at least two miles around the deck every morning.
- If you choose to structure your cruise this way, you will not risk gaining the "expected" seven to ten pounds.

weddings, company parties, conferences, etc.

- Contact the person in charge of food at least one week before the event. Special arrangements can usually be made with no additional cost to the host.
- Request a non-dairy, vegetarian plate. Those sitting around you will be eyeing your choice with envy!

breakfasts

basic
breakfasts

It is a cliché to say that eating a wholesome breakfast is important, but it's true. In the morning, our blood sugar level is low. We can either refuel the body with nourishing foods or attempt to run on stimulants like caffeine. This chapter offers a variety of breakfast suggestions. I am confident you will discover some that will work for you.

Whole grain cooked cereal, like *Oatmeal*, makes an ideal breakfast in cool weather. It does not need to be humdrum. Add other grains for variety. For sweetness, cook it with dried fruit or top with maple syrup. To add some crunch, sprinkle on *Savory Sunflower Seeds* or *Gomashio*. Finally, try dulse sea vegetable. It is not only delicious, it is remarkably high in calcium.

Other warming options include *Corn Grits*, *Mochi*, *Scotch Oats* and soup. Surprisingly, soup is a common breakfast food in many cultures. It is quick, filling and can be made ahead of time. Soup offers an abundance of vegetables and complex carbohydrates for energy. Particularly good choices are *Sweet Miso Soup* and *Millet Squash Soup*.

When the seasons change, our tastes change too. In warm weather we are more attracted to cold cereals and fresh fruit. Choose whole grain, naturally sweetened cereals like shredded wheat, puffed kashi or oatio's from the natural foods store. To add protein, pair with soy or rice beverage. My favorite is EdenBlend®.

Although a bowl of fresh fruit is appealing for breakfast, its simple sugar, fructose, will not sustain the body's activities for long. If you choose this for breakfast, bring along a healthy snack to avoid a mid-morning slump. Alternately, plan to eat an early lunch!

Another breakfast favorite is toast with peanut butter. However, if you are trying to lose weight, choose a low-fat spread like apple butter or natural fruit preserves. I especially like *Savory Tofu Spread* for its calcium and delicious flavor.

Lastly, breakfast foods are great for an occasional speedy dinner when you are too tired and hungry to cook. Cold cereal is instantaneous, toast with peanut butter is a quick fix and frozen muffins thaw quickly. The slightly bitter flavor of Roma®, a coffee alternative, perfectly complements the sweetness of muffins. Besides, it feels like a treat to turn the day upside down by eating breakfast last, instead of first!

cook's tips

- Set out the pot, cereal and measured water the night before to speed preparation in the morning.
- Make extra cereal to save yourself time the next day. Cooked cereal can be reheated in a steamer or in a saucepan with a little extra water.
- Save even more time by cooking *Overnight Oatmeal* in a thermos.
- For variety, combine several grains for cooked cereal. See *Beyond Brown Rice*.
- If you prefer cooked cereals with a very soft consistency, add an additional 1/2 cup of water to the recipe.
- For cooked cereals, substitute Spectrum Naturals® Canola Spread for butter and soy or rice beverage for milk.

oatmeal

This breakfast standard tastes so much better when prepared with organic rolled oats the "old-fashioned" way, in a pot on the stove.

ingredients

3 cups water

1 cup rolled oats

1/4 tsp. unrefined sea salt

directions

1. Pour the water into a medium pot and bring to a boil. Add the rolled oats and salt. Reduce the heat and simmer covered.
2. Place a flame tamer under the pot to prevent oats from scorching.
3. While getting ready for your day, simmer for 20-35 minutes, the longer the better.
4. Sprinkle with *Gomashio*, *Savory Sunflower Seeds* or diced, dried dulse for a salty taste. To sweeten, pour brown rice syrup, barley malt or raisins on top. Enjoy!

variations

- Substitute 1/2 cup kasha, millet, quinoa, amaranth or any other quick-cooking grain for 1/2 cup of the rolled oats.
- Add diced squash or other sweet vegetable in step #1.
- Add nuts and or dried fruit like raisins or apples in step #1.

cook's tip

- If you are not a morning person, make *Overnight Oatmeal*, page 41, in a wide-mouth thermos.

overnight oatmeal

If you are not a morning person, you can still enjoy a wholesome breakfast at home, work or while traveling. Overnight Oatmeal, made in a thermos, requires less than fifteen minutes to prepare the night before.

ingredients

1 cup rolled oats

2 1/2 cups boiling water

1/4 tsp. unrefined sea salt

directions

1. Dry-roast the oats in a hot skillet, over medium heat, until golden brown. Stir often to prevent burning. This adds a toasty flavor.
2. Pour hot tap water into a wide-mouth, 3-cup thermos to preheat it. Cover and allow to stand for 5 minutes.
3. Pour the water out of the thermos. Add the oats, salt and 2 1/2 cups of boiling water. Replace the stopper and lid. Wrap in a towel to keep warm. Oatmeal will "cook" overnight.
4. Serve sprinkled with *Gomashio* or diced, dried dulse for a salty taste.

variation

- To sweeten, add raisins in step #3.

cook's tips

- As a short cut, prepare rolled oats ahead of time by dry-roasting them in a large quantity. Allow to cool. Store in glass jars in the refrigerator or freezer.
- Prepackage individual portions of dry-roasted rolled oats and salt in sandwich-sized Ziploc® bags.
- When you stay at a motel or hotel, you can easily request hot water at a nearby coffee shop and make *Overnight Oatmeal* in your room.

scotch oats

yield: 2 generous servings

Also known as steel-cut oats, this breakfast cereal is less processed, heartier and more nutritious than rolled oats, but requires longer cooking. A pressure cooker reduces the cooking time to only fifteen minutes!

ingredients

3 1/2 cups water   1/4 tsp. unrefined sea salt
  1 cup steel-cut oats

directions

1. Bring the water to a boil in a pressure cooker. Add the oats and salt.
2. Over high heat, bring up to full pressure.
3. Place a flame tamer under the pressure cooker. Reduce the heat, maintaining high pressure for 15 minutes.
4. Quick-release the pressure by placing the closed pot under cold, running water.
5. After all the pressure has been released, remove the lid. Stir to incorporate any water remaining on the top.
6. Serve sprinkled with *Gomashio* or diced, dried dulse for a salty taste. To sweeten, pour brown rice syrup, barley malt or raisins on top.

variation

- Substitute 1/4 cup kasha, millet, quinoa, amaranth, couscous or teff for 1/4 cup of the oats.

lenore's natural cuisine

42

corn grits

Try this Southern-style breakfast for a gratifying change from oatmeal. Its warm, golden color and creamy texture will help start your day.

ingredients

1 cup corn grits

3 cups water

1/4 tsp. unrefined sea salt

directions

1. Whisk together the corn grits and 1 1/2 cups of the water in a bowl. Allow to stand for 3 minutes.
2. **Meanwhile,** boil the remaining 1 1/2 cups of water in a medium saucepan.
3. Pour the soaking corn grits (with the soaking water) into the pot of boiling water. Add the salt and stir vigorously over low heat until it becomes a thick porridge, about 10 minutes.

variations

- Top with maple syrup for a naturally sweet treat.
- Spoon warm, leftover corn grits into a rinsed shallow dish. Cool, cover and refrigerate until firm. For a delicious lunch see *Fried Corn Grits*, page 110.

maple
pecan pancakes

For a lovely brunch, treat yourself to these yummy pancakes. They are fast to make and the batter freezes well for later use.

wet ingredients

3 TBS. unrefined corn oil
1 TBS. maple syrup
1 cup soy or rice beverage
3⁄4 cup water

dry ingredients

1⁄2 tsp. unrefined sea salt
2 cups whole wheat pastry flour
1 TBS. Rumford® baking powder
1⁄2 cup pecans, toasted and chopped

directions

1. Combine the wet ingredients and the salt in a blender. Blend until uniform in color.
2. Combine the dry ingredients in a bowl and mix well with a whisk.
3. Pour the wet mixture into the dry mixture and briefly blend with a whisk.
4. For best results, refrigerate the batter until cold, about 20 minutes.
5. Add water, if needed, to make the batter thin and runny. Heat an additional 1⁄4 teaspoon of corn oil in a non-stick or heavy skillet.
6. Pour 1⁄3 cup of the batter into the hot skillet to make 1⁄4-inch thin pancakes. Cook until bubbles appear on the top surface and the pancakes appear dry around the edges.
7. Turn the pancakes over. Cook until golden brown on both sides.

variations

• To make fluffier pancakes, add 2 tablespoons of arrowroot powder to the dry ingredients.
• Substitute canola oil for corn oil.
• Substitute 2 tablespoons brown rice syrup for 1 tablespoon maple syrup.

cook's tips

- In place of 100% maple syrup, combine 1/4 cup brown rice syrup with 1/4 cup maple syrup. Or, combine 1/4 cup brown rice syrup with 1/4 teaspoon natural maple syrup flavoring. Heat gently and pour over the pancakes.
- To toast pecans, follow the *Savory Sunflower Seed* recipe, page 171.
- Top with apple sauce or canola spread.
- Plain pancakes at room temperature make a surprisingly delicious quick snack.
- The consistency of frozen pancake batter will not be as uniform as fresh batter. This will not affect the finished product. Simply stir with a whisk.

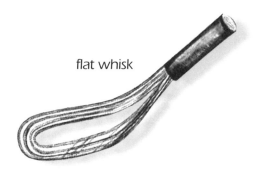

flat whisk

scrambled tofu

yield: 4 servings

This is an intriguing alternative to scrambled eggs. It is high in protein and calcium, without the drawbacks of animal products. Whether you prefer it plain, Western or Mexican style, it is sure to satisfy. Serve with toast.

ingredients

- 1/2 tsp. unrefined corn oil
- 1 onion, minced
- 1 carrot, minced or grated
- 1 celery stalk, minced
- 1 pound firm tofu, rinsed
- 1/2 tsp. turmeric, or more to taste
- 1/4 tsp. unrefined sea salt
- 1-2 tsp. shoyu or umeboshi vinegar, to taste
- 1 TBS. fresh parsley, minced, to garnish

directions

1. Heat the oil in a large, nonstick skillet. Sauté the onion until translucent, about 5 minutes.
2. Push the onion to one side of the pan. Sprinkle a few more drops of oil in the cleared space. Add the carrot to the pan and sauté for several minutes. Add the celery and sauté for another minute.
3. Crumble the tofu and add it to the vegetables. Add the turmeric and salt, then stir.
4. Add shoyu or umeboshi to taste. Cover to steam until the carrots are fork-tender, about 4 minutes. Stir once or twice.
5. Adjust seasonings and serve garnished with parsley.

variations

- Western style: omit the carrot, add 1/2 diced green pepper and one handful of sliced mushrooms.
- Mexican style: omit the carrot, add 4 ears of corn-off-the-cob and one red pepper in strips.

cook's tip

- To prepare tofu for marinating, compress it in a pickle press or between two cutting boards for 20 minutes. This expels excess water and allows more flavor to be absorbed by the tofu.

notes

soups

souper soups

Historically, out of necessity, cooks poured whatever ingredients were available into a pot of boiling water to create a meal for the family. Soup was born. It is my favorite food to cook any time of year. It is warming, nourishing and satisfying as well as wholesome, simple and convenient. Hot soup stimulates the appetite and relaxes the digestive system.

It is especially good for beginners to start with soup recipes because they are so forgiving. Any recipe can be successful with relative ease. They also fill up a menu quickly. Soup can be an impromptu meal, snack, travel food or even be used as a sauce over rice or noodles.

You can incorporate an ample portion of your daily vegetable requirement in soup. Bean soup is a bountiful, economical source of protein, fiber, iron, calcium, B-1 and niacin. It makes a satisfying and filling meal when served with cooked vegetables or a salad and crusty whole grain bread.

I make a steaming pot of soup weekly. It is waiting then, ready to warm, comfort and nourish. I hope it will do the same for you!

cook's tips
- Fresh spring or filtered water is recommended for cooking.
- Boiling water ahead speeds cooking time.
- Do not fill the pressure cooker more than half full when cooking beans. If it is filled higher than this, the pressure valve can become clogged by the beans' loose outer shells.
- Sautéing onions before adding to the soup pot adds flavor and depth. However, this extra step is not essential.
- To prevent beans from boiling over while cooking, keep the lid ajar.
- Add salt, miso, shoyu and vinegar at the end of cooking time when cooking bean soups. These ingredients harden bean skins and retard cooking if added sooner.

- A damp dishcloth held over the top of a closed blender prevents the hot mixture from spurting out.
- Bean soups thicken as they stand. Thin slightly with water and adjust the seasonings before serving.
- To prevent soup from splattering as you serve it, place a spoon upside down in the bowl.
- Store soup in wide-mouth canning jars. Glass, unlike plastic, is an inert material which is non-reactive with food. A bonus is that you can see what is inside.
- A stainless steel funnel makes filling jars a breeze.
- When freezing soups, allow 2 inches of "head" space at the top of canning jars to allow for expansion. This will avoid breakage.

red
lentil soup

For years, this has been the favorite soup of my beginning students. Many tell me that even their meat-and-potato eaters love it!

ingredients

6 cups water
1 cup red lentils
2 ears of corn, husked
1 6-inch strip kombu
1/2 tsp. unrefined corn oil
1 medium onion, diced small

2 carrots, cut into rounds,
  1/4-inch thick
3 celery stalks, diced small
3 TBS. sweet, white miso
1 TBS. fresh parsley, minced,
  to garnish, optional

directions

1. Bring the water to a boil in a large stock pot.
2. **Meanwhile,** pick over the lentils to remove debris and set aside.
3. Boil the corn cobs in the boiling water for 10 minutes. This makes a sweet soup stock. Remove the cobs and cool. Cut the kernels off the cobs and set aside.
4. Rinse the lentils through a strainer, then add them to the pot. Simmer uncovered for 15 minutes. Skim off foam that comes to the surface.
5. **Meanwhile,** cover the kombu with water and soak for 5 minutes. Then, cut it into 1/2-inch squares and add it to the pot.
6. **Meanwhile,** heat the oil in a nonstick skillet. Sauté the onion until translucent, about 5 minutes.
7. Move the onion to one side of the skillet. Sprinkle a few more drops of oil in the cleared space. Add the carrots to the skillet and sauté for several minutes.
8. Repeat step #7 with the celery. Add the sautéed vegetables and corn to the pot.
9. Place a flame tamer under the pot. Simmer covered until the lentils are soft and creamy, about 45 minutes.
10. Place a small amount of the hot soup in a small bowl, add the miso, whisk until smooth and return it to the pot. Serve garnished with parsley.

cook's tips
- Lay the corn cob horizontally on the board to slice off kernels with a minimum of mess.
- Use a Bash 'N Chop® to efficiently scoop up corn kernels and other vegetables.

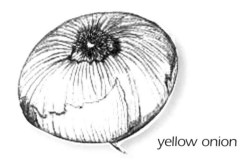

yellow onion

the ultimate
lentil soup

For many years I enjoyed this yummy soup at a Mediterranean restaurant in Arizona. I experimented and finally recreated it. I hope you enjoy it as much as I do. It freezes extremely well, so make the whole batch!

ingredients

4 cups green lentils
8 cups water
1 12-inch strip kombu
2 tsp. ground cumin
1 tsp. paprika
1/2 tsp. dried thyme
10 medium garlic cloves, minced
1/4 tsp. cayenne, optional

2 medium onions, diced small
2 bay leaves
3 celery stalks, diced small
3 carrots, cut into 1/2 rounds
3 TBS. barley miso
1 TBS. unrefined sea salt
3 TBS. mirin
1 TBS. fresh parsley, minced, to garnish

directions

1. Pick over the lentils to remove debris and set aside.
2. Bring the water to a boil in a large stock pot.
3. Rinse the lentils through a strainer and add them to the pot.
4. Simmer uncovered for 15 minutes, skimming off foam that comes to the surface.
5. **Meanwhile**, cover the kombu with water and soak for 5 minutes.
6. Cut the kombu into 1/2-inch squares and add it to the pot. Simmer for 30 minutes with the lid ajar.
7. Add the remaining ingredients, except the miso, salt, mirin and parsley. Replace the lid, keeping it ajar.
8. Place a flame tamer under the pot. Simmer until the lentils have completely dissolved, about 3-4 hours. Stir from the bottom every 20 minutes to prevent the soup from scorching. Add more water to thin the soup when it gets too thick.
9. Place a small amount of the hot soup in a small bowl, add the miso, whisk until smooth and return it to the pot. Add the mirin and salt. Stir and cook for 20 minutes.
10. Serve garnished with parsley.

cook's tips

- If you use red lentils, you will have crushed lentil soup. Red lentils are simply green lentils from which the hard outer shell has been removed.
- A bay leaf flavors bean soups and helps reduce gas. A Boston tradition is to make a wish if you find the bay leaf in your soup bowl. It has a strong flavor, so do not eat it!

garlic

green split pea soup

As a vegetarian, my mom left the ham out of this recipe. Job's tears, a wild barley seed, provides the depth and richness instead. It is her favorite split pea soup and it may become your favorite as well!

ingredients

1 2/3 cups split green peas	1 large carrot, cut into 1/2 rounds
7 cups water	
1 6-inch strip kombu	1 celery stalk, diced small
3 TBS. Job's tears	1/4 tsp. dried basil
1 large onion, diced small	1/4 tsp. unrefined sea salt
1 garlic clove, minced	3 TBS. shoyu, or to taste

directions

1. Pick over the split peas and Job's tears to remove debris and set aside.
2. Bring the water to a boil in a large stock pot.
3. Rinse the peas and Job's tears through a strainer and add them to the pot.
4. Simmer uncovered for 15 minutes, skimming off foam that comes to the surface.
5. **Meanwhile**, cover the kombu with water and soak for 5 minutes.
6. Cut the kombu into 1/2-inch squares and add it to the pot. Simmer for 1 hour with the lid ajar.
7. Add the remaining ingredients, except the salt and shoyu. Replace the lid, keeping it ajar.
8. Place a flame tamer under the pot. Simmer until the peas have completely dissolved, about 45 minutes. Stir from the bottom every 15 minutes to prevent soup from scorching.
9. Add the salt and shoyu. Simmer for 5 minutes to cook in the seasonings.

variation

- Substitute pearled barley for Job's tears.

cook's tips

- When boiling bean soups, the pot is vented by keeping the lid ajar. This prevents the soup from spilling over.
- Pea soup will thicken overnight. When reheating, add a little water.

carrots

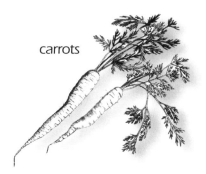

creamy cauliflower and chickpea soup

yield: 2 quarts

High in beta carotene, cauliflower is disguised in this soup by puréing it. Chickpeas add creamy heartiness.

ingredients

1 cup chickpeas
2 1/2 cups water
1 6-inch strip kombu
1 large cauliflower, cut into large chunks

1/4 tsp. sesame oil
1 small onion, diced small
1/3 cup sweet, white miso
1 TBS. fresh parsley, minced, to garnish

directions

1. The day before, pick over the chickpeas to remove debris and broken beans. Rinse the beans and place them in a large bowl. Cover with water, 2 inches above the level of beans and soak overnight. See cook's tip, page 129.
2. Rinse the chickpeas through a colander. Pour them into a pressure cooker with 2 1/2 cups of fresh water.
3. Bring to a boil. Cook uncovered for 6-8 minutes, skimming off foam that comes to the surface.
4. Add the kombu strip to the pot and lock the lid in place. Over high heat, bring up to full pressure.
5. Place a flame tamer under the pot. Reduce the heat, maintaining high pressure. Cook for 25 minutes.
6. **Meanwhile**, heat the oil in a nonstick skillet. Sauté the onions until caramelized, 15-25 minutes, the longer the better.
7. Steam the cauliflower in 2 cups water until fork-tender, about 7 minutes.
8. Quick-release the pressure by placing the closed pot under cold, running water.
9. After all the pressure has been released, remove the lid. Test the beans for tenderness. If they are not soft, replace the lid and simmer until the chickpeas are done.
10. Combine the cauliflower, chickpeas and miso in a blender. Blend until smooth. Return the purée to the pot. Heat gently for several minutes to marry the flavors.
11. Serve garnished with the caramelized onions and minced parsley.

variation

- Serve as a sauce over noodles or rice.

cook's tip

- It enhances the flavor of cauliflower to steam the entire head whole for 12 minutes before cutting it apart.

skimmer

millet
squash soup

This soup is soothing anytime. It also helps maintain an even blood sugar level, excellent for people with hypoglycemia.

ingredients

7 cups boiling water
1 small buttercup squash
1 large onion, diced small
1 cup millet

3 TBS. sweet, white miso, or
   more to taste
2 TBS. fresh parsley, minced,
   to garnish, optional

directions

1. Bring the water to a boil in a medium pot.
2. **Meanwhile**, remove blemished areas from the squash skin. Leave the remaining skin intact. Cut the squash in half lengthwise, from top to bottom. Scoop out the seeds. Trim away the stem and blossom ends. Cut it into 1/2-inch cubes and set aside.
3. Add the squash and onion to the pot.
4. Rinse the millet through a strainer and add it to the pot.
5. Place a flame tamer under the pot and reduce the heat to low. Simmer covered until the soup becomes creamy, about 40 minutes. Stir occasionally.
6. Place a small amount of the hot soup in a small bowl, add the miso, whisk until smooth and return it to the pot. Serve garnished with parsley.

variation

- Substitute butternut squash for buttercup.

cook's tip
- Leave the skin on vegetables and fruit to add fiber, texture and flavor to the dish. However, if you do not like squash skin, peel it off!

shiitake-leek miso soup

yield: 1 1/2 quarts

Dried shiitake mushrooms add an earthy flavor and color contrast to green leeks. They are reputed by traditional medicine to help dissolve fat and cysts. Adapted from Jeff Woodward's recipe in The Healing Power of Food.

ingredients

- 6 dried shiitake mushrooms
- 1 6-inch strip wakame
- 1/4 tsp. sesame oil
- 1 cup leeks, cut into 1-inch matchsticks
- 2 cups green cabbage, shredded
- 5 cups boiling water
- 3 TBS. brown rice miso

directions

1. Rinse the shiitake mushrooms, then place them in a small bowl. Cover with boiling water and soak for 15 minutes. Place a plate over the bowl to hold in the heat.
2. **Meanwhile**, cover the wakame with water and soak for 5 minutes. Then, cut it into 1/2-inch squares and set aside.
3. Cut off the mushroom stems and discard. Cut the caps into 1/4-inch strips.
4. Heat the oil in a medium pot. Sauté the leeks and mushrooms for 5 minutes.
5. Add the cabbage to the pot and sauté for 5 minutes.
6. Add the wakame and 5 cups of boiling water to the pot. Simmer covered for 30 minutes.
7. Place a small amount of the hot soup in a small bowl, add the miso, whisk until smooth and return it to the pot.

variations

- Substitute barley miso for brown rice miso.
- For added flavor, add 1/2 teaspoon of Herbamere® seasoning in step #6.

leek

sweet miso soup

Soup for breakfast! It sounds crazy, but once you try it, I think you will be hooked. Warm and nourishing, it gives you a better jump-start than any cup of Java, without the caffeine. Since we eat it everyday, we make enough for a week's breakfast. Serve it with sourdough bread or Moist and Hearty Muffins, page 77.

ingredients

8 cups water
1 6-inch strip wakame
1 small buttercup squash
1 medium onion, cut into thin 1/2 rounds

1 small daikon radish, cut into 1/2-inch rounds
6 TBS. barley miso, or to taste
1 scallion, thinly sliced, to garnish, optional

directions

1. Bring the water to a boil in a large stock pot.
2. Cover the wakame with water and soak for 5 minutes. Cut it into 1/2-inch squares and set aside.
3. **Meanwhile,** remove blemished areas from the squash skin. Leave the remaining skin intact. Cut in half lengthwise, from top to bottom. Scoop out the seeds. Trim away the stem and blossom ends. Cut the squash into 1/2-inch cubes and set aside.
4. Add the onion and wakame to the pot. Simmer uncovered for 5 minutes.
5. Add the daikon and simmer uncovered until fork-tender, about 5 minutes.
6. Add the squash and simmer uncovered until fork-tender, 5-8 minutes.
7. Reduce the heat so that the soup is no longer boiling.
8. Place a small amount of the hot soup in a small bowl, add the miso, whisk until smooth and return it to the pot. Serve garnished with scallion.

variations

- Substitute carrots, rutabaga, parsnips, cabbage or butternut squash for the buttercup squash.
- Add 1/2-1 cup diced daikon greens or other greens in step #6.
- Add 2 slices of fresh ginger in step #7.

cook's tips

- To make a one-pot breakfast meal, add leftover cooked rice, millet or noodles to the soup.
- Use an 8-inch chef's knife to cut through the dense skin of buttercup squash. Hold the squash securely on a cutting board, stem side up. Place the tip of the knife into the top of the squash and cut with a rocking downward motion. Repeat on the other side.
- To preserve the friendly bacteria and enzymes in miso soup, do not boil it when reheating. For the same reason, do not freeze it. It will keep refrigerated for one week.

daikon

summer
vegetable chowder

yield: 1 1/2 quarts

This light, vegetable-filled soup makes a complete meal when served with salad.

ingredients

2 cups water

1/2 tsp. unrefined corn oil

1 medium onion, diced small

2 carrots, cut into thin 1/2 rounds

2 celery stalks, diced small

1 garlic clove, minced

1 6-inch strip kombu

1 ear of corn, cut kernels off the cob

1/2 tsp. dried basil

1 bay leaf

1/2 tsp. unrefined sea salt

1 pinch white pepper

8 pods fresh fava beans

2 TBS. sweet, white miso, or to taste

directions

1. Bring the water to a boil in a medium pot.
2. **Meanwhile,** heat the oil in a nonstick skillet. Sauté the onion until translucent, about 5 minutes.
3. Move the onion to one side of the skillet. Sprinkle a few more drops of oil in the cleared space. Add the carrots to the skillet and sauté for 3-4 minutes.
4. Repeat step #3 with the celery and garlic, sautéing for 1 minute.
5. **Meanwhile,** cover the kombu with water and soak for 5 minutes. Then, cut it into 1/2-inch squares. Add the kombu, corn, sautéed vegetables and all the seasonings, except the miso, to the boiling water.
6. Simmer covered for 20 minutes. Add more water as needed.
7. **Meanwhile,** remove the fava beans from their pods and place in a bowl. Pour boiling water over them. Allow to stand for 30 minutes to loosen the skins. Next, place the beans in a bowl of cold water. Use the thumb and forefinger to rub off the bitter peel.
8. Add the beans to the pot and adjust the seasonings. Simmer for 5 minutes.
9. Place a small amount of the hot soup in a small bowl, add the miso, whisk until smooth and return it to the pot.

variations
- Substitute 1 cup frozen peas for the fava beans.
- Substitute 1 cup canned fava beans for fresh ones.

cook's tips
- Please do not be intimidated by the little-known fresh fava bean. Its heartiness and taste will delight and reward your adventurous spirit tenfold.
- Garlic becomes bitter if sautéed in oil for longer than one minute, so keep your eyes on the clock!

sweet yellow corn

creamy broccoli-squash soup

yield: 2 1/2 quarts

One day, it took forever to retrieve some bay leaves from a large pot of soup. I was determined to find an easier way. Securing the leaves inside a mesh tea ball was my joyful discovery. The tea ball even has a chain and hook so it can hang nicely from the edge of the pot! Use this tip when making this yummy vegetable soup.

ingredients

- 4 cups water
- 3 stalks broccoli
- 1 medium onion, cut into large chunks
- 2 medium garlic cloves, cut in 1/2
- 2 small yellow summer squash, cut into large chunks
- 1 tsp. unrefined sea salt
- 1 bay leaf
- 1/2 tsp. each dried basil, marjoram, thyme
- 2 pinches white pepper, optional

directions

1. Bring the water to a boil in a medium pot.
2. **Meanwhile**, cut off the very bottom of the broccoli stalks. Peel the stalks and coarsely chop them. Separate florets and reserve 1 cup for the garnish.
3. Add the onion, garlic, squash, salt, bay leaf and the broccoli, except the florets to garnish, to the pot. Simmer covered until the onion and broccoli are tender, about 15 minutes.
4. **Discard the bay leaf.**
5. Blend the soup in batches until smooth, pouring the puréed batches into a second pot.
6. Add the remaining ingredients to the puréed soup. Simmer covered for 10 minutes. Add the reserved florets the last 3 minutes of cooking time.

variation

- For a richer flavor, sauté the onions and garlic in 1/2 teaspoon of extra-virgin olive oil before adding them to the soup.

cook's tips

- Black pepper is known to irritate the intestines. Substitute white pepper, which is milder.
- For added flavor, use Herbamere®, an organic herb seasoning salt. Add 1/2 teaspoon for every 4 cups of water.
- Use a hand blender to reduce clean up.

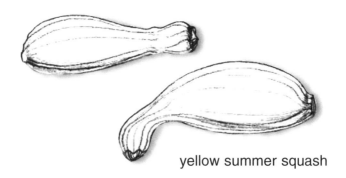

yellow summer squash

cream of
shiitake soup

This divine soup was inspired by a friend, Elaine King Gagné. Rice wine, called mirin, is used in place of sherry to round out the flavor. Although more involved than other recipes, it is worth the effort!

ingredients

10 dried shiitake mushrooms
2/3 cup rolled oats
4-5 cups water
1 6-inch strip kombu
1/2 tsp. sesame oil

1 medium onion, diced small
3 TBS. shoyu, or more to taste
1 TBS. mirin
1/4 toasted nori sheet, cut into
    strips, to garnish, optional

directions

1. Rinse the shiitake mushrooms then place them in a small bowl. Cover with boiling water and soak for 15 minutes. Place a plate over the bowl to hold in the heat.
2. **Meanwhile**, in a dry skillet, dry-roast the oats until golden brown, about 5 minutes. Set aside.
3. Strain the mushroom-soaking water into a bowl. Measure it and add water as needed to make a total of 5 cups of liquid. Pour it into a medium pot
4. Add the kombu strip to the pot and bring to a boil.
5. **Meanwhile**, cut off the mushroom stems and discard. Cut the caps into 1/4-inch strips. Set aside.
6. When the water comes to a boil, remove the kombu and reserve.
7. **Meanwhile**, heat the oil in a large, nonstick skillet. Sauté the onion until translucent, about 5 minutes. Set aside.
8. Add the oats to the boiling water and simmer covered for 30 minutes.
9. Pour the oat mixture into a blender and blend until smooth. Return the purée to the pot.
10. Add the onion, mushrooms, shoyu and mirin. Simmer covered for 20 minutes to soften vegetables and marry the flavors.
11. Serve garnished with toasted nori strips or minced fresh parsley.

cook's tip
*   Leftover kombu keeps refrigerated for 3 days. Otherwise, freeze it. Use it in any bean dish.

notes

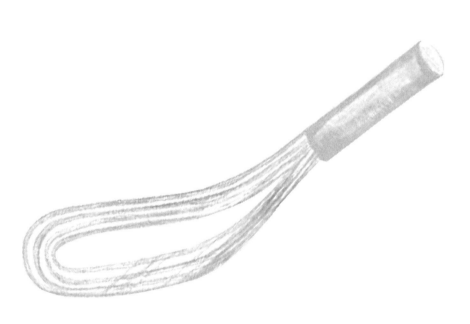

quick breads
and spreads

quick
breads and spreads

The aroma of muffins, cornbread and other quick breads fresh from the oven creates an ambiance of love, caring and home. Whether eaten for breakfast or added to dress up a simple meal, they are absolutely scrumptious. Best of all, they can be prepared in less than an hour with infinite variations.

You will discover a delightful taste difference when using wholesome ingredients like whole wheat pastry flour, canola oil, and maple and brown rice syrups. This is in sharp contrast with commercial baked goods, which are made with nutritionless white flour, so-called flavor enhancers, and high quantities of saturated fat and sugar. Rather than tasting intensely sweet and oily, these breads are hearty, deliciously moist and low in fat. Feel free to indulge.

What to spread on bread? Avoid saturated or hydrogenated fats like butter and margarine. Solid at room temperature, they clog arteries. Instead, use an unsaturated, non-hydrogenated spread like Spectrum Naturals®. It is made of canola oil and even tastes like butter! Buy it at your local natural foods store. Otherwise, you can make *Savory Tofu Spread* in less than ten minutes. It adds protein, calcium and a savory flavor. Lastly, for a non-fat bread topping, use natural fruit preserves.

cook's tips
- Begin by measuring all of the ingredients. Room temperature ingredients allow the batter to rise as soon as it enters the oven.
- Nuts are scrumptious, but high in fat. If I am eating those calories, I want to see them, so chop them coarsely!
- Add salt to the wet mixture to evenly distribute it throughout the batter.
- Before pouring gooey syrups into measuring cups and spoons, brush them with oil. Syrups will glide out more easily.
- Arrowroot powder can be substituted for egg replacer in any recipe in equal amounts.

- Use a blender to efficiently mix wet ingredients. This then allows you to combine the wet and dry ingredients, resulting in lighter baked goods.
- Sift flour through a standard mesh strainer to aerate it. This produces lighter baked goods.
- A whisk combines the wet and the dry ingredients more quickly and gently than a spoon.
- Over mixing tends to make a heavy muffin. Only stir until the flour is absorbed into the wet mixture. Small lumps will not ruin the batter.
- If the batter is too wet, add one tablespoon of flour at a time. If too dry, add one tablespoon of water at a time.
- Use a spring-action ice cream scoop to make uniform muffins fast.
- Using individual paper muffin cups is a sticky proposition. Because the batter sticks to the paper, I don't use them. Instead, I brush the muffin tins with oil.
- Near the end of the cooking time, pierce the center of muffins with a toothpick. When it comes out dry, the muffins are done.
- Allow the muffins to stand in the baking tins for 5 minutes after baking, then use a large spoon to guide them out.
- Place the muffins on a rack to cool completely before freezing in glass canning jars. To thaw, set on the counter for 10 minutes or warm in a steamer for 2 minutes.

blueberry muffins

yield: 10 muffins

Blueberries burst in your mouth in this sensational breakfast option. Moist and light, they make a scrumptious snack any time!

wet ingredients
1/4 cup canola oil
1 cup soy or rice beverage
1/2 cup maple syrup
1 tsp. natural vanilla flavor

dry ingredients
1/4 tsp. unrefined sea salt
1 1/2 cups whole wheat pastry flour
1/2 cup cornmeal
1 TBS. Rumford® baking powder
1/4 cup oat or wheat bran
2 TBS. EnerG® egg replacer
1 cup blueberries, rinsed

directions
1. Preheat the oven to 400°F.
2. Combine the wet ingredients and the salt in a blender and blend until uniform in color.
3. Combine the dry ingredients, except the blueberries, in a bowl. Mix well with a whisk.
4. Pour the wet mixture into the dry mixture and briefly blend with a whisk. Gently stir in the blueberries.
5. Fill oiled muffin tins to the top.
6. Bake for 25-30 minutes.
7. Muffins are done when golden brown and when a toothpick inserted in the middle comes out dry.

variations
- Substitute raspberries or blackberries for the blueberries.
- Substitute unrefined corn oil for canola oil.

cook's tips
- Buy a flat of unsprayed blueberries when they are in season. Freeze them, unwashed, in Ziploc® bags. You will have organic berries, even in the winter!

bran muffins

I wanted to recreate the bran muffins I ate back in the 60's at a New York City coffee shop, Chock Full O' Nuts®. With this recipe, you can too! The sweetness of the muffins is offset by the mild bitterness of Roma®.

wet ingredients

- 3 TBS. unrefined corn oil
- 1/4 cup maple syrup
- 2 TBS. brown rice syrup
- 2 TBS. barley malt syrup
- 1 tsp. brown rice vinegar
- 1 cup water

dry ingredients

- 1/4 tsp. unrefined sea salt
- 1 3/4 cups whole wheat pastry flour
- 1 1/3 cups wheat bran
- 1 TBS. Rumford® baking powder
- 1 TBS. EnerG® egg replacer

directions

1. Preheat the oven to 400°F.
2. Combine the wet ingredients and the salt in a blender and blend until uniform in color.
3. Combine the dry ingredients in a bowl and mix well with a whisk.
4. Pour the wet mixture into the dry mixture and briefly blend with a whisk.
5. Fill oiled muffin tins to the top.
6. Bake for 35-40 minutes.
7. Muffins are done when golden brown and when a toothpick inserted in the middle comes out dry.

variations

- Substitute arrowroot powder for egg replacer.
- Add 1/3 cup organic raisins or currants in step #4.
- Add 3/4 cup toasted and chopped pecans, walnuts or sunflower seeds in step #4.
- Substitute sesame oil for corn oil.

double corn muffins

These versatile muffins are great for breakfast, a snack or to accompany any meal. They are especially good with canned beans by Eden®, Bearito's® or Shari®, if you are in a hurry.

wet ingredients
- 3 TBS. unrefined corn oil
- 2 TBS. brown rice syrup
- 2 TBS. maple syrup
- 1 tsp. brown rice vinegar
- 1 cup water

dry ingredients
- 1/2 tsp. unrefined sea salt
- 1 1/2 cups cornmeal
- 1 1/2 cups whole wheat pastry flour
- 1 TBS. Rumford® baking powder
- 2 ears of corn, cut kernels off the cob

directions
1. Preheat the oven to 400°F.
2. Combine the wet ingredients and the salt in a blender and blend until uniform in color.
3. Combine the dry ingredients, except corn kernels, in a bowl. Mix well with a whisk.
4. Pour the wet mixture into the dry mixture and briefly blend with a whisk. Gradually add more water, as needed, to make a loose batter. Gently stir in the corn kernels.
5. Fill oiled muffin tins to the top.
6. Bake for 20-25 minutes.
7. Muffins are done when golden brown and when a toothpick inserted in the middle comes out dry.

variation
- Add 1/3 cup diced red peppers in step #4.

cook's tip
- Frozen organic corn kernels are available year-round in natural foods stores, packaged by Cascadian Farms®. Substitute one cup frozen for two ears of corn.

moist and hearty oatmeal muffins

These nutty and nutritious muffins freeze well and are a perfect on-the-run instant breakfast. Take a travel mug of Roma® or tea and you are set for the morning!

wet ingredients
- 1/4 cup canola oil
- 1/4 pound soft tofu
- 1 cup water

dry ingredients
- 1/4 tsp. unrefined sea salt
- 1 cup whole wheat pastry flour
- 2 cups rolled oats
- 1/2 cup sunflower seeds
- 1/2 tsp. cinnamon
- 1 TBS. Rumford® baking powder

directions
1. Preheat the oven to 375°F.
2. Combine the wet ingredients and the salt in a blender and blend until uniform in color.
3. Sift the flour through a single mesh strainer into a bowl.
4. Combine the remaining dry ingredients in the bowl. Mix well with a whisk.
5. Pour the wet mixture into the dry mixture and briefly blend with a whisk.
6. Allow the mixture to stand for 10 minutes to absorb the liquid. The desired texture resembles tuna salad. Add more water if needed.
7. Fill oiled muffin tins to the top.
8. Bake for 20-30 minutes.
9. Muffins are done when golden brown and when a toothpick inserted in the middle comes out dry.

variations
- Use an additional 2/3 cup water to replace the tofu.
- To make these muffins moister, chewier and even more wholesome, add 1 cup leftover rice or other cooked grain and 1/4 cup water in step #5.

cornbread

Since this cornbread is enriched with whole-grain brown rice, it makes for wholesome eating anytime. It is wonderful alone or as a perfect complement to baked beans and a salad.

wet ingredients

3 TBS. unrefined corn oil
1 3/4 cups water

dry ingredients

1 tsp. unrefined sea salt
3 cups coarse cornmeal
1 cup whole wheat pastry flour
2 TBS. Rumford® baking powder
2 1/2 cups cooked brown rice
1 TBS. black sesame seeds, to garnish, optional

directions

1. Preheat the oven to 350°F.
2. Combine the wet ingredients and the salt in a blender and blend until uniform in color.
3. Combine the dry ingredients, except the rice and sesame seeds, in a bowl. Mix well with a whisk.
4. Pour the wet mixture into the dry mixture briefly blending with a whisk.
5. Allow the mixture to stand for 5 minutes to absorb the liquid.
6. Stir in the cooked rice. The mixture should be thick and "squishy." Add more water if needed.
7. Press lightly into an oiled 8-inch square baking dish.
8. Smooth the top with wet hands. Pat the sesame seeds on top.
9. Bake covered for 30 minutes. A cookie sheet placed upside down over the baking dish makes a good cover.
10. Uncover. Bake 15 minutes longer. Cornbread is done when golden in color and when a toothpick inserted in the middle comes out dry.

variation

• Add a 4-ounce can of diced green chilies and corn kernels from 2 ears of corn in step #6.

notes

salads and
salad dressings

salads
and salad dressings

White iceberg lettuce smothered in an overpowering dressing is not my idea of a scrumptious salad. What comes to mind is a bed of vibrant, fresh, leafy greens accented with bright colors. Filled with vitality, vitamins and crunch, it is light, cool and appetizing.

Traditional medicine suggests that it is healthier to eat raw foods more frequently in warm weather and less often in cool weather. A large salad filled with "extras" can be the centerpiece of a warm summer's day meal. A crisp, small, green salad can balance a heavy meal in winter or complement a substantial grain, bean or pasta salad in summer. An effortless way to transform a simple bowl of greens to gourmet is to add mesclun. French for "a mix of greens," mesclun is a marvelous mixture of colors, shapes, flavors and textures. It is widely available in produce markets.

Lastly, what is a salad without dressing? Homemade salad dressings are lively and fresh, bearing no resemblance to oily, bottled dressings laden with artificial ingredients. In minutes, you can create a creamy, rich-tasting tahini dressing or choose extra-virgin olive oil as the foundation for an instant vinaigrette.

cook's tips
- To speed preparation, cut the carrots, cucumber or radish ahead of time. Store in plastic bags in the refrigerator.
- Romaine is the only lettuce that seems to stand up to being stored after washing. When spun in a salad spinner or blotted dry, it will keep almost a week in a plastic bag. Just before serving, tear leafy greens rather than cutting to prevent browning.
- Add extra salad ingredients and the dressing to lettuce just before serving for the liveliest presentation and the best taste.
- To make grain, bean and pasta salads visually appealing, cut all of the vegetables for each salad approximately the same size.

- It is more efficient to cook grain, bean and pasta ahead of time. It reduces preparation time and allows for cooling. Add the dressing just before serving.
- To reduce garlic's pungency, steam the whole, peeled clove for one minute before adding to salad dressings or any other recipe.
- Enliven grain, bean and pasta salads the next day by sprinkling a little umeboshi vinegar on top just before serving.
- Most grain and bean salads will keep refrigerated about five days.

leafy
green salad

A mainstay in your meal plan can be the humble, yet glorious, green salad. When composing a salad, I like to use one part strong-flavored lettuce to four parts mild lettuce. These strong-flavored, bitter varieties perk up the salad.

mild-flavored lettuce
bibb
boston
buttercrunch
green leaf
red leaf
romaine

strong flavored lettuce
arugula
dandelion
endive
escarole
mesclun
radicchio

extras
artichoke hearts
beans, homemade or
    canned
carrots, thinly sliced or grated
croutons
cucumbers, thinly sliced
fresh basil, cilantro or dill
nuts or seeds, toasted
olives, pitted
pasta, cooked
red onions, thinly sliced
red pepper, cut into 1-inch strips
red radish, thinly sliced
snow peas, cut into 1/3's on the
    diagonal

directions
1. Swish the lettuce in water until clean. If the produce is not organic, add a few drops of mild, natural soap to the water, see pages 14-15. Rinse thoroughly.
2. Spin or blot the lettuce dry. Tear it into bite-size pieces and place in a large serving bowl.
3. Add a colorful variety of extras.
4. Toss salad gently. Add a light sprinkling of salad dressing just before serving.

cook's tips
*   Avoid buying too much bitter-flavored lettuce which might not get eaten before it goes bad. Ask the produce staff to cut off a small portion of stronger-flavored lettuce for you. Or, buy mesclun by the ounce.

- Test commercial cucumbers to see if they are waxed. Scrape your fingernail along the cucumber skin. If it is waxed, peel it, unless you want paraffin clogging your intestines! Organic and farmer's market cucumbers are never waxed. The small variety known as gherkin, or pickle, is also never waxed, whether commercial or organic.
- Whether homegrown or store-bought, the hulls of sprouts often harbor bacteria or mold. I avoid them.
- To avoid a wilted salad, pour dressing only on the portion of salad you plan to eat immediately.
- Place leftover salad ingredients in a covered bowl. Refrigerate and add dressing just before serving the next day.

red radish

italian dressing

This tasty Italian dressing, made with very little oil, perks up salads and chilled vegetables.

ingredients

2 TBS. extra-virgin olive oil
1 TBS. brown rice vinegar
1 TBS. red wine vinegar
1 TBS. water

1 1/2 tsp. shoyu
1/4 tsp. dried oregano
1/4 tsp. dried rosemary

directions

1. Place all the ingredients in a glass jar and shake well. Refrigerate at least 1 hour for the flavors to marry.
2. Keeps refrigerated for about 1 month.

cook's tip

- For a smooth consistency, use dried, ground oregano or rosemary. However, the usual leaf variety will do.

lenore's natural cuisine

86

debbie's
instant vinaigrette

Reach for these handy ingredients when you want a speedy salad dressing. It is simple, but delicious over a beautiful salad.

ingredients

several sprinkles extra-virgin
    olive oil

several sprinkles balsamic
    vinegar

directions
1. Prepare a colorful fresh salad in a large bowl.
2. Sprinkle oil and vinegar to taste.
3. Toss gently and serve immediately.

variations
- Substitute umeboshi vinegar for the balsamic vinegar.
- For added flavor, include several leaves of fresh cilantro, basil, oregano or thyme, or a pinch of dried herbs in winter.

cook's tip
- My favorite brand of extra-virgin olive oil is L'estornell®, available at gourmet delis and grocery stores.

tahini-lime dressing

yield: 1/2 cup

This is a vibrant and tangy recipe by Meredith McCarty from her noteworthy cookbook, Fresh from a Vegetarian Kitchen.

ingredients

1/4 cup tahini

2 TBS. fresh lime juice

1 TBS. umeboshi vinegar

1 small garlic clove, minced

1/4 cup water

directions

1. Place all the ingredients in a blender. Blend until a smooth consistency is reached.
2. Keeps refrigerated for several weeks.

cook's tips

- To reduce garlic's pungency, steam the whole, peeled clove for 1 minute before blending.
- To make a dip, use less water.

tofu
dressing

While many dressings add taste without nutrition, this one will nourish you with calcium and protein. It also satisfies the craving for a creamy taste, without all the fat. Use it generously on salads, boiled vegetables, rice or noodles.

ingredients

1/4 pound soft tofu	2 TBS. tahini
1 TBS. sweet, white miso	1/2 fresh lime, juiced

directions
1. Refresh the tofu by steaming it for 4 minutes.
2. Combine the tofu, miso, tahini and lime juice in a blender. Blend until uniform in color.
3. Add water, as needed, to create a creamy and pourable dressing.
4. Keeps refrigerated up to 6 days.

variation
- Substitute lemon juice for the lime juice.

cook's tips
- I use Arrowhead Mills® tahini, because it is creamy, organic and not bitter-tasting like most other brands.
- When serving this dressing over boiled, organic vegetables, substitute the vegetable-cooking broth for the water. This adds flavor and nutrients.

tabouli

This classic Mideastern salad, based on Meredith McCarty's recipe in Fresh From a Vegetarian Kitchen, *is made with very little oil and no tomatoes. It is exceptionally high in iron and pairs up nicely with* Hummus-in-a-Hurry, *page 194 or* The Ultimate Lentil Soup, *page 54.*

salad

- 3 cups water
- 1 tsp. unrefined sea salt
- 2 cups coarse bulgur
- 2 cups cucumber,
  seeded and cut into
  1/4- inch pieces
- 4 cups minced, fresh parsley
- 1 cup scallions, thinly
  sliced

dressing

- 1/2 cup fresh lemon juice
- 1/4 cup extra-virgin olive oil
- 2 large garlic cloves, minced
- 1 TBS. shoyu, or more to taste
- 3 TBS. minced, fresh mint,
  optional

directions

1. Bring the water to a boil in a medium pot. Add the salt and bulgur. Simmer covered for 15 minutes.
2. Transfer to a large bowl. Fluff with a fork and allow to cool.
3. **Meanwhile**, whisk together dressing ingredients in a small bowl.
4. Add the remaining salad ingredients and the dressing to the bulgur. Mix gently.
5. Refrigerate at least 1 hour before serving.
6. Keeps refrigerated for about 3 days.

variations

- Substitute 1 teaspoon of dried mint for the fresh mint.
- Add 1/4 cup blanched and toasted, slivered almonds in step #4.

cook's tips

- It is healthier to use organic cucumbers. If only waxed cucumbers are available, peel off the skin to avoid ingesting the wax, which can coat the intestines and impair absorption of food.
- To remove cucumber seeds, cut the cucumber in half lengthwise. Use a spoon to scrape out the seeds. This step is not imperative, but seeds make the dish watery and give it a seedy texture. You decide!

brown rice salad

This is a cool, crunchy way to eat rice in the heat of summer. Serve with a leafy green salad.

salad

- 2 cups short-grain brown rice
- 3 cups water
- 2 pinches unrefined sea salt
- 2 ears of corn, husked
- 1⁄2 small bunch parsley, minced
- 1⁄2 cup sunflower seeds, toasted
- 1 red radish, thinly sliced

dressing

- 1 TBS. brown rice vinegar, or more to taste
- 1 TBS. umeboshi vinegar, or more to taste
- 1 TBS. mirin, or more to taste

directions

1. To pressure-cook rice, see page 100.
2. Spread the cooked rice in a large bowl to cool.
3. **Meanwhile**, steam or boil the corn until tender, about 10 minutes. Cut kernels off the cob and set aside.
4. Add the dressing ingredients to a small saucepan. Simmer for 2 minutes, then allow to cool.
5. Add the corn, parsley, sunflower seeds and dressing to the rice. Mix gently.
6. Serve garnished with red radish slices.

variation

- Pressure-cooked rice lends a hearty texture to this dish, but *Boiled Brown Rice*, page 106, will do.

cook's tips

- To toast sunflower seeds, rinse them through a strainer. Pour the damp seeds into a hot skillet. Toast over medium heat, stirring continuously with a rice paddle or wooden spoon. Seeds are done when they are golden brown and give off a nutty fragrance, about 10 minutes.
- Store extra toasted sunflower seeds in a glass jar in the freezer.
- Refrigerate the salad an hour before serving.

barley salad

yield: 2 quarts

Sweet, fresh corn and crunchy celery enliven this cool grain salad for summer. Only a small amount of oil is needed since umeboshi vinegar and mustard are so flavorful. Fresh herbs, garlic and scallion round out the flavor.

salad
3 1/2 cups water
1 1/2 cups pearled barley
  2 pinches unrefined sea salt
  2 ears of corn, cut kernels off
    the cob
  2 celery stalks, diced small
  2 scallions, thinly sliced

dressing
  3 TBS. extra-virgin olive oil
  3 TBS. umeboshi vinegar
  1 garlic clove, minced
1/4 tsp. dry mustard
  1 tsp. fresh basil, minced, or
    more to taste

directions
1. Bring the water to a boil in a medium pot.
2. **Meanwhile,** rinse the barley through a strainer. Add the barley and the salt to the boiling water.
3. Simmer covered 1 1/4 hours, with a flame tamer under the pot.
4. Spread the cooked barley in a large bowl to cool.
5. **Meanwhile,** steam the corn kernels and celery until tender. Set aside.
6. Whisk the dressing ingredients together in a small bowl until uniform in color.
7. Add the steamed vegetables, scallion and dressing to the barley. Mix gently.
8. Refrigerate at least 1 hour before serving.

variations
- Substitute fresh dill for the fresh basil.
- Substitute 1/4 teaspoon of dried dill for 1 teaspoon fresh dill. However, dried basil does not substitute well for fresh basil in this recipe.

cook's tip
- To reduce garlic's pungency, steam the whole, peeled clove for one minute before mincing.

wheat berry
dill salad

This festive, whole-grain salad combines chewiness and crunch to create a delightful dish. Umeboshi paste magically adds its zest. Serve with a leafy green salad.

salad
- 2 cups whole wheat berries
- 3 3/4 cups water
- 2 pinches unrefined sea salt
- 4 ears of corn, cut kernels off the cob
- 1/2 cup minced, fresh dill
- 1/4 cup sesame seeds, toasted

dressing
- 1 TBS. extra-virgin olive oil
- 3 TBS. umeboshi paste, or more to taste
- 1 TBS. shoyu

directions
1. Rinse the wheat berries through a strainer. Add them to a medium pot. Add the water and the salt. Bring to a boil.
2. Simmer covered for 1 1/2 hours with a flame tamer under the pot.
3. Spread the cooked wheat berries in a large bowl to cool.
4. **Meanwhile**, steam the corn kernels until tender, about 3 minutes.
5. Add the corn, dill and sesame seeds to the wheat berries. Mix gently.
6. Whisk the dressing ingredients together in a small bowl until uniform in color.
7. Add enough dressing to the wheat berry mixture to lightly coat the salad. Mix gently.
8. Refrigerate at least 1 hour before serving. Add more dressing if desired.

variation
- For added color, add 1 diced red pepper in step #5.

cook's tip
- A wheat berry is the whole, unprocessed kernel of the wheat plant. To shorten cooking time, pressure-cook the wheat berries and the salt for 45 minutes, then quick-release and proceed with step #3.

pickled cabbage

The crunch and sour flavor of this fermented dish add a fresh dimension to an otherwise plain meal. In addition, it is more easily digested than raw salad. Because it keeps at least ten days, it is easy to include with packed lunches.

ingredients

6 cups shredded cabbage

1 small carrot, cut into thin matchsticks

2 tsp. unrefined sea salt

directions

1. Place the vegetables in a large bowl, add the salt, then mix well. The cabbage will glisten, which means that the salt is drawing moisture from it.
2. Place the vegetables in a pickle press and screw on the lid. Apply pressure to the pressure plate to compress the vegetables.
3. Allow to stand on the counter for 1 hour. The liquid level should reach the level of the pressure plate. If it does not, add 1/2 teaspoon of salt and mix lightly. Repeat step #2. However, if there is more than 1 inch of liquid above the pressure plate, pour the vegetables into a colander. Rinse for 5 seconds, repeat step #2.
4. Leave the pickle press on the counter during fermentation, about 3 days. Every morning and night you must baby-sit your cabbage. Use a chopstick or knife to poke out the air bubbles along the inner walls of the pickle press. Note: you will not be able to remove all the bubbles.
5. After 3 days, taste the cabbage. If sour enough for your taste, refrigerate it. Otherwise, let it stand on the counter another day.
6. Squeeze out most of the liquid from the portion you are serving.

variations

• Add 1 thinly sliced green apple, radish or cucumber in step #1.

cook's tips
• Discard the outer, dark, bitter leaves of cabbage.
• Vegetables must stay below the liquid, see page 169.
• To save refrigerator space, store in a mini-pickle press.
• Taste the salad before serving. If it is too salty, rinse it for 5 seconds, then squeeze out the excess water.

sunomono

Cucumbers are one of the most cooling foods to eat in hot weather. Pickling renders them more alive and digestible. Japanese cuisine offers us this refreshing side dish.

ingredients

1 medium cucumber, peeled
and thinly sliced in rounds
1/4 tsp. unrefined sea salt
2 tsp. brown rice vinegar

1/2 tsp. brown rice syrup
2 tsp. black sesame seeds,
toasted, optional

directions

1. Place the cucumbers in a pickle press. Add the salt and mix gently. Replace and tighten the lid. Allow to stand for 30 minutes.
2. Squeeze out the excess liquid from the cucumbers, but do not rinse them.
3. Combine the brown rice vinegar and brown rice syrup in a small bowl. Add it to the cucumbers and toss gently.
4. Cover and let it stand one hour to marinate.
5. Serve garnished with black sesame seeds.
6. Keeps refrigerated about 3 days.

cook's tip

- For some odd reason, if you do not happen to own a pickle press, place cucumbers in a bowl. Insert a plate slightly smaller than the diameter of the bowl on top of the cucumbers. Place a jar filled with water on top of the plate to expel excess water from cucumbers. Doesn't it sound easier to buy a pickle press from a natural foods store or Asian market?

grains

glorious
grains

Why does a grain of brown rice planted in fertile soil flourish, while a grain of white rice planted in the same soil, wither? Refined grains are stripped of their fibrous hull and essential germ, leaving only the starchy endosperm with little nutritional value. The germ is the vital life force of the plant, without which it will not grow, let alone thrive. Nor will we.

All together, the parts of a whole grain provide essential nutrients and benefits. The germ provides vitamin E, small amounts of high quality oil and protein. Fiber acts like a broom to sweep clean the digestive system and arteries. Finally, the carbohydrate stabilizes the blood sugar level and boosts energy. Do not be fooled by enriched breads, pasta and white rice. Manufacturers enrich these lifeless foods by adding vitamins and minerals to convey the impression that they are wholesome. They are not.

In fact, grains in their natural state have been the cornerstone of mankind's diet throughout history. Grains grew easily, stored well and were easy to cook, requiring only water, salt and fire. Our ancestors simply added local foods like berries, fruits and vegetables to supplement this healthful diet. Today, in developing countries where people continue to eat this way, common modern diseases, including cancer, arthritis, asthma and heart disease, are virtually unknown.

Whole grains are not only beneficial to your body, but to your senses as well. The heavenly aroma of pressure-cooked brown rice will draw you to the kitchen. Its chewy texture and sweet flavor satisfy your body, mouth and soul. Top it with nutty *Gomashio* condiment for an exquisite combination. Finally, do not be concerned that you will be eating only brown rice. Traditional peoples from all over the world offer us an abundance of other grains to enjoy. Each whole grain will add its unique flavor and texture to your diet. For example, millet is creamy and comforting. Kasha is crunchy, nutty and warming. Wild rice is chewy and exotic. See *Beyond Brown Rice* for ways to enjoy these and many other grains.

cook's tips

- An ideal way to reheat grain is in a steamer. It requires less than one minute to restore dried-out, refrigerated rice to just-made perfection.
- Typically, whole grains comprise a large portion of a vegetarian diet. Buy certified organic. It is worth the additional cost.
- Buy grains from a store with a high turnover to ensure that they will be fresh. Fresh grains smell sweet, not musty or rancid.
- Store grains in glass jars or paper bags. Plastic will eventually impart its smell to stored grains. Keep in a cool, dry place like a basement or refrigerator.
- Grain moths appear in grain as clumps of cobwebs or full-grown moths. Discard or pour the infested grain through a colander outside and the moths will fly away. Rinse thoroughly and cook.
- Freezing grain for three days in glass jars or Zip-loc® plastic bags kills grain moths. Once out of the freezer, add a bay leaf to the stored grain to further discourage these pests.
- Label jars to help distinguish one grain from another if this is all new to you.
- To obtain maximum nutrients from grain, chew thoroughly. The enzymes in saliva initiate the digestive process. Without this step, digestion will be incomplete.
- It is best not to lift the pot lid while cooking rice or any other grain. There will be loss of water and, according to tradition, diminished food vitality.
- If water remains at the end of cooking time, cook uncovered 5 minutes longer. If the grain appears too dry, add 2 tablespoons of water and allow to stand covered, off the heat, for 5 minutes to absorb the extra moisture.

pressure-cooked brown rice

yield: 4 servings

The most delicious, nutritious way to prepare rice is to pressure cook it. Because rice becomes stickier this way, it encourages more chewing, which facilitates digestion. When you smell the sweet aroma of pressure-cooking brown rice, you know you are home. And there is no need to worry, since the new pressure cookers are much safer and easier to operate than your grandmother's. When you begin to use one, you will wonder how you ever cooked without it.

ingredients

2 cups short-grain brown rice
3 cups water

2 pinches unrefined sea salt

directions

1. Place the rice in a large bowl. Cover with water.
2. Stir the rice to cause the rice hulls and debris to float to the surface. Pour the debris off the side of the bowl with some of the rinsing water. Pour off the remaining water through a strainer. Repeat until the water is clear.
3. Pour the drained rice into a pressure cooker. Add 3 cups of fresh water and submerge the rice completely. To soften the rice, allow to stand 30-60 minutes before cooking.
4. Add the salt and lock the lid in place. Over high heat, bring up to full pressure.
5. Place a flame tamer under the pressure cooker. Reduce the heat, maintaining high pressure for 45 minutes.
6. Quick-release the pressure by placing the closed pot under cold, running water.
7. After all the pressure has been released, remove the lid. Allow the rice to stand for 5 minutes, covered with a bamboo mat or non-terry cloth towel.
8. Remove the rice with a wet spoon or rice paddle and place it in a rinsed bowl. This prevents the rice from sticking to the bowl and the spoon.
9. Serve sprinkled with *Gomashio*.

variation

• Substitute medium-grain brown rice for short-grain rice.

cook's tips
- An inexpensive rice-washing bowl facilitates step #2 and can be found in Asian markets.
- Do steps #1-3 in the morning. Rice can soak all day before cooking.
- If you do not have enough time to soak the rice, simmer it for 5 minutes in step #3.

pressure cooker

fried
rice

My mentor, Marcia Halpern, taught me this recipe when I first started cooking the macrobiotic way. I have not yet discovered a version that surpasses it in speed or taste.

ingredients

1/2 tsp. toasted sesame oil

4 slices fresh ginger, peeled, optional

6 scallions, cut into 1-inch pieces, on the diagonal

5 cups cooked brown rice

1 TBS. shoyu

1 TBS. mirin, optional

2 celery stalks, cut into 1-inch diagonals

2 TBS. water

directions

1. Heat the oil in a large, nonstick skillet.
2. Sauté the ginger for 2 minutes to flavor the oil. Add the scallions and cook for 1 minute, stirring constantly.
3. Remove the ginger and add the cooked rice. Sauté for about 8 minutes over medium heat, allowing the bottom rice to crisp.
4. Sprinkle 1/2 tablespoon each of the shoyu and mirin over the rice.
5. Flip the rice over with a spatula and crisp the other side. Repeat step #4.
6. Place the celery on top of the rice. Pour 2 tablespoons of water along the outer edges of the rice. Cover and steam for 3 minutes.

variations

- Substitute yellow or red onions for the scallions.
- Add 2 cloves of garlic, cut into matchsticks, in step #2.
- Substitute 1 carrot, cut into matchsticks, for the celery.
- If you love the taste of ginger as much as I do, cut it into matchsticks and do not remove it in step #3.

cook's tips

- 2 cups of raw brown rice yields 5 cups of cooked rice.
- Leftover, cooked rice works wonderfully in this recipe since it dries out in the refrigerator. Dried rice is a better texture than sticky, fresh rice for frying.
- A nonstick surface is ideal for sautéing. Unfortunately, most pans with a nonstick surface will eventually flake off into the food. Glass and stainless steel are poor conductors of heat and not well suited for this purpose. Cast iron is acceptable, but requires considerably more oil during sautéing and care to prevent it from rusting. Luckily, I discovered Scanpan® with its high quality, ceramic and titanium surface which will not flake off.

ginger root

sweet rice with chestnuts and adzuki beans

While studying at the Kushi Institute, a young couple taught me this intriguing recipe. The sweetness of the chestnuts and the red flecks of adzuki beans make this fall dish unforgettable. It is festive, yet easy to serve to company.

ingredients

1/3 cup adzuki beans
1/3 cup dried chestnuts
1 cup sweet brown rice

1 cup short-grain brown rice
3 1/2 cups water
1 6-inch strip kombu

directions

1. The day before, pick over the adzuki beans to remove debris and broken beans. Rinse the beans and place them in a large bowl. Cover with water, 2 inches above the level of beans and soak overnight. See cook's tip, page 129. Soak the chestnuts overnight in another bowl.
2. Place the sweet and short-grain rice in a large bowl. Cover with 2 quarts of water. Stir the rice to cause the rice hulls and debris to float to the surface. Pour the debris off the side of the bowl with some of the rinsing water. Pour off the remaining water through a strainer. Repeat until the water is clear.
3. Pour the drained rice into a pressure cooker. Add 3 1/2 cups of fresh water. Submerge the rice completely. To soften the rice, allow it to stand for 30-60 minutes before cooking.
4. **Meanwhile**, cover the kombu with water and soak it for 5 minutes. Then cut it into 1/2-inch squares and add it to the pot.
5. Drain the chestnuts and rinse the adzuki beans. Add these to the pot and stir.
6. Lock the lid in place. Over high heat, bring up to full pressure.
7. Place a flame tamer under the pot. Reduce the heat, maintaining high pressure for 55 minutes.
8. Quick-release the pressure by placing the closed pot under cold, running water.
9. After all the pressure has been released, remove the lid. Allow the rice to stand for 5 minutes, covered with a bamboo mat or non-terry cloth towel.
10. Remove the rice with a wet spoon or rice paddle and place it in a rinsed bowl. This prevents the rice from sticking to the bowl and the spoon. Serve sprinkled with *Gomashio.*

variation
- Substitute medium-grain brown rice for short-grain.

cook's tips
- If you have difficulty finding sweet brown rice, substitute short-grain brown rice.
- For the most attractive presentation, an additional step is required. After soaking, remove any residual chestnut skins and then cut the chestnuts in half.

dried chestnuts

boiled
brown rice

yield: 4 servings

Brown rice is a mainstay of a vegetarian diet. It is wholesome, easy to prepare and can be transformed into a variety of appealing leftovers. See Beyond Brown Rice, page 112.

ingredients

2 cups brown rice

4 cups water

2 pinches unrefined sea salt

directions

1. Place the rice in a large bowl. Cover with water.
2. Stir the rice to cause the rice hulls and debris to float to the surface. Pour the debris off the side of the bowl with some of the rinsing water. Pour off the remaining water through a strainer. Repeat until the water is clear.
3. Pour the drained rice into a medium pot. Add 4 cups of fresh water. Submerge the rice completely. To soften the rice, allow it to stand for 30-60 minutes before cooking.
4. Add the salt and bring the water to a boil.
5. Place a flame tamer under the pot, then reduce the heat. Simmer, covered, for 1 hour.
6. Remove from the heat. Allow the rice to stand for 5 minutes, covered with a bamboo mat or non-terry cloth towel.
7. Remove the rice with a wet spoon or rice paddle and place it in a rinsed bowl. This prevents the rice from sticking.
8. Serve sprinkled with *Gomashio*.

cook's tips

- An inexpensive rice-washing bowl facilitates step #2 and can be found in Asian markets.
- If you have not soaked the rice, simmer it uncovered for 5 minutes to soften the grains before adding the salt. Then, cook covered for one hour.
- Do steps #1-3 in the morning. Rice can soak all day before cooking.

millet with fresh sweet corn

yield: 4-6 servings

Brighten a summer's day with this simple, yet appealing grain dish. It is bursting with sweet corn, fresh off the cob.

ingredients

5 cups water

2 cups millet

2 pinches unrefined sea salt

2 ears of corn, cut kernels off the cob

directions

1. Bring the water to a boil in a medium pot.
2. **Meanwhile**, rinse the millet through a strainer. Drain.
3. Pour the millet, salt and corn into the pot.
4. Place a flame tamer under the pot and simmer covered for 40 minutes.
5. Remove the millet with a wet spoon or rice paddle to a rinsed bowl. This prevents the millet from sticking to the bowl and the spoon.
6. Serve sprinkled with *Gomashio*.

variation

- For a crunchier texture, add corn at the beginning of step #5. Allow to stand, covered, for 5 minutes to cook the corn.

cook's tips

- To enhance the flavor of domestic millet, dry-roast it in a skillet until it is light golden brown in color, about 8 minutes.
- The flavor of Japanese Kibi millet is superior to the domestic variety. See Mail Order Sources.

quick
and easy polenta

yield: 2 generous servings

The traditional procedure for making polenta is out-of-step with the busy cook of today. Who has time to stand over a pot stirring cornmeal for 45 minutes in order to prevent lumping? In her outstanding cookbook, The Complete Vegetarian Kitchen, *Loma Sass created this modern, express version.*

ingredients

3 1/2 cups water

1/2 tsp. unrefined sea salt

1 cup corn grits

1 tsp. extra-virgin olive oil

1/2 tsp. dried rosemary, optional

directions

1. Bring the water and salt to a boil in a pressure cooker.
2. Gradually sprinkle in the corn grits, stirring continuously with a spoon or whisk.
3. Stir in the oil and rosemary. Lock the lid in place. Over high heat, bring up to full pressure.
4. Place a flame tamer under the pot. Reduce the heat, maintaining high pressure for 5 minutes.
5. Remove the pot from the heat. Allow the pressure to come down naturally for 10 minutes. Quick-release the remaining pressure by placing the closed pot under cold, running water.
6. After all the pressure has been released, remove the lid. Stir the polenta to incorporate any water remaining on top. Allow to stand for 5 minutes to firm.
7. Serve in small bowls, sprinkled with *Gomashio.*

variations

- Substitute dried oregano for rosemary.
- Top with *Un-Tomato Sauce,* page 123.
- Alternatively, pour the cooked polenta into an oiled 9-inch pie plate to cool. When it is firm, cut into wedges. See *Fried Corn Grits,* page 110.

cook's tip
- Use either traditional white corn grits or yellow corn grits for its bright, sunny color.

millet
"mashed potatoes"

yield: 4 generous
servings

This classic macrobiotic dish is reminiscent of mom's mashed potatoes. Serve with a bean dish and greens. It also makes a warming and nourishing breakfast.

ingredients

3 cups water

1 cup millet

1 small onion, diced small

1/2 head cauliflower, cut into
    large chunks

1/4 tsp. unrefined sea salt

1 TBS. fresh parsley, minced,
    to garnish

directions

1. Bring the water to a boil in a pressure cooker.
2. Rinse the millet through a strainer and drain.
3. Add the onion, cauliflower, millet and salt to the pressure cooker. Lock the lid in place. Over high heat, bring up to full pressure.
4. Place a flame tamer under the pot. Reduce the heat, maintaining high pressure for 20 minutes.
5. Quick-release the pressure by placing the closed pot under cold, running water.
6. After all the pressure has been released, remove the lid.
7. Mash the millet in the pot with a potato masher.
8. Serve warm, garnished with parsley.

variation

•   For added pizzazz, add 2 teaspoons caraway seeds in step #3.

cook's tips

•   If using a saucepan rather than a pressure cooker, add an extra 1/2 cup of water to allow for escaping steam. Simmer, covered, for 45 minutes.
•   For a smoother texture, put the millet through a food mill in step #7 instead of mashing it.

grains

fried corn grits
with green onions

yield: 4 servings

If you have leftover cooked corn grits, this pleasing dish can be made in less than 5 minutes.

ingredients

1 cup corn grits
3 cups water
1/4 tsp. unrefined sea salt

1/2 tsp. unrefined corn oil
2 scallions, cut into 1-inch
strips on the diagonal

directions

1. Mix the corn grits with 1 1/2 cups of water in a large bowl. Allow to stand for 5 minutes.
2. **Meanwhile**, bring the other 1 1/2 cups of water to a boil in a medium pot.
3. Pour the soaking corn grits (with the soaking water) and salt into the pot.
4. Simmer uncovered until the corn grits become a thick porridge, about 5 minutes. Stir continuously.
5. Spoon into a rinsed, shallow dish. Cover and refrigerate until firm, about 1 hour.
6. Cut the polenta into squares or triangles.
7. Heat the oil in a large, nonstick skillet. Sauté the scallions until wilted, about 1 minute.
8. Move the scallions to one side of the skillet. Sprinkle a few more drops of oil in the cleared space. Add the corn pieces to the pan and sauté until golden brown on both sides.
9. Serve garnished with the sautéed scallions.

variation

• Top with a spoonful of *Savory Tofu Spread*, page 196. It is delicious!

cook's tips

• Make a double batch of corn grits in the morning. You can eat it for breakfast and then have leftovers to make this recipe the next day.
• Instead of frying, simply reheat leftover corn grits in a steamer. Serve sprinkled with *Gomashio*.

mochi

Mochi is sweet brown rice that has been steamed, pounded and laid in pans to dry. It is then vacuum-sealed and sent frozen to natural foods stores. Mochi is a whole grain which cooks in less than 15 minutes, making it excellent for breakfast or as a snack. Moreover, this versatile food can be melted over lasagna, made into waffles or used as croutons in salad or soup.

ingredients
   1/2 package mochi

directions
1. Preheat a large, nonstick skillet.
2. **Meanwhile**, cut the mochi into strips, squares or triangles.
3. Add the mochi to the skillet. No oil is necessary.
4. Cover and cook over low heat until the pieces puff up and the bottom turns a golden color, about 8 minutes.
5. Turn the mochi over. Cook covered until the bottom turns golden, an additional 6 minutes.
6. Eat immediately or it will become too hard to chew! If it does dry out, it can be steamed back into soft submission.

variations
- To make a chewy pancake, cut the mochi into 4 squares. Cut each square lengthwise, dividing it into 2 thin pieces. Cook as above, with the pieces touching each other. The edges will run together to form a pancake. You can enjoy these guilt-free, wholesome pancakes as often as you like.
- Grate mochi straight from the package. Sprinkle over casseroles, lasagna and other covered baked dishes. It will melt like cheese.
- Serve cooked cubes in soups or salads in place of croutons.
- Cut mochi into 3-inch squares. Bake in an oiled waffle iron until the waffle is firm and easily pulls away from the waffle iron, about 5 minutes.

beyond
brown rice

Each grain has its own nutrients, flavor and texture. For diversity, add other grains when cooking brown rice. Seeds, herbs and nuts also add a surprising touch.

brown rice variations
Cook other grains with rice in a 3:1 ratio. This translates to 1 1/2 cups of rice with 1/2 cup of another grain. Try the following:

amaranth	kasha
barley	millet
bulgur	quinoa
corn grits	sweet brown rice
couscous	teff
Job's tears	wild rice

grain variations
For a tasty change, try these variations with 2 cups of uncooked grain.

Sauté 1 small onion, diced, before adding the grain and water to the pot.

Cook with 1/2 teaspoon dried spice or herb like saffron or rosemary. Alternatively, add 1 tablespoon of fresh herbs after cooking.

Cook with 2-3 tablespoons of toasted sesame seeds.

Cook with a 2-inch piece of kombu instead of salt.

Cook with 1-2 sliced garlic cloves.

Cook with 2-3 slices of fresh gingerroot.

Top cooked grain with *Savory Sunflower Seeds*, page 171.

leftover brown rice variations

   Brown Rice Salad, page 91
   Sesame Rice Patties, page 192
   Rice Pudding, page 216
   Fried Rice, page 102
   Stir-Fried Rice and Vegetables, page 189
   Stir-Fried Rice with cooked greens
   Rice with *Creamy Pumpkin Seed Sauce*, page 187
   Rice with *Tahini Sauce*, page 184
   Rice with *Peanut Sauce*, pages 185 or 186
   Rice with *Chickpea Sauce*, page 182
   Rice with *Vegetable Sauce*, page 188
   Rice with *Curry Sauce*, page 190
   Rice with *Miso-Tahini Sauce*, page 183
   Rice with *Tofu Dressing*, page 89
   Add to *Moist and Hearty Oatmeal Muffins*, page 77
   Add to *Cornbread*, page 78
   A thick soup can be used as a sauce when ladled over rice.
   Rice with salad dressing, pages 88, 89, 159, 162, 164
   Add brown rice to any soup.
   Reheat brown rice in a steamer.
   Cook rice into a soft porridge for breakfast by adding a little
      extra water and umeboshi paste.
   Make a creamy soup, by blending 25% of the soup with 1 cup
      of cooked rice.
   Press rice into rice molds, available from Asian grocers.
   Stuff rice into baked squash.
   Fill a burrito with rice and leftover vegetables or beans.

pasta

pleasurable
pasta

If you are a busy person, this chapter is for you. Simple, quick and nutritious, a pasta meal can be put together in less than twenty minutes. Almost all pastas are an excellent source of complex carbohydrates, fuel to energize your daily activities.

While whole wheat pasta may be the healthiest choice, it is too heavy for most people to truly enjoy. I prefer wholesome noodles made from lighter whole-grain flours, such as artichoke, corn, kamut, quinoa, rice and buckwheat. Each has a distinct color, flavor and shape. Experiment to discover your favorites. Finally, semolina pasta, made from refined durum wheat, is the most popular, accepted and beloved of them all. My favorite brand is the readily available, DeCecco®. Although semolina pasta is not made from whole grain, it is fine to eat several times a week if you are eating whole grains on a daily basis.

Trendy Italian restaurants are everywhere, but I rarely patronize them. For a fraction of the cost, you can create a bistro in your own home. Simply light a candle, play soothing music and serve pasta in elegant dishes. Whether you are in the mood for *Lasagna* or *Instant Macaroni and "Cheese,"* these homemade pastas are sure to please. See Last-Minute Meals for more noodle dishes.

cook's tips
- The easiest way to cook noodles is in a pasta pot. It has a colander within the pot. Noodles are cooked in the colander and are easily removed and rinsed without breaking up. This is especially true for delicate lasagna noodles.
- Allow 4-8 ounces of dried pasta per person for a main meal (yield: 2-4 cups cooked).
- Experiment with a variety of pasta shapes such as farfalle (bow ties), fusilli (spirals) and penne (diagonally-cut tubes).
- To prevent clumping during cooking, allow 5 quarts of water for each pound (16 ounces) of noodles. A rolling boil works best.
- It is unnecessary to salt the water.

- Most noodle packages recommend a range of cooking time. Test the pasta for doneness at the shortest recommended cooking time. It should be al dente: tender, but firm. When cut, the noodle will be the same color throughout.
- Instead of adding oil to the pot, stir the pasta several times during cooking.
- Prewarm a large serving platter by placing it over the cooking pasta near the end of cooking time.
- Just before serving, prewarm individual bowls or plates by pouring hot water in them.
- Once cooked, immediately drain the pasta to prevent overcooking.
- Do not rinse the pasta after draining or it will become slick and sauce will not adhere to it. To prevent clumping, toss it immediately with the sauce. The exception is baked noodle dishes like macaroni and lasagna. For these dishes, rinse the noodles after boiling to prevent overcooking.
- Japanese pasta, such as udon, tends to be salty. Rinse through a colander to remove excess salt. Eden® Brown Rice Udon Noodles are my favorite.
- Store leftover sauce and noodles in separate glass jars in the refrigerator. To reheat the noodles, place them in a colander and pour boiling water over them.
- To add an authentic cheese flavor when serving pasta, sprinkle on Soyco® Lite & Less Grated Parmesan Cheese Alternative. Be aware, however, that this contains 30% casein, which is a skim milk powder product.

spaghetti with
mock marinara sauce

yield: 4 servings

Spaghetti is an American staple. I use Un-Tomato Sauce with its delicious blend of vegetables, as an alternative to traditional marinara sauce. Serve with a large salad and crusty sourdough bread, drizzled with olive oil.

ingredients

1 pound semolina spaghetti

3 cups *Un-Tomato Sauce*, page 123

directions

1. Fill a large stock pot with 5 quarts of water and bring it to a boil.
2. Cook the spaghetti until al dente, according to package directions.
3. Gently pour the cooked spaghetti into a colander in the sink.
4. **Meanwhile,** heat the *Un-Tomato Sauce* in a medium saucepan.
5. Place the spaghetti on individual plates and pour a generous 1/2 cup of sauce over each serving.

variations

- To please meat eaters, add crumbled *Tempeh Bacon*, page 143 or White Wave® Sloppy Joe Tempeh to the sauce.
- For a heartier dish, add cooked beans.

cook's tips

- Prepare *Un-Tomato Sauce* several days or weeks ahead and freeze in canning jars.
- To add an authentic cheese flavor, sprinkle Soyco® Lite & Less Grated Parmesan Cheese Alternative on top. Be aware, however, that this contains 30% casein, which is a skim milk powder product.
- Tomatoes can aggravate arthritis. However, if this is not a concern for you, substitute organic spaghetti sauce for the *Un-Tomato Sauce*.

spaghetti with gingered broccoli

yield: 4 servings

When visiting a friend, we decided to cook dinner together. All I found in her refrigerator was broccoli with some leftover, cooked spaghetti. This simple, but tasty dish came together quickly and has become a favorite of mine ever since.

ingredients

1 pound semolina spaghetti
1 bunch broccoli, stems peeled and diagonally sliced, florets separated
2 tsp. toasted sesame oil

1 4-inch piece fresh ginger, peeled and cut into matchsticks
3 large garlic cloves, minced
1 TBS. shoyu, or more to taste

directions

1. Fill a large stock pot with 5 quarts of water and bring it to a boil.
2. Cook the spaghetti until al dente, according to package directions.
3. Gently pour the cooked spaghetti into a colander placed in the sink. Rinse until cold and leave it in the colander.
4. **Meanwhile,** steam the broccoli until barely fork-tender, about 2 minutes. Set aside.
5. Heat the oil in a large, nonstick skillet or wok. Sauté the ginger and garlic for 1 minute.
6. Add the spaghetti and sauté until lightly golden, 3-5 minutes. Season with shoyu, to taste.
7. Add the broccoli and mix gently. Cover and heat through before serving, about 2 minutes.

variations
- Substitute asparagus for broccoli.
- For extra pizzazz, add 1/4 teaspoon hot sesame oil in step #6.

cook's tip
- To prevent shoyu from burning, sprinkle it on the food rather than on the pan.

kasha varnishkas

This traditional Jewish dish originates from the cold regions of Eastern Europe. Made with kasha and bow tie pasta, it is a hearty entrée that will warm you, too.

ingredients

8 ounces bow ties (farfalle)
2 tsp. unrefined corn oil
1 large onion, diced small
2 cups boiling water
1/4 tsp. unrefined sea salt

1 cup kasha (toasted buckwheat groats)
2 TBS. shoyu
1 TBS. fresh parsley, minced, to garnish

directions

1. Fill a large stock pot with 4 quarts of water and bring it to a boil.
2. Cook the bow ties until al dente, according to package directions.
3. Gently pour the cooked bow ties into a colander placed in the sink. Rinse the pasta until cold and leave it in the colander.
4. Heat the oil in a large, nonstick skillet. Sauté the onion over medium heat until golden brown, about 8 minutes. Leave the onions in the skillet, off the heat.
5. **Meanwhile**, combine 2 cups of boiling water, salt and kasha in the large stock pot. Simmer covered for 10 minutes.
6. Just before serving, pour boiling water over the bow ties to reheat them. Shake the colander to remove excess water.
7. Add the reheated bow ties, onion and shoyu to the hot kasha in the stock pot. Mix gently. Serve immediately, garnished with parsley.

variations

- For a nuttier flavor, substitute sesame oil for corn oil.
- For a spicier dish, substitute hot sesame oil for corn oil.

cook's tips

- Kasha lends a nutty taste when cooked with *Oatmeal*, page 40.
- Use a nonstick Dutch Oven to eliminate the need for the nonstick skillet. One less pan to clean!

instant
macaroni and "cheese"

yield: 4 servings

Try this nourishing rendition of a home-cooked classic. This comfort food will become a regular for anyone who tastes it!

ingredients

12 ounces corn macaroni
1 pound soft tofu
1/4 cup tahini
2 TBS. barley miso

1/4 cup boiling water
1 scallion, thinly sliced, to garnish

directions

1. Fill a large stock pot with 5 quarts of water and bring it to a boil.
2. Cook the macaroni until al dente, according to package directions.
3. **Meanwhile,** place the tofu in a strainer and submerge it into the boiling pasta water for 4 minutes to refresh it. Set aside.
4. Gently pour the cooked macaroni into a colander placed in the sink. Rinse the pasta until cold and leave it in the colander.
5. Mash together the tofu, tahini and miso in a suribachi. Slowly add enough boiling water to make a pourable sauce.
6. Just before serving, pour boiling water over the macaroni to reheat it. Shake the colander to remove excess water.
7. Pour the macaroni into a large serving bowl. Add the sauce and serve garnished with scallion.

variation

• Substitute artichoke macaroni for corn macaroni.

cook's tip
• Instead of a suribachi, use a food processor, fitted with a metal blade, to purée the sauce.

lasagna

yield: 9 generous servings

Typical vegetarian lasagna contains too much fatty cheese and acidic tomato sauce for my taste. For a more healthful, yet delicious version, use this recipe with its quick, low-fat tofu "cheese" and red sauce, made without tomatoes!

to assemble and cook

1. Make 1 recipe of *Un-Tomato Sauce*. This can be made ahead of time. See cook's tips. You can substitute organic tomato sauce for the *Un-Tomato Sauce*.
2. Make 1 recipe of *Tofu-Onion "Cheese,"* page 124. Set aside.
3. Preheat the oven to 350°F.
4. **Meanwhile,** fill a large stock pot with 5 quarts of water and bring it to a boil. Add 12 semolina lasagna noodles (3⁄4 pound). Cook until al dente, according to package directions. Carefully pour off the hot noodle water and fill it with cool water. Gently swish the noodles until cool. This prevents them from overcooking and breaking up. Carefully drain them, then pat them dry.
5. Spread 1 1⁄2 cups of *Un-Tomato Sauce* in a 9 x 13 baking dish.
6. Place 3 noodles lengthwise on top of the sauce.
7. Evenly distribute 1⁄4 of the *Tofu-Onion "Cheese"* over the noodles.
8. Repeat steps #6, #7, #8 three more times.
9. Pour 1 cup of the *Un-Tomato Sauce* over the last *Tofu-Onion "Cheese"* layer.
10. Optional: sprinkle 1⁄2 package of mochi, thinly sliced, over the sauce. For more about mochi, see pages 111 and 230.
11. Cover the mochi with the remaining sauce. This helps the mochi melt.
12. Bake covered for 30-40 minutes. A cookie sheet placed upside down over the baking dish makes a good cover. Uncover and cook 10 minutes longer.
13. Allow to stand for 5 minutes before serving.

cook's tip
- To add an authentic cheese flavor, sprinkle Soyco® Lite & Less Grated Parmesan Cheese Alternative on top of each serving. Be aware, however, that this contains 30% casein, which is a skim milk powder product.

un-tomato sauce

ingredients

1/2 tsp. extra-virgin olive oil

2 jumbo onions, cut into
large chunks

6 garlic cloves, peeled and cut
in 1/2

2 pounds carrots, cut into
large chunks

2 small beets, peeled and cut
into 1/4's

2 bay leaves

2 tsp. dried basil

1 1/4 tsp. dried oregano

1/8 tsp. dried thyme

3 TBS. barley miso, or
more to taste

1/4 cup umeboshi paste

directions

1. Heat the oil in a large stock pot. Sauté the onions until translucent, about 5 minutes. Add the garlic and sauté for 1 minute.
2. Add the carrots, beets and bay leaves. Add water to 1 inch below the surface of the vegetables. In this case, less is more!
3. Bring to a boil. Simmer covered for 1 hour, adding the basil, oregano and thyme during the last 15 minutes of cooking time.
4. **Remove the bay leaves**. Pour off the broth and reserve. Remove half of the beets and set aside.
5. Place the vegetables, miso and umeboshi paste in a blender. Blend, adding just enough broth to reach the desired consistency. Add the beets, one at a time, to simulate the color of tomato sauce.

variation

- Substitute organic tomato sauce for the *Un-Tomato Sauce* if you are not concerned about nightshade vegetables (see page 15).

cook's tips

- Place bay leaves in a mesh tea ball so that you can remove them easily before blending the sauce.
- Ground oregano creates a smoother sauce than the common leaf variety.
- Use boiling water in step #2 to save time.
- Prepare *Un-Tomato Sauce* several days or weeks ahead of time and freeze in canning jars. Use for spaghetti, pizza and soup.

tofu
onion "cheese"

ingredients

1/2 tsp. extra-virgin olive oil	1 pinch dried basil
3 onions, diced small	1/8 tsp. unrefined sea salt
2 TBS. water	1 pinch nutmeg
2 garlic cloves, minced	1 pinch dried oregano
1 pound soft tofu	1 cup plain mochi, grated or
2 TBS. tahini	thinly sliced, optional

directions

1. Heat the oil in a large, nonstick skillet. Sauté the onions until translucent, about 5 minutes.
2. Add the water and garlic. Cook covered to soften onions, about 10 minutes.
3. **Meanwhile**, mash the tofu in a suribachi or large bowl.
4. Add the tahini, basil, salt, nutmeg, oregano and 3/4 cup mochi to the tofu. Mash thoroughly. Reserve 1/4 cup mochi for the top layer of lasagna.
5. Add the onions to the tofu mixture. Adjust seasonings to taste.

variation

- Substitute 2 cups of chopped, cooked kale or collards or winter squash, etc. for the onions.

notes

beans, tofu and tempeh

bountiful beans
tofu and tempeh

The legume family includes beans, lentils, peanuts and split peas. All of these seeds grow in pods. Generally, they are all referred to as beans. By whatever name, they are hearty, nourishing and versatile. They make rich and luscious soups, sandwich spreads and cracker dips. They add texture, fiber and protein to casseroles and salads.

As if this were not enough, these little guys are packed with nutrients and health benefits. A mere half cup of cooked beans provides 25% of the daily requirement of fiber, 30% of folic acid, 15% of iron and 7 grams of protein. In fact, beans provide twice as much protein as grains. Moreover, this same half cup of beans can lower cholesterol and blood pressure, control blood sugar levels and maintain healthy intestines.

It is no wonder that most countries have a traditional bean dish as a nutritious and economical staple:

Cuba: black beans
India: split pea dahl
Indonesia: tempeh
Italy: cannellini beans
Japan: adzuki beans and tofu
Middle East: chickpea hummus and lentil soup
New Orleans: Cajun red beans and rice
U.S.A., Native Americans: kidney beans
U.S.A., New England: baked navy beans
U.S.A., southern regions: black-eyed peas

Soy foods, made from the humble soybean, have recently been hailed as the new wonder food. Although soybeans contain more protein than other beans, they are difficult to digest. Because of this, soybeans are transformed into fermented foods including tempeh, miso paste, and tamari or soy sauce. See the Glossary for more details. Tofu is also derived from soybeans and is particularly praised for its high calcium content. Some people think of tofu as a bland, tasteless food. But this is actually a cook's friend. Tofu will take on the flavor of whatever seasonings are used, allowing you to create scrumptious dishes. Examples of simple and appetizing tofu recipes are *Savory Tofu Spread* and *Tofu Dressing*.

Do not omit beans from your diet due to lack of time or planning. Natural foods stores now offer organic canned beans that are even cooked with kombu, making them more digestible. They are as low in calories and sodium as home-cooked beans. Rinse them for optimum flavor. While they may not be as delectable as your own, they are handy for last-minute meals.

With all these good qualities, you would think that everyone would be bean crazy. Yet, there is a drawback that no one wants to mention in public, flatulence. Why does this happen? Beans contain indigestible complex sugars, oliogosaccharides, which feed harmless intestinal bacteria. Before long, fermentation takes place and these bacteria emit gas, causing us do the same. Luckily, there are a multitude of remedies for this problem. Since none is a cure-all, try them alone or in combination to see what works for you.

cook's tips

- Purchase beans from a store with a high turnover to ensure they will be fresh. Beans dry out and become tough if stored too long. They are best if used within six months.
- Store beans in a cool place in non-plastic containers like paper bags or glass jars. Plastic containers will eventually impart a chemical taste to the beans.
- Before using, pick over beans to remove debris, small pebbles, clumps of dirt and broken beans.
- To wash beans, place them in a bowl. Cover with water. Rub beans between your hands and rinse. Repeat until rinse water appears clear. Pour rinse water over a white plate to make this easier to see.
- **Overnight soak:** cover with water, two inches above the level of dried beans. **Speedy soak:** place the beans in the pot you will be using to cook them. Cover with water, two inches above the level of the dried beans. Cover the pot and bring to a boil. Turn off the heat and allow to stand for one hour.

- After soaking, pour the beans through a colander to drain off the soaking water. Thoroughly rinse off the foam residue.
- Do not fill the pressure cooker more than half full when cooking beans. This prevents the pressure valve from clogging.
- To prevent beans from boiling over while cooking, keep the lid ajar.
- Do not add salt, miso, tamari, vinegar, citrus juice, mirin or tomatoes until the beans are soft. Adding salty and acidic ingredients will not allow beans to soften. When cooking beans in a pressure cooker, add these ingredients after the pressure has been released.
- Freeze leftover cooked beans in small portions so they can be a quick addition to any meal.
- **Remedies for gastric distress:**

  Soak beans, which eliminates 75% of indigestible oliogosaccharides (see above).

  Use a skimmer or slotted spoon to remove foam from the surface during the initial cooking: 5 minutes in an uncovered pressure cooker; 15 minutes in an uncovered stock pot.

  Add kombu sea vegetable to the cooking beans, which not only makes beans softer and more digestible, but adds calcium and other essential minerals to the dish.

  Add to the bean pot, aromatic herbs and spices such as bay leaves, ginger, cumin and curry.

  Begin by eating small, but steady servings of beans. Always chew your beans well.

  For a particularly delicate digestive tract, try eating beans only with vegetables. Avoid combining beans with fruit or grains. After soaking, boil beans 5 minutes and discard the water. Repeat two times before proceeding with the recommended cooking method.

  When all else fails, take Yes to Beans® with the first bite.

boiled chickpeas

If you do not have a pressure cooker, you can boil chickpeas. I do not recommended this for the busy cook as they require a minimum of three hours to become tender.

ingredients

2 cups dried chickpeas

7 cups water

1 6-inch strip kombu

3/4 tsp. unrefined sea salt

directions

1. The day before, pick over the chickpeas to remove debris and broken beans. Rinse the beans and place them in a large bowl. Cover with water, 2 inches above the level of beans and soak overnight. See cook's tip, page 129.
2. Rinse the chickpeas through a colander, then add them to a large stock pot with 7 cups of fresh water.
3. Bring to a boil, then cook uncovered for 15 minutes, skimming off foam from the surface.
4. **Meanwhile,** cover the kombu with water and soak for 5 minutes.
5. Cut the kombu into 1/2-inch squares and add it to the pot.
6. Place a flame tamer under the pot. Simmer with the lid slightly ajar, about 3 hours.
7. Check every 30 minutes. Add more water as needed to barely cover the beans.
8. When the beans are tender, add the salt. Simmer 10 minutes longer to cook the salt.

variation

- Substitute other beans for chickpeas. See The Bean Cooking Chart, page 250.

cook's tips

- *Pressure-Cooked Chickpeas* or organic, canned chickpeas are great time savers.
- Buy a pressure cooker!

pressure-cooked chickpeas

yield: 3 cups

Pressure-cooked chickpeas are a real time-saver. These creamy beans can be used to make Hummus-in-a-Hurry or added to soups and salads for extra protein.

ingredients

1 cup dried chickpeas

3 cups water

1 6-inch strip kombu

3⁄4 tsp. unrefined sea salt

directions

1. The day before, pick over the chickpeas to remove debris and broken beans. Rinse the beans and place them in a large bowl. Cover with water, 2 inches above the level of beans and soak overnight. See cook's tip, page 129.
2. Rinse the chickpeas through a colander, then add them to a pressure cooker with 3 cups of fresh water.
3. Bring to a boil. Cook uncovered for 5 minutes, skimming off foam from the surface.
4. **Meanwhile,** cover the kombu with water and soak for 5 minutes.
5. Cut the kombu into 1⁄2-inch squares and add it to the pot. Lock the lid in place. Over high heat, bring up to full pressure.
6. Place a flame tamer under the pot. Reduce the heat, maintaining high pressure for 25 minutes.
7. Quick-release the pressure by placing the closed pot under cold, running water.
8. After all the pressure has been released, remove the lid. If the beans are not tender, simmer until they are, then add the salt. Close the lid and allow to stand for 10 minutes, off the heat.

variations:

• Boiling chickpeas, page 131, is an option, but since they require a minimum of 3 hours to become tender, it is not recommended for the busy cook.
• Substitute other beans for chickpeas. See The Bean Cooking Chart, page 250.

cook's tips

- Do not fill the pressure cooker more than half full when cooking beans. This will prevent the pressure valve from clogging.
- Freeze cooked beans in small portions so they can be a quick addition to other dishes.

pressure cooker

macro
baked beans

A potluck favorite is baked beans. Bring this dish to your next gathering and watch it disappear.

ingredients

4 cups dried navy beans	2 medium carrots, cut into 1/2 rounds
8 cups water	
1 12-inch strip kombu	2 stalks celery, diced small, optional
1 tsp. unrefined sea salt	
1/3 cup barley miso	4 garlic cloves, minced
1/4 tsp. canola oil	3 TBS. prepared natural mustard
1 large onion, diced small	
	1/2 cup barley malt syrup

directions

1. The day before, pick over the navy beans to remove debris and broken beans. Rinse the beans and place them in a large bowl. Cover with water, 2 inches above the level of beans and soak overnight. See cook's tip, page 129.
2. Rinse the beans through a colander, then add them to a pressure cooker with 8 cups of fresh water.
3. Bring to a boil. Cook uncovered for 5 minutes, skimming off foam from the surface.
4. **Meanwhile**, cover the kombu with water and soak for 5 minutes.
5. Cut the kombu into 1/2-inch squares and add it to the pot. Lock the lid in place. Over high heat, bring up to full pressure.
6. Place a flame tamer under the pot. Reduce the heat, maintaining high pressure for 6 minutes.
7. Quick-release the pressure by placing the closed pot under cold, running water.
8. After all the pressure has been released, remove the lid. If the beans are not tender, simmer until they are, then add the salt and miso. Close the lid and allow to stand for 10 minutes, off the heat.
9. Drain the beans into a bowl, reserving the cooking water. Pour the beans into a baking dish and set aside.

10. **Meanwhile**, heat the oil in a nonstick skillet. Sauté the onion until translucent, about 5 minutes. Move the onion to one side of the skillet. Sprinkle a few drops of oil in the cleared space. Add the carrots, then the celery and sauté until tender. Add the garlic and sauté for 1 minute.
11. **Meanwhile,** preheat the oven to 350°F.
12. Add 2 tablespoons of water to the skillet and cover. Steam until the vegetables are soft, 3-5 minutes.
13. Add the vegetables, mustard and barley malt syrup to the beans. Stir gently. Add the reserved bean-cooking water to barely cover the beans. Bake uncovered until golden around the edges, 1 1/2-2 hours.

cook's tip
- Instead of cooking beans in a pressure cooker, simmer them uncovered in a large stock pot for about 1 1/2 hours, until tender. Use a flame tamer and skim off foam from the surface during the first 15 minutes of cooking time.

chef's knife

chili
sans carne

Who says that chili without meat can't be fabulous? This dish will convince even skeptics that vegetarian chili measures up.

ingredients

1 cup dried kidney beans	1/2 tsp. mild chili powder
2 cups water	1 TBS. barley miso
1 6-inch strip kombu	1 1/2 TBS. barley malt syrup
1/2 tsp. canola oil	3 cups *Un-Tomato Sauce,*
1 large onion, diced small	page 123
1 large celery stalk, diced small	2 TBS. scallions, thinly sliced,
6 garlic cloves, minced	to garnish
1/2 tsp. ground cumin	

directions

1. The day before, pick over the kidney beans to remove debris and broken beans. Rinse the beans and place them in a large bowl. Cover with water, 2 inches above the level of beans and soak overnight. See cook's tip, page 129.
2. Rinse the beans through a colander, then add them to a pressure cooker with 2 cups of fresh water.
3. Bring to a boil. Cook uncovered for 5 minutes, skimming off foam from the surface.
4. **Meanwhile**, cover the kombu with water and soak for 5 minutes.
5. Cut the kombu into 1/2-inch squares and add it to the pot. Lock the lid in place. Over high heat, bring up to full pressure.
6. Place a flame tamer under the pot. Reduce the heat, maintaining high pressure for 12 minutes.
7. Quick-release the pressure by placing the closed pot under cold, running water.
8. After all the pressure has been released, remove the lid. If the beans are tender, set aside. If not, replace the lid and simmer until the beans are tender.
9. **Meanwhile,** heat the oil in a large, nonstick skillet. Sauté the onion until translucent, about 5 minutes. Move the onion to one side of the skillet. Sprinkle a few more drops of oil in the cleared space. Add the celery, garlic, cumin and chili powder. Sauté for 1 minute. Transfer to the pressure cooker and stir gently.

lenore's natural cuisine

136

10. In a small bowl, whisk together the miso and barley malt syrup. Add the mixture to the *Un-Tomato Sauce* and add it to the pressure cooker. Stir.
11. Simmer with the lid ajar to heat and marry the flavors, 20-30 minutes.
12. Serve garnished with scallion.

variations
- Substitute other beans for the kidney beans.
- Substitute organic tomato sauce for the *Un-Tomato Sauce*.
- Add 1 cup of seitan, cut into 1/2-inch cubes, in step #11.
- Add 1/2 pound of crumbled *Tempeh "Bacon,"* page 143, in step #11.

cook's tips
- This dish tastes even better the next day, after the flavors have time to marry.
- Cook extra chili since it freezes so well. It makes a convenient meal when you are in a time crunch. Defrost in the refrigerator overnight.
- Serve with rice, *Double Corn Muffins*, page 76, or *Cornbread*, page 78. Add a fresh *Leafy Green Salad*, page 84, to complete the meal.

garlic

southwestern black-eyed peas

yield: 2 1/2 cups

These black-eyed peas are great as a side dish with wholesome bread, steamed vegetables or a salad. They also make a luscious filling for a Mexican-style burrito.

ingredients

1 cup dried black-eyed peas	1/2 tsp. ground cumin
3 cups water	3/4 tsp. mild chili powder
1 6-inch strip kombu	2 TBS. shoyu, or more to taste

directions

1. The day before, pick over the black-eyed peas to remove debris. Rinse the peas and place them in a large bowl. Cover with water, 2 inches above the level of peas and soak overnight. See cook's tip, page 129.
2. Rinse the peas through a colander, then add them to a pressure cooker with 3 cups of fresh water.
3. Bring to a boil. Cook uncovered for 5 minutes, skimming off foam from the surface.
4. **Meanwhile,** cover the kombu with water and soak for 5 minutes.
5. Cut the kombu into 1/2-inch squares. Add the kombu squares, cumin and chili powder to the pot and lock the lid in place. Over high heat, bring up to full pressure.
6. Place a flame tamer under the pot. Reduce the heat, maintaining high pressure for 8 minutes.
7. Quick-release the pressure by placing the closed pot under cold, running water.
8. After all the pressure has been released, remove the lid. If the peas are not tender, simmer until they are, then add the shoyu.

tofu
pate'

Thanks to Margaret Lawson for this recipe from her wonderful book, The Naturally Healthy Gourmet. *It is a gourmet appetizer when spread on crackers or toast.*

ingredients

2 TBS. barley miso

1 garlic clove, minced

1/4 cup tahini

1 pound firm tofu

1/4 cup fresh parsley, minced

3 TBS. scallions, thinly sliced

directions

1. Preheat the oven to 350°F.
2. Thoroughly mash together the miso, garlic and tahini in a bowl.
3. Rinse the tofu, pat it dry, then crumble it into the bowl. Add the parsley and scallions. Mix well.
4. Press the mixture into an oiled 8-inch square baking dish. Bake uncovered until golden brown, about 25 minutes.

cook's tip

• A suribachi makes step #2 easier.

parsley

millet-tofu casserole

This soothing, easy-to-digest casserole warms and comforts. Serve with crunchy, steamed broccoli for a pleasing color contrast.

ingredients

1 pound firm tofu

2 TBS. shoyu, or more to taste

1/4 cup water

1/2 tsp. sesame oil

1 large onion, diced small

2 stalks celery, minced

2 cups millet

5 cups boiling water

2 pinches unrefined sea salt

1/3 cup tahini

2 medium carrots, shredded

1/2 cup fresh parsley, minced

1/2 TBS. dried sage

directions

1. Rinse the tofu and pat it dry. Crumble it into a bowl. Add the shoyu and 1/4 cup of water. Marinate for 30 minutes.
2. **Meanwhile**, heat the oil in a large, nonstick skillet. Sauté the onion until golden brown, about 10 minutes. Transfer the onion to a large stock pot.
3. Add the celery, carrots, millet, boiling water and salt to the pot. Place a flame tamer under it. Simmer covered for 25 minutes.
4. **Meanwhile**, preheat the oven to 350°F.
5. Add the tofu, marinade, tahini, parsley and sage to the millet mixture. Stir gently.
6. Spoon the mixture into an oiled casserole dish. Smooth the top with a wet spatula.
7. Bake uncovered until golden brown, 20-30 minutes.

variations

- Use 1 cup of millet and 1 cup of quinoa instead of 2 cups of millet.
- For a richer taste, add 1/2 cup of tahini instead of 1/3 cup.

cook's tip
- If you use a Dutch oven to sauté and cook all the ingredients, it will make clean up faster.

baked
marinated tofu

yield: 4 servings

Marinating and baking tofu makes it delectable. It can then be added to stir-fries, salads and sandwiches, or eaten as a hot or cold snack. This recipe has been adapted from Vicki Chelf's recipe in her wonderful cookbook, Cooking with the Right Side of the Brain.

ingredients

1 pound extra-firm tofu
1 1/2 tsp. minced and peeled
    fresh ginger
1/4 tsp. toasted sesame oil

2 garlic cloves, thinly sliced
3 TBS. shoyu
3 TBS. water

directions

1. Rinse the tofu and pat it dry. Cut it into six 1/2-inch slabs. Place the tofu in a baking dish which has sides at least 2 inches high.
2. Whisk together the remaining ingredients in a small bowl. Pour the mixture over the tofu and marinate for 20-30 minutes.
3. Pour off the marinade, into a bowl, leaving the tofu in the baking dish. Set aside.
4. **Meanwhile**, preheat the oven to 375°F. Pour enough of the reserved marinade over each piece of tofu to cover. Bake for 15 minutes.
5. Spoon more marinade over the tofu and bake for 15 minutes.
6. Turn over each piece of tofu. Spoon the remaining marinade over the tofu. Continue to bake until golden brown and all the marinade is absorbed, about 15 minutes.
7. Baked tofu keeps refrigerated 5-7 days.

cook's tips

- If you cannot find extra-firm tofu, do the following: after rinsing the tofu, compress it in a pickle press or between two cutting boards for 20 minutes to expel excess water. This process helps the tofu retain its texture and allows more of the marinade flavor to be absorbed.
- Do not marinate tofu longer than 1 hour or it will become too soft and lose flavor.

sautéed
sesame tofu

Transform plain brown rice or noodles into a gourmet treat with the help of this crunchy tofu recipe.

marinade
- 2 tsp. toasted sesame oil
- 2 TBS. shoyu
- 1 TBS. water
- 1 TBS. brown rice vinegar
- 2 TBS. brown rice syrup
- 1/2 tsp. red pepper flakes, optional
- 1 TBS. scallions, thinly sliced
- 1 1/2 TBS. fresh cilantro, minced, optional

tofu, etc.
- 1 pound firm tofu
- 1 tsp. toasted sesame oil
- 1 TBS. sesame seeds, toasted, to garnish
- 2 TBS. fresh cilantro, minced to garnish, optional

directions
1. Combine the marinade ingredients in a small bowl.
2. Rinse the tofu, pat it dry, then cut it into 1/2-inch cubes or triangles.
3. Place the tofu pieces in a medium baking dish. Pour half the marinade over the tofu. Marinate for 30 minutes, basting several times.
4. Pour off the marinade. Set aside.
5. Heat the oil in a large, nonstick skillet. Add the tofu and sauté until golden brown, about 5 minutes on each side.
6. Add the marinade to the pan. Simmer until bubbling and hot, stirring occasionally. Taste and adjust the flavor. If too salty, add more brown rice syrup.
7. Serve the tofu and sauce over brown rice or cooked noodles. Garnish with sesame seeds and cilantro.

variation
- Substitute light sesame oil for the toasted sesame oil.

tempeh "bacon"

Replace high cholesterol, fatty bacon with this savory soy dish. It is easy to make and is surprisingly like the real thing. Adapted from Mary Estella's recipe in her classic, Natural Foods Cookbook.

ingredients

- 2 TBS. sweet, white miso
- 1/2 cup boiling water
- 1 tsp. prepared natural mustard
- 2 bay leaves
- 3 garlic cloves, thinly sliced
- 1/4 tsp. white pepper
- 1/2 pound all soy tempeh, cut into 1/4-inch X 2-inch X 4-inch strips

directions

1. In a small saucepan, purée the miso in the boiling water with a spoon or whisk. Add the remaining ingredients, except the tempeh. Stir gently.
2. Add the tempeh strips and simmer covered for 20 minutes.
3. Drain the tempeh strips and place them on an oiled baking dish. Discard the marinade.
4. Broil the tempeh until crisp and browned, 5-8 minutes. Turn over and broil for 5 minutes longer.

variation

- For juicier "bacon," add 1 teaspoon of toasted sesame oil in step #1.

cook's tip

- *Tempeh "Bacon"* is delicious as a snack or served with *Scrambled Tofu,* page 46. It is equally wonderful added to stews, sandwiches, stir-fries and salads.

tempeh "turkey" with zesty gravy

yield: 4 servings

This hearty dish will satisfy even hungry meat-eaters. Because tempeh is made from whole soy beans, it offers considerable fiber and valuable nutrients. An added bonus is that it is fermented, making it more digestible. It is adapted from Mary Estella's classic, The Natural Foods Cookbook.

ingredients

- 1/2 pound tempeh
- 1/2 tsp. toasted sesame oil
- 1 1/2 cups water
- 2 TBS. barley miso
- 1/2 TBS. prepared natural mustard
- 1 small garlic clove, minced

- 1 small onion, diced small
- 1/4 tsp. dried sage
- 1/4 tsp. dried thyme
- 1 pinch dried rosemary
- 1 TBS. kudzu, dissolved in 1/4 cup cool water

directions

1. Cut the tempeh into thin, bite-sized triangles.
2. Heat the oil in a large, nonstick skillet. Sauté the tempeh until golden brown, about 7 minutes on each side.
3. In a small bowl, whisk together the remaining ingredients, except the kudzu-water mixture. Pour the mixture over the tempeh.
4. Simmer covered for 15 minutes, stirring occasionally.
5. Add the kudzu-water mixture. Whisk over low heat until the sauce is translucent and thick, about 3 minutes.

cook's tip
- Toasted sesame oil best complements the flavor of tempeh in any tempeh recipe.

tempeh "reuben"

High in protein, this satisfying tempeh dish is great by itself or in a sandwich.

ingredients

1/2 tsp. toasted sesame oil

1/2 pound tempeh, cut into 1-inch strips

1 tsp. prepared natural mustard

1 tsp. barley miso

1/3 cup water

2 garlic cloves, minced

1 TBS. mirin

4 cups shredded green cabbage

1 cup sauerkraut with juice

5 TBS. uncooked plain mochi, thinly sliced, optional

directions

1. Heat the oil in a large, nonstick skillet. Sauté the tempeh strips until golden brown, about 5 minutes on each side.
2. In a small bowl, whisk together the mustard, miso and water. Pour the mixture over the tempeh.
3. Add the garlic, mirin, cabbage and the sauerkraut with its juice. Mix gently.
4. Simmer covered for 20 minutes. Add water as needed.
5. **Meanwhile**, preheat the broiler or the oven to 350°F.
6. Transfer the mixture to a 2-quart casserole dish. Sprinkle mochi over the top.
7. Melt under the broiler or bake covered until golden brown, about 25 minutes.

cook's tip
- Using a Dutch oven to sauté and cook all the ingredients will make clean up faster.

vegetables

vivacious
vegetables

Unfortunately, many vegetables never make it off the plate. Too often, they are tasteless, overcooked and uninteresting. This chapter will transform vegetables from ordinary to enticing. You will discover delightful ways to prepare them so that they will fly off the plate.

Steamed or boiled just right, vegetables are crisp and fresh-tasting. Stir-fried in minimal oil, they satisfy the desire for fats. Baked, they become rich, caramelized and warming in the winter. Whether center stage or on the side, vegetables will nourish your body, mind and waistline, too. Low in fat, you can freely indulge in an abundance of luscious vegetables. Packed with fiber, they give you a full feeling without the calories.

Vegetables are a gold mine of nutrition. Surprisingly, seeds and pods are high in protein. Common examples are peas, corn and lima beans. One cup of fresh peas is packed with as much protein as a large egg, without the fat and cholesterol. In addition, they are rich in zinc, iron, calcium and B vitamins.

Traditional medicine classifies vegetables into three groups: leafy green, ground and root. Often neglected, leafy greens are a remarkable source of nutrients. For example, one cup of cooked collard greens contains 234 milligrams of calcium. That is only five milligrams less than a glass of milk! However, unlike milk, leafy greens are not mucous-forming, which can aggravate allergies and asthma. In addition, they do not contain the antibiotics, steroids and hormones commonly fed to cows. Greens act as cancer-fighting warriors with weapons of beta carotene, anti-oxidants and chlorophyll. Collards, kale, broccoli and other greens contain more vitamin C than citrus fruit.

Ground vegetables also contain cancer-fighting properties. This group includes brussel sprouts, cauliflower and cabbage. The sweeter varieties like squash and onions, satisfy the sweet tooth, maintain blood sugar levels and nourish the middle organs: the liver, spleen and pancreas. Traditional medicine believes that by nourishing these organs, the body becomes relaxed, reducing stress and worry.

Roots include familiar vegetables like carrots, yams and turnips. Less known are parsnips, rutabaga and burdock. These starchy foods comfort us like mom's mashed potatoes, only they are healthier. If your head is in-the-clouds, traditional medicine prescribes these grounding vegetables. We, like them, become rooted to the earth.

Choose from all three categories. Each offers unique nutritional properties for your health. Try *Stir-Fried Exotic Greens*, *Roasted Garlic Parsnips* or *Vegetable Medley with Tahini-Poppyseed Sauce*. Relish them all!

cook's tip
- Store vegetables in the refrigerator in tightly-closed plastic bags. Evert-Fresh Bag®, a green, reusable produce bag, extends vegetables' shelf life.
- Rather than store yams, onions, garlic and winter squash in the refrigerator, keep them in a cool, well-ventilated area.
- Ideally, wash organic vegetables just before cooking to preserve nutrients. However, if time is a constraint, it is better to wash vegetables early in the day rather than eat frozen ones or none at all!
- If vegetables are not organic, fill a sink with several inches of water. Add a few drops of a mild, natural, coconut-based soap, such as Shaklee® Basic H®. This emulsifies oily pesticides from the surface of produce. Scrub the vegetables until clean then rinse well.
- Cut each vegetable into pieces of the same size for even cooking. For variety, choose different cutting techniques, see page 243.
- Save time and maintain highly beneficial fiber by not peeling vegetables. There are two exceptions: tough outer skin, like broccoli stalks or butternut squash; or waxed skin, like most supermarket apples, cucumbers, bell peppers and rutabagas.

- Waxing improves a supermarket's profit margin by creating a longer shelf life for vegetables. Unfortunately, waxing does not improve our shelf life. Paraffin clogs the small intestines, making it more difficult to absorb nutrients.
- For sautéing, heat the oil only to the sizzling point. This happens when a few drops of water sprinkled onto the hot oil begin to sizzle. Do not allow the oil to reach the smoking point. Food cooked in smoking oil creates free radicals. Scientists believe that these free radicals cause cancer, arthritis and premature aging. Deep-fried foods are extremely unhealthy.
- Do not sauté garlic longer than one minute or it will become bitter.
- Heat and oxygen destroy vitamins B and C. Cook vegetables only until fork-tender and bright in color.
- Different variables such as size, age and density of the vegetable make it challenging to give exact cooking times. Although I have included cooking guidelines, page 250, keep a granny fork handy to test vegetables for doneness.

collard greens

boiled
collard greens

A staple in any healthful repertoire, collard greens are high in calcium, iron and vitamin C. They are terrific plain or sprinkled with a natural vinegar.

ingredients

1/2 large bunch collard greens   4 inches water

directions

1. Bring the water to a boil in a medium pot.
2. **Meanwhile,** thoroughly swish greens in water until clean. Be sure to remove all of the dirt especially from the stems.
3. Cut out the stems. Slice away the dried ends. Slice the stems into long, thin diagonals. Cut the leaves into 2-inch pieces.
4. Add the stems to the pot and submerge completely. Boil until tender, 3-8 minutes.
5. Remove the stems with a skimmer or slotted spoon to a colander. Cover with a bamboo mat or non-terry cloth towel to keep warm.
6. Repeat steps #4 and #5 with the leaves. Boil until tender, 3-6 minutes.
7. Serve immediately.

variation

- Substitute other bitter greens such as mustard, turnip or rapini for collard greens.

cook's tips

- Like most bitter greens, collards taste best when boiled rather than steamed. This decreases bitterness.
- If greens are organic, be on the look out for tiny, green aphid bugs. Add salt to the water when washing greens with aphids.

steamed vegetables

A steamer pot or stainless steel steamer insert is a kitchen necessity. You will use it every day to prepare and reheat vegetables this healthful way.

ingredients
3 cups vegetables, of choice

directions
1. If the vegetables are organic, scrub them thoroughly with a brush and then rinse them off.
2. If the vegetables are not organic, fill a sink with several inches of water. Add a few drops of mild, natural soap. Scrub the vegetables until clean and rinse well. See pages 14-15.
3. Cut the vegetables into bite-sized pieces. Place them in a steamer basket over 2 cups of boiling water.
4. Steam covered, until the vegetables are fork-tender and bright in color, 3-10 minutes. Serve immediately.

cook's tips
- Organically grown vegetables are full-flavored. You will seldom need sauces or condiments. This means less work for you, too.
- Steaming: allow enough room in the steamer basket for the steam to freely circulate and cook all the vegetables. When removing the pot lid, tilt it away from you to avoid burning yourself.
- Arrange the vegetables attractively on a platter with each vegetable representing a spoke of a wheel. Place the green beans, then carrots, cauliflower, broccoli, yellow squash and so on. Serve a dip, such as *Tofu Dressing*, page 89, or *Tahini-Lime Dressing*, page 88, in a small bowl in the center of the platter.

approximate cooking times for common vegetables, in minutes

- Asparagus - 5
- Broccoli, florets and stems - 3
- Cabbage, shredded - 3
- Carrots, thinly sliced - 4
- Cauliflower, florets - 8
- Daikon, thin 1/2 rounds - 6
- Green beans - 8
- Onion, thin 1/2 rounds - 5
- Summer squash, 1/4-inch slices - 3
- Winter squash, 1-inch pieces - 7

broccoli

stir-fried
exotic chinese greens

yield: 2 servings

For variety and exotic flair, make these delicate and delicious Chinese greens often! Chinese broccoli is particularly lovely with its edible, yellow flowers.

ingredients

1/2 tsp. toasted sesame oil
1/2 pound Chinese broccoli, cut
   into 2- inch pieces

1/2 tsp. shoyu
1 TBS. water

directions

1. Thoroughly swish the greens in water until clean. Place in a colander to drain.
2. Heat the oil in a large, nonstick skillet or wok.
3. Add the greens and stir-fry for 1 minute.
4. Drizzle with shoyu and water. Stir-fry until wilted and bright green, about 1 minute. Serve immediately.

variations

- Add 1/4 tsp. of mirin in step #4.
- Add a few drops of hot sesame oil in step #4.
- Substitute yu choy, shanghai or baby bok choy for Chinese broccoli.

cook's tip
- You will find Chinese broccoli, also known as Gai Lan, in Asian or well-stocked produce markets. Ask the grocer to find them for you.

steamed
sweet corn

Steaming requires less water than boiling, so your kitchen will be cooler when making this summer bounty. For a complete meal in less than twenty minutes, serve with Grilled Vegetables, page 165, and a Leafy Green Salad, page 84.

ingredients
8 ears corn on-the-cob

directions
1. Husk the corn, then brush off the corn silk.
2. Place a steamer insert in a large stock pot. Add 2 inches of water and bring to a boil.
3. Place the corn in the steamer basket.
4. Steam until tender, about 10 minutes.

variation
- Boil the corn until tender in a large stock pot filled with water for about 10 minutes.

cook's tips
- For the sweetest flavor, buy fresh corn as close to cooking time as possible.
- Nylon, corn silk brushes are inexpensive and available at kitchen gadget stores.
- In place of butter, use Spectrum Naturals® Canola Spread. Alternatively, lightly spread umeboshi paste over corn for a salty, sour contrast.
- A large, pasta pot facilitates cooking ears of corn.

steamed kale with savory-sesame dressing

yield: 2-4 servings

Kale is high in calcium and delightfully delicious when served with this four-flavor dressing. Or, for an instant alternative, sprinkle umeboshi or brown rice vinegar on top.

ingredients

1 TBS. shoyu

1 TBS. water

1 TBS. unhulled sesame seeds, toasted

1 TBS. fresh lemon juice

1 tsp. grated fresh ginger, juiced

1 bunch kale

directions

1. Combine the shoyu and water in a small saucepan. Simmer over low heat for 3 minutes. Remove from the heat. Stir in the sesame seeds, lemon and ginger juices. Set aside.
2. Place a steamer basket over 2 cups of water and bring to a boil.
3. **Meanwhile,** thoroughly swish the greens in water until clean. Pay special attention to the stems.
4. Cut out the stems. Slice away the dried ends. Slice the stems into long, thin diagonals. Cut the leaves into 2-inch pieces.
5. Place the stems into the steamer basket. Steam until tender, 3-8 minutes.
6. Remove the stems to a colander. Cover with a bamboo mat or non-terry cloth towel to keep them warm.
7. Repeat steps #5 and #6 with the leaves. Steam until tender, 3-6 minutes.
8. Place the kale in a large serving bowl. Add the dressing and serve immediately.

variation

• Substitute bok choy or Chinese cabbage for the kale.

cook's tips

- Discard the yellow, decaying leaves which lack vitality and sap yours! Choose fresh, bright green, organic vegetables whenever possible.
- To effectively shred ginger, use a ginger grater. Asian and natural foods stores carry porcelain or aluminum ginger graters, although I prefer the stainless steel variety.
- To make ginger juice, place grated pulp into the palm of the hand. Squeeze out the juice by making a tight fist. Do this over a strainer so that no bits of pulp falls into the juice.

kale

ambrosial
asparagus

yield: 4 servings

My assistant, Sian Yardley, taught me this sensationally simple spring delight. Asparagus comes alive in this dish, with its heavenly fusion of fruity olive oil and savory parmesan.

ingredients

1 pound young asparagus
1 tsp. extra-virgin olive oil

1 tsp. Soyco® Lite & Less
Parmesan Cheese Alternative

directions

1. Rinse the asparagus and break off the bottom ends.
2. Place a steamer basket in a large stock pot. Add one inch of water and bring to a boil.
3. Place the whole asparagus, bottom end down, in the basket.
4. Steam until tender, about 7 minutes.
5. Serve sprinkled with olive oil and Parmesan Cheese Alternative.

variations

• Cut the asparagus into 1 1/2-inch pieces and use a smaller steamer pot.
• Substitute real parmesan cheese for Soyco® Lite & Less. If you do choose to eat diary, treat yourself to the highest quality, best-tasting Parmigiano Reggiano, available at Italian grocers and gourmet food stores.

cook's tip

• A pasta pot cooks asparagus to perfection.

asparagus

green beans with sesame-miso dressing

yield: 4-6 servings

These savory green beans are a snap to make and are great to serve to company. Tart lemon juice, sweet mirin and the complexity of miso are married in this delightful recipe from Jan Belleme's Culinary Treasures of Japan.

ingredients

1 pound young, tender green
beans, cut off stem ends
2 TBS. unhulled sesame seeds
2 TBS. barley miso

1 TBS. mirin
1 TBS. brown rice syrup
1 tsp. fresh lemon juice

directions

1. Steam or boil the green beans until tender and bright green, about 8 minutes.
2. **Meanwhile**, toast the rinsed sesame seeds in a dry skillet. The seeds are done when they are golden brown, give off a nutty fragrance, pop frantically and crush easily between the thumb and ring finger, about 7 minutes. Stir constantly to prevent them from burning.
3. Crush the seeds in a suribachi.
4. Add the remaining ingredients, except the green beans, and mix well.
5. Gently toss the cooked green beans in the suribachi until evenly coated with the paste.
6. Serve either hot or at room temperature.

variation

- Substitute steamed broccoli for the green beans.
- To save time, omit crushing the seeds in step # 3. Simply mix the dressing ingredients together in a small bowl.

cook's tip
- For visual appeal and added texture, do not remove the pointed tips of green beans. Steam whole or cut into 1/3's, on the diagonal.

baked
garnet yams

yield: 2-4 servings

Sweet, nutritious and easy-to-make, I bake these yams several times a month in cool weather. The leftovers are perfect for snacks and lunch.

ingredients

    2 garnet yams

directions

1. Preheat the oven to 400°F.
2. Scrub and rinse the yams. Pierce with a fork 2 or 3 times.
3. Place the yams on a cookie sheet or baking dish. Bake them until fork-tender, 45-60 minutes, depending on their size.

cook's tips

- Although there is confusion about sweet potatoes and yams, most of the time what is sold as a yam is really a sweet potato. In any case, the sweetest is the dark red garnet.
- Leftover yams can be sliced into 1/3-inch rounds. Sauté the rounds in a few drops of corn or canola oil until brown and sweetly caramelized, about 5 minutes on each side.

yams

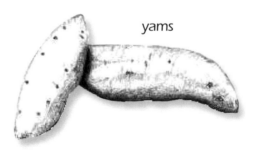

roasted
garlic parsnips

yield: 6 servings

This recipe unlocks the sweetness of parsnips with a hint of fragrant garlic. Guests love this simple, holiday side dish. They always come back for more.

ingredients

- 1 pound young parsnips
- 1 TBS. extra-virgin olive oil, or more to taste
- 6 garlic cloves, thinly sliced

- 1 pinch unrefined sea salt
- 1 pinch nutmeg, optional
- 1 TBS. fresh parsley, minced, to garnish, optional

directions

1. Preheat the oven to 350°F.
2. Scrub and rinse the parsnips. Cut them into 1/2-inch chunks.
3. Sprinkle the oil in a covered baking dish. Add the parsnips, garlic and salt. Stir gently to coat.
4. Bake covered until the parsnips are fork-tender, about 30 minutes. Stir occasionally.
5. Uncover and broil to lightly brown the parsnips, about 5 minutes.
6. Sprinkle nutmeg and parsley on top to garnish.

variations

- Substitute onions, carrots, rutabaga or yams for parsnips.

granny fork

vegetable medley with tahini-poppyseed sauce

yield: 6-8 servings

You will love serving this beautiful vegetable dish to company. The rainbow of vegetables is complemented by a flavor-packed sauce.

vegetables

- 1 small head cauliflower, cut into florets
- 2 small yellow squash, cut into spears
- 1 small head broccoli, stems peeled and diagonally sliced, florets separated
- 2 large carrots, cut into spears

sauce

- 4 TBS. tahini
- 1 TBS. sweet, white miso
- 1 garlic clove, blanched
- 1/4 tsp. ginger juice, page 157
- 2 TBS. poppy seeds, toasted

directions

1. Fill a large stock pot with 3 quarts of water and bring it to a boil.
2. Cook each vegetable until tender and bright in color, page 153. As each vegetable is cooked, place it in a colander. Cover with a bamboo mat or non-terry cloth towel to keep them warm. Reserve about a cup of cooking water.
3. **Meanwhile,** add the sauce ingredients to a blender. Blend until uniform in color, adding the vegetable cooking water as needed to reach the desired consistency. Pour it into a bowl or small pitcher.
4. Arrange the vegetables on a large platter and serve with the sauce.

variation

- Add one raw red pepper, cut into strips.

cook's tips

- Cook lighter colored vegetables first. This prevents them from being stained by the cooking water from darker colored vegetables like carrots.

joe's mixed stir-fried greens

yield: 2 servings

The strong flavor of arugula needs balancing. My husband, Joe, achieves this by adding sweet onions and pungent garlic. Since Joe was my student in cooking class, I am happy to see that he really learned the basic principles after all!

ingredients

2 cups arugula, cut into 1-inch pieces

1/4 tsp. extra-virgin olive oil

1 medium onion, cut into thin 1/2 rounds

3 garlic cloves, thinly sliced

1/2 small head green cabbage, shredded

1 tsp. water

1 tsp. shoyu

directions

1. Thoroughly swish the arugula in water until clean. Place in a colander to drain.
2. Heat the oil in a large, nonstick skillet or wok. Add the onion and sauté until translucent, about 5 minutes.
3. Move the onion to one side of the skillet. Sprinkle a few more drops of oil in the cleared space. Add the garlic and sauté for 1 minute.
4. Add the cabbage and sauté for 3 minutes.
5. Add the arugula and water. Sauté until wilted, bright green and almost tender, about 2 minutes.
6. Drizzle with shoyu. Sauté for 1 minute then serve immediately.

variations

- For a milder dish, add 1 cup of kale, bok choy or other greens in step #1.
- Substitute rapini for arugula.
- Top with toasted pine nuts for crunch.

cook's tip

- Arugula is available in well-stocked produce markets.

leeks and cauliflower with emerald goddess dressing

yield: 4-6
servings

I include this tangy recipe in my Beyond Beginnings Cooking Series to introduce an unfamiliar, yet lively vegetable, the leek. It has become a favorite because its flavors explode in the mouth. Elaine Gagné taught me this recipe many years ago.

ingredients

- 1/2 leek, cut into 1/3-inch diagonals, white and green parts separated
- 1/2 small head cauliflower, cut into florets
- 1 garlic clove, cut in 1/2
- 2 scallions, minced
- 1/4 cup fresh parsley, minced
- 2 TBS. tahini
- 1 TBS. umeboshi paste, or more to taste
- 1 small lemon or lime, juiced

directions

1. Steam the garlic for 1 minute, then place it in a blender.
2. Steam the cauliflower until fork-tender, 8-10 minutes. Place it in a serving bowl.
3. Steam the leeks, greens and whites separately, until tender, but not mushy, 2-3 minutes. Place in the serving bowl.
4. Add the remaining ingredients, except the cauliflower and leeks, to the blender. Blend, adding water as needed, to make a pourable dressing.
5. Pour the dressing over the cauliflower and leeks. Mix gently.
6. Serve at room temperature or refrigerate and serve chilled.

variation

- Spoon *Emerald Goddess Dressing* over steamed broccoli, a leafy green salad, rice or noodles.

cook's tip
- Unlike bok choy and other greens, the green part of leeks seems to take longer to cook than the white section.

grilled vegetables

Grilled vegetables are an exciting change from the ordinary. Make them anytime of year using seasonal vegetables. I like to use a grill pan on the stove rather than dealing with an outdoor grill. These colorful vegetables will transform a grain burger on a bun into a guest-worthy meal. Make a simple and satisfying summer lunch or dinner with a plate of grilled vegetables, corn on-the-cob and salad.

ingredients

- 1 tsp. extra-virgin olive oil
- 1/4 tsp. shoyu
- 1 pinch dried oregano
- 1 broccoli stalk, stem peeled and diagonally sliced, no florets
- 1 small red onion, cut into 1/4-inch thick rounds
- 1 red pepper, cut into 1/2 rounds, 1/4" thick, optional
- 1 yellow summer squash, cut into 1/4-inch rounds

directions

1. Preheat the grill pan.
2. Combine the olive oil, shoyu and oregano in a small bowl.
3. Using your fingers or a pastry brush, rub a little of this mixture onto the vegetables.
4. Place the vegetables on the grill pan. Cook until the onion is translucent, other vegetables are fork-tender and the seared ridge marks appear on all, about 4 minutes on each side. Serve immediately.

variations

- Substitute yellow onion for red.
- Substitute zucchini for the yellow squash.
- Add carrots.

cook's tips

- Alternatively, cook outdoors on a grill.
- Grilled vegetables are delicious served rolled up in a chapati.

snacks and
condiments

savory snacks and condiments

We do not need to feel guilty about snacking. Many of us need something to eat while on-the-go to boost energy. Unfortunately, most available snacks are simple carbohydrates which will not sustain us for long. Plan to keep these nutritious alternatives on hand:

- Fruit, preferably organic
- Sourdough bread (see pages 17-18) with peanut butter
- Rice cakes with peanut butter
- Natural popcorn, such as Bearitos®
- Cold cereal with soy or rice beverage
- Carrot sticks
- Organic Vegan Food Bar™
- Hot soup
- Homemade muffins
- Homemade cookies
- *Lenore's Nutty Seed Mix*
- *Blueberry Couscous Cake*

Gomashio enhances the taste of grain and almost any other dish you choose to sprinkle it on. Brown rice is not the same without it!

Pickles have played a key role in traditional diets for many reasons. Their friendly bacteria help to digest food, cleanse the liver, encourage a sluggish appetite and fight off unfriendly bacteria. Best of all, they add pizzazz to any meal.

In the traditional process of fermentation, food is submerged in a salt water solution, or brine. This produces pickles which remain edible for several months. Many peoples from around the world continue to use this method to make pickles and prevent food from spoiling.

cook's tips

- To produce crisp pickles, use firm, fresh vegetables.
- To facilitate fermentation, use thinly sliced vegetables.
- Vegetables must stay below the pressure plate even when refrigerated. If not submerged in the salt water solution at all times, food particles can become moldy.
- A mini-pickle press simplifies pickle preparation and storage.

gomashio

yield: 1 cup

Any grain comes alive with this nutty, mildly-salty condiment, pronounced "go-ma-shee-o." It is high in calcium and fiber, and I never tire of sprinkling it on brown rice.

ingredients

1 TBS. unrefined sea salt

1 cup + 2 TBS. unhulled
sesame seeds

directions

1. Preheat a large, nonstick skillet.
2. Dry-roast the salt over medium heat until it becomes shiny and has released its chlorine smell, about 2 minutes.
3. Pour the salt into a suribachi. With a wooden pestle, grind the salt into a fine powder.
4. **Meanwhile**, rinse the seeds through a strainer, then immediately pour them into the hot skillet. Dry-roast until the seeds are dry and golden in color, about 7 minutes. Stir continuously with a wooden spoon or rice paddle to prevent the seeds from burning.
5. Add the seeds to the ground salt in the suribachi. While still warm, grind the seeds and salt together with an even, circular motion until about 90% of the seeds are crushed.
6. Place a small portion of the condiment in a tightly sealed glass or ceramic container for table use. Store the remainder in the refrigerator to keep it fresh.

variation

- For children, substitute 1 teaspoon unrefined sea salt for 1 tablespoon.

cook's tips

- Sesame seeds are toasted when they are golden brown, give off a nutty fragrance, pop frantically and crush easily between thumb and ring finger.
- Gomashio so enhances the taste of grain that it is well worth the $25 investment in a grooved, ceramic suribachi bowl. In addition, this bowl is useful for making sauces, dressings and spreads. It is available in natural foods stores, Asian grocery stores and through mail order catalogues, page 247.

savory
sunflower seeds

yield: 2 cups

When I was making the transition to a vegan diet, I found I was missing crunch in the food. This recipe from the Kushi Institute was the answer. These delectable seeds can be sprinkled on oatmeal, added to grain salads, used in my Nutty Seed Mix or eaten alone as a snack.

ingredients

2 cups sunflower seeds
1 TBS. shoyu

1 TBS. water

directions

1. Preheat a large, nonstick skillet.
2. **Meanwhile**, rinse the seeds through a strainer, then immediately pour them into the hot skillet. Dry-roast until the seeds are dry and golden in color, about 7 minutes. Stir continuously with a wooden spoon or rice paddle to prevent the seeds from burning.
3. Combine the shoyu and water in a medium bowl. Pour the hot seeds into the bowl and stir to coat.
4. Pour the seeds through the strainer. Return the drained seeds to the hot skillet. Discard the remaining shoyu-water mixture.
5. Continue to dry-roast the seeds on low heat until dry and crunchy, about 8-12 minutes.

variation

- Substitute any seeds or nuts for sunflower seeds.

cook's tips

- Allow the seeds to cool completely before refrigerating or freezing in a glass jar.
- Buy sunflower seeds that are gray in color. A yellow coloration indicates old age and rancidity. All seeds and nuts become rancid fairly quickly once their hard outer shells are removed. It is best to refrigerate or freeze them during storage.

lenore's
nutty seed mix

yield: 2 cups

I always have this instant, high-energy snack stored in small packets in my car. Crunchy, colorful and wholesome, this mix will satisfy your hunger pangs.

ingredients

1/2 cup pumpkin seeds
1/2 cup almonds
1/2 cup sunflower seeds
1/2 cup bulk sesame sticks, optional

1/4 cup salted peanuts
1/4 cup organic raisins, optional
1/2 cup baked oriental rice snacks, optional

directions

1. Preheat a large, nonstick skillet.
2. **Meanwhile**, rinse the pumpkin seeds through a strainer, then immediately pour them into the hot skillet. Dry-roast until the seeds are dry and golden in color, about 7 minutes. Stir continuously with a wooden spoon or rice paddle to prevent burning. Pour the seeds into a large bowl.
3. Repeat step #2 with the almonds and then with the sunflower seeds.
4. Add the remaining ingredients to the bowl. Mix well.

variation
• Substitute dried cherries for raisins.

cook's tips
• Toast the nuts and seeds ahead of time. Freeze in glass jars.
• Keep only a few packets of this mix in the car. Refrigerate or freeze the remaining mix to prevent rancidity.

terrific
turnip pickles

yield: 1 1/2 cups

To add sparkle to any meal, serve naturally-fermented pickles such as these. They add a salty, sour, pungent and crunchy note to any menu.

ingredients

1/3 cup shoyu

1/3 cup water

2 medium turnips, cut into
 thin 1/2 rounds

directions

1. Simmer the shoyu and water in a saucepan over low heat for 5 minutes. Allow to cool.
2. Place the turnips in a clean, dry glass jar. Pour the cooled liquid over the turnips to just cover them.
3. Place a smaller jar, filled with water, inside the first jar. This keeps the vegetables submerged under the liquid. Allow to stand on the counter to ferment for about 3 days.
4. Every morning and night use a chopstick or knife to poke out the air bubbles.
5. After 3 days, taste the pickles. If they are sour enough for your taste, refrigerate them. Otherwise, allow the jar to remain on the counter for another day.
6. Serve 2 or 3 pickles with lunch and dinner.
7. Pickles will keep refrigerated about 1 month.

variations

- Substitute other hard vegetables for the turnip, such as daikon, carrots, rutabaga, winter squash, peeled broccoli stalks or cabbage cores.

cook's tip

- Not only do these pickles set off the meal with a burst-in-your-mouth flavor, they add three of the five tastes to make a meal complete. For more details, see Cravings and The Five Tastes, pages 29-30.

dill brine pickles

These cheerful, orange pickles perk up the visual appeal on an otherwise plain platter.

ingredients

2 cups water

3⁄4 TBS. unrefined sea salt

3 carrots, cut into thin slices

1 sprig fresh dill

directions

1. Bring the water to a boil in a small saucepan. Add the salt. Boil until the salt has dissolved, about 3 minutes. Allow to cool.
2. Place the carrots in a clean, dry glass jar. Pour the cooled liquid over the carrots to just cover them. Place the sprig of dill on top of the carrots.
3. Place a smaller jar, filled with water, inside the first jar. This keeps the vegetables submerged under the liquid. Allow to stand on the counter to ferment for about 3 days.
4. Every morning and night use a chopstick or knife to poke out the air bubbles.
5. After 3 days, taste the pickles. If they are sour enough for your taste, refrigerate them. Otherwise, allow the jar to remain on the counter for another day.
6. Serve 2 or 3 pickles with lunch and dinner.
7. Pickles will keep refrigerated about 1 month. A cloudy appearance of the liquid is normal.

variations
- Substitute thinly sliced cauliflower and red radish for carrots.
- Substitute 1⁄4 teaspoon dried dill for fresh dill.

notes

last-minute
meals

last
minute meals

In a hurry? This chapter is reserved for you! All of these recipes can be prepared in less than half an hour. Delight in pasta smothered with chickpea, tahini or peanut butter sauce. Bite into a quick mini-pizza, or create a healthy version of the old stand-by, soup and a sandwich.

The key to quick cooking is to minimize preparation time. Pasta, organic canned beans and fresh steamed vegetables are perfect for creating fast meals. Another time saver is to make extra grain and beans to use in other recipes. For example, pressure-cook a large pot of chickpeas. Sprinkle some in salad or soup and use the rest to make hummus the next day. This principle works particularly well with rice. There are more than two dozen ways to use leftover rice in *Beyond Brown Rice*, page 112.

You can expedite cooking in other ways. Invest in a few, essential kitchen tools like a food processor, a steamer pot and a Bash N' Chop®. These are enormous time-savers. Moreover, by keeping food staples on hand, you can make almost every recipe in this chapter. See the cook's tips.

Finally, keep a list on the refrigerator of your favorite quick meals. When you cannot think of something fast to cook, choose a wholesome option from your list.

cook's tips
- When beginning to cook, put a teapot of water on to boil. You will have boiling water at your fingertips.
- If you do not have a nonstick or heavy saucepan, use a flame tamer under your pot when cooking sauces.
- In place of a suribachi, use a blender when making sauces. Alternatively, whisk ingredients together in a mixing bowl.
- See also Pasta cook's tips, pages 116-117, for pasta cooking guidelines.
- **Staples in the cupboard**
  Organic canned beans: chickpeas, kidney
  A variety of dried pastas

Kombu, wakame

Organic canned soups

Shoyu, mirin, umeboshi vinegar and paste, kudzu

Onions, garlic

- **Refrigerator staples**

Oils: canola, corn, sesame, toasted sesame, extra-virgin olive

Maple syrup, brown rice syrup

Soy cheese slices

Fresh vegetables: carrots, green cabbage, scallions, broccoli, fresh ginger

Peanut butter, tahini

Barley miso, sweet white miso

Salad ingredients, see page 84

Cooked brown rice

Homemade soups

- **Freezer staples**

Whole wheat English muffins and sourdough whole wheat bread, sliced

Pumpkin, sunflower and sesame seeds

Un-Tomato Sauce, page 123

Cooked beans

Homemade soups

- **Essential kitchen tools**

(see Cook's Tools for details)

Blender, food processor

Colander

Pots: Dutch oven (4- to 6-quart/medium), 10- or 12-inch nonstick skillet, 8-quart stock pot

Food scraper (Bash N' Chop®)

Several sharp knives

Knife sharpener

Steamer pot, essential for cooking and reheating leftovers

Grip-EZ™ peeler

Skimmer

Wooden or polyethylene cutting board

pressure-cooked
green split pea soup
yield: 2 quarts

Would you believe split pea soup in thirty minutes? Warming, filling and tasty, this soup is sure to become a favorite. Serve with crusty bread and a salad.

ingredients

2 cups split green peas
1 tsp. canola oil
2 medium onions, diced small
1 6-inch strip kombu
2 garlic cloves, minced
1/2 tsp. dried thyme
1 bay leaf

2 carrots, cut into 1/4-inch rounds
6 1/2 cups boiling water
2 TBS. pearled barley
1 tsp. unrefined sea salt
2 TBS. barley miso, puréed in 1/4 cup water

directions

1. Pick over the peas to remove debris and set aside.
2. Heat the oil in a 6- or 8-quart pressure cooker. Sauté the onions until translucent, about 5 minutes.
3. **Meanwhile**, cover the kombu with water and soak for 5 minutes. Cut it into 1/2-inch squares and set aside.
4. Add the garlic and thyme to the onions. Sauté for 1 minute.
5. Add the kombu, bay leaf, carrots and boiling water to the pressure cooker.
6. Rinse the peas and the barley through a strainer and add them to the pot.
7. Lock the lid in place. Over high heat, bring up to full pressure.
8. Place a flame tamer under the pot. Reduce the heat, maintaining high pressure for 20 minutes.
9. Quick-release the pressure by placing the closed pot under cold, running water. If the peas are not soft, simmer until they are, then add the salt. Close the lid, and allow to stand for 5 minutes, off the heat.
10. Place a small amount of the hot soup in a small bowl, add the miso, whisk until smooth and return it to the pressure cooker.
11. Serve hot. This soup will thicken as it stands, so add a little water when reheating.

variations
- Substitute Job's tears for pearled barley.
- To reduce the cooking time, do not sauté the onions, garlic and thyme. Simply add them to the pressure cooker in step #5.

cook's tip
- Rinse legumes such as split peas and lentils just before cooking. This prevents them from sticking to the strainer.

pressure cooker

pasta with chickpea sauce

yield: 4 servings

This unusual and simple peasant meal is creamy and sweetly satisfying. It has rustic appeal, particularly when the onions and carrots are sautéed. Adapted from Margaret Lawson's recipe in The Naturally Healthy Gourmet.

ingredients

- 1 pound pasta, of choice
- 1 15-ounce can organic chickpeas
- 1 medium carrot, coarsely chopped
- 3 TBS. onion, coarsely chopped
- 2 TBS. tahini
- 1 1/2 TBS. umeboshi vinegar
- 3/4 cup water
- 1 TBS. fresh parsley, minced, to garnish

directions

1. Fill a large stock pot with 5 quarts of water and bring it to a boil.
2. Cook the pasta until al dente, according to package directions.
3. Gently pour the cooked pasta into a colander placed in the sink. Rinse until cold and leave in the colander.
4. **Meanwhile**, add the remaining ingredients, except the parsley, to a blender. Blend until smooth.
5. Pour the mixture into a small saucepan. Simmer over low heat for about 5 minutes.
6. Just before serving, pour boiling water over the pasta to reheat it. Shake the colander to remove excess water.
7. Place the pasta on individual plates. Pour a generous 1/4 cup of sauce over each serving. Serve garnished with parsley.

variations

- Add 1/2 cup of minced parsley in step #4, reserving 1 tablespoon for the garnish.
- For a richer sauce, sauté the onions and carrots while pasta is cooking.

pasta with miso-tahini sauce

yield: 4 servings

Jazzed up with ginger, this delightful sauce also pairs wonderfully with rice or steamed vegetables. Adapted from Jan Belleme's recipe in The Culinary Treasures of Japan.

ingredients

1 pound pasta, of choice	1 TBS. mirin
1/4 cup sweet, white miso	2 tsp. ginger juice, optional
1/4 cup tahini	1 garlic clove, minced
1/2 cup water	1 scallion, thinly sliced, to
2 TBS. brown rice vinegar	garnish

directions

1. Fill a large stock pot with 5 quarts of water and bring it to a boil.
2. Cook the pasta until al dente, according to package directions.
3. Gently pour the cooked pasta into a colander placed in the sink. Rinse until cold and leave in the colander.
4. **Meanwhile,** combine the miso and tahini in a small saucepan. Simmer over low heat, whisking in a little water at a time to create a smooth sauce.
5. Whisk in the remaining ingredients, except the scallion. If the sauce becomes too thick, add a little water. If too thin, simmer several additional minutes to thicken. Adjust the seasonings.
6. Just before serving, pour boiling water over the pasta to reheat it. Shake the colander to remove excess water.
7. Place the pasta in a large serving bowl and add the sauce. Serve garnished with scallion.

variation

- Add a pinch of dried tarragon or thyme in step #5.

cook's tip

- To juice fresh ginger, it must first be grated. A fine-toothed ginger grater works best. Place shredded ginger in the palm of the hand. Squeeze the pulp over a strainer to prevent bits from falling into the sauce. One tablespoon of grated ginger yields approximately 1 teaspoon of juice.

noodles with tahini sauce

yield: 4 servings

This sauce transforms everyday noodles into gourmet. It offers a blend of sour, sweet and pungent tastes.

ingredients

1 pound udon noodles
2 garlic cloves, coarsely chopped
1/3 cup tahini
2 TBS. shoyu
1 tsp. maple syrup

1 TBS. brown rice vinegar
1/2 cup water
1/4 tsp. hot chili oil, optional
1 scallion, thinly sliced, to garnish

directions

1. Fill a large stock pot with 5 quarts of water and bring it to a boil.
2. Cook the noodles until al dente, about 10 minutes.
3. Gently pour the cooked noodles into a colander placed in the sink. Rinse until cold and leave in the colander.
4. **Meanwhile**, crush the garlic in a suribachi. Add the tahini, shoyu, maple syrup and vinegar. Whisk until the mixture becomes uniform in color.
5. Pour the mixture into a small, nonstick or heavy saucepan. Simmer over low heat, adding water by the spoonful. Whisk well after each addition until a smooth consistency is reached.
6. Add the hot chili oil to taste, a few drops at a time.
7. Just before serving, pour boiling water over the noodles to reheat them. Shake the colander to remove excess water.
8. Place the noodles in a large serving bowl and add the sauce. Serve garnished with scallion.

variations

- Substitute 2 teaspoons of brown rice syrup for the maple syrup.
- Substitute kukicha twig tea for the water.
- Substitute soba noodles for udon noodles.

cook's tip
- Purée sauce ingredients in a blender instead of in a suribachi.

peanut sauce over udon noodles

yield: 4 servings

This popular Asian dish will also please the American palate with its cherished ingredient, peanut butter. Vinegar and shoyu balance the oil in peanut butter, making it more digestible and more delicious.

ingredients

1 pound udon noodles	1 1/2 tsp. brown rice vinegar
1/3 cup peanut butter	1 TBS. shoyu
1 tsp. umeboshi paste	1/2 cup water
1 tsp. mirin, or to taste	1 scallion, thinly sliced, to garnish
1 tsp. umeboshi vinegar, or to taste	

directions

1. Fill a large stock pot with 4 quarts of water and bring it to a boil.
2. Cook the noodles until al dente, about 10 minutes.
3. Gently pour the cooked noodles into a colander placed in the sink. Rinse until cold and leave in the colander.
4. Pour the remaining ingredients, except the water and scallion, into a small, heavy saucepan or double boiler. Simmer over low heat for 15 minutes, gradually whisking in water, as needed, to make a slightly runny consistency.
5. Just before serving, pour boiling water over the noodles to reheat them. Shake the colander to remove excess water.
6. Place the noodles in a large serving bowl and add the sauce. Serve garnished with scallion.

variations
- Substitute strong kukicha twig tea for the water.
- Substitute almond butter for the peanut butter.

cook's tip
- Salty shoyu, pungent scallion and sour vinegar balance the oil in peanut butter.

udon noodles with quick peanut sauce

yield: 4 servings

This lively sauce uses garlic and ginger to add pizzazz. It will become a favorite quick meal for everyone in the family!

ingredients

1 pound udon noodles
2 TBS. peanut butter
1/3 cup boiling water
2 TBS. shoyu
2 tsp. brown rice vinegar
2 tsp. maple syrup
1/8 tsp. ginger powder

1 small garlic clove, minced
1 tsp. kudzu, dissolved in 1/4 cup cool water
1 scallion, thinly sliced, to garnish

directions

1. Fill a large stock pot with 4 quarts of water and bring it to a boil.
2. Cook the noodles until al dente, about 10 minutes.
3. Gently pour the cooked noodles into a colander placed in the sink. Rinse until cold and leave in the colander.
4. Place the remaining ingredients, except the kudzu-water mixture and scallion, in a blender. Blend until uniform in color.
5. Pour into a small, nonstick or heavy saucepan. Simmer over low heat for 10 minutes, stirring occasionally. Whisk in additional water as needed to reach the desired consistency.
6. Whisk in the kudzu-water mixture. Stir over low heat until translucent and thick, about 5 minutes.
7. Just before serving, pour boiling water over the noodles to reheat them. Shake the colander to remove excess water.
8. Place the noodles in a large serving bowl and add the sauce. Serve garnished with scallion.

variations

• Substitute 1/8 teaspoon granulated garlic for the garlic clove.
• Substitute 4 teaspoons of brown rice syrup for the maple syrup.

cook's tip

• Salty shoyu, pungent scallion and sour vinegar balance the oil in peanut butter.

rice with creamy pumpkin seed sauce

yield: 2 servings

This snappy sauce works well over reheated brown rice or noodles. It also works well as a dip or poured over vegetables. Make it ahead of time to serve later.

ingredients

1/3 cup pumpkin seeds
1 tsp. shoyu
1 tsp. fresh lemon juice
1/4 cup water

3 cups cooked brown rice
1 scallion, thinly sliced, to garnish

directions

1. Rinse the seeds through a strainer, then add them to a hot skillet. Dry-roast the seeds over medium heat, stirring continuously so that the seeds cook evenly. They are done when they begin to pop and are golden in color, about 7 minutes.
2. Place the seeds in a blender. Add the shoyu, lemon juice and water. Blend, adding water as needed, to reach the desired consistency.
3. If time allows, let the sauce stand for 20-30 minutes to achieve a creamier consistency.
4. Place the rice on individual plates. Pour the sauce over each serving and garnish with scallion.

variations

- Substitute kukicha twig tea for the water.
- Substitute umeboshi or brown rice vinegar for the lemon juice.
- Serve hot or cold.

pasta with
vegetable sauce

This is a way to put a complete meal on the table in record time. Bursting with flavor and color, this recipe will become part of your basic repertoire.

ingredients

1 pound pasta, of choice

1/2 tsp. sesame or extra-virgin olive oil

2 onions, cut into thin 1/2 rounds

1 small head green cabbage, shredded

2 carrots, cut into matchsticks

2 tsp. shoyu

2 tsp. umeboshi paste, puréed with a little water

1 tsp. toasted sesame seeds, optional, to garnish

directions

1. Fill a large stock pot with 5 quarts of water and bring it to a boil.
2. Cook the pasta until al dente, according to package directions.
3. Gently pour the cooked pasta into a colander placed in the sink. Rinse until cold and leave in the colander.
4. Heat the oil in a large, nonstick skillet or wok. Add the onions and sauté until translucent, about 5 minutes.
5. Add the cabbage, carrots, shoyu and umeboshi purée. Sauté until the cabbage is wilted and the carrots are fork-tender, about 5 minutes.
6. Just before serving, pour boiling water over the pasta to reheat it. Shake the colander to remove excess water.
7. Place the pasta in a large serving bowl. Spoon the vegetables over the pasta. Serve garnished with sesame seeds, if desired.

variations

- Add a large garlic clove, cut into matchsticks, in step #4 (after you sauté the onions) and sauté for 1 minute.
- Add 1 inch of peeled ginger, cut into matchsticks, in step #4 (after you sauté the onions). Sauté for 1 minute.

stir-fried rice and vegetables

yield: 4 servings

This meal will become a mainstay. Keep extra rice in the refrigerator and all the other ingredients on hand, as they will stay fresh for several weeks.

ingredients

1 tsp. toasted sesame oil
1 large onion, diced small
1 2-inch piece fresh ginger, peeled and cut into matchsticks
4 garlic cloves, cut into matchsticks

1/4 head green cabbage, shredded
2 carrots, cut into matchsticks
2 stalks broccoli, stems peeled and diagonally sliced, florets separated
4-5 cups cooked brown rice
1-2 TBS. shoyu

directions

1. Heat the oil in a large, nonstick skillet or wok. Add the onion and a sprinkle of shoyu. Sauté until translucent, about 5 minutes.
2. Add the ginger and garlic. Sauté for 1 minute.
3. Add the cabbage, carrots and a sprinkle of shoyu. Sauté for 3 minutes.
4. Add the broccoli stalks and a sprinkle of shoyu. Sauté 1 minute.
5. Add the rice. Sprinkle with shoyu to taste. Drizzle 2 tablespoons of water into the skillet. Cover and steam until the rice is heated, about 3 minutes.
6. Drizzle another tablespoon of water into the skillet. Add the broccoli florets. Cover and steam until the broccoli turns bright green and is fork-tender, about 3 minutes.

variations

- For a fiery dish, substitute hot sesame oil for toasted sesame oil.
- Substitute 1 pound of cooked noodles for the rice.

cook's tip

- Leftover cooked rice works wonderfully in this recipe since it dries out in the refrigerator. Dried rice is a better texture than sticky, fresh rice for frying.

rice smothered
with curry sauce

Savory and rich, yet easy to prepare, this wonderful dish is perfect for company. Serve with a plate of colorful steamed vegetables.

ingredients

1 1/2 TBS. sesame oil
1/3 cup whole wheat pastry
  flour
1-2 garlic cloves, minced
1 tsp. curry powder
1 tsp. unrefined sea salt

1 TBS. shoyu
1 1/2 cups water
4 cups cooked brown rice
1 scallion, thinly sliced, to
  garnish

directions

1. Heat the oil in a large, nonstick or heavy saucepan. Add the flour, stirring constantly, until all the oil is absorbed by the flour, about 5 minutes.
2. Add the garlic, curry and salt. Lightly brown for about 3 minutes.
3. Combine the shoyu and water. Gradually add it to the pan, whisking to prevent lumps.
4. Simmer uncovered, stirring frequently, until the desired consistency is reached, about 10 minutes.
5. **Meanwhile,** reheat the rice in a steamer.
6. Place the rice on individual plates. Pour a generous 1/4 cup of the sauce over each serving and garnish with scallion.

variation

• For a creamier sauce, substitute 3/4 cup soy or rice beverage for 3/4 cup water.

mini
pizza

In a rush? While the muffin is toasting, make a simple salad to go with this speedy pizza.

ingredients

1 whole wheat English muffin

2-3 TBS. *Un-Tomato Sauce,*
    page 123

1-2 soy cheese slices

directions

1. Split open the English muffin with a fork. Toast the muffin.
2. Spread the sauce on top of both halves.
3. Place the soy cheese slices over the sauce.
4. Broil on low for 5 minutes to melt the "cheese." Serve hot.

variations

- Substitute organic tomato sauce for *Un-Tomato Sauce.*
- Substitute 2 tablespoons *Savory Tofu Spread,* page 196, for the soy cheese slices.
- Add steamed or sautéed vegetables in step #3. Good choices are sliced onions, summer squash and broccoli florets.
- Add marinated artichoke hearts, cooked beans or sliced olives in step #3.

sesame
rice patties

yield: 10 patties

These golden, crunchy patties make a terrific last-minute meal. All that you need on hand are leftover rice and toasted sesame seeds.

ingredients

6 cups pressure-cooked
  brown rice

3 TBS. barley miso

1/2 cup sesame seeds,
  toasted

1 tsp. toasted sesame oil

directions

1. Reheat the rice in a steamer.
2. Place the rice in a bowl. Add the miso and mix well.
3. With wet hands, form patties with 1/2 cup of the mixture.
4. Place the toasted sesame seeds in a plate, then roll the patties in the seeds.
5. Heat the oil in a large, nonstick skillet. Sauté the patties until golden brown on each side, about 5 minutes.

cook's tips

*   Pressure-cook 2 cups of short-grain brown rice with 3 cups of water to yield 6 cups of cooked rice.
*   To ensure firm patties, compact the mixture well, as you would a snowball. Then flatten the patties with open hands, using your thumbs to firm the edges.

grilled soy cheese sandwich

yield: 4 sandwiches

This alternative grilled "cheese" sandwich will fool almost everyone. If you are not a mustard or sauerkraut fan, omit them. This fills the bill for a quick lunch on the weekend.

ingredients

8 ounces soy cheese slices

8 slices naturally leavened bread

2 tsp. prepared natural mustard, optional

4 TBS. sauerkraut, optional

1 tsp. Spectrum Naturals® Canola Spread

directions

1. Place the soy cheese slices on the bread.
2. Spread mustard and/or sauerkraut on top of the soy cheese.
3. Place the other slice of bread on top. Spread Spectrum Naturals® Canola Spread on the outside surfaces of the sandwich.
4. Place the sandwiches on a griddle, waffle iron or nonstick skillet. Cook covered until the bread is golden brown and the soy cheese is melted. Serve hot with a pickle on the side.

cook's tips

- If you are avoiding dairy, be aware that soy cheese contains 30% casein, which is a skim milk powder product. Nevertheless, my favorite soy cheese is Soyco® Veggy Singles™ Swiss Cheese Alternative.
- For more facts about bread, see What It's All About, page 17-18.

hummus
in-a-hurry

Looking for a party-pleaser or a quick meal? This high-calcium, easy spread can be served as a dip with rolled romaine lettuce leaves, pita bread or lavosh. For an instant lunch or dinner, stuff it into whole wheat pita bread with shredded lettuce.

ingredients

2 large garlic cloves
2 stalks celery, coarsely
　chopped
1/2 cup fresh lemon juice
1 15-ounce can organic
　chickpeas, rinsed

1/4 cup tahini
2 tsp. shoyu
1 pinch cayenne, optional
4 pepperocini, to garnish,
　optional

directions

1. Purée the garlic, celery and lemon juice in a food processor or a blender.
2. Add the rinsed beans, tahini, shoyu and cayenne. Blend until smooth and creamy.
3. Serve garnished with pepperocini.

variation

- Garnish with a sprinkle of extra-virgin olive oil and paprika.

cook's tip
- A food processor is the best choice for puréing hummus. A blender will do, but may require additional liquid, causing the spread to have a thinner consistency.

celery

lenore's natural cuisine

194

tofu
"egg" salad

This healthful version of classic egg salad is wonderful served on a bed of lettuce or in a sandwich.

ingredients

1 pound firm tofu
1 TBS. orange juice, freshly squeezed, or more to taste
1 TBS. shoyu
1/4 tsp. unrefined sea salt
1/4 tsp. turmeric

3 TBS. Vegenaise®, vegan mayonnaise
1 celery stalk, minced
2 scallions, thinly sliced
1/2 small onion, minced

directions

1. Refresh the tofu by steaming it for 4 minutes.
2. Crumble the tofu into a suribachi or mixing bowl.
3. Add the orange juice, shoyu, salt, turmeric and Vegenaise®. Mix well.
4. Add the remaining ingredients and mix gently.

variation

• Substitute water for the orange juice.

scallion

savory tofu spread

This quick, savory, high-calcium spread is a memorable alternative to margarine or butter. High in protein and low in fat, it can be added to a salad instead of cheese. Try it as a substitute for cream cheese on a bagel.

ingredients

1/2 pound soft tofu

1 TBS. tahini, or more to taste

2 TBS. barley miso, or more to taste

directions

1. Steam the tofu for 4 minutes.
2. Crumble the tofu into a suribachi or mixing bowl.
3. Add the tahini and miso. Mix well, adding a few tablespoons of water, as needed, to make a creamy consistency.
4. Store refrigerated in a glass jar. Keeps one week.

variation

- Add a pinch of dried oregano, basil, thyme or dill in step #3.

cook's tip

- To store the extra 1/2 pound of tofu, leave it in the tofu container or a glass jar covered with fresh water. Change the water every other day. It will keep for one week. When it starts to turn pink and has a rotten smell, throw it away!

notes

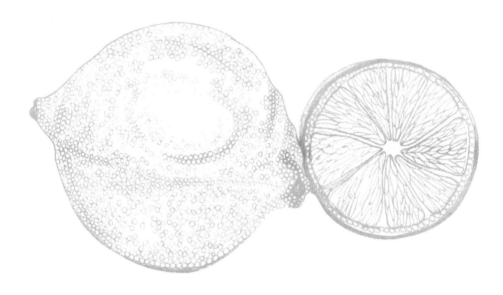

desserts

delectable
desserts

Most of us love to celebrate with the sweetness and decadent richness of desserts. The challenge is finding a way to indulge without creating more stress and dis-ease in our lives. What you will find in this chapter are luscious recipes made with guilt-free ingredients.

Successful baked desserts require oil for texture, sweetener for pleasure and, occasionally, nuts for crunch. Canola oil is a healthful alternative to butter and vegetable shortening. Brown rice syrup and barley malt are used instead of refined sugar, *see* pages 18-19. Whole wheat pastry flour is substituted for bleached white flour, see page 72. If you are eating well most of the time, feel free to splurge on these low-fat treats. As a final touch, drink Roma® grain *"Coffee"* with dessert. Its mildly bitter flavor perfectly complements sweets.

If you do not like to bake, there are other sensual dessert options. Europeans make a habit of enjoying the most wholesome dessert of all, fresh fruit. Since most fruits are heavily sprayed with pesticides, buy organic. You can also indulge in creamy, non-dairy puddings and ice cream alternatives like Sweet Nothings® and Soy Dream®.

Consider the seasons when choosing desserts. While cold *Strawberry Mousse* is appealing on a hot summer day, cookies fresh from the oven are enticing in winter. Storing homemade cookies in the freezer ensures there will be yummy, wholesome treats available anytime.

Finally, allow several weeks for your taste buds to become accustomed to the simple natural sweetness of brown rice and maple syrups. Many of us are addicted to the drug-like quality of white sugar. An assistant at our school, a professionally trained baker, loved conventional desserts. However, after a month of abstinence from refined sugar, even she no longer craved them. Join us in healthful decadence!

cook's tips

- Begin by measuring all of the ingredients. Room temperature ingredients allow the batter to rise as soon as it enters the oven.
- Nuts are scrumptious, but high in fat. If I am eating those calories, I want to see them, so chop them coarsely!
- Add salt to the wet mixture to evenly distribute it throughout the batter.
- Before pouring gooey syrups into measuring cups and spoons, brush them with oil. Syrups will glide out more easily.
- Use a blender to efficiently mix wet ingredients. This then allows you to gently combine the wet and dry ingredients, resulting in a lighter dessert.
- Sift flour through a standard mesh strainer to aerate it. This produces lighter baked goods.
- A whisk combines the wet and the dry ingredients more quickly and gently than a spoon.
- Over mixing tends to make a heavy baked product. Only stir until the flour is absorbed into the wet mixture. Small lumps will not ruin the batter.
- If the dough or batter is too wet, add one tablespoon of flour at a time. If it is too dry, add one tablespoon of water at a time.
- To prevent baked goods from sticking, line the pan with parchment paper.
- Use a spring-action cookie scoop, like a mini ice cream scoop, to make uniform cookies fast.

- Unless you have a convection oven, switch the cookie sheets from the top to the bottom, halfway through the baking time. This prevents uneven baking.
- Near the end of cooking time, pierce the center of baked goods with a toothpick. When the toothpick comes out dry, they are done.
- Allow cakes to set up in the baking pan for 5 minutes after baking to facilitate removing them.
- Place cookies on a rack to cool completely before freezing in glass jars. To thaw, set on the counter for 2-3 minutes. Refrigerated, they will stay fresh for about 5 days.

baked apples

yield: 4–8 servings

These juicy baked apples ooze with a sweetness and crunch that is hard to resist.

ingredients

4 apples, organic
1 TBS. barley miso
2 TBS. tahini

2 TBS. walnuts, coarsely
   chopped
1/2 cup water

directions

1. Preheat the oven to 375°F.
2. **Meanwhile**, wash and core the apples.
3. Purée the miso and tahini in a suribachi or whisk them together in a small bowl.
4. Add the walnuts. Mash with a fork or leave chunky, if you prefer.
5. Divide the filling into 4 parts. Spoon it into the center of each apple.
6. Place the filled apples in a baking dish. Pour the water around the apples to steam-bake them in the oven.
7. Bake, uncovered, until fork-tender, about 20 minutes.

cook's tip

- If you do not have an apple corer, slice the apples in half, then remove the core. Place the halves skin-side down and proceed with the recipe.

mom's
oatmeal cookies

yield: 2 dozen cookies

I cannot think of cookies more comforting than these. They remind me of cold winter afternoons in the kitchen with mom.

wet ingredients

- 1/4 cup canola oil
- 1/4 cup maple syrup
- 1/4 cup brown rice syrup
- 1/2 cup water
- 1 tsp. natural vanilla flavor

dry ingredients

- 1/4 tsp. unrefined sea salt
- 1/4 cup organic raisins, optional
- 2 cups rolled oats
- 3/4 cup whole wheat pastry flour

directions

1. Preheat the oven to 350°F.
2. Add the wet ingredients and the salt to a blender. Blend until the mixture becomes uniform in color.
3. Combine the dry ingredients in a bowl and mix well. Pour the wet mixture into the dry mixture and briefly blend with a whisk.
4. Allow the dough to rest for 5 minutes. This allows the rolled oats to soften. Gradually add more water, as needed, to make a loose batter.
5. Drop the dough from a cookie scoop or a tablespoon onto 2 oiled cookie sheets. Press flat with a wet fork or the back of a spoon.
6. Bake for 20-25 minutes, until golden brown and crispy on the bottom.
7. Allow the cookies to firm up on the cookie sheet for 5 minutes before removing with a spatula to a cooling rack.

cook's tip

- To plump raisins, cover them with boiling water and allow them to soak while assembling the other ingredients. Drain and reserve the raisin-soaking water. Substitute it for plain water in the recipe.

pecan
oatmeal cookies

yield: 21 cookies

Pecans add a rich crunchiness to these festive oatmeal cookies and they make an attractive holiday gift. These are the cookies that our dear friend, Chris Smith, makes every year for Christmas!

wet ingredients

- 1/3 cup canola oil
- 1/4 cup barley malt syrup
- 1/2 cup brown rice syrup
- 1 tsp. natural vanilla flavor
- 1/2 cup water

dry ingredients

- 1/4 tsp. unrefined sea salt
- 2 cups rolled oats
- 1 cup whole wheat pastry flour
- 1/2 cup pecans, toasted and coarsely chopped
- 21 pecan halves, to garnish

directions

1. Preheat the oven to 350°F.
2. Add the wet ingredients and the salt to a blender. Blend until the mixture becomes uniform in color.
3. Combine the dry ingredients, except the pecan halves, in a bowl and mix well. Pour the wet mixture into the dry mixture and briefly blend with a whisk.
4. Add the 1/2 cup of chopped pecans and stir gently.
5. Drop the dough from a cookie scoop or tablespoon onto 2 oiled cookie sheets. Press the cookies flat with a wet fork or the back of a spoon.
6. Gently press one pecan half into each cookie.
7. Bake for 20-30 minutes, until golden brown on the bottom.
8. Allow the cookies to firm up on the cookie sheet for 5 minutes, before removing them with a spatula to a cooling rack.

walnut-lemon shortbread

yield: 28 cookies

This shortbread crumbles with sublime sweetness in your mouth. Fresh lemon adds a tantalizing sparkle. They are a delectable finale to a special meal.

wet ingredients
1/3 cup canola oil
1/3 cup maple syrup
2 tsp. natural vanilla flavor
1 tsp. natural lemon flavor
2 TBS. water

dry ingredients
1/4 tsp. unrefined sea salt
1 1/4 cups rolled oats
1/2 cup walnuts, toasted
1 cup whole wheat pastry flour
1 TBS. grated lemon rind

directions
1. Preheat the oven to 350°F.
2. To make oat flour, place the rolled oats in a blender. Blend until a flour-like consistency is reached. Pour the flour into a mixing bowl.
3. To grind the walnuts, place them in a spice or coffee grinder. Process until a paste is formed. Alternatively, crush them in a suribachi.
4. Combine all of the dry ingredients in the bowl. Mix well with a whisk.
5. Combine the wet ingredients and the salt in the blender. Blend until uniform in color.
6. Pour the wet mixture into the dry mixture and briefly blend with a whisk. Add water or flour, as needed, to make a stiff dough.
7. Roll out the dough to 1/4-inch thick. Cut it into 1 x 2 inch rectangles. Using a spatula, transfer the pieces to an oiled cookie sheet.
8. Bake for 15-25 minutes, until golden brown on the bottom.
9. Allow the shortbread to firm up on the cookie sheet for 5 minutes, before removing to a cooling rack.

cook's tip
- Wipe the spice or coffee grinder clean before grinding the walnuts.

pumpkin
spice cookies

These spiced gems, reminiscent of pumpkin pie, are chock full of nuts and flavor. I begin to crave them around Thanksgiving every year.

wet ingredients

1/3 cup unrefined corn oil
1/2 cup maple syrup
1/4 cup barley malt syrup
1/2 cup brown rice syrup
1 1/2 tsp. natural vanilla
    flavor
  2 cups canned pumpkin

dry ingredients

1/4 tsp. unrefined sea salt
1 cup rolled oats
2 cups whole wheat pastry
  flour
1 tsp. cinnamon
3/4 tsp. nutmeg
1/2 tsp. allspice
1/2 tsp. ground cloves
1 cup nuts or seeds, toasted
  and coarsely chopped,
  optional

directions

1. Preheat the oven to 350°F.
2. Combine the wet ingredients and the salt in a blender. Blend until uniform in color.
3. Dry-roast the oats in a hot skillet over medium heat until golden brown. Stir often to prevent burning. Pour them into a mixing bowl.
4. Add the remaining dry ingredients to the oats and mix well.
5. Pour the wet mixture into the dry mixture and briefly blend with a whisk. Gradually add water or flour, as needed, to make a loose batter.
6. Drop the dough from a cookie scoop or tablespoon onto 2 oiled cookie sheets. Press the cookies flat with a wet fork or back of a spoon.
7. Bake for 30-35 minutes, until golden brown on the bottom.
8. Allow the cookies to firm up on the cookie sheet for 5 minutes, before removing them to a cooling rack.

variations

- Add 1/2 cup of currants or raisins in step #5.
- Substitute 3 cups of steamed buttercup squash for canned pumpkin, omit 1/4 cup maple syrup and add 1/4-1/2 cup water.

chocolate
chip cookies

yield: 3 dozen cookies

Yum, yum, yum! Here is my version of the much-loved chocolate chip cookie! You will be astonished when you taste these cookies made without dairy, refined sugar or white flour. You will have to hide them in your freezer.

wet ingredients
- 1/3 cup canola oil
- 1/4 cup brown rice syrup
- 1/3 cup maple syrup
- 1 tsp. natural vanilla flavor
- 3/4 cup water

dry ingredients
- 1/4 tsp. unrefined sea salt
- 1 1/2 cups whole wheat pastry flour
- 1 1/2 cups rolled oats
- 1 tsp. Rumford® baking powder
- 1 tsp. arrowroot powder
- 2/3-1 cup Sunspire® Chocolate Chips
- 1/2 cup walnuts, coarsely chopped, optional

directions
1. Preheat the oven to 350°F.
2. Combine the wet ingredients and the salt in a blender. Blend until uniform in color.
3. Combine the dry ingredients, except the chocolate chips and walnuts, in a bowl and mix well with a whisk.
4. Pour the wet mixture into the dry mixture and briefly blend with a whisk. Gradually add water, as needed, to make a loose batter.
5. Add the chocolate chips and walnuts and stir gently.
6. Drop the dough from a cookie scoop or tablespoon onto 2 oiled cookie sheets. Gently press the cookies flat with a wet fork or the back of a spoon.
7. Bake for 10-15 minutes, until golden brown on the bottom.
8. Allow the cookies to firm up on the cookie sheet for 5 minutes, before removing them to a cooling rack.
9. Do not eat up all the cookies the first day you bake them!

variation
- If you prefer a sweeter taste, substitute Tropical Source® for Sunspire® Chocolate Chips.

lenore's natural cuisine

208

double chocolate chip cookies

yield: 3 dozen cookies

Luxuriate in the sensual chocolate taste of these wonderful cookies. You will be surprised how easy they are to make.

wet ingredients

- 1/3 cup canola oil
- 1/3 cup brown rice syrup
- 1/3 cup maple syrup
- 1 tsp. natural vanilla flavor
- 2 TBS. Roma®, dissolved in 2/3 cup boiling water

dry ingredients

- 1/4 tsp. unrefined sea salt
- 2 1/2 cups whole wheat pastry flour
- 1 cup rolled oats
- 1/3 cup natural cocoa powder
- 1/2 tsp. Rumford® baking powder
- 1 tsp. arrowroot powder
- 1 tsp. grated orange rind
- 2/3 cup Sunspire® chocolate chips
- 3/4 walnuts, toasted and coarsely chopped, optional

directions

1. Preheat the oven to 350°F.
2. Combine the wet ingredients and the salt in a blender. Blend until uniform in color.
3. Combine the dry ingredients, except the chocolate chips and walnuts, in a bowl and mix well with a whisk.
4. Pour the wet mixture into the dry mixture and briefly blend with a whisk. Gradually add water, as needed, to make a loose batter.
5. Add the chocolate chips and walnuts and stir gently.
6. Drop the dough from a cookie scoop or tablespoon onto 2 oiled cookie sheets. Gently press the cookies flat with a wet fork or the back of a spoon.
7. Bake for 10-15 minutes, until golden brown on the bottom.
8. Allow the cookies to firm up on the cookie sheet for 5 minutes, before removing them to a cooling rack.

cook's tip

- For a smoother consistency, substitute rolled oats flour, page 230, for the rolled oats.

fabulous brownies

Everyone loves these wonderful brownies. It is hard to believe they are not the real thing. Sian Yardley, my British assistant, describes these gems as rich, chocolatey and "scrummy!"

wet ingredients

- 1/4 cup canola oil
- 1/2 cup brown rice syrup
- 1/4 cup maple syrup
- 1 tsp. natural vanilla flavor
- 1/2 cup water

dry ingredients

- 1/4 tsp. unrefined sea salt
- 2 cups whole wheat pastry flour
- 1 1/2 tsp. Rumford® baking powder
- 1/3 cup natural cocoa powder
- 3/4 cup walnuts, toasted and coarsely chopped, optional

directions

1. Preheat the oven to 350°F.
2. Combine the wet ingredients and the salt in a blender. Blend until uniform in color.
3. Combine the dry ingredients in a bowl and mix well with a whisk.
4. Pour the wet mixture into the dry mixture and briefly blend with a whisk. Gradually add water, as needed, to make a loose batter.
5. Pour the batter into an oiled 8-inch square baking pan
6. Bake for 45 minutes or until a toothpick comes out clean and dry. If you prefer a soft and gooey, fudge-like consistency, bake for only 30-35 minutes.
7. Allow the brownies to set up in a baking pan for 5 minutes. Cut into squares and serve.

variations

- Add 1/2 cup peanut butter and 1 teaspoon cinnamon in step #4.
- Add 3/4 cup Sunspire® chocolate chips in step #4.

cook's tip
- Brownies freeze well, stored in a glass jar.

guilt-free chocolate fudge

Who would imagine you could make a healthy version of fudge? We can thank Margaret Lawson, author of The Naturally Healthy Gourmet, *for this remarkable confection. The secret to mimicking the texture of fudge is to store these sweets in the freezer. It takes only minutes to defrost these squares of chocolate heaven.*

ingredients

1/2 cup water
1/4 cup agar flakes
  1 pinch of unrefined sea salt
1/4 cup maple syrup
1/4 cup Sweet Cloud® brown
   rice syrup
1/2 cup natural cocoa powder

1/3 cup tahini
1 1/2 TBS. kudzu, dissolved in
   1/4 cup cool water
1 TBS. natural vanilla flavor
1/2 cup walnuts, toasted and
   coarsely chopped, optional

directions

1. Pour the water into a medium saucepan. Stir in the agar flakes and the salt. Bring to a boil, then lower the heat to simmer for about 5 minutes.
2. Add the maple syrup, brown rice syrup, cocoa and tahini. Simmer for 3 more minutes, stirring constantly with a whisk.
3. Add the dissolved kudzu. Stir constantly until the mixture thickens and becomes translucent, about 3 minutes.
4. Remove from the heat. Stir in the vanilla and the walnuts.
5. Pour the fudge into an 8-inch square dish and freeze, covered, for 1 hour. Cut into 24 squares.

variations

- Substitute almond butter for the tahini and almonds for walnuts.
- Substitute carob for the cocoa powder.

cook's tip

- Fudge freezes well in a quart glass jar. Separate the fudge squares with small pieces of waxed paper.

crispy
rice treats

These sweet, chewy delights are enjoyed by children and adults alike.

wet ingredients

- 1 tsp. sesame oil
- 2 TBS. peanut butter, or more to taste
- 3 TBS. barley malt syrup
- 3 TBS. brown rice syrup
- 1 pinch unrefined sea salt
- 1 tsp. natural vanilla flavor

dry ingredients

- 3 cups brown rice crispy cereal

directions

1. Add the oil, peanut butter, sweeteners and salt to a medium saucepan. Warm over low heat, stirring well.
2. Remove the saucepan from the heat and stir in the vanilla. Gently fold in the cereal until it is completely coated.
3. Spoon the mixture into a 6 x 8-inch glass storage container. With wet hands, press the mixture firmly into the glass container. Score it into 16 squares, then refrigerate it until firm.
4. Separate the squares with pieces of wax paper and store refrigerated.

variations

- Add 1/2 cup of chopped nuts, raisins or both in step #2.
- Substitute almond butter for the peanut butter.
- Add 1/3 cup of chocolate chips in step #2.

flan
custard

Feel free to indulge in this divinely sweet and delicate custard. It is as delectable as the classic version without the fat, dairy and refined sugar.

ingredients

2 cups soy or rice beverage
1/3 cup brown rice syrup
2 TBS. agar flakes
1/4 tsp. unrefined sea salt
1/4 tsp. ground cinnamon

2 TBS. kudzu, dissolved
  in 1/4 cup cool water
2 tsp. natural vanilla flavor
1/4 tsp. natural almond flavor

directions

1. Pour the soy or rice beverage, brown rice syrup, agar flakes and salt into a small saucepan. Simmer until most of the flakes have dissolved, about 8 minutes, stirring occasionally.
2. Add the cinnamon and the dissolved kudzu. Stir constantly until the mixture thickens and becomes translucent, about 5 minutes.
3. Whisk in the vanilla and almond flavors.
4. Pour the mixture into a rinsed glass or ceramic dish. Refrigerate covered until firm, at least one hour.

variation

• Add 1/4 teaspoon of rum flavor in step #3.

cook's tips

• For a silky consistency, press the mixture through a fine strainer at the end of step #3.
• For preparation of puddings, I recommend EdenBlend® for its smooth, creamy consistency, milky color and excellent flavor.

strawberry mousse delight

A superb cook and a fellow student from the Kushi Institute, Elainie Gagné, created this fabulous light and creamy strawberry mousse. It only tastes decadent! This is a summer party pleaser.

almond milk ingredients
1/4 cup almonds
1 cup boiling water
1 pinch unrefined sea salt

remaining ingredients
1/4 cup brown rice syrup
2 TBS. agar flakes
1 pinch unrefined sea salt
1 pint fresh strawberries
1/2 lemon, juiced
1/2 lemon rind, grated
1 tsp. natural vanilla flavor
2 TBS. kudzu, dissolved in
    1/4 cup cool water

directions
1. To make almond milk, add the almonds, water and the salt to a blender. Blend until puréed, then strain. Discard the pulp.
2. Combine the almond milk, brown rice syrup, agar flakes and another pinch of salt in a medium saucepan. Simmer until the agar flakes have dissolved, about 8 minutes, stirring occasionally. Pour the mixture into a blender.
3. **Meanwhile**, wash the strawberries, then remove the stems. Set aside 4-6 small, unblemished berries for the garnish. Add the remaining strawberries to the blender with the almond milk mixture.
4. Add the lemon juice, lemon rind, vanilla and the dissolved kudzu. Blend for 1 minute.
5. Refrigerate covered for 1 hour.
6. Whip the mixture with a hand mixer. Refrigerate for 1 more hour until firm.
7. Spoon into individual bowls and serve garnished with a strawberry.

variations
- Substitute 1 cup of soy or rice beverage for the almond milk.
- Substitute raspberries for strawberries.

almond amazake pudding

yield: 4 servings

Amazake, a sweet rice drink, has a luscious milk shake consistency. Available refrigerated or frozen in most natural foods stores, it makes a wholesome pudding in a jiffy.

ingredients

- 1 pint almond amazake
- 4 TBS. kudzu, dissolved in 1/3 cup cool water
- 1 pinch unrefined sea salt
- 1/2 tsp. natural vanilla flavor
- 4 almonds, toasted, cut in 1/2 to garnish

directions

1. Heat the amazake in a small saucepan until it boils. Add the dissolved kudzu and the salt.
2. Whisk until thick, about 3 minutes. If the pudding is not thick enough, add an extra tablespoon of kudzu, dissolved in 3 tablespoons of cool water.
3. Remove from the heat. Add the vanilla and whisk again. Pour the mixture into serving dishes, garnished with almonds. Allow the pudding to set up for about an hour. Serve warm or cold.

variations

- Substitute 1 teaspoon of almond flavor for the vanilla flavor.
- Substitute another amazake flavor for the almond amazake.
- Top the pudding with almond crunch: 3 tablespoons of toasted and chopped almonds mixed with 1 teaspoon brown rice syrup.

flat whisk

rice
pudding

This is a sweet way to use leftover brown rice. If you keep amazake on hand in the freezer, you can make this comforting treat anytime.

ingredients

1 cup amazake
2 cups cooked brown rice
1/8 tsp. unrefined sea salt
2 TBS. currants
1/4 tsp. cinnamon, optional

1/2 tsp. natural vanilla flavor
1/4 tsp. grated lemon rind
1/4 cup walnuts, toasted
and coarsely chopped,
optional

directions

1. Combine the amazake, cooked rice, salt, currants, and cinnamon in a medium saucepan.
2. Place a flame tamer under the saucepan. Cover and simmer for 5 minutes, stirring occasionally.
3. Stir in the vanilla, lemon rind and walnuts. Simmer for 1 more minute before serving.

variations

- Substitute sunflower seeds for the walnuts.
- Substitute raisins for the currants.

cook's tip

- Raisins are dried grapes which are heavily sprayed with pesticides. Opt for organic.

indian pudding

The gentle sweetness of amazake, a rice drink, teams well with cornmeal to create an earthy delight. Make this pudding in fall and winter to warm your body and soul.

ingredients

1 cup cornmeal
1 1/2 cups water
2 cups amazake
1/4 tsp. unrefined sea salt
1/4 cup barley malt syrup
1/2 tsp. cinnamon

1/2 tsp. ginger powder
1 tsp. grated lemon rind
1 tsp. natural vanilla flavor
1 TBS. sunflower seeds,
    toasted, to garnish

directions

1. In a medium, heavy, nonstick pot, dry-roast the cornmeal over low heat. Stir constantly until golden and fragrant, about 5 minutes.
2. When the cornmeal cools, add the water and whisk well.
3. Add the amazake, salt, barley malt syrup, cinnamon and ginger. Simmer, covered, over low heat for 45-50 minutes. Use a flame tamer to prevent scorching. Whisk occasionally.
4. Just before serving, whisk in the lemon rind and vanilla. Serve the pudding hot, garnished with sunflower seeds.

variations

- To increase sweetness and add texture, add 1/2 cup of currants or raisins in step #3.
- To make a richer-tasting pudding, add 1/4 cup of tahini in step #3.

cook's tip
- Spoon leftover pudding into a covered glass dish. After it cools, cut it into slices and serve it garnished with toasted sunflower seeds.

poppyseed cake

This is a tender and moist cake, enlivened with fresh lemon zest and crunchy poppy seeds.

wet ingredients
- 1/4 cup canola oil
- 1/4 cup unrefined corn oil
- 3/4 cup Sweet Cloud® brown rice syrup
- 1 1/3 cup soy or rice beverage
- 2 tsp. natural vanilla flavor

dry ingredients
- 1/4 tsp. unrefined sea salt
- 3 1/4 cups whole wheat pastry flour
- 1/4 cup chickpea flour
- 1 TBS. cinnamon
- 1 tsp. nutmeg
- 3 TBS. poppy seeds
- 1 lemon rind, grated
- 2 tsp. Rumford® baking powder

directions
1. Preheat the oven to 350°F.
2. Combine the wet ingredients and the salt in a blender. Blend until uniform in color.
3. Sift the pastry flour through a mesh strainer into a bowl. Add the remaining dry ingredients to the bowl and mix well with a whisk.
4. Pour the wet mixture into the dry mixture briefly blending with a whisk. Gradually add water, as needed, to make a loose batter.
5. Pour the batter into a 9-inch, oiled cake pan and bake for 40-45 minutes.
6. The cake is done when a toothpick inserted in the middle comes out dry and the cake is golden in color.
7. Allow the cake to set up in cake pan for 5 minutes. Place it on a rack to cool.

variations
- Substitute 1/4 cup of EnerG® egg replacer or arrowroot powder for the chickpea flour.
- Spread *Lemon Icing*, page 220, over the cooled cake.
- Substitute amazake for the soy or rice beverage.

cook's tip

- Chickpea flour can be found in Italian grocery stores and well-stocked natural foods stores. Its oil content helps to bind the cake.

blueberry couscous cake with lemon icing

yield: 8-12 servings

A cake made in twenty minutes without flour, oil or sugar? It's true! Lemon icing adds a tart edge, balancing the cake's sweetness. Blueberry couscous cake is good any time of day. Sometimes we even eat it for breakfast!

cake ingredients

2 3/4 cups water
2/3 cup brown rice syrup
1 pinch of unrefined sea salt
2 cups couscous
1 lemon rind, grated
1 tsp. natural vanilla flavor
1 cup blueberries

icing ingredients

1/3 cup water
2 TBS. Sweet Cloud® brown rice syrup
1 pinch unrefined salt
1 1/2 TBS. kudzu, dissolved in
1/4 cup cool water
1 small lemon, juiced

cake directions

1. Add the water, brown rice syrup and the salt to a medium saucepan. Bring to a slow boil.
2. Add the couscous and stir occasionally with a wooden spoon until thickened, 7-8 minutes. Remove from the heat.
3. Stir in the lemon peel and vanilla. Gently fold in the blueberries, reserving 2 tablespoons for the garnish.
4. Pour the mixture into a 2-quart ceramic or glass dish which has been rinsed with water. With wet hands, compress the mixture and smooth the top surface. Allow the cake to firm up for about an hour before icing it.

icing directions

1. Add the water, brown rice syrup and the salt to a small saucepan. Bring to a slow boil.
2. Add the dissolved kudzu and the lemon juice. Stir constantly until the mixture thickens and becomes translucent, about 3 minutes.
3. Pour the icing over the cake, smoothing it evenly. Garnish with the reserved blueberries.

variations

- Substitute other sliced fruit, like raspberries, strawberries, apples, peaches or pears for the blueberries.

"coffee"

Roma® is an instant grain beverage with a slightly bitter taste. This taste complements the sweetness of desserts and breakfast foods. Besides, it's low in calories and caffeine-free! Make a "café latté" by adding warm soy or rice beverage.

ingredients

6 cups boiling water
2 TBS. Roma®, or more to taste

1 tsp. natural vanilla flavor
1 sprinkle cinnamon to garnish, optional

directions

1. Pour all of the ingredients, except the cinnamon, into a blender. Blend until frothy, less than a minute.
2. Pour the mixture into tall mugs, sprinkle with cinnamon and enjoy!

variations

- Other coffee alternatives are Sip®, Bamboo®, Pero®, Yannoh® and Cafix®. However, my personal favorite is Roma®.

cook's tip

- I like to add the creamy richness of EdenBlend® to make "café latté."

appendix

glossary

The majority of these foods are available at natural foods stores. If you cannot find something, check the mail-order list. The quality of ingredients is of paramount importance for outstanding flavor.

Adzuki Bean, Azuki Bean [ad-zoo-kee, ah-zoo-kee] Adzuki beans are small, sweet, purple-colored beans, reputed to be diuretic and highly beneficial to the kidneys.

Agar, Agar-Agar [ah-gahr] This sea vegetable is also known as kanten. It contains a complex starch that acts as a gelling agent. Used in desserts, it is a healthful alternative to gelatin, which contains ground horse's hooves and other animal parts.

Amaranth [am-ah-ranth] Amaranth is a cream-colored seed, the size of a poppy seed. It was once the prized food of the Aztecs. Amaranth is a high-energy endurance food, offering more calcium and protein than milk.

Amazake [a-mah-sah-kee] Amazake is a sweet, fermented rice drink high in nutrients. It contains complex sugars, so it supplies the body with long-lasting energy. It has the consistency of a milk shake and is available in a variety of flavors, including almond, mocha java, vanilla bean, hazelnut and original. You can find it in the freezer or refrigerator section in natural foods stores.

Arrowroot Powder This tropical root yields a white starch which is used to thicken sauces. Once thickened, the arrowroot mixture becomes clear. Be aware that over stirring can cause the sauce to become thin again. Arrowroot is high in calcium and is nutritionally superior to cornstarch. However, there is a third alternative that I prefer, kudzu. See Kudzu. In her award-winning book, *The New Whole Foods Encyclopedia*, Rebecca Wood recommends the following substitutions: 1 tablespoon arrowroot powder for 2 1/4 teaspoons cornstarch or 1 1/2 tablespoons flour.

Baking Powder Baking powder is used as a leavening agent to make baked goods rise. Unfortunately, most commercial brands contain unhealthful aluminum compounds. Buy aluminum-free brands such as Rumford®.

Balsamic Vinegar [bal-sah-mihk] This Italian vinegar is aged in wooden barrels. It graces foods with its rich color and complex flavor, which is both sweet and sour.

Barley Malt Syrup This syrup is similar to molasses in taste and appearance. It is made by cooking sprouted barley until it becomes a sweet syrup. Its primary component is maltose, a complex sugar, which provides longer-lasting energy than sweeteners made of simple sugars.

Bragg® Liquid Aminos Made from soybeans, Bragg® Liquid Aminos is an unfermented alternative to tamari. It is not a personal favorite, but you may want to use it if you are avoiding fermented foods.

Brown Rice Syrup This thick, amber-colored syrup is commonly used to sweeten desserts. Traditional rice syrup is produced by combining whole, sprouted barley with cooked brown rice. In contrast, domestic brands use extracted barley enzymes instead of whole barley to produce the syrup. This affects the overall quality and taste. Meredith McCarty, author of *Sweet and Natural*, recommends Sweet Cloud® brown rice syrup because it is still made traditionally. Refrigerate rice syrup after opening.

Brown Rice Vinegar Imported from Japan, brown rice vinegar has a smooth, mild flavor. Buy brands that are traditionally brewed. This means that the vinegar has been fermented for approximately one year, assuring superior quality.

Bulgur Wheat, Bulgar, Bulghur [buhl-guhr] Bulgur consists of wheat kernels that have been steamed, dried and crushed. It has a nutty flavor and cooks much faster than whole wheat kernels. Although available in coarse, medium and fine grinds, I usually choose the coarse variety for its chewy texture. Store in the refrigerator or freezer.

Canola Oil [kan-oh-luh] Extracted from rape seed, canola oil is lower in saturated fats than any other oil. Because it has a neutral taste, it is a great choice for baking. Refrigerate after opening. See also Spectrum Naturals® Canola Spread.

Chestnuts Even though chestnuts are less than ten percent fat, they offer a rich, sweet taste. They are available fresh in the fall or dried year round. Refrigerate dried chestnuts to keep grain moths at bay.

Chickpeas   Chickpeas, also known as garbanzo beans, have a delicious, sweet flavor. While most other beans weigh in at 0.5% fat, chickpeas contain 2.6%. This makes them rich and creamy.

Chocolate   Conventional chocolate bars contain refined sugar, milk products, chemical additives and hydrogenated fats. For a healthier alternative, choose organic, non-dairy chocolate bars that are sweetened with unrefined sugar cane juice. For baking, use a natural, unsweetened cocoa powder which is typically dairy-free.

Chocolate Chips   Sunspire® makes guilt-free chocolate chips. They are dairy-free and are sweetened with malted grains. Tropical Source® chocolate chips are also dairy-free, but they are sweetened with unrefined sugar cane juice. Many people cannot tell the difference between these and the "real" chocolate chips.

Corn Grits and Cornmeal   Both made from dried, ground corn, these foods are often confused with each other. Corn grits are coarse and are used to make cooked cereal and polenta. Cornmeal is finer and is used to make muffins and cornbread. Both must be kept refrigerated to prevent rancidity.

Corn Oil   This oil has a buttery flavor, so I occasionally like to use it in baking and when I use corn as an ingredient. However, it is not as healthful as canola oil and tends to make baked goods heavy.

Couscous   [koos-koos] This quick-cooking grain is made from steamed semolina wheat, which has been oven-dried. It is best stored in the refrigerator.

Currant   [kur-uhnts] A currant is a dried Zante grape. It resembles a tiny, dark raisin, but has a tangy edge. They are perfect for baking since they hold their shape better than raisins.

Daikon   [dye-kon] Sweet and pungent, this long, white radish has great healing properties. According to traditional medicine, it aids in the digestion of fat and protein and is effective against many bacterial and fungal infections. I like to add it to miso soup.

Dulse   [duhlss] This tasty sea vegetable is particularly delicious cooked in oatmeal. Before cooking, remove the small shells that are often found clinging to it.

EdenBlend® EdenBlend®, my replacement for milk, is a combination of organic rice and soy beverages. I prefer it over rice milk or soy milk, since it is lighter in color and taste and has complementary proteins.

EnerG® Egg Replacer EnerG® is a vegetarian and gluten-free egg substitute. For those avoiding nightshade vegetables, be aware that it does contain potato starch. Alternatively, you can substitute an equal amount of arrowroot powder.

Florets This term refers to bite-sized pieces cut from the heads of broccoli or cauliflower.

Garlic A pungent food, garlic is famous for its healing powers. It is reputed to be antibacterial, anticarcinogenic and antifungal. It is also known to lower blood pressure and cholesterol. See *The Healing Power of Food* for a complete list of health benefits. To easily remove the papery skin, set the clove on a hard surface. Place the flat side of a chef's knife blade against the clove and lightly smash with the side of the fist. This will cause the skin to break away. Separate individual cloves and cut off the root end. To prevent wooden cutting boards from absorbing the strong flavors of garlic and onions, wet the board before cutting them. I mince garlic instead of pressing it, since this texture works better in most dishes. Sauté garlic for only one minute or it will become bitter. Store leftover cloves in a cool, dry place. If there is a green sprout in the center of the garlic clove, discard it. It is old and will taste bitter. You can increase the anti-carcinogenic benefits of garlic if you cut it and allow to stand for 10 minutes before cooking it.

Gingerroot This pungent vegetable is superb in stir-fries and dressings. According to traditional medicine, it increases circulation, stimulates digestion and is an effective remedy for motion sickness. To effectively shred ginger, use a ginger grater. Asian and natural foods stores carry porcelain or aluminum ginger graters, although I prefer stainless steel. To make ginger juice, place grated pulp into the palm of the hand. Squeeze out the juice by making a tight fist. You might want to do this over a strainer so that no bits of pulp accidentally fall into the juice. Store fresh ginger in the refrigerator in a paper bag. Slice off the shredded edge when you are ready to reuse it.

Gomashio [goh-mah-shee-o] Gomashio is a condiment made from toasted, crushed sesame seeds and unrefined sea salt. It is a perfect accompaniment to grains and other foods.

Hato Mugi Barley [hah-to moo-gee] See Job's Tears.

Herbamere® This organic herb seasoning can be used to make an instant vegetable stock to boost the flavor of soups. Use one half teaspoon per quart of water. Note that it contains salt, so adjust your own recipes accordingly.

Hot Sesame Oil This oil is extracted from toasted sesame seeds and red chili peppers. It imparts a fiery edge to stir-fries.

Job's Tears Job's tears, also known as hato mugi, is a pearl-shaped grain with a hearty, chewy texture. Traditional medicine believes that it helps reduce arthritis symptoms, urinary problems, cysts and tumors. Combine with other grains or add to soups. My favorite use for these little gems is in *Green Split Pea Soup*, page 56. Pick over for stones and bits of hulls. Soak at least an hour before cooking. See Mail Order Sources.

Kanten [kan-tehn] See Agar.

Kasha [kah-shuh] Kasha is toasted buckwheat. It is amber in color and has a wonderful, nutty flavor. Plain buckwheat tends to be bland unless you toast it yourself. Related to rhubarb, buckwheat is not a true grain, even though it is cooked like one. Nor is it related to wheat. Buckwheat is gluten-free and, therefore, excellent for people with allergies. Its warming nature makes it popular in cold places like Siberia and Michigan! Buckwheat is rich in protein, iron and vitamins E and B complex. In addition, buckwheat has 100% more calcium than any grain and has all eight essential amino acids, rare in the true grain family. Kasha is best stored in the refrigerator.

Kombu [kohm-boo] Kombu is a dried sea vegetable, also known as kelp. It was the original MSG, acting as a natural flavor enhancer. When cooked with beans, it makes them easier to digest.

Kudzu [kood-zoo] This root starch is used as a thickening agent in sauces and icings. First, dissolve it in cool water. Then, cook it until thickened and translucent, about five minutes. According to traditional medicine, kudzu is beneficial to the intestines and stomach. It is also used to make blood more alkaline and to relieve acute muscle pain. Kudzu has more medicinal properties than arrowroot powder and has double the thickening power. One tablespoon of kudzu thickens one cup of liquid. See Arrowroot Powder.

Kukicha Twig Tea [ku-kee-cha] This low-caffeine tea is naturally sweet, especially when it's organic. High in minerals, it is made from the stems and twigs of tea bushes.

Kuzu See Kudzu.

Legumes [lehg-yoom] This plant family includes beans, lentils, peanuts and peas. All grow in pods and are high in protein. They are generally referred to as beans.

Maple Syrup On average, 40 gallons of maple tree sap are required to produce one gallon of maple syrup. It is sold in various grades. AA grade is perfect for dressings and sauces. B grade is often used for baking. Keep in mind that maple syrup is made up of simple sugars, so it is not as healthful as brown rice syrup. Refrigerate after opening.

Millet [mihl-leht] Gluten-free, millet has more iron than any other grain. It helps balance blood sugar levels and is one of the few grains which is alkaline. Japanese Kibi millet is so sweet and tasty that it is well worth the time and money to send for it. See Mail Order Sources.

Mirin [mihr-ihn] This heavenly, traditional cooking wine is imported from Japan. It is made from sweet brown rice, koji and water. Its light, sweet taste balances the flavors of strong condiments like shoyu, miso and vinegar. Common commercial brands are almost always chemically brewed and sweetened with sugar. Buy only naturally brewed varieties, available at natural foods stores.

Miso [mee-soh] Miso is an aged, fermented soybean paste made from cooked soybeans, salt and usually a grain. The two main types of miso are dark and light. Dark commonly refers to barley miso, which has been aged for at least two years. It has a salty taste and is used in dark-colored soups, gravies and stews. Light miso has a sweeter taste because it contains less salt and is fermented for less time. It is used in light-colored soups and sauces. Regardless of the type, unpasteurized miso contains friendly bacteria, high quality protein and digestive enzymes. Since digestive enzymes are destroyed by high heat, do not boil after adding miso to the dish. Store miso in the refrigerator.

Mochi [moh-chee] Mochi is cooked, sweet brown rice that has been pounded and formed into flat cakes. It is a superb, wholesome snack or breakfast food, since it offers long-lasting energy. Traditionally, mochi is considered excellent for pregnant and lactating women. It is available in the freezer or refrigerator section in natural foods stores.

Mustard, Prepared Natural This prepared condiment is made of dried mustard seeds mixed with vinegar and spices. Stoneground mustard has a lovely flavor and a rustic feel.

Nuts Store shelled nuts in the refrigerator or freezer, otherwise they will become rancid. To toast nuts, preheat a large, nonstick skillet. Rinse nuts through a strainer and pour into the hot skillet. Dry-roast until nuts are dry and light brown in color, about eight minutes. Stir continuously with a wooden spoon or rice paddle to prevent burning.

Oat Flour Oat flour can be made fresh at home. Simply place rolled oats in a blender and blend until a flour-like consistency has been reached, about one minute.

Olive Oil This fruity oil is frequently used in salad dressings and pasta dishes. High in vitamin E, olive oil is one of the most stable vegetable oils. The term extra-virgin means that the oil comes from the first stage of mechanically-pressed olives. This is in contrast to later extractions when chemicals and heat are used, destroying flavor and trace nutrients. I store it in the refrigerator to preserve its flavor and freshness, but keep a small amount by the stove.

Olives Olives are either green or black. The green ones are simply unripened black olives. Regardless of the type, the tastiest olives are those that have been naturally cured in a salt solution. My favorite olive, Kalamata, can be found in most ethnic markets and natural foods stores.

Oregano I prefer dried, ground oregano which imparts a smooth consistency to any dish, unlike the common, coarse leaf variety.

Pasta While whole wheat pasta may be the healthiest choice, it is too heavy for most people to truly enjoy. I prefer wholesome noodles made from lighter, whole-grain flours, such as artichoke, corn, kamut, quinoa, rice and buckwheat. Each has a distinct color, flavor and shape. Semolina pasta, made from refined durum wheat, is the most popular variety. My favorite brand is the readily available DeCecco®.

Peanut Butter Commonly thought of as a nut, a peanut is actually a legume. Although high in oil, peanut butter is also high in protein with no cholesterol. While natural peanut butter contains only peanuts and salt, commercial brands contain sugar and many chemical additives for marketing appeal. A significant drawback to peanut butter is that a carcinogenic mold, aflatoxin, is commonly found on peanuts grown in damp conditions. Buy only brands which are certified to be free of aflatoxin, such as Arrowhead Mills®. Keep refrigerated.

Pepper Black pepper is considered an irritant to the intestines. I substitute its milder sister, white pepper, in dishes that call for pepper.

Polenta [poh-lehn-tah] Polenta is the Italian name for traditional porridge made from cornmeal. For a speedy version made in the pressure cooker, see *Quick and Easy Polenta*, page 108.

Pumpkin Seeds Pumpkin seeds are not from a pumpkin, but rather from a South American squash. They are not only a good source of Omega-3 fatty acids, zinc, iron and calcium, but contain 29% protein. They are the most delicious when dry-roasted. See Nuts for dry-roasting instructions.

Quinoa [keen-wah] Quinoa is grown in the high valleys of the Andes. It was the staple food for the Incas because it thrives under the most rugged conditions. Quinoa, like amaranth, is a member of the goosefoot family, rather than being a true grain. It is easy to digest, quick-cooking and acts as a high-energy endurance food. As an added bonus, it has the highest protein content of any grain. It contains all eight essential amino acids, including lysine, which is rarely found in the plant kingdom. Rinse thoroughly before cooking to remove the bitter saponin coating.

Radicchio [rah-dee-kee-oh] This is the Italian name for red chicory.

It is a mildly bitter, bright purple vegetable that looks like a miniature red cabbage. Radicchio is often used to perk up the flavor and color of leafy green salads.

Rice, Brown Brown rice is a whole grain, with only the inedible, outer husk removed. It is a good source of B vitamins, minerals, carbohydrates and fiber. In cool weather, I pressure-cook short-grain rice. In warmer weather, I often boil brown basmati, the most aromatic long-grain variety.

Rice Milk Just as you would imagine, rice milk is a beverage made from rice. Check the package label for ingredients, as all rice milks are not made from whole brown rice. See EdenBlend®.

Rice, Sweet Brown Sweet brown rice is more glutinous, higher in protein and sweeter than regular brown rice. It is traditionally made into mochi. You can cook it with other grains for a sweet change. See *Mochi*, page 111, and *Beyond Brown Rice*, page 112.

Rolled Oats These are whole oat groats that have been flattened between rollers in order to shorten cooking time. See also Oat Flour.

Roma® Roma®, an instant grain cereal beverage, is made from chicory and roasted malt barley. It is caffeine-free and has a robust, full-bodied taste. With only ten calories per teaspoon, Roma® is an excellent coffee substitute. See "*Coffee*," page 221. Other brands of instant grain cereal beverages are Bamboo®, Cafix®, Pero® and Sip®.

Rutabaga [roo-tuh-bay-guh] Surprisingly, this vegetable is a cross between turnip and wild cabbage. It is large and round with a light yellow and purple skin. It tastes slightly sweet and is high in fiber. Supermarket rutabagas are almost always waxed, so peel off the skin.

Sauerkraut Sauerkraut, a naturally-fermented condiment, is made from cabbage and salt. It contains friendly bacteria which aid digestion. Buy only the refrigerated, unpasteurized variety. All other sauerkraut is pasteurized, which destroys its beneficial bacteria and zingy flavor.

Scallions Scallions, also known as green onions or spring onions, conveniently keep for several weeks in the refrigerator. Keep them on hand for a fresh, green garnish for soups and pasta.

Sea Salt Unrefined sea salt is pure sea salt that has been hand-harvested and air-dried. It contains all the trace elements found in sea water with no chemical additives. The best natural sea salt brands are Muramoto®, Lima®, Celtic® and Si®.

Sea Vegetables Also known as sea weed, sea vegetables are the most plentiful food on earth. They draw bountiful trace minerals from the sea brine in which they grow. These are essential for the body's health. For example, two tablespoons of sea vegetables contain eight to ten times more calcium than a cup of milk. Sea vegetables also boast an astounding 30% protein. In addition, researchers report that sea vegetables help reduce blood cholesterol, prevent thyroid deficiencies and remove metallic and radioactive elements from the body. Dried sea vegetables do not require refrigeration.

Sesame Oil This light, nutty-flavored oil can be used in all cooking styles.

Sesame Seeds Sesame seeds have a slightly sweet, nutty flavor. They are remarkably high in calcium and they contain more iron than liver and more protein than nuts. Unhulled sesame seeds offer more nutrients than the hulled variety. Black sesame seeds can be an attractive garnish, but only purchase them from a reputable natural foods store. Asian stores typically sell imitation black seeds that have been dyed. Store sesame seeds in the refrigerator or freezer.

Shiitake Mushrooms [shee-tah-kay] According to traditional medicine, dried shiitake mushrooms help dissolve fat, cysts and cholesterol, and act as a blood cleanser. They are also delicious. To prepare, soak dried mushrooms for several hours before cooking. They can be left to soak for up to eight hours. Or, pour boiling water over them and soak for fifteen minutes. Trim off and discard the stems.

Shoyu [shoh-you] Shoyu is the Japanese name for naturally-fermented soy sauce. Made from soybeans, roasted wheat and salt, it is fermented in wooden kegs for at least eighteen months. While shoyu does not require refrigeration, a lacy, white mold may appear on the surface. It is a harmless fermenting agent. Skim it off and simmer the shoyu for five minutes. To prevent it from returning, refrigerate it. See Tamari and Soy Sauce.

Soba [soh-buh] Soba refers to Japanese noodles made from 100% buckwheat flour or a combination of buckwheat and another flour.

Soy Milk Soy milk is a beverage with as much protein as whole cow's milk, but one-tenth of the chemical residues, one-third of the fat, fewer calories and no cholesterol. Moreover, it is packed with essential B vitamins and has about ten times more iron than its dairy counterpart. A drawback is that it is darker in color than cow's milk. I recommend EdenBlend® instead. I also suggest that it be mixed with cow's milk during a transition to a non-dairy diet.

Soy Sauce Soy sauce is a generic term for a dark, salty sauce made by fermenting boiled soybeans with roasted wheat or barley and salt. When traditionally made, a long aging process imparts a rich, complex flavor. Commercial soy sauce, on the other hand, is quickly made and chemically modified. It contains corn syrup and artificial flavors and colors. Soy sauce does not require refrigeration. See Tamari and Shoyu.

Spectrum Naturals® Canola Spread This spread is non-dairy, non-hydrogenated and is made with pure canola oil. It has a buttery taste without the cholesterol. This is what I recommend to everyone as a healthful alternative to butter or margarine.

Squash There are two distinct categories of squash: summer and winter. The most popular summer varieties are zucchini and yellow squash. Winter squash are my favorite, because they are so sweet. They include buttercup, kabocha, butternut, sweet dumpling and delicata. Less sweet are acorn and spaghetti squash. No matter what the variety, the more dense the squash, the sweeter it is.

Sweet Potatoes Sweet potatoes are not related to white potatoes or yams. True yams are tubers of a tropical climbing plant. In spite of this, dark sweet potatoes are often referred to as yams. While sweet potatoes come in several varieties, garnet yams are my favorite. They have dark red skins and are intensely sweet, almost like candy.

Tahini [tah-hee-nee] Tahini is made from ground, hulled sesame seeds. It is sometimes referred to in recipes as sesame tahini. It has a nutty flavor and is high in calcium. Be careful when choosing a brand. Canned tahini is often bitter, grainy and thick. I prefer Arrowhead

Mills® raw, organic tahini, which has a creamy texture and a delicate flavor.

Tamari [tuh-mah-ree] Traditionally, the liquid by-product of miso production was called tamari. Today, it refers to a wheat-free soy sauce made with traditional processing methods. I prefer the full-bodied flavor of shoyu, although tamari is a good choice for people with wheat allergies. Tamari does not require refrigeration.

Tea Popular black tea, such as orange pekoe, is made from the leaves of the tea-shrub. Black tea contains, on average, half as much caffeine as coffee. Green tea, although reputed to be healthful, contains the same amount of caffeine as black tea. A better choice is herbal tea, which is made of an infusion of herbs, flowers and spices. Celestial Seasonings® offers innumerable choices. Also, try kukicha twig tea and caffeine-free teas like Good Earth® Original Sweet and Spicy Caffine-free Herb Tea and Traditional Medicinals® Ginger Aid® Tea. See Kukicha Twig Tea.

Teff Teff is a minuscule cereal grain. A staple in Ethiopia, it has a mildly sweet and nutty flavor. Teff is a good source of complex carbohydrates and is higher in protein and calcium than most other grains.

Tempeh [tehm-pay] Tempeh is a fermented soybean product originating from Indonesia. It boasts 50% more protein than hamburger and is cholesterol-free. It has a hearty texture and is an excellent source of energy. Its distinct flavor is complemented by strong seasonings such as ginger, garlic, vinegar and mustard. Try steaming, grilling or sautéing it in a few drops of oil. Tempeh is available in the freezer or refrigerator section in natural foods stores.

Toasted Sesame Oil This rich, dark oil is extracted from toasted sesame seeds. Its divine fragrance and nutty flavor enhance stir-fries.

Tofu Made from soybeans, tofu is rich in calcium and is a cholesterol-free protein source. According to oriental medicine, tofu is reputed to have a cooling nature and is beneficial to people who have high blood pressure. Traditionally, cooling tofu was never an ingredient in cold desserts. People with a delicate digestive tract would be better off not eating sweet, oily desserts made with tofu.

When prepared this way, it can cause digestive problems.

Tofu has a blandness which makes it a versatile ingredient, readily absorbing other flavors. It comes in smooth, white cakes in two basic varieties. Soft tofu has a higher water content than firm tofu and is used for making soups and creamy sauces. In contrast, firm tofu is used for stir-frying, baking and grilling. Compress firm tofu in a pickle press or between two cutting boards for twenty minutes to expel excess water. This process allows additional flavor to be absorbed by the tofu.

Both kinds of tofu are usually found refrigerated in the produce department or dairy case at grocery stores and always at natural foods stores. I prefer refrigerated tofu over the variety that is packaged in an aseptic box. To store leftover tofu, leave it in the container covered with fresh water. If the water is changed every other day, the tofu will keep for one week. When it starts to turn pink and smells rotten, throw it away.

Udon [ew-dohn] These thick, Japanese wheat noodles look like fettuccini. Since they are made by traditional methods, they are of high quality. My favorite variety, brown rice udon, contains 30% brown rice flour.

Umeboshi Paste [ew-meh-boh-shee] Umeboshi paste is made from puréed umeboshi plums. It adds a salty, sour taste to salad dressings and sauces. It is wonderful lightly spread on corn on-the-cob.

Umeboshi Plums These bright pink plums have a salty, sour flavor. They are considered a natural antibiotic and are exceptionally high in iron. Umeboshi plums are made from unripe plums, salt and shiso leaves. They are fermented in a wooden keg for one year. Refrigeration is not required. See also Umeboshi Vinegar and Paste.

Umeboshi Vinegar Umeboshi vinegar is a by-product of umeboshi plum production. This salty, sour condiment is delicious sprinkled on salad and steamed greens.

Vanilla Vanilla, an aromatic bean pod of the orchid, is processed in a number of ways for use as a flavoring. Vanilla extract contains 35% alcohol. Vanilla flavor, on the other hand, is made with a glycerin base rather than alcohol. Purchase only natural vanilla flavor or extract as others are of questionable quality. Artificial vanilla is made from sugar, alcohol, artificial color and vanillin, a by-product of paper making. I use my old bottle of artificial vanilla to keep the refrigerator smelling heavenly. Pour a small amount of artificial vanilla on a damp dishcloth to wipe down the inside walls of the refrigerator.

Vinegar, Natural Natural vinegar refers to a delightfully salty, sour condiment which is naturally fermented for about a year. This is in sharp contrast to commercial vinegar, which is chemically fermented overnight. See Balsamic Vinegar, Brown Rice Vinegar and Umeboshi Vinegar.

Wakame [wah-kah-meh] Wakame is a dried, quick-cooking sea vegetable, most often used in miso soup. See Sea Vegetables.

Wheat Berry A whole wheat berry is the unprocessed wheat kernel with all its nutrients intact.

Whole Wheat Pastry Flour Whole wheat pastry flour is made from finely ground, soft, spring wheat berries. Since it has a lower gluten content than bread flour, it produces lighter baked products.

Wild Rice Wild rice, with its impressive nutty flavor and chewy texture, is not from the rice family. Rather, it is a long-grain marsh grass, native to the Great Lakes area. It has more protein, minerals and B vitamins than barley, oats or wheat.

Zest Also known as peel, zest is the colored, outer-layer of skin on citrus fruit. Avoid grating the white underskin as it is bitter. It is best to use organic whenever possible to avoid wax, dyes and pesticides.

colander

flame tamer

chef's knife

pressure cooker

double steamer
(assembled)

double steamer
(open)

cook's tools

Although my mother hosted many fine dinner parties, she was not a fan of kitchen tools and gadgets. But I am! If you invest in these tools, you will shorten your time in the kitchen and have more fun cooking. Most tools are available in kitchen gadget stores. If you have difficulty finding any of these items, contact our website (www.lenoresnatural.com).

I prefer stainless steel cookware to aluminum. I avoid chemical coatings like Teflon® and Silverstone® which eventually flake off into the food. Instead, I stock my kitchen with nonstick Scanpan® pots and skillets. They are coated with titanium metal and are virtually indestructible.

I avoid storing food in anything plastic, as it has been shown to impart its chemicals into the stored food. The exception is a non-leaching, polycarbonate bottle by Nalgene® and New Wave Enviro Products®. Glass, on the other hand, is inert and completely see-through so you know what is inside.

Lastly, I remove anything from kitchen drawers, cabinets and counter tops that I do not want, use or love. This makes space for more efficient tools, pots and gadgets.

basic tools checklist
- ❏ Blender
- ❏ Brush (sisal) To scrub vegetables.
- ❏ Colander (stainless steel)
- ❏ Cookie Sheets
- ❏ Cutting Board (wood or high density polyethylene; clear acrylic boards dull knives)
- ❏ Cutting Board Mat (nonskid shelf liner) To stabilize cutting board.
- ❏ Dishcloths Instead of sponges. Change daily.
- ❏ Flame Tamer To distribute heat under pots of cooking beans and grains to prevent burning. Available at hardware stores.
- ❏ Funnel (wide-mouth)
- ❏ Jars (wide-mouth quart) To store cooked and uncooked food.
- ❏ Knife (6-inch chef's or rectangular Japanese vegetable knife)

suribachi   angled   bash n' chop®
             wooden spatula

dutch oven   lunch tote   granny fork
              thermos

miso strainer   grater   pickle press

- ❏ Knife Sharpener (Firestone® Two-stage)
- ❏ Measuring Cup (2-cup glass)
- ❏ Measuring Spoons Set
- ❏ Mixing Bowls (nesting, stainless steel) For vegetable preparation.
- ❏ Pressure Cooker (4-quart for 1-2 people; 6-quart for 3-4 people; 8-quart for 6 or more people; preferably non-jiggle top)
- ❏ Saucepan (2-quart/small)
- ❏ Skillet (10- or 12-inch, nonstick or cast iron)
- ❏ Slotted Spoon (a large spoon with holes) To remove vegetables from cooking water and foam from cooking beans.
- ❏ Spatula (angled wood)
- ❏ Spatula (Rubbermaid®)
- ❏ Spoons (wooden)
- ❏ Steamer (double) To steam vegetables and reheat rice, all in one pot.
- ❏ Stock Pot (8-quart stainless steel) Also known as a soup pot.
- ❏ Stove (gas) The optimal heat source for cooking is natural gas.
- ❏ Suribachi and Wooden Pestle A grooved, ceramic crushing bowl for making gomashio and sauces.
- ❏ Timer
- ❏ Vegetable Peeler (large, soft handle)

additional tools checklist
- ❏ Apple Corer
- ❏ Bash n' Chop® To efficiently scoop sliced vegetables from the board.
- ❏ Blender (hand-held)
- ❏ Cookie Scoop
- ❏ Dutch Oven (5-quart)
- ❏ Ginger Grater
- ❏ Granny Fork To test when vegetables are cooked.
- ❏ Knife (8-inch chef's)
- ❏ Lemon Reamer
- ❏ Lunch Tote Thermos To carry soup, grain and vegetables.
- ❏ Measuring Cups (1- and 4-cup glass)
- ❏ Measuring Spoons (additional sets)
- ❏ Miso Strainer To efficiently purée miso into soups.

- ❏ Muffin Scoop
- ❏ Pasta Pot
- ❏ Pickle Press To compress vegetables and facilitate fermentation.
- ❏ Salad Spinner
- ❏ Skimmer To remove foam from cooking dried beans and to remove vegetables from cooking water.
- ❏ Soup Ladle
- ❏ Spatula (angled, wooden)
- ❏ Spatula (silicon)
- ❏ Spoonula (Rubbermaid®)
- ❏ Strainer (fine mesh) To wash fine grains and seeds.
- ❏ Sushi Mats (bamboo) To cover cooked food to keep it warm.
- ❏ Timer (triple)
- ❏ Tongs (9-inch metal or wooden) To serve salads, pastas, etc.
- ❏ Trivet
- ❏ Turner (2- X 4-inch stainless steel)
- ❏ Whisk (flat)
- ❏ Wok (nonstick)

skimmer

stainless steel
spatula/turner

sushi mat

pasta pot

flat whisk

cutting
methods

florets and matchsticks

shredded

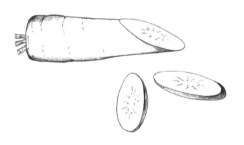

diagonal cut

half-rounds and matchsticks

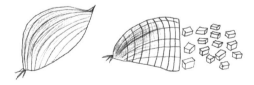

diced

half-rounds

recommended reading

Colbin, Annemarie. *Food and Healing*. New York: Ballantine, 1986.

Dufty, William. *Sugar Blues*. New York: Warner Books, 1975.

Ferré, Carl. *Pocket Guide to Macrobiotics*. Freedom, CA: The Crossing Press, 1997.

Heindenry, Carolyn. *Making the Transition to a Macrobiotic Diet*. Garden City Park, NY: Avery Publishing Group, 1985.

Herbst, Sharon Tyler. *The New Food Lovers Companion*. Hauppauge, NY: Barron's Educational Services, Inc., 1995.

Jack, Alex. *Let Food Be Thy Medicine*. Becket, MA: One Peaceful World Press, 1998.

Kushi, Michio. *The Macrobiotic Way*. Garden City Park, NY: Avery Publishing Group, 1984.

Kushi, Michio. *Holistic Health Through Macrobiotics*. New York: Japan Publications, 1993.

Lair, Cynthia. *Feeding the Whole Family*. San Diego, CA: LuraMedia, 1994.

Mattson, Robert. *The International Macrobiotic Directory*. Oakland, CA. (510) 601-1763.

McDougall, M.D., John. *McDougall's Medicine-A Challenging Second Opinion*. Clinton, NJ: New Win Publishing, Inc., 1986.

Oski, M.D., Frank. *Don't Drink Your Milk!* Brushton, NY: Teach Services, 1996.

Pitchford, Paul. *Healing with Whole Foods*. Berkeley, CA: North Atlantic Books, 1993.

Robbins, John. *Diet for a New America*. Tiburon, CA: H.J. Kramer, 1998.

Robbins, John. *The Food Revolution*. Red Wheel/Weiser, 2001.

St. James, Elaine. *Simplify Your Life*. New York: Hyperion, 1994.

Stanchich, Lino. *Power Eating Program*. Miami, FL: Healthy Products, Inc., 1989.

Turner, Kristina. *The Self-Healing Cookbook*. Grass Valley, CA: Earthtones Press, 1987.

Weil, M.D., Andrew. *Eight Weeks to Optimum Health*. NewYork: Random House, 1997.

Wood, Rebecca. *The Whole Foods Encyclopedia (new and revised)*. New York: Penguin, 1999.

Zipern, Elizabeth and Williams, Dar. *The Tofu Tollbooth*. Woodstock. NY; Ceres Press, 1998.

newsletters
and magazines

Good Medicine, Physicians Committee for Responsible Medicine, Suite 404, 5100 Wisconsin Avenue NW, Washington, DC 20016.

Macrobiotics Today, George Ohsawa Macrobiotic Foundation, 1994 Myers Street, Oroville, CA 95966.

Natural Health: The Guide to Well-being, 17 Station Street, P.O. Box 1200, Brookline, MA 02147.

Nutrition Action Healthletter, Center for Science in the Public Interest, CSPI, Suite 3000, 1875 Connecticut Avenue NW, Washington, DC 20009.

Simple Living Oasis, 4509 Interlake Ave. N. PMB 149, Seattle, WA 98103-6773, www.simpleliving.com

Vegetarian Times, 4 High Ridge park, Stamford, CT 06905.

recommended cookbooks

Albert, Rachel. *Cooking with Rachel.* Oroville, CA: George Ohsawa Macrobiotic Foundation, 1989.

Baum, Lenore. *Sublime Soups: Vegetarian Soups and Quick Breads.* Farmington Hills, MI: Culinary Publications, 2002.

Chelf, Vicki Rae. *Cooking with the Right Side of the Brain.* Garden City Park, NY: Avery Publishing Group, 1985.

Colbin, Annemarie. *The Natural Gourmet.* New York: Ballantine Books, 1989.

Estella, Mary. *Natural Foods Cookbook.* New York: Japan Publications, 1988.

Kushi, Aveline and Esko, Wendy. *Changing Seasons Cookbook.* Garden City Park, NY: Avery Publishing Group, 1985.

McCarty, Meredith. *American Macrobiotic Cuisine.* New York: St. Martin's Press, 1986.

McCarty, Meredith. *Fresh from a Vegetarian Kitchen.* New York: St. Martin's Press, 1989.

McCarty, Meredith. *Sweet & Natural, More Than 120 Sugar-Free and Dairy-Free Desserts.* New York: St. Martin's Press, 1999.

Lawson, Margaret. *The Naturally Healthy Gourmet.* Oroville, CA: George Ohsawa Macrobiotic Foundation, 1994.

Madison, Deborah. *Vegetarian Cooking for Everyone.* New York: Broadway Books, 1997.

Sass, Lorna J. *Lorna Sass's Complete Vegetarian Kitchen.* New York: Hearst Books, 1992.

Sass, Lorna J. *Great Vegetarian Cooking Under Pressure.* New York: William Morrow and Company, 1994.

Sass, Lorna J. *Short-Cut Vegetarian Cooking.* New York: Quill, 1997.

Sass, Lorna J. *The New Soy Cookbook.* San Francisco, CA: Chronicle Books, 1998.

Turner, Kristina. *The Self-Healing Cookbook.* Grass Valley, CA: Earthtones Press, 1987.

mail order sources

natural foods and supplies

Gold Mine Natural Foods
7805 Arjons Drive
San Diego, CA 92126
(800) 475-3663

Kushi Institute Store
P.O. Box 7
Becket, MA 01223
(800) 645-8744

Lenore's Natural Cuisine
www.lenoresnatural.com
cookbooks, Dutch ovens, nonstick skillets, woks, pressure cookers and water purifiers.

organic produce and prepared food

Diamond Organics
P.O. Box 2159
Freedom, CA 95019
(800) 922-2396

South River Miso
South River Farm
888 Shelburne Falls Road
Conway, MA 01341
(413) 369-4057

Maine Coast Sea Vegetables
Franklin, Maine 04634
www.seaveg.com
(207) 565-2907

vegan cruise menu

breakfast suggestions
old-fashioned oatmeal
corn grits
buckwheat pancakes with pure maple syrup
whole wheat waffles with pure maple syrup
whole wheat English muffins, toast and bagels
roasted grain cereal beverage (Roma®, Cafix® or Pero®)

lunch suggestions
bean or vegetable soups
Greek salad (no cheese)
hummus
tabouli
leafy green salad with balsamic vinaigrette
corn on-the-cob
whole wheat bread, drizzled with extra-virgin olive oil
pasta salad
steamed, roasted or grilled vegetables

dinner suggestions
stir-fried brown rice and vegetables
polenta with vegetables
pasta with pesto sauce
pasta with olive oil and garlic
couscous vegetable stew
wild rice pilaf
steamed, roasted or grilled vegetables
herbal tea

grain cooking

grain cooking - boiling method

grain (1 cup dry)*	water (cups)	cooking time (minutes)
barley, pearled	3	75
bulgur	1 1/2	15-20
corn grits	3	15-20
kasha	2	15
millet	2 1/2	30-45
oats, rolled	3	15-30
quinoa	3	20
rice, brown	2	60

* 1 cup dry grain yields approximately 3 cups cooked grain. For complete cooking instructions, see pages 99 and 106.

brown rice - pressure-cooking method

brown rice (1 cup dry)*	water (cups)	pressure cooker size (quarts)	yield (cups)
1	1 1/2	5	3
2	3	5	6
3	4 1/2	5	9
4	5	5	12
5	6 1/4	5	15
6	7 1/2	5	18
7	8 3/4	8	21
8	10	8	24
9	11 1/4	8	27

For complete instructions, see page 100.

bean and vegetable cooking

bean cooking

bean (1 cup dry) *	boiling water (cups)	boiling cooking time (minutes)	pressure-cooking water (cups)	pressure-cooking cooking time (minutes)	yield (cups)
adzuki	to cover	60	3	6	3
black (turtle)	4	90	3	11	2
chickpeas (garbanzos)	4	180	3	25	2 1/2
kidney	3	90	3	10-12	2
lentils (green or brown)	3	60-120	3	10	2
lentils (red)	3	45	3	5	2
pinto		180	3	5	2
white (navy, great northern, lima)	3 1/2	120	3	7	2 1/4

Soak 8 hours before cooking. For complete cooking instructions, see pp. 51,129-132

vegetable cooking - steaming method

fresh vegetable	approximate cooking time (minutes)
asparagus	5
broccoli, florets and stems	3
cabbage, shredded	3
carrots, thinly sliced	4
cauliflower, florets	8
daikon, thin 1/2 moons	6
green beans	8
onions, thinly sliced	5
summer squash, 1/4-inch rounds	3
winter squash, 1-inch pieces	7

For Cooking instructions, see page 152.

index

Sublime
Soups: Vegetarian Soups and Quick Breads

For centuries, the family meal has centered around a steaming pot of soup. *Sublime Soups* makes it easy to continue this tradition, even with today's busy lifestyles. In fact, soup even tastes better the next day! Let Lenore show you how easy it is to build nutritious and satisfying low-fat meals around soup, quick breads and salad.

Tempting recipes with:

- No milk, butter, eggs, sugar or cholesterol – just great taste!
- An easy way to incorporate vegetables into your meals
- Even meat-eaters will love these hearty soups and stews
- Your meals will be a success with Lenore's great recipes
- So much better than soup from a can!
- Otabind® lay-flat binding
- 176 pages, 7" x 10"

Baum's engaging, straightforward style informs, but does not overwhelm. She provides step-by-step instruction for over 100 scrumptious recipes with less than 15% fat and no dairy products or refined sugar. They will help you lose weight, increase your energy and feel satisfied!

"If you are looking for delicious and healthy recipes with a macrobiotic slant, Sublime Soups *is the answer."*
-John Robbins, author of *Diet for a New America* and *The Food Revolution*

"Lenore has mastered the art of wholesome and satisfying dairy-free cuisine. It's a pleasure to make and share her luscious soup-and-muffin combinations like Red Lentil Corn Chowder *and* Secret Sweet Potato Muffins. *Simple and sublime are a taste-full combination I think everyone will find irresistible."*
-Meredith McCarty, author of *Sweet and Natural, More Than 120 Sugar-Free and Dairy-Free Desserts*

**Sublime Soups:
Vegetarian Soups and
Quick Breads**

available for $19.00 (postpaid)
www.lenoresnatural.com

Sublime Soups, simmered to perfection...

Opera in History

Herbert Lindenberger Opera in History

FROM MONTEVERDI TO CAGE

STANFORD UNIVERSITY PRESS

STANFORD, CALIFORNIA

Stanford University Press
Stanford, California

© 1998 by the Board of Trustees of the
Leland Stanford Junior University

Printed in the United States of America

CIP data appear at the end of the book

Acknowledgments

This book received most of its final revisions in a Romanesque tower built around 1100 A.D.: the tower is all that remains today of the church of San Pietro, the rest of whose site now holds the Villa Serbelloni overlooking Lake Como at Bellagio. This tower existed half a millennium before the composition of the first opera around 1600. Reading through my manuscript, I was aware that the mere four hundred years since the beginnings of opera constitute a shorter period than that between the construction of the tower (now modernized to accommodate a computer and central heating) and the meetings of that group of Florentine intellectuals who dreamed of a union of words and music that would restore the conditions of ancient tragedy. Many thanks to the Rockefeller Foundation for giving me a month of the most generous hospitality at the villa.

So many friends and colleagues have contributed to the ideas of this book—sometimes even in chance conversations—that a full list would take several pages. I single out the following for providing expert advice in their specialties: Helen Brooks, Andrew Culver, Barbara Gelpi, Philip Gossett, Laura Kuhn, Donald Reiman, and Peter Selz. Joseph Frank, Marjorie Perloff, and Brian Stock were all kind enough to look over individual chapters and to encourage me to forge ahead with this project. Special thanks are due to the core members of the Opera Studies workshop at Stanford: James Aldrich-Moodie, Karol Berger, Thomas Grey, Stephen Hinton, and Paul Robinson; I also thank the Stanford Humanities Center for sponsoring this workshop. Helen Tartar, humanities editor at Stanford University Press, deserves special gratitude for pushing me to undertake the book in the first place. I also acknowledge the helpfulness of Marshall Brown and Paul Hernadi, who, as referees for the Press, defined the purpose and method of the book more precisely than I had been able to do myself. As with my earlier book on opera, my wife, Claire F. Lindenberger, contributed immeasurably to this study through our discussions during opera intermissions and while listening together at home; it is, in fact, difficult to remember just who suggested what idea to whom.

Early versions, now heavily revised, of Chapters 3, 5, and 8 appeared, respectively, in *The Wordsworth Circle, Comparative Drama,* and *John Cage: Composed in America* (Chicago: University of Chicago Press, 1994). For Chapters 4 and 7 I drew several paragraphs from essays contributed, respectively, to the forthcoming volume of the *Cambridge History of Literary Criticism* on European Romanticism and to the journal *Modern Judaism.* I am grateful to the Arnold Schoenberg Institute for making the composer's manuscripts available to me.

H.L.

Contents

Figures

A Note on Abbreviations and Translations

The following abbreviations are used for frequently cited editions:

AGS   Adorno, Theodor. *Gesammelte Schriften*. Ed. Rolf Tiedemann. 20 vols. Frankfurt: Suhrkamp, 1970–86.

BBS   Brecht, Bertolt. *Stücke*. 14 vols. Frankfurt: Suhrkamp, 1953–67.

BGH   Burney, Charles. *A General History of Music: From the Earliest Ages to the Present Period (1789)*. 2 vols. New York: Dover, 1957.

CC   Kostelanetz, Richard. *Conversing with Cage*. New York: Limelight Editions, 1988.

DCH   Smith, A. J., ed. *John Donne: The Critical Heritage*. London: Routledge & Kegan Paul, 1975.

HA   Hegel, G. W. F. *Aesthetics: Lectures on Fine Art*. Trans. T. M. Knox. 2 vols. Oxford: Clarendon Press, 1975.

MSL   Shelley, Mary. *Letters of Mary Wollstonecraft Shelley*. Ed. Betty T. Bennett. 3 vols. Baltimore: Johns Hopkins University Press, 1980–88.

PSL   Shelley, Percy Bysshe. *Letters of Percy Bysshe Shelley*. Ed. Frederick L. Jones. 2 vols. Oxford: Clarendon Press, 1964.

WGS   Wagner, Richard. *Gesammelte Schriften*. Ed. Julius Kapp. 14 vols. Leipzig: Hesse und Becker, n.d. [ca. 1914].

WM   Weill, Kurt. *Musik und Theater: Gesammelte Schriften*. Ed. Stephen Hinton and Jürgen Schebera. Berlin: Henschelverlag, 1990.

All translations are my own unless otherwise indicated in the Works Cited.

Opera in History

Prelude Opera Books

Books on opera constitute a breed of their own. Like books on film and sports, they are generally composed not simply to satisfy fans' desires for the background knowledge they believe they need to pursue their avocations. Just as important, they provide vicarious renderings at home of much-cherished spectator experiences possible only within a communal setting.

The characteristic habitat of the opera book is the so-called opera shop, a distinctly commercial-minded institution that in recent decades has attached itself to opera houses throughout North America (and to a degree even in Europe) to provide at least partial relief from the deficits inevitable to this nonprofit art form. Anybody entering one of these shops is unlikely to note the book section at first sight but will instead see tables arrayed with a wide variety of artifacts: ballpoint pens with as many musical notes imprinted on them as their quite limited space will allow; coffee mugs picturing the "Three Tenors"; cocktail napkins with the opening bars of "La donna è mobile"; green T-shirts with "I love opera!" printed in red and red T-shirts with "I love Luciano!" in green; coloring books of famous scenes designed for those who, one hopes, will fill up the opera house a half century hence; Belgian chocolates with images of only the thinnest among present-day divas on the box; calendars with the Marschallin's grand third-act entrance reproduced for October, Radames's triumphal entry for November, and Butterfly's suicide to end the year.

Should older operagoers feel disconcerted by the commercial aura surrounding what they long considered a lofty form of art transcending monetary considerations, they might note the reminders in letters mailed to subscribers that any ticket they purchase pays for less than half the cost of a performance they attend. Certainly once they get past the garish items at the front of the shop they will come across more earnest matter: shelf after shelf of videotapes and videodiscs of operatic performances. And if they venture still further they will likely find the largest display of all: compact discs of virtually every opera one has ever heard of and of others whose titles, indeed even whose composers, seem totally new. These CDs feature not only the commercial recordings one sees in ordinary shops but also performances that had long circulated as "pirated" tapes, gathered by aficionados on small recorders hidden inside their jacket pockets.

Not until operagoers reach the back of the shop will they likely discover the book section, which has been relegated there to reserve the store's most accessible area for the high-markup items. Still, most of the books on display have been selected with the company's deficit in mind. There is never a shortage of sumptuous coffee-table books—for example, a book featuring photographs from the Metropolitan's early-twentieth-century "Golden Age"; or albums of Callas in both her personal and professional capacities (the boundaries sometimes proving hard to distinguish); or any number of books whose glossy photos of stage productions match the sumptuousness of the books themselves.

One can also find books of a less decorative but equally entertaining character. A favored genre is the collection of operatic anecdotes—everything from backstage gossip about the machinations of great stars to catastrophic stage mishaps, as when some necessary prop like a goblet, swan, or weapon failed to appear in time to motivate the sublime musical moment the audience was awaiting. There are also memoirs of famed sopranos and tenors (though rarely of baritones and basses, who do not exercise charisma enough to arouse curiosity about their private lives) ghostwritten in a breezy manner that screens out whatever does not suit the public image they wish to preserve.

Also included will be books with genuinely useful information—whatever spectators may need to follow an opera without feeling lost or bored and then forced to pretend they understand something they haven't the faintest idea about. The opera guide is like the travel guide one buys for help in finding the right museums and churches while dutifully touring abroad. Although it gives some basic dates (composer's birth, first performance, often first American performance) whose relevance has been dictated by long-standing convention, most of its space is taken up with narrating plots: who disguises herself in whose clothes, who swears love to whom, who dies by what means, and in which particular act this action occurs. Like the travel guide, the opera guide is generally of little help in explaining how to approach a work's music, what precisely to look for, how to become committed to this particular opera. Again like the travel guide, the opera guide usually consists of repackaged information (reworded sufficiently to fend off plagiarism suits) long available in other books.

By contrast, books devoted to individual composers ordinarily mix biographical detail with studies of individual operas—the history of their composition and initial rehearsals (for earlier operas these were often one and the same phenomenon), their principal musical themes (reproduced for those who care to hammer them out on the piano), their relation to some play or novel that they took off from (but which, we note, they have generally altered beyond recognition). And then there are the even more specialized books by learned musicologists, books too narrowly focused for the ordinary operagoer—on, say, the changes in a particular aria form between 1690 and 1740, or the use of folk material in German opera of the early nineteenth century—but whose publisher (usually some university press as deficit-plagued as the opera company) is hoping to recoup its investment through operagoers' long-demonstrated zeal to enhance their aesthetic experience.

What was long in short supply was the sort of book that asked larger questions about the nature of opera—for example, what precisely separates opera from other musical and dramatic forms, or what role opera has played within the history of European culture. My first book on opera, *Opera: The Extravagant Art* (1984), set out deliberately to fill this gap; when the *TLS* reviewer (in an otherwise condescending article) began with the words, "At last, a serious book about opera,"[1] I recognized I had achieved my goal. That book was conceived originally as a kind of "poetics of opera," and in fact I long thought of turning this conception into the title. Yet as I reached the final third of the manuscript early in the 1980s, the new, historicizing mood affecting humanistic study came to take hold of my project. In my final chapters I found myself moving from the more formal questions that had dominated the book up to that point—for instance, how does opera differ from nonmusical drama? or, how does the relationship of composer and librettist constitute a distinct form of authorship?—to a more specifically historical area of inquiry. Thus, I suggested that *Aida* embodied what at its time counted as the new science of archaeology, or Wagner's *Ring*, the new science of philology. To cite another example, I portrayed the opera house as a site variously used at different times for the display of royal power and for newly "arrived" segments of society to advertise their hard-won status.

A subsequent book that I wrote to illustrate the uses of historical method in contemporary literary study, *The History in Literature* (1990), extended these perspectives, though with a focus on literature rather than on opera. Yet one chapter, entitled "The History in Opera," sought to show how operas on historical subjects—*La clemenza di Tito, Khovanshchina,* and *Moses und Aron,* together spanning almost a century and a half—gave voice to different philosophies of history and established quite distinct relationships with their audiences in their own and in later times. I soon recognized that the perspectives suggested there needed further development, and the result is the present book.

The main title of this volume deliberately reverses the nouns in the title of the earlier chapter. My concern in these endeavors is a search for new ways of thinking about the relation of history to aesthetic phenomena. And my interest here is the ways that history has found itself *in* works of art as well as in the processes by which art is made; I am correspondingly interested in how an art form such as opera can be contextualized within those various narratives that we package under the name *history*.

When somebody writing a description of my work misnamed my last book *The History* of *Literature*, I recognized how readily my intentional playing with prepositions could be misunderstood to yield a more conventional appellation. Certainly writing the history *of* an aesthetic form, whether of literature or of opera, would be a most uncongenial task. Doing the history "of" a form is something that the nineteenth century, that evolution-oriented time, could undertake with confidence but that nobody can today without considerable skepticism. Indeed, at several points the present book seeks to expose the narrative strategies that past operatic histories have used and, more important, to uncover the motives (usually unbeknownst to their authors) behind these strategies.

Since I have placed the terms "history," "literature," and "opera" in unexpected combinations with one another, the reader may wonder if a still unused title, "The Opera *of* History" might suggest a project to be pursued. A study of this sort could, after all, analyze the rituals, the histrionics, the operatic antics practiced by leaders from pharaohs, Roman emperors, and absolutist kings down to the dictators of our own century who have sought to breathe their charisma upon a gullible world. Such a book might look quite appealing in the opera shop, but I do not intend to author it.

Despite the skepticism I have been voicing about conventional ways of organizing, thinking, and writing history, it will be evident from this book's subtitle, *From Monteverdi to Cage*, that I have not abandoned a chronological ordering of the subjects I take up. Yet within individual chapters I have found it necessary to move back and forth in time. For example, two chapters—those on Monteverdi and Rossini—are organized largely as studies of these composers' reception from their own time to the present. For example, Monteverdi, unperformed and almost forgotten from soon after his death until the twentieth century, emerges here as a creation of early modernism, while Rossini, most of whose significant work was equally forgotten, emerges as a creation of our current postmodern age. In writing about both composers, I found that I could best flesh out my own historical narratives by treating the composers not in isolation but rather in juxtaposition with contemporary figures in other arts—Caravaggio and Donne with Monteverdi, Shelley with Rossini—whose oeuvres have endured similar fates. In studying the changing perceptions of artists over long stretches of time, we gain an understanding quite different from what we see when we remove their creations from their historical contexts.

Although the figures and the works come up in something close to chronological sequence, readers will not be able to discern a sustained historical narrative. The history they will find here consists of discrete moments in the life of that institution we label opera; and it may well be, as I suggest in Chapter 4, that the only factor authorizing the word "opera" to name works from 1600 to the present is the persistence of that allied institution called the opera house, within which these works are performed. Moreover, the discrete moments of operatic history on which this study concentrates may well strike readers as somewhat removed from what have long counted as the most celebrated, most canonical achievements in the form. To be sure, I devote Chapter 5 to one of the acknowledged peak moments in the development of opera, namely, Wagner's *Ring des Nibelungen*. Yet the *Ring* emerges here as what I call a "nineteenth-century artifact," deeply implicated in such concerns of its time as the philological reconstruction of a national past and the shaping of a new community bound together by means of a uniquely new theatrical experience. This chapter, one might say, seeks to estrange the *Ring* a bit from those interpretations stressing its universalizing power, its mythological inventiveness, its success in "transcending" temporal matters. And although the succeeding chapter, on orientalist settings and musical coloring in opera, contains examples from canonical works such as *Aida* and *Carmen*, it seeks above all to demonstrate how composers from the eighteenth century to the present have created ideologically distinct contexts in which some non-European "other" might entertain, and often tantalize, their audiences.

Whereas the chapters on Monteverdi and Rossini juxtapose artists in different media who were contemporaries, Chapter 6 juxtaposes three distinct moments (each of them a century apart) in the European appropriation of supposedly "Eastern" musical and visual materials—from the militant, threatening Orient of the late eighteenth century through the sexualized Orient of a century later and thence to the multicultural East-West accommodations of recent opera. Indeed, if there is any method governing this book as a whole, it might be described by the term "significant juxtaposition," by means of which seemingly disparate categories—for example, composer and painter, militancy and sexuality, opera-as-art and opera-as-institution—are brought into dialogue with one another to illuminate each from an unaccustomed point of view.

As I have already indicated, this study is mainly built around composers and works outside what most operagoers will take to be the mainstream. The Handel presented here is not the Handel of *Messiah* or of the instrumental works but the composer of operas in a once-popular form (*opera seria*) now so remote from us that we are scarcely able to understand their greatness when we adapt them to the conditions of the modern opera house and, just as important, when we hear them with the expectations of an aesthetic alien to them. In the same way Monteverdi, who, despite the enormous prestige he has gained within the twentieth century as the first major opera composer, lends himself even less than Handel to performance in large houses by singers trained for the reigning canon. Yet Monteverdi, unlike Handel, pursued a concept of opera as a developing drama, as a vehicle for words that suggest and shape music, a concept that, although his example remained unknown to composers until the present century, has constituted the prevailing notion against which the most influential critics and theorists have evaluated individual composers and works. John Cage's single intrusion into the world of opera, the collage he entitled *Europeras 1 & 2*, suggests how a systematic postmodernist subversion of this prevailing aesthetic at the same time demonstrates its long-standing power.

Not only is operatic history marked by conceptions of form that shift between music-drama and number-opera, it is also marked by varying attitudes toward this form as "serious" art and as popular entertainment. Opera as serious art is not necessarily synonymous with opera as music-drama—though it is in Wagner's example. Monteverdian music-drama, by contrast, assumes its "high" and its popular form through the circumstances of the distinct venues—court performance and commercial theater—for which individual works were commissioned. Indeed, the lines of demarcation between what we have viewed as art and popular culture have changed considerably during the four centuries in which operas have been composed. Chapter 4 examines the discussions of opera to be found in various philosophies of art written during the time that art came to be viewed as an autonomous activity distinct from other, more lowly areas of endeavor; within these treatises one notes a continual nervousness about the status of an art form such as opera that is difficult to locate firmly within either the aesthetic or the popular realm. Indeed, the merchandise in the opera shops I described testifies to the continuing presence of the most blatantly commercial objects within a supposedly noncommercial sanctum committed to the practice of high art.

Chapter 7, on *Moses und Aron* and *Aufstieg und Fall der Stadt Mahagonny*, confronts two seemingly opposite works emanating from the same time and place—the first a music-drama uncompromising in its commitment to serious art as the latter was defined in early twentieth-century culture, the second an attempt to refashion elements drawn from popular culture to create a new art form embodying the librettist Brecht's emerging concept of epic theater; the first, moreover, an expression of political sentiments drawn from the right wing of Zionism, the second, of a Marx-inspired vision of an imagined land run by greed—yet each of these works in its own way helping shape the image of Weimar culture emerging today. Unlike the other chapters, which practice a more or less traditional form of argument, this chapter is organized as a series of alphabetically ordered "entries" as a means of better demonstrating how the issues taken up in the rest of the book—for example, of opera as high or as popular culture, as music-drama or as number-opera, as removed from or involved with history—play themselves out in two seemingly antithetical modernist works that share the same year and place.

If this book seems organized more like a number-opera than like a full-fledged music-drama, it should also be evident that a series of persistent concerns cuts across the individual chapters—for example, the changing ways that the operatic canon has been recreated at different times; how narratives have been shaped to explain the history of opera; how opera has shifted between a high and a popular form and how the lines defining high and popular have themselves shifted; how the political purposes that operas have sometimes served become blurred with time, or how we come to read political meanings into works distinct from those that earlier audiences perceived.

Above all, much of the book seeks to show that, however much we may think that we can reconstitute operas in their original condition, the works we experience reflect and define ourselves at least as much as they do these works' creators and the eras of their creation.

Since the publication of my earlier book on opera a number of other books have appeared that are at once original in their focus, interdisciplinary in the perspectives they bring to bear, and wide-ranging enough about periods and composers to satisfy the general reader. All of us working in the field have felt the power of one much earlier text, Joseph Kerman's *Opera as Drama* (1956). I still remember the exhilaration I experienced when, as a graduate student, I read chapters of this book in a journal before their publication as a book: here was an approach to opera that commanded more intellectual respect than that of any other modern-day study and that, even when you disagreed with its judgments, provoked you into seeking plausible rebuttals. If I often seem critical of Kerman's book in this book as well as in the earlier one, this is because of its standing as an influential predecessor text, many of whose assumptions need to be reconsidered in the different intellectual climate of our present time.

Both Kerman's and my own approaches to opera have been shaped by the particular systems of literary criticism prevailing at the times we wrote our books. *Opera as Drama* is a product of the so-called New Criticism, the reigning movement of the mid-century, a movement that stressed the critic's need to make value judgments in order to teach readers to discriminate between works that achieve artistic greatness and those that supposedly pander to popular taste. My own two books on opera come out of more recent critical models—for example, theories of literary reception, of narrative, of how what we call art is entangled within the social contexts in which it is produced and consumed. As with my first book of literary criticism, *On Wordsworth's 'Prelude'* (1963), which looked at a single poem from a number of critical approaches, I have felt shameless here in imposing a variety of models upon a single cultural object, the history of opera.

The most enterprising books on opera of recent years are all marked by a desire to approach opera from new angles of vision, to place the form within contexts with which it had not previously been linked. In *Opera and Ideas* (1985), Paul Robinson, a distinguished intellectual historian, demonstrates how a number of celebrated works express the tensions that characterize their times. In *Unsung Voices* (1991), Carolyn Abbate borrows techniques from deconstruction and narratology to question the literary and musical cohesion that certain key operatic works and passages have claimed. And in *Opera: Desire, Disease, Death* (1996), Linda and Michael Hutcheon, a literary theorist and medical specialist in chest diseases, respectively, observe the intersections between opera and medicine within such works as *Carmen* and *Parsifal*, as well as in those famed operas about the deaths of tubercular women. Opera is obviously emerging as a central site to bring together observers from fields of inquiry that must long have seemed unrelated to one another. Since opera has thrived from its beginnings as a collocation of otherwise distinct art forms, it seems only appropriate that diverse intellectual disciplines join each other to promote its understanding. And just as it is scarcely a generation or two since the novel received the serious treatment traditionally accorded to poetry by literary critics, so opera is only now emerging as a topic for serious study commensurate with literature and the other major forms of art.

Chapter One

Monteverdi, Caravaggio, Donne: Modernity and Early Baroque

When the Metropolitan Opera redecorated its interior in 1903 as the result of a fire a decade before, the names of six composers—Gluck, Mozart, Beethoven, Wagner, Verdi, and Gounod—were inscribed on the proscenium.[1] Of these six, only the last three had played a dominant role in the repertory as it existed in fin-de-siècle New York. Gounod's *Faust*, though revived only sporadically today, was at that time the most popular opera in most opera houses west of the Rhine. Even though Verdi did not yet count as "high" art in the way that Wagner did (the latter having in fact helped create that distinction we still make between high and low musical art), these two composers provided a large proportion of the active repertory. Wagner even received three times the performances accorded Verdi during the Met's first twenty years.[2] The fifty-five performances of the three Mozart operas that the Met had staged by this point in its history constituted too small a number to justify the presence of their composer's name on the basis of audience preference; Meyerbeer and Bizet easily outpaced Mozart by this criterion. The twenty-two performances accorded Beethoven's only opera were so few during this period that even those newly emerging composers Mascagni and Puccini— if it were popularity that mattered—should surely have had precedence over Beethoven on the proscenium. Obviously it was the prestige of Mozart's and Beethoven's names, and of the Germanic musical tradition as a whole, that motivated their inclusion.[3]

Yet the presence of Gluck among this select company demands special explanation today. Because the one Gluck opera staged at the Met received a mere five performances during this whole twenty-year period, audience demand evidently was not a consideration. Whereas the place of Mozart and Beethoven on the proscenium can be explained by the fact that they counted as major composers not simply of operas but of a multitude of other musical forms, Gluck remained primarily an opera composer, indeed, the founding father of opera as the succeeding two centuries came to define the form. If Beethoven was long thought to be the composer who "freed" music as a whole, Gluck, as I discuss in Chapter 4, occupied a special role in the history of the form. He was the composer who had liberated opera from its domination by the singer, who had restored a high-mindedness to what had supposedly become a vulgar form, and, above all, who had reasserted the dramatic principle central to opera theory when the form was invented around 1600. Despite the large output of operas composed throughout Europe during the century and a half before Gluck instituted his celebrated reform, these works, together with the various aesthetic principles upon which they were based, disappeared from audience consciousness during succeeding generations. Indeed, even the knowledge of what opera during its first century sounded and looked like was pretty much lost in subsequent centuries.

From our present vantage point Monteverdi deserves recognition on the proscenium as opera's founding father as surely as did Gluck, who himself, like his contemporaries, doubtless had no idea of how his predecessor had sought to reconcile the needs of drama and music. For no continuing tradition, whether in the form of stylistic influence or critical commentary, issued from Monteverdi's work in a way similar to the poetry, painting, and even nonmusical theater of his time. This chapter will focus upon the critical fortunes of Monteverdi's operas as a means to understand the ways that operatic canons have been shaped and reshaped, once-grand reputations destroyed and rehabilitated, in comparison with those in two other arts, poetry and painting. The omission of some of the most popular composers of the day from the Metropolitan's proscenium, and the subsequent relegation of the once-adulated Gounod to the sidelines of the international repertory, attest to a peculiar instability that marks the history of opera—and not simply that early moment in the history of opera about whose critical fortunes this chapter is concerned. What was once inscribed in stone (or at least in plaster) for audiences to ponder while they gazed at the old Met's sumptuous décor has not even survived physically, for the proscenium, together with the whole building, was itself torn down after the company's move uptown to Lincoln Center in 1966.

Surprisingly little is known even today, despite the most considerable research efforts, about Monteverdi's operas. For one thing a good bit of his work has been lost, with only three operas remaining extant—*Orfeo* (Mantua, 1607), *Il ritorno d'Ulisse in patria* (Venice, 1640), and *L'incoronazione di Poppea* (Venice, 1643). His authorship of the second of these was, in fact, long disputed. We know the titles of several other large-scale works that are lost but which are known to have been performed: *Arianna* (Mantua, 1608), of which only the heroine's lament survives; *Andromeda* (Mantua, 1620); *Proserpina rapita* (Venice, 1630); and *Le nozze d'Enea con Lavinia* (Venice, 1641). Other lost operas once ascribed to Monteverdi, for example, *Adone* (Venice, 1639), are no longer listed within the Monteverdi canon. A few short stage works like the *Ballo delle ingrate* (Mantua, 1608) and the *Combattimento di Tancredi e Clorinda* (Venice, about 1624) survive because the composer included them in the last volume of madrigals published during his lifetime. Of other works, both large and small scale, we know titles—*Le nozze di Tetide* (1616–17) and *La finta pazza Licori* (1627)—but our knowledge is based solely on Monteverdi's letters, and there is no evidence that these were even completed, let alone performed. The generic designations for musical drama were still so fluid in Monteverdi's time that the three extant operas bear the diverse labels of *favola in musica* (*Orfeo*), *dramma per musica* (*Ulisse*), and *opera reggia* (*Poppea*).

Even for these three operas the problems deriving from textual transmission are formidable. *Orfeo* was the only one published in Monteverdi's time, indeed in two editions (1609 and 1615). As a court opera it could conceivably bring sufficient honor to its sponsor, Duke Vincenzo of Mantua, to motivate its publication. Yet *Arianna*, composed a year after *Orfeo* for the marriage festivities of the ducal heir, Francesco Gonzaga, to whom *Orfeo* had been dedicated, was never honored with publication. Only its heroine's lament has come down to us, for Monteverdi, aware of the great fame it had quickly achieved, published it in three forms—its operatic version, a five-part madrigal, and a sacred setting in Latin, in which the plaint of the mythological character is transformed into Mary's lament for her son.

Since Venetian opera in the seventeenth century counted as a quickly consumable form similar to Elizabethan drama and the films of the early twentieth century, the preservation of its scores was casual at best. Not only did Monteverdi's two last operas remain unpublished for two and a half centuries, but the manuscripts on which our knowledge is based are records of performances by touring companies that took place after the composer's death in 1643. Recent scholarship even suggests the strong hand of collaborators in *Poppea* and argues that its most celebrated operatic number, the final duet between Nero and Poppea, was likely drawn from an opera by another composer.[4]

The uncertainties surrounding the texts of Monteverdi's operas are mirrored as well in our knowledge of how precisely they were meant to be performed. Of the three extant operas only *Orfeo*, prepared as it was for publication, provides solid information about its instrumentation.[5] The manuscripts of the two Venetian operas give only the barest of instrumental lines—with the result that performers in our own time have opted for a wide variety of solutions ranging from the large modern orchestra to small groups of early instruments that keep as literally as possible to what the manuscripts imply. Since research into the performing practices of the Venetian theaters of the 1630s and early 1640s indicates that producers sought to save money on players in favor of extravagant stage machinery, it is likely that the first audiences of *Ulisse* and *Poppea* experienced these operas by means of a minimal orchestral accompaniment quite foreign to the largeness of sound that later centuries have come to associate with opera.[6]

I stress these varied uncertainties to note the precariousness attending the transmission of the operatic past, above all those operas composed during the first century in which the form flourished. Among those activities that we customarily bunch together as the "arts," only dance has resisted preservation and dissemination in a more radical way than music. Except for a few figures such as Palestrina and Allegri, whose compositions were institutionalized within the Roman Catholic church, composers did not enjoy the classical status that had long since been granted to poets and painters. The notion that a composer of an earlier age can and should be performed for listeners in later times dates to the later eighteenth century, when Handel's oratorios (though emphatically not his operas, as I show in Chapter 2) were enshrined as foundation stones of English musical life.[7] By this time, Monteverdi's achievement—not only his operas but also the church music and the books of madrigals whose publication he himself had supervised—was long forgotten.

Yet in his own time Monteverdi counted as a towering figure. As musical director of the church of San Marco in Venice during the latter part of his life, he occupied a lofty public position that few if any composers after him were ever granted. Even before his first opera he had become an object of controversy when the music theorist G. M. Artusi publicly attacked the harmonic deviations from the practices of sixteenth-century contrapuntalists in his madrigals. In an exchange that sounds familiar to those who have witnessed the battles between conservatives and avant-gardists in the various arts during the last century or two, Monteverdi justified his supposedly harsh sounds by announcing what he named a *seconda prattica*—a new form of musical practice suitable to what he termed modernity, a second practice, moreover, that would replace the first practice that had previously constituted musical orthodoxy.[8]

Although *Orfeo* experienced no known performance history between its initial production and the twentieth century, it achieved considerable fame in its time. In an age in which operas were not normally repeated after their early performances, the now-lost *Arianna* was actually revived in Venice during the composer's old age. Its lament not only spawned a whole genre of Arianna laments by other composers, but the descending tetrachord of its accompaniment became a recognizable emblem of operatic laments in general for much of the century.[9] To judge from the statement that "there has not been any house with theorbos or harpsichord which did not also possess the lament [of *Arianna*],"[10] Monteverdi's name quickly became what we would today term a household word.

Within the development of operatic form, Monteverdi was the dominant figure in two quite distinct styles of early opera—the courtly mode at the beginning of the century and the public mode diffused a whole generation later by means of the Venetian theaters. Both through his own late works and through the many operas of his student Francesco Cavalli he left his imprint on mid-seventeenth-century operatic style—even if this style, given the unreliability of textual transmission, soon gave way to another, markedly different style.[11] His few theoretical pronouncements—above all, his defense of the primacy of word over music in the controversy with Artusi and his later explanation of the expressive effects he sought in the *Combattimento*—are as crucial to the history of the aesthetics of opera as the later pronouncements of Gluck, which themselves (and doubtless without Gluck's direct knowledge of his predecessor) make similar claims for the centrality of the verbal text in musical drama.

Yet within a generation after his death an understanding of Monteverdi's achievement was lost to history. With the development of what came to be called *opera seria*, opera in Italy assumed a new form in which an alternation of arias and recitatives, as Chapter 2 elaborates, made vocal virtuosity primary over the expressivity that had been essential to Monteverdi's aesthetic. And just as important for his reputation, the shortness of historical memory that characterized the institutional life of opera during its first century ensured that Monteverdi's work would need to await a time more assiduous than his own in preserving earlier forms of music. This loss of historical memory is evident, for example, in the preface that John Dryden wrote in 1685, little more than a generation after Monteverdi's death, to the libretto of an opera in English, *Albion and Albanus*. Dryden recognizes the primacy of the Italians in the form, who, as he puts it, have "brought to perfection this sort of Dramatique Musical Entertainment."[12] Though hoping to describe the origins of opera for his readers, he gives up by admitting, "I have not been able by any search, to get any light either of the time, when it began, or of the first Author." Dryden cites rumors that opera was suggested to the Italians by their observing the feasts of Spanish Moors and goes on to mention, quite correctly, that "Their first *Opera's* seem to have been intended for the Celebration of the Marriages of their Princes, or for the magnificence of some general time of Joy." Certainly this describes the occasions not only of Monteverdi's early operas for the Mantuan court but, even earlier, for the operas of Peri and Caccini presented at Medici festivities in Florence. Dryden does not supply the names of composers, librettists, or even particular occasions. All such matters by his time belonged to some dim historical past.

Yet the beginnings of opera were never totally forgotten. When Count Francesco Algarotti wrote his influential *Essay on the Opera* (1755) to advocate a reform similar to the one that Gluck was to institute a few years later, he looked back to early opera as constituting some sort of utopian past in which "the poets were themselves musicians" and in which music and poetry were "twin siblings."[13] However, the knowledge of this past was at best hazy to him. Algarotti credits Jacopo Peri, the composer of *Euridice* (Florence, 1600), as "inventor of the recitative" and mentions Ottavio Rinuccini, the librettist not only of Peri's opera but of Monteverdi's *Arianna*.[14] Algarotti never names Monteverdi, in whose time libretti easily survived the music that was composed for them. Doubtless Algarotti's knowledge of Peri came not from hearing the music itself but from the preface that the composer had written to justify his subordinating music to speech in the *Euridice*. Exemplary though the operatic past may have seemed to Algarotti during the mid-eighteenth century, the discontinuity of tradition allowed little real knowledge to survive. Yet despite the obscurity into which Monteverdi, as well as early opera as a whole, had fallen by the eighteenth century, a few references to him can be found, of which the most sympathetic may well be the account in a famous handbook of counterpoint by the composer and theorist Giambattista Martini, *Esemplare di contrappunto fugato* (1774). Martini reproduces and analyzes examples by many of the famed sixteenth- and early seventeenth-century composers including Monteverdi, who is represented by two madrigals and an a capella Agnus Dei. In his commentary Martini reminds the prospective student of Monteverdi's once-great fame, recounts the controversy with Artusi, and then points out dissonances that, unlike Artusi, he defends for their ability to give "expression to the words."[15]

The sympathy that Martini accorded Monteverdi's deviations from the rules was by no means present in those great pioneering (and also rival) histories of music produced in late-eighteenth-century Britain by Charles Burney (1776–89) and John Hawkins (1776). The very fact that two such projects—both of which trace the history of music back to antiquity—would even be undertaken testifies to the new curiosity about the past that marked their time. Yet, as the treatment of Monteverdi shows, what we would today consider a proper historical understanding of the past had to await a later time. Both Hawkins and Burney depend on already-published sources for what they know of Monteverdi—which means the madrigals, some church music, and only *Orfeo* among the operas. For his discussion of the origins of opera Burney simply quotes—for several pages—an early-seventeenth-century witness, Giovanni Battista Doni, and even excuses himself for his dependence on what he calls "second-hand intelligence" (*BGH*, 2: 511–14). Both Burney and Hawkins also quote passages from *Orfeo*, but largely to disapprove of elements that do not conform to the musical practice of their own time. "A specimen of recitative music, in the form in which it was originally composed," Hawkins tells us, "cannot at this day but be deemed a curiosity."[16] Burney, though citing Martini's defense of Monteverdi's liberties in the madrigals, was unable to stomach what he took to be the even greater liberties of *Orfeo*—for example, a succession of fifths in Proserpina's plea, an "*unprepared* seventh" (Burney's italics) and seconds that he assumes "would be as unpleasant to other ears as my own" (*BGH*, 2: 517, 519).

The lack of empathy for a past style of art evident in Hawkins's and Burney's statements about Monteverdi no longer holds for the few existing nineteenth-century accounts of his achievement. The public by this time still had had little or no opportunity to hear what the music sounded like. Not only were there no new editions of *Orfeo* until 1881 (or even a single printed edition of the last two operas, which remained in manuscript until the twentieth century), but an intimate work such as *Orfeo* could scarcely have fit the repertory of any opera house at a time that largeness of sound and of spectacle was becoming the rule—nor did the institutions of musical life accommodate the type of the madrigal ensemble that proliferated during the mid-twentieth century. Yet the new historical attitude toward all the arts that developed preeminently in Germany during the nineteenth century sought to recover the past on its "own terms." In an account of Monteverdi published in 1834 that was uncommonly sympathetic for its time, Carl von Winterfeld, though noting the "awkwardness and rigidity of the modulation" in the *Arianna* lament, also stressed the "strength of passional expression" of this once-celebrated piece.[17] The influential Belgian music historian F.-J. Fétis in his *Biographie universelle des musiciens* (1835–44) was among the first to treat Monteverdi as one of the major figures in the history of music—a figure whom Fétis, using a characteristic nineteenth-century term, describes as of "fecund genius," and whose founding role in the creation of modern tonality he claims has not been understood by any music historian.[18]

By the end of the nineteenth century, well before his work had become familiar once again to the public, Monteverdi's importance had become acknowledged by a biographical account published in a musicological journal in 1887;[19] even earlier, the music historian August Wilhelm Ambros, using a phrase with which Arnold Schoenberg a generation later was to describe his own break with the past, credited Monteverdi with "emancipating the dissonance" from its hitherto strict constraints.[20] Yet Monteverdi's music, like that of nearly all other composers before him, became the privileged territory of scholars and antiquarians whose claims for its greatness the lay public and even performers, if they consulted these specialists' writings at all, had to accept on faith. It is characteristic of the dimness with which the past was perceived that when Georg Gervinus, the founding father of German literary history, outlined a genealogy of opera in 1868, he barely mentioned Monteverdi at all but instead highlighted the role of Peri (whose contribution Gervinus was evaluating more from his Preface to *Euridice* than from his music) together with those of Gluck and Wagner in creating the tradition of music-drama.[21]

Consider the fortunes of Monteverdi in relation to those of two almost exact contemporaries who practiced in media able to reach their public without having to be realized in public performance. Both the careers and the later reception of the painter Caravaggio (1571–1610) and of the poet John Donne (1572–1631), born within five years of Monteverdi, parallel those of the composer in surprisingly similar ways. Each was immensely famous in his time. Each developed a distinctly new and identifiable style, a style that, in each instance, situated itself against an earlier, more "idealizing" mode. Each created what we view today as a distinctly dramatic, even theatrical form of representation.[22] The work of each of these figures was charged with being "harsh" or "rough" both in its own time and in subsequent centuries. Each could be said to have fathered a school—or at least to have exerted so strong an imprint on his followers that he left a decisive mark on the history of his particular art form. Each also suffered a period of neglect lasting centuries—yet, as I shall later show, each also emerged as one of the founding heroes of modernism.

As we read the opening stanza of Donne's "The Canonization"—

For Godsake hold your tongue, and let me love,
  Or chide my palsie, or my gout,
My five gray haires, or ruin'd fortune flout,
  With wealth your state, your minde with Arts improve,
    Take you a course, get you a place,
    Observe his honour, or his grace,
  Or the Kings reall, or his stamped face
    Contemplate, what you will, approve
    So you will let me love.[23]

—we note at once the colloquial language, into which the poet rushes headlong without preparing the reader; the deliberately harsh meters—"my fíve gráy háires"—in which the piled-up accents strain against the norm of the standard iambic mode; the overt intrusion of the world of court politics—"get you a place, / Observe his honour"—into the supposedly closed world of love poetry. Similarly Monteverdi must have jolted his early listeners with the striking dissonances that occur without warning near the opening of Arianna's lament (see Figure 1).

Caravaggio's *Crucifixion of St. Peter* (Figure 2) must likewise have struck its early viewers in Santa Maria del Popolo as something shockingly new in painting. Note the absence of spectators to portray their emotions about the event, as in that earlier painting of the same subject by Michelangelo (Fig-

FIG. 1 The opening bars of Monteverdi's *Lament of Arianna* (madrigal version). The dissonances are marked x. Reprinted from Monteverdi, *Madrigali*, p. 107.

ure 3), with its crowd of awestruck onlookers. Note the helplessness, even confusion, of Caravaggio's old man, whose role as founder of the church could scarcely be guessed at here; note as well Caravaggio's dramatic lighting, whose origin remains uncertain and whose starkness undercuts conventional notions of what should constitute beauty in painting; or note the presumed concentration on the physical process of hoisting the cross rather than on the plight of the martyr; or the claustrophobic effect created by the figures arrayed so closely to the front of the canvas; or the sheer awkwardness of the illuminated pale orange buttocks of the otherwise obscure figure beneath the cross. "Hard to conceive a more dehumanized treatment of the subject," Bernard Berenson, puzzled and fascinated at once by Caravaggio, wrote of this painting.[24]

All three artists, moreover, situated themselves confrontationally against an elegant earlier style—Donne against the smooth rhythms of the Petrarchan love poetry of the late sixteenth century; Monteverdi against the contrapuntalists who followed the codes laid down by Zarlino more than a half century before; Caravaggio against the deliberately decorative, decorous, and often nondramatic quality of late Mannerist painting. All three, as well, exercised such authority in their time that their example quickly kindled the work of others. Since Donne's own heyday it has been common to speak of a group that flourished in England during the first half of the seventeenth century

FIG. 2. Caravaggio, *Crucifixion of St. Peter*. Rome, Santa Maria del Popolo. Courtesy, Alinari / Art Resource, New York.

FIG. 3. Michelangelo, *Crucifixion of St. Peter*. Cappella Paolina, Vatican Palace, Vatican State. Courtesy, Alinari / Art Resource, New York.

and that included such Donne-inspired though also quite distinct voices as George Herbert, Abraham Cowley, Richard Crashaw, and Andrew Marvell—with a branch extending even to the Netherlands, where Donne was translated and imitated. Of these three artists, Caravaggio, unbeknownst to him, achieved the most international reach: his blatantly new realism, which observers from the start labeled *naturalista*, and his chiaroscuro technique were imitated not only by those immediate followers traditionally called Caravaggeschi—for example, the Neapolitan Carlo Saraceni, the Spanish-Neapolitan José Ribera, and the Dutch Hendrik Terbrugghen and Gerrit van Honthorst—but in a looser sense by such major figures of the early seventeenth century as Francisco Zurbarán, Diego Velázquez, Rembrandt, and Jan Vermeer. Though Monteverdi cannot be called the father of a school in quite the manner of the other two, he was quickly imitated by other composers, above all in the series of Arianna laments (as well as laments by other characters) that followed his own,[25] while his theoretical pronouncements—especially his description of the *stile concitato*, the agitated style he created in the *Combattimento*—left a model for later theorists who sought to link musical devices to the expression of specific emotions.[26]

All three, despite the controversies they engendered, also inspired enormous respect in their time. Monteverdi was a presence in a multitude of households, as I have mentioned, through the infectiousness of the Arianna lament, and, as the only one of the three to reach old age, he was able to exercise a long-continuing authority by means of his office at San Marco. Although only a handful of Donne's poems had been published by the time of his death in 1631, his work circulated widely in manuscripts passed along among coteries,[27] and borrowings from and allusions to his still unprinted work can be found in many poems and dramas of the time.[28] Although Caravaggio never had students of his own, his work excited such curiosity that young artists from various countries came to Rome to view his canvasses in the years immediately after his death and adapted his radical new style to their own ends; artists even voyaged to Malta to see the *Beheading of John the Baptist* that he painted there after fleeing a murder charge in Rome.[29]

Yet this adulation was not to last. Thanks in part to the brevity that characterized music's institutional memory, Monteverdi's work and, indeed, the aesthetic he had practiced was eclipsed by the increasing demand for vocal virtuosity in late-seventeenth-century opera. Although Donne and his followers were the dominant poetic voices in England for two decades after his death (indeed, his major impact came posthumously because of his refusal to publish his verses during his lifetime), in the last half of the century a new poetic style came to eschew the roughness of meter and the reconditeness of subject matter that the school of Donne had cultivated. The more classically oriented values associated with a rival mode, the so-called school of Jonson (Jonson himself greatly respected Donne even if he once remarked in conversation that the poet "for not keeping of accent deserved hanging" [*DCH*, 69]), came to shape the work of the succeeding generation, whose most potent voice was Dryden. Though starting out himself as an imitator of Donne,

Dryden marked the break with what had become a style of the past by giving the latter a name, what we still today call the metaphysical style: "He affects the Metaphysicks," Dryden wrote, "not only in his Satires, but in his Amorous Verses, where Nature only shou'd reign" (*DCH*, 151).[30] (Like the names of many period styles such as "baroque," "impressionism," and "cubism," this one was initially created as a term of disparagement.) Similarly, the dominant painters of the mid- and late seventeenth century adopted a more classical-minded, less harsh style than that emanating from the school of Caravaggio. The latter's rival painters, the Carraccis, with their at once decorative and heroic (and, one might add, less disturbing) qualities, offered an alternative model that, unlike Caravaggio's, left its mark on European painting for at least a century and a half.

Although the work of all three figures experienced an abrupt decline in prestige and influence after the mid-seventeenth century, neither Donne nor Caravaggio languished in an obscurity comparable to that of Monteverdi. The difference between poet and painter, on the one hand, and composer, on the other, lies in the quite diverse ways that their work and the aura they exercise can be kept alive. In this sense everything militates against the preservation of music in relation to other arts. In his history of seventeenth-century music, Lorenzo Bianconi even speaks of a decline in music publishing throughout Europe for economic reasons after 1620.[31] Not only was the availability of musical scores limited, but changes in performing style quickly made the instruments and voices associated with an earlier style obsolete. The virtuoso voices that the public came to demand later in the century would scarcely have seemed challenged by or interested in the style that Monteverdi's music offered.[32] Indeed, the preservation of his final operas in manuscript may well be credited not to any continuous performing tradition but rather to the fact that it had become fashionable during the century for individuals to collect manuscript scores as well as musical instruments—the latter of which have enabled us to know what earlier instruments must have sounded like.[33]

By contrast, the writings of Donne and the paintings of Caravaggio remained the subject of commentary, even if of a negative bent, during the several centuries in which they suffered comparative neglect. Literature has remained an ongoing institution since antiquity, with the result that even when writers get demoted they maintain their institutional membership. When Dryden, in the letter complaining about Donne's "affecting the Metaphysicks," likened the poet's critical fortunes to those of Horace (*DCH*, 152), he in effect asserted the continuity of tradition over millennia. Moreover, since books of poetry are considerably more accessible than scores—both physically and in the number of consumers capable of using them—an out-of-favor poet such as Donne was available in a way that a composer of his time simply was not. During Donne's heyday, from the first edition of his poems in 1633 through 1669, his poems were printed or reedited seven times. Still another edition, based on that of 1669, was printed as late as 1719.[34] Coleridge, one of Donne's few genuine admirers during his long period of critical disfavor, annotated a copy of the 1669 edition that he had borrowed from Charles Lamb.[35] For those without access to these old editions, generous selections of the work of earlier English poets, including Donne, could be consulted in a series of multivolume anthologies—for example, those of John Bell (1779), R. Anderson (1793), and Alexander Chalmers (1810)—that sought to enshrine a national literary tradition.[36] As an art of words, literature breeds more words—even if only commentary upon itself—to a degree that music and the visual arts simply do not. It is instructive, for instance, that interest in the history of Donne's reputation has generated at least two monographs, a goodly number of articles, including a whole issue of a journal, plus a 500-page collection of commentaries on his work from his own time until the late nineteenth century—that is, before the major revival of Donne even got going![37] By contrast, scholarly inquiries into the history of Caravaggio's and Monteverdi's reputations are meager at best—generally a few pages or a short chapter within a larger book on these figures.[38]

The difference in our perception of a literary figure and a visual artist, on the one hand, and of a composer, on the other, manifests itself in the images that scholars have created to depict these figures' relationships to the thought of their time. Donne and Caravaggio have both been shown participating in or commenting upon the most advanced areas of thought. Donne's concern with the implications of the new science at the turn of the seventeenth century is evident in some of his most famous poems, above all, in "The Anniversaries," and modern scholarship has documented this concern in great detail.[39] An ambitious recent study of Caravaggio has linked the painter with "libertine" elements in the Roman church of his time and argued for a connection between the naturalism of his painting and that of such contemporary thinkers as Giordano Bruno, Galileo, Tommaso Campanella, and Bacon.[40] Monteverdi has been linked not so much to the newer strains of his time but to the traditional humanistic thought of the Renaissance; whatever new "thinking" is to be found in his operas has been credited to his librettists.[41] Even Claude Palisca, in a pioneering essay that connects changes in musical practice and theory with the empirical attitude of the new sciences, stresses that Monteverdi never wrote the theory he had promised to justify his new practice and credits the theoretical advances in music to philosophers such as Mersenne, Descartes, and the Galileis (both father and son).[42] Can it be that the representational orientation of poetry and painting leads the practitioners of these arts—or at least their modern interpreters—to seek out connections with the more advanced verbalizations of their time? And does the nonverbal art of the musician, even when he is setting the words of others, render him dumb?

All this is not to say that the circulation of and commentary upon a poet's texts or a painter's works ensured the acclamation of his art. Few if any of the writers we respect today have received the opprobrium heaped on Donne for a century and more after his poems were composed. As late as 1798, Nathan Drake, employing musical terminology that could easily be mistaken for Burney's condemnation of Monteverdi a few years before, wrote, "It is scarce possible for a human ear to endure the dissonance and discord of his [Donne's] couplets" (*DCH*, 258). Earlier in the eighteenth century the poet Matthew Prior voiced the general disapproval of his age toward Donne's style by describing his verses as "too dissolute and wild" and coming "very often too near Prose" (*DCH*, 187). The most famous condemnation is of course that of Samuel Johnson, who, writing less specifically of Donne than of the metaphysical poets as a group, condemned not only their style but, in one of the most memorable passages within all English criticism, denounced what he took to be their whole poetic project: "The most heterogeneous ideas are yoked by violence together; nature and art are ransacked for illustrations, comparisons, and allusions; their learning instructs, and their subtilty surprises; but the reader commonly thinks his improvement dearly bought, and, though he sometimes admires, is seldom pleased" (*DCH*, 218).[43]

The fact that literary criticism was an ongoing activity meant that even a mode of writing deemed worth condemning could in fact be kept alive. When Alexander Pope undertook the task of rewriting two of Donne's satires to suit the tastes of his own day, he was, in effect, giving them a continued life. Consider the following example from Pope's reworking of Donne:

mee thought I saw
One of our Giant Statutes ope his jaw
To sucke me in; for hearing him, I found

DONNE:

That as burnt venome Leachers do grow sound
By giving others their soares, I might growe
Guilty, and he free[44]

I fear'd th'Infection slide from him to me,
As in the Pox, some give it, to get free;

POPE:

And quick to swallow me, methought I saw
One of our Giant *Statutes* ope its Jaw![45]

What Pope has accomplished here is to adapt one of the reigning styles of a century before to the dominant style of his own time. One notes his careful avoidance of Donne's notorious series of stresses ("búrnt vé-nome," "dó grów sóund," "míght grówe / guíl-ty") as well as of Donne's habit of running a line over from one couplet to the next ("might growe / guilty"). Nobody could accuse Pope's lines, as eighteenth-century critics accused those of Donne, of being mistakable for prose. Moreover, Pope renders Donne's graphic image of lechers spreading venereal disease more decorous by using the more general term "pox" and eliminating the sores. Despite the closeness with which Pope follows Donne here (much more so than throughout most of his reworking of his predecessor), these two passages belong to quite distinct sonic worlds. It is as though Handel had rewritten Arianna's or Penelope's lament as a da capo aria accompanied by an orchestra of his own time.

Just as Donne survived changes in style and sensibility through the ability of literature as an institution to preserve its past, so Caravaggio survived equally powerful changes by means of the institutional channels that had been established in European painting ever since the High Renaissance. Beginning with Vasari's *Lives of the Artists* (1550), the collection of short biographies of notable artists had flourished as a continuing genre in Italy. As a result, even painters deemed out of date were memorialized with anecdotes about their lives (which, in Caravaggio's case, offered the opportunity to recount his murder of a rival on the racket court), with descriptions of their individual works, and with information about where these works could be found. Since most of Caravaggio's paintings were commissioned for churches, they remained in place for travelers to view even during the centuries in which he was out of fashion. As a result, his paintings would often be mentioned in travelers' accounts of Rome and, as tourism increased during the eighteenth century, included in guidebooks. Moreover, even though illustrated coffee-table artbooks are a recent innovation, Caravaggio's images could be seen in engravings as well as in copies painted by others, above all, those made by art students who had been assigned the replication of pictures in Roman churches.[46]

The basic issue determining the reigning attitude toward Caravaggio was evident already during his time of greatest fame, the early decades of the seventeenth century. As one of his contemporaries, Giovan Battista Agucchi, put it disparagingly, "He has abandoned the idea of beauty, intent only to seek out likeness."[47] Agucchi sought to place Caravaggio's innovation historically by comparing him to an ancient artist, the naturalistic Greek sculptor Demetrius. Yet as long as the Renaissance notion persisted that the visual arts must give order to the natural world by means of certain principles of so-called beauty—and this notion persisted in one form or another until the late nineteenth century—Caravaggio was characterized as the artist who turned his back upon the aesthetic that Raphael and Michelangelo had legitimated and that, in Caravaggio's own time, was represented preeminently by his rival An-

FIG. 4. Caravaggio, *Entombment*. Pinacoteca, Vatican Museums, Vatican State. Courtesy, Scala / Art Resource, New York.

FIG. 5. Cézanne, watercolor copy of Caravaggio's *Entombment*. Photo, Bernheim-Jeune, Paris.

nibale Carracci. Just as Monteverdi was charged with ugliness for his harmonic violations and Donne for his tampering with meters, so Caravaggio was attacked for his refusal to embellish nature (we today would of course call the supposedly unmediated nature in his art still another artistic "construction"). Poussin went so far as to claim that Caravaggio "had come into the world to destroy painting."[48] One of the most influential collections of artists' lives, the *Vite* of Pietro Bellori (1672), though mindful of Caravaggio's fame and of the fascination that his life and his work had aroused, claimed that he had "neither invention nor decorum nor design nor knowledge of the science of painting" and that "once the model was removed from his eyes, his hand and his mind remained empty."[49] Bellori deflected much of his attack onto Caravaggio's followers, who, he claimed, since they had rejected the authority of the ancients and of Raphael, displayed their indecorousness in their search for "filth and deformity," their depiction of "wrinkles and skin defects" as well as of "knotted fingers and diseased-afflicted limbs." Had it been customary for later artists to repaint famous pictures in the way that Pope rewrote Donne, one can well imagine how Caravaggio's work might have been transformed—more precisely, "beautified"—beyond recognition: the wrinkled forehead of the man at the upper left of the *Crucifixion of St. Peter* would have been smoothed over and the buttocks at the lower left illuminated less conspicuously and reduced to more decorous proportions. Indeed, it is in the sketches and engravings that later artists made of famous works—in Caravaggio's case, for example, Fragonard's sketch of the London *Supper at Emmaus* or, most strikingly, Cézanne's nearly abstract watercolor of the Vatican *Entombment* (see Figures 4 and 5)—that we see how a later aesthetic can come to terms with an earlier one.[50]

However one came to terms with Caravaggio, his originality was beyond dispute. The same Count Algarotti whose essay on opera ignored Monteverdi and cited Peri as the founding father of music-drama later wrote an essay on painting (1762), in which he rightly calls Caravaggio "the real author" of chiaroscuro, though he also calls him "the Rembrandt of Italy" as though to honor him by reference to his own follower, who was by now much more prestigious.[51] Although Caravaggio remained visible in the various lives of painters and in Luigi Lanzi's much-read history of Italian painting (1789), his name is omitted entirely from the most powerful treatise on painting of the eighteenth century, Sir Joshua Reynolds's *Discourses*, delivered during the 1780s and early 1790s to students at the Royal Academy. As the most eloquent and comprehensive defense of the classical tradition in painting, this book has much to say about painters such as Raphael, Titian, and the Carraccis—yet, as I show later, its refusal even to allude negatively to Caravaggio was to play a role in the latter's revival more than a century afterwards.

Whereas the few discussions of Monteverdi during the nineteenth century, as I have shown, emanated mainly from specialized historians of music—and without the ready availability of scores, let alone live performances—Donne and Caravaggio remained subjects that were much discussed, whether from a positive or negative point of view. Coleridge's enthusiasm for Donne, though known to his friends, expressed itself in notes that were not published until well after his death. The public "rehabilitation" of Donne could be said to begin with an anonymous essay of 1823 in the *Retrospective Review*, a journal that displayed the new historical spirit by concentrating on reconsiderations of the past. Yet just as Winterfeld in 1834 would feel the need to mention Monteverdi's "awkwardness" while attempting to champion him, so this rehabilitative essay admits that "almost every beauty we meet with [in Donne] goes hand in hand with some striking deformity . . . so completely *irritating* to the imagination" (*DCH*, 328, author's italics).[52] It is clear that Donne's style, though even more "irritating" to eighteenth-century readers than to this writer, was too far removed from the new romantic mode to be assimilated easily. When Thoreau wrote, "Donne was not a poet, but a man of strong sense" (*DCH*, 391), he placed Donne's matter over his music and thus perpetuated the topos of the poet's "unpoetic" roughness of style. Despite many nineteenth-century uses of his work, in the form not only of criticism but of allusions and epigraphs in poems and novels, Donne's sounds remained an issue no matter which side one took. If Hazlitt could assert that Donne's "thoughts are delivered by the Caesarean operation" (*DCH*, 310), Emerson could claim to read "these Donnes and Cowleys and Marvells with the most modern joy" (*DCH*, 303). The Tennyson-inspired *Golden Treasury* omitted him entirely from its first edition of 1861—yet Browning, who himself cultivated harshness of sound like no other major poet of his century, championed Donne to the point that he became the dedicatee of the first large new edition of Donne's poetry (1872).[53]

Similarly, the topos that Caravaggio sacrificed art in favor of nature persisted throughout nineteenth-century descriptions of his work. This attitude dominates the various depictions of Caravaggio's paintings in Jacob Burckhardt's *Cicerone* (1855), the travel guide whose judgments of what was worth viewing in Italy—and also of how it was to be evaluated—carried its author's prestige as the great cultural historian of his time. Although Burckhardt is able to appreciate those early canvasses of Caravaggio that retain some of the "harmony" of the painter's Venetian predecessors, he expresses horror at the way Caravaggio relishes dragging "a sublime and ideal" subject such as the conversion of Paul into the "trivial and commonplace"; or at the "naturalism" of the beheaded Medusa, whose expression, he tells us, could as well have resulted from a tooth extraction.[54] Burckhardt's attack on Caravaggio's naturalism has a more timely purpose than other such attacks during the preceding two centuries, for it serves explicitly to comment upon the new naturalism emerging in literature as well as in art and, in particular, in the painting of Courbet. "Modern naturalism in the narrower sense begins in the most strident [*grell*] way with Michelangelo Amerighi da Caravaggio":[55] Burckhardt thus opens his discussion in such a way that the solemn northern European tourists dependent upon his cultural guidance could not fail to get the point. The word *grell* (crude, shrill, strident), which Burckhardt uses on several occasions in connection with Caravaggio (and which can refer both to sound and sight), has much the same function as do "dissonant" and "harsh" when applied to Monteverdi and Donne.

Yet Caravaggio's works possessed an attribute that, unlike anything in Monteverdi and Donne, was deemed in tune with one aspect of late-eighteenth- and early-nineteenth-century sensibility. The very chiaroscuro that, in Caravaggio's hands, threatened traditional principles of good composition also created an atmosphere of gloom that gave pleasure to viewers nurtured on graveyard poets and Piranesi's prison prints. Thus, Lanzi's history of art, though careful to set up the usual caveats ("we must not look in him [Caravaggio] for correct design, or elegant proportion"), also speaks of "his sombre genius" and of the "enchantment" emanating from the fact that "his figures inhabit dungeons . . . his backgrounds are always dark."[56] Lord Byron's reference in *Don Juan* to "gloomy Caravaggio's gloomier stain" invokes a topos that rivals the one about the painter's artless naturalism.[57] For those who eschewed the Caravaggian gloom, his art remained outside the great tradition of painting as surely as it had for the classicist Reynolds. It is scarcely surprising to find the light-obsessed Ruskin associating the "brown and grey" of Rembrandt, Caravaggio, and Salvator Rosa with the "vulgar, dull, or impious" and, in another context, calling the last two artists "worshippers of the depraved."[58]

The fascination that Caravaggio was beginning to awaken was voiced repeatedly in the various travel writings and histories of art by Stendhal. Although Stendhal's judgments were sometimes secondhand—to the point of literally reproducing Bellori on Caravaggio's lack of invention and decorum[59]—Stendhal could also admire the way that Caravaggio cultivated the lowly and even the ugly as a means of expressing his boredom with the elegant imitation of Raphael and the ancients expected of painters in his time. Stendhal characteristically uses the terms "energy" and "energetic," for example, when, in a guide to Roman churches, he cites the "crude but energetic peasants" who fill up two of Caravaggio's St. Matthew canvasses.[60] Yet there are two other terms, *assassin* and *scélérat* (villain), that recur in Stendhal's accounts of Caravaggio. "Ce grand peintre fut un scélérat," he likes to remind his readers[61]—as though suggesting that our knowledge of Caravaggio's criminality is intrinsic to our response to his paintings. Two of the features that had been present throughout the various short biographies of Caravaggio— his capital crime and the unpleasantness of his personality—quite easily accommodated themselves to the new image emerging in Stendhal's time of what constituted an artist. And it is not surprising that Caravaggio's life was the subject of some now-forgotten novels and dramas in French and Italian during the heyday of romanticism.[62]

One might wonder what Stendhal, who wrote almost as extensively about music as about art, would have made of Monteverdi had he known his works. Among Stendhal's writings I have found only a single reference to Monteverdi, whom he mentions in passing in his biography of Haydn. To indicate his disapproval of a voice part that Haydn's brother added to the purely instrumental *The Seven Last Words of Christ*, Stendhal speaks of "a Herculean labor, which would have terrified a Monteverdi or a Palestrina."[63] Unlike Caravaggio, whose work was physically present to Stendhal during his Italian travels, these composers' names are simply labels for two luminaries from some legendary and none-too-familiar past. Had the music of Monteverdi's time been available to Stendhal, he would even have found Caravaggio's particular crime embodied in a famous composer, Prince Carlo Gesualdo, who murdered his wife (not, like the painter, a rival in a sporting match) and whose provocative lack of tonal definition, moreover, would have proved considerably more disconcerting to the nineteenth century than Monteverdi's dissonances.[64]

Within the context of this chapter it seems noteworthy that at one point Stendhal, admitting himself "obsessed with a mania for comparisons," lists a group of painters and opera composers whom he playfully presents as "corresponding" to one another.[65] For example, Raphael is made to correspond to both Pergolesi and Cimarosa, and Michelangelo, quite aptly, to Handel. Stendhal's list illustrates, among other things, the quite different time-spans governing the available knowledge of earlier painting and music during his own time: whereas the painters go back well over three centuries to Leonardo da Vinci, the composers are all drawn from the eighteenth and early nineteenth centuries. Interestingly, Stendhal pairs Caravaggio with Gluck in this list. Did Stendhal, who gave no explanation for this particular correspondence, link them because of the sharp break with the past that both had made to create new styles in their respective media? Possibly—but more likely, to judge from some chance remarks about the difficulties that each of them posed in holding a viewer's or a listener's attentions, Stendhal may simply have found them rather austere and demanding for his particular tastes, which tended to seek out more immediately sensuous delights in the various arts.[66]

Throughout my own discussion of correspondences between Monteverdi, Donne, and Caravaggio, I have thus far left out the name of a major literary figure who was as contemporaneous with Monteverdi as the other two. I refer of course to Shakespeare, born three years before Monteverdi and, like the latter, a practitioner of a medium designed for performance. Like Monteverdi in his Venetian operas, Shakespeare took no responsibility for publishing his productions designed for the Elizabethan popular stage; both men authorized only their work written within the more "prestigious" genres—the composer, his books of madrigals, some church music, and one of his court operas; the playwright, only his two early narrative poems. Yet despite the textual uncertainties of Shakespeare's plays—uncertainties that have kept a multitude of editors occupied since the early eighteenth century and have now become a problem for computers to reckon with—Shakespeare has had a continuing performance history since the seventeenth century in England and, since the late eighteenth and early nineteenth centuries, in most other countries. Certainly during the early part of this history Shakespeare's plays challenged the reigning classical canons as sharply as the work of the three figures whose afterlife I have been tracing. Within the context I have sought to establish, the surviving power of Shakespeare tells us something of the crucial difference between musical and nonmusical theater. Even if Monteverdi's operas had been available, they would not likely have had a continuing performance history, for opera does not adapt itself to changing conditions of representational style to the degree that spoken theater can. Despite the continuity of interest they have aroused over time, Shakespeare's plays have been subject to the most fundamental changes in acting style, scenic production, and literary interpretation. For a long while they were even revised mercilessly to suit the needs and tastes of the time—most notoriously, of course, in the happy ending attached to *King Lear* in the 1680s and used in performance on the English-speaking stage until well into the nineteenth century. Still, despite all the changes to which they can be subjected, Shakespeare's plays have remained recognizably their author's work in a way that no opera could with comparable changes in musical scoring.

But Shakespeare also fulfilled a particular role that could not easily have fallen to a composer or a painter: for nearly three centuries, no matter how "irregular" his language and his dramatic structure were taken to be, he has served as a foundation stone for defining and embodying British national culture. However much a particular culture may idolize its artists and composers, this role has been reserved during recent centuries for practitioners of the written word such as Dante, Cervantes, and Goethe in their respective nations: it is as though only a verbal art form can fully express national aspirations. Yet during the nineteenth century, outside his own national domain Shakespeare also played another role, for the very irregularities that had once made his work suspect became a prime means by which the classical system within both art and literature—the very system that had impeded the understanding of Donne and Caravaggio, not to speak of Shakespeare himself—was questioned in the name of the new romanticism. Stendhal, whose journalistic pursuits took him across the various arts before he had composed the novels for which he is most remembered today, himself participated in this battle. In his polemic *Racine et Shakspeare* (1823), he attacked the classicism of the greatest dramatist in his own language in favor of a foreign writer who symbolized what Stendhal's generation took to be the wave of the future.

The classical status held today by the three figures whose critical fortunes I have been tracing through history was not, like Shakespeare's, achieved during the romantic period but awaited a much later time. Monteverdi, Donne, and Caravaggio are in fact the classics of modernism—one might even say the creations of what we call early modernism. At the start of the twentieth century each of them underwent the sort of reexamination necessary within each of their respective art forms to ground the relevance of their work. Monteverdi's *Orfeo* received a live performance—its first since the composer's own time—in Paris in 1904, with *L'incoronazione di Poppea* following a year later.[67] The paintings associated with Caravaggio became the subject of serious investigation within that scientifically minded new discipline of art history, which, concerning itself with matters such as the development of his style and the authenticity of particular paintings attributed to him, established and defined the Caravaggio canon.[68] Donne's poems appeared in 1912 in an elaborate and equally scientifically minded critical edition based on his original manuscripts.[69] A musical performance, the establishment of a canon, a critical edition—these were the public gestures necessary within each art form to provide the setting within which new critical interpretations and assessments could be made.

Even before the Paris performance of *Orfeo*, C. Hubert Parry's discussion of Monteverdi's style in a 1902 volume of the *Oxford History of Music*, though it claims to speak of the composer's first audience, suggests the frame of mind with which listeners have come to hear the music in our own century. After reproducing and analyzing the composer's dissonances in the first eleven bars of the *Arianna* lament, Parry writes of "a kind of strain upon the nerves which certainly ministered to the excitement of sensibility which is said to have been aroused in the audience at the first performance." As though anticipating the shocks to the ear that would issue from composers such as Strauss, Stravinsky, and Schoenberg during the next decade, Parry goes on to write, "The crowding of so many features which were quite unfamiliar to the audience into such a short passage was like a defiant manifesto." Parry's keen historical sense also encouraged him to place Monteverdi in much the same position that we would still grant him today—as founder of a musical mode "which passed through Monteverdi's pupil Cavalli into France . . . , arrived at one important crisis in Gluck's work, and culminated in the works of Wagner and his recent followers."[70] This juxtaposition of Monteverdi, Gluck, and Wagner to form a genealogy of musical dramatists obviously seems more accurate to us than the genealogy that appeared on the Metropolitan Opera's proscenium at about the same time.

The *Orfeo* of 1904, though done in concert form and cut drastically by its adapter and conductor, the composer Vincent d'Indy, struck certain of its listeners as a revelation, if one can judge from those reviewers who championed it—among them the novelist Romain Rolland, who, a decade before, had dis-

cussed Monteverdi with considerable sympathy and knowledge in his doc-
toral dissertation.[71] From the point of view of the present argument, the concluding lines of another reviewer, Louis Laloy, seem especially pertinent: "I
know scarcely any works more humane and more exalted than the *Orfeo*, and
it is not without reason that the criticisms aimed at the *Orfeo* . . . resemble
those aimed at *Pelléas*. The two works should displease the same spirits."[72]
Laloy was himself a vigorous defender of Debussy's harmonic innovations
and, in particular, of *Pelléas et Mélisande*, which had premiered only two years
before the *Orfeo* performance[73]; in addition to the strange harmonies that listeners would have heard in Monteverdi and Debussy, Laloy may also have
recognized in *Orfeo* that overwhelming sense of stasis that so offended (and
still offends) in *Pelléas*. As so often in the course of modernist polemics, the
revival of an earlier artist becomes linked inextricably to the reception of a
controversial new one. With Debussy's innovations fresh in audiences' ears,
Monteverdi's music evidently did not need to wait for the more jarring sonic
violations to be heard, say, in *Salome* (1905) or *Erwartung* (1909) to make its
particular point.

In 1905, about the time that art historians were starting to examine the Caravaggio canon seriously, the young art critic Roger Fry produced an edition
of Reynolds's *Discourses* illustrated with reproductions of various paintings
discussed in this classic work. In what one might call a typical act of modernist defiance, Fry (who, a few years later, was to introduce contemporary
French painting to Britain) included a picture by an artist conspicuously missing from Reynolds's lectures—Caravaggio. In the commentary accompany-
ing this illustration, the *Entombment* (Figure 4), Fry declares, "It is extraordinary that, treating so much as he does of Italian art of the seventeenth century, Reynolds does not mention Caravaggio either for blame or praise in the
whole of the Discourses, though he mentions him occasionally in his notes
on a Journey in Flanders. And yet there is hardly any one artist whose work is
of such moment as his in the development of modern art."[74] Fry proceeds to
point out not only how critical Caravaggio was to the major Spanish painters
of the seventeenth century, but, even more important to his own concerns,
"The art of the nineteenth century is continually marked by an unconscious

return to his point of view. Manet, for instance, goes back rather to him [Caravaggio] than to Velasquez." The affinity, "unconscious" though it may have been, that Burckhardt disparagingly pointed out between Caravaggio and the realist art of his time, now achieves a positive assessment. Indeed, Fry goes on to hail Caravaggio as "the first modern artist; the first artist to proceed not by evolution but by revolution; the first to rely entirely on his own temperamental attitude and to defy tradition and authority."[75] Just as Fry must have discovered Caravaggio's modernity through his own experience with recent artists such as Manet, so Roberto Longhi, the foremost Caravaggio exponent and scholar of the succeeding generation, tells of encountering the earlier painter's significance for his own time while viewing Courbet at the Venice Biennale in 1910.[76]

Although the Donne revival had begun during the nineteenth century to a degree that the Monteverdi and Caravaggio revivals had not, the edition issued by Herbert Grierson in 1912 is generally credited with drawing the attention of readers and poets to his work.[77] The most articulate of Donne's advocates was the young T. S. Eliot, who, in a 1921 review of an anthology of metaphysical lyrics that Grierson had recently published, within the course of a few pages transformed the label "metaphysical poets" from what he calls "a term of abuse" to a model for a mode of writing so successful in its time— above all in its ability to "devour any kind of experience"—that all subsequent English poetry, from Milton to Eliot's immediate predecessors, seemed to Eliot a woeful falling off.[78] Like Laloy in his juxtaposition of Monteverdi with Debussy, or Fry, of Caravaggio with Manet, Eliot ends his review with a quotation from a recent French Symbolist poet, Jules Laforgue, whom, through his irony and combination of "simple phrasing" and "obscure words," we are meant to view as "nearer to the 'school of Donne' than any modern English poet."[79]

The modernity that we have learned to read into Monteverdi, Caravaggio, and Donne—indeed, the modernity by means of which we have defined them for ourselves in the first place—does not imply that they have necessarily served to influence the modern artists working within their respective media. Although Eliot's poetry shows the impact of Donne and his contemporaries, his work was more directly shaped by Laforgue, Baudelaire, and other recent French poets. Rather, one should speak of the metaphysicals as helping to legitimize the sharp break with eighteenth- and nineteenth-century poetic language and aesthetics that Eliot and his generation sought to effect. Likewise, although Monteverdi has been favored by many modern composers (including those, like Gian Francesco Malipiero, Hans Werner Henze, and Luciano Berio, who edited his work or adapted his operas for performance), his music served less as an influence than as a means to legitimize a rejection of the refined harmonic languages that developed between his and their times.

Although the naturalist Caravaggio would not seem a direct influence on the abstract painting that became dominant during the very years of his revival, his own sharp break with classicist art provided a model, to use Fry's words, both for "defying tradition and authority" and for allowing art to present objects in a "squalid" light (as Fry put it) instead of having to idealize them. In short, Caravaggio offered twentieth-century artists an example to justify practices that the general public often refused to consider suitable for what it deemed art. Indeed, by mid-century Caravaggio had come to speak with such immediacy that even so pure an abstractionist as Mark Rothko could acknowledge his impact on his own later work, which, as he told the art historian Peter Selz, could rethink the earlier painter "but without the narrative."[80] The presence of narrative in Caravaggio did not pose a problem for one of the major abstractionists of the generation after Rothko, namely Frank Stella, who situated Caravaggio as the centerpiece of his Harvard Norton lectures of 1983–84. For Stella, Caravaggio's radical reshaping of the Italian painting of the preceding century—what Stella calls his "declaration of a truly independent space for painting"—becomes part of Stella's own polemic to renew American abstraction after its supposed decline around 1970. When we read Stella's description of Caravaggio's achievement as "a lifetime involvement in the creation of projective, spherically informed pictorial space," we quickly grasp the affinities he must have felt between the earlier painter's style and his own three-dimensional, mixed-media works of the late 1970s and 1980s.[81]

In an essay published in 1917, the same year as his first and quite contro-versial volume of poems, Eliot, in a statement that has itself become canonical within critical discourse in English, theorized about the way literary canons were reshaped: "What happens when a new work of art is created is some-thing that happens simultaneously to all the works of art which preceded it. The existing monuments form an ideal order among themselves, which is modified by the introduction of the new (the really new) work of art among them."[82] As a result of his own new way of writing—his ironic voice, his col-loquial language, his bizarre allusions—Eliot suggests that the existing mon-uments have been reordered, that a new canon of poetry has replaced, or at least modified (to use his own, more diffident term) the view of poetry that prevailed during the preceding century. The establishment of a central place for Donne in English poetry, for Caravaggio in painting, for Monteverdi in music, was thus to be seen as a natural, perhaps even inevitable consequence of the advent of modernist languages in the various arts.

Yet Monteverdi has still, nearly a century after his first modern performances, to establish his centrality for those calling themselves operagoers. One won-ders how many opera houses, if they were to memorialize the past with busts of the great composers or with names carved upon the proscenium, would find room for Monteverdi. By no stretch of the imagination can one speak of Monteverdi as a "popular" composer even in the late 1990s. Except for a con-cert performance of *Orfeo* that took place on its stage in 1912, the Metropoli-tan Opera has not to date produced a Monteverdi opera. A list compiled of the 100 operas most frequently performed worldwide among some 252 com-panies and festivals during 1988 and 1989 includes only one of his three extant operas, *L'incoronazione di Poppea*, and it ranks no higher than 71; indeed, only one other opera before Gluck, Handel's *Giulio Cesare*, even made it to this list, some six notches below *Poppea*. All six composers included on the Metropol-itan proscenium in 1903, even the supposedly fast-fading Gounod, appear considerably higher on the list than Monteverdi and Handel. The once-so-rarely-performed Mozart was at the top of this recent popularity contest, with

Le nozze di Figaro number one and a total of four Mozart works among the highest-ranking ten! Beethoven's single opera was up to number 14, and even Gluck's *Orfeo et Euridice* stood at 46, still well above Monteverdi.[83]

If Monteverdi's operas have not yet fully established themselves for the operatic public, the long-playing record and later the compact disc and video-tape and -disc have made them easily available for those who care to listen. People wanting to see them staged live are more likely to encounter them at festivals and smaller venues such as Glyndebourne and Glimmerglass than at the major opera centers. Even the nonoperatic works of Monteverdi have suffered from the difficulty of absorbing them within institutionalized musical life, which tends to be based around specialized groups and individuals such as the symphony orchestra, the string quartet, the individual lieder singer. Within this spectrum Monteverdi, together with his Renaissance predecessors, has become the property of college-based madrigal singers and professional early-music groups, the latter usually so narrowly focused that they often devote themselves to no more than a century or two of music within a broad time frame running from Hildegard of Bingen down to Bach. Despite the considerable success of the early-music movement, audiences attending these events are still nearly as specialized as the practitioners themselves— with the result that members of the general music public, even those who pride themselves on recognizing a particular late Beethoven quartet or a Mahler symphony after only a few bars, may often never have heard such landmark Monteverdi madrigals as "Lamento della ninfa" or "Zefiro torna."

By contrast, Caravaggio and Donne had become thoroughly institutionalized for the museum-going and reading publics by the mid-twentieth century. In painting, the retrospective exhibition has within our century become a prime means for persuading a potentially reluctant public of a painter's centrality. A Florence exhibit of 1922 devoted to seventeenth- and eighteenth-century art placed Caravaggio within a historical context and gave him the attention needed to assure him the canonical status for which the art-historical scholarship of the preceding decades had laid the groundwork. A Milan exhibit of 1951 devoted to him and his followers and a 1985 show in New York and Naples demonstrated his centrality within that twentieth-century appellation, the baroque, that students learn in their college art-history surveys. Donne's exemplary status was confirmed through the fact that the New Criticism, the reigning movement in Anglo-American literary criticism from the 1940s until the 1960s, adapted what it took to be the poetics of Donne and the metaphysicals—mediated as it was by Eliot—as its own general poetics for literature as a whole; indeed, for vast numbers of college students during this period (and even after) the analysis of a Donne poem became the model of what any poem any time should be. It scarcely seems accidental that one of the foundation texts of the New Criticism used as its title *The Well Wrought Urn*, a phrase drawn from "The Canonization," which itself in effect became the canonical text of this critical movement.[84]

The Monteverdi whom we *do* hear, during the still sporadic intervals in which he appears in the opera house, is doubtless remote from what his first audiences experienced. The most obvious and unavoidable difference lies in the fact that not only Monteverdi but all composers of *opera seria* down to the early Rossini normally utilized castrati in major roles. Although Monteverdi's Orfeo was a tenor and his Caronte a bass, the female parts of his first opera were likely sung by castrati, as were the two rival male lovers in *Poppea*.[85] Every modern production must perforce choose a substitute voice for the castrato, whether by means of a female singer, a countertenor, or a male voice that has been lowered an octave—and with the obvious resulting musical and textual distortions. The minimal instrumentation of the Venetian operas creates considerable difficulty in reconciling the desire for "authentic" performance with the policies of the standard opera companies. When the San Francisco Opera, for example, performed the two Venetian operas, it opted for the distinctly inauthentic sounds of a modern orchestra and of large-scale voices trained for a later form of opera. Doubtless a performance closer to Monteverdi's original conditions would have been acoustically too subdued in a cavernous house such as San Francisco's, as well as politically explosive if some six or seven early-music instrumental specialists sought to displace the unionized orchestra.

Moreover, to judge from recorded versions of *Poppea* spread over the last four decades, one notes the most profound changes not only in the choices made for the range of the singers and for the size and makeup of the instrumental ensemble but also in their basic musical style. These were the very decades during which the early-music movement created a revolution in performance practices. The earliest recording I have heard, from a Zurich production of the early 1950s conducted by Walter Goehr, not only uses a modern orchestra and a male singer for Nerone but also opts for a style that sounds early romantic. The famous Glyndebourne production of the early 1960s, arranged and conducted by Raymond Leppard, was shameless in the romantic effects it sought out with its tremulous modern strings and voices, the latter including low voices for the castrato roles of Ottone and Nerone. When the Nikolaus Harnoncourt version appeared in 1974, it seemed like the latest development in the re-creation of early opera, for it employed female voices and countertenors for the castrato roles as well as period instruments, though with a thicker and more varied instrumentation than the Venetian theaters had likely used. A more recent recording, based on a London production of 1988 by Richard Hickox, employs not only similar voices but takes a strictly bare-bones approach to the instrumentation, with most of the singers accompanied by no more than one or two instruments at a time. Satisfying though this recording seems to our latest hearing practices, it is probably much too chamberlike to be workable at any of the larger opera houses, and like other recent performances of Monteverdi's other works, it foregrounds its dissonances to a greater degree than earlier performances. To ensure productions of early operas satisfying to the most contemporary tastes, an enterprising company would need to build an intimate theater (analogous to the small recital hall for chamber music that one often finds next to the large symphony hall) with appropriately selected voices and instruments.

Obviously it is difficult for us to get back to what must have been the "real" Monteverdi. The problem is compounded by the visual elements shaping contemporary opera production, which, even when seeking musical authenticity, often opts for radical theatrical reinterpretation—as, for example, in Jean-Pierre Ponnelle's Zurich productions in the late 1970s of the three Monteverdi operas, which were set not in their "original" locales but in a repressive seventeenth-century court. To hear the "real" Monteverdi one might be best off—especially if one is aware of the latest research in early performing practices—simply to hum or sight-read the scores, however much the texts we have of the Venetian operas may deviate from Monteverdi's "intentions." Similarly, one may well get to the "real" Shakespeare less from performances (what with the propensity of contemporary directors to use, say, Victorian or modern dress and scenery) than from reading the texts, however much these may differ from Shakespeare's lost manuscripts and whatever changes he may have authorized for different performances. (The search for the individual author's original intentions is an obsession we have inherited from a conception of authorship that goes back no longer than the later eighteenth century—long after figures such as Monteverdi and Shakespeare had hidden their traces.) It may also be that we get to the "real" creator most surely within those media that are not dependent upon performance for their re-creation. Among the creators I have discussed in this chapter, surely Donne and Caravaggio (despite the restorations his paintings have undergone over the years) should pose fewer barriers than Monteverdi and Shakespeare for experiencing their work in its immediacy.

But we also have come to recognize this desire to reexperience the art of the past "as it really was" as a naive form of historicism. A series of lively articles during the 1980s and early 1990s by two musicologists, Laurence Dreyfus and Richard Taruskin, both also experienced early-music practitioners, questioned the pretensions of the early-music movement to reconstruct the past and argued, in turn, that so-called authentic performances are part and parcel of musical modernism, whose own program of shocking complacent ears with new sounds this movement seeks to emulate.[86] I might add that modernity imposes itself in still another way in our experience with the art of the past, for our awareness of modern art itself helps shape our perceptions of the past. In hearing the voice of Monteverdi during the twentieth century, we also hear the voices of Debussy, Stravinsky, and their successors; in reading Donne today, we also hear Browning, Eliot, and any number of poets who have deliberately "roughened up" their language and sought to emulate his dramatic immediacy; in approaching Caravaggio, we carry with us the perceptual apparatus suggested by the innovations of Courbet and Manet.[87]

Throughout this chapter I have treated these figures from a distant past as masters of comparable status, regardless of the differences in the media within which they worked. The Metropolitan Opera's gesture, nearly a century ago, of inscribing the names of the six supposedly canonical composers was a statement that the great operatic creators were to be honored in much the same way that the great authors in the culture of the West have been honored since antiquity. Certainly before the late eighteenth century it would have seemed presumptuous to grant composers so lofty a degree of authorial authority.

Indeed, the realities of operatic production throughout much of the history of opera suggest that often the composer's status was highly questionable, that the hierarchies among the various specialists—composers, librettists, star singers, impresarios, directors, designers—who have come together to create an opera have adapted themselves to changing conditions. In late-eighteenth- and early-nineteenth-century Italy the impresario exerted such power that Rossini, despite the acclamation accorded him from a young age, was treated almost as a lackey as he traveled for years from city to city to fulfill his deadlines for new scores.[88] Moreover, the many operas from various times and places that were designed with the strengths and limitations of particular singers in mind testifies to the power of the performer—even with a Handel or a Mozart setting the text—to give shape to the music. The very title of Stendhal's set of biographies, *Vies de Haydn, de Mozart et de Métastase*, indicates the reverence in which the celebrated poet-librettist was held. In fact, these composers were only two among a multitude who set some of Metastasio's same texts as many as thirty or forty times, while the praise that Stendhal metes out to him is commensurate with that granted to Haydn and Mozart. Those two recent John Adams operas, *Nixon in China* and *The Death of Klinghoffer*, from their very conception were the joint products of a team that, besides the composer (who, by contemporary custom, still received top billing), included the librettist Alice Goodman; the director Peter Sellars, who supplied his own collection of singers and supposedly instigated the project in the first place; and the choreographer Mark Morris, who designed the dances for his own troop. When the score of *Der Rosenkavalier* was first published with the label as "A Comedy for Music by Hugo von Hofmannsthal, with music by Richard Strauss," the librettist was pitting his prestige as foremost man of letters in the German-speaking world against Strauss's equivalent prestige as foremost composer. If Hofmannsthal won that skirmish, Strauss in fact had the last word, for in his final opera, *Capriccio*, he not only wrote his own libretto (with some help, to be sure, from his conductor, Clemens Krauss) but built the whole plot around the problem of whether the librettist or the composer has primacy in opera.[89]

These differing views of a composer's relative role are evident in Monteverdi's two distinct phases as a composer of opera: whereas the title page of *Orfeo* features his name in large type, with that of the dedicatee, the ducal heir Francesco Gonzaga (in effect his impresario), in smaller type, in the collaborative, profit-minded world of the Venetian theaters the need for the continuous production of new works left Monteverdi's last operatic achievements nearly lost to posterity. One might add that Monteverdi's own insistence on the primacy of word over music as a central tenet of the *seconda prattica*—a tenet already implied in the theorizing of the Camerata and in the first Florentine operas—can be interpreted as a threat to whatever hegemony a composer might later claim.

By the twentieth century Monteverdi had earned his rightful place as founder of that tradition of opera-as-drama that passed through Gluck and Wagner and, indeed, through most of the composers who have been accorded the highest prestige in histories of music. Yet one might remember that there exists another tradition—what is called the number-opera as opposed to the music-drama—whose quite different aesthetic we have come to reassess of late. I speak of that long-deprecated line represented by Handel, Rossini, Bellini, the early Verdi, and in the next century by Stravinsky and Weill—a line that, moreover, has underplayed so-called dramatic values in favor of sheer musical exuberance and the sometimes shameless display of vocal virtuosity. Chapters 2 and 3, in focusing upon the first two of these figures, will analyze and situate historically the aesthetics underlying their work. In view of such competing genealogies, and in view as well of the challenges posed to the composer's primacy in that collaborative endeavor we call opera, the canons we establish of opera composers will likely never seem quite as stable as those projected for poets and painters. Among all the art forms except for dance, opera most strikingly calls into question the notion of authorship. Some future proscenium inscribing the names of opera's most honored practitioners might, unlike the Metropolitan's list of nearly a century ago, demand quite different criteria for selection, with a Callas or a Pavarotti competing for space with Verdi, or even with a director such as Wieland Wagner vying with his illustrious grandfather.

Chapter Two

Handel and the Poetics of *Opera Seria*

The names glorified on the proscenium of the old Met at the turn of the twentieth century—Gluck, Mozart, Beethoven, Wagner, Verdi, and Gounod—do not simply articulate a canon but, like any canon, suggest a narrative about operatic history. Thus Gluck, however little he may have been performed, could serve as a foundation stone for that tradition of opera in which the drama motivated and justified the music and that, one could assume, was carried on by the other names decorating the theater. If one consults the standard histories of opera of the early twentieth century, one notes brief accounts of the Florentine Camerata, of the experiments of Peri and Monteverdi with recitative, of the unique direction taken by Lully and his successors in France, and, before these histories can get on with their eulogies of Gluck, of the supposedly unfortunate direction that Italian opera took for well over half a century in the form known as *opera seria*. "It is not surprising to find that the librettists were unable to treat their subject in a worthy manner," one reads in Arthur Elson's 1901 history, "and the composers cared little or nothing about suiting their music to the dramatic emotion of the words." Elson goes on to conclude that "opera had degenerated into a set of contrasted vocal forms, as definite as the group of instrumental movements that constituted the suite."[1] Or, to cite another popularly written history of the same decade, "The favorite form of entertainment in these degraded times was the pasticcio, a hybrid production composed of a selection of songs from various popular operas, often by three or four different composers, strung together regardless of rhyme or reason."[2]

The words "degenerated" and "degraded" in these two accounts of *opera seria* quickly reveal an evolutionary historical bias, one already evident in their subtitles, "A Sketch of the Development of Opera" and, even more blatantly, "Giving an Account of the Rise and Progress of the Different Schools." Monteverdi, whose music was still too unfamiliar at the start of the century to attain a major place in these histories, appears briefly in these books as one who anticipated the ideal of music-drama only to have this ideal betrayed during the century following his death. For each of these authors, Gluck's achievement becomes the first major step in a development that culminates in the work of Wagner and Verdi. The latter two, in fact, are honored with photographs in Elson's book—Verdi's as frontispiece, Wagner's pasted on the cover.

Indeed, the special place Elson accorded Wagner as *primus inter pares* seems wholly appropriate, for the evolutionary model of musical drama that long dominated the history of music emanates directly from his own critical writings. For Wagner the history of opera can be defined by the liberation of the dramatic element from the hegemony of the individual aria, and, in particular, from the willfulness of the singer intent on displaying his or her vocal prowess by means of the aria. "As long as arias are composed," he wrote in *Opera and Drama* (1851), "the basic character of [opera] will always reveal itself in purely musical terms" (*WGS*, II: 39). For Wagner, at least at this particular stage of his thought, drama and music remained in contention with one another to the degree that performers insisted on maintaining their autonomy from the composer. In this same treatise Wagner defined Gluck's "celebrated revolution" as the "rising up of the composer against the arbitrariness of the performer" (*WGS*, II: 27). Throughout Wagner's early theoretical writings, which I treat in greater detail in Chapters 4 and 5, the reader remains aware that the history of opera will culminate in the triumph of the dramatic principle within Wagner's own works, above all those he began to compose after the completion of *Opera and Drama*.[3]

Wagner's strategy of defining a specific approach to operatic composition as central and, just as important, of designating a founding father was of course a way of legitimating his own practice or, more precisely, what he intended to make his practice in *Der Ring des Nibelungen*. Indeed, Wagner's attempt to establish a particular narrative of operatic history as the *only* plausible narrative is typical of the ways that historians of the various art forms have initiated the reigning narratives within their respective forms. Thus Boileau, writing at the end of the seventeenth century, justifies the newly triumphant mode we have come to call French classicism by dismissing poets from earlier centuries as crude and barbaric and crowning François Malherbe as founder of the new dispensation:

> Enfin Malherbe vint, et le premier en France,
> Fit sentir dans les vers une juste cadence:
> D'un mot mis en sa place enseigna le pouvoir,
> E reduisit la Muse aux regles du devoir.[4]

> Finally Malherbe came and was the first in France
> To make felt a just cadence in verse,
> Taught the power of a word put in its place
> And reduced the muse to the rules of duty.

However minor a place we now ascribe to Malherbe's poetry, it was not until well into the nineteenth century that once-famous poets such as Villon and Ronsard could again find a spot within the pantheon of French letters.

Similarly, Giorgio Vasari created what for long counted as the reigning narrative of art history by privileging that form of pictorial representation which began with Giotto as its founding father and culminated in the work of Vasari's teacher Michelangelo and, by implication, in Vasari's own painting: "He [Giotto] alone, although born among inept artists, revived through God's grace what had fallen into an evil state and brought it back to such a form that it could be called good."[5] Despite the success of modern art historians in opening viewers' eyes to other modes of representation such as those of medieval painters as well as those of non-Western artists, it is remarkable how strong a hold Vasari's story, which was created some four and a half centuries ago, has maintained on the art-going public's notions of how painting developed in time.

Wagner's particular story has maintained a similar dominance, as one can see from Joseph Kerman's long-influential *Opera as Drama* (1956), whose very title echoes that of Wagner's own treatise and whose bald statement, "The period between Monteverdi and Gluck can also be called the dark age of opera,"[6] goes beyond Wagner only to the extent that it allows Gluck to share his founding role with the only recently rediscovered Monteverdi. Although Monteverdi's own theory and practice of musical drama was unknown to either Gluck or Wagner, it could easily be accommodated to the great tradition. Just as the Enlightenment thinkers needed a concept of some dark, not-yet-enlightened age to define and celebrate the achievements of their own age, so historians of the arts, at widely differing times, have constructed images of periods to contain painters who had not yet learned to convey an illusion of reality; or of poets whose language was too rough-hewn to circulate safely among civilized readers; or of composers like Monteverdi whose harmonies were jarring to cultivated ears or, like Handel, who encouraged singers to display their talents shamelessly at the cost of whatever drama they were purportedly performing.

The power of Wagner's narrative to shape our perceptions of operatic history can be seen even in the work of those musicologists whose own scholarly efforts have been devoted to excavating and defending the products of the so-called "dark age of opera." In his *Short History of Opera,* a book that has long counted as the standard reference history in English, Donald Jay Grout, himself an editor of Alessandro Scarlatti's operas, includes two detailed chapters on *opera seria* that seek to arouse sympathy for the form, above all in the hands of its major practitioners. Yet Grout's adherence to the principle of the primacy of drama over music pushes him into a certain defensive posture regarding even those composers he most respects. Writing of coloratura passages in a Handel aria, for example, Grout defends the composer by claiming that Handel "seldom employed such passages solely for display; they spring naturally from the tension of the music or from some obvious image in the text." One suspects that Handel would have felt surprised to learn that he had succeeded in reining in the improvisatory proclivities of his singers. Moreover, in full knowledge that one cannot defend the characters in Handel's operas in the same way one treats those of Wagner or the later Verdi, Grout describes the most famous figures in these operas as "universal, ideal types of humanity, moving and thinking on a vast scale," and he calls upon the romantic doctrine of genius when he praises the music that Handel wrote for his characters as "the incarnation of a great soul."[7] Although his chapter on Gluck, which directly follows those on *opera seria*, presents a far more historically nuanced account of this composer than one finds in the turn-of-the-century histories from which I quoted earlier, it is also clear that Gluck's reform works represent a type of opera he can discuss without apology, indeed, with considerable enthusiasm; above all, since Gluck provided a new starting point from which later developments could be anticipated, this composer justified the very writing of a history such as Grout's.

Similarly, the most distinguished Handel scholar of our time, Winton Dean, has tried to accommodate his subject's operas to a notion of musical drama that would have seemed foreign to audiences of the time. To defend the idea that Handel's operas are not, like other *opere serie*, a succession of unconnected arias, he stresses the composer's close attention to the key relationships within a particular work but quickly admits that "if this [phenomenon] is barely perceptible to listeners without perfect pitch, it still operates at a subliminal level."[8] Unlike Grout, who does not try to find specificity in Handel's characters but calls them "universal, ideal types of humanity," Dean seeks to show how a characterization can be built up by a succession of disparate arias. Calling the Cleopatra of *Giulio Cesare* "the equal of Shakespeare's, and one of the most subtly drawn characters in opera," he analyses each of her eight arias and her final duet with Caesar as part of a narrative that gradually reveals the intricacies of her gradually developing character, by turns "flippant," "kittenish," "confident," and "basically optimistic," yet with "unsuspected depths of suffering."[9] For eighteenth-century audiences, for whom any aria represented the expression of a particular *Affekt* or emotion regardless of the "character" giving voice to it, Dean's account can only be viewed as an ahistorical apologia for Handel specifically directed to modern audiences with expectations formed by the Gluck-Wagner tradition.

The powerful hold that this tradition has maintained throughout the last 150 years has allowed, in fact encouraged, writers on opera to assimilate within its confines large areas of operatic history that Wagner himself would have shunned. Wagner's own attitude toward *opera seria* is neatly encapsulated in a dismissive remark aimed at Mozart's *La clemenza di Tito*, doubtless the last major work in that form: "Mozart knew the tragic muse only under the mask of the Metastasian *opera seria*: rigid and dry" (*WGS*, 13: 285). Although defenders of the form such as Grout and Dean sought to accommodate it as best they could to the Wagnerian model, many other areas of operatic history, including some toward which Wagner felt considerable hostility, have turned out to fit comfortably within his framework. Certainly most of the significant operas written after Wagner by composers from otherwise distinct musical cultures are readily assimilable within this tradition—until, as I shall show in later chapters, composers such as Stravinsky and Weill challenged this tradition by returning to the so-called number-opera and, even more conspicuously, until postmodern composers such as Philip Glass and John Cage undermined the very aesthetic that had long sought to link music and words to one another.[10]

Among Wagner's contemporaries and predecessors, many of whom Wagner viewed as outside the mainstream he was defining for himself, a number have since established their credentials as practitioners of music-drama. Although Wagner and his disciples would never have granted Verdi a place within this category, in the course of the twentieth century his last two operas, *Otello* and *Falstaff* (both composed after Wagner's death), came to be defined as successful attempts to achieve music-drama by means other than Wagner's. Indeed, during the last two or three decades even Verdi's earlier work, including some of his operas from the 1840s, has been interpreted as a serious and continuing development toward the formal solutions he reached at the end of his long career. By means of the dramatic interpretations of Maria Callas, those operas that we label *bel canto* and that were long relegated to obscurity through the triumph of the Wagnerian aesthetic have come to seem far more compatible with this aesthetic than the proponents of Wagnerism would ever have allowed. If *opera seria* has resisted such accommodation (despite the efforts of its defenders), the other dominant eighteenth-century Italian genre, comic opera, above all the Mozart–Da Ponte operas, in which the genre culminated at the end of the century, could, by means of its often intricate ensembles, its easily definable character-types, and its forward-moving plots, provide examples of music that serves the needs of drama. Once Monteverdi's work had become known in our own century, both his practice and his theory could be linked to the Gluck-Wagner aesthetic to provide an ongoing if also sometimes interrupted tradition of musical drama extending some four hundred years.

In view of the dominance of this tradition, it is no wonder that one of the foremost historians of eighteenth-century Italian opera, Reinhard Strohm, begins a book by naming the subject of his inquiry "an artistic phenomenon that has become quite strange *[fremd]* to us and that needs neither our polemics nor our apologies."[11] Except for Handel's operas and an occasional *opera seria* by Vivaldi or Pergolesi, the form has attracted early-music performers less than most areas of music before the later eighteenth century. In almost every respect the conventions associated with *opera seria* seem at odds with those that audiences have come to associate with opera since the triumph of the Wagnerian aesthetic. For one thing, an individual *opera seria* does not, from a later point of view, enjoy the type of autonomy that came to be ascribed to operas as individual works of art. As with much early music, the score of an *opera seria* provides essentially a template that the individual singer would feel free to embellish.[12] Moreover, composers customarily designed their music to meet the needs not of the drama as a whole, or even the words of a text, but rather of the abilities and desires of particular singers.[13] Operatic scores were treated as virtually disposable items: except for Handel's operas, a relatively small percentage of *opera seria* scores was even preserved for posterity. During its heyday, the first half of the eighteenth century, *opera seria* functioned as an international system with houses from St. Petersburg to London, from Hamburg to Naples, presenting ever-new scores composed to a relatively limited canon of librettos. In fact, much that we know of these operas derives from the librettos, which, serving as they did as crutches for the audience in the way that supertitles assist current-day operagoers, were preserved in numerous printed copies while the musical scores, if they were kept at all, generally remained in manuscript.[14] Moreover, given the economics of the international system, in which composers were paid considerably less than singers and even than scene designers, and in which the work of a few prestigious librettists such as Apostolo Zeno and Metastasio was much in demand, an impresario usually found it more advantageous to commission a new score to a respected libretto than to stage a score that was not even available in print and that had been designed for a different set of singers altogether.[15]

Our modern notion of a work's autonomy is antithetical to *opera seria* in a still more fundamental way: not only were operatic scores easily disposable items, but an individual score, even when it was revived or played in a new venue, would contain wholly new arias designed to meet the needs and the whims of particular singers. Not only that, but a "new" score was often full of borrowings from other composers or from the composer's own earlier operas, cantatas, and masses. If Handel is particularly notorious for the extent of his borrowings, this may only be because, as the composer of those early *opere serie* most revered today, his working habits have been subjected to considerable scholarly scrutiny.[16] To the extent that our notion of musical drama—inherited with varying points of emphasis from Monteverdi, Gluck, and Wagner— assumes some ideal wedding of words and music, the very idea that a composer would regularly adapt earlier tunes, sometimes their harmonic embodiments as well, to new words would seem a form of aesthetic deception. (Gluck, one might add, mined from his own *opere serie* for his reform operas—an appropriate enough gesture for someone who had been trained and had worked for many years in the older system.)

No aspect of *opera seria* indicates the gap separating music and words more tellingly than the pasticcio, a form that flourished down to Rossini's time, when the stature newly accorded the individual composer demanded the acknowledgment of single authorship. A pasticcio, as its name implies, mixed arias from a number of operas, usually from a diverse group of composers, and adapted them to a particular libretto that, in most instances, had had no previous relationship to these arias. Handel's *Elpidia* (1725), or, more precisely, this composer's arrangement of *Elpidia*, for which he composed only the recitatives, contained arias by Vinci, Sarri, Orlandini, and Capelli (plus several that are still unidentified)—with new arias from different composers, or different ones from the same composers, being added the following season to accord with changes in the cast.[17] If *opera seria* in general undermines any dogmas about the necessary relationship of words and music, the pasticcio, through its indiscriminate mélange of tunes drawn from a multitude of sources, foregrounds the very arbitrariness characteristic of operatic form through a long period of its history.

Not that such matters went unnoticed at the time. Polemics about opera make up a goodly amount of eighteenth-century discourse on aesthetic matters. The two operatic "wars" in eighteenth-century France, the Guerre des Bouffons in the early 1750s between the proponents of Italian comic opera and of French opera and, a generation later, a second Franco-Italian war between the proponents of Gluck and Niccolò Piccinni, are simply the most celebrated battles among many others that took place within the various capitals in which opera flourished. Specialists in English literature have generally been more familiar with Joseph Addison's satirical remarks on the scenic effects that supposedly overwhelmed the drama of Handel's first opera for London, *Rinaldo*, than with the opera itself: "On seeing an ordinary Fellow carrying a Cage full of little Birds" on a London street, Addison is told that these "are Sparrows for the opera. . . . They are to enter towards the end of the first Act and to fly about the Stage."[18]

In his satire of 1720, "Il teatro alla moda," Benedetto Marcello (who himself composed instrumental and church music but at most one or two operas, if he authored any at all) provided later adherents of Wagnerian music-drama with ample evidence to support a negative view of eighteenth-century taste. Thus, observing the lack of significant relationship between words and music in the operas of his time, he ironically tells the would-be composer "that happy and sad arias should alternate throughout the opera, from beginning to end, regardless of any meaning of text, music, or stage action." If Addison complained of the incompatibility of serious drama with the need to impress audiences with stage effects, Marcello put his finger on virtually every vice with which *opera seria* has been charged. Not only does he stress the gap between words and music, but, even more emphatically, he makes fun of the way composers fawn over the performers for whom they design their scores.

Thus, the composer is told to "speed up or slow down the tempo of the arias according to every whim of the singer and . . . swallow all their impertinences, remembering that his own honor, esteem, and future are at their mercy. For that reason he will change, if desired, their arias, recitatives, sharps, flats, naturals, etc."[19]

Count Algarotti, as I indicate in Chapter 1, contrasted the operatic abuses he witnessed in the mid-eighteenth century with the ideals that flourished in Florence about 1600 when the form was born out of the supposed union of words and music. For Algarotti the separation of words from music manifests itself most conspicuously in the violation within *opera seria* of the classical standard of verisimilitude: "In arias expressing anger . . . verisimilitude is taken beyond its limit," Algarotti writes; "when a man in a fit of rage stands and waits with his hands on his belt until the aria's ritornello is finished, how can he vent the passion seething within his heart?"[20]

The frequency of accounts such as these would seem to confirm Wagner's narrative of operatic history. Yet one might also note that these complaints manifest a conflict between two institutions with distinct standards—on the one hand, the institution of literature, or letters as the eighteenth century would have called it, and, on the other, the institution of theater. Most of the critical writing on opera that has come down to us speaks from the point of view of letters, for which the then-reigning classical values of verisimilitude, decorum, and rationality remained paramount. But the institution of theater represented a different set of values and, indeed, does so down to the present day. From the theatrical point of view the effects of the moment are primary, whether those of the star castrato who overwhelms the audience with his seemingly superhuman ornamentation or of the scenic designer who achieves comparably overwhelming effects as palaces collapse amid thunder and lightning. (One could define the achievement of Wagner and of the later Verdi by means of the reconciliation they were able to create, in their differing ways, between the demands of literature and theater.) *Opera seria* throughout its heyday existed in a tension between these two poles, with theatrical effect the priority of most of the audience and with standards in letters represented not simply by critics such as Algarotti but by the major librettists. It is significant that the most famous librettists, Apostolo Zeno and Metastasio, were also responsible for instituting classicizing ideals—the former, for instance, by eliminating the comic subplots of seventeenth-century opera, the latter by not only regularizing a number of conventions (the exit aria, among others) that had developed earlier but also by demonstrating through the quality of his language that a librettist could count—as Metastasio still does—among the classic poets in Italian.

If the attacks on *opera seria*, both in its own time and in subsequent centuries, have left a negative image for posterity, one might also consider the contrasting view expressed in the following paragraph from Charles Burney's *General History of Music*:

> Between the year 1725 and 1740, the musical drama in Italy seems to have attained a degree of perfection and public favour, which perhaps has never been since surpassed. The opera stage from that period being in possession of the *poetry* of Apostolo Zeno and Metastasio; the *compositions* of Leo, Vinci, Hasse, Porpora and Pergolesi; the *performance* of Farinelli, Carestini, Caffarelli, Bernacchi, Babbi, la Tesi, la Romanina, Faustina, and Cuzzoni; and the elegant *scenes* and *decorations* of the two Bibienas, which had superseded the expensive and childish machinery of the last century. *Dancing* was at this time likewise substituted in serious operas, to the coarse farces between the acts, called *Intermedj*, or *Intermezzi*; and it was about this period that *Balli* were first composed analogous to the incidents of the piece, which they enlivened and embellished without assuming such a degree of importance as robs the poet, composer, and performer, of their due rank and attention in every musical drama. (*BGH*, 2: 927)

Burney wrote these lines about a half century after what he took to be the golden age of opera. His knowledge of seventeenth-century opera, as I indicated in the last chapter, was limited by the paucity of scores (though Burney avidly consulted manuscript scores when he could find them). His knowledge of the opera of his own century was prodigious. Many of the persons cited in the paragraph above were personal acquaintances whom he came to know either in London or on his musical travels on the Continent.

Note first that Burney, at both the beginning and the end of the paragraph, uses the term "musical drama" to designate opera. Though quite familiar at the time he was writing with Gluck's reform operas and appreciative of their dramatic forcefulness on the stage, he did not, like Wagner and subsequent historians, single these out as exemplary models of drama to serve as cornerstones of some future operatic history. Note as well the order in which he lists the personnel responsible for opera: first the poets and then, in descending order, the composers, singers, and scene designers. As a historian and devotee of music, Burney granted the poets top billing according to the conventions of the time: when he remarked in his history that the phrase "composed by Signor Hasse" on a playbill of 1736 was "the first time I ever perceived the composer of an opera named in the advertisements and bills of the day" (*BGH*, 2: 804), he was simply acknowledging the primacy that the institution of letters granted to poets. The intermezzi of which Burney speaks disdainfully—with a classical bias that treated farce as far below a tragic action—count in later operatic history as the beginnings of a tradition culminating in the comic masterpieces of Mozart and Rossini.[21] Even the ballets, which he hails as improvements on the intermezzi, retain a subordinate position in his hierarchy—to the point that he leaves the names of dancers and choreographers unmentioned.[22] Above all, one must note that Burney views *opera seria*, a genre that was not only much criticized in its time but has often since been treated as an unfortunate episode within operatic history, with a respect reserved for only the highest forms of art.

Burney's omission of Handel's name from the above list of composers derives from the fact that at this point in his narrative he was writing specifically about opera performed in Italy. Actually Handel, who by the time of Burney's history (1776–89) was revered as a national classic, receives a more detailed treatment than any other composer in Burney's book.[23] Handel's work in opera fits easily within the international opera system of the early eighteenth century, for the management of his theaters, his relations to his personnel, and the formal shape he gave his operas were all comparable to the mode of organization to be found in other opera centers throughout Europe (except of course in France, which cultivated its own distinct system).[24] His nearly forty *opere serie* (depending on how one counts uncompleted or lost scores), not to speak of the pasticci he concocted to display arias from other composers' operas, fully share the form's conventions and are vulnerable to the same objections leveled at the work of lesser composers. Indeed, during his own time Handel, like his contemporary Bach, came to seem retrograde in comparison with younger composers, for the musical style of his London operas, composed from 1711 to 1741, had been formed during the five years he spent in Italy immediately preceding his move to London. Even his librettos, ordinarily rewritings of texts that sometimes went back to the preceding century, would not have seemed up-to-date from a Continental point of view. He used or, more precisely, adapted texts by Metastasio for only three operas—and then principally to satisfy a demand to meet the latest fashion.[25] Burney, despite his great admiration for Handel, regularly points out whether a particular aria is stylistically out of date.[26] *Opera seria*, like any aesthetic form, changed over time, with the conventions that Handel took for granted giving way to newer modes; by the end of the century, as we know from Mozart's reworking of an old Metastasian libretto, *La clemenza di Tito* (1791), the succession of individual arias that had marked the earlier style had been replaced by a mixture of arias and larger ensembles, while the three-part da capo aria had been superseded by a two-part structure.[27]

Yet whatever the differences, whether in style or in quality, between Handel's *opere serie* and those of his younger contemporaries, the very strangeness that later audiences have found in the form itself has created a barrier to the understanding and proper recognition not only of a major part of Handel's oeuvre but also of some of the most powerful music produced during what we have come to call the baroque era. I am not concerned here with Handel as a composer of oratorios. The oratorio, to which he devoted himself increasingly during his last three decades, has assimilated itself far more readily to later traditions of music-drama than the operas. With its far greater reliance on chorus and varied ensembles than his operas; with its vernacular texts, the vast majority of which were based on familiar biblical themes; with its relatively smaller dependence on vocal virtuosity (if only because Handel used English rather than imported singers); with its deliberate cultivation of a middle-class public rather than the aristocratic audience that had supported the opera; with its continued performing history, above all of *Messiah*, since Handel's own time[28]—with all these factors in its favor, the oratorio is readily accessible not only to listeners attuned to the operatic traditions established by Wagner and Verdi but also, because of its concert format, to audiences with too antitheatrical a bias to stomach staged opera of any sort.

Indeed, for those to whom Handel's oratorios, despite their baroque style, seem to offer a "natural" form of musical expression, his *seria* operas must seem "artificial" in the extreme. All art, of course, is wrought out of artifice, but certain forms, notably *opera seria*, seek to foreground this artifice. Because all opera pretends that people engaged in singing are actually only speaking to one another (or to themselves), its artifice is immediately evident to a degree found in few other forms of art. One could interpret the celebrated operatic reforms of Gluck and Wagner, together with the theories of musical drama voiced at the form's beginnings, as a means of concealing opera's tendency to display, sometimes even to flaunt, its artifice through the insistence that music demonstrate its responsibility to the individual words or to the overall drama to which it is supposedly giving expression.[29]

The predominant role of the castrato, who played a large proportion of the heroic figures and male lovers in *opera seria*, is perhaps the most conspicuous manifestation of the form's high artifice.[30] When we look today at prints of *opera seria* scenes, the strangeness of the form is striking even without audible evidence, for the castrati, owing to their peculiar endocrine balance, look abnormally tall in comparison with the other singers (as Figure 6 amply shows).[31] Handelian *opera seria* could in fact be characterized by its very avoidance of verisimilitude. When the right castrato was not available, Handel customarily composed (or, in the case of already existing scores, transposed) his major male parts for female voices.[32] Moreover, the plotting of *seria* operas is designed above all for the display of vocal prowess—with the result that a particular work consists mainly of a succession of harpsichord-accompanied recitatives (*recitativo secco*) and orchestra-accompanied arias. The rare intervals within a particular opera when we hear a recitative with orchestral accompaniment (*recitativo accompagnato*) simply call attention to the relative importance of this passage. Duets are so infrequent (usually near

FIG. 6. Caricature, possibly based on Hogarth, of two castrati, thought to be Senesino and Gaetano Berenstadt, with the soprano Francesca Cuzzoni in Handel's *Flavio* at King's Theatre, London, 1723. Courtesy, Victoria and Albert Museum, London / Art Resource, New York.

the end of the opera, sometimes also near the end of an earlier act) that the variety they create gives the modern listener a sense of relief. A quartet such as the one Handel wrote for the final act of *Radamisto* is so rare that it strikes us as a special occasion. Choruses are likewise rare, and they issue not from a large group of voices, as in the oratorios, but from the dramatis personae of the opera, ordinarily no more than six or seven in all; most often the only chorus comes at the end of the opera, to which it gives a literally resounding closure.

The peculiarly central role played by the aria within *opera seria* works to augment the impression of artifice. Librettists designed their plots so that a singer could exit directly after finishing an aria, with the presumption that the exit would be accompanied by applause; the result is that the opera is made up of a succession of brief scenes with as many twists and turns of plot as are needed to "motivate" the aria and its required exit. Moreover, as I have indicated, the aria does not "express" a particular character who is "developing" in the course of the opera but rather a particular emotion or *Affekt*—for example, declarations of rage, of constancy, of tender love, of desire for divine intervention.[33] In addition, the alternation of different emotions that, regardless of the larger narrative being staged, determines the organization of an *opera seria* often seemed to violate common sense even in the form's heyday, as one can see from Marcello's ironic statement, quoted earlier, advising composers to disregard the text in order to keep "happy" and "sad" arias succeeding one another. Yet Marcello's German contemporary, the influential theorist Johann Mattheson, could seriously insist on such alternation since, as he put it, "We are playing with sounds, not with words."[34]

Perhaps the strangest aspect of the *opera seria* aria from a later point of view is its da capo or *ABA'* structure, in which, after a relatively long *A* section and briefer *B* section (with orchestral ritornellos interspersed), the *A* section returns with even more ornamentation than the singer gave it the first time around. About the only arias that were not in da capo form were those called cavatinas, which consisted of the *A* part alone and tended to occur near the beginning of an act. Since the aria does not express a developing character, and since the da capo form is essentially circular, with the final section looking back upon, in fact embroidering, the first, the aria remains a kind of isolated phenomenon that does not function as part of a developing dramatic whole but is related to other arias, if at all, by means of the sharply differing rhythms and expressive means appropriate to a particular *Affekt*.

By virtue of the autonomy of the individual aria in *opera seria*, a contemporary audience's experience was markedly different from a later audience's experience with music-drama. Precisely how did an eighteenth-century audience hear an opera? Up to now I have stressed the satirical accounts, those that were motivated by literary biases and that pointed to the excesses and incongruities resulting from a form designed to create the maximum theatrical effect. For a more sympathetic account, I turn to one of Burney's many detailed analyses of Handel's operas, in this instance *Amadigi* (1715). Burney, though he knew Handel personally during the latter's old age, did not arrive in London until 1744, by which time Handel no longer produced opera (*BGH*, 2: 1007). As a result, he based his descriptions of the operas on his extensive study of manuscript scores, on accounts he researched in London newspapers, and on his memories of arias sung at concerts.

Amadigi, one of several "magic" operas by the composer that offered considerable opportunities for spectacular scenic effects, was one of Burney's favorite Handel operas, with "more enchantment and machinery . . . than I have ever found to be announced in any other musical drama performed in England" (*BGH*, 2: 697). But his admiration extended to far more than the staging (which he of course had not known at first hand), for he concluded his analysis by remarking that the opera contained "more invention, variety, and good composition, than . . . any of the musical dramas of Handel which I have yet carefully and critically examined" (*BGH*, 2: 698). Yet his manner of analyzing what he calls a musical drama is far different from what an opera critic of the last century and a half would give the public. I quote at length from Burney's description of the second act:

> The first air in the second act, *Sussurate, onde vezzose*, is an admirable *cavatina*, accompanied by two common flutes, two violins, tenor, and base. The bright and brilliant tones of the violins playing in octaves, from which so many pleasing effects have lately been produced, seems to have been first discovered by Handel in the accompaniment to this song, which must have delighted and astonished every hearer, more than seventy years ago. The second air in this act, *S' estinto e l' idol mio*, is, in my opinion, one of the finest which Handel ever produced in his best and most masterly style: the pathetic subject, the natural and pleasing imitations in the instrumental parts, the richness of the harmony, the affecting modulation, particularly in the second part; but above all, the strain of sorrow which runs through every passage of the voice-part, all conspire to render it one of the most perfect compositions of the kind with which I have been acquainted. The next air, *T' amai quant' il mio cor*, begins in a sublime style of cantabile, and in the second part is painted all the rage and fury which could be excited in an offended knight errant, and expressed by the voice and action of such a performer as Nicolini. In the succeeding air the lady, not to be behind-hand with the hero in rage, tries "to out Herod, Herod." The imitations in the accompaniments of the first violin and base only, have all the spirited effect of a crouded score.
> (*BGH*, 2: 696–97)

Burney's concerns here include a number of diverse matters, above all the technical means employed by Handel to achieve his musical effects. As a historian of music, Burney is always on the lookout for evidence of innovation, which he finds here in violins playing in octaves to accompany the cavatina at the start of the act. But he also points out where precisely the composer is musically successful, as when he notes the "imitations," the "richness of the harmony," and the "affecting modulation" of the second aria. Moreover, he keeps his reader informed of the particular performers for whom Handel designed his operas, in this instance the castrato Nicolini, who played the title role. Yet nowhere in this analysis, or in any analysis of the time that I have encountered, are we given a sense of the individual arias as parts of a dramatic whole. Burney's rival historian of music, John Hawkins, does not, like Burney, even describe the contents of individual operas, as Burney does in considerable detail, but concentrates on the external circumstances surrounding Handel's career—for example, his rivalry with Bononcini, his problems with his individual singers, and the rivalries among the latter.[35] For Burney, an aria is successful, whether in its composition or performance, only to the extent that it successfully expresses a particular emotion or *Affekt*, for example, the "strain of sorrow which runs through every passage of the voice-part" of the second aria. The only relationship a particular aria has to other arias is that of contiguity: thus, Handel has juxtaposed the hero's rage aria with a rage aria by the heroine Oriana, and Burney defines this relationship by means of a familiar literary allusion.

Indeed, by alluding to Hamlet's advice to the player not to "out-Herod Herod," Burney underlines the high degree of artifice that audiences expected in *opera seria*, however much they may have been moved by the emotion they were hearing expressed. The singer and the music are clearly defining an emotion of the moment and not a character functioning within a larger drama. To be sure, Handel commentators from Burney through Dean have stressed the ways that Handel played with his inherited form—for example, the violins playing in octaves that Burney praises in the passage on *Amadigi* above; or the quartet in *Radamisto* and, earlier in that opera, the aria in which Zenobia switches back and forth between *Affekte* as she alternately addresses the hero and the villain; or the trio, immediately followed by a series of truncated arias, in the middle of *Tamerlano*'s second act. Yet these innovative touches simply tell us how original and inventive Handel could be even while working within a long-established form; they do not suffice to portray him as working toward the evolution of music-drama in the ways that Gluck and Wagner later did.

The large gap separating *opera seria* from the type of musical drama that modern audiences have come to expect is particularly evident if we set a Handel score next to, say, an example of Verdi's later phase. Consider, for instance, the glaring differences between two operas—both with strongly political themes—such as *Giulio Cesare* and *Simon Boccanegra*. *Giulio Cesare* is doubtless the best known among Handel's operas in our own century, at least if one can judge from the number of productions it has received.[36] It follows the usual conventions of Handelian opera—to the point that any deviation from the norm, in this instance the use of an opening chorus and, later, of a melody from a Cleopatra aria to accompany a dialogue between Cesare and his servant in the Mount Parnassus scene, stand out conspicuously. To create a more dramatic contrast one could of course juxtapose *Giulio Cesare* to a late Wagner score. Yet *Simon Boccanegra*, as an Italian opera that is still, for the most part, divided into discrete numbers, can show how a composer absorbing the newer aesthetic of music-drama can transform individual numbers to suit his own purposes.[37] *Simon Boccanegra* is of particular interest here, for the final version (1881), a radical revision of an opera composed and first presented twenty-four years before, displays distinct stages in Verdi's approach to dramatic form.[38]

Except for choral passages at the beginning (a relative rarity) and at the end, *Giulio Cesare*, like other *seria* operas, consists of an alternation of individual arias and recitatives, with duets only at the end of the first act and before the closing chorus.[39] The revised *Boccanegra* consists largely of small ensembles—six duets, a trio, and a quartet—with only a single aria each for the principals and no formal aria at all for the titular hero. In the development of Italian opera from Rossini to Verdi, the duet became a means of overcoming the isolation of the individual aria. And it is precisely in the course of the various duets in this opera that most of the dramatic action takes place, as when Boccanegra discovers his long-lost daughter during their first-act duet. By contrast, the action in *opera seria* does not even occur in the arias but in the recitatives that link them together; the arias here function to display the performer's emotional reactions to what had been enacted in the preceding recitative. The two duets between the baritone Boccanegra and bass Fiesco, one in the prologue, the second at the end of the opera, work to bring the drama's issues full circle: thus, the first presents the conflict, at once personal and political, between the corsair hero and the aristocrat whose daughter bore him a child, while the second, with the hero dying and Fiesco reduced to tears, culminates in a reconciliation bringing the whole dramatic action to conclusion.[40] It is in these duets, above all, that both Boccanegra and Fiesco emerge as what, in a play or a novel, we would call "complex" and "round" characters.

Moreover, in their disposition of voice ranges no two operas could sound more different than *Giulio Cesare* and *Simon Boccanegra*. Like Handel's other *seria* operas, *Giulio Cesare* stresses the high voices—whether for castrati or women singers—with only two relatively small parts (one even without an aria) for low voice. In a performer-centered aesthetic such as Handel's the opportunities for spectacular ornamentation are considerably greater among the high voices than the lower ones, which are generally reserved for villains or confidants. Although Verdi ordinarily divided his voices according to the system prevailing in nineteenth-century Italian opera—with the soprano and tenor reserved for heroine and hero, the mezzo-soprano and lower male voices for the villainous, the older, or the less successful characters—in *Simon Boccanegra*, though still reserving soprano and tenor for the young lovers, he left much of the significant drama to the two baritone voices and the one bass voice, with only one of these lower voices playing a villain, while the other two (including Boccanegra himself), though older than the other characters, are the most dramatically compelling figures in the opera. The very lack of vocal variety through long stretches becomes in effect a means of giving the opera the somberness that distinguishes it from other Verdi operas. The individuality that this opera achieves through its disposition of voices is paralleled by its particular local color: with its Genoese setting and as its hero a figure who made his mark as a corsair, at several points in the opera Verdi is intent upon evoking the presence of the sea—for example, in the orchestral intro-duction to Amelia's act 1 aria and in another brief orchestral seascape accom-panying Boccanegra's words "Il mare! Il mare!" in act 3. Although Handel's operas differ according to the number of comic and magic elements that the *seria* form is forced to accommodate, they do not cultivate local color in the way that a late-nineteenth-century opera is able to do; a *Giulio Cesare* in the nineteenth century, as Chapter 6 makes clear, would surely have included the sort of "orientalist" music found in a more famous opera that was also set in ancient Egypt, Verdi's *Aida*. (Contemporary productions of Handel, to be sure, find their own ways of embodying local color: witness, for example, the Paris Opéra's 1997 *Giulio Cesare*, which, though thoroughly faithful to Han-del's musical score, visually displays the detritus of pop orientalism in its brightly colored masks and mummy cases, gilded toy pyramids, and a heroine whose hairdos self-consciously mimic those of such film Cleopatras as Theda Bara and Elizabeth Taylor.)

The revisions that Verdi made to his long-forgotten score of *Simon Boc-canegra* with the help of Arrigo Boito, who was later to prepare the librettos of *Otello* and *Falstaff*, show him exploring a newer form of drama. For one thing, he eliminated or transformed the cabalettas still to be found in the opera's 1857 version. In early-nineteenth-century opera the cabaletta played some-thing of the role of the da capo section of an *opera seria* a century before: the cabaletta served to display a singer's vocal prowess, though, unlike the da capo aria, it did not repeat earlier music but instead moved the action forward by contradicting or supplementing what the first, usually slower section of the aria was voicing. By mid-career Verdi, as he moved increasingly toward an aesthetic that stressed dramatic integration and economy, had become em-barrassed by the cabaletta, which, to the extent that it called attention to the performer's virtuosity, undercut the character's function within the progressing drama.

But the most telling revision in *Simon Boccanegra* from the point of view of the present argument is Verdi's insertion of a wholly new scene, the Council Chamber, at the end of the first act. Here, in as dramatically powerful a set of events as any composer ever packed into twenty minutes, Verdi devises a whole spectrum of musical situations to reveal such diverse dramatic moments as the quelling of a revolutionary mob, the rescue of the heroine from abduction, and the denunciation of the conspiratorial villain. The scene contains no formal arias or other traditional forms except for a brief concertato; it is as though the materials of earlier Italian opera had been condensed and fragmented to achieve a maximum of dramatic tension. Just as important, in the passage in which Boccanegra quiets the mass, Verdi provides a model of how music can create the most eloquent political rhetoric. Indeed, at certain moments, for example, at the lines "E vo gridando pace! / E vo gridando amor!" Verdi's music fuses nobility and generosity with an intensity similar to those passages in Beethoven's *Fidelio* that we honor with the term *Humanitätsmusik*.

Both *Giulio Cesare* and *Simon Boccanegra*, like most operas supposedly based on historical events, mix "actions of state" with a "love interest" plot. Yet whereas in a nineteenth-century opera such as *Simon Boccanegra* the lovers tend to inhabit a world separate, even protected, from that of the political actors, in *opera seria* the lovers generally are also the public figures engaged in political action. Thus, Cesare's arias can alternate readily between his emotional reactions to Cleopatra's enticements and to the Egyptian conspiracy threatening him. Since characters in *opera seria* exist for the diverse emotions their arias can give voice to, they are no more "stable" than the emotional spectrum covered by the arias. By contrast, the characters in *Simon Boccanegra* remain "consistent," and the changes we note, above all in Fiesco, who moves from enmity toward Boccanegra to ultimate forgiveness, are meant to suggest what critics praise with the term "growth." Indeed, in the revised first-act duet between Fiesco and Gabriele, the former sings a brief and moving benediction that works to soften the harsh image he had presented in his duet with Boccanegra in the prologue. Even the love interest in *Simon Boccanegra* is better integrated with the political theme than in many nineteenth-century operas: here the class conflict between aristocrats and plebeians is reflected in the relationship between the lovers, whose marriage at the end comes to signify a reconciliation between the warring parties—or, more precisely, the raising of a lower order to a higher rank to which its "natural" nobility should entitle it.

These differences in political resonance between the two operas point to a fundamental difference in the literary systems from which each composer's librettos drew their situations. Handel's plots, besides borrowing from Renaissance romance, above all Ariosto, for his "magic" operas, often derive from earlier theatrical sources such as French seventeenth-century drama and Venetian and French opera librettos of the same period. *Giulio Cesare*, in fact, comes ultimately from a Venetian libretto of 1677;[41] the small comic part for Cleopatra's servant Nireno reveals its origin in a style that had not yet banished comic elements. As an art form under royal and aristocratic sponsorship, *opera seria*, together with the older works that it adapts, presents a world seen from an uncomplicatedly ruling-class point of view. The torments undergone by a ruler in love (performed by a castrato or a female singer) are not only intended to evoke the audience's sympathy but are resolved by the mandatory happy ending in which shaky thrones achieve stability at the same time that rightful lovers (usually with the ruler among them) are reunited.

Verdi's operas, quite in contrast, are products of the ideology governing the romantic dramas from which he took his plots: Shakespeare (at least the Shakespeare constructed by the romantics), Schiller, Byron, Hugo, the younger Dumas, and two Scott/Byron/Hugo-inspired Spanish dramatists, the Duke of Rivas and Antonio García Gutiérrez, the latter of whom supplied the story of *Simon Boccanegra* (as he had earlier that of *Il trovatore*). Unlike the ruling-class biases guiding the political actions of *opera seria*, the biases behind certain Verdi operas favored lowly characters with largeness of soul (Rigoletto, Azucena, Violetta) as well as those oppressed peoples (the Hebrews of *Nabucco*, the Scots of *Macbeth*, the Flemings of *Don Carlos*, the Ethiopians of *Aida*) with whom mid-nineteenth-century Italians could identify. Not only in Verdi but throughout later nineteenth-century opera, as Chapter 6 shows in more detail, the audience's sympathy is directed principally to the "other," whether in the guise of woman, of Oriental, or of some oppressed political group. Even a drama so centered around royalty as *Don Carlos* becomes, as Paul Robinson has demonstrated in detail,[42] an indictment of nineteenth-century *Realpolitik* (to the extent that *Giulio Cesare* displays victorious Romans outwitting their Egyptian hosts, it could be called a celebration of *Realpolitik*). The corsair Doge in *Simon Boccanegra* proves in the course of the opera that the high office he had been granted by the populace is matched by a nobility demonstrated musically and dramatically both in his paternal tenderness to his daughter (a persistent Verdi *topos*) and in his skill in calming an unruly crowd.

If I have stressed Verdi's dramatic achievement at the cost of Handel's seemingly undramatic method of organizing an opera, this simply reflects the fact that the type of music-drama represented by Wagner and the later Verdi has remained the norm—despite some postmodernist challenges—by which we judge operas of earlier eras. The aesthetic that stands behind Handelian *opera seria* is in fact so foreign to the aesthetic governing what we call music-drama that one wonders how the revival of Handel's operas during the twentieth century has ever achieved as much success as it has.

Although Handel's operas had stopped being performed even before the composer died, unlike the many *seria* operas of his time whose scores were either lost or left languishing in libraries, collections of arias from individual operas were readily available in published form for performance in the home or at concerts. By the mid-nineteenth century Handel had become so established a classic as a composer of oratorios and instrumental music that the operas, though remaining unperformed until our own century, were included by Friedrich Chrysander in his monumental edition of the composer's works (1858–1902). Even for much of the twentieth century, however, if one heard Handel's operatic music at all, it was usually in the form of a single aria inserted near the beginning of a vocal recital. To judge from my own experience, as often as not the favored aria was "Lascia ch'io pianga" from *Rinaldo*, usually performed without the da capo, indeed without proper ornamentation, and with the singer's and the piano accompanist's phrasing more suitable to a Brahms lied than to a baroque composition. For the many audiences whose only exposure to Handelian opera took this form, a Handel aria was a frankly boring experience, certainly little more than a warm-up for the headier nineteenth-century fare to come.

Still, by the early twentieth century, with the renewed interest in baroque music (of which the Monteverdi revival I describe in Chapter 1 was a part), Handel's operas had already received their first stagings in more than 150 years. It is no coincidence, as I point out in Chapter 7, that this revival took place simultaneously with the revolt against Wagnerian music-drama instituted by composers such as Busoni, Stravinsky, and Weill, all of whom attempted to give a new life to the number-opera, a form long deemed thoroughly obsolete. The Handel revival began in Germany directly after the First World War through the efforts of an art historian, Oskar Hagen, who initiated regular Handel festivals in Göttingen and supervised performing editions that he deemed accessible to the audiences of his time. As we look back at these early revivals, indeed, even at those taking place until a relatively short time ago, it is clear that the sharp differences between Handel's aesthetic and that of the mainstream repertory have forced productions to accommodate themselves to expectations of audiences nurtured on Wagner and Verdi.[43] As with the changing approaches to Monteverdi's *L'incoronazione di Poppea* described in Chapter 1, during the last two decades one can trace an increasing willingness, in the interest of authenticity, to risk introducing performing practices quite foreign to the audience's experience. Producers of Handel operas, like those who staged or recorded *Poppea*, were reluctant until quite recently to entrust the male roles originally intended for castrati to the only high voices available today, namely, countertenors or female singers. (It hardly mattered that the same audiences were willing to accept a female Cherubino, Oscar, or Octavian, because these "pre-adult" men also functioned within a lighthearted context; a high voice for rulers like Monteverdi's Nerone or Handel's Giulio Cesare would be something else again.) Again, as with Monteverdi productions, Handel revivals long utilized the opera-house orchestra, whose large forces, tremulous strings, and smooth-sounding modern wind instruments become uncomfortable to listen to once one has heard the same scores performed by early instruments in an orchestra of the same size and composition as the composer's.

Yet Handel revivals also face obstacles of a different and less easily resolved sort from those of Monteverdi's operas. Whereas Monteverdi, with his flexible recitative, composed a form of music-drama quite compatible with the aesthetic of Gluck, Wagner, and Verdi, the foreign aesthetic of *opera seria* has often led producers to violate the music to an unacceptable degree. The transposition of Monteverdi's Nerone or Ottone to baritone or tenor was bad enough, especially in the way it changed the musical effect of these characters' duets with female performers; yet to make Cesare—as well as the other Handel heroes—a baritone, as Hagen did in his edition, is to alter the music in a fundamental way, for a lower voice lacks the flexibility for the complex ornamentation necessary to the arias Handel composed for his heroic figures. (One might add that during the first half of the twentieth century both the female and the male singers rarely if ever commanded a proper knowledge of the ornamentation necessary for *opera seria*.) Moreover, since *seria* operas are quite long, with arias designed to accommodate their original performers' techniques (not to speak of their bargaining power with the impresario) modern productions have often been radically cut. (Audiences willing to sit through an uncut *Tristan* or *Meistersinger* were evidently less patient with Handel.) But the habit of lopping off whole arias is perhaps less musically damaging than the pruning that characteristically took place *within* an aria in early Handel revivals. In the interest of dramatic "economy," arias were often reduced to the *A* sections alone, with the result that the *B* section and the da capo, not to speak of the ornamentation demanded within the latter, would be kept to a minimum. Though economy of this sort may be part of the aesthetic of later music-drama, it works to suppress the richness and extravagance central to one's experience of Handel.

Despite the many Handel operas that have been revived in one form or another since the 1920s, they have rarely been done in the major opera houses except within the German-speaking countries. The first Handel opera to be performed at the Metropolitan was *Rinaldo*, mounted in 1984 around a celebrated singer, Marilyn Horne, who also created the occasion for the mounting of *Orlando* at a number of other houses. More often than not, Handel productions have provided an opportunity for "secondary" houses such as the English National Opera and the New York City Opera, both of which did much-publicized productions of *Giulio Cesare*, to display their knack for exploring new operatic territories. Yet one wonders if the traditional opera house is the proper place at all for Handel today; with its resident orchestra of modern instruments, it seems no more appropriate to Handel than it is to Monteverdi. As it turns out, Handel's operas are becoming by and large the stuff of early-music groups, who, with their period instruments and their singers trained in the performing practices of Handel's time, are more likely to bring these operas to life today than companies for which the Mozart-through-Strauss repertory remains the norm. The performances of Handel operas conducted (and sometimes recorded) since the 1980s by a new generation of conductors—for example, John Eliot Gardiner, René Jacobs, Nicholas McGegan, and Marc Minkowski, all with a special commitment to baroque practice—have offered listeners sounds so distinct from what they heard before that earlier recordings now come to seem unbearable.

Even with the vocal and instrumental authenticity that is fast becoming *de rigueur*, in one important respect the very strangeness I have attributed to *opera seria* works against its realization on the modern stage. The dramatic aesthetic guiding Handel and his contemporaries seems irreconcilable with the expectation of audiences that singers "act" their roles while they are engaged in singing. The long and self-contained arias that make up the bulk of an *opera seria* simply do not lend themselves to the sort of stage action that audiences accustomed to later music-drama demand. To judge from my own experience watching a number of live productions and videotapes of Handel operas, directors are often so intent on filling up the long musical stretches with body movements, props, and interminable stage business that one all too often feels distracted from the music. The high artifice central to *opera seria* is scarcely appropriate to attempts such as these at simulating verisimilitude. How, after all, can one stage the da capo? Should the singers repeat the gestures and blocking they employed in the *A* Section, even exaggerate them to accompany the increased vocal ornamentation that marks their restatement of that section? Should their faces keep trying to repeat the expressive features with which they accompany a particular line of verse? (*Opera seria* arias usually consist of no more than four to eight lines, most of which, especially in the *A* section, must be repeated a number of times.)

Peter Sellars's production of *Giulio Cesare*, prepared for Brussels in 1988 and later issued on videotape, illustrates the dilemmas a director of a Handel opera must confront. On the one hand, this production is reasonably complete, and it is musically "authentic" to the extent that it used singers with high voices (including two countertenors) in the same roles to which Handel had assigned these voices. The production, to judge from the videotape, not only included an aria for Nireno that Handel added for a revival but retained the da capo sections throughout. Sellars's only significant compromise with musical authenticity came in his use of a modern orchestra. As with his other opera productions, Sellars's musical faithfulness was accompanied by his customary attempt to create a modern reinterpretation of the text, in this instance an American imperialist incursion into a corrupt, decadent Near Eastern land. Although the production displayed Sellars's usual interpretive brilliance, it also showed how precarious it is to fill every Handelian musical moment with dramatic interpretation. The show was full of props—including a snake, a garden hose, the *New York Times*, and a bag full of dollars—to keep the audience's attention from flagging during the long arias. Two of Sesto's arias were accompanied by detailed visual portrayals of his bleeding. Sellars's habit of filling up the music with constant, often frenetic visual action is only an extreme example of one that directors all too easily fall prey to when they ground an opera's action in some real, discernible world that they hope their audiences should be able to recognize.

Not that we could ever go back to the conditions of Handel's own productions. However successful we may be in restoring earlier musical practices, we shall never recapture the thrill of the castrato voice, which, as far as one can tell from early accounts, cannot be matched in its peculiar timbre and sheer power by the countertenor and the soprano. These latter can only compensate as best they can for an irretrievable loss.[44] Yet the resources of modern stage technology allow us to outdo the ambitious efforts of baroque scene designers in creating the enchantments specified in Handel's "magic" operas, as well as the wonders of Mount Parnassus or the harbor of Alexandria in *Giulio Cesare* (the latter shown in Figure 7), or the collapse of the Asia-to-Europe bridge in *Serse*.

F I G . 7. The harbor scene at the end of *Giulio Cesare*, Theater am Gänsemarkt, Hamburg, November, 1725. Courtesy, Thames and Hudson.

Within an aesthetic such as Handel's, which is built on the psychology of individual emotional moments rather than on the psychological interiority of individual characters, it seems vain to seek the sort of realism we expect in later opera. Despite the efforts of many modern directors to apply this approach to Handel, the "consistency" or "growth" with which singers characterize the major personages of, say, *Simon Boccanegra* or *Der Rosenkavalier* is quite out of order in *opera seria*. In our own time, in which an earlier realism in the various arts has given way to the artifices lumped together under the umbrella term *postmodern*, the frank and high artifice of *opera seria* can perhaps find a meeting ground with its contemporary descendant. Indeed, the artifices of Handelian *opera seria* have more in common with those of John Cage's collage opera, *Europeras 1 & 2*, whose aesthetic I place within operatic history in Chapter 8, than they do with the dramatic methods underlying the operatic canon that developed during the intervening two and a half centuries. In an age that has come to believe that in real life character is constructed (and reconstructed) at will, why should stability, consistency, and essentiality be deemed necessary for characters in fictional situations and, above all, in opera of all things? And in an age that has toyed with the theory that one's gender is constituted through the manner in which one performs before the world,[45] is there anything unnatural in an art form refusing necessarily to match the singer's "own" gender with the voice range that she or he projects?

Though Handel's achievement as a composer of opera is clearly antithetical to the later tradition of music-drama, this is not to say that his operas are undramatic: indeed, as one listens to a good performance, one realizes that Handel is one of the most dramatic of composers. His is not, however, the Aristotelian type of drama that drives forward toward some inevitable end (Handel could not have given us a *Trovatore* or a *Ring*), nor is it the drama of a particular individual's growth and development (he could not have given us a Boris Godunov or a Marschallin). Rather, it is the drama inhering in the individual aria or in the collision of contiguous arias (as in Burney's observation, cited earlier, of one character "out-Heroding Herod" when two rage arias collide in *Amadigi*).[46] As in all good opera, it is a drama that is defined above all by the music, a drama that we experience in the musical power generating a particular and familiar *Affekt*—the music of mourning evoked by Radamisto's aria "Ombra cara"; of constancy, by Oriana's "Affannami, / Tormentami" in *Amadigi*; of seduction, in Cleopatra's "V'adoro, pupille." If Handel's particular mode failed to enter what was only much later defined as the mainstream history of opera, the authority that the music exerts when convincingly performed may itself help reconfigure this history.

Chapter Three

Rossini, Shelley, and
Italy in 1819

Nothing but their year of birth—1792—provides a common ground between two such disparate personalities as Gioacchino Rossini and Percy Bysshe Shelley; indeed, the composer's birth on February 29, which allows him to share a birthday year only every four years with the English poet, suggests the tenuousness of any relationships that one might seek to link these figures. Certainly 1819 was an annus mirabilis for both Rossini and Shelley. For the former this year marked the composition of three operas that have been revived only in recent years and that all derive from quite diverse texts—*Ermione* (an operatic setting of Racine's *Andromaque*), *La donna del lago* (from Scott's early verse romance), and *Bianca e Falliero* (from a French historical tragedy of 1798 by Antoine van Arnhault). For Shelley this was the year that brought the completion of *Julian and Maddalo* and *Prometheus Unbound*, as well as *The Cenci*, *The Mask of Anarchy*, *Peter Bell the Third*, and "Ode to the West Wind."

Yet the antitheses one can draw between Rossini and Shelley, which are captured in Figures 8 and 9, are tantalizing in the extreme. The intense, delicate, vegetarian Shelley would never have stomached those heavily livered concoctions—*tournedos Rossini, poularde Rossini*, and *oeufs pochés* and *oeufs brouillés Rossini*—that have assured the composer a place in the international culinary canon not wholly incommensurate with his place in the musical canon. Indeed, after their fleeting, chance, and only encounter (in Naples early in 1819) the bon vivant Rossini responded to a companion's description of Shelley as "looking very much like a man of genius" with the line, "I thought he looked very much like a *mezzo-morte, un etico* [a man half-dead, a consumptive]."[1]

FIG. 8. Rossini as sketched by Sir Thomas Lawrence, probably about 1823. Courtesy, Edward T. Cone, Princeton, New Jersey.

In the very year that the political radical Shelley railed against the moribund George III in his great sonnet "England in 1819," Rossini composed a cantata celebrating the recovery from illness of *his* monarch, Ferdinand I of Naples (also, incidentally, his employer). And some four years later, after Shelley had died, Rossini composed one of his most sparkling scores, the only re-

FIG. 9. Shelley in a watercolor painted by his friend Edward Ellerker Williams, probably in 1822. Courtesy, The Pierpont Morgan Library (1949.3).

cently rediscovered and published *Il viaggio a Reims*, to honor the coronation of the last French Bourbon king, Charles X.

In drawing such striking contrasts between Rossini and Shelley, we must remember that the only reason we even think of the two figures as comparable is that our modern concept of artistic creation—encompassing, as it does, the making of music, literary texts, and visual artifacts with a single term—is able to include at once an expatriate English gentleman poet and a hardworking artisan in what, to cite the title of a book describing working conditions in opera at the time, has been called the Italian "opera industry."[2] Once we grant this broad concept of art, Rossini and Shelley are doubtless the most notable artists who also happened to be born in the year 1792. The apparent incommensurability between their careers is evident from a complaint about Rossini made by Mary Shelley soon after arriving in Rome from Naples early in 1819: "Nothing is heard in Italy now but Rosini [sic] & he is no favourite of mine—he has some pretty airs—but they say that when he writes a good thing he goes on copying it in all his succeeding operas for ever and ever—he composes so much that he cannot always be called on for something pretty & new."[3] Rossini's habit of reworking passages from earlier works was of course nothing new in the history of music, for many of the composers we still respect today, as I point out in Chapter 2 with regard to Handel's working habits, had no compunction about recycling their own and indeed other people's work under their own names. If Rossini was more notorious for repeating himself than his predecessors, this doubtless stemmed from the financial need the composer felt to accept new commissions whether or not he had the time to provide wholly new scores. Thus, a hurriedly composed fourth opera dating from 1819, *Eduardo e Cristina*, was essentially a pasticcio, consisting mostly of numbers drawn from his own (but not, like eighteenth-century pasticci, from other composers') previous works—though these works presumably had not yet been heard in Venice, for one of whose theaters it was prepared. Not that Shelley did not sometimes rework and repeat earlier writings: for example, the passage from the "Defence of Poetry" about poets as legislators was borrowed from the earlier "Philosophical View of Reform," but since the latter was unfinished and unpublished when he wrote the "Defence," this scarcely counted as a self-plagiarism according to the rules governing the literary domain.

In social and institutional terms Shelley's career resembled those of Italian writers such as Manzoni and Leopardi much more than Rossini's career resembled that of any Italian author of his time. Whereas writers generally

came from the educated classes and often had private means at their disposal, composers, like painters, still belonged to the artisanal class and, more
often than not, came from families that performed similar work. Rossini's
father, for instance, was a brass player and his mother an opera singer.
(When writers derived from other writers, the former were usually authors'
daughters such as Maria Edgeworth and Mary Shelley.) Moreover, Rossini's
role as a functionary within the opera industry was scarcely analogous to
that of a writer who could cultivate his independence. During the years in
which he established his international fame Rossini moved constantly from
one city to another at the behest of whatever impresario hired his services.
The composer within this system subordinated himself in varying ways to
the singers for whose particular ranges and talents he designed his numbers
and to the impresario upon whose whims and financial resources his creativity was dependent. Rossini's role was perhaps comparable to that of the
dramatist in the Elizabethan theater or to the director of Hollywood films
during the thirties—and like the productions that resulted from these collaborations, Rossini's and his contemporaries' operas were designed for immediate consumption, with little regard for their fame or even for their
preservation. By contrast, the preface to *Prometheus Unbound* is uttered with
the assurance of one who expects his product to assume a classic status analogous to those models he cites—*Paradise Lost* as well as the Aeschylean version of *Prometheus*.

If we trace the activities of the two figures during the year 1819, the differences between the situation of an opera composer and of a poet quickly become evident. About the only thing they had in common that year is that
they were immensely productive and that both of them moved a good bit
from one Italian site to another in the course of the year. During January and
February 1819 both in fact resided in Naples, though the only concrete evidence we have that the Shelleys heard a Rossini opera there is a note in
Mary's journal about attending one of the early performances of *Ricciardo e
Zoraide* on December 13 of the preceding year.[4] It was apparently this performance that elicited Shelley's description of the San Carlo theater, where Rossini served as music director, as "very beautiful," with the subsequent obser-

vation that the boxes were "so dear and the pit so intolerable that I fear we shall visit it but seldom" (*PSL*, 2: 69). The Shelleys' letters from the smaller Italian cities often indicate visits to the opera and ballet, though the only other Rossini performance that we know they attended together was the first London production of *Il barbiere di Siviglia* on March 10, 1818, the night before their departure for Italy.[5]

By 1819 Rossini was not only world-famous, but he had also achieved a degree of security through his directorial position in Naples, which had counted as the musical capital of Europe for several generations. Rossini's professional life—quite unlike Shelley's—cannot be separated from his personal life. Thus, during his Neapolitan period, which extended from 1815 to 1822, he composed his soprano roles for the great Spanish singer Isabella Colbran, who was the mistress of the Naples impresario, Domenico Barbaja, but who later became his own mistress and, still later (by which time her voice was failing), his wife. Barbaja also controlled the gambling concession at the opera, with the result that opportunities for sumptuous productions often motivated the choice of texts. After deploring the expense of the boxes, Shelley declared that at the San Carlo "the scenery exceeds any thing of the same kind in theatrical exhibition I ever saw before."[6] For instance, during the succeeding year the San Carlo mounted at least two productions, one of them Rossini's setting of *The Lady of the Lake*, which allowed for what must have seemed an exotic display of Scottish scenery and costumes.

During the early months of 1819 Rossini's Neapolitan schedule included new productions (which always involved some recomposition) of his earlier operas *Armida* and *Mosé in Egitto*; in fact, Moses' prayer, today the most famous number in the latter opera, was added for the 1819 revival. In addition he prepared his cantata celebrating the king's recovery (within five days of its performance on February 20 the king was evidently well enough for Shelley to report "a spectacle little suited to the antique & Latonian nature of the place—King Ferdinand in a winter enclosure watching to shoot the wild boars" [*PSL*, 2: 77–78]). During this period Rossini was also composing his new opera *Ermione*, which did not open until late March, by which time the Shelleys had moved to Rome. But the composer also moved on soon after this opening, for despite his relative security in Naples he was still taking commissions for operas in other houses throughout the peninsula.

April saw him in Venice, where he hastily gathered together various numbers from earlier operas to complete *Eduardo e Cristina*, described by Byron in a letter as "a splendid Opera . . . by Rossini—who came in person to play the Harpsichord." Byron tells us something of the composer's immense fame at the time with these lines: "the People followed him about—crowned him—cut off his hair 'for memory'[;] he was Shouted and Sonnetted and feasted—and immortalized much more than either of the Emperors."[7] In May Rossini was in Pesaro, his birthplace on the Adriatic, which his itinerant musical family had left when he was six and which has become central to the revival of his work in recent years because of its summer Rossini festival. What was intended as a homecoming for its famous citizen in the Pesaro theater on May 24 turned into a near-riot instigated by the Princess of Wales (later the unfortunate Queen Caroline), who lived nearby with her Italian lover and whom Rossini had apparently snubbed on an earlier occasion by refusing to come to one of her parties.

In their common disdain for members of the English royal family one can note a certain affinity between the composer and the author of "England in 1819." Not so in their attitudes toward other European royalty, for even before his return to Naples in June a Rossini cantata was performed there in honor of the Austrian emperor Francis I, whose visit to Rome on his way down was witnessed by Mary Shelley, who wrote that "our English blood would . . . boil over" at the "insolence" of his guard "rudely pushing the people back with a drawn sword" (*MSL*, 1: 93). Soon after Rossini's return to Naples, he met a young French composer, Desiré-Alexandre Batton, who suggested *The Lady of the Lake*, which Rossini read in a French translation and quickly chose to fulfill his next assignment for the San Carlo. Though not a success its first night in September, the opera quickly caught on and, though buried after the mid-nineteenth century among his many forgotten operas, became the first of the 1819 works to emerge during the recent Rossini revival. As though this opera were not enough to fill out the year, after its opening Rossini went off to Milan, where in November or December he may have met (or may not have met, depending on which of the two men one believes)[8] his future biographer and eulogist Stendhal and where, before the year out, he mounted still another new opera, *Bianca e Falliero*. For this work he composed a largely original score but cheated a bit at the end, at which point he simply transferred (to a new set of words) the brilliant finale for soprano from *La donna del lago*.

If Rossini's movements in 1819 were determined by his working assignments, Shelley's were determined by a variety of factors—his own as well as his child William's need for healthful climates, Mary's new pregnancy, their desire to witness the antiquities and sublime scenery that Italy had to offer, and, perhaps most important of all, a certain restlessness apparently necessary to his writing and his psychological equilibrium. Certainly Shelley's productivity that year, despite the constant resettling, the death of William in June, and the birth of Percy Florence in November, seems as impressive as Rossini's.

The exigencies of *Bildung* accompanied his writing throughout the year. The brief Neapolitan period included trips to Pompeii and Herculaneum and a strenuous excursion to the temples of Paestum besides visits to galleries to view pictures. Spring was spent in Rome, where he wrote the middle two acts of *Prometheus*. Shelley explicitly connected the setting with the process of composition in the work's preface, in which he credits the ruins of the Baths of Caracalla and "bright blue sky of Rome" with inspiring the drama. On the darker side, Shelley's encounter with the portrait of Beatrice Cenci in the Palazzo Colonna set off *The Cenci*, a drama whose style is more radically different from *Prometheus* than that of any two Rossini operas of 1819 is from the other. After William's death, summer was spent just outside Leghorn, where the isolation of a glass tower favored such diverse activities as completing *The Cenci* and responding to the Peterloo massacre by composing *The Mask of Anarchy*. Autumn took the Shelleys to Florence, where Mary bore the child Percy Florence, who was not only to carry that city's name but was also to be the only child of theirs to survive to adulthood. During this time her husband produced works as generically distinct as "Ode to the West Wind,"

Peter Bell the Third, and the "England in 1819" sonnet and began the never-to-be-completed treatise "A Philosophical View of Reform."

Although cultural historians today link Rossini and Shelley by means of the common denominator "romantic artist," the more one charts their movements the more the differences between them seem incommensurable. And perhaps most obviously so in their political stances. The image of Shelley the radical colored readers' views of his work long after his death, while Rossini's role as a functionary within one of the most successful business operations of his day makes whatever political views he may have nurtured seem irrelevant. But Shelley's politics within the Italian world in which he spent his most productive years are of little consequence. We know he took some interest in the activities of the Carbonari, but he had too little contact with the "natives" during those years to play any role in whatever revolutionary ferment took place against the reactionary governments of the various places he resided in. Indeed, the post-Napoleonic condition of the variously restored Italian states in 1819 was of considerably less interest to Shelley than the condition of England, to whose reform some of his most passionate poetry and prose was dedicated that year. Moreover, the personal oppression exercised upon Teresa Viviani, the addressee of *Epipsychidion*, written the following year, attracted Shelley's imagination in a way that the oppression of the Italian people in general never could. In fact, his attitude toward the common people was no more sympathetic than that of a Coriolanus, and, like Shakespeare's character, he complained vehemently of the bad breath emanating from Italian mouths. For Shelley there were, as he put it,

> two Italies; one composed of the green earth & transparent sea and the mighty ruins of antient times, and aerial mountains, & the warm & radiant atmosphere which is interfused through all things. The other consists of the Italians of the present day, their works & ways. The one is the most sublime & lovely contemplation that can be conceived by the imagination of man; the other the most degraded disgusting & odious. (*PSL*, 2: 67)

However much sympathy Shelley felt for the victims at Peterloo, his political imagination was not kindled by the Italians he saw around him. It is not surprising, I might add, that the above quotation literally invokes the Wordsworthian sublime—"interfused through all things"—and is followed immediately by Shelley's observation that "young women of rank actually eat—you will never guess what—*garlick*."

Although Shelley's revolutionary sympathies have always been a commonplace of literary history, the precise political meanings one can read into his major poetry, above all, into *Prometheus Unbound*, have covered a wide range, from his biographer Richard Holmes's political reading of the play as "a symbolic story of man's liberation from tyranny"[9] to M. H. Abrams's Christian humanist interpretation dating from about the same time.[10] To ask what sympathies Rossini had either for the revolution or for the fate of the oppressed people is scarcely a relevant question, for the professional role he chose to pursue left him neither the leisure nor the opportunity to express himself in the way that a poet could. Yet his work was subjected to political interpretations even while he was at the height of his powers. The famous opening words of Stendhal's biography, written in 1823—"Napoleon is dead; but a new conqueror has already shown himself to the world"[11]—suggest the revolutionary context within which we are meant to place Rossini.

Still, Stendhal is unable to make any substantive claims for Rossini's political activism. At one point, when listing Rossini's works, Stendhal includes a "patriotic hymn" supposedly written in 1820 in support of the Neapolitan revolt that forced the king to grant a constitution until the Austrians moved in to restore absolute monarchy; whether or not such a piece was ever written, no record exists of any manuscript or performance. When listing this hymn, Stendhal even draws an analogy to the sad fate of an earlier operatic composer, his beloved Cimarosa, who had been sentenced to death (though never executed) for collaborating with the invading French in 1799; at another point, when excusing Rossini for refusing to condemn the evil actions of the small-town mayor in his opera *La gazza ladra*, Stendhal describes the composer as "an extremely cautious man, and clearly mindful of the fate of Cimarosa."[12] Whatever cautiousness Stendhal may have read into his musical Napoleon, the young Heine, traveling through Italy in 1828, discovered what he took to be the esoteric meaning behind Rossini's comic operas, whose music and plots, according to Heine, expressed a desire for freedom from foreign powers that must be kept hidden from the sentries standing guard in the theaters.[13]

The striking differences one notes between Rossini and Shelley, above all in their political stances, seem perhaps less interesting to us today than the attempts of their expositors to absorb them into their own systems of value. Whether we create a revolutionary or a conservative image for Rossini that extends beyond his compositional methods; or whether we speak of a radical or a platonic or a skeptical or a humanist Shelley, or several of these at once, we are primarily reading ourselves, or at least the biases of whatever community with which we seek to identify.

As we look backward on the history of their reception, their careers suggest some striking similarities—similarities of a sort one does not find if one simply compares them as working artists. Both Rossini and Shelley achieved the height of their fame during the first half of the nineteenth century; both suffered a considerable period of neglect, even opprobrium, during which time they held on at best to sharply reduced spots in the musical and the literary canon; and both have returned only in recent years to challenge the critical principles by which we determine our aesthetic tastes. Similarly to the reception of the three baroque artists I discuss in Chapter 1, the respective fates of Rossini and Shelley in musical and literary history can tell us a good bit about the workings of cultural institutions.

Stendhal's crowning of Rossini as a new Napoleon indicates the mythical status that the composer achieved early in his lifetime. Indeed, Rossini remained a living myth throughout his long life even after musical taste had shifted in directions antithetical to his aesthetic. Shelley, dying early, was the stuff that multiple myths are made of, as one can see from the many (and often conflicting) biographical accounts that appeared for several generations after his death.

No practitioner of the arts ever received international adulation as powerfully and also as early as Rossini, whose *Tancredi* dates from the first of his *anni mirabili*, 1813, when he was only 21. By the time the Shelleys had come to Italy the title figure's entrance aria—"Di tanti palpiti"—was firmly entrenched within what we today call popular culture. Doubtless the most ubiquitous tune of the early nineteenth century, it was sung, according to Stendhal, by "everyone from the humblest gondolier to the proudest lord of the land."[14] Both the Shelleys complain independently in letters from Leghorn in 1819: writing of farm laborers, Mary tells Marianne Hunt, "They sing not very melodiously but very loud—Rossini's music—*Mi revedrai ti revedro*" (*MSL*, 1: 102–3), while her husband, writing to Hogg, speaks of "the vine-dressers . . . singing all day *mi rivedrai, ti revedrò*, but by no means in an operatic style" (*PSL*, 2: 105). The tune left so powerful an imprint that, more than a half century after its composition, it—and, indeed, the whole Rossini style—could be parodied in the chorus of tailors entering before the song contest in *Die Meistersinger*.

Though Rossini's music could impose itself on the public to the point of annoyance, throughout the world of letters it received a level of praise that one rarely hears of relatively recent artistic work. Thus, Schopenhauer uses Rossini as his key example to illustrate the power of music, which, in *The World as Will and Representation*, finished in 1818, looms as the highest of the arts. Music, to the extent that it is nonrepresentational, represents the will itself: "If music tries to stick too closely to the words, and to mould itself according to the events, it is endeavoring to speak a language not its own. No one has kept so free from this mistake as Rossini; hence his music speaks its *own* language so distinctly and purely that it requires no words and therefore produces its full effect even when rendered by instruments alone."[15] It seems extraordinary that a composer who was never far from the smell of greasepaint should be singled out for his ability to transcend representation. Yet hyperbole of this sort often occurs in contemporary accounts; to cite still another German philosopher, one need only read the ecstatic letters that Hegel sent his wife reporting on the Rossini performances he attended in Vienna in 1824—indeed, he dallied in Vienna as long as he could to keep attending more.[16]

Shelley too achieved a mythical status in the years following his death—though not so universally or unequivocally as did Rossini, who, as I mentioned earlier, could be likened to emperors by Stendhal and Byron. With Shelley there always remained the touch of scandal—political, religious, sexual—which itself of course added to the myth, endowing his life and his writing at once with the ability to generate some hitherto undiscovered *frisson*. The young Browning's apostrophe to the figure he labelled "suntreader" attests to that larger-than-life quality which characterized Shelley in the eyes of his followers. Note the following statement, written well after Browning had attempted to shed Shelley's voice from his own poetry: "I would rather consider Shelley's poetry as a sublime fragmentary essay towards a presentment of the correspondency of the universe to Deity, of the natural to the spiritual, and of the actual to the ideal, than I would isolate and separately appraise the worth of many detachable portions which might be acknowledged as utterly perfect in a lower moral point of view, under the mere conditions of art."[17] However fragmentary or uneven Shelley's actual literary production, for Browning he occupies a place analogous to the Napoleonic Rossini evoked by Stendhal, who otherwise managed to carp a good bit about what he saw as the composer's imperfections. Unlike Rossini, whose adulation derived from a single source, namely his extraordinary musical inventiveness, Shelley appealed to people on a number of grounds, only one of which was his artistry as a poet. Shelley also commanded such distinct publics as radical workers on the Continent, for whom *The Mask of Anarchy* counted as a sacred political text, and readers eager for every scrap of scandal that the poet's surviving friends were able to reveal (sometimes also make up) in print.

How, after exercising such magnetism upon the world, did Rossini and Shelley fall as decisively from grace as they did? By the early twentieth century, only one Rossini opera, *Il barbiere di Siviglia*, remained in the repertory. Orchestral concerts featured the overtures to otherwise forgotten titles, and American children growing up in the 1930s and 1940s had no idea that the music introducing their favorite radio western, *The Lone Ranger*, came from the overture to a once-revered grand opera, *Guillaume Tell*. Scores that once inspired the awe of the civilized world languished unsung in unreliable editions—and some, like the recently resurrected *Il viaggio a Reims*, had not even been printed. Meanwhile Shelley continued to be published, lectured on, commented upon—if only because the university departments of English whose mission it was to preserve past poets were so large and so hungry for tasks to perform that they managed to keep Shelley in view. But despite the continued popularity of *Il barbiere* and the overtures, and despite the innumerable books on Shelley that helped keep the institution of English literary study going, those who sensed a greatness in either the composer or the poet found themselves so firmly on the defensive that they often chose not to express their opinions at all.

However different their media, the work of both figures was looked upon as something suitable for the less enlightened, for those members of the public who could be labeled as not quite mature in their tastes. Note the following statement from Arthur Elson's now-forgotten history of opera, published in 1901 and from which, in Chapter 2, I quoted a remark dismissing eighteenth-century *opera seria*: "The music of Rossini and the Italians of his time errs in presenting successive chord-relations that are too simple, and at times affect those who possess a refined sense of harmony about as a problem in the multiplication table would appeal to a student in quaternions."[18] A comparable disparagement of Shelley can be found in a source that is still much remembered, T. S. Eliot's Norton lectures of 1932–33: "An enthusiasm for Shelley seems to me . . . to be an affair of adolescence: for most of us, Shelley has marked an intense period before maturity, but for how many does Shelley remain the companion of age?"[19] Just as Eliot used Donne as a positive example to legitimate modernist poetics, as I indicate in Chapter 1, so he uses Shelley here to voice the antiromanticism central to this poetics. Soon after Eliot's pronouncement, F. R. Leavis sought to administer the coup de grace to Shelley's earlier reputation with his comment on the famous lines from *Adonais* beginning "life like a dome of many-coloured glass": "The famous imagery is happily conscious of being impressive, but the impressiveness is for the spellbound, for those sharing the simple happiness of intoxication."[20] For Leavis, Shelley's writings have been relegated not only to Eliot's audience of adolescents but also to those older folk shameless enough to want their reading to work like a drug.

At an earlier time one might have sought to answer comments such as these directly—or even to accept them—but I prefer to place them within a historical context. And one way of placing them would be to say that by the time these statements were uttered the techniques needed to perform the works both of Rossini and of Shelley had been lost. As far as Rossini is concerned, I refer here to that florid mode of singing that today we call *bel canto*, which gradually died out during the nineteenth century as a result of the simpler, more direct, seemingly more "natural" and "expressive" style of singing that developed, in differing ways, in the operas of Verdi and Wagner. In an analogous manner Shelley demanded techniques of reading that readers were able to command until at least the beginning of the twentieth century—that is, as long as there were poets such as Dante Gabriel Rossetti, Swinburne, and the early Yeats whose linguistic configurations kept these techniques in the public's reading repertory.

With the loss of these performing techniques by singers and readers alike, other arguments developed to justify the considerably lower niches to which both Rossini and Shelley were assigned in their respective canons. To the extent that "naturalness" and "expressiveness" became valued in both opera and poetry, one could easily point to the artifice and the corresponding lack of verisimilitude in their work. Elson's turn-of-the-century history of opera complains of the lack of "dramatic fitness" in Rossini and his school, and it refers in particular to the "trivial vocalises" of the aria "Bel raggio" from *Semiramide*, a piece that managed to outlast the opera for which it was composed as long as sopranos such as Adelina Patti were around to show off their older techniques on the concert platform.[21] It has been characteristic of operatic histories and handbooks until quite recently to speak of the dramatic absurdities of Rossini's *seria* operas—which make up about half his oeuvre—while at the same time justifying his elaborate vocal style when it appears in his *buffa* operas (above all in *Il barbiere di Siviglia*), in which, after all, absurdity is what the whole thing is supposedly all about.

Leavis also uses lack of verisimilitude as a central argument in his case against Shelley. In particular, he cites the storm images in "Ode to the West Wind":

Thou on whose stream, 'mid the steep sky's commotion,
Loose clouds like Earth's decaying leaves are shed,
Shook from the tangled boughs of Heaven and Ocean,
Angels of rain and lightning.

Leavis asks, "In what respects are the 'loose clouds' like 'decaying leaves'? The correspondence is certainly not in shape, colour or way of moving. . . . What again, are those 'tangled boughs of Heaven and Ocean'? They stand for nothing that Shelley could have pointed to in the scene before him."[22]

Just as opera, during the later nineteenth century, had cultivated a naturalistic form of drama that left Rossini obsolete, so the attempts of early- and mid-twentieth-century poets in English to achieve a certain naturalness and transparency of language not only made Shelley an unsatisfactory model but even made him a poet one needn't take too seriously. Although these changes in musical and poetic style were crucial to the changing status of both figures, one might note that each of them could conveniently be pitted by critics against an older contemporary to whom positive values might be attributed. Thus, Leavis sets Shelley against Wordsworth, comparing some lines from "Mont Blanc" with the latter's Simplon Pass passage in *The Prelude*. Whereas Shelley has only a "weak grasp upon the actual," Wordsworth grounds his sublime language in his "grasp of the outer world," with the result that (and here Leavis clearly echoes Eliot on objectives correlative) "he [Wordsworth] seems always to be presenting an object . . . and the emotion seems to derive from what is presented."[23] Thus the poetic language favored during the critic's time becomes legitimated by the contrast Leavis draws between Shelleyan excess and the sobriety of his distinguished predecessor.

Similarly music historians have characteristically pitted Rossini against his musical predecessor Beethoven, a few of whose works Rossini came to know after the latter was already established as a composer. The evaluative distinctions that have persisted between the two were already evident at Rossini's single meeting with Beethoven in 1822 when the latter advised him to keep away from tragic opera: "But look, *opera seria*—that's not the Italians' nature," Beethoven pronounced; "they don't have enough musical science to deal with true drama; and how could they acquire it in Italy?" Beethoven saw Rossini to the door with the admonition that he stick to comic opera. "Above all, make a lot of *Barbers*" were supposedly his last words, which, as it turned out, became accurate predictors about where Rossini was to stand in the musical canon until quite recently.[24] The history of music (or what Beethoven here called musical science) has in effect been the property of Germans—of the famous composers themselves and of their later collaborators, the musicologists. Rossini clearly did not fit their paradigm, and this despite the fact that the innovations he introduced—in matters such as his famous crescendos, his rethinking of the structure of arias and ensembles, his attempts (none too successful) to curb the improvisation of individual singers—were crucial to the development of nineteenth-century Italian opera. Yet Robert Schumann's characterization of the Rossini-Beethoven encounter—"The butterfly crossed the path of the eagle, but the latter turned aside in order not to crush it with the beating of his wings"[25]—gives some indication of the Germanic contempt that has been heaped on Rossini ever since his own time.

With his considerable command of languages and past knowledge, Shelley surely had more "literary science," to use an analogy to Beethoven's phrase, at his disposal than did Wordsworth. But Wordsworth conveyed an image of literary authority such as Shelley could never have done. Indeed, the particular images that posterity has chosen to construct for both Rossini and Shelley are bound to place them at a severe disadvantage to the images we retain of a heroic Beethoven, on the one hand, and of a gravely wise Wordsworth on the other. Our contemporary slang term "flaky" helps characterize these images— though in differing ways—for each of the two later masters. And certainly both of them contributed a good bit to making themselves vulnerable. Shelley's political rashness, his hysteria, his flouting of sexual mores made him an easy target for continued attacks of which Matthew Arnold's celebrated phrases, "What a set!" and "*ineffectual* angel, beating in the void his luminous wings in vain," have proved particularly telling.[26] Rossini's reputation as a joker, his role as master of a fashionable Paris salon, together with his gourmandizing and the laziness that characterized the whole second half of his life—these were all quite incompatible with the earnest professionalism and the sense of mission expected of serious composers during the nineteenth century. Moreover, when, in his interview with the much younger Wagner, he excused himself for his lack of musical training and subordinated his talents to those of the German masters from Bach through Beethoven, we recognize that his customary good-humored modesty allowed him to play into that German myth of progress that refused him a major place in the history of music.[27] Indeed, when Wagner, long before the interview, referred disparagingly to Rossini's "narcotic-drunken melody" (*WGS* 11: 42), one notes the same tactic of questioning an artist's seriousness that Leavis used when he characterized some of Shelley's most famous lines as appropriate only for those seeking intoxication.

Then how should we deal with our perceptions of Rossini and Shelley today in our new, so-called postmodern time? How do we account for the fascination many of us have discovered for their virtuosity, their extravagance, their outrageousness? The wrong tactic would be to defend them on more traditional grounds. It has become usual to point out the stylistic experimentation and growth characteristic of Rossini's Neapolitan operas, for instance, his introduction of the chorus in the overture to *Ermione*[28]; or, to cite some rare praise from a pivotal figure in the German tradition, one might note the compliment Wagner paid Rossini for drawing music out of the text in the "Sois immobile" passage of *Guillaume Tell*.[29] Or one could mention Rossini's keen interest, during his post-operatic retirement, in the recent Bach revival—an interest manifested not only in his study of the Bach-Gesellschaft edition but also in the contrapuntal passages to be found in his late *Petite Messe solennelle*.[30] Yet none of these compliments could make a Beethoven or a Wagner out of Rossini, who, despite the impetus he gave to subsequent Italian and French opera, refused to display the earnestness and the unrelenting rigor characteristic of the major German composers.

Similarly, it seems futile to attempt to reconcile Shelley with frameworks that do not easily accommodate him. It may be well and good to show that Leavis lacked a solid grasp of Tuscan weather when he attacked "Ode to the West Wind,"[31] but the poem is not likely to find new advocates simply because it shows more verisimilitude than it did before Leavis took after it. Donald Davie's attempt to locate an urbanity similar to that of his fellow Movement poets of the 1950s in passages of *Julian and Maddalo* and "The Sensitive Plant" may seem quite convincing,[32] but if these urbane moments are all that we should value in Shelley, why bother with him at all? From quite another intellectual quarter, in the 1950s Northrop Frye and the young

Harold Bloom brought out a mythopoeic Shelley who, though he encompassed more ground than other recently rehabilitated Shelleys, is scarcely the Shelley with whom we can make contact in our own time.[33] *The Triumph of Life* has been an especially favored piece for those who have come to praise Shelley—for example, the aging T. S. Eliot, who tried to undo the fierceness of his earlier attack by finding *The Triumph* a decorous tribute to his own hero, Dante,[34] or the various Yale critics who in 1979 collectively brought out their big guns to demonstrate what this poem could reveal about their own methods.[35]

Where would we find the Rossini and the Shelley with whom we can make contact in the 1990s and who, one hopes, will not prove ephemeral after our current tastes have worn themselves out? The Rossini and the Shelley of our time are above all performing figures who speak out in diverse voices no one of which has any special authority nor reveals the essentials of its creator nor of the voice it purports to represent. Let us think of "Ode to the West Wind" not simply as the record of a prophetic voice, as its more receptive readers from its own time up through the Beat poets wanted to read it, but let us see it instead as the artifice of an actor-prophet performing his prophecy—and with a shamelessness he in effect acknowledges by knocking himself down upon the thorns of life to bleed.

And what shall we say a Rossini aria represents or expresses? Certainly not an individual character the way that a late Verdi or Mozart aria does, but rather it expresses a character type or more precisely a voice type—the basso parlante or the basso profundo or the trousered mezzo. Or it expresses the particular singer for whose range and vocal peculiarities it was composed and whom later singers have learned to imitate. Or, as in the baroque style out of which Rossini developed, and whose aria style I discuss in Chapter 2, it expresses a particular *Affekt*, essentially an emotional pose—prayer, revenge, sexual longing—that, added together with the succession of such poses making up the opera as a whole, simulates some possible emotional cycle. Or it expresses a display of such compelling virtuosity that the boisterous social activity characteristic of the theater in his time will calm down briefly for its duration.

Note these lines, which constitute the cabaletta of the aria with which the soprano concludes *La donna del lago*:

Fra il padre e fra l'amante	With my father and my lover
oh quel beato istante!	oh what a blessèd moment!
Ah! chi sperar potea	Ah! who could hope
tanta felicità!	for such happiness!

These final words of Elena have no analogy in Scott's poem, in which Ellen's happiness must be taken on faith in accordance with the gentle passivity she has demonstrated throughout.[36] But in Rossini's operas the female voices (whether they impersonate male or female characters) maintain an aggressiveness quite in keeping with the flexibility they can enjoy in comparison with male voices. Moreover, Rossini often chose to end his operas—above all, those, like *La donna del lago*, composed for Isabella Colbran—with a showpiece for a female voice. No attempt is made here, as it was in Monteverdi and Gluck, or later would be in Wagner and in much nineteenth-century Italian opera, to give the illusion that the music emanates directly from the words themselves, the illusion that operatic expression constitutes some ideal fusion of text and sound. Quite the contrary, for excess and repetition display themselves as Rossini's guiding procedures. Each of these four short lines is sung at least five times, with line three appearing ten times and the final line only one time less. The words *istante* and *felicità* receive additional repetitions—and *istante* with lengthy ornamentations that challenge the common notion of what constitutes an instant of time. One could, of course, mount a mimetic argument that all this conspicuous excess provides some plausible imitation of jubilation. But a similar excess of means and a similar jubilation conclude a goodly number of Rossini's operas, and these include operas both in the comic and the *seria* genre, with the soprano (sometimes more properly mezzo-soprano) role assigned to a wide variety of women that include the title characters of *L'italiana in Algeri*, *La Cenerentola*, *La donna del lago*, and *Zelmira*.

In a hurry to complete a new opera for Milan, *Bianca e Falliero*, in December, 1819, Rossini, as I indicated earlier, simply transferred the music from

Elena's finale, composed for Naples just three months before, to Bianca's finale, which not only served a new soprano and a new audience but also used a new set of words to suggest jubilation. Looking back at these and other solo finales—at least with the voices of present-day Rossini singers in our ears—we hear them not so much as expressions of particular texts or even of emotional stances such as jubilation but as assertions of a purposeful, sometimes even aggressive playfulness that constantly reminds us that it is speaking a world we can label simply "Rossini" and, when persuasively performed, that we can even call "performance" or "opera-in-general."

And what does a Shelley passage such as the following express?

> It is impossible to read the productions of our most celebrated writers, whatever may be their system relating to thought or expression, without being startled by the electric life which there is in their words. They measure the circumference or sound the depths of human nature with a comprehensive and all-penetrating spirit at which they are themselves perhaps most sincerely astonished, for it [is] less their own spirit than the spirit of their age. They are the priests of an unapprehended inspiration, the mirrors of gigantic shadows which futurity casts upon the present; the words which express what they conceive not; the trumpet which sings to battle and feels not what it inspires; the influence which is moved not, but moves. Poets and philosophers are the unacknowledged legislators of the world.[37]

This passage is of course familiar as the grand finale to "A Defence of Poetry," written in 1821, though I quote its earlier version as it appeared in "A Philosophical View of Reform," composed (though never completed) between December 1819 and spring 1820. It scarcely matters whether these lines are about both poets and philosophers, as they explicitly are here, or about poets alone, as they are in their second embodiment. Nor does it matter much that the context for the earlier version is political, and that of the later version poetical. Moreover, though these lines technically count as prose rather than verse, they call attention to themselves as a manifestation of poetry similar to the poetry Shelley himself, in the "Defence," attributes to Roman law, which he finds superior to what formally counted as Roman verse.

Like a Rossini cabaletta, this passage is notable for its performativity, the earnest playfulness with which it builds repetitively and with increasing intensity to its final assertion. The hyperbolic voice we hear penetrating through the words calls attention to itself as formidably as a singing voice that seeks to amaze us with its capacity for intricate runs. Though repetitive, the passage jolts us constantly with its terms drawn from the discourse of the sublime—"electric life," "astonished," "gigantic"—together with its ability to tease us with phrases drawn from widely varying forms of religious and philosophical discourse, "all-penetrating spirit," "trumpet which sings to battle," "moved not, but moves." If pressed to declare what precisely all this expresses, we can opt for some sort of historical statement about the role of the poet in the romantic era or simply claim that it represents an attitude, say, of awe, or wonder, or whatever word we choose from our own repertory of sublime terms.

Although I began this chapter by stressing the gap that separates Shelley and Rossini, it should be evident by now that I am proposing a certain rapport between them, not perhaps in what they themselves were (whatever that may mean) or even in how their earlier readers and listeners perceived them—but rather in how we today have come to apprehend their work. Certainly for many of us a new Rossini and a new Shelley have emerged in the course of our own experience with music and poetry. Once we grant their newly reborn presences, one wants to ask what precisely has made it possible to feel enthusiasm for two figures so long neglected, even sometimes despised among those whose opinions counted in the world.

Perhaps I should approach the problem from another direction and ask, what precisely is the originary moment from which we can date the new Shelley and Rossini we have been discovering in recent years? Originary moments, of course, are nothing more than markers we insert into the narratives we concoct to account for and legitimate the tastes we enjoy and seek to propagate among others. For the sake of such legitimation let me suggest the origin of our contemporary Rossini in Marilyn Horne's first performance of the trouser role of Arsace in *Semiramide* in Los Angeles on January 29, 1964. Horne at least assigned a special relevance to this performance in an interview during the 1992 New York Rossini birthday celebration, and this was corroborated in that interview by Philip Gossett, who cited Horne's example as a prime motivating factor in his own work uncovering and editing the manuscripts of the many forgotten Rossini operas.[38] Indeed, the whole style of Rossini performance today, whether or not it authentically restores the style prevalent in Rossini's own day, could be said to derive from Horne and from several later singers, notably Cecilia Bartoli, who have worked within the tradition she has established. And although connoisseurs of historic voices can doubtless cite earlier singers in our century—for example, Conchita Supervia and Jennie Tourel—who anticipated Horne in restoring certain Rossini roles for the mezzo coloratura, it was Horne who recreated a whole succession of Rossini characters—many from long-forgotten operas—with an authority that legitimated the composer's style in a way that had not been possible since Rossini's own time.

If one must seek a similar moment to situate the way we are coming to read Shelley today, one might look back to a much earlier date, namely the performances of *The Cenci* that Antonin Artaud staged in Paris in 1935, using a condensed French prose translation of Shelley's play and combining it with elements from Stendhal's narrative on the same subject.[39] Doubtless the actual Shelley text that we know mattered little—not only because the performances were in a different language, but above all because spectacle and subtext dominated whatever actual text one assigns to the poet we know as Shelley. "The gestures and movements in this production are just as important as the dialogue," Artaud explained, adding that "the lighting effects, like gesture, will also stand for a language." As for the sonic effect, he maintained, "The audience will find themselves in the centre of a network of sound vibrations," and went on to describe 30-foot-high bells diffused by loudspeakers from the four corners of the auditorium, including a recording he had made of the great bell of Amiens cathedral.[40] Artaud quite clearly anticipated the electronically manipulated performances common within contemporary theater—performances that usually display the same lack of piety toward the literary texts they are enacting as Artaud's production. To provide a special irony to my designation of the Artaud *Cenci* as an originary moment, one might note that it appeared at precisely the same time that Leavis declared, "*The Cenci* is very bad and . . . its badness is characteristic [of Shelley]."[41] From what we know of the production, it sounds pretty much like what we today would label a post-modern appropriation by a director bent on extracting as much violence and excess as he can from the text—to the point that the very badness that Leavis so deplored becomes a feature in which the production positively exults.

The Artaud *Cenci*, in historical retrospect, also helps illuminate a central aspect of Shelley that made him difficult to approach during the long period in which transparency of language and economy of expression reigned as central literary values. I refer to the operatic quality that characterizes a good bit of his work—and by operatic I include such matters as its extravagance, its cultivation of excess, indeed a certain shamelessness that causes embarrassment to those who, throughout the long history of opera, have actively resisted whatever spells the medium has sought to exercise upon its beholders. In this light one might call *Prometheus Unbound* the preeminent opera-without-music in English; certainly such a judgment would allow readers who reject the work to account for their attitude without more need for explanation. The very fact that Shelley attached the generic label *lyrical drama* to *Prometheus Unbound* suggests his operatic intentions, for, as Stuart Curran has demonstrated, this term was used during the early nineteenth century for "any serious dramatic effort containing music, from opera to choral drama."[42] But Shelley is operatic throughout his writings—though, except for the generic designation he gave to *Prometheus Unbound*, he did not himself pursue such analogies to explain his own work.[43] At one point in his letters, however, he uses an analogy from opera to describe the extravagant prose with which a negative review of *The Revolt of Islam* by John Taylor Coleridge concludes: "I was amused, too, with the finale [of the review]; it is like the end of the first act of an opera, when that tremendous concordant discord sets up from the orchestra, and everybody talks and sings at once."[44] Of all the Rossini operas we know that Shelley had attended when he wrote these words, *Il barbiere di Siviglia*, whose first-act finale can still strike its listeners as the ultimate musical realization of calculated confusion, comes directly to mind. Doubtless Shelley, who preferred Mozart to all other composers, would not have recognized an analogy between the operatic qualities of Rossini and those I ascribe to his own work.[45] Indeed, calling Rossini operatic at all would seem a ridiculous tautology. Yet many of the qualities that distinguish Rossini from earlier opera composers—his crescendos, the complications he introduced in his ensembles, his constant upping of the ante of what is allowable within the bounds of musical decorum—were decisive in creating the image audiences perceive of what constitutes opera. It was Rossini above all who made it possible to modify the word "opera" with the adjective "grand," first through the intensifying techniques of his Italian operas and then through the example of his final contribution to the genre, *Guillaume Tell*, which established many of the conventions intrinsic to what the French came to call *grand opéra*.

By now it may seem that I have been postulating some spirit of the age, give or take a few years around 1819, in which those qualities we define as operatic—extravagance, excess, and a general indifference to referentiality in favor of performative values—could be said to define the artistic production of the age. Although the phrase "spirit of the age" goes back at least to Hume,[46] the notion did not exert its power until a later generation, and Shelley himself demonstrates this power in the passage above when he grants philosophers and poets the ability to speak "the spirit of their age." Frankly, I do not know if ages have spirits or even what sorts of boundaries one should attach to the term we invoke when we say "age." But I *do* know that others as well as I have come to respond to Shelley and Rossini in recent years as we did not a generation ago. Whatever spirit we may attribute to our own so-called postmodern time, it is significant that we have grown impatient with the older models of literary and musical history that relegated figures such as Shelley and Rossini if not quite to the dustheap at least to some limbo, with the result that suspicion could be cast upon anybody who dared to admire them unduly. When Artaud describes Shelley's language as "resembling a summer night bombarded with meteors,"[47] or when Michael Davidson locates a postmodern Shelley in the poet's transgressions across the boundaries separating text and life,[48] or when Michael Palmer finds his own postmodern Shelley in the "defiant poetic excess" of *Epipsychidion*,[49] we may find some analogies to the superhuman vocal feats we seek to hear in present-day Rossini performers, whose manner has been characterized as a "stylized and allegorical form of vocalization."[50]

Just as the three baroque artists I treat in Chapter 1 can be called the creations of early-twentieth-century modernism, so Rossini and Shelley may well turn out to be among the most vital creations of and even models for our current fin-de-siècle postmodernism. From our present vantage point it is as though the very qualities that a Leavis could cite to beat down Shelley—his "weak grasp on the actual," his confusion of tenor and vehicle, his intent to intoxicate his readers with the impressiveness of his performance—these qualities, like those that traditional musicology has cited to keep Rossini in his place—his repetitiveness, his loudness, his failure to advance musical form in accordance with the prevailing German model—seem rather beside the point in an age that takes its aesthetic cues from the likes of John Cage, the Language poets, Philip Glass, and the various forms of poststructuralist theory circulating within the intellectual marketplace. Many of these vices, in fact, turn out to be the virtues by which we come to define ourselves. It once seemed natural, for instance, to attack the lack of naturalness in the sort of art that came from a Rossini or a Shelley: yet in an age that has rejected the term "natural" as an unnatural and thoroughly social construction, nothing need seem more natural than anything else, and nothing need seem valuable simply because it is pronounced natural. As so often in the history of the various arts, we revaluate the past in order to legitimate what we seek to produce, indeed what we today conceive ourselves essentially and naturally to be.

Chapter Four

Opera Among the Arts
Opera Among Institutions

About 1805, at virtually the halfway point in the history of opera, the philosopher Friedrich Schelling chose to conclude his *Philosophy of Art* with a statement about opera (a form hitherto unmentioned in his treatise) in relation to Greek drama:

> The most perfect combination of all the arts, the union of poetry and music through song, of poetry and painting through dance—and these synthesized with one another: this represents the most fully created manifestation of theater, namely the theater of antiquity. Today we have only a caricature of this theater, namely *opera*, which, if it commanded a higher and nobler style of poetry as well as of the remaining rival arts, could most directly lead us back to the performance of that ancient drama which combined music and song.[1]

In one sense this statement is simply a recapitulation of what the theoretical founders of opera had speculated more than two centuries before when they proposed the new form as a restoration of the ideals and practices of Greek drama. Yet Schelling speaks of the form in what he took to be its present, fallen state, a "caricature" of the ancient model it was supposedly to succeed and emulate. At the same time this concluding statement voices a hope for the future: as his conditional verb indicates, if the various arts that opera brings together assume a "higher and nobler style," it "could" lead us back to that long-lost ideal genre.

Schelling's sharp distinction between opera's high potential and the degradation into which he claims it has lapsed is emblematic of the uneasy status that opera has occupied among the various art forms throughout its history. On the one hand, opera is idealized as that form which, in its power to unite "all" the arts, or at least a goodly number of them, has the capacity to generate more pleasures than any single art alone. Aristotle himself had already employed this "more-is-better" argument in asserting the preeminence of tragedy over epic: "Tragedy has everything that epic has (it can even use its metre), and moreover has a considerable addition in the music and the spectacle, which produce pleasure in a most vividly perceptible way."[2] On the other hand, opera as an art form has often been castigated for reasons such as its impurity—the very criterion for which it has most often been praised—its refusal to honor such classical virtues as unity and verisimilitude, its entanglement in a world of commerce, and, often in connection with the last-named reason, its willingness to compromise itself for the sake of immediate effect.

This chapter seeks to provide some historical contexts for the varying ways in which opera has been evaluated and culturally placed. How has it been viewed in relation to some of the individual art forms that it supposedly brings together? How has it been related to other musical forms? How can we speak of opera as an institution, and how, through the collaboration of composers and librettists, is opera implicated in that more venerable institution we call literature?

The curt dismissal of opera at the end of Schelling's philosophy of art is fairly typical of the way that the form was treated (when it was treated at all) in systems of aesthetics. The aesthetics treatise is a genre that has flourished most notably among German thinkers, beginning with Alexander Baumgarten's Latin work *Aesthetica* (1750–58), whose title gave a name to what was to become a significant branch of philosophy. Down to our own time the aesthetics treatise has remained a recognizable and continuing genre with its own set of conventions and with later examples building self-consciously on their predecessors. In many instances the treatise has served as a means of filling out a larger philosophical system, as it did for Kant, Schelling, and Hegel. The development of the aesthetics treatise coincided with the development of a new conception of the role of art within human thought: the conception that, as

Kant's 1790 *Critique of Judgment* and its successors proclaimed, art occupies its own, autonomous domain distinct from other forms of activity.

It is characteristic of these treatises to provide a compendium of the various genres and media that make up this newly mapped out aesthetic realm and, indeed, to provide evaluative judgments of their relative worth. As the genre developed, the various art forms often came to shape a universe of their own (a world of art distinguishable from other areas of activity) by means of mutual correspondences. In Schelling's tightly argued treatise, for example, music, painting, and the plastic arts (the last in their most general sense) correspond, within the more limited realm of the plastic arts themselves, to architecture, bas-relief, and sculpture, respectively.[3]

Opera, when it appears within these classification systems, is generally viewed as a form that ideally should create a union of the various arts, in the spirit of the Schelling remark quoted at the start of this chapter. An earlier treatise, J. G. Sulzer's *General Theory of the Fine Arts* (1771–74), which is organized as a kind of dictionary of aesthetic terms [*Kunstwörter*], contains a detailed entry on opera that envisions the form as "capable of being the greatest, most important of dramatic forms because all the powers of the fine arts are united." But Sulzer quickly adds that opera has "abandoned the path of nature," that even the best operas are compromised by vices such as an inappropriate fit between words and music, the demands of singers, and an inordinate use of scenic display. "Contemptible as opera may be in its customary disfigurement, . . . so important and honorable it might become," Sulzer concludes his entry, for "no work of art can create opera's liveliness of effect," with "eye and ear and imagination, all tension-springs of the passions brought into play at the same time."[4]

By the time that Sulzer wrote his entry, this view had already become a topos in discussions of opera. Sulzer refers at several points to Count Algarotti's influential *Essay on Opera* of 1755, which, as I indicate in Chapters 1 and 2, elaborated an image of opera's decline from its origins together with a hope for its reform. On the first page of his essay, Algarotti declared that "the most attractive elements of poetry, of music, of mime, of dance, and of painting, are all happily combined in opera," but on the very next page he accounted for the form's present-day woes by comparing it to that favorite eighteenth-century image, the machine: "As with machines, so with opera—the more complex they are, the more likely they are to go out of order."[5] It scarcely seems accidental that Sulzer cites Gluck's preface to *Alceste* as a positive example given his predilection for Algarotti, since Algarotti's essay was in the forefront of the mid-eighteenth-century discussions of opera that stood behind Gluck's reform. But whereas Algarotti's essay attributed the failure of opera in his time to the difficulty of keeping its various component arts in "concurrence" with one another, Sulzer specifically assigns the blame for the form's degradation to the cultures within which it thrives: thus, in northern Europe, the problem lies in the courts that serve as opera's sponsors, while in Italy, with its more commercially based houses, artistic considerations must be compromised to please the crowds who make opera financially viable.

However much the major aesthetics treatises may differ in their individual classifications and evaluations, they promulgate a view of art free of the cultural entanglements that Sulzer finds ruinous to the opera of his time. Throughout its history, opera has seen shifts in its relationships to the various spheres within which it participates—aesthetic, commercial, and sometimes both at once. Later in this chapter I discuss those relationships, but explicating them first requires a broader historical contextualization. My concern here is to show how the conception of art that developed in German thought in the eighteenth and early nineteenth centuries scarcely accommodates opera at all; at best it projects opera as a form that, after a brief flowering during its early days, may conceivably achieve aesthetic status in some utopian future.

When opera is mentioned in aesthetics treatises, it is generally treated as a category of music rather than of drama, the latter usually being subsumed under the rubric of poetry. It is striking that until Schopenhauer's treatise of 1819, in which music emerges as the highest of the arts, poetry was granted pride of place in the aesthetic pantheon. To the extent that opera is defined as music, it shares in the limitations traditionally attributed to music. Kant, who in fact has nothing to say about opera in the *Critique of Judgment*, placed music low within the aesthetic hierarchy, associating it with "sensations" rather than intellect, which he attached to that considerably higher art, poetry. Music for Kant is "more a matter of enjoyment than of culture," and at one point he cites "a certain lack of urbanity" about music, comparing its effects to the odor spreading from a perfumed handkerchief.[6]

Kant's bias against the intellectual limitations of music is still discernible a generation later in Hegel's far more sympathetic and detailed treatment of music in his posthumously published lectures on aesthetics. Hegel's classification of the arts, like his classifications of historical periods in his *Philosophy of History* and of modes of consciousness in his *Philosophy of Mind*, is organized according to the historical stages that particular forms represent. Within the Hegelian aesthetic system, architecture is the representative form of the earliest stage, what Hegel calls the "symbolic" or primitive era. Sculpture represents the second, "classical" stage, while painting, music, and literature, in hierarchically ascending order, are the arts of the "romantic" stage, which here refers to the whole post-classical period and which is characterized by a subjectivity and inwardness unknown to earlier moments of civilization.

It is significant that in Hegel's system, as in most other systems, literature remains firmly at the top of the hierarchy, whether or not the arts are analyzed as timeless categories or, as in Hegel, in historical terms. Yet music, on account of the inwardness it manifests, stands higher than painting, its immediate neighbor in the hierarchy. "The real region of [a composer's] compositions remains a rather formal inwardness, pure sound," Hegel writes, "and his immersion in the topic [from a literary text] becomes not the formation of something external but rather a retreat into the inner life's own freedom, a self-enjoyment, and, in many departments of music, even an assurance that as artist he is free from subject-matter altogether" (*HA*, 2: 895). Within the framework that Hegel establishes here, opera obviously must be valued for its music rather than for its text or even for some union of music and text. "The text is the servant of the music," Hegel declares at one point in his discussion (*HA*, 2: 934) in obvious defiance of the still-quite-prestigious principle that Gluck had voiced to defend his practice in his reform operas. "We understand little or nothing of the text," Hegel writes at another point, "especially in the case of our German language and its pronunciation. Therefore it is after all an unmusical trend to put the main emphasis of interest on the text" (*HA*, 2: 901). In view of the unimportance of the libretto in his conception of opera, it is scarcely surprising that Hegel shows little patience with recitative as against aria; he even notes how Italian audiences pay scant attention to recitative in their opera houses. Yet Hegel is also impatient with what he calls the "characterization in detail" that he associates with "our strict German musical intellect" (*HA*, 2: 948, 949), which he distinguishes from the unself-consciousness of Rossini; indeed, he even rejoices in his observation that "often Rossini is unfaithful to his text and with his free melodies soars over the heights" (*HA*, 2: 949).

As I point out in Chapter 3, Hegel was entranced by some Rossini performances he attended in Vienna. Indeed, Rossini is among the very few composers that Hegel so much as names in his lectures on aesthetics. Yet his characterization of Rossini as unconcerned with subject matter ultimately suggests something negative to Hegel. At another point, though without giving specific names, Hegel expresses a certain condescension toward composers for their refusal to be much concerned with content and ideas in favor of purely musical structures and even adds gratuitously that "very talented composers frequently remain throughout their life the most ignorant and empty-headed of men" (*HA*, 2: 954). This negative aspect of music comes to the fore much more clearly in the final section of Hegel's lectures in his discussion of drama, which he views as the highest of the literary genres. Having reached this latest stage in his dialectic, Hegel can now look back at opera as a distinctly lower species of drama. From this point of view the external "visible magnificence" of opera comes to correspond to a "subject-matter . . . utterly devoid of any intellectual connection" (*HA*, 2: 1191). Though here he names *Die Zauberflöte* as the best "artistically worked out" example of the genre, he closes his discussion with the remark that opera at best "puts us in the mood we have in reading one of the Arabian Nights" (*HA*, 2: 1192). Doubtless Hegel was able to let himself go when, in his role as tourist, he attended the Rossini operas in Vienna; once he put on his mantle as philosopher, however, he felt forced to forsake the more frivolous pleasures offered by opera and the literature of fantasy.

Although we consider Hegel's system opposed to that of Schopenhauer in all matters of philosophical importance, their approach to opera manifests a striking similarity. Schopenhauer did not, like most German philosophers, leave a separate treatise on aesthetics, but—because the role of art was central to his philosophy as a whole—he included his discussion of the various arts within his central work, *The World as Will and Representation*. For Schopenhauer, quite in contrast to other philosophers, who generally privileged literature as the highest of the arts, music occupies top place within the hierarchy. Schopenhauer's enthronement of music represents the culmination of speculations about the special place of music, above all of instrumental music, that began in the 1790s in the influential musical discussions of Ludwig Tieck, Wilhelm Wackenroder, and E. T. A. Hoffmann.[7] Within Schopenhauer's larger system, music becomes the central means—together with the practice of renunciation—for escaping the torments of the will, that metaphysical principle of flux and turbulence that rages through all things. Music provides us with a kind of absolution, and Schopenhauer virtually deifies music by calling it the "innermost kernel preceding all form," something that gets us to the "heart of things," the "universalia ante rem" that is at once the "universalia in re."[8] And here one can note where Schopenhauer coincides, if ever so briefly, with his rival Hegel: for both of them, the text to which music may be set has little relevance to the experience of the music itself. Composers too much concerned with a text betray the spirit of music; Schopenhauer, in fact, castigates Haydn, the only composer he names besides Rossini, for trying to make sounds imitate natural objects in *The Seasons* (1: 263–64). Schopenhauer, again like Hegel, defies the principle behind Gluck's reform by stipulating that the text should be written to fit the music rather than the other way around, for words are a "foreign extra of secondary value" (2: 448). And again like Hegel, Schopenhauer was entranced by Rossini, whose "music speaks its *own* language so distinctly and purely that it requires no words at all" (1: 262, italics Schopenhauer's).

Among the few philosophers of art who took opera seriously as an independent category was Friedrich Theodor Vischer, whose 1857 treatise came at the end of the century of serious theorizing about that new category, the arts, that began with Baumgarten. For Vischer as for his master Hegel, poetic drama remains the highest of the arts, yet opera occupies its own terrain within his system as a blending of drama and music in which both forms reinforce one another to express feeling (*Gefühl*).[9] Vischer's theory of opera is narrow and normative, with *Don Giovanni* serving as the ideal model, for it displays "the poetry of feeling" (1117). A few other operas, principally Gluck's reform operas, meet this standard, with *Le nozze di Figaro* criticized for "too much action" and *Die Zauberflöte*, for "too little action" (1113, 1114). History-based operas such as *Les Huguenots* and *La clemenza di Tito* are so tied to an actual world that they belong to drama more than to opera (1119–20). Once a generic category becomes reified within a system, as opera does within Vischer's, it hardens to the point that its only use is to help explain the system—or at least the particular tastes of its author.

In a much more fundamental sense than Vischer's, another theory, which appeared in 1850, served as the real culmination of German thinking about the relationship of the arts. Unlike the other treatises I have discussed thus far, it is not by a philosopher at all, nor does it employ the subtle, restrained language characteristic of these treatises. I refer to Wagner's tract *The Artwork of the Future*, written in a heated rhetorical manner more suited to the political realm in which Wagner had actively participated during the preceding years than to the aesthetic domain to which he was now transferring his energies both as theorist and practicing composer. Written at the height of Wagner's enthusiasm for Ludwig Feuerbach, to whom the text was dedicated, it rejects the high abstractions of earlier philosophy and instead invokes its attachment to that concept of the "human" characteristic of Feuerbach. Yet despite its frequently "unphilosophical" tone, *The Artwork of the Future* stands as heir to a century of theorizing about the nature, sources, and divisions of art.[10] Like the earlier treatises, it projects a world of art that stands apart from other modes of activity. Yet this world for Wagner does not exist in a timeless realm but as the product and expression of what he calls the people (*Volk*).[11] Here Wagner is building on Hegel's historicization of artistic forms as well as manifesting the nationalist ideology that had been developing during the same period as the new ideology of autonomous art; indeed, part of Wagner's achievement in his tract is to link these ideologies together.

Just as earlier treatises had projected art as a realm independent of the everyday world, so Wagner defends the autonomy of art by contrasting it with what he calls fashion (*Mode*; *WGS*, 10: 65–67), which, though his argument remains abstract throughout, he associates with attributes such as "custom," "egoism," and "unnaturalness." As in the earlier treatises, much, in fact, most of Wagner's discussion centers around the individual forms and genres of art. The three principal forms—principal because for Wagner they are purely human (*reinmenschlich*), created by human beings without the need for nonhuman materials (*WGS*, 10: 74)—are dance, music, and poetry. One might note that the last two of these three correspond to the two highest of Hegel's three "romantic arts." Unlike his predecessors Wagner does not view art as a finished product but speaks rather of the "capability" of creating and expressing art (*Kunstfähigkeit*; *WGS*, 10: 74). One notes here the stress on activity, which implies performance on the part of creator and performer, and, not least important within this politically motivated theory, on the part of the communal audience. The subsidiary arts, separated from the principal ones through their need to utilize nonhuman materials, encompass architecture, sculpture, and painting, the first two corresponding to the arts of Hegel's earlier periods, the third, to the first and lowest of Hegel's romantic arts.

Among the three principal arts, poetry, and in particular poetic drama (again as in Hegel and indeed in most aesthetic theorists before Wagner), occupies the top of the hierarchy. Here Wagner projects the ideal ages in which poetic drama achieved its apogee, fifth-century Greece and Elizabethan England (both examples echoing the canonization of these two periods a half century before in German romantic criticism); in both instances Wagner proposes a genre originating in the spirit of the *Volk*, who at the same time are transformed into the audience that experiences the genre. Tragedy in fact at one point is called a people's drama (*Volkskunstwerk*; *WGS*, 10: 111). Wagner's idealization of poetic drama, and of tragedy in particular, is the springboard from which he is then able to project a rebirth of the genre in the form of that new union of the various arts in which his argument culminates.

If one is surprised to find a composer placing drama "above" music, it may seem even more surprising that Wagner's discussion of music as an art includes only the briefest allusions to opera. The opera aria at one point is revealed to be a degeneration of the folk song, and opera as an institution becomes associated with the world of "fashion" (*WGS*, 10: 97–98). Wagner's long section on music centers not around any vocal form but around the symphony, which emerges as the highest manifestation of musical form, above all through the examples of Haydn, Mozart, and Beethoven (97–98). Wagner here shows himself as the heir to the deification of instrumental or absolute music that, as I indicated earlier, goes back to the speculations of the early German romantics.[12] Indeed, here and in the discussion of Greek and Elizabethan tragedy in the following section Wagner cunningly sets up a genealogy that legitimizes and in effect celebrates his own later practice of fusing symphony with poetic drama. The disparagement (or neglect) of opera evident throughout the history of German aesthetics serves Wagner quite advantageously, for he can reject opera at least as strongly as his predecessors at the same time that he proposes a new form that lies wholly within the precincts of that higher mode called "art."

As Wagner moves toward proposing his new union of the various arts, he returns to opera briefly to seek out models that may serve, in effect, as precursors. The names he comes up with are Gluck and Mozart, the same ones who provided positive examples of operatic art (when such examples were invoked at all) within earlier treatises (*WGS*, 10: 129–30). As a result, the genealogy he creates for his own musical dramas (still uncomposed at the time of this tract) can encompass the classical symphony, the major tragedies of drama's two highest ages, and the operas of the two earlier composers who possessed the seriousness appropriate to what had come to count as art.

The actual union that Wagner proposes is by no means a neutral composite of the arts but one in which the various arts are subsumed under drama, a notion quite in keeping with the pride of place that drama plays in Wagner's and most of his predecessors' hierarchies of the arts. "The highest collective work of art is drama," he writes; "it can only reach its *full potential* if *every form of art* is present in its *highest intensity*" (*WGS*, 10: 158, italics Wagner's). Since the concept of "people" (*Volk*) is central to Wagner's theory both as the origin of art and as the public to which art must communicate, the people's need comes to authorize the proposed union: "Each individual form of art is able to reveal itself to the *full understanding* of the collective public only by means of a joint communication with the remaining art forms within the domain of drama, for the purpose of each individual art form is fully realized only in the working together of all art forms to achieve mutual understanding with one another" (*WGS*, 10: 158, italics Wagner's). Thus the three principal forms, dance (broadly conceived to include gesture and stage movement in general), music, and poetry join the three subsidiary forms to establish the new composite form. Architecture will find an obvious role in the design of an ideal theater (the realization of Bayreuth was still a quarter century in the future), and painting will find its natural niche in stage décor. Even sculpture has a place, if only in the sense that the performer will work in the spirit of the sculptor "in the manipulation and management of his actual body" (*WGS*, 10: 162).

Wagner's crudely stated theory would be of relatively little interest if it were not supported by the example of the great musical works that followed in its wake, not to speak of the radical shift in the history of opera that these works made possible. Yet this theory is also heir to a whole century of thinking about the nature of art—its origins, its value among other human endeavors, its divisions and their worth in relation to one another. Even the notion of the *Gesamtkunstwerk*, so closely associated with Wagner's theory and practice, can be seen as the culmination of a desire for a union of the arts that goes back to the beginnings of the form and that was voiced repeatedly during the century before Wagner.

Yet Wagner came to change one important aspect of his theory. Whereas drama was the genre within which the remaining arts came together in *The Artwork of the Future*, ultimately music was to take over the reins. This shift was not simply the product of an artist whose vocation had always been that of a composer (no matter what his pretensions to making drama), but above all it came out of a new philosophical allegiance, namely, to the work of Schopenhauer. Although *The World as Will and Representation* had been published in 1819, it did not achieve a wide readership until the 1850s, after Wagner had published *The Artwork of the Future* and its companion work, *Opera and Drama*, which together were intended to lay the theoretical groundwork of his practice. At the suggestion of the poet Georg Herwegh, Wagner read Schopenhauer in 1854. If Wagner's espousal of drama as the highest art represented a continuation of mainstream aesthetic theory, his new enthusiasm for Schopenhauer led him not only to champion what had been a dissenting voice on the ordering of the arts but also, as I point out in Chapter 5, to change the ending of *Der Ring des Nibelungen* from an earlier Feuerbachian optimism to a Schopenhauer-inspired pessimism.[13] Once Wagner's aesthetic allegiance had taken this new turn he could speak of his works not as music-drama (a term he rejected because, among other things, it made music sound secondary) but as "deeds of music made visible" (*WGS*, 13: 123).[14] The ultimate triumph of music as *primus inter pares* within this union of the arts is confirmed in the subtitle, *Out of the Spirit of Music*, that Wagner's sometime disciple Friedrich Nietzsche gave to his *Birth of Tragedy* (1872), the most influential statement of the nature and effect of art in the later nineteenth century.

Wagner's rejection of opera in its traditional forms was echoed in a particularly emphatic way when Nietzsche, in a passage of *The Birth of Tragedy* that prepares his own celebration of Wagner's achievement, denied opera the crucial argument for justifying its preeminence as an art form, namely, its self-representation as the rebirth of Greek tragedy.[15] Nietzsche directs his critique at the theorists and practitioners who created the *stile rappresentativo*: by giving text primacy over music, the operatic founding fathers were catering to what he called a "nonaesthetic need" totally foreign to the "Apollinian and Dionysian impulses" that, earlier in his book, Nietzsche had described as central to the experience of Greek tragedy.[16] When Nietzsche describes this style as "an alternation of emotionally impressive speech . . . half sung with interjections which are wholly sung" (115), it is doubtful that he had actually examined the earliest operatic scores, which cultivate recitative with relatively little hint of full song. Yet this alternation of recitative and song is of course central to the later history of opera, which Nietzsche condemns not simply as "nonaesthetic" but as "the birth of theoretical man" (116), as "Alexandrian cheerfulness" (118), and as "Socratism" (119), all of which Nietzsche views as key attributes of his own degenerate age and which he seeks to surmount through his example of Greek tragedy as the experience of Apollinian and Dionysian impulses.

Nietzsche uses Schiller's essay *On Naive and Sentimental Poetry* (1795) as a historical model to support his rejection of the purported rebirth of Greek tragedy in the guise of opera. Applying Schiller's scheme, Nietzsche argues that whereas Greek tragedy was a product of the "naive," of a relation with "the heart of nature" in its immediacy (117), early opera was an attempt to recapture this immediacy by an act of will, just as, to use Schiller's own examples, Virgil or Milton's attempts at epic were the willed efforts of modern, "sentimental" (or, more properly translated, self-reflective) poets to invoke the immediacy of Homer in a world that no longer made possible Homer's direct relation to nature. The genre to which Nietzsche assigns opera is the idyll, which in Schiller's argument is one of the characteristic genres available to the modern poet. The idyll for Schiller celebrates the restoration of an image from a primitive age, or, to cite one of Schiller's examples, Milton's image of primal innocence in the Garden of Eden. This restoration for Schiller is at best a simulation, and his essay throughout expresses an ambivalence, regretting the loss of a past condition at the same time that it seeks to accept the limitations of the present.

Whereas Schiller's theory sought to renew the confidence of modern writers (and, by implication, his own self-confidence in his role as poet) who despaired of emulating the great writers of the past, Nietzsche stresses the false confidence inherent in any attempt such as that of opera's founders to simulate a lost primordial state. "The features of the opera do not by any means exhibit the elegiac sorrow of an eternal loss," he writes, "but rather the cheerfulness of eternal rediscovery, the comfortable delight in an idyllic reality which one can at least always image as real." Having unmasked this falseness, Nietzsche heightens his rhetoric to express his disgust: "In this process one may some day grasp the fact that this supposed reality is nothing but a fantastically silly dawdling, at which everyone who could . . . compare it with actual primitive scenes of the beginnings of mankind [scenes such as those that Nietzsche, earlier in his essay, had envisioned in describing the horrendous experience of the ancient Greek audience] would be impelled to call out nauseated: Away with the phantom!" (118) In view of Nietzsche's later writings, we can recognize this critique of opera not simply as a contribution to aesthetics but as a statement about his culture. Opera, or at least its pre-Wagnerian variety, here is associated with the false optimism, the Socratic rationalism, the "Alexandrian flatteries" (118) he finds characteristic of his own decadent age. It is significant, for instance, that §19 of *The Birth of Tragedy*, from which I have been quoting, begins with the statement, "We cannot indicate the inner modern content of this Socratic culture more distinctly than by calling it *the culture of the opera* [*die Kultur der Oper*]" (114, italics Nietzsche's). As a form that makes grand aesthetic pretensions but that Nietzsche considers "nonaesthetic" at its core, opera thus becomes the first major example in Nietzsche's writings of the decadence that he finds endemic within modern culture and that his subsequent philosophy attempts to overcome.

Yet one can find opera attacked as an inferior art form long before Nietzsche's critique in *The Birth of Tragedy*, indeed, well before the aesthetic treatises I discussed in the preceding section. One can cite, for instance, Saint-Évremond's well-known letter of 1678 to the Duke of Buckingham complaining of the "fatigue" that opera induces, of its "ridiculousness," of its inability, unlike tragedy, "to elevate the Soul, or . . . form the Mind"[17]; or one can cite, as I do in Chapter 2, the composer Benedetto Marcello's hilarious satire of 1720, *Il teatro alla moda*, with its colorful examples of singers, librettists, composers, and designers exercising their egos to plague the life of the opera impresario and compromise whatever artistic product might result from their mutual collaboration; or one can cite the countless descriptions throughout the eighteenth century of raucous, inattentive audiences at performances in which star singers do whatever they please regardless of what composers or librettists ever had in mind. Among the reasons for the growing prestige of nonvocal music since the early nineteenth century is the fact that the number of aesthetic compromises necessary to perform this music is radically less than that required for opera; although what came to be called absolute music demands concrete realization in an auditorium as surely as opera, most of the variously competing interests—rival singers, dancers, designers, as well as librettist in the case of new operas—could simply be eliminated.

Wagner's most striking example of the abuses within the "culture of the opera" is his depiction of his onetime benefactor Meyerbeer as the quintessentially commercial composer who depends on what Wagner memorably calls "effects without causes" for the *coups de théâtre* that keep his audiences enthralled.[18] In the essay "Richard Wagner in Bayreuth," Nietzsche's final acclamation of his master before his break with him, the disciple acknowledges how Wagner had begun his career within Meyerbeer's aesthetic and only later had "his eyes opened to the 'artistic devices' the artist was virtually obliged to employ in order to achieve success with the audience." Out of his despair at recognizing his error, Wagner, according to Nietzsche, came to understand the nature of "modern success, the nature of the modern public and the whole mendacious nature of modern art [*Kunst-Lügenwesen*]." As a result of this recognition, Wagner, who had "started out with such a tremendous error and who so uncritically and guilelessly pursued the most revolting form of his art," ultimately found his own way and discovered "that he was still a composer, still an artist—indeed, that he had only now become one."[19]

The sharp dichotomies that Nietzsche and, before him, Wagner himself set up between what can and should count as art and non-art highlight a continuing problem in discussions of opera in relation to other forms of art. If the French grand operas for which Meyerbeer serves as Wagner's chief whipping boy rank in operatic history as particularly oriented toward monetary success, one must also remember that opera, since within a generation of its foundation, has been at least partially (and, in many instances, even mostly) dependent upon financial support from its immediate audience. With the establishment of the first Venetian theater for opera in 1637, opera must surely rank as the first market-driven musical art. And although aristocratic or royal support helped sustain it to varying degrees in its subsequent venues, the perceived need to offer immediate pleasure to its public—whether in the form of superhuman vocal display, bewitching stage illusions, or startling turns of plot—remained central to its institutional survival. Combine this need with the fact that it has always been a composite art form—demanding the collaboration of artists representating different métiers with often conflicting agendas (not to speak of the agendas of those who oversee its financing)—and it scarcely seems surprising that it has often fallen short of meeting whatever standards of art have reigned in a particular time and place.

Wagner, as it turned out, provided an alternative to opera's inability to live up to the standards of what had come to be defined as art. If opera as an institution was incapable of producing and sustaining art, Wagner would create his own institutional framework in which he could control those competing forces that militated against what he saw as artistic integrity. His first step was to become his own librettist, which meant that he eliminated the most glaring difficulty a composer faced in establishing control over his product. At the same time he retheorized opera to provide it with a rationale compatible with his notion of art. In founding his own theater at Bayreuth (see Figure 10), Wagner was able to bypass the competing wills of the diverse talents necessary to realize a performing art, for at Bayreuth, even if his theater could operate only sporadically as a "festival" occasion, he could exercise the individual control that a nonperforming artist such as a poet or painter ordinarily wielded over his work.

The result was a one-man institution intended as an alternative to what he viewed as that corrupt institution—a network of competing interests ultimately dominated by the paying public and well-heeled patrons—that defined opera in his day. In Bayreuth he would wield total control over all the resources that go into the production of opera. The darkened auditorium, the orchestra hidden beneath the stage, the singers and designers all subservient to the master—all these attest to an imperial authority beautifully encapsulated in Nietzsche's image of Wagner appearing like Alexander the Great as he rode back to the center of Bayreuth after he had laid the cornerstone to the Festspielhaus in 1872.[20] The power that Wagner sought to exercise, indeed, often succeeded in exercising, is perhaps suggested by two juxtaposed images, the first (Figure 11) a photo of an adolescent Nietzsche at the time that his hero-worship for Wagner began, the second (Figure 12), Adolph Menzel's caricature of the master supervising a rehearsal of the *Ring* during the year before Bayreuth opened. Only in the nineteenth century, with its peculiarly

FIG. 10. The Bayreuth Festspielhaus as painted in 1873 from architectural plans before it was actually completed. Courtesy, Richard-Wagner-Archiv, Villa Wahnfried, Bayreuth.

elevated conception of art, can one imagine a composer compared to what Hegel would have called a "world-historical" figure; and just about the same time, as I point out in Chapter 3, Stendhal opened his book on Rossini saluting him as a new Napoleon. As it turned out, Wagner's imperium endured a good bit longer than Alexander's, at least to the extent that the festival he founded to enshrine his so-called musical deeds is still, a century and a quarter after the cornerstone was laid, controlled by his direct descendants (even if he could not, given his limited vision, have approved of the productions they authorize today).

Yet the Wagnerian institution has its own corruptions, as an older Nietzsche came to realize after attending the first Bayreuth festival in 1876 and seeing the master pandering to those powerful personages who had made the new institution financially possible in the first place.[21] However one may evaluate the artistic integrity of Wagner's enterprise, the handful of works

FIG. II. Nietzsche at seventeen in 1861, the year he first expressed his reverence for Wagner in a letter to his mother and sister. The two men did not meet until 1868. Courtesy, National-Archiv der Richard-Wagner-Stiftung, Bayreuth.

FIG. 12. Wagner conducting a rehearsal in 1875 of the first *Ring* in preparation for the opening of the Bayreuth Festspielhaus the following year. Chalk sketch by Adolph Menzel. Courtesy, Richard-Wagner-Archiv, Villa Wahnfried, Bayreuth.

mounted during the now-annual summer festival have represented only a small fraction of the performances that Wagner's operas have received over the years. Otherwise they have had to make their way as part of the general repertory of opera houses throughout the world—with singers, directors, designers, and impresarios exercising their usual self-interest, regardless of the aesthetic consequences, just as they do for the operas of Donizetti, Verdi, and Puccini.

Nietzsche's reference to Wagner as a new Alexander the Great, or Stendhal's to Rossini as another Napoleon, masks the fact that throughout most of the history of opera, the composer, as I stress in Chapter 1, has not counted unambiguously as the creator of his work. In the separate roles assigned to librettist and composer (except for those occasions when composers such as Berlioz and Wagner fulfilled both roles) the librettist has often commanded more prestige than the composer. To put it another way, although a certain adulation has been directed at major opera composers ever since Monteverdi's time, librettists have been granted a special status different from and in certain ways higher than that accorded to the composers whom they supplied with words. One remembers Hegel's reference to the "many talented composers" who were also "the most ignorant and empty-headed of men." By the same token Hegel and other aesthetic theorists (except of course Schopenhauer and his much-later followers) generally placed literature higher than music—not to speak of painting—in their hierarchies of the arts. One could surely speak of a bias in favor of the verbal characterizing those who determine status within the arts.

If one examines the backgrounds of the operatic canon's creators, one quickly finds that librettists occupy a niche on the social and educational scale that, at least up to the twentieth century, has been deemed higher than that occupied by their musical collaborators. The seeming incommensurability in the careers of Rossini and Shelley with which I began Chapter 3 represents a gap between two institutions, music and literature, both with their own traditions, missions, and biases. Composers, as often as not, had musicians as parents (Bach, Mozart, Beethoven, Rossini), and when their fathers came from other backgrounds, the latter scarcely counted as "elevated": Handel, for instance, was the son of a barber-surgeon, Haydn of a wheelwright, Gluck of a forester, Verdi of an innkeeper.

The training that a composer received, though often quite rigorous, did not stray beyond the bounds of music. By contrast, librettists generally came from more highly educated families and, as practitioners of a verbal art, could claim a more wide-ranging education than their musical partners. To cite the librettists of Monteverdi's three extant operas, Alessandro Striggio (*Orfeo*) was a nobleman and diplomat, and Giacomo Badoaro (*Ulisse*) and Francesco Busenello (*Poppea*) not only came from prominent Venetian families but were members of the Accademia degl' Incogniti, a literary circle in which the composer for whom they wrote, despite his great fame at the time, would scarcely have been welcome. In the eighteenth century Metastasio, though an adopted child, was raised by a jurist and had himself studied law before taking up literature. Gluck's foreword to *Alceste*, one of the canonical pronouncements in the history of operatic theory, is thought to have been drafted by the composer's verbally more skillful librettist Ranieri Calsabigi.[22] Lorenzo da Ponte, for all his roguishness, had taught literature in a seminary before his brief encounter with Mozart and, indeed, ended his life teaching Italian to college students in the United States. Imperious though Verdi could be toward his various librettists, the latter generally counted as more "educated" in their particular worlds: Francesco Piave, for example, had studied rhetoric and philosophy, and Antonio Somma had practiced law. Even during the twentieth century, long after music had come to rival literature in the hierarchy of the arts, a study of the correspondence between Richard Strauss and Hugo von Hofmannsthal shows the composer playing the role of a bumpkinish bourgeois while the librettist takes full advantage of his august role as man of letters.

Music bows to literature in still another sense: whereas the literary work exists as a text that can be consumed by a large number of people, music, to be experienced, is dependent upon performance, and above all on the interpretations of diverse individuals. To be sure, there have been times when a relatively large part of the educated class was able to read scores and try them out on the keyboard, but this is certainly not true in our own time. Whereas literary classics have retained their own life within the educational system, the musical classics have always occupied a relatively peripheral place in schools. During the Middle Ages, for instance, music, which was treated as one of the four mathematical arts called the quadrivium, belonged to a category different from that of the three verbal arts—grammar, dialectic, and rhetoric—making up the trivium. While the study of music was essentially theoretical, with Pythagorean notions of harmony rather than actual musical works the center of focus, students of the verbal arts traditionally drew their examples from whatever literary works exercised authority at a particular time.

Even those verbal arts created to be performed, most notably oratory and drama, have circulated since antiquity in written texts that maintain a life separate from the performances in which they originated or, as with drama, with which they get revived on later occasions. The text of a drama can count as a literary work just as a lyric poem or a novel does, and it can be experienced by large numbers of readers in private; by contrast, the score of an opera is accessible to only those few who have developed the skills to read it adequately. And while a poetic drama may "gain" something when spoken by live actors, a competent reader can bring the intricacies of its language to life more fully than even a well-trained reader of scores can recreate the roulades of a singer from the page (if, indeed, they were even written out at all by the composer).

Although I have spoken of opera throughout this chapter as an entity in the singular, this in no way denies the differences in style and effect among operas composed even during identical periods of time. From the later seventeenth century, when French opera was founded, until at least the early twentieth century it was customary for commentators on and historians of opera to speak of particular national styles or schools (the latter term being analogous to the techniques of painting practiced in individual places). No two styles of opera sound as radically different to the ear, or look as different to the eye, as the French and Italian styles of the later seventeenth and the early eighteenth centuries. With its ceremonious fusion of dance and music, its dependence on an understated and flowing vocal line, and its mythological themes, French opera as realized by Lully and, even several generations later, by Rameau scarcely occupies the same generic territory as its contemporaneous Italian counterpart, with its alternation of aria and recitative, its vocal display, its castrati, and its stories purportedly drawn from history. Indeed, these two forms (despite Lully's Italian origins) on first hearing seem almost as far apart as either do from the so-called Peking opera, a highly conventionalized form originating in the late eighteenth century and given the term "opera" by Westerners simply because, like its Western equivalents, it presents a drama by means of song accompanied by instruments—though its song bears less resemblance to the aria of European opera than it does to that amalgam of speech and music that Schoenberg developed under the name *Sprechstimme*.[23] It is scarcely an accident that the two famed operatic "wars" of eighteenth-century France—the Guerre des Bouffons of the early 1750s and the Gluckiste-Piccinniste battle a generation later—revolved around the relative worth of the French and the Italian styles. In the nineteenth-century repertory, no two styles look more distinct than those practiced by Wagner and Verdi during the 1850s. Or, to anticipate the argument of Chapter 7, how does one account for the same generic term used for two works, both composed in late Weimar Germany around 1930, that are as diverse in style and in the audiences for which they were intended as Schoenberg's *Moses und Aron* and Weill's *Mahagonny*?

And yet the term "opera" has maintained its hold for fully four centuries over a wide spectrum of works that have in common merely the fact that they enact a play by means of instrumentally accompanied song. Among musical forms only the mass, sustained as it has been by the authority of religious institutions, has had a longer continuing tradition. (I assume here that those long-standing genres we call the "song" and "fantasia" are too much individually defined by place, period, and composer to exhibit the same continuity.) Despite the diversity of national and period styles the generic designation "opera" and its cognates in various languages have persisted throughout the form's four centuries. Opera sometimes of course sports a qualifying adjective such as *buffa* or *comique*—or, to cite the special term that Wagner attached to

Lohengrin, romantische Oper—to indicate its particular genealogy. The word *Singspiel,* which includes such repertory items as *Die Entführung aus dem Serail* and *Die Zauberflöte,* circumvents the term to signal the use of ordinary speech between arias. And certainly the earliest works claimed for operatic history employed their own generic terminology: the Caccini *L'Euridici composta in musica in stile rappresentativo* (1600) announces the new style in its title, while the Monteverdi *Orfeo,* called *favola in musica,* stresses the narrative over the music quite in keeping with the composer's theory of the relation of words to music. There are of course occasional designations such as *dramma giocoso* (*Don Giovanni, Così fan tutte, Il viaggio a Reims*), *Bühnenweihfestspiel* (*Parsifal*), *commedia lirica* (*Falstaff*), and *Komödie für Musik* (*Der Rosenkavalier*) that avoid the word "opera" altogether.

From an institutional point of view, what holds together that mixed bag of works called operas is the fact that they are performed in theaters especially dedicated to them. Ever since the first public house opened in Venice in 1637, opera has been associated with specific buildings in the various sites in which it takes place. The opera house, one might say, frames and differentiates the events that transpire within it as surely as the church frames the mass. To be sure, in many smaller cities opera, nonmusical drama, and ballet share quarters; outside the anglophone domain, in fact, the ballet company is usually part of the opera, supplying the dances written into operatic scores while also offering independent performances without speech or song. Yet despite such arrangements, the generic boundaries of opera remain evident. In larger centers since the eighteenth century the boundary has often been marked by the presence of a separate house for lighter fare such as the Paris Opéra Comique. The recent phenomenon of Viennese operettas and early Broadway musicals making their way into the opera house in no way destroys the generic boundary but simply points to the fact that newer forms of light fare—for example, rock-inspired musicals—now come to mark opera's lower boundary.

As though to mark a higher boundary, the concert hall developed in the course of the nineteenth century to offer a supplementary and, for those dedicated to that new concept of absolute music, an alternative institution. In cities large and generous enough to support still another theater one finds the small recital hall, which, assigned as it is to those less sonorous forms, chamber music and lieder, demarcates a still higher boundary. It is significant that the concert and the recital hall, through the absence of a capacious stage as well as of backstage areas, can avert the scenic and histrionic distractions associated with opera. Yet opera has so embedded itself within European culture that it has sometimes invaded precincts consecrated to a supposedly higher form of music: note, for instance, how those two nonoperatic composers and virtuosi, Chopin and Liszt, customarily regaled their audiences with their fantasias and sets of variations drawn from the operas popular in their day. In his "Réminiscences de Don Juan" (1841), for example, Liszt plays upon his audiences' familiarity with such tunes from *Don Giovanni* as the champagne aria and "La ci darem la mano," which, wholly without scenic or vocal display, emerge in the recital hall with a dramatic flair that make their embodiment within the opera house seem tame by comparison. And as Charles Rosen has recently suggested, Liszt's audiences would have experienced this piece within an even larger frame of reference, namely, their knowledge that the composer and performer of this piece was himself a breathing reincarnation of Mozart's hero.[24]

Opera displays its institutional identity not simply in the venues that it inhabits but also in the interchanges that transpire among these venues. Since the late seventeenth century there has existed an international system whereby singers, composers, librettists, designers, and orchestral musicians have moved from one opera house to another. During much of this time the system was dominated by the reigning Italian style of the moment, with Italian-language companies (though often using the talents of non-Italian composers) resident within a triangle defined by London, St. Petersburg, and Naples. Over two centuries before jet travel allowed singers to move from one production to another each month or two, audiences inside this triangle could experience some of the world's most celebrated voices within the course of several seasons. Despite the repeated complaints from proponents of operatic reform about the aesthetic abuses to which the form was being subjected, the system retained a self-sustaining power that often stifled attempts at change. Within Italy in the late eighteenth and early nineteenth centuries an impresario-dominated and commercially motivated system kept the system's various participants (including great composers such as Rossini and Verdi) moving frantically and subserviently among the various operatic centers to satisfy the system's needs.[25] The demands of a complex system, above all one that is as driven by political and economic forces as opera has been throughout much of its history, are not necessarily compatible with the notions of what constitutes art that developed in the age of the great aesthetic treatises.

In our own time, the interchange of personnel that has long served to give opera an identity has, with the technological changes of recent decades, proceeded with far greater intensity and rapidity than before. Not only do musicians move freely about the globe, but so do sets and costumes—with the result that directors and designers play a more crucial role in defining the audience's experience of opera than they have before. The operatic exchanges in our time have also helped create a peculiar phenomenon—the new opera specially commissioned by a whole consortium of companies throughout the operatic world. Critics have long bemoaned the fact that the creation of new operas—at least new operas that the public might clamor for—gradually came to a halt early in the twentieth century, with the result that the repertory consisted of classics of the past, with an occasional new opera dutifully smuggled in despite the expected displeasure of the audience. Yet a number of new operas—one thinks of John Adams's *Nixon in China* and *The Death of Klinghoffer*, several Philip Glass operas, and others by far lesser composers—have turned out to please more than to threaten their audiences. Like Italian operas in Rossini's and the young Verdi's time, these operas tend to be impresario-activated: one or more opera directors bring together a team of talents representing the various arts that constitute opera, with the result that the music once again becomes only one and often not even the most important component within the fabrication. Many of these operas, like the two Adams pieces mentioned above, are based on recent news events (quite in contrast to the distant historical themes of *opera seria*), and some recreate famous books (*Les Liaisons dangereuses*, *McTeague*) or the biographies of celebrated personages (John Ruskin, Harvey Milk, Mohandas Gandhi) whose lives excite popular curiosity. Generally the composers are considerably below the stature of an Adams or a Glass—though no worse, one suspects, than the many composers setting Metastasian texts during the heyday of *opera seria*. If projects such as these, together with postmodern challenges to the tradition such as John Cage's collage opera, typify the form at the close of the twentieth century, operatic creation today seems a far cry from Wagner's *Ring des Nibelungen*—that monumental, four-evening-long attempt to ground opera as the loftiest imaginable art whose unique place in the history of the various arts is the subject of the next chapter.

Chapter Five

Wagner's *Ring* as Nineteenth-Century Artifact

Suppose that Wagner had died in 1853, exactly thirty years before his actual death. At this point he would have left behind at least three operas that count for us as major works: *The Flying Dutchman*, *Tannhäuser*, and *Lohengrin*. Most important for the ideas I hope to develop in this chapter, he also would have left behind the libretto for another set of operas, namely the *Ring*. Early in 1853 he had fifty copies of this libretto printed privately for friends. Had he died at the time it would surely have been necessary for some propagandist to enter the scene and call attention to the importance of Richard Wagner as a cultural phenomenon. After all, throughout the thirty years of which we have just deprived him, Wagner, among other activities, himself assumed the role of propagandist for his own works—and, one might add, with the most considerable success.

If, let us say, someone other than Wagner had convinced the world of the worth of Wagner's completed operas,[1] scholars would no doubt have made a big thing of the *Ring* text—to the point, surely, of trying to extrapolate what might have happened musically in those unfortunately never-to-be-composed works. At least they would have found the musical sketches that Wagner had made early in the composition of the text—though it is unlikely they could have reconstructed the musical style we now associate with Wagnerian music-drama.[2] Certainly Wagner would have left a number of tantalizing theoretical writings, above all *The Artwork of the Future* and *Opera and Drama*, from which one might have made some informed guesses about the direction in which the composer was going. Indeed, these writings possess such suggestive power—as the extensive use to which I have put them in Chapter 4 should demonstrate—that they might well have goaded some other composer to move in this particular direction.

Yet one still wonders what posterity might have made of the 1853 *Ring* text. This text, let me explain, is very close to the *Ring* libretto that the real-life Wagner subsequently set to music. Except for minor verbal changes here and there, plus some rewriting of the first act of *Siegfried*, the only substantive change that Wagner made, as I point out later, was in the ending. But my concern at the moment is what we would make of the text if we did not have the completed musical score. Would the text be taken seriously by literary scholars? Would those ordinary readers who enjoy reading plays want to include *Der Ring des Nibelungen* among the pile of Shakespeare, Racine, and Ibsen dramas they make their way through? Even more telling, would theaters, even those state-subsidized German theaters not subject to the financial risks experienced by companies in the English-speaking world, be tempted to realize Wagner's text on the stage?

It would be hard, I admit, to answer these questions in the affirmative. Without the musical dimension that Wagner intended for his text, the *Ring* would excite little interest for readers or theatergoers. I make this statement in full knowledge that Wagner doubtless attributed a literary value to his text in addition to its role as part of the whole musical-dramatic complex in which it was eventually to take part. After all, he saw fit to print it for his friends and to give occasional readings of it. Although it is unlikely, if we lacked the music, that we would appreciate the text today for its literary value, we might still recognize it as a strange curiosity, something unlike any other opera libretto. Indeed, I can well imagine that the *Ring* libretto might retain a minor place in German literary history simply because it seeks a new linguistic mode to recapture the spirit of a lost national past. Whereas Wagner's earlier operas used a fairly conventional language, with the rhyme, meters, and diction characteristic of the poetry of their day, even a cursory look at any page of the *Ring* text tells us that we are facing what must be called a serious literary experiment.

I open at random to Wotan's words just before the entrance to Valhalla:

Abendlich strahlt	Evening rays flood
der Sonne Auge;	the sky with splendour;
in pracht'ger Gluth	those glorious beams
prangt glänzend die Burg:	shine there on my hall.
in des Morgen's Scheine	In the morning radiance
muthig erschimmernd,	bravely it glistened,
lag sie herrenlos	standing masterless,
hehr verlockend vor mir.	proud, awaiting its lord.[3]

Note the alliterations—*pracht'ger* and *prangt*, *herrenlos* and *hehr*, *Morgen's* and *muthig*. Note also the abrupt shifting of the places where one would expect to hear accents: instead of alternating stressed and unstressed syllables, as German poets (including even the anonymous poet of the Middle High German *Nibelungenlied*) had done for centuries, Wagner has used an entirely different metrical system, and we hear "in des MORGen's SCHEINe MUTHig erSCHIMMernd." Moreover, the words that Wagner chooses are based as much as possible on Germanic root words, and he avoids Latinate forms with equal fervor. Anybody reading this text in 1853 would have known at once that these lines are different from the style of German opera librettos (including those for Wagner's own earlier operas) and from the styles that German lyric and dramatic poets had been cultivating. Wagner's educated readers would also have recognized that he was consciously imitating the sound of early medieval heroic poetry—in particular the alliterative and accent-based verse of the Old Norse *Poetic Edda*.[4]

Wagner's metrical experiment, bold though it may be, is of course a manifestation of the medievalism that marks much of the painting and architecture as well as the writing of the nineteenth century. What he attempted to do with language in the *Ring* is analogous to the experimentation of a great English religious poet, someone far removed in sensibility, though not in time, from Wagner. I refer to Gerard Manley Hopkins. Note the conspicuous alliterations, the strange accent patterns, and the predominantly Germanic diction of these lines from "The Wreck of the Deutschland," a poem of the mid-1870s:

It dates from day
Of his going in Galilee;
Warm-laid grave of a womb-life grey;
Manger, maiden's knee;
The dense and the driven Passion, and frightful sweat.[5]

Both Wagner's and Hopkins's passages would have seemed strange to their first readers. Like Wagner with the first version of the *Ring*, Hopkins circulated his poems only among friends, one of whom, Robert Bridges, finally arranged for their publication at the end of the First World War, some thirty years after his death. In the work of both Wagner and Hopkins, one notes an attempt to challenge the reigning conventions of the poetry of their time, as well as to get literally to the roots of their respective languages. For both poets had faith that by invoking and evoking an earlier form of their language they could get at the roots of *things* as well as of words. Wagner even discussed alliteration in *Opera and Drama*—written during the very years in which he was preoccupied with the *Ring* text—and he expressed his faith that an alliterative poetic language, together with an attempt to select words that revealed their ancient roots, could create an immediacy of communication with its listeners impossible within those styles that derived from later moments in the history of culture.[6]

My juxtaposition of Wagner with Hopkins may seem unfair. Both passages certainly read like bold experiments even today, and a first exposure in each instance is likely to put the reader off. Yet as one absorbs Hopkins's verse, it comes to read with a rightness that one associates with the greatest poetry. The same cannot be said for Wagner's verse, fascinating though his experimentation with language may be. If Wagner had left nothing more than the 1853 text for us, it is hard to believe that we should have seen it as much more than that—a fascinating experiment. After many readings I must say that, unlike Hopkins's poetry, it does not manage to acclimate itself to the ear. The difference in quality between the two poets can be explained not simply by reference to value terms such as the word "greatest" that I just invoked (though I am personally convinced that Hopkins was a far better poet than

Wagner), but also by the fact that whereas Hopkins's example helped shape much twentieth-century poetry in English (one thinks above all of poets such as W. H. Auden, Dylan Thomas, and John Berryman), Wagner's verbal experiments, quite unlike his musical experiments, remained essentially a dead-end within the history of German poetry.

Yet while I read through Wagner's lines I know I can bring them to life simply by letting my ear simulate the music he later wrote for them; and it is no accident that those lines that seem most readable on their own are precisely those whose musical settings are most memorable. As with nearly all librettos, the text of the *Ring* simply is not complete without the music. I suspect that the praise we customarily mete out to certain librettos—and the *Ring* libretto has elicited a high degree of praise over the years[7]—derives largely from our admiration for the music that was composed for them and for the total dramatic complex that music, words, and stage action have come to achieve in actual performance. Even those librettos that are very readable on their own—one thinks above all of the ones that Hofmannsthal wrote for Strauss—would probably count as fairly minor if also quite respectable affairs within a purely literary canon.[8]

Thus far I have stressed the significance of the *Ring* text as an experiment with poetic language—an attempt to restore the linguistic forms of the early Middle Ages to poetry and, as a consequence, to communicate structures of emotion that Wagner associated with this earlier period to his own time. Even if this experiment is not successful without the music that Wagner later wrote for the text, it also links Wagner to certain ways of thinking that we now see as central to his time. During the early nineteenth century the great works of medieval Germanic literature, both those written in Old Norse and in Middle High German, became known to readers for the first time since these earlier linguistic forms had ceased being used. Indeed, by looking at Wagner's text without the music, we are able to see with special clarity how rooted the *Ring* is within the culture of its own time.

The early nineteenth century in Germany was the great age of what we call philology—a field of inquiry that comprised at once the history of languages and of the literary artifacts that survived in these languages. To be a philologist in the early nineteenth century was to be at the forefront of knowledge—something like being a molecular biologist during the last decade or two, or an atomic physicist in the 1930s or 1940s. During the half century before Wagner completed his *Ring* text a number of philologists— names as legendary in the field as Jacob Grimm and Eduard Lachmann— had edited and annotated the Old Norse and Middle High German writings on which Wagner based his text, and many of them had also provided translations into modern German so that the general reader could experience these works. Wagner, I might add, made some attempt to master the early languages, though he is also known to have used these translations as cribs. Standing behind the *Ring* are an uncommonly wide variety of diverse texts stretching across several centuries of writing from Iceland to Germany. The principal texts from which Wagner drew his materials are the Middle High German epic the *Nibelungenlied*; two Old Norse heroic prose sagas, the *Völsungasaga* and *Thidrikssaga*; and both the *Prose Edda* and the *Poetic Edda*. But Wagner was not simply seeking out narrative situations—he also displayed an uncommon intellectual curiosity about the world in which these situations took place.

Philology in the early nineteenth century was what we would today call "area studies," for it encompassed not simply the language or literature of an area but its customs, its religion, its mythology, its general history. Wagner did not content himself with merely reading what we call "primary texts," but he read just as avidly in the scholarly literature that was fast accumulating during his day, including commentaries such as Jacob Grimm's *Deutsche Mythologie* and *Geschichte der deutschen Sprache* and Lachmann's *Zu den Nibelungen*. Considerable effort has gone into uncovering Wagner's own role as a philologist—to the point that we now know which books he owned and which he borrowed from the Dresden Royal Library while he was working on the *Ring* libretto.[9] Many key ideas that made their way into the *Ring* did not originate in Wagner's "literary" sources but in the scholarship he read about these sources: for instance, the central role of Wotan's spear was likely suggested by a passage in Wilhelm Müller's *Geschichte und System der altdeutschen Religion*, while his linking of Siegfried's death with the fall of the gods may well come from a passage in Lachmann's *Zu den Nibelungen* that challenges this very linkage by an earlier commentator![10] If Wagner himself, despite his lack of academic training, played the role of philologist, then his own achievement in creating the *Ring* has itself spawned a whole philological industry: indeed, the long series of source studies of the *Ring* goes back at least to 1875, almost a decade before the composer died and a year before the first performance of the whole tetralogy.[11]

Let us step back a moment and ask what it must have meant to dig up the national past, to seek a special significance in the way a Wotan established his rule or a Siegfried sought to give new life to his ancestors' fading empire through his own exemplary and heroic deeds. What we see here is an extraordinary faith in the significance of national experience at its earliest stages, indeed at its point of origins. This was a peculiarly nineteenth-century idea—something that earlier, multinational composers such as Handel, Gluck, and Mozart could never have conceived—and one that Wagner, in writing the *Ring*, participated in, experienced, and propagated to the fullest. Within the framework of this idea a modern individual's imputed ancestors of a millenium before, together with the world they inhabited, achieved a new and privileged status.

To those who read the old sagas and epics as they were being reprinted and translated, the world embedded in them must have seemed more "natural" than their own nineteenth-century world. In the course of the preceding century people had projected a dichotomy between what they saw as nature and what they saw as culture. The most fervent propagandist of this gap was doubtless Rousseau, who, a century before Wagner, made people question the value of the cultural forms that defined their own, seemingly advanced stage of civilization. In the late eighteenth century Herder built on the dichotomy between nature and culture elaborated by Rousseau to provide a justification for cultural identity that was at once historical and "natural." Herder popularized the view that the people sharing a particular language retained deep cultural bonds with one another and that these bonds could best be understood through the recovery of the early cultural products of this people, for example its folk songs and its folk epics.[12]

By the early nineteenth century ideas such as Rousseau's and Herder's had become major factors guiding and motivating the way serious people thought. To get back to the roots of one's national past was to know oneself better; it meant tapping something that seemed more authentic, more elemental than what could be experienced within the all-too-complex cultural forms of the modern world. The early nineteenth century thought not only in terms of origins, but also about where they could later lead: to grant a special privilege to one's origins is also to place a special emphasis on the evolutionary process that leads from these origins to where we are today.

"Origin" and "evolution" are key nineteenth-century concepts, and it is no accident that the most famous of all books tracing evolutionary process should have the word "origin" in its very title. In this sense the *Ring* text, even without its music, is a work that we can now see as very much a product of its time. Within this text Alberich's theft of the gold is the originary moment from which a long series of later events will be generated. These later events then come to constitute the evolution of the human race—or that segment of the race, in this instance the Nordic-Germanic segment, that happened to matter most to nineteenth-century Germans and, if we note the centrality that Wagner achieved within the cultural program of the Third Reich, to Germans until the mid-twentieth century as well.

We can thus see Wagner's reworking of his Old Norse and Middle High German sources as an attempt to embody this new attitude toward origins on both what could be called a "micro" and a "macro" level. On a micro level he evokes early Germanic man by means of his strange linguistic experiment— through the alliterative verse forms, the archaic language ("in prächt'ger Gluth / prangt"). On a macro level Wagner realizes this idea in the way that he organizes his material—beginning as he did with the beginning, as the Rhine maidens guard their gold, and then taking his plot down its multigenerational evolutionary path.

It is significant from this point of view that Wagner had not originally planned a tetralogy. He started in 1848 with an early form of the text we now know as *Götterdämmerung*, then called *Siegfrieds Tod*. Before that he had drafted a prose scenario of what was later to be all four plays, and in this scenario he had started with a description of Alberich's theft and had gone on to tell many, though by no means all of the events that were to follow in its wake.[13] Only after writing the first version of *Siegfrieds Tod* did he recognize that it wouldn't do simply to start at the end of the story and present earlier events in retrospective form—as classical drama had customarily done. Rather he would have to tell his story by starting with the origins themselves. And thus he worked backwards, moving on to write the text of *Siegfried* before he got to *Das Rheingold* and *Die Walküre*.

By the time he was done with the text in 1852 it was clear that this would be no ordinary opera. Wagner had of course announced in one of his theoretical writings during the preceding year that he was going to write no more operas.[14] But whatever the musical or dramatic form that the *Ring* was to take, one fact stands out. By encompassing four evenings instead of one, and by speaking out on matters such as the origins and the evolution of the nation, the *Ring*, in its largeness of scope and its cultural pretensions, seeks out a place for itself different in kind from that of any opera libretto written before it. The one earlier form that the *Ring* does bring to mind is what we have customarily called "epic," and I shall attempt to characterize Wagner's undertaking in light of what this term might have meant to him and his age. Despite the fact that the *Ring* retains the outward form of drama, Wagner's decision to shift from the retrospective form of narrative that originally characterized *Siegfrieds Tod* to one that enacts events widely spaced in time in their chronological order represents in effect a movement from a dramatic to an epic mode of narration. As such, Wagner's project challenges the generic identity that all earlier forms of opera, however different their other aesthetic premises, had taken for granted.

Before writing further of the *Ring*'s relation to epic, I will digress briefly to speak of the centrality that those works labeled epic have come to claim within Western culture. It is no accident that until recently every American university course on the "great" works of the past had to include one of the two Homeric epics, either the *Iliad* or the *Odyssey*, as well as Virgil's *Aeneid*. Both Homer and Virgil in their varying ways have been made to stand at the head of the epic tradition in the West. When we speak of the great epics we do not refer simply to long poems that tell stories—though length and a narrative mode of presentation are central to any definition of the epic. Our understanding of earlier epics encompasses considerably more than these elements, for it must also include the type of stories that epics tell and, at least as important, the type of relationship that the epic poet attempts to establish with his listeners or his readers. The major ancient and medieval epic poets, at least as they have come to be perceived since the late eighteenth century, saw themselves in a special relation to their communities, to whom they were seen imparting knowledge of their own national past and whose future direction and stability their poems intended to influence. Their role within the community often radiated something that would strike us today as a religious aura. In certain respects they came to be seen as comparable to the Hebraic prophets; even if these epic poets did not engage in lamentation as overtly as did the prophets, the role they played was considerably closer to that of these prophets than it was to that marginal role that people calling themselves poets play in our society today. The traditional epic poet's special relation to his community is something that Wagner remained keenly aware of, and one cannot fully understand what he was attempting in the *Ring* without noting that he himself sought to renew and continue this role.

Although I have linked Homer and Virgil as epic poets, and although for most of two millennia they have been lumped together by critics, one must remember that well before Wagner's time readers had become aware of the great differences in the conditions under which they wrote—differences that would of course affect the kinds of relationships they could establish with their later audiences. Since the mid-eighteenth century we have come to think of Homer as a poet of a far more "primitive" age than that of Virgil. The Virgil who emerged during the eighteenth century was a sophisticated urban poet who, in his attempt to help stabilize the new regime of his patron, the emperor Augustus, used the conventions and narrative method of the Homeric poems to celebrate and legitimate the ancient Roman past. Like the Homeric poems, many of the early medieval narratives that Wagner read and admired radiated a certain primitive power. They told of heroic feats and of vengeance for unspeakable deeds with an unself-conscious ease impossible within the more sophisticated literature that an urban society would produce. Thus the *Aeneid*, however well it may imitate the heroic deeds of the Homeric poems, came to be read as a more civilized and self-conscious work than its models. Similarly, the anonymous *Beowulf* and the *Nibelungenlied*—works that were not revived until after Homer and Virgil had become separated into radically different categories of epic—exercise their primitive power in a manner that their later imitators, among them of course Wagner, could never hope to emulate.

Not that the writing of even a Virgilian epic was still possible in Wagner's time. During and after the Renaissance, poets in the newly emerging vernacular literatures had sought to emulate Virgil by telling the stories of their own peoples in a deliberately lofty language, the most successful of these efforts doubtless being Camões's *The Lusiads*, on the heroic doings of his countryman Vasco da Gama. Otherwise the Renaissance Virgilian epics that remain central within the literary canon—the *Gerusalemme* of Tasso and Milton's *Paradise Lost*—are centered in the community of Christianity rather than of nation (though Milton had originally planned a national, Arthurian epic). Yet both recapture much of the territory that earlier epics had cultivated—by their encyclopedic range, by their attempt to impart wisdom to their respective communities, and by their formal, lofty tone.

By the nineteenth century, although poets throughout Europe often hoped to restore the heroic dimensions of the great epics of the past, they also recognized that such an effort was not only fraught with difficulty but perhaps could never be brought properly to fruition. Why, many have asked, had it become impossible to create a great long poem that could rival the epics of the past? Had the high style of language necessary to create a heroic poem simply worn out to the point that it sounded mannered, or that it came across as a tissue of clichés? Could heroic deeds solemnly told no longer seem plausible in a world organized according to the new economic and social arrangements that the industrial revolution had brought about?[15] Whether one puts the question in traditional literary terms or sets it within a larger social context, it goes without saying that the type of poem represented by Homer, Virgil, Milton, or by such anonymous medieval epics as *Beowulf*, the *Song of*

Roland, and the *Nibelungenlied* was no longer possible after the Enlightenment. (It does not seem accidental that by the mid-nineteenth-century, Virgil and Camões's epic themes could be realized not in literary but in operatic terms, that in fact the very years that witnessed the composition of the *Ring* also witnessed the composition of those two epic-minded French operas *Les Troyens* and *L'Africaine*.)

When poets after the Enlightenment sought to emulate the epic writers of the past, they were forced into compromises that badly undercut the traditional values and conventions of epic. Wordsworth, for example, though attempting to renew the possibilities of epic, ended up celebrating not the deeds of heroic martial figures but the heroism of the individual consciousness. As a result, his major long poem, *The Prelude*, to which he referred as his poem about the growth of a poet's mind, contains little of the outside world, but remains essentially a spiritual autobiography.[16] And Byron's epic poem, *Don Juan*, gave new vitality to the form by using a comic method to question not only the traditional epic conventions but also the very value of heroism.[17]

It has often been said that by the nineteenth century, once poetry could no longer support heroic matter, the epic impulse moved into that relatively new genre, the novel, above all into the novels of Sir Walter Scott. Despite the unheroic matters Scott was forced to tell because of the conventions that prose narrative imposes, he nevertheless sought to renew the national and communal functions of epic in his long series of novels based on the history of his native Scotland. The young Wagner had in fact been attracted to the heroic potential of the historical novel—if not precisely to the example of Scott, at least to that of his imitator Edward Bulwer-Lytton, whose novel *Rienzi* he had turned into a French-style *grand opéra*. Many years later, while working up the energy to begin the composition of *Siegfried*, Wagner sought relaxation by reading both Byron and Scott. But relaxation rather than inspiration—for in view of the compromises that both Byron and Scott made in order to renew epic tradition, one doubts that Wagner could have noted an analogy to his own efforts in their work.

By Wagner's time, the difficulties that writers encountered in their attempts to renew epic had already been confronted theoretically by Hegel. In his lectures on aesthetics, Hegel proposed that a particular genre such as epic does not exist in some ideal, timeless realm but, as I indicate in Chapter 4, is instead rooted within a particular historical milieu. Thus epic appears within Hegel's theory as the major literary genre within what he calls the "classic" period of art as against, on the one hand, the "symbolic" or "primitive" period, and, on the other hand, that postclassical time that Hegel variously labels "Christian," "romantic," and "modern." Hegel's ideal model for epic remains the Homeric poems, which he analyzes as rooted in a "general world-situation" that can never be recaptured at a later time.[18] Hegel's systematic historicizing of the genres (not only those we label "literary" but those within all the arts) presents a theoretical justification of the difficulties that poets and readers alike had come to feel in continuing the life of epic and other forms that had seemed to flourish and to peak at earlier stages of civilization. From the point of view of the present chapter, it is significant that Hegel singled out the *Nibelungenlied* (at the time of his lectures considered by many a central text for inspiring the emerging German national consciousness) as unsuitable for epic treatment in his own time, for the world in which it is rooted, according to Hegel, "has no longer any living connection whatever with our domestic, civil, legal life" (*HA*, 2: 1057). One might also note that despite Hegel's evident disdain for the *Nibelungenlied* (as well as for another of Wagner's major sources, the *Poetic Edda* [*HA*, 2: 1101]), Hegel concedes that "the whole collision [of the *Nibelungenlied*] is rather tragic and dramatic than completely epic" (*HA*, 2: 1103).

If Hegel, in effect, suggests the suitability of the Nibelung matter for dramatic rather than epic treatment, another philosopher of aesthetics, Friedrich Theodor Vischer (whose theorizing about opera I treat in Chapter 4), in an essay of 1844 entitled "Proposal for an Opera," went so far as to provide a scene-by-scene outline of a possible opera on the theme. For Vischer the German operatic tradition from Gluck through Weber had failed to produce a work that was at once heroic and national in character. Although the *Ring* in no sense followed Vischer's specific scenario (which, after all, was based on only one of Wagner's sources, the *Nibelungenlied*), Vischer's vision of a heroic, national drama that could utilize music to communicate directly with a modern audience and to soften those crude, medieval aspects of the story that had disturbed Hegel today reads like an uncanny prediction of the project that Wagner was soon to conceive.[19]

The movement from epic to drama (and thence to opera) suggested in these remarks by Hegel and Vischer was itself anticipated in a work of the late eighteenth and early nineteenth centuries with which Wagner was much preoccupied throughout his life. I refer to Goethe's *Faust*, a text that an uncommonly large proportion of nineteenth-century composers attempted to set to music in one form or another[20] and on which Wagner in his youth started to write a symphony (though the one movement he completed in 1840 ended up simply as his *Faust* "overture"). Like earlier epics, *Faust* is encyclopedic in scope—to the point that in its long second part its dramatic form can barely contain the masses of material that Goethe sought to accommodate. It is significant that although Goethe had once tried unsuccessfully to write an epic on Achilles, the genre he exploited in *Faust* was not the long narrative poem but a sprawling form of poetic drama. Indeed, it scarcely seems accidental that the term "operatic" has frequently been applied to characterize what must have seemed to its early readers a conspicuous deviation from classical dramatic form. It is as though by Goethe's time the traditional concerns of the epic could best be accommodated in some dramatic mode of presentation—dramatic but not necessarily theatrical form, for *Faust*, above all its second part, was in its time very much a reader's play. Not until well after its completion—and only after staging techniques had liberated themselves from too literal a dependence on the dramatic text—could it acclimate itself to the German theater.

Certainly *Faust* could scarcely count as heroic in the old epic sense: Franz Liszt's designation of *Faust* as a "philosophical epic," made at the time he was composing his own *Faust* Symphony (and while Wagner was working on the *Ring*) suggests the difficulties in establishing its generic status.[21] However one might classify this work, the nineteenth century clearly viewed the character Faust's strivings as a peculiarly modern mode of heroism. Wagner was himself taken by the dedication to significant action suggested by Faust's pronouncement "Im Anfang war die Tat" (in the beginning was the deed), a line from the play that Wagner quotes twice in the introduction he wrote in 1862 for the first publication of the *Ring* since its private printing nine years before (*WGS*, 2: 128, 132). A decade later, when Wagner suggests the phrase "ersichtlich gewordene Taten der Musik" (deeds of music made visible) as a possible alternative to the generic term *Musikdrama* (*WGS*, 13: 123), he is doubtless playing on the Faustian motto. Still, fascinated though he was by *Faust*, Wagner also expressed some grave reservations about its hero, whose embracing of external, worldly experience as opposed to inward experience went against his own emotional and metaphysical grain.[22] In one sense, however, Goethe's poem shares a certain common ground with the *Ring*, for both culminate in a grand-style, nineteenth-century flourish that represents a peculiarly modern, secularized form of redemption.[23] Yet Goethe's dramatic poem, unlike the *Ring*, which inhabits a lofty domain allowing relatively little variation of tone, introduces a wide array of forms by means of which it strikes its readers as witty, mercurial, often even improvisatory in nature.[24] Although it opened up a whole new genre of what one could call a panoramic form of drama,[25] the direction it suggested was not—despite the thematic connections between *Faust* and the *Ring*—the one that Wagner chose to follow.

If Goethe demonstrated one direction in which some traditional concerns of epic could manifest themselves in dramatic form, a much earlier dramatic poem suggested a transformation of epic materials much closer to the type of experience that Wagner sought to create for his audience in the *Ring*. I am thinking of Aeschylus's trilogy the *Oresteia*, a work that Wagner sought to emulate in the *Ring*.[26] Like traditional epic, the *Oresteia* tells its audience the story of its own people, and it organizes this story in a way designed to show its relevance to the audience's present concerns. As a cycle of plays, it obviously could serve as a model for the *Ring*; and whether or not Wagner actually modeled the *Ring* after it, one might remember that he labeled his own work "für drei Tage und einen Vorabend," as though, despite the fact that the latter actually encompasses four distinct entities, to remind us that he sought to revive the Greek idea of a trilogy. Moreover, the language of the *Oresteia*, as Wagner encountered it in Johann Gustav Droysen's contemporary translation, is lofty and heroic in a way that the language of *Faust* or of Scott's novels could not strive to be. Above all, Wagner could view the *Oresteia* as a work that did not, like the operas and plays of his own time, merely seek to entertain, but rather as one that could create a communal bond with its audience, above all by evoking a religious dimension. And just as important, by viewing (and also representing) himself as renewing the work of a Greek dramatist, Wagner was actively participating in that century-long movement—beginning with Winckelmann's studies of Greek sculpture and culminating in Nietzsche's Wagner-inspired celebration of Greek theatrical experience—which sought to make modern German culture the privileged and direct heir to the achievements of ancient Greece.

For Wagner to renew the possibilities of epic thus meant to create a work analogous to the *Oresteia*, a work that would reawaken the audience's national Germanic consciousness as Aeschylus's drama had played upon what Wagner took to be the Greek national consciousness. It would represent events of the greatest magnitude—heroic deeds, acts of vengeance, threats to the communal order, and attempts to restore this order. The *Oresteia* could also serve as a model in the sense that it did not, like epic narratives, rely on words alone, but that its actions were embodied in scenic terms and that they also used musical resources—though Wagner had no way of knowing what Greek choral chants could really have sounded like. To find his equivalent national materials Wagner had merely to go to the newly revived Old Norse and Middle High German tales about the Germanic gods and the fortunes of their descendants. Not only did Wagner retell these tales, but by imitating the accentual and alliterative verse that he found in the Old Norse poetic versions he also sought to recapture their heroic tone.

Yet what Wagner's audiences saw as heroic in the *Ring* did not actually come from the language of the texts he wrote. Heroic language could not be convincingly achieved simply by the philological reconstruction that Wagner practiced in writing his libretto. If Wagner had really died right after publishing his text in 1853—to return for a moment to the supposition with which this chapter began—we might have granted him considerable respect for his antiquarian activities, but we would never have seen him, as we do today, as the artist who, more fundamentally than any other in the nineteenth century, successfully renewed the possibilities of traditional epic. What is missing in the 1853 text is of course the music. And to give this text its proper heroic dimension Wagner had at his disposal a musical language and structure inherited not from earlier opera, but, as Joseph Kerman pointed out in his pioneering book on opera, from the symphony in the form it had been given by Beethoven.[27] If Wagner succeeded in restoring the heroic dimension of literature at a time that those who practiced the literary arts had pretty much abandoned this dimension, he did so by fusing a fascinatingly diverse group of elements—the traditional epic poem, the national Germanic themes and the linguistic forms of early medieval heroic tales, the religious and communal experience of the Aeschylean tragic trilogy, and the grandeur and solemnity of the Beethoven symphony.

After more than a century of productions the *Ring* has acclimated itself so successfully within our consciousness that we can easily forget how unique and strange this fusion of diverse elements actually is. There was nothing intrinsically common to these elements—Greek tragedy, early Germanic heroic tales, national epics, Beethoven's symphonic form—except perhaps the nineteenth-century notion that each element expresses itself in a sublime style, that each, in fact, invokes a mode of thinking distinctly higher than that associated with everyday life in modern middle-class society.

Yet in combining these elements, Wagner obviously created something new, something that nobody could ever confuse with the originals that they imitated or sought to transform. In adapting symphonic form to his dramatic needs, Wagner of course took this form in an entirely new direction, one that could be said to undercut most of the aesthetic premises on which it had been founded. Similarly with his use of his literary materials. If one reads the various medieval sources that Wagner used for the *Ring*, one will be struck far less by similarities than by how different these sources look in their new nineteenth-century embodiment. For example, Wagner's method of telling a story is entirely different from that of his medieval sources, however different these may be from one another. In the *Ring* Wagner supplies some sort of psychological motivation—whether or not we judge it plausible—for every significant action of every character. And if the motivation is not always fully comprehensible in the 1853 text, he later saw to it that his music filled in the psychological gaps.

Everything in Wagner's *Ring* happens in a closely linked chain of cause and effect: Alberich steals the gold because he is greedy and because he feels the Rhine maidens treat him badly, and his theft generates a whole series of actions that make up the plot of the whole tetralogy. Not so in the sources, in which psychological motivation simply does not exist in its modern sense (or even in the ancient Greek sense that Wagner would have learned from his study of Aeschylus's plays), but in which people and symbols and actions simply come and go—often without what we would consider adequate preparation or explanation. The fact that we call the work the *Ring* and that Wagner gave it the title *Der Ring des Nibelungen* is itself an indication of the cohesion that Wagner, unlike his sources, sought to give his story. In the sources we find only occasional rings, and they have no necessary connection with one another. Although the Brünnhilde of the *Nibelungenlied* has a ring that Siegfried steals while wooing her for Gunther, this ring has no connection with a fateful ring owned by a dwarf in one of Wagner's other sources, the *Poetic Edda*. Thus, the ring in Wagner symbolizes not only such large concepts as greed, power, and fate, but, just as important, it symbolizes the tight narrative cohesion and deterministic structure that in Wagner—and emphatically not in his sources—serves to make sense of the whole.

Moreover, however much Wagner hoped that his audiences would experience their Germanic past by hearing the alliterated Germanic root words of his text, one very much doubts that the language they heard helped them make contact with this past any more than it would help those modern audiences in various countries who clamor for tickets whenever a *Ring* cycle is announced. Nor would these root words help the German audience any more than they would a modern American one in achieving an immediacy with their referents as Wagner hoped. What Wagner reconstructed in his text was a private poetic language, one that, though purportedly based on older and related versions of the language his countrymen spoke, is an act of artistic autonomy and a rejection of existing forms of expression that clearly anticipates the various linguistic experiments, a generation later, of Hopkins, Rimbaud,

FIG. 13. The first Siegfried, Georg Unger, Bayreuth Festspiele, 1876. Courtesy, National-Archiv der Richard-Wagner-Stiftung, Bayreuth.

and Mallarmé—to the point that if we had nothing of the *Ring* except for the 1853 text we should be tempted to attach the label "hermetic" to an artist who longed above all to make his work communicate with his public.

Indeed, the communal experience of the ancient Greek theater that Wagner sought to renew turns out not to have much in common with what the *Ring* actually succeeded in doing. However well the early Bayreuth audiences may have boned up on the medieval myths from which the music-dramas derived, these myths could not have had the easy familiarity for them that the Greek myths surrounding the Trojan wars had for the Athenian audiences at the Dionysian festival. Indeed, given the strong classical education that Wagner's German middle-class audiences enjoyed until fairly recently, one suspects that these audiences felt a deeper intimacy with Agamemnon and Electra than they did with the ancient Odin (that is, Wotan) or Siegfried. Or perhaps I should put it another way: if his original audiences did not quite feel these myths in their blood, his own achievement served to bring these myths into the German consciousness in the peculiarly nineteenth-century form he gave them, a form epitomized in the rough-hewn, distinctly nonclassical Siegfried of Figure 13; and it is no accident that many late-nineteenth-century Germans (among them, inappropriately enough, my own Orthodox Jewish grandparents) would give their sons names such as Siegmund and Siegfried.

All of this is only to say something that was obvious all along—namely, that Wagner is very much of the nineteenth century and that the *Ring*, however much it invokes and reworks the literary past, is a work very much of its own time. Even when it seems to borrow the forms and themes of the past, Wagner gives these forms and themes a peculiarly nineteenth-century and also, one might add, a personal coloring. Certainly one can find an incestuous relationship between brother and sister in the *Völsungasaga*. But Signy, the original of Sieglinde in the latter work, disguises herself before going to bed with Siegmund, and her motive for joining him is not romantic love but the desire to bear a son of their strain who will be able to avenge their father's death.[28] By contrast, the incest we witness in *Die Walküre* is very romantic, as the ecstatic nineteenth-century Sieglinde gazing at her triumphant brother

FIG. 14. Sieglinde looks rapturously at her brother Siegmund as he holds the sword Nothung, which he pulled out of the tree trunk at the end of *Die Walküre*, act 1. Leipzig production of 1878. Courtesy, National-Archiv der Richard-Wagner-Stiftung, Bayreuth.

in Figure 14 makes clear; in fact, to judge from the music as well as the text, it is one of the most passionate relationships within the whole history of opera.

Yet incest was a romantic theme for several generations before Wagner, for example in the Gothic novel and in Byron's poetry (not to speak of his life); above all, incest served to titillate its audiences by invoking a universally acknowledged taboo and by the consequent questioning of the value of present-day social conventions that a powerful taboo of this sort can represent in a particularly striking way. Like much nineteenth-century literature and art, the *Ring* continually expresses a rebelliousness against authority, and in this sense it stands at an extreme remove from eighteenth-century *opera seria*, which had celebrated the authority of rulers. Moreover, the *Ring* often manifests this rebelliousness by examining transgressions that occur within personal relationships. The incest of *Die Walküre* is only one such transgression, a single though extreme instance of that violation of the marriage bond which we also see in the adulterous relationships of Wotan and later of Siegfried.

Adultery, as we know, is one of the central obsessions of the nineteenth-century novel, and as literary critics have come to realize in recent years, this obsession was not simply the lurid gossip about private life that novelists employed to tantalize their readers, but it was also a means of talking about the breach of contracts in a larger sense: the transgression that we call adultery thus became representative of other transgressions that could tell us something about the nature of modern society.[29] Within our present context it seems significant that during the very years in which Wagner was composing the music for *Das Rheingold*, *Die Walküre*, and the first two acts of *Siegfried*, Flaubert was writing that great novel about adultery, *Madame Bovary*. One hesitates to name Wagner's and Flaubert's projects in the same breath—for what after all can a work with the heroic, mythical dimensions of the *Ring* have in common with a realist novel that shocked its early readers by means of the frankness with which it confronted the grubbiest details of ordinary middle-class life? If the mid-nineteenth-century novel took the low road, opera in that period, by narrating its concerns in musical form and by representing characters of lofty social status costumed in ways far removed in time from the world of the audience, emphatically sought out the high road.[30] Yet the deeper concerns that we find in operas of this time, and certainly in the *Ring*, are closely related to those of the great novels—above all the transgression against traditional authority, symbolized as it is in both forms by the violation of the marriage contract.

Yet by opting for the high road, the *Ring* could confront certain problems of its time more directly than could the domestically centered novel. I think of Wagner's concern with the nature of power, above all the relation of power to economic greed. The whole complex drama that transpires between Wotan and the Nibelungs, or between Siegfried and the Gibichungs, points to some central concerns of the time that the novel, to the extent that it concentrated on figures lower on the social scale than those in opera, was forced to approach in a different way. However much we may feel that George Bernard

Shaw, in *The Perfect Wagnerite*, exaggerated the socioeconomic meaning of the *Ring*, we must also grant that relatively early within the history of Wagnerian reception Shaw pointed to a central area of significance from which academic commentators even to this day have largely shied away. Similarly, however strong feelings many may have against directors who change the décor and the stage directions specified by a composer, Patrice Chéreau's attempt to locate the *Ring* in the nineteenth-century, central-European social milieu in which it was composed can be taken as an act of contemporary literary criticism that attempts to read a work of art against the world out of which it came.[31] Indeed the considerable gap between the heroic dimensions of the *Ring* and the often unpleasant facts it lays bare about money, sex, and power is itself part of the fascination that radiates from the work and that also locates the *Ring* squarely in a world that often covered up its seamier aspects with the most sublime gestures.

Besides the larger statements one can make about the relation of the *Ring* to the social and economic world of Wagner's time, one can also chart some specific areas that point to the events of his time. Indeed, the changes he made in the ending to the *Ring* are themselves indicators of his changing views of the world—or, to put it in somewhat more precise terms, of changes in the world that also brought about changes in the way that an artist such as Wagner viewed this world. The 1848 scenario and the first version of *Siegfrieds Tod* end on a note quite consonant with the revolutionary politics that Wagner practiced during that politically fateful year.[32] After Brünnhilde's death and the return of the ring, the lower order of Nibelungs are liberated from their bondage in much the same way that the revolutionists of the time sought to liberate the equivalent lower orders of their own time. Indeed, the whole ending celebrates a triumph, for Valhalla in these early versions remains intact and will in fact receive the freshly immolated ex-Valkyrie and her recently murdered consort Siegfried. According to the final stage direction, Siegfried and Brünnhilde are seen moving together through a glowing sky— an optimistic, romantically triumphant ending that has far less in common with the way Wagner ultimately resolved his tetralogy than it does with the ending of (dare one say it?) *La fanciulla del west*.

By the time Wagner published his text in 1853, the revolutionary ardor of 1848 had long since passed, and Napoleon III was firmly ensconced as French emperor. Now the ending of the *Ring* takes a different turn: instead of a liberation of the masses and a transformation of Valhalla, the latter is destroyed, and Wotan and the gods all go to their doom. The framework in which we see the events moves from the level of politics to that of personal ethics. Brünnhilde, just before her death, celebrates the coming triumph of love and the breaking of those institutions that impede this triumph. If Wagner is still a revolutionist at this point, he remains so purely through the hope that the ending expresses for a new order of personal relations.

Yet even this ending was not to be the last word. In the following year Georg Herwegh, Wagner's fellow refugee in Zurich, introduced him to the writings of Schopenhauer, and as a result the composer found a rationale for his postrevolutionary feelings of disillusion (one could also argue that Schopenhauer could have provided a rationale for the disillusion already quite evident in Wagner's operas of the 1840s). The triumph of love that Brünnhilde proclaimed in the printed text—combined as it was with a confident prediction that what Wagner called the "iron rule of hypocritical custom"[33] would soon reach its end—now, in fact, gives way, in words added in 1856, to the quietism and resignation that Wagner discerned in Schopenhauer's *The World as Will and Representation*, a book that was published 37 years before but, as it turned out, was just the right tonic for the composer at this disillusioned moment of history.[34] Brünnhilde now speaks of "trauernde Liebe" (mourning love) and "tiefstes Leiden" (deepest suffering)—though, at Cosima's behest, Wagner never set these added words but decided instead to let the orchestral passages that conclude *Götterdämmerung* do whatever new ideological work was needed.[35]

I mention these changes to stress how firmly the *Ring*, despite its seemingly distant setting, was embedded in the world of its time. Yet I do not mean to say that the *Ring* simply "reflects" the historical forces surrounding it. Classic works do not "reflect" history so much as they make history—not necessarily political history (though they play their role in this too), but what we have come to call the history of culture, and above all that branch of it that some call the history of consciousness. The things that great works such as the *Ring* teach us are not necessarily what past times were really like or how particular events in the real world motivate the events we see rendered in art. Rather, art provides us with a framework for rethinking the times in which they were created, or deciding what is peculiar and unique to these times in contrast with other times, and above all for connecting things that, to the inhabitants of these earlier times, must have seemed to belong to alien orders.

The *Ring*, like many of the great novels of the time, has helped define the mid-nineteenth century for us; perhaps one might even say it has helped create a mid-nineteenth century for us. To put it another way, the *Ring* provides us with a focal point through which we can bring together and make mutual sense out of some quite diverse nineteenth-century events and problems—for example, if I may cite again some of the phenomena I discussed earlier in this chapter, the enthusiasm for what people took to be the early medieval Germanic world, or the difficulties encountered by artists in renewing the epic tradition, or the fascination with origins and the need to make tight cause-and-effect narrative connections, or the preoccupation with incest and adultery as modes of transgression, or an artist's need to rethink the ending of his work as he rethinks his attitude toward the historical events taking place around him.

The old notion that art reflects history grants too passive a role to the work of art, at least to a seminal work such as the *Ring*. Moreover, the historicity I have sought to locate in the *Ring* lies not simply in the nineteenth-century image that it conjures up but in the meanings it has accumulated through more than a century of interpretation both on the stage and in the study.[36] When I attend a *Ring* cycle I hear both the voice of an otherwise lost nineteenth-century world as well as the long succession of later significations that have stamped themselves upon it—for example, Nietzsche's condemnation of Wagner as "der Künstler der *décadence*" (the artist of decadence) for allowing Schopenhauer's pessimism to compromise the ending of *Götterdämmerung*;[37] or Adorno's reading of Alberich and Mime as caricatures of Jews;[38] or Hitler's statement in his notebooks, "Young Siegfried, well known from my time at the Linz Opera; Wagner's piece showed me for the first time what blood-myth [*Blutmythos*] is";[39] or Wieland Wagner's suppression of the traditionally Germanic visual effects in his Bayreuth *Ring* after World War II;[40] or Chéreau's presentation of the Rhine maidens as whores prancing about a hydroelectric dam. Even while thinking myself spellbound at a *Ring* performance I confess that I do not erase the photo-images in my memory of Hitler paying his respects to Wagner's descendants at their shrine in Bayreuth.[41] Through an examination of the *Ring*'s many entanglements past and present all these strikingly diverse matters can assume connections with one another—can, in fact, build up a larger image to which we then attach the name *history*.

Chapter Six   Opera / Orientalism / Otherness

When Puccini's *Turandot* received its first staging in China early in 1996, the opera's setting was moved westward from the country in which it was being performed to what a reviewer for a U.S. newspaper took to be "a kingdom on the Silk Road."[1] Changes of setting have of course been frequent in operatic productions during our present, director-dominated age, most notably perhaps in Peter Sellars's relocations of *Don Giovanni* and *Le nozze di Figaro* from the Spain of their source texts to the present-day South Bronx and to midtown Manhattan respectively. Yet geographically restaging a work whose supposed rootedness in an ancient culture has been central to its production history is clearly an attempt to "de-sinify" the opera. "To me Turandot is undoubtedly a Western character," the production's director, Xu Xiaozhong, said, adding that "a Chinese princess would never have been as cruel as Turandot" but would instead "have been kind, obedient and conservative."[2] Since Xu presumably left Puccini's music intact—just as Sellars and other iconoclastic recent directors have ordinarily refused to tamper with the operatic scores or librettos they were rethinking—one wonders if his Beijing audience heard the Italian composer's pentatonic runs as expressive of their own culture or simply as something vaguely East Asian, for Puccini had, after all, teased his listeners with pentatonic tunes as a means of depicting the Japan of his earlier opera *Madama Butterfly*.

Whatever biases about national character stand behind Xu's artistic decisions, his transfer of locales might be termed an instance of "occidentalism," by means of which certain notions—for example, the idea that a princess can behave cruelly—have become attributed to the culture of some Western other.

To be sure, a Western audience would surely view an operatic setting on the Silk Road as something intrinsic to the Orient, indeed, even further to the East than those Near Eastern settings of many popular late-nineteenth-century operas to whose exotic ballet sequences and Arab-flavored musical style we have come to attach the term "orientalism."

Two decades have passed since Edward W. Said published the book whose title transformed this term from a seemingly neutral reference to the research that scholars performed on the history and culture of much of the non-Western world to an ideologically loaded one, one that characterized the inhabitants of that world as passive, backward, and hypersexual. As Said explained early in his book, orientalist discourse assumes a basic rationality within the West, while portraying the oriental character in a manner that, although it posits certain positive aspects, lays its stress on the negative ones: thus, to cite the words of a social scientist applying Said's insights, the Orient appears within this discourse as "strange, exotic and mysterious, but also as sensual, irrational and potentially dangerous."³ For most of its history the word "orientalist" simply referred to those who studied the cultures of Islam and of the Asian landmass, while the "ism" referred to their professional activities. To be sure, artistic products were sometimes associated with the word, as when Byron appropriated it in *Beppo* not only to refer to the type of romance he had composed in earlier years but also to rhyme with the word "sentimentalism":

> How quickly would I print (the world delighting)
> A Grecian, Syrian, or *Assy*rian tale;
> And sell you, mix'd with western sentimentalism,
> Some samples of the finest Orientalism.⁴

In its influence upon humanistic study *Orientalism* is doubtless unrivaled by any book produced in the Anglo-American cultural domain during the last generation. Yet although Said directed his polemic above all at the biases underlying the production of supposedly scholarly knowledge by the West about the East, its most conspicuous effect has been upon the way we have come to interpret the various art forms seeking to represent the non-Western world— above all, the Near East—to Western audiences. Said himself recognized what he called "two aspects of Orientalism"—first, "the discipline by which the Orient was (and is) approached systematically, as a topic of learning, discovery, and practice," and second, an aspect that exists outside formal institutions of learning and consists of what Said calls "that collection of dreams, images, and vocabularies available to anyone who has tried to talk about what lies east of the dividing line."[5] This is the Orient that for centuries has fueled the West's imagination, whether in the private reveries of individuals or in the works of art in various media that fed these reveries and that in turn fed new works of art. In view of the clichés about the Orient that have been exposed in the wake of Said's study, one is scarcely surprised to find this long-familiar vocabulary used in connection with Near Eastern music as early as 1751, in a French treatise on "oriental music" by Charles Fonton that was not published in full until the 1990s. Though Fonton praises this music for its "sad" and "touching" quality, it emerges as "like its nation, soft and languorous, without forcefulness or vigor, and without the liveliness and soul of our music."[6]

Even those who know of Said's book only by word of mouth have developed a consciousness of orientalist presences they encounter regularly in a whole range of art forms. Who has not muttered the word "orientalism" when reading, or seeing, or hearing a lyric, say, from Goethe's *Westöstlicher Diwan* or Hugo's *Les Orientales*; a prose romance such as Beckford's *Vathek* or a verse romance such as Byron's *Bride of Abydos*; an Ingres *baigneuse* pictured in a harem or a Delacroix genre scene sketched in Algeria; or the temple ritual sending Radames off to his conquests in *Aida* or the Philistines doing their bacchanalian romp in *Samson et Dalila*? Even brief allusions to orientalist discourse in works that would otherwise seem to stand outside it remind us of the power that orientalism has exercised upon the imagination during recent centuries. To cite a literary character known for her especially lively imagination, Emma Bovary, whose wide early reading included romantic orientalist tales, chose the name Djali for her dog, allowed the merchant Lheureux to play upon her consumer greed with shawls from Algeria, and chose Turkish incense from an Algerian shop in Rouen to accompany her lovemaking with Léon Dupuis. Even in these brief allusions we recognize the same fixation upon the Near East that her author manifested in such overtly orientalist texts as *Salammbô* and *Hérodias*, as well as in his meticulously detailed account of his sexual encounters with Kuchuk Hanem, the reigning courtesan of the upper Nile at the time of his Egyptian journey.[7]

It seems small wonder that Said's book has generated a veritable industry of scholarly investigation within all the arts. The orientalist discourse that Said uncovered in earlier historical scholars, social scientists, and writers is fast being supplanted by a discourse dedicated to exposing manifestations of orientalism wherever these may be found. Within English studies alone the orientalizing tendencies discovered in long-familiar writers have reshaped their images within literary history, while once-little-read writers exploiting Eastern themes have become the subjects of serious inquiry. The orientalism of Byron's four "Turkish tales" constitutes the argument of a full-length volume, while another volume, suggestively entitled *British Romantic Writers and the East: Anxieties of Empire*, not only covers much the same ground with Byron but also includes sections on the Orient-induced opium taking of De Quincey and on the more "positively" directed orientalism that Shelley manifests, above all, in *Prometheus Unbound*.[8] The use of a title such as *Orientalism and Modernism*, though this book is more accurately described by its subtitle *The Legacy of China in Pound and Williams*, suggests how fashionable it has become to search for evidences of orientalism in a range of periods.[9] An epistolary writer such as Lady Mary Wortley Montagu, once relegated to the fringes of literary history, has assumed a more central role in eighteenth-century studies not only through her gender but also through the vivid, firsthand descriptions in her letters of harem life in Constantinople.[10] Within the French eighteenth-century canon, Montesquieu's *Les Lettres persanes* now rivals the same author's *L'Esprit des lois* in importance. An enterprising recent book, *Critical Terrains*, subtitled *French and British Orientalisms*, manages to cover some of the more celebrated orientalist literary terrains from Lady Mary and Montesquieu through Flaubert, E. M. Forster, and down to those recent French theorists such as Kristeva and Barthes who have carved out their own Orients.[11]

Although scholarship in literature is a much larger-scale industry than that in the other arts, the search for orientalism in painting and music is fast coming to rival that in literature. The study of visual orientalism, above all in French nineteenth-century and early twentieth-century painting, has manifested itself not simply in art-historical essays and monographs but in museum exhibitions.[12] Orientalism has emerged as central to much of the so-called program music of the same period; indeed, just as the current fascination with orientalism (which could be said to supplant the fascination with the Orient itself a century ago) has spawned art shows, it has also created a reassessment of orientalist music—to the point that a record company in 1991 initiated a series entitled "Les Brises d'Orient" with a long-forgotten, once-influential work, Félicien David's Berlioz-inspired "Ode-symphonique" *Le Désert* (1844), in which a tenor performs a supposedly "authentic" version of the Islamic muezzin's call to prayer. But it is opera above all—with its ability to mark orientalist traces at once by visual, textual, and audible means—that we are coming to recognize as a crucial example of Said's thesis. Said himself, in his later book, *Culture and Imperialism,* has used *Aida* as a means of describing the entanglements of orientalism and imperialism within the late nineteenth century, while the musicologist Ralph P. Locke has portrayed *Samson et Dalila* as exemplary of the orientalism that shaped much French opera of the period.[13]

What do we make of the special hold that the Orient has maintained over opera during much of the form's history? What historical distinctions can one suggest among the effects that operatic orientalism has exercised upon audiences in different times and places? What does orientalist opera tell us about the nature of opera as a popular art form? To what degree is it appropriate to assign a political program to the various forms of art that we dub orientalist? And how is the oriental "other" related to other modes of otherness projected in opera?

Consider three distinct moments of orientalist opera, each a century apart. My first examples, one "serious," the other "comic," are Gluck's *Iphigénie en Tauride* (1779) and Mozart's *Die Entführung aus dem Serail* (1782). Both belong to that genre we call the captivity narrative, within which personages from a civilized world—the world of the imputed audience—have been held captive by what the audience is to see as a barbarous force. As Said argued in

Orientalism, the confrontation of a supposedly civilized West against barbarous Asians has been a staple of European writing since Aeschylus's *Persians* and Euripides's *Bacchae*.[14] In the captivity narratives that shape these two
operas of the late eighteenth century, this confrontation could be taken for
granted as a dramatic convention by means of which composers literally cap-
tivate their listeners with that exotic form of music immediately recognizable
as the *alla turca* style.[15] As Thomas Bauman, in his study of Mozart's *Entführung*, has shown, this music, which bears only the most tangential relation
to actual Arabic or Turkish music, was derived from the military music played
by Janissary bands imported from Turkey by European armies during the
eighteenth century; the music was identifiable to its audiences partly by its
characteristic percussion instruments—triangle (itself not even an authentic
Turkish instrument), tambourine, cymbal, and bass drum—and by certain
rhythms and harmonies.[16]

In transforming Euripides's *Iphigenia in Tauris* into an opera, Gluck and
his librettist Nicholas-François Guillard maintained the distinction between
Greek and barbarian that had prevailed in ancient tragedy. Having been saved
by Artemis from sacrificial death on the island of Aulis—the event drama-
tized both in Euripides's other Iphigenia play and in Gluck's earlier opera,
Iphigénie en Aulide—the heroine serves as a priestess under the protection of
Thoas, king of the Scythians, the tribe occupying what later became known as
the Crimean peninsula. Bound to the service of Thoas, the heroine is forced
to participate in sacrificing one of two Greek strangers, who turn out to be
her brother Orestes and his companion Pylades and who ultimately work
with her to secure their freedom by murdering the barbarian. Although the
musical style of Thoas himself is scarcely distinguishable from that of the
other characters, all of whom present themselves in the high-minded style
characteristic of Gluck's reform operas, the king's Scythian followers sing and
dance a musical language in the contemporary Turkish mode. The music associated with modern Turks could of course not have flourished in ancient
Scythia: what mattered was the fact that the *alla turca* music connoted barbarism. As an account of the opera in its own time made clear, the Scythians'
music transported its hearers into a primitive world: "The dance air is rela-

tive to the situation and perfectly renders the barbaric joy of these savages, who enjoy the execution of these unfortunate [strangers] in advance. The author has mixed his instruments with cymbals, a triangle and muffled drums. This strange sound should transport spectators into the world of cannibals dancing around the stake to which their victim is tied."[17] As a recent study of eighteenth-century "musique à la turque" makes clear, the Scythian dances in the two *Iphigénie*'s served as model for a long tradition of oriental operatic scenes from Mozart through Meyerbeer.[18]

The barbaric joy cited here indicates that the fascination excited by Gluck's Turkish music derived from that larger fascination with primitive rites and customs so common within European culture during the later eighteenth century. With its ability to convey its meanings by sight and sound at once, opera, together with ballet (another site for primitivist representations), was uniquely suited to rousing an audience's desire to experience exotic, non-European cultures. In his influential *Essay on Opera* Algarotti had recommended Montezuma as an ideal subject for opera because "the magnificence and strangeness of America would create a striking contrast with Europe."[19] But Algarotti, as a result of reading Norden's *Travels into Egypt*, also suggested ancient Egypt as a prospective operatic site: "What can be more majestic and awful (not to mention the pyramids) than the ruins of Memnon's palace that tower along the banks of the river Nile, or that ancient city Thebes with its hundred gates; all of which, thanks to Norden's accurate work, the public can now enjoy?"[20] As though Mexico and Egypt were not enough, Algarotti goes on to recommend China as an operatic site.[21]

To the extent that the primitive world—whether in the guise of ancient Scythians or Egyptians, recent Aztecs, or current-day Turks—seemed warlike and sublime, it offered a certain *frisson nouveau* to jaded Europeans. Moreover, the *alla turca* music, with its loud percussive effects, its brisk rhythms, simple harmonies, and rapid alternation between major and minor, could offer brief respites from the expectations that an audience brought to the standard classical style of the time. But "Turkish" music found uses that went considerably beyond the depiction of primitive people on the stage. For example, the final movement of Mozart's A major piano sonata, K. 331, marked *alla turca*, offers all the satisfactions of an alternative to the reigning style without being tied to a specific text—though doubtless its listeners and performers could readily imagine the sounds of the military bands in which this mode of music making originated.

"Turkish" music also served as a means of representing at least one culture, that of China, to which Europe granted a degree of respect that it did not grant Turks or primitives. Gluck's brief court entertainment for Empress Maria Theresa, *Le Cinesi* (1754), set to a Metastasio text created for an earlier Austrian ruler two decades before, opens with an overture employing the same percussive effects that audiences associated with Turkish music. Whereas in the early twentieth century Puccini would distinguish the Far from the Near East by means of the pentatonic scale that marks large portions of *Madama Butterfly* and *Turandot*—with only miminal distinctions to separate the two Far Eastern cultures he was representing[22]—Gluck simply counted on long-familiar auditory signs to suggest a non-European world. Yet the elegant sets produced for the piece, together with the work's highly cultivated characters (who gently parody the principal Western dramatic genres) belong to that quite nonprimitive world of *chinoiserie*, whose refined rococo sensuality offered still another stylistic alternative among the arts of the eighteenth century.

Although a serious opera such as *Iphigénie en Tauride* allowed only brief opportunities for the *alla turca* style, a comic opera such as Mozart's *Die Entführung aus dem Serail* could exploit both the dramatic and musical possibilities in East-West cultural confrontations to a considerably greater degree. *Die Entführung* contains two large roles for its Islamic characters, the nonsinging Pasha Selim, who holds the European heroine captive, and his servant Osmin, the most musically memorable orientalist figure in eighteenth century opera. If Selim shows sufficient nobility to let his captive, Constanze, go free with her Spanish suitor, Belmonte, who has tricked his way into the harem, this may be due to the fact that the Pasha is himself ultimately revealed as a European whose ethical instincts, despite his conversion to Islam, betray his Western origins. But one could also look at the reconciliatory ending of this opera in another way: whereas Belmonte's father had been responsible for Selim's banishment into the oriental world, the latter, speaking in his acquired role as an Islamic chief, displays the ability to forgive cruel European behavior.

Although Pasha Selim's noble conduct complicates an easy orientalist reading of Mozart's text, Osmin's actions display the various negative traits that Europeans associated with Muslims at the time: boastful, loud, lascivious, and vengeful up to the end, Osmin, like the great scapegoat characters in traditional comedy, angrily turns his back on the reconciliation scene in which the opera culminates.[23] Audiences accustomed to the increasingly higher volumes with which music came to bombard listeners' ears after Mozart's time are not likely to realize how overwhelmingly loud Osmin's arias, as well as the orchestral music passages composed *alla turca* (and which were played by a special military band), must have seemed in the composer's day.

But Osmin is only one among a succession of grossly comic orientalist figures peopling operas as late as Rossini's Mustafa in *L'italiana in Algeri* (1813). His immediate predecessor is the dervish Calandra in another operatic captivity narrative that happened to be set in different languages, and in different national styles as well, by two other major germanophone composers, Gluck and Haydn. Gluck's *La Rencontre imprévue, ou les Pèlerins de La Mecque* (1764), which was immensely popular in its time and from which Mozart was even accused of plagiarizing for *Die Entführung*, employs the spoken dialogue of French *opéra comique*, while Haydn's *L'incontro improvviso* (1775), little known in its day since it was composed as an Esterházy court entertainment and not even published until our own time, uses the recitative of Italian comic opera. In these two works (for which the Italian librettist Karl Friberth simplified the original text's plot line), the more "civilized" characters within the East-West confrontation are not precisely Europeans but Persians, while the barbarians who keep the Persian princess imprisoned are Egyptians. The character named Osmin in these operas, unlike his namesake in Mozart's text, belongs to the civilized group, while the star barbarian is the dervish Calandra, who in both operas mouths nonsense language—"Castagno, castagna / Castrato, castrato, castrata / Farapisache" in Gluck—with the loudness and vulgarity of Mozart's Osmin. The percussive effect of "Turkish" music punctuates both Gluck's and Haydn's operas at various moments; a Chinese ballet in

Gluck's opera, like the overture to *Le Cinesi*, utilizes the same percussion instruments that by convention signaled Easternness to audiences of the time.

The stereotype of the grossly comic Near Easterner goes back at least a century before these examples to the ceremonial scene that Lully composed for Molière's *Le Bourgeois Gentilhomme* (1670), a *comédie-ballet* whose hero is "honored" with the title *mamamouchi*, and whose Turkish representatives invoke Mahomet while engaging in grotesque "contortions and grimaces" and mouthing a garbled Italian much like the sounds emitted a century later by Gluck's and Haydn's dervishes. Lully's music, which calls for "instruments à la turque" without stipulating precisely which instruments were to be played, sounds considerably like the "Turkish" music of the next century, whereas his standard style bears no resemblance to the classical style of Gluck or Haydn.[24]

In view of a convention that appears at such widely spaced moments in time, one may wonder what continuing significance these representations of Turkish otherness may have had for their audiences. When *Le Bourgeois Gentilhomme* was first performed, the Ottoman Turks still posed an active threat within Europe; it was not for another thirteen years, in 1683, that they besieged Vienna for the last time, though the French viewed them as potential allies in containing the Hapsburgs. Molière and Lully's Turkish ceremony was likely motivated by the curiosity aroused by the presence of a Turkish delegation to Paris during the year preceding its first performance.[25] By the late eighteenth century, however, though still occupying southeastern Europe, the Turks had become a considerably weakened power. The major threat that they posed by then was that ancestor of current-day terrorism, namely pirating, an activity that could at once arouse the anxieties represented in captivity narratives such as those of Gluck and Mozart and then alleviate these very anxieties by the liberation of the European characters at the end. The operatic Turk, together with the brash music surrounding him, could serve at once as a source of amusement and confirm an audience's notion of European civility and cultural superiority.

If we look forward to the later nineteenth century, operatic orientalism assumes an entirely different character. We move from a male- to a female-centered Orient, from the harshness of military music to the mellifluousness of

Arab-flavored melismas, from the East as a place of threat and force to one of softness and passivity, from a cavalier attitude toward dramatic or musical verisimilitude to an attempt to create the illusion of geographical authenticity. Between Gluck and Mozart, on the one hand, and the heyday of operatic orientalism, on the other, one can cite a succession of events within political, intellectual, and literary history: Napoleon's invasion of Egypt; the *Description de l'Égypte*, that multivolumed project initiated by Napoleon to create a compendium of knowledge about a long-ignored civilization; the popular representations of the Near East in Byron's jaded oriental heroes and in the exotic, evocative images shaping the lyrics of Hugo's *Les Orientales*; and the various imperialist expansions ranging from the French seizure of Algeria to Russia's occupation of the Islamic lands to its south and southeast.

Consider the distinct forms of orientalism in two works of the early 1870s, Bizet's *Djamileh* (1872) and Verdi's *Aida* (1871). Bizet's little-known one-act opera, once championed by Mahler and Richard Strauss, contains the essential elements of late-nineteenth-century musical orientalism in paradigmatic and also masterly form—the exaggerated melismas in the heroine's ballad about a girl's longing for an Indian king, the harmonic and rhythmic imitations of Arabic forms to establish the Near Eastern local color, the percussive effects (above all of the triangle and the tambourine) that a century before had suggested military threat and now help create a seductive world in which sexual passions may be both aroused and fulfilled.[26] According to Eduard Hanslick's 1898 account, the best parts of the opera are those that evoke the local color of the Near East, those in which "the composer has perceived and given shape to the soul of the Orient."[27]

Distantly based on the final pages of Musset's Byronically self-conscious narrative poem *Namouna*, Bizet's opera de-ironizes its source much as Tchaikovsky's *Evgeny Onegin* was to de-ironize its Pushkin original. Its simple plot charts its heroine's success in tricking the hero Haroun, who, accustomed to a succession of women to each of whom he grants only a single encounter, is tricked into accepting her a second time by means of her disguise; by the end of the opera, the oriental hero's promiscuous habits are converted into a monogamy that accords with its Western audience's professed sexual code.

The presence of Djamileh's coconspirator Splendiano, echoing the comic Arabic servant of late-eighteenth-century opera, works to remind us of the huge gap between the latter form and the enchanting musical orientalism dominating Bizet's opera. In its brief, hour-long duration, *Djamileh*, with a light-handed charm that few of Bizet's fellow composers could match, displays some key conventions of operatic orientalism in its time: the establishment of an exotic place by easily recognizable musical means, the heroine's lament at her powerlessness, and her ability to amend and control her situation by means of seductive song and dance. Above all, Djamileh radiates a powerfully sexualized and specifically "oriental" femininity manifesting itself—as operatic performance allows to a degree that an orientalist painting or literary work could never do—as a singing and dancing body.

The orientalism of *Aida*, a work of considerably greater proportions whose international popularity has never waned since its early performances, is of a more complex and problematic sort. Indeed, in response to Said's use of this opera to illustrate the entanglements of orientalism and imperialism, Paul Robinson has questioned whether the term "orientalism" is even appropriate to this opera: what Verdi was really concerned with in *Aida*, Robinson argues, was not the politics of current-day or ancient Egypt, but the relationship between Italy and the Hapsburg monarchy from which Italy had just liberated itself.[28] Verdi, he reminds us, never sought out the subject matter of *Aida* as he did that of his other operas but was commissioned to compose it by the Egyptian ruler, the Khedive Ismail, who was prepared to turn to Gounod or Wagner if Verdi turned him down. Whatever Verdi's own notions about the essential content of his opera, operagoers since its earliest performances tend to note the exotically "oriental" sound of the music (not to speak of the exotic look of the décor) even if, as Robinson reminds us, the orientalizing music encompasses only a small part of the score. (With very few exceptions, notably *Djamileh*, the orientalizing music of nineteenth-century operas is generally confined to a few episodes, usually of a ceremonial nature.) As Hanslick, writing within a year or two of the premiere put it, "Verdi applies national coloring to his music with great skill . . . in the dances and temple chants [with the] peculiarly whimpering melody of Orientals, with their aug-

mented fourth and diminished sixth, their scant harmony and simple, for-
eign-sounding instrumentation."[29] Just as Gluck had used an approximation
to the contemporary Near East to depict his ancient Scythians, Verdi resorts
to the orientalist conventions of his time to define an Egyptian culture that
knew a distinctly different music.

Yet Hanslick in this essay also speaks of "two original Egyptian motifs"
that Verdi employed in the temple scene at the end of the first act.[30] Whether
Hanslick thought these to be ancient or modern Egyptian, what is significant
here is the fact that during the nineteenth century composers came to seek,
and audiences to expect, a certain historical authenticity in what was being
depicted on the stage. Early in the century Carl Maria von Weber, for example, could boast of finding "original" non-Western tunes—a Chinese one published in the eighteenth century for his *Turandot* overture (1809) and a Near
Eastern one for his orientalist opera *Oberon* (1826).[31] This illusion of authenticity could be achieved in sets and costumes more readily than in music; Said,
for instance, links the set designs for the original *Aida* to the sketches included in the Napoleonic *Description de l'Égypte*.[32] Getting back to ancient
Egyptian music was a considerably greater problem than reconstituting its visual artifacts, many of which, after all, were still in Egypt for all to see. Verdi's
publisher Giulio Ricordi encouraged the composer to read a section on Egyptian music in a general history of music written by the Belgian composer and
historian François-Joseph Fétis, who reproduced what he took to be typical
ancient Egyptian scales. An Egyptian flute in a Florence museum supposedly
provided evidence of what the music sounded like, and Verdi even visited the
museum to examine the flute, which he deemed "but a pipe with four holes
like our shepherds have" and thus too primitive for a modern operatic performance.[33] But in the triumphal scene Verdi did include a long, straight
trumpet like those pictured in ancient Egyptian paintings, though we now
assume that this trumpet was of Roman rather than Egyptian origin.[34]

In an earlier book I discussed *Aida* as a product of the "new archeology"
of the nineteenth century, just as, in Chapter 5, I spoke of Wagner's *Ring des
Nibelungen* as a product of the new philology.[35] If the philology of the time
was primarily nationalist in character, the archeology, above all in France,

combined nationalism with an imperialist mission. Though both *Aida* and the *Ring* in performance establish the illusion of autonomous works of art independent of the contexts within which they were created, it is difficult, in view of our present-day knowledge of these contexts, to experience the stage illusions they strive for without also feeling aware of the often unresolved social and cultural tensions underlying them. To grapple with these tensions, Said has suggested what he calls a "contrapuntal interpretation" not only of *Aida* but of a host of other nineteenth- and early-twentieth-century works that he takes up in *Culture and Imperialism*.[36] On the one hand, the audience hears the opera "itself" in all its musical and dramatic splendor, and, on the other, it remains aware of a whole cast of characters "outside" the opera who instigated and helped shape its composition and production: Khedive Ismail, technically viceroy to the Ottoman emperor, but very much his own ruler within Egypt, which was at that time the most economically progressive part of the empire; Paul Draneht, a Greek Cypriot who had played a key role in negotiating the construction of the Suez Canal by a European consortium and who happened as well to be the impresario of the new opera house for which *Aida* was commissioned; and finally Auguste Mariette, a Frenchman who counts as one of the founding fathers of Egyptology, who had lived in Egypt since 1850 doing excavations, and who, with the financial help of Ferdinand de Lesseps, the builder of the canal, had founded the first major museum of ancient Egyptian artifacts. It was this last-named character, Mariette, who concocted the scenario of the opera—from sources still not incontrovertibly established[37]—that was submitted to Verdi.

However much Verdi may have thought himself to be dramatizing the political tensions generated within the Risorgimento (tensions which underlie many of his earlier operas, no matter what their purported settings), to the extent that *Aida* was the product of the committee named here, it served to offer legitimacy and fame (not least of all because of the composer's high status within European culture) to a Near Eastern ruler of a backward and not-yet-independent country. Egypt owed its quick rise to the cotton trade, which had temporarily lost its North American base as a result of the Civil War; as a result of this prosperity and the recent opening of the Suez Canal, he clearly

FIG. 15. The Cairo Opera House (1869–1971), photographed shortly before its destruction by fire. Photo, John Ross.

felt the need to display his success in material terms that the Western world could observe. Figure 15 shows the opera house that the Khedive had built in the neo-Renaissance style then fashionable for public buildings in Europe. By building such a structure and situating it strategically at the confluence of Cairo's poor native quarter and the modern, Western-style city he had constructed, he could at once claim the prestige accruing to a European monarch and display his link with an ancient, archeologically reconstructed Egypt that became glorified in Verdi's opera and that contrasted starkly with the bedraggled, still underdeveloped land he had inherited.

Such are the complexities that entangle the student of *Aida* today. Whether or not one chooses to call the opera orientalist, *Aida* more than any earlier opera except for Meyerbeer's *L'Africaine*, its immediate predecessor, helped to inspire the Eastern local color (both Near and Far Eastern, as well as South Asian) cultivated within the many orientalist operas that dominated the world's stages until well into the twentieth century.[38] Yet if we go more than a century forward to our own time, it is clear that the operatic Orient visible in recent works is scarcely orientalist in any earlier sense. In that compendium of earlier operatic styles, *The Ghosts of Versailles* (1992), John Corigliano presents a crude parody of both the eighteenth- and nineteenth-century versions of orientalism. Near the end of the long first act a giant effigy of one Soleyman Pasha appears on the stage accompanied by long-familiar orientalist percussion effects and plaintive woodwind melismas, while the strings play a version of the muezzin's call and veiled dancers go through their predictable gyrations. A fat, aged diva in the guise of a veiled Near Eastern siren named Samira is carried in to mouth such clichés as "The fragrance of jasmine," "The warmth of the desert," and "The beauty of the moon." Just as Flaubert, in his descriptions of his Egyptian journey, mingled reminders of Near Eastern dirt and disease with his more erotic details, so this scene seeks to expose the dark underbelly of orientalism: "In every house there is a cesspool," Samira sings at one point and at another, "He beat me, wept, stole my water and then complained." The scene ends with Samira leading a group of male dancers in drag in a gross caricature of late-nineteenth-century orientalist divertissements. "The Arab/Islamic world, quite bad enough in its present morass, is degraded still further by this utterly silly and confusing scene," Said wrote in his role as music reviewer.[39]

Precisely two centuries after Gluck's and Mozart's captivity narratives, both of which proclaimed the triumph of Western ethical values over those of the supposedly barbaric East, Philip Glass in *Satyagraha* (1980) created a kind of reverse orientalism by celebrating the legacy of what he took to be a peculiarly Eastern idea, namely, the nonviolent civil disobedience conceived and practiced by Mohandas Gandhi.[40] Glass set his opera in South Africa at the turn of the century in order to concentrate on Gandhi's formative years as a political figure leading his fellow South African Indians in passive resistance to the British regime that had denied them their rights. Like most of Glass's works for the stage, *Satyagraha*, whose title means "truth-force" (a term that Gandhi had used for the title of a book) is more oratorio-like than traditionally operatic, ceremonial rather than dramatic in the usual sense. It consists of a series of tableaux charting key moments in Gandhi's South African career—Gandhi addressing his followers, leading the crowd in defiance of the British government, conducting a prayer meeting. In what could be called a theatrical collage, the events surrounding Gandhi's life are juxtaposed with images of mythological battlefields suggesting the Bhagavad Gita, certain of whose passages are quoted at length in the libretto in their original Sanskrit. Indeed, the whole opera is sung in Sanskrit, with the passages supplied by the librettist, Constance deJong, translated back into this ancient language, whose effect is not to evoke some exotic Orient but, like the Latin of Stravinsky's *Oedipus Rex*, to establish a formal distance between the audience and what it witnesses on stage. The collage effect is heightened even further by three figures who literally hover over the set, one for each of the three acts. These figures—two Western, one Eastern—all have particular affinities with Gandhi: Leo Tolstoy, chosen because his social ideas influenced Gandhi; the latter's Indian contemporary and friend, the poet Rabindranath Tagore; and Martin Luther King, who sought to transfer Gandhi's ideas and methods to a Western political context.

Just as the Sanskrit words refuse to elicit the romantic responses characteristic of an earlier orientalism, so the minimalist style associated with Glass resists granting its audiences the sensual pleasures of nineteenth-century orientalism. Yet in its own way Glass's style, in *Satyagraha* as well as in his other compositions, is more genuinely a product of Eastern influence than most of the music we dub orientalist. For Glass in his formative years, as he explains in detail, was closely associated with the Indian sitar player Ravi Shankar and himself spent considerable time in India seeking alternatives to the Western styles he had learned in his conservatory years as a serialist and later as a student of Nadia Boulanger. As Glass explains it, "In Western music . . . you take a length of time and slice it the way you slice a loaf of bread. In Indian music (and all the non-Western music with which I'm familiar), you take small units, or 'beats,' and string them together to make up larger time values."[41] The resulting style would scarcely sound "oriental" or even specifically Indian to a Western listener unless the latter had been informed of Glass's particular interests. For one thing, *Satyagraha* uses a conventional opera orchestra, nor does it seek to exploit the instrumental effects used by earlier orientalist composers. Yet Glass always remains mindful of the Eastern origins of his music; thus, in explaining the chaconne harmony in the first scene of *Satyagraha*, he points out its derivation from flamenco guitar music, adding that "this particular form of Spanish folk music was introduced into Spain by gypsies who, it is believed, originated in India."[42]

If Glass propounds the superiority of Eastern spiritual values in *Satyagraha*, his fellow minimalist composer John Adams, in *The Death of Klinghoffer* (1991), seeks a reconciliation between East and West, both of which he treats in as evenhanded a way as is conceivable in retelling a recent historical event surrounding an Arab terrorist attack on a ship full of American tourists and the consequent killing of an innocent Jewish passenger. As a work that confronts the conflicting values of profoundly separate political and religious cultures, *The Death of Klinghoffer* is doubtless the paradigmatic opera of the age of multiculturalism. Though cast like *Satyagraha* in the form of a historical drama, *The Death of Klinghoffer* is just as ceremonial and oratorio-like as the former in the effects that it creates; it may well be that the minimalist style, with its endlessly repetitive melodies and slow changes of harmony, has a built-in ceremoniousness whatever composer may employ it.

If the earlier work seeks to celebrate the values of its Eastern hero as superior to those of the West, *Klinghoffer* clearly wants to mediate between two cultures in seemingly irreconcilable conflict. As Said has written in a review of this opera, "As you sit there watching this vast work unfold, you need to ask yourself how many times you have seen any substantial work of music or dramatic or literary or pictorial art that actually tries to treat the Palestinians as tragically aggrieved, albeit sometimes criminally intent, people."[43] Although some Jewish reviewers complained of the opera's lack of political balance,[44] the dramatic method employed by the librettist, Alice Goodman, herself of Jewish background, from the beginning displays its aspiration to give equal weight to the opposing sides of one of this century's most bitter political and cultural conflicts. Thus the opera opens with two moving choruses, the first of displaced Palestinians, the second of exiled Jews. Each chorus presents the plight of its own people in strikingly parallel ways. But whereas the chorus of

Jews contains no trace of local color in its music, the Arab chorus, as well as a later aria sung by a member of the terrorist group, is characterized by the melismas that audiences since the early nineteenth century came to recognize as referring to the Near Eastern world. A melisma is even used to shape the term "Allah" when uttered by the ship's Western captain. Much as earlier composers since at least Weber have acknowledged the non-European sources consulted for their orientalist music, Adams has named Abed Azrié, a Syrian composer whose songs he listened to while composing one scene, and he also mentions wanting "to convey a sense of 'otherness' . . . if only to point up the fear of the unknown that must have gripped these American and European tourists [but] at no point did I try to imitate Arabic music. . . . What I did instead was to develop certain harmonic and melodic modes that were dedicated to one group and not shared by another."[45] Whatever the degree of actual imitation, an audience accustomed to the long tradition of Near Eastern musical reference quickly recognizes the locale signified by Adams's modes. Yet what seems particularly meaningful about the Near Eastern coloring of this music is that it never suggests the sexuality or the glamour of nineteenth-century orientalist opera, nor does Adams, despite the narrative he tells of terrorist activity, ever use this coloring, as Gluck and Mozart did in their *alla turca* numbers, to suggest threats of violence. Adams's is an orientalism stripped of its traditional meaning, if indeed we can call it an orientalism at all.

Indeed, as with *Satyagraha*, the ceremoniousness suggested by the minimalist style works to distance audiences from the rawness of the historical events being enacted before them.[46] And it scarcely seems surprising that both Adams and Peter Sellars, who directed the initial production, cite the Bach passions as models for their endeavor.[47] By a strange paradox, one might say, Adams and his team encourage us to impose a historical distance on a work extraordinarily close in its audiences' memory—some five or six years—to actual events they had read about in their newspapers or watched on the television news in October 1985. Even the team's preceding work, *Nixon in China* (1987), another operatic lesson on current events, offered a longer retrospect— in this instance, fifteen years—upon its historical source. Although most non-comic operas since Monteverdi's *L'incoronazione di Poppea* have at least purported to present a historical narrative (however false the narrative may be to what annotators of opera program notes tell us the "real" history was), this narrative has ordinarily been located in some distant past beyond the initial audience's personal memories. In *Klinghoffer* Adams plays upon our contemporary skepticism toward stereotypes about the "other" to offer a coup de grace, as it were, to that long tradition of operatic orientalism that inspired a succession of great composers to some of their most enticing (and, from a present-day point of view, also most provocative) passages.

A Chinese composer, Bun-Ching Lam, has recently provided a new musical approach to the East in a chamber opera, *The Child God* (1993), whose dramatis personae are shadow figures enacting an ancient legend about the adventures of a hero who slaughters gratuitously but is ultimately saved through a vision of a Chinese paradise. The dragon-killing early in this tale may remind the audience of an earlier operatic hero whose creator took two long evenings to spin out the salient moments in his life. Yet while Wagner devoted an unprecedented massiveness of sound and duration to develop his character Siegfried, Lam surprises us by condensing her tale to a 25-minute opera with the most minimal of forces—the Chinese string instruments called the *zheng* and the *pipa*, a bass clarinet that encompasses a large range of pitches, and percussion; moreover, the listener rarely hears more than two instruments playing at once. A narrator speaks the story in English while accompanied by instruments in the traditional manner of the *mélodrame*. As the shadow figures enact the heroic events, the "characters," all of them enacted by a single singer, perform in Chinese, with the vocal style varying from a kind of *Sprechstimme*, which exploits Chinese speech patterns much as Schoenberg exploited German ones, to aria-like passages in which the tonal properties of Chinese words help shape the musical line. The Chinese text alternates the composer's own writing with Chinese classical poems.

Just as Adams in *Klinghoffer* seeks to balance the political interests of East and West, so Lam, raised in the Far East but trained in Western music, mediates between musical styles, mixing a contemporary, multinational Western idiom with specifically Chinese features: the pitch intervals of Chinese speech, recognizably Chinese drum rhythms, the plucking of strings. Although Lam's use of the pentatonic scale will at first remind listeners of Puccini's two East Asian operas, she employs this scale primarily as a familiar way of referring to China. She does not seek to give us local color in the manner that Puccini and his nineteenth-century predecessors sought to do: whereas these earlier composers had used color to transport their audiences into some imaginary East, to convince them of the authenticity of that Eastern space they placed on stage, Lam's opera maintains an ironic distance from whatever Orient it may be conjuring up, a distance guaranteed, as it were, by such features as the English narration and the fact that the actions are performed not by the singers but by shadow figures.

When Steve Reich in *The Cave* (1993) introduces a passage about Abraham chanted from the Torah and in the next act places a traditional chant about the same ancient character from the Koran, we hear the "authentic" voices of the Near East to a degree that earlier orientalist operas did not realize. But these chants constitute only a brief part of Reich's opera, which consists of meditations on the nature of Abraham and his family uttered by individuals (real people whose statements in interviews make up most of the libretto) drawn from various cultures—Israeli, Palestinian, and ultimately modern American—that look back to Abraham as a common ancestor. Unlike Adams, Reich does not dramatize a political confrontation between these cultures; rather, as the librettist, Beryl Korot, put it in the notes issued with the recording, "We attempted to steer away from the politics of the . . . Arab/Israel conflict" and focus instead on "the culture and religion of these peoples."[48] Whereas each of the first two acts is devoted to one of the Near Eastern groups, the third act is based on interviews with Americans—including some well-known artists and thinkers—who meditate on the same sacred figures but with considerably less involvement than the Israelis or Palestinians ("Abraham Lincoln High School," the sculptor Richard Serra answers when asked "Who is Abraham?"). Through its long passages of spoken matter based on the interviews; its lack of narrative; its use of video clips; its percussive sounds from the everyday world; its mixture of taped and live sound; and its singing voices, which deliberately avoid vibrato and are modeled on the style of preoperatic vocal music—by means of all these novel features *The*

Cave makes works such as *Satyagraha* and *The Death of Klinghoffer* look quite traditionally operatic. From the standpoint of the present chapter it seems particularly significant that so radical an attempt as Reich's to rethink the materials, the structure, and the musical style of opera should focus upon the cultural confrontation of East and West—even if not explicitly politicized—a concern central to the history of opera for well over two centuries.

If recent composers such as Glass, Adams, Lam, and Reich have succeeded in desensualizing the Orient, one should also note that however different the forms that orientalist opera has taken over the past two centuries, the Orient has continued to provide an icon for various modes of "otherness"—the otherness of supposedly less advanced cultures, of gender, of forbidden social practices. Philip Brett, in a study tellingly entitled "Eros and Orientalism in Britten's Operas," has shown how Benjamin Britten employs Eastern-colored music to identify quite nonoriental male figures with homoerotic longings—for example, Peter Quint in *The Turn of the Screw* and Oberon in *A Midsummer Night's Dream*, both in pursuit of young males like those whom the composer himself was known to seek out—while he later assigned gamelan music to Tadzio, the boy pursued by the aging hero of *Death in Venice*.[49] Richard Taruskin has identified what he calls "the orientalist trope denoting sensuality (*nega*)" beginning as early as Glinka's *Ruslan and Lyudmila* (1842); continuing in Borodin's *Prince Igor* (first performance, 1890), whose seductive "oriental" deep contralto heroine, Konchakovna, performs her love duet a third below her Russian tenor partner; and evident even in the love theme that Tchaikovsky composed for his nonoperatic and otherwise nonoriental tone poem *Romeo and Juliet* (1869).[50] As one notes from these examples, the music that audiences learned to associate with the Orient has come to refer to matters that are only peripherally true of particular geographic locales but that all, in one way or another, stand outside what was perceived as the dominant culture.

The range of reference within orientalist music is especially evident in Bizet's *Carmen*, which, unlike *Djamileh*, the Bizet opera immediately preceding it, is not set in what we would today term the Orient. But Spain could claim special oriental status during the nineteenth century. In the most powerful theoretical formulation defining orientalist art of the time, Victor Hugo's preface (1829) to his lyric collection *Les Orientales*, Spain becomes oriental by virtue of its partially non-European heritage: speaking of the cultures that influenced his "reveries" and "thoughts" during the composition of these poems, Hugo cites "Hebraic, Turkish, Greek, Persian, Arabic, even Spanish, for Spain is still the Orient; Spain is half African, Africa is half Asiatic."[51] In the wake of Hugo's consecration of Spain as an orientalist site, one notes a long tradition of exotic visions of some mythical Spain—from Mérimée's story *Carmen*, out of which Bizet's librettists drew their text thirty years later, to such diverse artifacts as Manet's bullfighter, the Spanish-flavored instrumental pieces of Tchaikovsky, Rimsky-Korsakov, and Ravel, even the attempts of early-twentieth-century Spanish composers such as Albéniz, Granados, and De Falla to build on foreign hispanizing music in order to exoticize their own national heritage.

It scarcely seems surprising that Nietzsche, in seeking expression for his revulsion toward Wagner, should turn to *Carmen*, which he praises in terms consonant with Hugo's image of Spain: for Nietzsche, *Carmen* offers an "African serenity," a "more southern, brown, burnt sensibility," to contrast with what he sees as the "sick," northern art of the composer-poet whom he had earlier served as a disciple. "Il faut méditerraniser la musique," he writes in French as though for a moment having to shun his own, too-northern language. But if *Carmen* represents a healthy form of art in contrast with Wagner's, for Nietzsche it nonetheless exhibits traits long associated with orientalism, above all the uninhibited sensuality and violence—its treatment, for example, of "love as fatum, as *fatality*, cynical, innocent, cruel"—that he comes to praise it for, that, indeed, came to be the medicine he prescribed to counter the sickness he associated with Western decadence.[52] But *Carmen*, as Susan McClary has shown in detail in her full-length study of Bizet's last opera, manifests multiple levels of otherness. As a gypsy the heroine represents a racial other as defined by nineteenth-century audiences; as a factory worker she represents a class that had never been as graphically defined in earlier opera; as a woman she represents the seductive power, the destructiveness and ultimately the vulnerability with which her gender came to be depicted in operas of her time; and in the musical styles of her set pieces—the "Habañera," for instance, based as it is on an actual Cuban song—she calls attention to a popular music-hall culture quite at odds with the culture of the opera house for which Bizet composed her music.[53]

If Spain can count as orientalist territory in nineteenth-century art, one must also acknowledge varying degrees of orientalism within *Carmen*. Exotic though the bullfighter Escamillo may be, the non-gypsy characters of the opera appear distinctly European in relation to the "oriental" heroine and her gypsy friends. The bland Michaela, both in her dramatic function and in her musical style, provides a striking contrast to Carmen, who brings down the European hero by means of her seductive otherness. As such, *Carmen* can count as one among a succession of late-nineteenth- and early-twentieth-century operas that enact a cultural confrontation between East and West. Unlike the eighteenth-century captivity narratives I described earlier, whose central figures are Westerners outwitting their Eastern captors, these operas focus the sympathies of their audiences upon a figure who is both oriental and female.

The model for these confrontations was doubtless Meyerbeer's posthumous *L'Africaine* (first performed in 1865), whose heroine Sélika is at once of East Indian origin and monarch of an island off the African coast, though she had also been brought to Portugal as a slave (see Figure 16, in which Rosa Ponselle suggests her abject and racially ambiguous condition). The Aeneas-like hero, Vasco da Gama, must ultimately reject her (as his Virgilian model rejected Dido) to take up his higher destiny, which here means both pursuing his conquests for Portugal and linking up with a more "appropriate" partner, the well-blooded European and distinctly less interesting Inès. Meyerbeer's opera, like David's cantata *Le Désert*, actually contains only a few passages that its audiences would have perceived as orientalist music, notably an exotic ballet on Sélika's island, Vasco's famous aria extolling the tropical setting, and a soothing lullaby that Sélika sings to the sleeping Vasco as, earlier in the opera, he languishes in a Portuguese prison. Meyerbeer's librettist Eugène Scribe gave Vasco a rival suitor for Sélika, her fellow native Nélusko, whose trickiness and unreliability retain the negative stereotypes of the oriental in order that the heroine may receive the audience's wholehearted sympathy. Indeed, her unambiguous preference for the white hero over somebody of her own kind must surely have ennobled her for audiences of the time. The opera culminates in an immolation scene, in which Sélika, rejected by Vasco and herself rejecting Nélusko, stands on a promontory watching her heroic lover sail off with his white bride and sings herself to death inhaling the poisonous flowers of a native plant, exotically named the mancinilla. In her death the audience could experience at once the plight of the abandoned colonial other and the necessity that the imperialist project (at its height among the British and French at this time) must roll on whatever its human cost. *L'Africaine*, like most of Meyerbeer's operas in French, remained a repertory staple until well into the twentieth century—yet much the same pattern of meanings can be found in a contemporaneously composed work, Berlioz's *Les Troyens* (1858), which, though scarcely known in its time, spells out its imperial theme even more explicitly than Meyerbeer's opera: at the end we are made to witness a vision of the future Rome above the pyre of Dido, toward whom, in her final agonies, we had directed our sympathy.

One can map out a sequence of East-West confrontations with settings progressively further East: Delibes's 1883 *Lakmé* represents the pathos of a Brahmin priest's daughter in love with a British officer (see Figure 17, in which Lily Pons, though reluctant, unlike Ponselle, to darken her skin, shows off the splendor of her oriental regalia) and who, like Meyerbeer's Sélika, kills herself by means of an exotic plant—in Lakmé's case, the datura. Another two decades later Puccini composed *Madama Butterfly* (1904), which moves to the easternmost site that could be termed "oriental" and whose pathetic heroine chooses a meticulously detailed Japanese suicide ritual (depicted by Claudia Muzio in the cover illustration) that, even after almost a century, rarely fails to reduce its Western audiences to tears. By the time of *Butterfly* the balance between Eastern and Western characters that Meyerbeer's opera had maintained shifted to favor the oriental heroine unequivocally (foolishly trusting though she may be) while the Western hero, despite the passionate love music assigned to him, is eventually exposed as little more than a shallow cad, with the heroine's bland Western rival's role reduced (increasingly so as Puccini revised the score) to the point that she appears on stage only to enable

FIGS. 16 and 17. Two versions of the operatic oriental "other": Fig. 16 (*left*), Sélika (Rosa Ponselle), and Fig. 17 (*right*), Lakmé (Lily Pons). Courtesy, Culver Pictures and The Metropolitan Opera Archives, respectively.

the heroine to recognize her husband's betrayal. One might note that the likely model for Puccini's Pinkerton was recently identified as the naval officer William B. Franklin, who eventually became a Wall Street broker, who lived until 1942, and whose name in the opera suggested the original character's given names.[54] How much compassion might he have expended upon the hapless heroine whenever he joined other members of his class at the Metropolitan to hear this opera about his early adventures?

With each of these operas one notes an increased proportion of orientalizing music. Although earlier composers such as Félicien David and Meyerbeer had been sparing in the amount of exotic flavor they doled out to their audiences, their successors found such music a commodity considerably in demand; similarly, orientalizing visual artifacts had become commercially profitable items in the course of the nineteenth century. Indeed, the commodifying possibilities of orientalist music recently became evident in a strikingly new way when, over a century after the composition of *Lakmé*, the Eastern-sounding music of the first-act duet between Lakmé and her slave Mallika was broadcast *ad nauseam* in the advertisements of an international airline to lure its captive listeners to purchase distant Eastern voyages.

The orientalizing moments in late-nineteenth- and early-twentieth-century operas are often those that, among critics intent upon guarding music as a form of high art, have given opera the reputation of pandering to audiences for the sake of commercial success. The ballet sequences displaying brazenly contorted bodies accompanied by correspondingly brazen orientalist orchestral music serve to reveal, indeed, to underscore the popular nature of opera.[55] Nobody would begrudge a commercially ambitious composer such as Massenet the orientalist purple patches within a number of his operas, yet similar passages are present, above all in the ballets, of operas by composers with otherwise "serious" aesthetic pretensions. Saint-Saens's *Samson et Dalila*, originally conceived as an oratorio, reveals itself near the end as shamelessly theatrical in its Bacchanale. Such great Russian operas as *Khovanshchina* and *Prince Igor* have long been known in the non-Russian world mainly through their purple patches—the Persian and Polovtsian dances, respectively—performed regularly at pops concerts. Analysts of the once-avant-garde *Salome* have characteristically apologized for the intrusion of so flagrantly "vulgar" a piece as the heroine's Dance of the Seven Veils;[56] but the avant-gardism of this opera cannot be separated from its orientalism, which, as Sander L. Gilman has shown, is intimately connected to Strauss's depiction of the Jews in the opera in the guise of East European Jewish types—and all of this designed for the consumption of liberal Westernized Jews who could watch this opera congratulating themselves on their cultural superiority to their Eastern brethren.[57]

Even so aesthetically uncompromising a work as Schoenberg's *Moses und Aron* sports its own orientalist purple patch in its dance around the golden calf; although the composer's twelve-tone method does not provide him a musical code that audiences could easily recognize as orientalizing, the rigid rhythms of this "dance" music (the composer himself referred to it as the "most primitive program music"),[58] together with the stage directions calling for an orgy of drunkenness, four naked women to be knived to death by their priests, and various other unspeakable practices associated with the Orient give an unmistakable signal of the tradition to which it belongs. Once one notes the persistence of this tradition, one must add that even the supposedly high-minded Wagner wrote his own purple patches, though not with the overtly orientalizing music of his successors: one can cite, for instance, the Bacchanale that Wagner composed for the Paris version of *Tannhäuser* in 1861 to satisfy the Opéra's requirement for a ballet, or, to name an even more blatant example, the flower maidens in *Parsifal*, whose allures Syberberg exposed in his 1982 film of this opera by reducing them to whores.

The late-nineteenth-century focus upon the plight of oriental women serves not only to highlight a fascination with racial otherness but also to suggest a connection between racial and gender otherness. In nineteenth-century noncomic operas, and well before the East became a favored setting, the central tragic figure was generally the soprano. In my earlier book on opera I referred to these works as successors to Christian martyr plays.[59] If one notes the great mad scenes within those operas whose period style we have come to label *bel canto*, or the great monologues uttered in their final scenes by later heroines as diverse as Violetta, Didon, Sélika, Isolde, Brünnhilde, and Elektra, it is clear that the central female figure has become the prime site upon whom the audience can lavish its feelings of pity and terror. The very title of Catherine Clément's pioneering feminist study, *L'Opéra, ou la défaite des femmes* (*Opera, or the Undoing of Women*), indicates the special martyr role that has been reserved for operatic heroines since the early nineteenth century. When Meyerbeer's Sélika and her successors take over this role, their racial specificity simply makes more explicit the subordinate role to which women in general were subjected and to which opera has sought (quite literally, in fact) to provide a voice.

The oriental woman thus becomes a figure for woman in general. As Said has put it, "Orientalism is a praxis of the same sort, albeit in different territories, as male gender dominance, or patriarchy, in metropolitan societies." The conflation of female and Oriental in nineteenth-century art scarcely seems accidental, for, as Said goes on, "The Orient was routinely described as feminine, its riches as fertile, its main symbols the sensual woman, the harem, and the despotic—but curiously attractive—ruler. Moreover Orientals, like Victorian housewives, were confined to silence and to unlimited enriching production."[60] It is significant, for instance, that such temporal art forms as opera and the novel should seek out methods for breaking the silences to which women were confined in the nineteenth century. Whereas the novel, by means of interior monologue, developed a method for exploring the inner voices of, say, an Emma Bovary or an Anna Karenina, opera could count upon the convention that a character—however silent she might appear in so-called real life—may give actual and often even overpowering voice to her emotions.

Once the historicity of orientalism has become evident, one must ask how this insight may affect our experience of orientalist art. Is one to distance oneself from this art to the point that one no longer cares to engage with it? Certainly a reading of Said's book when it first appeared provided so powerful a shock of recognition that some readers felt tempted to reject those works of art created within that mode of Western discourse that Said defined as orientalism. Similarly, early feminist criticism that exposed the male-conceived images of women in literature and film sometimes seemed to imply that many revered works no longer needed to be taken seriously.

Said himself has obviously felt the need to clarify and refine the arguments of *Orientalism*, for he has published two retrospective essays, the first nearly a decade after publication of the book, the second still another decade later.[61] In the second of these essays he stresses that his intention had not been to essentialize either the "East" or the "West" but to examine how a particular image of the Orient had become constructed over the past two centuries in European scholarship and descriptive writing. In *Culture and Imperialism*, a book published between these two essays to expand *Orientalism*'s argument, he attempts to formulate what he calls "an alternative both to a politics of blame and to the even more destructive politics of confrontation and hostility."[62] In his approach to earlier works of art this alternative takes the form of what

Said calls contrapuntal interpretation, by means of which, as I indicated in the discussion of *Aida* above, one maintains a kind of double awareness, experiencing the work at the same time that one views it (in this particular instance) within the orientalist/imperialist context in which it was shaped.

Is it really possible for opera audiences to distance themselves historically from the aesthetic experience they should supposedly be having in the opera house? In Chapter 5 I suggest that, while witnessing the *Ring*, it is possible to alternate moments of feeling spellbound with an awareness of what today seem such politically reprehensible practices as Wagner's attempt to embody the new, nationally oriented philology and his imputed caricatures of Jews in the guise of Nibelungs. Paradoxically, however, it is precisely the new aesthetic associated with Wagner that sought to bully an audience into total attentiveness to the work at hand. Once he had darkened the auditorium and made spellbinding central to one's musical and dramatic experience, it was not only difficult but, indeed, heretical to resist the passivity to which Wagner reduced his audience. Must we suppress our critical faculties in order to engage with music? Must we accept the silence and obedience imposed upon an audience by the Wagnerian aesthetic? Surely the eighteenth-century Italian opera house (to cite an extreme example), with its chaotic comings and goings in the boxes, its technological inability to allow lighting to separate the performance from an audience's social activities, would have proved more conducive than the post-Wagnerian house to the critical engagement with opera I put forward here.[63]

This engagement would not, however, include what Said calls a "politics of blame." To read the art of the past in order to find scapegoats for our present-day ills is a futile task, whatever temporary therapeutic effects it may offer. Indeed, blame is not a satisfactory means for keeping readers, or listeners, or viewers of art attentive for very long. A genuine historically based aesthetics would encourage us to rethink the common wisdom that has accrued over the years about long-familiar works. It would ask us to reframe the questions we ask ourselves about these works, to attempt to locate the most appropriate contexts within which to ponder their meaning, their formal properties, and the power they exercise upon us. And it would ask us, as well, to make our own decisions about how and when and to what degree we will allow them to exercise this power.

How, then, might one approach the extravagant orientalist fantasies of later-nineteenth-century opera? In watching the dances of the Nubian slaves in Amneris's private rooms, or the revels that precede Samson's knocking down the pillars, or Salome's stripping of her veils (often, these days, to reveal the singer's bare body, for better or worse), we quickly recognize that behind these images of some mythical and ancient Near East there stand the sexual desires of a repressed culture that transferred these desires to a place distant and powerless enough to allow free interpretive access. When we hear the explorations into new musical modes and rhythms in these passages, we also recognize the needs that listeners felt for new sonic territories to spice up standard period styles that had come to sound conventional—just as these new orientalist territories would all too soon themselves count as conventional! And each time we experience a radically new setting for a well-known opera, as in the non-China to which *Turandot* was moved in the example with which I began this chapter, we must ask what this shift may tell us about our own, present-day cultural biases—or at least of those prevalent within that theatrical profession to which we entrust our productions.

And if we feel a certain embarrassment today at the kitsch we see and hear in the purple patches of operas we deem otherwise intellectually respectable, we may ask ourselves if there is not a certain popular element, even a "vulgarity" inherent within the whole of, say, *Samson* and *Salome*, indeed, also of *Aida*. Or, to put it another way, we may ask whether the lines of demarcation we set up to separate "high" from "popular" art must be located elsewhere in opera, especially during the nineteenth and early twentieth centuries, than they are in other, more intimate and less publicly directed forms of music. Indeed, as I attempt to show in Chapter 7 by juxtaposing two works of about 1930, a twelve-tone music-drama and a traditionally organized "number" opera building upon popular musical forms, these lines of demarcation are not always as clear as we may think.

Chapter Seven

Moses und Aron, Mahagonny, and Germany in 1930: Seventeen Entries

ANTITHESES

> They [*Mahagonny* and *Moses und Aron*] shaped the twin foundations of whatever viable opera the future might yet hold in store.
>
> —Alexander Ringer,
> *Arnold Schoenberg: The Composer as Jew*

From a review by W. W. Göttig of the "Dance Around the Golden Calf," performed in Darmstadt on July 2, 1951, a few days before Schoenberg's death, and the only part of *Moses und Aron* to receive a performance during the composer's lifetime:

> Arnold Schoenberg's musical language discloses itself to the listener's understanding only with great difficulty: in its fully unconventional diction, which refuses to make concessions, it remains a book with seven seals if one does not have the piano reduction or, even better, the full score at hand. To be sure, one recognizes strong and moving thematic ideas and monstrous eruptions from the orchestra that pile up to create powerful structures of sound, delicate lyrical resting places—but in their total impression they become obliterated by the harshness and inflexibility of the frequent (we shall say it bluntly) ear-torturing cacophony.[1]

From a review in *Die Scene* by H. H. Stuckenschmidt of the first performance in Leipzig on March 9, 1930, of *Aufstieg und Fall der Stadt Mahagonny*:

> [Weill] dissolves the action into song-type episodes and thus creates hauntingly melodic operatic numbers. Not only the most attractive high points—such as the "Alabama Song," the ballad "The dice roll the way you have cast them," or the magnificent "Cranes" love duet—but also linking passages have been worked with loving detail and are often modelled directly on pre-classical (Handelian) examples. . . . The work forms a climax in the operatic history of the age.[2]

TABLE 1. Antitheses

	Schoenberg, *Moses und Aron*	Weill, *Aufstieg und Fall der Stadt Mahagonny*
Date of Composition	1930–32 (unfinished), revised until composer's death in 1951	1927–29, revised until 1931
Librettist	Composer	Bertolt Brecht
First Performance	1954 (radio); 1957 (stage)	1930
Mode of Organization	Throughcomposed music-drama	Number-opera
Musical Style	Twelve-tone	Mixed, from neoclassical to popular music, and drawing on direct quotation and stylistic allusion
Setting	Ancient Jews on way to Palestine	An imagined contemporary America
Sources	Bible; unfinished play *Der biblische Weg*	No known outside source, but with passages drawn from earlier Brecht poems and plays
Ideological Framework of Libretto	Zionism (conservative wing)	Marxism
Relation to Composer's Earlier Style	At least as complex	Increasingly simple
Implied Audience	Fit audience though few	Large range of theatergoers
Contemporary Reception	Unfinished, unperformed	Multiple productions, considerable success, loud right-wing protests
Status Within Present-Day Canon	Immense respect, occasional productions	Increasing respect, occasional productions

AVANT-GARDE

If anybody were asked today which of these two works—*Aufstieg und Fall der Stadt Mahagonny* or *Moses und Aron*—was perceived in its time as the more avant-garde, the answer would surely be Schoenberg's twelve-tone opera rather than that jazz-influenced succession of easily digestible songs and ensembles concocted by Bertolt Brecht and Kurt Weill. Certainly Schoenberg would have assented to this judgment. Of the music composed for *Die Dreigroschenoper* (1928) Schoenberg was recorded as saying, "So what has he [Weill] accomplished? He's made us a gift once again of three-quarter time."[3] There is no reason to believe that Schoenberg's opinion of *Mahagonny* would, despite the latter's operatic pretensions, have been much different. From the avant-gardist Schoenberg's point of view, Weill's development as a composer was clearly retrograde.[4] Though never in the Schoenberg camp, Weill, like a number of his neoclassical contemporaries, had, before his collaborations with Brecht, earned a degree of respect from the older composer. Yet once Weill had begun to play with popular musical forms and, even worse from Schoenberg's point of view, to advertise his desire to make contact with the contemporary public, the gap between the two composers had become insuperable.

Schoenberg's avant-gardism was based on an aesthetic of difficulty, one that assumed—or at least hoped—that audiences would eventually become reconciled to his compositions once they had heard them sufficiently to get accustomed to their complexities. In early 1930, a few months before starting the composition of *Moses und Aron*, Schoenberg published a piece entitled "My Public," whose opening sentence reads, "Called upon to say something about my public, I have to confess: I do not believe I have one."[5] To the extent that the concept of avant-garde could encompass only those who baffled, confounded, or alienated the listening public, there was no way to include Weill—or, for that matter, his many contemporaries such as Milhaud, Hindemith, even Stravinsky during his neoclassical phase, all of whom sought a means of communication with audiences.

Yet the young Theodor Adorno, himself a former composition student of Alban Berg and also one of Schoenberg's most fervent and articulate defenders, extended the notion of what constitutes the avant-garde to encompass

FIG. 18. Kurt Weill and Lotte Lenya in 1929. Courtesy, The Weill-Lenya Research Center, Kurt Weill Foundation for Music, New York.

Schoenberg and Weill at once. In one of several early accounts of *Aufstieg und Fall der Stadt Mahagonny*, Adorno wrote, "Outside of the antithetically opposed operas of the Schoenberg school, I know of no work that fits the concept of the avant-garde more strictly and satisfactorily than *Mahagonny*" (*AGS*, 19: 193). Adorno argues powerfully for the seriousness with which *Mahagonny* employs its materials, even though his later fulminations against jazz and the culture industry in general would suggest him as an improbable advocate of a work that has consciously absorbed commercially oriented music. Behind its "primitive façade," Adorno tells us, *Mahagonny* belongs among "the most complex of modern works" (*AGS*, 19: 194). Not that it makes fun of the popular forms it uses: for Adorno, Weill's quotations of "salon music are not to be understood as literary parody" but as "a dialectical criticism of the music of the past" by means of montage (*AGS*, 18: 36–37). Note not only the Marxist

FIG. 19. Schoenberg, self-portrait, 1929. Courtesy, Lawrence
and Ronald Schoenberg and Nuria Schoenberg-Nono and © VBK,
Vienna, Europe, 1997.

locution "dialectical criticism" but above all the word "montage," which, with
its reference to Eisenstein's film technique, ties Weill's opera to the most enterprising artistic experiments of the 1920s. (Brecht had himself used the film-
inspired term in his notes to the opera [*BBS*, 3: 167].) For Adorno *Mahagonny*
achieves its modernity in an opposite way from that of Schoenberg's work,

for instead of abandoning assimilable melodies, it draws its material from "the decaying remains of nineteenth-century light music" (*AGS*, 19: 193). If Schoenberg gave up the chords familiar within the traditional tonal system, Weill employs them to demonstrate that these "chords have lost their power and can no longer create form" (*AGS*, 17: 121).

For Adorno Weill's achievement goes far beyond its formal concerns but lies as well in the social relevance it displays: thus, in an essay on contemporary opera, Adorno links *Mahagonny* with his teacher Berg's *Wozzeck* as a model work to legitimate modernist operatic style through the "understanding of society" that it shows (*AGS*, 19: 478). (In one of his reviews of *Mahagonny* Adorno had even defended the presence of French operettas within the Frankfurt repertory in order "to fill the coffers and thus enable productions of *Mahagonny* and *Wozzeck* to take place" [*AGS*, 19: 190]). *Mahagonny*'s claims to modernity extend beyond its text to its performance history; thus, using the characteristic language of Western Marxism of the 1920s, Adorno can refer to Lotte Lenya's portrayal of Jenny in the 1931 Berlin production as an "allegory of reification" (*AGS*, 19: 277).

Adorno's interest in Weill as an exemplar of avant-garde art did not outlive the Weimar Republic. Whereas in Adorno's later writings, the music of Schoenberg and his disciples came to define the avant-garde to the exclusion of less difficult composers, Weill's career as a successful composer of Broadway musicals during the latter's American years cast him as a representative of that culture industry which for Adorno was by its very nature antithetical to what could count as serious art.[6] Yet we can also look back at Adorno's sympathetic early accounts of *Mahagonny* to mark its place in that historical terrain that we have come to label "high modernism." The sounds from popular culture that well up in *Mahagonny*—the droning saxophone, the cabaret voices, the blues and fox-trot rhythms—find their analogies in other forms of the time: in the "Shakespeherian Rag" of *The Waste Land*, Gerty Macdowell's sentimental effusions in *Ulysses*, the newspaper cutouts in the collages of Picasso and Braque, the grotesque representations of the entertainment underworld in Max Beckmann. All these images, whatever their popular origins, have been framed by their creators to count as high art, whether in the pages of a novel or volume of poems, a picture hung on the wall, or an opera that, like *Mahagonny*, was designed for consumption in that most earnest of aesthetic establishments, the opera house.

BRECHT / WEILL

Of all the composer / librettist collaborations, only Verdi / Boito, Stravinsky / Auden, Strauss / Hofmannsthal, and Mozart / Da Ponte, perhaps also Lully / Molière, exude as fine an aura for us today as the collaboration between Brecht and Weill (Figure 20). In looking back at the great operas of the past, we generally make excuses for the libretto: *Fidelio* maintains its luster despite its awkward text, the great middle-period Verdi operas despite their narrative absurdities, the *Ring* despite its pretentious poetry. There are of course those operas whose composers set their texts (even if drastically cut) directly from famous plays—Debussy / Maeterlinck, Strauss / Wilde, Berg / Büchner, Berg / Wedekind—but these were by no means collaborations, for within this genre, commonly called *Literaturoper*, the librettist had no opportunity to talk back. And then there are those literary-minded composers who, from Berlioz and Wagner down to Schoenberg in *Moses und Aron*, chose to be their own librettists and resolve internally the considerable tensions inherent in any attempt to wed text to music.

But why do we say Brecht / Weill when we ordinarily privilege the composer's name in operatic collaborations? Doubtless this has to do with the relative reputations of these two parties at the time that the two major works they created together—*Die Dreigroschenoper* and *Aufstieg und Fall der Stadt Mahagonny*—were rediscovered after being forgotten for two decades. (The full score of *Mahagonny* did not even turn up until the early 1950s, several years after the death of the composer, who himself did not have access to it once he had left Germany.) Whereas Brecht emerged during the 1950s as one of the century's central dramatists—perhaps even *the* central dramatist—Weill at the time of his death in 1950 was remembered chiefly as the practitioner of a commercial form, the Broadway musical, that was not assumed to "endure" in the manner of classical music. Not until well into the 1970s did a serious reassessment of Weill's place in the history of twentieth-century mu-

FIG. 20. Brecht and Weill in 1928. Courtesy, The Weill-Lenya
Research Center, Kurt Weill Foundation for Music, New York.

sic begin. The result has been not only an interest in his works with Brecht but also in his instrumental and vocal works before the relatively brief collaboration with Brecht; indeed, in recent years some of Weill's Broadway musicals have even been revived *within* the opera house. Any analysis of the Brecht / Weill collaboration must also note the role of a third party, Brecht's sometime lover and longtime assistant, Elisabeth Hauptmann, who today is given a major responsibility for the texts of *Die Dreigroschenoper* and *Der Jasager*, both of which are based on translations she did from sources in English (a language she commanded far better than did Brecht) but also for those two *Mahagonny* numbers, the "Alabama" and "Benares" songs, memorable, beyond their music, for their charmingly nonnative English.[7] Certainly it would not be inaccurate to entitle the present entry Brecht / Hauptmann / Weill; in fact, the text of *Mahagonny* in Brecht's collected plays lists as collaborators [*Mitarbeiter*] "E. Hauptmann, C. Neher [the set designer], K. Weill" (*BBS*, 3: 168).

The Brecht / Weill collaboration began in 1927, when the two men, who circulated within the same circles in Berlin, were drawn together through Weill's attraction to the group of poems about the mythical city of Mahagonny included in Brecht's recent collection of poems, *Hauspostille*. They quickly discussed the possibility of an opera, toward which they created a half-hour entertainment, the so-called *Mahagonny Songspiel*, staged, in a program together with short operas by Milhaud, Hindemith, and Toch, at the prestigious Baden-Baden Chamber Music Festival in 1927. Work on the longer *Mahagonny* opera was interrupted by a number of collaborative pieces in varying genres: the enormously (and unexpectedly) successful *Dreigroschenoper*, the cantata *Berliner Requiem* (1928), the radio cantata *Der Lindberghflug* (1929), several individual songs, and the play with music *Happy End* (1928), for which Brecht claimed only to have written the lyrics, allowing Hauptmann to claim the rest under a pseudonym. Weill later listed these earlier collaborations with Brecht as "building stones" toward the opera *Mahagonny* (*WM*, 79–80). After the *Lehrstück* (didactic play) *Der Jasager* (1930) the collaboration yielded relatively little—except for some songs and most notably the ballet *Die sieben Todsünden* (1933), which was written for Paris after both men had left Germany.

Although the other celebrated composer / librettist collaborations, as the Strauss / Hofmannsthal correspondence amply shows, had their share of tensions, once *Mahagonny* had been launched, the clashes between Brecht and Weill made any further large projects impossible.[8] Doubtless Brecht's self-serving financial deals with Weill were part of the problem, and one can speculate that Brecht, unlike Hofmannsthal, was too imperious to collaborate long-term (as he later did with lesser composers such as Hanns Eisler and Paul Dessau) with a composer who was his artistic equal. In any event, by the time of the rehearsals for the Berlin production of *Mahagonny* in 1931, Brecht and Weill were fighting with one another in public,[9] and by 1933, during the composition of *Die sieben Todsünden,* Weill could write his lover Erika Neher, "After having worked with Brecht for a week I am more than ever of the opinion that he is one of the most repulsive, unpleasant characters on the face of the earth."[10] As an ironic afternote one might mention that during the early 1940s, when Brecht was an impoverished refugee in the United States and Weill an affluent member of the culture industry, the former sought to interest the latter in setting the music for two plays, but at the insistence of the composer's wife, Lotte Lenya, he was refused.[11]

Within the context of operatic history, what seems most significant about this illustrious though brief collaboration is less the personal conflicts than the fact that both the librettist and the composer claimed the primacy of his particular medium. Whereas Gluck / Calsabigi and Wagner / Wagner (the latter at least in his theoretical writings of the 1850s) accepted the subordination of music to text, the statements published separately by Brecht and Weill made their divergent biases clear. Even before the premiere Weill, for example, published three statements insisting that the epic-theater form, with its discrete episodes, enabled a composer to concentrate on musical form without constantly having to seek a musical means to propel the plot forward. "The content of the opera *Aufstieg und Fall der Stadt Mahagonny,*" Weill wrote in one of these statements, "made possible a construction according to purely musical laws" (*WM,* 77). As though in direct response to Weill's claims, Brecht's "Notes to the Opera *Aufstieg und Fall der Stadt Mahagonny,*" which were subsequently to count as his major pronouncement on the nature of epic theater, award primacy to the work's message. The same dramatic method that Weill credits with allowing a composer free musical rein becomes the writer's means for ensuring that his audience is forced to think about what he has to say. And it scarcely seems accidental that Brecht's growing attachment to Marxist thought coincided with the years of his collaboration with Weill.[12] By the time the work was produced in 1930, Brecht felt thoroughly committed to the didacticism inherent within the system of ideas he had espoused. A Marxist coloring is evident throughout the "Notes" to the opera: whereas in traditional theater "Thought determines being," in epic theater "Social being determines thought" (*BBS*, 3: 267). He insists, above all, on *Mahagonny*'s function to change society (*BBS*, 3: 276), while the music's role in this endeavor is not to "serve" the text, as in traditional music-drama (the term "serve" had been used in this sense by Monteverdi, Gluck, and Berg) but to "communicate" this text, to "interpret" it, to "take stands" (*BBS*, 3: 268–69).

Not that these conflicting stands were to be the last word on the relation of words and music. In Strauss's final opera, *Capriccio*, which premiered in Munich during World War II (an opera that neither Brecht nor Weill likely ever knew, let alone would have approved of) the conflict of librettist and composer becomes the overt subject of the work. Serving largely as his own librettist, Strauss / Strauss conjures up some of the most sumptuous music he ever prepared for the soprano voice (music that Brecht would have dismissed as the ultimate in what he called the "culinary" nature of traditional opera) to tell us at the end that the conflict cannot possibly be resolved.

CRISES

Armed revolts
    mid-March 1920: Wolfgang Kapp putsch
    November 8, 1923: Adolf Hitler beer hall putsch
Assassinations
    January 15, 1919: Karl Liebknecht and Rosa Luxemburg, leaders of
      Spartacus
    February 21, 1919: Kurt Eisner, prime minister of Bavarian workers'
      republic
    June 24, 1922: Walter Rathenau, German foreign minister

February 23, 1930: Horst Wessel, Nazi youth, shot on Berlin street,
later cast as a martyr

Birth / Death

November 9, 1918: republic proclaimed

January 30, 1933: Hitler appointed chancellor

Elections

September 14, 1930: Nazis elected as second largest party

July 31, 1932: Nazis elected as largest party

November 6, 1932: Nazis, despite some losses, retain hold as largest
party

Finance

June 1919: Treaty of Versailles imposes harsh reparations on Germany

Second half of 1923: devastating inflation

October 1929: American stock-market crash sets off international
economic crisis resulting in increasing and massive unemployment
in Germany

Opera

May 1930: "Peculiar opera-crisis," Theodor Adorno writes of the
Frankfurt Opera's inability to satisfy its "retrograde public" with the
"good old" *L'Africaine* of Meyerbeer, which the management assumed was the sort of opera that this public wanted (*AGS*, 19: 177)

March 6, 1931: After months of discussion of the "Berlin opera crisis"
(*WM*, 93), the Kroll Opera, which since 1927 had served as the home
of experimental new operas as well as iconoclastic productions of
classic works, in which, moreover, two short Schoenberg operas had
been performed in 1930 and in which Weill hoped (unsuccessfully)
to present *Mahagonny*, is ordered closed under right-wing pressure[13]

July 8, 1932: "To resolve the financial crisis of the opera," Weill writes
in a newspaper symposium entitled "Wirklich Opernkrise?" (Is there
really an opera crisis?), "one would have to lay hold of the widest
public spectrum, which means not limiting oneself to the specialized
opera public" (*WM*, 104)

ELITE / POP

The antitheses between *Moses und Aron* and *Mahagonny* appear particularly
sharp in the diverse attitudes their composers expressed about the audiences
they were addressing. Schoenberg was clearly composing for an elite audience

that he realized did not yet exist. Shortly before he began *Moses und Aron*, in an essay entitled "The Future of Opera," Schoenberg spelled out a belief prevalent among many modernist artists that serious art is incompatible with popular approval. "Art and success will yet again have to part company," he writes, claiming "it is self-evident that art which treats deeper ideas cannot address itself to the many." Rather, art is to address an elite capable of processing these ideas: "The minority that can understand deeper things will never let itself be satisfied wholly and exclusively by what everyone can understand."[14] The context within which Schoenberg voiced this frank elitist bias was one in which the nature and future direction of opera were being debated vigorously, above all in Berlin, where Schoenberg had moved from Vienna in 1926 to succeed the recently deceased Ferruccio Busoni to the prestigious chair of composition at the Prussian Academy of Fine Arts. (Figure 21 shows Schoenberg conducting for the Berlin radio around 1930.) On the other side of this operatic battle were those younger composers like Paul Hindemith, Ernst Krenek, and Kurt Weill, who sought to create contemporary forms of opera (*Zeitoper*, to cite a coinage of the time) that not only utilized settings from modern life but introduced musical and theatrical forms associated with popular culture in order to communicate with new audiences who were hostile or indifferent to traditional opera.

Among the advocates on the popular side of the debate none was more articulate than Kurt Weill. Both in his correspondence and in his many journalistic activities, Weill repeatedly insisted on the composer's need to find musical forms to woo audiences in a way that the older operas, above all those in the Wagnerian tradition, were unable to do. Writing to his publisher in 1927 as he was moving from the *Songspiel* version to the full-length *Mahagonny*, Weill speaks of "a completely new form of stage work . . . evolving, one that is directed to a different and much larger audience and whose appeal will be unusually broad."[15] This new audience would contrast with the traditional public, which is made up of a "closed-off group of people who seem to stand outside the larger theater public" and who live, as Weill turns to English for a proper phrase, in "splendid isolation" (*WM*, 55). Although this new type of work has hitherto been represented mainly in nonmusical the-

FIG. 21. Schoenberg conducting his own works at the Berlin Radio, around 1930. Courtesy, The Arnold Schoenberg Institute.

ater—above all, Weill tells us, in the earlier work of Brecht—he now hopes to create a new type of opera to tap the large audience attracted to nonmusical theater.[16] A year later Weill concluded his essay entitled *Zeitoper* with a vision of a "simple, naive listener who is not tied to preconceived assumptions or traditions, a listener who carries with him a healthy disposition schooled in work, sports, and technical expertise" (*WM*, 50).

What is striking about these two views of audiences is that both reject the opera public of their time and seek instead to cultivate an entirely new sort of listener. Since, to cite Adorno's words, "the goal and ideal of [Schoenberg's] music was traditionalist and tied to the bourgeois faith in authority and culture" (*AGS*, 14: 249), he felt it incumbent on himself to train an elite to experience his work. By contrast Weill sought to reach out to a public that, though clearly possessing some educational qualifications, did not carry along the traditional baggage belonging to high culture. Just as Adorno had viewed *Mahagonny* and the operas of the Schoenberg school as two distinct paths pursued by the avant-garde of his time (*see* AVANT-GARDE), so the British composer Constant Lambert could write in 1933, as *Mahagonny* was briefly making its way across the stages of Europe, "Even those who do not find Weill's music sympathetic must realize that he symbolizes the split that is taking place not between highbrow and lowbrow, but between highbrow and highbrow."[17]

Indeed, the more closely one examines the careers of these two composers, the less absolute one finds the seemingly irreconcilable disparity that separates them. If one asked anybody which of the two wrote music for the cabaret, only Weill, whose song style was strongly influenced by the cabaret music of his time, would come to mind. As it turns out, Weill never wrote for an actual cabaret, while Schoenberg in the earliest years of the century had composed a series of songs for the first of the celebrated Berlin cabarets, Ernst von Wolzogen's Überbrettl (the *über* having been inspired by Nietzsche's then-popular concept of the *Übermensch*).[18] To be sure, Schoenberg composed these songs purely for the money, nor did he assign opus numbers to them, nor were most of them even performed at the time. Yet Schoenberg's *Pierrot lunaire* (1912), despite the difficulties imposed by its atonality, its complex musical structures, and its use of *Sprechstimme* in place of the ordinary singing voice, breathes the air of the cabaret as well as that of an older popular institution, the *commedia dell'arte*, that was exciting the interest of modernist artists at the time;[19] in fact, *Pierrot* was much admired by so antithetical a spirit as Stravinsky and hailed on several occasions by that other antithetical spirit Kurt Weill as the greatest masterpiece of contemporary music.[20]

Schoenberg even composed a *Zeitoper* of his own, the autobiographical *Von heute auf morgen* (1930), which, like Strauss's *Intermezzo* (1924), tells an anecdote about suspicions (unjustified) of spousal infidelity. Despite its ringing telephone, its saxophones, and its occasional suggestions of jazz rhythm—all of these unmistakable signs of the style that Weill and his contemporaries cultivated—its twelve-tone method militates against any possibility that *Von heute auf morgen* might woo the large audience that Weill succeeded in reaching. When working in a nonmusical form, however, Schoenberg had no compunction about communicating with this audience: *Der biblische Weg*, the play he wrote in 1926–27 and that supplied the germ of *Moses und Aron*, would, if it had ever been performed or even published, have proved an easily consumable product in a way that his musical compositions after his break with tonality emphatically were not (even the occasional tonal compositions he wrote after this break could not communicate to the degree that Weill's works did). That Schoenberg sought out Max Reinhardt to produce this play indicates his desire to be associated with a director who had been cultivating a mass audience since early in the century.

Just as Schoenberg's music eschewed the approval of all but his chosen few, Weill's musical style during the late 1920s underwent a degree of simplification in order to communicate more readily. The "Alabama Song," for example, shed some of its dissonances and shifted from *Sprechstimme* to straight song when it was transformed from the *Songspiel* of 1927 to the operatic version of 1930.[21] Not that Weill was in any way content to view himself as a commercial composer. When Hans Heinsheimer, who in his capacity as head of the opera section at Weill's publishing house, Universal-Edition, asked him to free himself from his "industrial artistic endeavors" and to return to "deeper and more substantial musical creations," Weill protested that he had no desire at all to adapt to the taste and mentality of the provincial operagoers that his editor evidently had in mind; indeed, right after *Mahagonny*'s Leipzig premiere Weill boasted that the hostile demonstrations proved that he had not only chosen the correct path but that he had accomplished something truly innovative.[22]

In recent years the once-formidable boundary between elite and popular art has begun to break down. For example, Steve Reich, in an interview occasioned by his opera *The Cave* (1993), remarked that he found Weill "very relevant" to his work "because we are living in a time when the lines between what is high art and what is going on in the street are, thankfully, drawn closer together."[23] As I show in Chapter 8, John Cage's *Europeras 1 & 2* are dedicated to questioning many of the aesthetic assumptions central to the form since its beginnings. And it also seems quite appropriate that the songs

Schoenberg prepared for the Überbrettl should be coupled on a compact disc with his short opera, the fiercely atonal *Erwartung*, both works sung with equal and total conviction by Jessye Norman.

EPIC THEATER

Epic theater is to traditional theater what number-opera (*q.v.*) is to music-drama (*q.v.*). Brecht worked out his concept of epic theater in a series of pronouncements beginning with the "Notes to *Mahagonny*," a document that now occupies a canonical spot in the history of dramatic theory analogous to texts such as Hugo's "Preface to *Cromwell*," Corneille's *Discourses*, and, to cite the theory that Brecht later came to identify as the polar opposite of his own, Aristotle's *Poetics*. In the "Notes" the concept is expanded to include what Brecht calls "epic opera," here exemplified by *Aufstieg und Fall der Stadt Mahagonny*. Brecht's vaunted theory challenged the tightly knit plot characteristic of dramas in the classical tradition and sets up an alternative tradition consisting of figures such as Marlowe, Shakespeare, Büchner, and Wedekind, all culminating, not surprisingly, in the work of Bertolt Brecht. This theory insisted, moreover, on preventing audiences from identifying with the characters on stage and instead asked them to step back and think about the issues that the author had raised in the course of the play. By now we have gained sufficient perspective on Brecht to realize that, instead of identifying with characters, we were being asked to identify with the thought of the author, whose cunning rhetoric directed our thinking precisely where he intended it to go.

Although Weill had distanced himself from Brecht by the time of "Notes to *Mahagonny*," the latter's theory of drama, at least to the extent that it sought an episodic form of play, consorted well with Weill's experiments with operatic structure. Like his teacher Busoni, Weill was looking for an alternative to the tightly plotted music-dramas associated with Wagner and the composers throughout Europe following in his wake. For Busoni and Weill this alternative structure took the former of episodic, loosely connected individual musical numbers.[24] As a result of practicing this method Weill was able to give precedence to music over text. But Brecht was cultivating his own episodic method to accomplish something quite the opposite, namely to keep his audiences from being hypnotized by the stage illusion and instead to pay attention to ideas being vented within the text.[25] It was small wonder that, despite their common goal of loosening dramatic structure (as well as provoking their audiences), this celebrated collaboration could not last.

The goals of epic theater as well as of number-opera were about the last thing that Arnold Schoenberg cared to achieve. The work that immediately preceded *Moses und Aron*, *Der biblische Weg*, is a carefully plotted narrative centered on the final crisis in the life of Schoenberg's hero, Max Aruns, and is intended to be a portrait of the founder of Zionism, Theodor Herzl, or rather a portrait of what might have befallen Herzl if he had been able to lead his followers to a territory in east-central Africa that the British government had tentatively offered to the Jews in 1902. Quite in contrast to Brecht's unheroic heroes, Aruns is expected to gain the audience's sympathy as he progresses toward his tragic death. In the opera that succeeded this play, Schoenberg separated the two components of his hero's name, which in the play had merged the two Biblical figures around whom the opera is centered. The opera presents two contrasting figures, the stern, uncompromising Moses, who gains our sympathy, or at least our awe, and his glib, compromising brother Aron, who, even though his rhetoric may temporarily sway us as it does the Jews whom he is leading during Moses' absence on Sinai, must ultimately be rejected. As a dramatic text this opera is as classically plotted and as classically austere as such earlier reworkings of Biblical matter as Racine's *Athalie* and *Esther* and Alfieri's *Saul*.

It is scarcely surprising that Schoenberg reacted unfavorably to Brecht's "Notes," to which he added some notes of his own. Commenting on Brecht's claim that in "epic opera" music plays a "mediating" role ("die Musik vermittelt" [*BBS*, 3: 268]), Schoenberg asks how this is possible "since he who mediates cannot possibly take a position of his *own* but instead must take his place between two each of whom *insists* on a different position."[26] For Schoenberg it was inconceivable that an author or composer could claim not to take a position. But Schoenberg's skepticism toward Brecht was not simply an aesthetic issue but above all political. The composer's conservatism was well known, as Alfred Keller, a Swiss student who worked with him in Berlin between 1927 and 1930 has testified: "He [Schoenberg] was strictly conservative. And as for us students, he always [said] that we were communists. He said to me, 'You are a red.'"[27] In contemplating "Notes to *Mahagonny*," Schoenberg's political antennae must have told him that epic theater was clearly the property of the left.

GENEALOGIES

Aesthetic genealogies are the reverse of family genealogies. Whereas the latter move forward from a few common ancestors to the diverse progeny they have spawned, the former progress backward from a singular entity labeled a work of art to a multitude of earlier works that, however little their creators may have recognized their mutual affinities, come to resemble a family that the later member has retrospectively begotten, defined, legitimated.

As a mixed genre, opera, composed at once of tonal and verbal substances, has the capacity to generate the most disparate ancestral voices. Thus, *Moses und Aron* establishes kinship among the likes of Theodor Herzl, *Salome*, and Bach (see Genealogy 1). A work such as *Mahagonny*, whose librettist and composer, unlike *Moses und Aron*, came together with sizable, already-existing households, creates a large, unruly, but by no means dysfunctional family out of Charlie Chaplin's *Gold Rush*, Büchner's plays, Paul Whiteman's band, Weber's *Freischütz*, and Handelian *opera seria* (see Genealogy 2).

GENERIC BOUNDARIES

Every significant work of art (so runs the common wisdom) questions, expands, even violates the boundaries of the genre to which it belongs. As truisms go, this one may be useful, but like all truisms it lacks historical specificity. Some periods are more genre-threatening than others, and during the 1920s artists in varying media across Europe remapped generic boundaries with something of the same zeal with which the diplomats meeting in 1919 in Versailles reconfigured whole continents.

Opera was no exception. The very concept of *Zeitoper* (*see* ELITE/POP) suggests a questioning of the conventions long assumed within the medium.

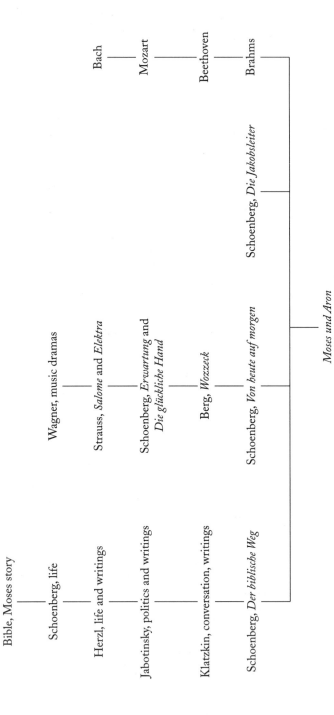

GENEALOGY 1. Schoenberg, *Moses und Aron*

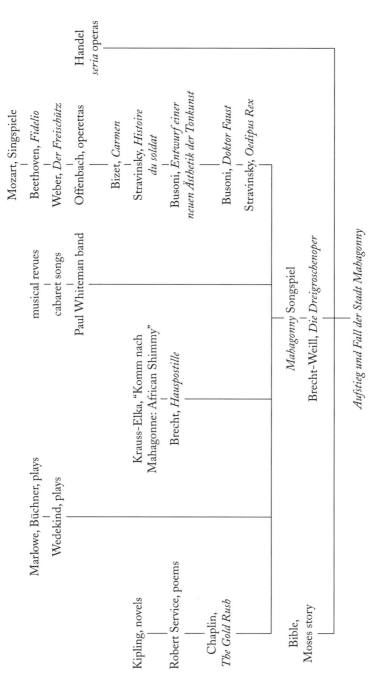

GENEALOGY 2. Weill and Brecht, *Aufstieg und Fall der Stadt Mahagonny*

Since the traditional opera audience expected costumed portrayals of places far away in space or time, the introduction of the sounds and sights of contemporary life—telephones, factories, jazz clubs, the living quarters of ordinary people of the time—was intended to create shock effects within the opera house. Even the *verismo* operas of the 1890s had ordinarily distanced themselves in time or place from the lives of their urban audiences. Although neither of the two operas around which this chapter is centered can be labeled a *Zeitoper*, each composer had already produced an opera within this genre— *Der Zar läßt sich photographieren* and *Von heute auf morgen*—before proceeding to *Mahagonny* and *Moses und Aron*.

Yet the latter two works violate generic boundaries in ways other than showing their audiences a local, familiar world. Weill, for instance, frequently mentioned the strong impact that Stravinsky's generically unclassifiable *L'Histoire du soldat* had made upon him and fellow composers. "What Stravinsky is doing in *L'Histoire du soldat*," Weill wrote in 1926, "may well count as the mixed-genre form that will most surely be taken up in the future; located on the border between drama, pantomime, and opera, this piece displays such predominantly operatic elements that it may emerge as fundamental for one direction of contemporary opera" (*WM*, 29–30, and see also 229, 240). With Brecht's visual projections and the intrusions of the narrator, not to speak of the popular musical forms that Weill played with in *Mahagonny*, the work clearly inhabits the borderlines that traditionally marked opera off from other media.

In his attempt to reach a new and larger audience Weill was obviously on the lookout for ways to frustrate spectators' expectations of what constituted opera. Indeed, in its early productions the question was often raised whether the work belonged more appropriately in the opera house or the commercial theater and whether it was to be performed by trained opera singers or by actors who, like Lotte Lenya, Weill's wife and the most celebrated of all the *Mahagonny* Jennys, also happened to sing. As Weill wrote to his conductor friend and former pupil Maurice Abravanel before the first performance, "*Mahagonny* is for singers. An opera for singers. To cast it with actors is absolutely impossible."[28] Adorno, having seen the production in the Frankfurt Opera, complained that the later Berlin production, which took place in a commercial theater, despite his admiration for Lenya's portrayal, created a "diminished" version of the piece, which as he insisted, "belongs in the opera house" (*AGS*, 19: 276–77). And although *Mahagonny* is normally performed today in the opera house, its "in-between" generic status, to employ a term used by Weill of *L'Histoire du soldat*, remains part of audience consciousness. Since the first part to be composed presumably included the pieces that formed the *Songspiel* of 1927, the larger *Mahagonny*, despite the ensembles that gave it a more discernibly operatic character, keeps teasing its listeners with the possibility that, like that popular vehicle, the musical revue, it is chiefly a collection of memorable songs.

If *Mahagonny* never fully loses the character of a revue, *Moses und Aron* retains something of its origin in oratorio, a form that, in the hands of its first major practitioner, Handel, was developed as a counter-genre to opera. From 1927 until mid-1930, when Schoenberg's publisher rejected his proposal for an oratorio, the composer had intended to use the oratorio form for the material. Although he rewrote the text for its operatic version, the latter—in the huge role assigned to the chorus and in its overwhelmingly solemn tone—hovers restively between the two genres.[29]

Yet *Moses und Aron* challenges our conception of opera as a genre in a more fundamental way than in its oratorio-like elements, which it shares with earlier works such as *La Damnation de Faust* and *Samson et Dalila*. Even after repeated hearings, the extensive use of *Sprechstimme* throughout the score remains astonishing: except for one brief spot of three lines, the hero with whom we are to sympathize does not sing at all but expresses himself in a mode of discourse that Schoenberg had developed early in his career and that reminds us constantly that it does not belong to what we ordinarily consider either speech or song.[30] Indeed, it is not only Moses who is assigned *Sprechstimme* but also the voice of God speaking in chorus in the guise of the Burning Bush. Since the "real" operatic singing comes from the gullible populace and above all from Aron, whom we are to reject for his deceptiveness and political opportunism, the composer would seem to be voicing a certain antioperatic bias toward the genre within which he is supposedly working. In a searching essay on *Moses und Aron* Adorno notes the anomaly that Schoenberg "employs the most sensual of all musical forms [namely, opera] for the extremely non-sensual idea" he is embodying (*AGS*, 16: 459). For the traditional operagoer with a narrow conception of what counts as opera, the harsh sounds with which Moses repeatedly declares himself inarticulate, or the pop-music rhythms that keep *Mahagonny* moving along ("an overwhelming amount of jazz," the composer Malipiero complained after an early performance[31]), may often prove intolerable.

HISTORICAL CONTEXT

How does one set an opera within its appropriate historical context? Since its earliest performances *Mahagonny*, despite its supposedly American setting, has been linked inextricably with the sociohistorical world of Germany at the end of the 1920s. "The city of Mahagonny is a representation of the social world in which we live, projected from the bird's eye perspective of a genuinely liberated society," Adorno wrote the year of its premiere (*AGS*, 17: 114). In his foreword to the production book for the first production, Weill used the word *Gleichnis*, which means at once "image," "simile," or "parable," to remark that the opera provides "an image [simile, parable] of contemporary life" (*WM*, 78). In 1948, near the end of his life—and before the full score had even turned up—Weill discouraged the idea of a production at La Scala because "*Mahagonny* . . . was very much an expression of the decade after the First World War."[32] Not only did he see the work as "expressing" its particular decade, but this very fact made it seem too time-bound, and as an alternative he suggested *Street Scene*, his most recent composition for Broadway, to the La Scala management. If we move ahead again nearly half a century, we hear another composer similarly voicing the relationship of work and context, but in an altogether positive spirit. In a 1992 interview advocating Weill as a model for contemporary composers, Steve Reich speaks of *Mahagonny* as a "masterpiece . . . that completely captures its historical time, not some other imaginary historical time. It doesn't capture the time of Mozart or Wagner or Verdi, it captures the Weimar Republic."[33]

All of these statements, which carry the authority, respectively, of an influential music critic, of the composer himself, and of a major contemporary composer, take for granted two notions: first, that a work can "represent," "image," "capture," or, to cite a slightly more active word, "express," a particular time and place; and second, that this time and place are a kind of given, a stable entity (however unstable its political structures may have been) that allows it to be reflected in a recognizable way. In the accounts of 1930 cited above, this entity is simply "the social world in which we live"; once this entity had vanished into the past, it became "the decade after the First World War," after which it has hardened into a concept called "Weimar" (*see* WEIMAR NOSTALGIA). Moreover, in these statements the opera itself seems to play a passive role as a repository, or at best an intermediary, of images to be captured of some external world. To be sure, Adorno also speaks of *Mahagonny* as "the first surrealist opera" and of Weill as "the representative of musical surrealism" (*AGS*, 17: 119; 18: 749), acknowledging that this manifestly unrealistic piece must resort to a certain distortion in order to represent its world to us.

Yet can we not grant the opera a more active role in creating the reality it supposedly expresses? In Chapter 5 I suggest that *Der Ring des Nibelungen*, together with a number of novels of that time, helped "define," even to "create" a concept of the mid-nineteenth century for us. Similarly, what we have come to call "Weimar culture" has been exemplified for us by a limited canon of works—for example, *Die Dreigroschenoper* and *Mahagonny*, paintings by Max Beckmann and Otto Dix, and films such as *The Cabinet of Doctor Caligari* and *The Blue Angel*. When Weill and Adorno asserted the documentary function of *Mahagonny*, they were in effect depending on the opera to help crystallize a hitherto not fully articulated account of what their world was all about—or at least a particular segment of that world, which, as it turned out, would eventually help shape the cultural entity called Weimar. Yet Weill at one point let on his ambition to make his work create its age, as it were: "It [*Mahagonny*] seeks to configure [*gestalten*] our time in its definitive form," he wrote to his publisher early during the composition of the opera.[34] Today when we hear such much-repeated lines out of context as "I tell you, we must die!" from the "Alabama Song," or "Denn wie man sich bettet, so liegt man" from the first and third act finales, we automatically link them in our minds to what we take to be "Weimar." To be sure, scholarly inquiry has considerably expanded the configuration that Weill and Brecht created, as one notes from the several hundred short texts comprising the major source book on the period.[35] Yet within the popular imagination Weimar remains the site shaped by *Mahagonny* and a surprisingly short list of loudly irreverent fellow provocateurs.

And what of *Moses und Aron?* Why do we not ordinarily link it to the Weimar within which it was composed? It is not enough to say that, fragment that it remained, it was not published or heard until the 1950s (*Mahagonny*, for that matter, was not heard until that time after its brief initial success just before the Nazi victory). The phenomenon known as Schoenberg encompasses a considerably longer *durée* than that of Weimar. The context that *Moses und Aron*, for instance, defines has to do with matters such as the history of Zionism, the myth of the artist's role during the late nineteenth and early twentieth centuries, the use and misuse of language in a politically volatile time (*see* LEADERSHIP; ZIONIST OPERA).

LEADERSHIP

Aesthetic Leadership

Several years before he left Vienna to assume his professorship in Berlin, Schoenberg, in his role as leader of what has since become known as the Second Viennese School, founded the Society for Private Musical Performances in order to provide hearings of contemporary music by a wide variety of composers practicing throughout Europe. To avoid the disapproval that the new music often encountered in newspapers and from heckling members of the audience, Schoenberg's society barred criticism from the press and limited its audience to the group's members. In a statement after his arrival in the United States, Schoenberg, writing in a language still relatively new to him, justified his actions as leader of the society:

> I was a kind of dictator, 1920, in a musical society, erected by myself in my ideas and on the whole very successful. Suddenly there arose a strong opposition to my plans, instigated by some political extremists. Fruitlessly I tried to convince them, fruitlessly I showed that the idea would break down if they continued with their

opposition, but fast arose the danger that they could gain a majority against my principles. I did not resign. On the contrary, I did something which under other circumstances could be called illegal: I dissolved the whole society, built a new one, accepted only such members who were in perfect agreement with my artistic principles and excluded the entire opposition. There were some sentimentalists who considered it wrong, but it was the only healthful means of avoiding the encroachment of non-artistic principles upon artistic ones. Right or wrong—these principles were my country.[36]

Like Wagner, Marx, and Freud, those other founders of discourse, and like those dictators of the time whose own discourse he employs here, Schoenberg did not easily tolerate opposition to his leadership. As he put it the following year, "In artistic life a leader is never called to answer."[37]

Political Leadership (fictive form)

Schoenberg explained his actions as the leader of the Society for Private Musical Performances to provide a positive example of leadership in contrast with that of Theodor Herzl, who, together with the latter's followers after his death, had failed to take advantage of an opportunity to create a Jewish state early in the century when the British government had offered the territory then called Uganda (today's Kenya) for that purpose. If Herzl, according to Schoenberg, had not been willing to compromise, and if his followers had not allowed themselves to be "outvoted" by those Zionists opposing the Uganda project, the Jews would at least have possessed a state, even if it was not in Palestine, the homeland for which the anti-Uganda delegates were holding out.[38]

Herzl's dilemma had earlier provided Schoenberg with the opportunity to examine the difficulties befalling a leader in his play, *Der biblische Weg (see* EPIC THEATER*)*. The play is centered around a Herzl-like hero, Max Aruns, who, unlike his model, succeeds in establishing a Jewish state in Africa. One could describe this play, which Schoenberg never managed to have produced or even published, as a speculative exercise in what might have happened had Herzl proven resolute and dictatorial enough to get the Uganda project underway.[39] *Der biblische Weg* takes the form of a conspiracy play, for the hero's doom is plotted in the course of the drama by several of his followers who betray him at the behest of those outside forces—Jewish financiers and the proponents of Palestine as the only Jewish homeland—that have remained hostile to the formation of an African colony. It also assumes the traditional form of a martyr play, for the conspiracy against Max Aruns culminates in his murder by a group of angry colonists whose supplies have been cut off by the conspirators. As with most martyr plays, the audience is made aware of the martyr-hero's ultimate vindication, for directly after Aruns's death a deus ex machina in the form of his follower Guido arrives to announce that the conspirators' plot has been thwarted, food supplies restored, and the colony's future assured.

The tragic conflict within Schoenberg's hero, which is suggested at once by his name, stems from the fact that Schoenberg tries to combine the two brothers Moses and Aron within a single person. Whereas his Moses side is visionary and uncompromising, his Aron aspect is practical, corrupting, indeed "political" in the negative sense of that word. Shortly before the crowd kills him, a prophetic figure, David Asseino, appears before Aruns to interpret in a new way the Biblical analogy that stands behind the play. The problem with Aruns, as Asseino defines it, is that the leader has sought to combine two incompatible types, the contemplative and the practical man, the spiritual and the material, in a single person. As his very name implies, he has, according to Asseino, tried to fuse the two antithetical leaders of the Exodus, Moses and Aaron:

> Max Aruns: you are trying to be Moses and Aron in a single person! Moses, to whom God granted the idea but refused the power of speech; and Aron, who could not grasp the idea but who could reproduce it and move the masses. Max Aruns, you who knew how to interpret the word of God in so modern a way, couldn't you understand why God did not unite both powers within a single person?[40]

After Aruns's martyrdom at the hands of angry Jewish colonists, Guido, who plays the role of the Joshua to his master's Moses, shifts the play's frame of reference from a political to an overtly religious level: "As with any ancient people, so it is our calling to spiritualize ourselves. To tear ourselves loose from

every material thing." In one of the play's final passages, Guido explicitly lays
the groundwork for *Moses und Aron*, in which Schoenberg reflects on the nature of religious leadership: "We have still another goal: We must all learn to
reflect upon the idea of the one, the eternal and the unrepresentable God."[41]

Religious Leadership

Moses und Aron, the libretto of which, though originally in oratorio form, was
drafted the year after Schoenberg completed *Der biblische Weg*, literally picks
up where the play left off. Thus, the opera's opening line—"One, eternal, om-
nipresent, invisible, unrepresentable God"—spoken, or, more precisely,
"speech-voiced" by Moses in that jarring, uncanny vocal style, repeats those
awesome divine attributes that Guido (and Aruns before him) had pronounced at the end of the play. Indeed, these attributes had been recited by
others at earlier moments in the play just as they will be repeated, literally as
an article of faith, at crucial moments within the opera.

By bifurcating the hero of the play into the two component figures who
comprise the opera's title, Schoenberg is able to shift the conflict from one
within a single persona to one between two separate figures who represent
wholly opposing sets of values. Thus, Moses' harsh bass *Sprechstimme* is made
to contrast with Aron's slick tenor coloratura. In Moses, Schoenberg presents
the religious visionary who, though chosen by God, lacks the verbal skill to
communicate directly with his people, and in Aron he presents a political
demagogue who is so rhetorically gifted that, in encouraging the people's desires to assert their autonomy, he leads them in the climactic Golden Calf
scene to violate the ban against polytheism and the representation of deity.
The musical resources at the composer's disposal allow Schoenberg to distinguish between the two brothers with a sharpness that would not be possible
in spoken drama. Whether or not, as one commentator has suggested,[42]
Schoenberg had Hitler specifically in mind when he created Aron, the audience quickly recognizes a peculiarly modern type of rhetorician who can make
most anything happen by means of his linguistic skill.

It is significant that Schoenberg sometimes deliberately lapses into what he considered a vulgar musical style for the passages associated with Aron and the crowd, above all for the Golden Calf scene, of which, in the course of composition, he wrote to his disciple Anton Webern, "Its expressive power generally remains no higher than that of the most primitive program music; and its 'beauty' seems hateful to me in its petrified mechanical quality."[43] Several years later, in a less self-condemning tone, Schoenberg, recognizing the centrality of this scene, justified its manner as something essentially "operatic": "And here my piece is at its most *operatic*—what it should be after all."[44] It is ironic, but also not surprising, that the scene has proved to be the most easily accessible part of the opera for audiences. Yet the sense of sublimity that Schoenberg achieves in the music associated with Moses, though perhaps less accessible at first hearing, works ultimately to overwhelm and defeat the more ornate, overtly operatic music associated with the material realm. As a result, one could call *Moses und Aron* a kind of anti-opera, one that utilizes "operatic" elements precisely in order to undercut them and to assert the triumph of a higher spiritual force.

In view of this gesture toward transcendence, which characterizes *Moses und Aron*, it is little wonder that commentators on the opera have approached it primarily from a religious point of view. As Adorno writes in an essay significantly entitled "Sacred Fragment: On Schoenberg's *Moses und Aron*": "The Wagnerian sphere of the passions is not that of theology, which is the sphere within which *Moses und Aron* moves" (*AGS*, 16: 466–67). Two monographs devoted to the opera, one of them bearing the title *Divine Word and Magic*, center around the religious message emanating from the work.[45] Schoenberg himself went to great effort to encourage this approach: "The content and its treatment are purely religious-philosophical," he wrote to his disciple Josef Rufer shortly before his death.[46] The remark to Rufer was occasioned by his irritation at a discussion of *Moses und Aron* by the musicologist Gerald Abraham in a recent edition of *Grove's Dictionary of Music*. Abraham had allegorized the conflict between spirit and matter in personal terms as "the artist's struggle to express in intractable material the ideal conception in his spirit (or both inextricably confused)," and he went on to trace this struggle to "the inner conflicts of Schoenberg's tortured and enigmatic mind."[47] "Partly nonsense, bring-

ing in the artist this way," Schoenberg comments disdainfully on this interpretation; "that refers to the end of the nineteenth century, but not to me."[48]

Yet Schoenberg's denial of an autobiographical dimension within the opera
(which had not even been performed when Abraham wrote his comment) is
doubtless less a true statement than a response to a musicologist whom he
perceived as hostile. When, early in the composition of the opera, Alban Berg
had asked if his Moses was based on a particular literary model such as
Strindberg's play about Moses, Schoenberg denied this and confessed instead
that "Everything I have written bears a certain similarity to myself."[49] Indeed,
the Moses analogy is implicit in a comic anecdote that Schoenberg liked to
tell about himself. As a conscript during the First World War he was asked,
after his name was called up at roll call, if he happened to be the "controversial composer," to which he replied hesitantly, "Yes, somebody had to accept
the job, nobody wanted it, so I volunteered."[50] Just as the Moses of Schoenberg's opera was reluctant to accept his mission ("Ask not thy servant to be
thy prophet," Moses protests in his first speech) to carry out the divine will, so
the Schoenberg of this anecdote implies that, like it or not, he was the one
whose lot it became to lead others along the difficult, but inexorable, path of
music history. And just as, within the confines of the opera, Moses suffers a
defeat as a result of the Jews' returning to idolatry at Aron's behest, so
Schoenberg has had to endure the sufferings inherent in the true prophet's
role. But of course we know that Moses had history on his side and that his
idealism would ultimately prevail. When Schoenberg announced his development of the twelve-tone scale to his disciples with these words, "Today I
have discovered something which will insure the superiority of German music for the next hundred years,"[51] we, or at least Schoenberg, can recognize
that he is heading us toward some promised musical land.

Political Leadership (real-life form)

With the completion of act 2 of *Moses und Aron* at the end of 1932 and Hitler's
assumption of power on January 30, 1933, the composer increasingly felt the
call—similar to that of his operatic hero—to assume the role of leader to the
Jewish people. Consider the following statements, each a few years apart:

1. 1934—from a letter addressed to the prominent American rabbi, Stephen Wise:

> But please don't misunderstand me. I have no political ambition. My ambition could have been able to find complete fulfillment on music paper, if I ever had any ambition at all. I strive only for the ignominious honor of being able to give up my life for the existence of the Jewish people. And only, if no more suitable person is found, above all no one younger and healthier than I only then, in order not to shirk a recognizable duty, would I want to step forward.[52]

Schoenberg goes on to elaborate that a leader is needed to "negotiate and make the terms" for the sake of establishing a Jewish nation, but before the lot should fall to him, he suggests Rabbi Wise himself or Albert Einstein, a figure with whom Schoenberg had long identified as someone whose intellectual achievements had been misunderstood by the public.[53]

2. 1938—from "A Four-Point Program for Jewry," a manuscript centered on the idea of "obtaining a land to which the Jewish people can migrate,"[54] that also includes the passages on Herzl and on the Society for Private Musical Performances described earlier:

> Only such men who are ready to die for their ideas should attempt to play a role in the fate of their people. . . . Why did Brutus and Varus kill themselves when they had lost? Justice asks the life of a man whose fault it is that people suffer or die who trusted him—he cannot simply withdraw and become a private person.[55]

Employing a traditional Plutarchian model, Schoenberg interrupts his detailed discussion of how to create a Jewish nation to expostulate on the triumphs and pitfalls of leadership.

3. 1946 or 1947—from the manuscript entitled "The Jewish Government in Exile (Broadcast)":

> I will speak to you, saying
>   Here I am, Arn[old] Sch[oenberg], the president of the Gov[ernment] in exile of the Jewish Nation on a ship which I received through the generosity of Pr[esident] Tr[uman], the Am[erican] Government and the Am[erican] People.[56]

Fashioning himself the head of a new Jewish state, Schoenberg addresses the radio audience of Jews for whom this speech was evidently intended by describing himself attended by representatives of the "great Powers" and "all the second greatest nations" as well as "prominent Jews" and "also many notables of non-Jewish race." The longtime acknowledged leader of the musical avant-garde has here emerged, in a manner appropriate to a ceremonial scene within an opera, as the leader of the first Jewish state since Biblical times. If this scene seems farfetched, one might remember that in 1952, several years after a real Jewish state had been established, Schoenberg's friend Einstein was actually offered the Israeli presidency, a job he happened to turn down. Just before his death the year before Schoenberg had happily settled for the less lofty post of honorary director of the Israel Academy of Music.

MARXIST OPERA

"Igor Stravinsky was present on the same evening [of the Frankfurt *Mahagonny* production] that we were, and on being asked his opinion, replied socratically with another question: 'After seeing *Mahagonny*, have you become Bolsheviki?'"

Anna and G. Francesco Malipiero[57]

"They misunderstood the whole thing in Leipzig. They thought it was satire which it isn't; and it has nothing to do with communism. It's the story of Sodom and Gomorrah."

Kurt Weill[58]

Can one speak of Marxist opera? If we mean an opera that is subjected to some form of Marxist analysis (whether by the director or a critic), almost anything in the operatic canon would provide fair game. Theodor Adorno, for example, once reviewed *Don Pasquale* to illustrate how the up-and-coming middle class represented by the young lovers revolts against the feudal older generation (*AGS*, 19: 209). Yet long before the creation of opera—indeed, as far back as Greek New Comedy—the countless plays centered around young people resisting the blocking strategies of their elders could just as easily lend themselves to this mode of analysis. And if one desires a clever Marxist take on *Moses und Aron*, one could look at the victory of Moses over his brother as an attempt to use the mystifications of religion as a means to manipulate and assume power over a gullible and unruly populace.

But it is *Mahagonny* that, like no other major opera, presents itself as a text shot through with Marxist categories, images, points of view. These categories are evident, for example, in the phrase "Social being determines thought" that Brecht included in his chart (*AGS*, 3: 267) distinguishing the epic theater he was proposing from traditional drama (*see* BRECHT/WEILL). One could go on to point out a variety of Marxist notions permeating Brecht's text—human relationships defined by means of monetary relationships (to the point that the hero is executed for his impecuniousness), America as the site of capitalism in its rawest manifestation. Walter Benjamin allegorized one of Brecht's *Mahagonny* lyrics, "Gott in Mahagonny," to show how "the anarchy of bourgeois society is an infernal one. For those caught up in [this society] there is nothing that can inspire greater terror for them."[59] This is Marxism clearly in its critical phase and not the celebratory mode that was to dominate art during the forthcoming period in the Soviet Union.

The composer, as we know, did not share his librettist's increasingly doctrinal rigidity, and his insistence on the primacy of musical form in his own pronouncements on this opera may lead us to underestimate the sheer political force that his music exercised. In its often sardonic tone; in the irreverence suggested by the sounds it emits in that bourgeois sanctum, the opera house; in its deliberate derangement of both traditional and contemporary musical forms such as the waltz and the fox-trot, Weill establishes a critical perspective upon the world that its audiences (whatever their political allegiances) could readily associate with commodity capitalism. Indeed, *Mahagonny* was a work whose political resonance was marked from the start, as one notes from the presence of Brown Shirts in the streets for the Leipzig premiere and the subsequent riot inside the theater that the Nazis instigated. Except for the Paris version of *Tannhäuser* in 1861, none of the operas still remembered today can boast so dramatic a disturbance on its opening night. Adorno, writing in 1930 (long before our current phrase "political correctness" had been formulated), found the Nazi stink-bomb demonstrations at a Frankfurt performance a clear sign that *Mahagonny* represented a "correct mode of consciousness" (richtiger Bewußtseinsstand, *AGS*, 19: 194), and in a later essay on the social role of music he described Weill's as the "only music with social-polemical impact today" (*AGS*, 18: 750). There was no place for this work, one might add, in postwar, Soviet-occupied Europe, not even—except for a reworked version with little of Weill's original music[60]—in Brecht's own theater in the former East Berlin.

MUSIC-DRAMA

Just as Wagner dismissed Mozart's *La clemenza di Tito* and the genre of *opera seria* to which it belonged as relics of the *ancien régime* (*WGS*, 13: 285) so Wagnerian music-drama was perceived by the new composers of the 1920s as a relic of a distant age. To be sure the Wagner canon still flourished actively not only in all the German opera houses but above all in the shrine that the master had set up in Bayreuth to conserve his art in perpetuity. Quite in contrast to the constantly shifting challenges to earlier art that characterized opera in Berlin around 1930, time had been made to stand still in Bayreuth. The book-length Bayreuth program guide prepared for visitors to the 1930 summer festival is a veritable exercise in hagiography. That spring had marked the death of the composer's widow, Cosima, whose obituary in the program is accompanied with a photo of her hearse leaving the Festspielhaus.[61] The composer's son, Siegfried, who served both as festival director and as one of its conductors, receives praise in the guide as a composer "for the originality of his art," which, "though based on Richard Wagner's doctrine, . . . is wholly individual."[62] As it turned out, only four months after the death of his mother Siegfried Wagner died suddenly at 61 in the midst of the festival.

That same year Bayreuth also commemorated the centennial of the conductor Hans von Bülow, who, as the husband from whom Richard Wagner appropriated Cosima, has been assigned the role of St. Joseph in the family myth and who in the program guide is extolled as the musician who would have held the line against such evils as "the pursuit of jazz and trash" of the present day, with "mediocrity and Americanization taking over."[63] Reading these words, one realizes what outrage a work such as *Mahagonny* must have aroused that year among the aesthetically conservative. About the only novelty Bayreuth could advertise in 1930 was the fact that it had hired its first non-German conductor, namely Arturo Toscanini, whom the festival program honored with an essay on Wagner and Verdi; it is scarcely surprising to find that whereas Wagner has nothing but disparaging words about Verdi, the latter praises Wagner in a hagiographical manner wholly consonant with the rest of the guide.[64] As for the master himself, the vocation of composer that created his fame seems insufficient to define his cultural role, which, in an article about his relation to Schopenhauer, is duly elevated to that of a philosopher, and in this role Wagner is depicted as creating "a metaphysics in sound that sees into the heart of things and surpasses every other means of expression."[65]

The form of music-drama by means of which Wagner had sought to snuff out what had long been known as opera exercised so powerful an effect (even for those who did not, like his heirs in Bayreuth, attempt to keep his art embalmed) that it was not until the 1920s that composers such as Busoni, Stravinsky, and Weill managed to mount a serious challenge to this form (*see* NUMBER-OPERA). The aesthetic of difficulty that characterizes the compositions of the Schoenberg school has its roots in Wagnerian music-drama, which, with its endlessly evolving melodies and its leitmotifs, did not, like earlier opera, encourage easy listening but forced listeners to prepare themselves in advance and, during the performance, to assume the role of active interpreters. (Despite the fact that anti-Wagnerians from the later Nietzsche to Brecht accused Wagner of drugging his audiences into passivity, Wagnerites took great pride in the intellectual efforts they claimed that the music demanded.) Such post-Wagnerian composers as Massenet and Puccini, who sought to comfort their audience more than the Wagnerian aesthetic called for, limited their Wagnerism to the sounds from the orchestra and to a simplified form of the leitmotif, and they proved shameless enough to interrupt the musical flow with operatic arias that audiences could hum their way home with and that their performers could show off in the concert hall.

The most serious attempt to renew music-drama came at the turn of the century in works such as *Pelléas et Mélisande* (1902) and *Salome* (1905), each of which suggested a distinct and new direction yet also, at least for their earliest listeners, compounded the difficulties that Wagner had built into the form. Soon after the acclaimed premiere of *Wozzeck* (1925), which was at first taken as a complete break with earlier tradition, the 25-year-old Kurt Weill, whose own first opera had not yet been performed, sought to ring the death knell for music-drama, to which he firmly tied Berg's composition: for Weill *Wozzeck* becomes "the grandiose conclusion to a development that leads from Wagner's *Tristan* through Debussy's *Pelléas* and Strauss's *Elektra* to his [Berg's] wholly negative art" (*WM*, 209). If one reveals that Weill also happened to admire *Wozzeck* and that elements of *Mahagonny* may have influenced Berg's subsequent opera, *Lulu*, this is only to say that a composer's strong feelings about a formal tradition do not necessarily coincide with his taste for individual works within that tradition.

However innovative *Moses und Aron* may seem in its *Sprechstimme*-thundering hero and its development from a single twelve-tone row, it fits comfortably within the tradition of Wagnerian music-drama, to whose leitmotifs and mode of constructing larger scenes it gives a new life.[66] In discussing *Moses und Aron* as a Wagnerian *Gesamtkunstwerk*, Adorno calls the composer a "naive artist" in Schiller's sense of that term, by which he means that "even while surpassing all his contemporaries in the consequences he drew about musical composition," Schoenberg "never put into question what constitutes an opera any more than he questioned what makes for music at the present time or what is a 'master'" (*AGS*, 19: 484). Comfortable though he must have felt working within the larger Wagnerian structure, Schoenberg remained far removed from the time-warped Bayreuth establishment,[67] which at that time would have rejected him at once for his Jewishness and for his musical iconoclasm. During the composition of *Moses und Aron* Schoenberg, in one of his frequent attempts to relate himself to musical tradition, listed Bach, Mozart, Beethoven, Brahms, and Wagner as the composers from whom he had learned the most about composition; yet he makes clear that Bach and Mozart were more important to him than the other three.[68] Still, the spell that Wagner cast upon him was sufficiently strong that, when addressing a Jewish group in Los Angeles in 1935, Schoenberg excused the master's anti-Semitism for being "mild" in comparison with the "harsh" form it took in the hands of his followers.[69]

1930   "The turning point came only in 1930."   Walter Laqueur, *Weimar: A Cultural History, 1918–1933*

Month	Politics	Operatic Politics	Opera
January	Jan. 23: Wilhelm Frick, first Nazi in a state cabinet, appointed cultural minister in Thuringia		
February	Feb. 23: Horst Wessel, Nazi youth, killed on Berlin streets, later cast as martyr		Feb. 1: Schoenberg's *Von heute auf morgen* premieres at Frankfurt Opera
March	Mar. 28: Brüning appointed German chancellor	Mar. 9: Nazi Brown Shirts instigate riot at *Mahagonny* premiere	Mar. 4: Krenek's *Leben des Orest* premieres at Kroll Opera, Berlin; Mar. 9: Brecht/Weill *Mahagonny* premieres at Neues Theater, Leipzig; performed later that month in Brunswick and Kassel
April			Apr. 1: Cosima Wagner dies in Bayreuth at 92; Apr. 10: Schoenberg writes Berg of intention to compose *Moses und Aron* as an opera
May			May 5: Claudel/Milhaud *Christophe Colombe* at Berlin Staatsoper; May 25: Antheil's *Transatlantic* premieres at Frankfurt Opera

Month	Politics	Operatic Politics	Opera
June	June 30: Final evacuation of Allied troops from Rhineland		June 7: Schoenberg's *Erwartung* and *Die glückliche Hand* as double bill at Kroll Opera, withdrawn after three and four performances, respectively June 23: Brecht/Weill *Der Jasager* premieres at a Berlin school
July	July 16: Brüning invokes emergency powers under Article 48		July 17: Schoenberg known to be composing music of *Moses und Aron* in Lugano July 22: Toscanini conducts *Tannhäuser* at Bayreuth, followed by *Tristan* the next night
August			Aug. 4: Siegfried Wagner, Richard Wagner's only son and director of the Bayreuth Festival, dies at 61 Aug. 5: Schoenberg acknowledges autobiographical nature of his *Moses* to Berg Aug. 22: Schoenberg finishes act 1, sc. 2
September	Sept. 14: Nazis emerge as second largest party in parliamentary elections		

(continued)

1930, continued

Month	Politics	Operatic Politics	Opera
September	late Sept.: Wilhelm Frick orders Oskar Schlemmer's Bauhaus paintings destroyed		Sept. 30: Schoenberg close to end of act 1
October		Oct. 20: Nazis interrupt second performance of *Mahagonny* in Frankfurt with stink bombs; productions scheduled later that year in other German cities canceled.	Early Oct.: Schoenberg, now in Merano, working slowly on end of act 1, then interrupts work to return to Berlin Oct. 16: *Mahagonny* opens at Frankfurt Opera
November			Schoenberg holds private class in Berlin, including foreign composers such as Henry Cowell and Marc Blitzstein
December	Dec. 4: Nazis riot at Berlin opening of *All Quiet on the Western Front* Dec. 25: State of emergency declared		Dec. 6: Schoenberg writes Adorno suggesting latter write a dictionary of music theory along historical lines Dec. 10: Brecht/Eisler *Die Maßnahme* premieres at Großes Schauspielhaus, Berlin

NUMBER-OPERA

Just as Wagner's concept of music-drama defined itself against the prevailing number-opera, so the revolt against Wagner and the form with which he was associated relegitimated what was thought to be the long-since-vanished number-opera. To cite Weill's own words from an article justifying his practice in *Mahagonny*, "The principle of number opera has been revived in many musical works in the last few years as a reaction to music drama" (*WM*, 71). The groundwork for this revival had been laid as early as 1907 in a theoretical essay by Busoni, *Entwurf einer neuen Ästhetik der Tonkunst*, which challenged the Wagnerian notion of music as the expression of characters' emotions in favor of "the old opera, which in a closed number condensed and brought to musical conclusion the mood aroused by a dramatically moving scene."[70] Years later, appropriately enough, Weill became Busoni's pupil in Berlin. Although Busoni's operas and Stravinsky's *Oedipus Rex*—the latter with its ornate arias sung in Latin and separated by spoken narration in the vernacular—had already offered challenges to the tightly interwoven structure of music-drama, Weill introduced a new element, the popular song, as the central block out of which an opera could be built. In his one-act opera *Der Zar läßt sich photographieren* (completed in 1927), he had created a "Tango Angèle," which was foregrounded from the rest of the score through the fact that it was performed not by live musicians but by a phonograph record to which the actors listen on stage. With *Die Dreigroschenoper* and *Mahagonny* the song—always referred to in German with its anglophone name (though pronounced "zonk" by Germans) in acknowledgment of the influence of American popular music—becomes the central unit with which the opera is put together. "He [Weill] created the modern song," an advertisement for sheet music stated in large type in 1929. The Weill-type song thus claims a uniqueness that makes it different at once from the traditional high-culture lied and, in its playing with models drawn from commercial entertainment of the day, from the supposedly folk-inspired songs of German *Singspiele* such as *Die Zauberflöte* and *Der Freischütz*. Yet the generic name, *Songspiel*, given to the 1927 version of *Mahagonny*, advertises the affinities that Weill and Brecht felt for that earlier genre.[71]

Early in the composition of *Mahagonny* Weill announced to his publisher, "I am replacing the bravura aria with a new kind of hit song."[72] Almost two years earlier Weill had written that, in seeking a means to cut the tie with music-drama, he and others of his generation recognized that only by returning to "absolute music" could they find "their way back to genuine opera" (*WM*, 29). The concept of absolute music, as I point out in Chapter 4, had been developed a century before as a means of isolating a "higher" realm of purely musical forms against those more popular idioms such as opera and oratorio that remained tied to verbal texts. It seems a strange irony in the history of aesthetics that, in order to reassert the primacy of music over word, Weill should not only invoke what had earlier served an antioperatic purpose but that he should do so by drawing his models not from high but from popular culture. The popular roots of *Mahagonny* extend even to the name of the mythical city, which Brecht drew from an American-inspired German song of 1922, "Komm nach Mahagonne," subtitled "African Shimmy."

The significance of Weill's return to individual musical numbers was stressed from the start not simply by the composer himself but by those analyzing his work. Perhaps to remind audiences of the seriousness with which Weill treats the popular materials upon which he drew, an essay by Ernst Latzko included in the program notes for early productions of *Mahagonny* points out the many traditional forms—recitative, arioso, finale, cantus firmus, sonata, chorale, rondo, not to speak of song—that make up the opera's various numbers. "The music does not seek to express, but to be nothing but music," Latzko writes in an obvious jab at music-drama.[73] But Latzko also draws an analogy between *Mahagonny* and Handel's *opere serie* to show that for both Weill and Handel the dramatis personae are not meant to seem like real people but are "representatives of categories."[74] It scarcely seems accidental that Handel should appear as a model, for during the very decade that composers sought to dismantle music-drama, Handel's operas were receiving their first performances since the composer's lifetime (though in what we today would call "inauthentic" versions) at the annual Göttingen Handel festivals. The characters of *Mahagonny*, like those of Handel's operas, are notable for their lack of character in the usual literary sense of the term. But one might push the Handel analogy further. In Chapter 2 I point out that individual Handel arias are not to be taken as expressions of a character but of what was called an *Affekt*—for instance, venting rage, affirming one's constancy, pleading for love. Similarly the various *Mahagonny* numbers do not so much "characterize" their particular singers as produce the occasion for a varied succession of musical forms. Indeed, as Adorno remarked on hearing Lotte Lenya perform pieces from Weill's *Happy End* on the radio in 1930, Weill's songs are easily "interchangeable from one work to another" (*AGS*, 19: 173) or even within a single work, as with "Denn wie man sich bettet" being sung in *Mahagonny* at various times by Jim and Jenny. Handel, of course, as well as that later number artist Rossini, was notorious for interchanging his arias freely among his operas. In *Mahagonny*, instead of arias based on the *Affekte* conventionalized by baroque theory and practice, we find a series of specific forms—fox-trot, waltz, march, fugue, chorale—each of which an audience may associate with certain emotional stances from their uses in earlier musical works; yet there is often no relation between these earlier uses and what Weill is actually doing with these forms. Indeed, one frequently notes a deliberate disjunction between the stage action and the associations that a particular form has for an audience. Thus, Jakob Schmidt sings to a waltz rhythm as he dies from overeating, while the men entering to found the new city of Mahagonny perform to a fox-trot.[75]

To the extent that a large proportion of Weill's numbers are based on dance rhythms, the proper analogy may be not so much the earlier opera as the baroque instrumental suite, whose succession of once-popular dance numbers such as allemande, sarabande, minuet, and gigue parallel the musical action of *Mahagonny*. Although popular dances were still voiceless in earlier times, in the cabarets and musical revues of the Twenties that supplied Weill's models the dances had become thoroughly vocalized.

Weill was by no means the first modern composer to build an opera self-consciously out of traditional short musical forms. In *Wozzeck*, the most powerful attempt to renew music-drama during the decade before *Moses und Aron*, Alban Berg, as he revealed in a short essay several years after the premiere of the opera, had created each of his scenes as a distinct musical element such as the passacaglia, march, fugue, or invention.[76] And yet no two operas could be more different in the spirit with which *Wozzeck* and *Mahagonny* use these forms: whereas Berg, invoking the Wagnerian notion that the music merely serves the drama, did not expect (or even want) his audience to recognize the particular musical genres out of which his opera was built, Weill knew that his dance rhythms could be identified immediately even, indeed, *especially*, by those who have never set foot in an opera house.

SCHOENBERG/WEILL

What if the 19-year-old Kurt Weill had journeyed to Vienna, as we now know that he briefly intended to do, to study composition with Arnold Schoenberg?[77] Would he have accepted discipleship in the way that Alban Berg and Anton Webern had committed themselves heart and soul to the master? (When Berg quietly attended rehearsals of the Vienna *Mahagonny* production, which left its marks on *Lulu*,[78] he made sure not to let his presence be known to Schoenberg.) Or might Weill, like Schoenberg's Berlin pupils Hanns Eisler and Marc Blitzstein, have left the fold to pursue more socially oriented musical forms? (Blitzstein, as it turned out, was responsible for adapting *Die Dreigroschenoper* for American audiences of the 1950s and, as a result, laying the groundwork for the reassessment of Weill's long-forgotten German period.) Or might Weill, like Schoenberg's Los Angeles pupil John Cage, have moved the avant-garde so far forward that, as I argue in Chapter 8, he left Schoenberg guarding the rear?

How, in view of the reverence that Weill regularly showed in print for Schoenberg—"leader of the boldest, most daring movement in modern music" (*WM*, 204), "the composer who pointed the way for contemporary music" (*WM*, 225)—do we account for Schoenberg's contemptuous dismissal of Weill, not simply the remark about Weill's returning us to "three-quarter time" (*see* AVANT-GARDE) but his telling Virgil Thomson in 1933 that Weill's "is the only music in the world in which I find no quality at all?"[79] Was it simply Weill's change to a more popular style after his first operas, which Schoenberg, after all, had admired? Was it the leftist political orientation that Schoenberg noted in the composer's collaboration with Brecht? Was it his ire at Weill's seeming lack of "seriousness" in a newspaper piece about himself that Weill published in 1928?[80] How could he then continue to dismiss Weill when he defended George Gershwin as an "artist" and "innovator" to those who questioned the latter's credentials as a "serious composer"?[81]

And what does one make of Adorno's dismissal of Weill after 1932? Why, for instance, did he publish a less-than-gracious obituary notice in which he took back most of his early admiration for *Mahagonny*,[82] which he had once been able to view as comparable to his own teacher Berg's *Wozzeck*? Was it simply because of Weill's gradual movement toward what Adorno saw as the culture industry? Or was it Adorno's sensitivity to the feelings of Schoenberg, whose most articulate defender he turned out to be, above all in *Philosophie der neuen Musik* (1949), in which the confrontation that Adorno set up between the rigorously avant-garde Schoenberg and the commercial-minded Stravinsky buttressed the high esteem in which the former was held for decades thereafter? (Schoenberg, according to his son-in-law Felix Greißle, "did not get along with him [Adorno] very well. . . . He did not like people to talk too much about music, . . . and Teddy Adorno used to talk too much.")[83] Or was it because Weill "wrote Wiesengrund [the patronymic that the latter had used in his early days before opting for his Italian mother's maiden name] a letter which he won't forget for some time," a letter in which he evidently expressed his resentment at Adorno's interceding for Brecht to gain Weill's assent to a black production of *Die Dreigroschenoper*?[84]

Is it ever possible to separate aesthetic judgment from personal feelings?

WEIMAR NOSTALGIA

Period nostalgia takes specific generic forms depending on the historian who happens to shape and feed this nostalgia. In the mid-nineteenth century Burckhardt's newly created Renaissance, with its larger-than-life figures who invented what Burckhardt called "individualism," assumed the form of a heroic poem.[85] More recently Carl Schorske's fin-de-siècle Vienna, coming as it did at the start of the Vienna craze, took the shape of an ironic comedy, though with a dose of *Angst*—in a chapter at the end called "Explosion in the Garden"—emanating from the young Schoenberg's music and paintings and from

Oskar Kokoschka's paintings and plays.[86] But Weimar, in whatever historian's hands it emerges, inevitably assumes the form of tragedy.

Note how John Willett, for instance, adopts the traditional critical discourse about the structure of tragedy: "The cultural-political reaction which killed it was built into the new Republic from the start, asserting itself unmistakably in the years up to 1924, and thereafter merely dormant but in no sense eradicated. . . . Never in our century has the gale of history blown so strongly as it did down the wind-tunnel of those fifteen years."[87] Here, in terms such as "built into," "unmistakably," "dormant," we are made to see Weimar's tragic end as inevitable just as Aristotle had seen the end of his character Oedipus.

Or note the five subtitles—quite plausible as names for the successive acts of a tragedy—in Peter Gay's brief history of Weimar appended to his book *Weimar Culture*:

I.   November 1918–July 1919: A Time of Troubles and Foundations
II.   August 1919–December 1923: The Time of Troubles Continues
III. December 1923–October 1929: The Golden Twenties
IV.   October 1929–May 1932: The Beginning of the End
V.   June 1932–January 1933: Into Barbarism[88]

Here the six years comprising the third act present that brief deception about a possibly happy ending that tragic writers often embedded halfway through before reminding us that we should have foreseen the inevitability of a tragic conclusion.

Or note Walter Laqueur's use of Aristotelian language to explain that "the turning point came only in 1930 when the effects of the Great Depression were felt and when the coalition of democratic forces fell apart."[89] Here, as in all the many recent books on Weimar,[90] our attraction to those fatal fifteen years derives from our hindsight that the peripety of which Laqueur speaks was the initial, though also inexorable, move toward a catastrophe the enormity of which no fictive tragedy—and certainly no opera—could ever hope to record.

ZIONIST OPERA

Can one speak of Zionist opera? With its ancient Biblical setting *Moses und Aron* certainly does not deal overtly with the issues central to the Zionist movement of the twentieth century. What we *do* know is the Zionist context surrounding the work—Schoenberg's fascination with the personality and the writings of Theodor Herzl;[91] his interest in the work of two Zionist thinkers, Vladimir Jabotinsky and Jakob Klatzkin, the latter of whom he consulted at the time he was composing the opera; and, above all, the play *Der biblische Weg*, whose obsession with the nature and problems of leadership was transferred to the opera (*see* EPIC THEATER; LEADERSHIP).

But surely such seemingly "extrinsic" facts cannot justify attaching so specific a label as "Zionist" to a work of art that, unlike the frankly political play that preceded it, seeks to rise above contemporary partisan issues and to enact instead a lofty image of human conflicts playing themselves out in some distant mythical time. Yet it is precisely such distancings that raise our suspicion these days about the motives and meanings underlying a work. Indeed, in the very process of seeking to rise above contemporary concerns, *Moses und Aron* discloses attitudes of mind that easily accord with these concerns.

If one reads the works of the Zionist thinkers who most attracted Schoenberg—as well as Schoenberg's writings on Jewish issues—one notes a certain absoluteness of vision, an unwillingness to compromise, a distinct hostility, in fact, directed toward those of their followers who talked of compromise. Jabotinsky, for example, was the leader of the so-called Revisionist faction of Zionism during the 1920s that pursued a hard, relatively inflexible approach to Jewish nationalism and that, long after Jabotinsky's death in 1940, left its marks on those parties in current-day Israel advocating an expansionary policy.[92]

Klatzkin's much-read book, *Probleme des modernen Judentums*, which entered its third edition the year that Schoenberg consulted him and also began composing his opera, sought to mold the Jewish people into a "living folk-organism" that would give up its attempts to assimilate within the Diaspora and heroically assert its nationhood on Palestinian soil.[93] Klatzkin occasionally cites Moses when he needs to invoke an authority for the solutions he prescribes to the problems of present-day Jews. For example, to counter those who warn against antagonizing non-Jews for fear of stirring up anti-Semitism, Klatzkin reminds his readers that "when Moses sought to liberate his people from Egyptian servitude, the leaders of the enslaved Jews groused that Moses had worsened our condition, had raised the Pharaoh's suspicions against us and put a weapon against us in the Egyptians' hands." But Klatzkin counters this argument with the reminder that "Moses refused to consider such matters, for it was not his business to relieve people's material needs but rather to pursue his mission of redemption."[94]

Like the Moses in Klatzkin's example, Schoenberg's Moses refuses to give in, as his brother Aron does, to his people's immediate desires, which in the opera assume the form of a return to idolatry. In the first scene of *Moses und Aron* the somber sounds from the Burning Bush—intoning in *Sprechstimme* just as the hero does—inform the latter of his mandate to free his people and enforce the monotheism that, whatever the hardships they may endure, is central to fulfilling their destiny as God's chosen people. What the opera subsequently enacts is a crisis in nation building as Aron, who, during Moses's absence on Mount Sinai, proves unable to curb the people's desires and, in an act of political expediency, allows them to return to their multiple gods. Although Schoenberg waits until the third act, whose music he never got around to composing, to explain the magnitude of Aron's offense, the nature of the crisis is clear enough from the first two acts. With historical hindsight the audience of course knows that the monotheism Moses was empowered to enforce ultimately prevails and that the Jews will make it to the land they had been promised. Similarly, Zionist thinkers of Schoenberg's time warned against making the sorts of compromises that would divert Jews from the task of creating the nation presumably destined for them.

As a drama of crisis *Moses und Aron* resembles those interludes in the great national epics of the past in which the people's or its leader's mission is temporarily diverted from its destined course by sexual and material temptations. As a tale of a crisis that is faced and then overcome, the opera celebrates the foundation of a nation in something of the way that Smetana's *Libuše* (1881) dramatizes the foundation of Prague in mythical times. Like Smetana's opera, composed while the Czechs lived under Austrian rule, *Moses und Aron* was composed before the establishment of Israel as a state. And like Smetana's opera, which is offered on ceremonial occasions in Prague to celebrate nationhood, *Moses und Aron* retains a solemn, oratorio-like character and might well, if the cultural authorities deemed its music sufficiently accessible, play a similar role within current-day Israel.

Yet within the history of opera it also looks back to another tradition, the clash between West and Orient that I describe in Chapter 6. Schoenberg's "Dance Around the Golden Calf," as I mention there, can be viewed within that long line of orientalist purple-patches going back to Salome's Dance of the Seven Veils and the Bacchanale in *Samson et Dalila*. In the sensuality and violence of this dance, the Jewish crowd has been turned by Aron's false leadership into the oriental other—though of course when it returns to its rightful course it will reassume its assigned role as advocate of what have come to be called Western values against the still idolatrous peoples surrounding them. As such *Moses und Aron* stands as the last of the grand imperialist operas that, going back to *L'Africaine* (the product of another Jewish composer, though one who must have excited Schoenberg's contempt), today demand a certain critical distance from the values they were once able to propagate with unself-conscious abandon.

Might one also speculate that another opera, one that also contains a character named Moses (who sports the nickname Trinity and even briefly masquerades as God at the end), suggests a critical perspective that we can take upon Schoenberg's work? It is an opera upon which Schoenberg would have heaped his scorn, it is by still another Jewish composer, and it happens to be contemporary with his own. It also implicitly echoes the exodus from Egypt to the promised land, which now assumes the guise of that city of sin named Mahagonny.[95] Yet if Weill and Brecht's opera can be used to unmask the spiritual pretensions of Schoenberg's, by the same token *Moses und Aron*, with the religious mission it renders so overwhelmingly in its high-style musical discourse, may also serve to unmask the materialist pretensions that make *Aufstieg und Fall der Stadt Mahagonny* so quintessential an example of what we take to be Weimar culture.

Chapter Eight

Regulated Anarchy:
John Cage's *Europeras 1 & 2*
and the Aesthetics of Opera

Anybody glancing through the reviews of Cage's *Europeras 1 & 2*, first performed by the Frankfurt Opera in December 1987, will note the frequency with which the term "parody" is employed to categorize the composer's intentions. As a Swiss newspaper put it, "The *Europeras 1 & 2* present us with a parody of opera that brings to a head and thereby exposes the pretense, the artificiality and, if you will, the falseness governing this genre," and, after describing examples of the dramatic musical actions taking place onstage, the review concludes by asking whether this production was anything "more than an expensive joke."[1]

Certainly it is understandable that a European opera audience, and professional music reviewers in particular, would experience the *Europeras* as parody. For one thing, even in Germany, where John Cage was far better known than in his own country, the operagoing public is none too likely to approach his work with the openness to new experience that he could expect from the altogether different public that frequents avant-garde events. Moreover, as the form that today could be called "the last remaining refuge of the high style,"[2] opera easily invites self-parody. "The closer opera gets to a parody of itself," Theodor Adorno wrote in "Bourgeois Opera," his most important (though also none too friendly) commentary on the medium, "the closer it is to the principle most inherent to it" (*AGS*, 16: 24). Often this parodistic component appears overtly in the subjects that composers choose, for example in works such as Mozart's *Der Schauspieldirektor* or Strauss's *Ariadne auf Naxos*, both of which expose operatic pretense by examining the process by which an opera is created or rehearsed; or, to cite a more subtle, indirect form of parody, in those arias within comic opera—for instance, Fiordiligi's "Come scoglie" in *Così fan tutte*—that imitate the text and musical form of *opera seria*.[3]

It is scarcely any wonder that traditional operagoers listening to two arias at once with singers in costumes deliberately inappropriate to each aria should view Cage's primary purpose as making cruel fun of cultural objects that have long maintained a sacred aura for them. After all, the opera house, centrally placed and luxuriously outfitted as it is in most European cities, has traditionally counted as the primary sanctum for high art. Even Christopher Hunt, who brought the Frankfurt production of *Europeras 1 & 2* to the Pepsico summer festival in Purchase, New York, in 1988, claimed that the work "takes the whole history and scope of an art form—European opera—and shows how ridiculous it is and says goodbye to it, like putting a period at the end of the sentence."[4] In an interview with Joan Retallack in 1992, Cage confirmed that when the Frankfurt Opera commissioned the work, the company officials—though certainly not Cage himself—intended the *Europeras* to mark the death of the form.[5] Yet, as Barbara Zuber, a German musicologist, put it in evident response to those who saw Cage's work as heaping ridicule on operatic tradition, "Though a person might be justified in guessing a parody here, he has not at all understood the concept behind this opera."[6]

The debate about whether or not the *Europeras* constitute parody assumes the commonplace notion of that term as a work's attempt to ridicule or to satirize an earlier work. If, on the other hand, we define parody in broader terms to mean what Linda Hutcheon has called a peculiarly twentieth-century mode, a "process of revising, replaying, inverting, and 'trans-contextualizing' previous works of art,"[7] then the *Europeras* could well be seen as an extension of modernist parody beyond even what Cage's predecessors had been aiming for. Indeed, the whole modernist notion of parody as the appropriation and expansion of earlier materials—and without necessarily subjecting these materials to ridicule—echoes the method of the so-called parody masses by, say, Josquin des Prés and Palestrina, who self-consciously constructed their polyphonic works out of earlier segments that they themselves or earlier composers had employed.

What is it the *Europeras* are attempting to say? Precisely how are the aesthetic principles of the traditional opera public alien to the Cagean aesthetic that has produced this extravagant theatrical romp? Is the alienness that separates these two aesthetics perhaps what endows Cage's Frankfurt creation with such force and fascination? And how does this creation provide a special perspective upon the various assumptions voiced by theorists of opera since the beginnings of the form?

I start with a description of the "action" and the "contents" of the *Europeras*.[8] One should preface these remarks with the statement that there is no single *Europera*, that since Cage empowered his singers to choose favorite arias from many operas for any single production, every production featuring a new set of singers has contained a correspondingly new set of arias and accompaniments. The Frankfurt Opera production of 1987 was entitled *Europeras 1 & 2*, with *1* being essentially a first act lasting an hour and a half, and *2* a second act, with a new set of singers and arias, lasting 45 minutes. Cage, who did not like the large-scale structuring implied by a division into acts, preferred to think of each segment as a separate opera—hence the numbers 1 and 2. After their production at the Pepsico festival, *Europeras 1 & 2* were performed in Zurich in 1991, but the subsequent versions, all of which bear higher numbers in their titles, are essentially concert operas that employ recordings and a small number of singers; although they use lighting, they are without costumes or décor. *Europeras 3 & 4*, produced in London and taken to Berlin, Strasbourg, and Paris in 1991, was followed the next year by *Europera 5*, premiered in Buffalo and performed in a number of cities in Europe and the United States.[9] In view of the difference in scale and resources, the later *Europeras* are essentially chamber works, while *Europeras 1 & 2*, however distorted they may strike a traditional opera audience, remain firmly within the genre we call grand opera. Every new production thus contains its own "text"—though regulated within the strict parameters Cage set up to govern the whole enterprise.

For *Europeras 1 & 2*, Cage used nineteen singers supposedly representing all known operatic voice ranges, with ten singers in 1 and nine in 2.[10] Each performer was asked to choose a group of arias that could be completed in no more than thirty and no less than twenty minutes. Several renditions took place at once. In my own audiotape of *Europeras 1 & 2* I can discern the Prize

Song from *Die Meistersinger* juxtaposed with "Che farò senza Euridice?" from Gluck's *Orfeo* and Méphistophélès's Serenade from Gounod's *Faust* set against two arias from different acts (and by different characters) of *Le nozze di Figaro*. My tape of *Europeras 3 & 4*, which introduces a piano, an instrument not present in the earlier work, at one point includes the piano playing the final moments of *Norma* against "Dich teure Halle" from *Tannhäuser* and the Flower Song from *Carmen*. Identifying a familiar aria is not always easy—partly because two or more arias are going on at once but also because the orchestral accompaniments have nothing to do with the arias being sung.

Although the orchestral accompaniments were drawn largely from the list of operas whose arias the singers were presenting, only fragments of accompaniments (and these are in no way tied to the arias as they are being sung), all chosen by means of chance operations, were actually performed. No conductor was in charge (a matter that apparently dismayed Gary Bertini, the director of the Frankfurt Opera, who had thought he would himself be conducting the opera he had commissioned from Cage), but all players remained on their own watching a digital clock to be sure that they kept within the time-brackets designated for each fragment. Cage here employed the same method he used in *Music for . . .* , a work of the same period in which each player operates independently by simply minding the clock. As with this latter work, although a musician would play the same part from performance to performance, the leeway allowed within the time-brackets makes each performance unique; by contrast, the singers, in order to avoid unplanned collisions on the stage, were expected to coordinate their singing with one another in the same way at each performance. The *Europeras 1 & 2* orchestra, consisting of twenty-four musicians with only five string players, sounds overwhelmingly brassy and percussive. The fragments assigned to a particular instrument have no necessary relation to one another except that they have been chosen by chance operations from some portion of that same instrument's part in the original score. Only occasionally does one recognize an accompaniment, and as often as not it is a Wagnerian leitmotif one hears—for example, Alberich's curse against a baritone singing the "Largo al factotum" or Wotan's sword motif set against another part of the same Rossini aria.

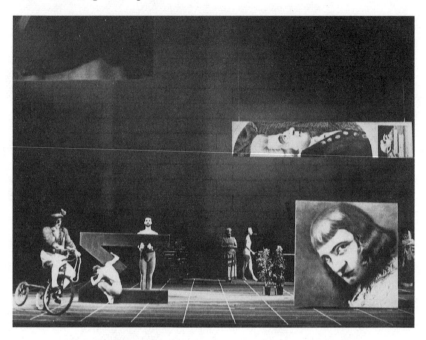

FIGS. 22 and 23. Two scenes from *Europera 2*. Fig. 22 (above): *Middle right*, truncated sideways image of Mozart. *Lower right*, Beniamino Gigli as Romeo in Gounod's opera. The letter *M*, as tall as the singer standing on it, is being moved in all possible positions, while another singer rides an enlarged tricycle. Photo, Beatriz Schiller; courtesy, The John Cage Trust. Fig. 23 (opposite): *Upper left*, lower neck of the composer Bellini. Singer climbs ladder while zeppelin advertises *Europera 3*, the next opera in the series. Photo, Mara Eggert; courtesy, The John Cage Trust.

Cage's use of chance operations in the *Europeras* achieved a complexity beyond any of the methods he had applied since he had begun composing with chance operations around 1950.[11] For one thing, as in his other work of the 1980s, he now had a computer at his disposal to provide electronic enhancement to the *I Ching*, which he had earlier employed, as it were, by hand. By means of an elaborate computer program devised by his assistant Andrew Culver, Cage determined not only the parameters within which the orchestral players were to operate, but also how to utilize such other traditional oper-

atic elements as stage lighting, scenic backgrounds, costumes, and actions and props. One could speak of each of these elements as creating a regularized set of internal relations by means of chance operations that determine matters such as sequence and timing. Yet each element maintains its independence and refuses to be integrated with any other.

Each of these elements, moreover, functions according to its own rationale. The rule behind the costuming, for example, is that all periods of civilization must be represented and that the singers must change costume from aria to aria. Yet no necessary relation exists between what a "character" sings and what she or he wears: Don Giovanni could be dressed as a medieval monk or Orfeo as a rake. In order to call primary attention to the singers, Cage intended the costumes to remain the most conspicuous visual elements of the work, while the constantly changing stage flats (their order and timing determined, of course, in advance by chance operations) remained in black and white. The visual categories governing the 57 images used in *Europeras 1 & 2* were limited to singers, composers, animals, and operatic set designs of the past. The photographs and drawings that the flats reproduced were cropped to sizes determined by chance operations so that only truncated versions of the original images could be viewed (see Figures 22 and 23).

The computer program that established the lighting likewise left no room for human intentionality in illuminating whatever was going on in the opera, whether aurally or visually. Thus the stage could be lit up and darkened at predetermined intervals that had nothing to do with the actions going on. As Culver describes it, "The electrical activity composed for each light was composed without attention to the concurrent activity of any other light: each light is a soloist."[12] Similarly the props that the singers used and the actions they performed while delivering their arias were determined in advance but without regard to the relation of these props or actions to the aria. Cage employed chance-determined page numbers referring to an unabridged dictionary, in which he located words that would suggest particular actions to him, and further chance operations decided the time-brackets available for these actions. Note, for instance, the following direction for a series of actions:

> Singer is brought in in a zippered container bag shaped like an igloo, half-spherical. As aria is begun, bag is unzippered. Assistants, at end, zipper bag up and take it offstage. Moving blindfolded but unassisted. The letter I is revealed to be the letter Z. Assistant puts large, costume donkey or rabbit ears on singer. Singer is brought in in a gondola, barge, or other sailing boat. Artificial, oversized mynah bird, with flying ability and built-in sound equipment who caws out names of opera composers, i. e. "Verdi, Verdi," "Monteverdi," etc. Works way unassisted slowly on all fours.[13]

The regulated anarchy transpiring onstage extended to still another institutional feature of opera, namely the synopses of plots characteristically distributed to the audience. Cage prepared not a single synopsis for *Europeras 1 & 2* but twelve sets of two synopses, with each member of the audience receiving one pair of the twelve available pairs of stories (one synopsis for *Europera 1*, the other for *Europera 2*). Sentences and phrases were drawn from pre-existing synopses of standard operas, then scrambled by chance operations to the point that one opera can merge with another in midsentence. Just as two composers so widely separated in time and style as Monteverdi and Verdi could be brought together (as in the quotation above) simply because of the sound repetitions in their names, so the segments of unrelated and widely differing operatic plots could be juxtaposed at random. Here, for instance, is the first synopsis in one of the two sets together with my own attempts (placed within brackets) at identifying the sources (question marks indicate my uncertainty about a particular source):

> He, unhappy at her apparent indifference to him [*La traviata?*] brings her captive [*Il trovatore?*] to the Temple of the Holy Grail [*Parsifal*]. Another man also loves her [this could be from countless operas], accusing her of witchcraft [*Un ballo in maschera*]. She expresses [?] but a lifeless automaton [*Les Contes d'Hoffmann*]—who should have reported to jail for a minor offense [*Die Fledermaus*]. Disguising himself [countless possible operas again] in exchange for her love [*Il trovatore?*], they are condemned as traitors [*Les Dialogues des Carmélites?*]. Conveniently, he flees to an inn on the Lithuanian border [*Boris Godunov*].

On the syntactic level this synopsis maintains a high degree of coherence. Indeed, in view of the fact that operagoers do not have high expectations that the plot summaries they read in their programs have much relation to the "real" world, one needs to read with some attention before realizing that on the semantic level the synopsis makes no sense at all.

The brief illusion that syntactic coherence can hide the semantic incoherence that the audience finds in the various synopses handed out before the *Europeras* is perhaps emblematic of the blind faith that opera can count on from those who feel committed to what we today call high culture. Among the various theatrical and musical genres, opera has traditionally exercised a special cultural authority throughout Europe as well as in urban centers outside Europe. An opera, one might say, is something more than a particular artifact combining theater with music; every opera implicitly suggests the larger institutional framework within which it participates. Not only does the opera house in European cities occupy a special site (in some cases even physically connected to the royal palace), but the tradition of the monarch's box at the center in the houses built in earlier centuries suggests its traditional connection with state power.[14] Opera houses often display a sumptuousness that in medieval times could be found only in palaces and cathedrals.[15] In our own, more democratic time, it sometimes seems anachronistic that the form has survived at all, indeed that in recent years it has achieved an uncommon degree of popularity. As one commentator put it,

> The innate conservatism of so many opera productions, the fêting of the star singer over the music, the little rituals that attend on each performance, the whole hierarchical organisation of singers and conductor, the existence of productions some twenty years old in an opera house's repertoire . . . all these work towards the continued establishment of opera as, not the most youthful art-form, but the oldest, the most fixed, and the most serving the interests of conservatism.[16]

When John Cage was invited to stage an opera for Frankfurt, he must have been keenly aware how distant the aesthetic associated with opera was from his own aesthetic—a fact not lost on the company officials who expected him to ring the medium's death knell. Through the confrontation of these two aesthetics, as it turned out, the commission afforded him an ideal opportunity to put his ideas to work in his own way. The very process of having to work with an opera company—even one, like the Frankfurt Opera, whose dramaturgs, Heinz-Klaus Metzger and Rainer Riehn, were already committed to the avant-garde and to Cage in particular—brought out all of Cage's anti-institutional fervor. In a newspaper interview a few days before the opening he spoke out openly: "At first they tell me that everything that I want simply will not work. Then I insist on it, and some of this finally gets realized. But we can't change institutions. The anarchistic view is this: Institutions can't be changed. They're wrong by nature."[17] The anarchism that Cage voiced here should not hide the fact that the anarchistic impulses within his own aesthetic were complemented by a strong regulatory impulse. Anybody who glances at the complex computer program set up for the lighting of *Europeras 1 & 2* will note that, despite the chance operations on which it is based, it looks at least as elaborate and regulated as the lighting programs used in any modern opera house. Producing *Europeras 1 & 2* allowed two strong forces to collide—on the one hand, the seemingly unbending will within that ancient institution we call opera and whose supposed corruptions had been the target of reform-minded thinkers such as Algarotti, Gluck, Wagner, and Nietzsche in earlier centuries; on the other, an equally powerful will (hidden though it may have been by the polite, good-natured demeanor that Cage characteristically displayed toward the world) of a figure determined to impose his own anti-intentionalist, anti-institutionalist convictions.

As institutional critique, *Europeras 1 & 2* clearly follows in the line of *4'33"* (1952), that once-scandalous work whose first performance showed a tuxedoed pianist walking to his instrument, lifting the cover, sitting on the piano stool for the precise period indicated in the title, and then closing the piano, bowing, and leaving for the wings. Both *4'33"* and Cage's Frankfurt "opera," for neither of which he "composed" a single chord or even note, attempt to comment on the social context of art—not in a theoretical statement, as many a contemporary academic critic has sought to do, but within the very context upon which he is commenting. Though Cage in his earlier days generated music presumably played by tuxedoed musicians going about their business much like the supposed performer of *4'33"*, nobody would have expected him to compose for the opera house.

Indeed, the attitude he had long displayed toward opera was indifferent and even unfriendly—though, as he told Joan Retallack in an interview, he had always retained an affection for *Don Giovanni*, which he approached by means of Kierkegaard's interpretation. Until he arrived in Frankfurt for rehearsals two months before the opening of the *Europeras*, he had rarely attended opera, whose vibrato vocal style had long put him off. It is clear that he had considerably less acquaintance with most of the works excerpted in the arias of *Europeras 1 & 2* than the devout opera fans clamoring for scarce tickets at the major houses or buying CDs of arias sung by the latest superstar. When asked what operas he had heard in his youth, he answered, "The only one I heard was *Aida.* . . . . That's Verdi, isn't it?"[18] During those two months, however, he attended a number of performances of various operas in Frankfurt and, according to Retallack, found himself surprised and delighted at what he heard, above all by *Falstaff,* whose "complexity" and "extreme musicality, with fugues and everything toward the end," he particularly admired.[19] Indeed, one wonders if Cage sensed an analogy between the musically controlled confusion of this final scene and the regulated anarchy governing his own work in rehearsal at the time. Not only *Falstaff,* but *Pelléas et Mélisande* and his one-time teacher's *Moses und Aron* came to excite his enthusiasm once his interest in opera had been kindled.

Still, despite his newfound interest in opera, Cage also expressed his hostility toward the social system he associated with the form, which he saw as out of touch with the realities of contemporary life: "Opera in the society is an ornament of the lives of the people who have. I don't feel that so much with my work [*Europeras 1 & 2*], but with more conventional operas, it's clearly an ornament that has no necessary relation to the 20th century."[20] Needless to say, Cage must also have seen the musical "content" of *Europeras 1 & 2* as thoroughly conventional. For practical reasons arias and accompaniments from operas still under copyright in Germany were excluded from the production—with the consequence that not a single work composed during the twentieth century was represented (the latest was *Tosca,* which premiered in January 1900). Not unexpectedly, the "favorite" arias presented by the various singers were thoroughly canonical, well known to opera listeners throughout the world except for those by a couple of German composers (Nicolai and Lortzing) whose canonical status is limited to their homeland. The arias selected encompassed the whole history of opera in several languages, including even a work as early as Purcell's *Dido and Aeneas,* though, quite in accord with audience taste, all but a few came from the century-long span beginning with the late Mozart operas. These were precisely the arias familiar enough to make an opera audience feel comfortable to a high degree—and with the result that the incongruous orchestral and scenic contexts within which they were placed doubtless induced a correspondingly high degree of discomfort.

The conflict between John Cage's aesthetic and the aesthetic we associate with European opera of course extends far beyond such institutional matters. Throughout its four-century history as an art form, opera, despite many changes in musical and theatrical styles, has maintained an uncommon continuity in the intentions that it has defined for itself. One might cite the following intentions, each of which can be pitted against the aesthetic we have come to associate with John Cage: (1) a pretense of mimesis, often manifested in a claim that the music reflects the words (not to speak of the referents in the real world to which the words supposedly point); (2) an attempt to unify various genres into some larger totality; (3) a cultivation of dramatic progressions, whether within individual arias, as in number-opera, or in the work as an integrated whole; and (4) a sustained effort (except in most comic operas) to express passion and achieve grandeur and thence to transmit these qualities to its audience. Cage's achievement in the *Europeras* may be viewed as a critical examination and undermining of each of these intentions.

Note, for instance, the rigorously antimimetic program governing the *Europeras*. Since its inception, opera has always sought to tell some story, whether from myth or history. Yet from the moment that the members of the audience at the *Europeras* sit down to read the synopses in their programs, they recognize that Cage has frustrated mimesis at every point. Once the "action" begins, characters appear in costumes that are likely to have nothing to do (unless chance operations should accidentally establish mimesis for a brief interval) with the already-familiar arias they are singing, and neither the costumes nor the arias have anything plausibly to do with the actions they are performing or the props they are using. One could, in fact, speak of a four-way frustration of mimesis.

Moreover, Cage has systematically challenged the traditional operatic claim of achieving a union of words and music. It is significant that since opera's beginnings (in fact, even in the writings of the Florentine Camerata, which provided the form with a theoretical grounding even before the first operas were composed), this claim has been repeatedly asserted (often in reaction to composers who violated the principle) by such central theorist-practitioners as Monteverdi, Gluck, Wagner, and Strauss.[21] Even a composer such as Kurt Weill, who, as I point out in Chapter 7, sought to restore the primacy of music over word, still took for granted that the two elements bore a significant relationship with one another. Cage, by contrast, sought to undo that relationship entirely. In his longtime role as the music director of Merce Cunningham's dance company, Cage insisted that music remain independent from dance movements. "Rather than the dance expressing the music or the music the dance," he once said, "the two could go together independently, neither one controlling the other" (*CC*, 104). By the same token, one can hardly imagine his buying into the word/music ideology central to the European opera aesthetic. Yet since the *Europeras* retain their singers' favorite arias precisely as they were written, the audience is barraged throughout the evening with specimens purporting to embody this aesthetic. The incongruous contexts within which these arias appear both visually and aurally, however, serve to make one question if there ever even *was* a "natural" fit of words and music.

Another feature central to the aesthetic governing opera is the presence within a single work of several art forms—poetry, music, scenery, dance. Wagner's notion of a *Gesamtkunstwerk* that would bring together the various arts that had once flourished harmoniously in Greek tragedy is only a late, theoretically worked out version of an idea of totality present in much operatic practice since the beginnings of the form. Anybody present at a performance of the *Europeras* would witness all the art forms available to theatrical representation (including dance, whose role in the work I have not mentioned), but, rather than functioning in tandem with one another, they are of course totally scrambled.

Just as the traditional opera aesthetic insists on bringing the various arts together in a totality, so it also privileges dramatic action. Like other theatrical styles, opera—with such notable exceptions, as I pointed out in earlier chapters, of eighteenth-century *opera seria* and the revived number-opera of the 1920s—cultivates a forward-moving dramatic development, and opera composers, whether in individual arias and ensembles or in a work as a whole, have employed all the technical resources available in whatever style was at their disposal to find a means of building and sustaining dramatic tension. In the *Europeras*, just as the traditional union of words and music in the individual arias teases the audience with the possibility that the music will speak some meaning, so the dramatic climaxes toward which the arias move (and which the singers develop with considerable fervor), tease us with constantly rising expectations that, because these arias are sung simultaneously with other arias seeking similar climaxes and heard against accompaniments that refuse to accompany them, consistently refuse to be adequately met. Moreover, the powerful closure to which audiences are accustomed in opera (even an *opera seria*, with its leisurely dramatic development, was expected to close with an emphatic chorus) is wholly absent from the *Europeras*, each of which ends abruptly when the stipulated time is up.

Finally, one might note Cage's subversion of the traditional operatic goal (evident as early as the theory and practice of Monteverdi) of expressing and transmitting passion. No serious art form has dedicated itself as assiduously as opera to the grand gesture—one in which the performers conduct themselves as though moved in the most earnest and inspired way and in turn seek to affect the audience with the emotions that they claim to possess. Cage characteristically displayed an acute resistance when asked to feel moved, as one notes in an anecdote about a performance of *Messiah* he attended with a patronizing companion who asked him, "Don't you love the 'Hallelujah Chorus'?" After he balked, she asked, "Don't you like being moved?" to which he replied, "I don't mind being moved, but I don't like to be pushed" (*CC*, 234). Certainly the individual arias of the *Europeras* make the traditional pretense of embodying passion and of infecting others with passion. Yet to listen simultaneously, say, to Orfeo's lament for his lost Euridice and to the Flower Song from *Carmen*, as one might in the *Europeras*, is to put the aesthetic of opera in question.

To the extent that the *Europeras* offer a critique of the highest-style theatrical form available within European culture, they implicitly set up an encounter between this culture as a whole and Cage's concept of some alternative mode of living. The very title of the work suggests a transatlantic confrontation: "Europe's Operas," distinctly not those that *we* might be producing; or, to take this notion a step further, as Laura Kuhn suggests, "Your Operas," but certainly not *ours*.[22] This confrontation gains special relevance when one notes that it could never have taken place in a major American opera house as it did in a German one. How does one explain the paradox that Cage's distinctly un-, even anti-European experimentalism excites not only admiration but also active sponsorship in a European cultural center? The easy answer is that the economics of cultural production allow things to be done on the Continent as they cannot be done in Cage's home country: the state subsidies available in many European countries give cultural organizations there a freedom that they do not enjoy in the United States, where cultural events depend almost wholly on the financial sponsorship of local subscribers and donors, who generally impose a conservative aesthetic on the programming for which they feel they are footing the bill. Yet one suspects still another motive for the fascination that John Cage has exercised for many years not only in Germany but throughout Europe and also in Japan: Cage's unbending experimentalism may well strike a more tradition-bound community as a refreshing New World barbarity that, even when it is challenging an older aesthetic, offers a promise of cultural renewal.

The Europe-America antithesis gains special resonance if we place it in relation to the role that Arnold Schoenberg came to play retrospectively for Cage. If Kurt Weill, as I indicated in the preceding chapter, in 1930 offered a striking alternative to the aesthetic represented by Schoenberg, the alternative that Cage offered his former teacher is considerably more radical. Although Cage studied with Schoenberg for only a brief period during the mid-1930s, the latter's impact, at once positive and negative, did not become clear until years later, once Cage had constructed the phenomenon we know today as John Cage. One might interpret the name "Arnold Schoenberg" within the terms of this construction to signify "Old World master" and the name "John Cage" to mean "New World successor." Note Cage's often retold story of how Schoenberg came to accept him as a pupil despite Cage's lack of funds. "Will you devote your life to music?" Schoenberg asked him (*CC*, 4), after which Cage formally committed himself. The story belongs to what one might call the "artistic-succession" genre, in which some canonical older master passes the mantle to a potentially canonical younger one; Emerson's words, "I greet you at the beginning of a great career,"[23] in response to Whitman's sending him a copy of the first *Leaves of Grass*, stand as the classical model within the genre.

Even though Cage never knew Schoenberg well, the parallels in their careers are striking. Both broke so sharply with the musical past that they remained highly controversial figures even in their old age. Both also distinguished themselves as visual artists—Schoenberg as a painter and Cage as a printmaker—and both have shown themselves to be masters of the written word independent of their musical attainments.[24] Yet Cage's recountings of his relationship with his master reveal some crucial tensions. Though Cage clearly revered him ("I worshipped him like a god" [*CC*, 5]) Schoenberg also represented an obstacle to be overcome, and this obstacle became defined for Cage in geographical terms. One notes the conflict particularly in a review that Cage wrote in 1965 of a volume of Schoenberg's letters. Calling the review "Mosaic," Cage wove Schoenberg's own words into his narrative by using italics to quote his former teacher, as in this passage:

> He was a self-made aristocrat. *I wonder what you'd say to the world in which I nearly die of disgust.* Becoming an American citizen didn't remove his *distaste for democracy and that sort of thing.* Of former times when a prince stood as a protector before an artist, he writes: *The fairest, alas bygone, days of art.*[25]

Note the glaring contrasts in this "mosaic" that Cage has pieced together: the Old World "aristocrat" who looks back nostagically to some "prince-protector" to sponsor his "art" has been relegated to a New World "democracy" that excites his "disgust." Cage deliberately defines his contrast of old and new worlds with recognizable clichés—both those from Schoenberg's own mouth and those that Cage, as representative of the New World, reads into his former master.

Compared with the *Europeras*, Schoenberg's major attempt at opera, *Moses und Aron*, seems to look back at least as much to the "bygone days" for which he longs in the quotation above as it does to the future. Despite its obvious iconoclasm—its composition out of a single tone row and its use of *Sprechstimme* instead of song for its hero—*Moses und Aron*, as I indicate in Chapter 7, strikes us today as a rigidly determined score whose dramaturgy, despite its advanced musical style, does not move substantially beyond the mode established long before in Wagnerian music-drama.[26] Regulation without the mitigating Cagean anarchy, one might say. When juxtaposed with Schoenberg's opera, the *Europeras*, despite deriving all their sounds from the European operatic canon, look and sound as though out of another world altogether. "Even though the subject is European, the conventions are Oriental" (*CC*, 132), Cage said while planning *Europeras 1 & 2*. Whether or not one can properly call these conventions "oriental," Cage discovered a means of defamiliarizing his European subject to the point that the work is constantly advertising its break with tradition.

Despite disrupting a centuries-old tonal method, Schoenberg, by contrast, steadfastly claimed to be continuing the European musical tradition. "Bach did this with these four notes," Cage remembered Schoenberg saying in the process of instruction, and "Beethoven did this, Brahms did this, Schoenberg did this!" (*CC*, 9). Whereas Schoenberg proudly names forebears going far back in time (though, significantly, not beyond German-speaking lands) Cage's ancestors belong largely to the modernist world. The title of his mesostic text, "James Joyce, Marcel Duchamp, Erik Satie: An Alphabet," advertises a genealogy that encompasses practitioners in the three major arts of the immediately preceding generation.[27] For Cage, the only important forebears of a more distant past remained Thoreau as well as certain ancient sages—Meister Eckhart and various Eastern philosophers—who occupied a timeless realm for Cage quite in contrast to the historical succession of composers in whose direct line Schoenberg situated himself. Schoenberg is the only German and, in fact, one of the few *composers* in Cage's genealogy, which includes not only persons whom one would classify as "artists," but also charismatic thinkers such as D. T. Suzuki, Buckminster Fuller, and Marshall McLuhan.

Cage's need to position himself in relation to Schoenberg gains special meaning if we remember that around 1950, at the very moment that Cage took his bold leap into composing by means of chance operations, the serialism that derived from Schoenberg became the favored mode among the most advanced composers on both sides of the Atlantic. As a result, Cage's mode did not count for much in official circles, above all among music professors, for whom Schoenberg and those who claimed to be extending his method reigned supreme. It was not, in fact, until serialism had worn itself out that Cage's achievement of taking composition a significant step beyond Schoenberg came to be acknowledged—and, with an irony I touched on earlier, more emphatically in Germany than in Cage's own country.[28]

Perhaps the most telling moment in Cage's reminiscences of Schoenberg is not one that he witnessed directly but rather heard somebody else report: "Someone asked Schoenberg about his American pupils, whether he'd had any that were interesting, and Schoenberg's first reply was to say there were no interesting pupils, but then he smiled and said, "There was one," and he named me. Then he said, 'Of course he's not a composer, but he's an inventor—of genius'" (*CC*, 6). The very contrast that Schoenberg is drawing here suggests a sharp dividing line between a European and a purportedly American view of creativity: being a composer means practicing creativity in the European mode—that is, dedicating oneself to the perpetuation of some form of "high art"—while being an inventor means tinkering with new, not traditionally artistic materials and envisioning relationships with audiences outside the usual institutional channels. From a European point of view in Schoenberg's time, invention would have seemed a peculiarly American vocation—witness such famed examples as Alexander Graham Bell and Thomas Edison, as well as (in an analogy that would not have been lost on Schoenberg) the not-so-famed John Milton Cage, father of his erstwhile pupil.[29]

Viewed as an "invention" rather than as a traditional "work of art," the *Europeras* emerge as objects that those choosing to attend them can themselves observe, contemplate, and examine without the emotional commitment that opera has traditionally demanded of its consumers. Although the purported composer of *Europeras 1 & 2* did not "create" a single note, the larger conception, together with the method by which the whole thing became assembled, was very much the invention of John Cage, who officiated over the rehearsals as resolutely as most any opera composer of the past. In his role as inventor re-using materials that were ready-at-hand (he had originally wanted to use costumes already in the Frankfurt Opera's inventory), Cage was continuing the work of his friend Marcel Duchamp, whose readymades provided a visual precedent for the auditory collage that constitutes the musical content of the *Europeras*.[30]

Once we view the work as something to be tinkered with—whether by its maker or its consumers—it loses whatever autonomy it had within the terms of the older aesthetic and, in effect, comes to "spill over," as it were, into the everyday world. The continuity between the *Europeras* and this world was brought home to me while I was preparing to write this chapter. I was driving from Stanford to San Francisco to attend a performance of Handel's opera *Ariodante*, to be performed in a former warehouse by apprentice singers from the San Francisco Opera. In the car I had been playing my tapes of *Europeras 1 & 2*. As I approached the makeshift theater, whose outer walls lacked soundproofing, I could hear two of the singers warming up with arias from the opera they were about to perform; in addition, several members of the orchestra were practicing recognizably Handelian passages. For a few moments I believed I was still immersed in the *Europeras*, for the noises I was hearing—Handel's music scrambled so that all the individual musicians were on their own—were no different in kind from those on the tape (except that all originated from the same opera). When the "real" opera began a little later, it took some effort to readjust myself to an older aesthetic that demanded a frame of mind totally at odds with the experience of Cage's work—except, of course, that *Ariodante*, as an example of *opera seria*, did not cultivate the sustained dramatic development of most later opera. This incident, let me add, served to remind me that Cage's many attempts—both in the *Europeras* and in other works—to undermine this earlier aesthetic did not consist simply of negative critique, but that they also were challenging his listeners to attend to and to attune themselves to sounds they might otherwise have dismissed as irrelevant or annoying.

The radicality with which Cage's aesthetic has been able to rethink the history and nature of opera is particularly evident when we compare the *Europeras* with the many iconoclastic productions of classic operas that have aroused the ire of critics and audiences during the last two decades. I think, for instance, of Chéreau's staging of *Der Ring des Nibelungen* for the Bayreuth centennial of 1976, in which, as I mention in Chapter 5, Wagner's Rhine maidens appeared as prostitutes guarding a nineteenth-century hydroelectric dam; or of Peter Sellars's readings of the Mozart/da Ponte operas, in which *Così fan tutte*, for example, is transferred from its elegant eighteenth-century setting to a contemporary diner.[31] On the surface the unexpected costuming in which long-familiar operatic characters appear should seem in tune with the method employed by Cage in the *Europeras*. Yet in all these so-called postmodern stagings, the original text (usually in the original language as well) and the vocal and instrumental music remain inviolate. Only the costumes and scenery confound one's expectations; those in the audience who feel offended by the changes wrought upon some beloved work are free to shut their eyes, after which they will hear exactly the same musical sounds and words to which they have been long accustomed. Cage's audience, on the other hand, has no way of escaping his provocative aural bombardment.

Chéreau's, Sellars's, and their various colleagues' interpretations are precisely that—interpretations. However much they may try to shock the opera-going public, they also seek, in a serious and sustained manner, to make contemporary sense out of an older text. Once the spectators have accustomed themselves to what the director is attempting, the experience of the opera is not much different from that of any conventional performance. I can testify that after repeated viewings of videotapes of several such productions, the director's new interpretations come to gain the same authority that earlier, less iconoclastic stagings did. Cage, quite in contrast, did not practice nor invite interpretation. In the *Europeras*, indeed throughout his later work, he tried to frustrate any desire by the audience to find coherence and "meaning" in the texts or noises laid before them. Indeed, even the contemporary sense of parody as an appropriation of past art to a new context is difficult to apply to the *Europeras*, for parody, even in this postmodern usage, implies some sort of interpretative gesture on the part of author or audience; the method of the *Europeras* is such that as soon as one feels tempted to make sense out of what one sees and hears on the stage, the ground is pulled out from under. Parody, I might add, also involves some form of mimesis, whether of some earlier artistic discourse or of something discernible within the real world; and mimesis, as I have indicated, is what Cage sought assiduously to avoid. This is not to say that the audience is not expected to experience comic effects from the heterogeneous materials colliding in the *Europeras*. Cage, in fact, was reported laughing a good bit as he watched the rehearsals and, in a program note for the performances of *Europeras 1 & 2* at the Pepsico festival, referred to the work as "comic . . . in the spirit of *Hellzapoppin*."[32]

Not only do the *Europeras* question the aesthetic of opera more radically than the stagings of iconoclastic recent directors but they also challenge this aesthetic in a way different from such celebrated postmodern new operas as those of Philip Glass and John Adams. The work of both these composers uses so-called minimalist orchestral effects that pretend to have nothing to do with the dramatic action enacted on the stage and often not even with the words being sung. Yet despite these effects Adams's *Nixon in China* and Glass's *Satyagraha* affect their audiences as quite traditional attempts at historical drama—the former as a titillating parody of still-living politicians, the latter as a message-loaded plea for all the various causes that its hero, Mohandas Gandhi, stood for. (It is scarcely surprising that both these works, unlike the *Europeras*, have made their way into major American opera houses.) Only Glass's first opera, *Einstein on the Beach*, performed in collaboration with Robert Wilson, would seem to approach the Cage aesthetic. With its refusal to develop a narrative, its conspicuous separation of the music from the words and actions going on, its use of an electronic synthesizer in place of traditional instruments, *Einstein* still seems one of the more radical challenges to traditional opera mounted by an American. Yet with repeated hearings the music and the words that might have first seemed incompatible come to sound made for one another; and the political message, despite the lack of plot, is scarcely less loaded than the message that Glass was later to deliver in *Satyagraha*.[33] Although John Cage always insisted that art is socially situated, one could not imagine him delivering the sort of message one finds in Glass. Among recent experimentations with operatic form, only Steve Reich's multimedia *The Cave*, which eschews narrative even more resolutely than *Einstein on the Beach* and utilizes the sort of nonvibrato voice that preceded the invention of opera, questions the aesthetics of opera in a manner commensurate with Cage's challenge.

The experience of listening to tapes of the *Europeras*, I might add, is somewhat deceptive, for repeated hearings, as with repeated viewings of the Chéreau *Ring* or hearings of *Einstein on the Beach*, work to freeze the performance: even the unaccustomed sounds juxtaposed with one another in the *Europeras* come to seem wedded to one another once you have heard them enough. (Cage himself balked at listening to recorded performances, whether of his own or of other composers' pieces.) Yet since the various instrumentalists are instructed to work within their individual time-brackets, no two actual performances could possibly produce the same "score." Writing of the many Cage compositions that allow latitude to individual performers even when performing with one another, Dieter Schnebel has claimed, "Cage's music is basically one for soloists, or one might almost say: for solipsists—one plays solo, alone, for oneself."[34] A string player who recorded *Music for . . .* , which, as I mentioned earlier, employs time-brackets similar to those of the *Europeras*, has described the difficulty that a professional musician faces trying to go it alone in order to carry out the inventor Cage's "do-it-yourself" method: "You're always feeling tempted to coordinate your notes with those of the musicians around you," he reported in conversation, "and then you have to keep reminding yourself that Cage expects each instrument to be on its own." To guard his players from such temptations in this piece, Cage instructed them to stay widely apart physically—to the point of having them spill out from the stage into the auditorium.

Yet the anarchy suggested in these statements is by no means complete but remains regulated within parameters determined in advance. Explaining the way that his method in *Music for . . .* extends the possibility of individual autonomy beyond what he had done before, Cage spoke of a "togetherness of differences—not only differences in ranges, but differences in structure" (*CC*, 123–24). Though the listener, as well as the performer, is more likely to be aware of differences than "togetherness," it is significant that Cage felt the need to employ the latter term—perhaps suggesting that the anarchic tendencies he unleashed are subsumed under some ultimate conception of community. Speaking of Indian music at one point, he indicated several devices needed "to hold improvisation together," and, directly after, he made a general statement that can refer at once to the aesthetic and to the social realms: "I believe in *dis*organization; but I don't see that in terms of non-participation or isolation, but rather precisely as a complete participation. Those rules of order must have been put there in order, as we say, to hold things together" (*CC*, 259). The more one reads Cage's descriptions and justifications of his procedures, the more aware one becomes how powerfully his social views—combining as they do individuality with participation, difference with togetherness—have at the same time shaped the aims and methods of his artistic production.

The regulated anarchy within which Cage's musicians operate in his later work applies as well to the activity of the audiences who attend his performances. In earlier chapters I wrote of how the opera audience, at least since the later nineteenth century, was expected to sit passively in a darkened hall and submit itself to the emotional demands of the music; by contrast, Cage's audiences are encouraged—within the parameters established by the composer—to pursue a new kind of attentiveness, one that, for example, heeds the sounds "outside" the work itself as scrupulously as it does those produced by the official performers. Cage once said that "my own best piece, at least the one I like the most, is the silent piece," namely *4'33"*, and he used this example to chastise audiences: "What they thought was silence [in *4'33"*], because they didn't know how to listen, was full of accidental sounds. You could hear the wind stirring outside during the first movement [in the first performance]" (*CC*, 65). The individuals constituting a properly trained audience would free themselves from the usual institutional constraints and let their minds wander according to the various sounds (and sights) presented to them. Doubtless they will sometimes allow themselves a certain inattentiveness—somewhat like that condoned among the audiences attending traditional Japanese drama, one of Cage's models. They are not tempted with expectations of something about to come, whether a climactic moment or the closure that has customarily been necessary to inform them that their musical experience has achieved some final meaning.[35] Above all, they would not be molded into a single mass reacting collectively, and unthinkingly, to a composer's or a conductor's manipulations—precisely the accustomed annual experience of *Messiah* that Cage disappointed his companion by resisting.

Within the larger context of Cage's work these new arrangements he ad-

F I G . 2 4 . John Cage during a conference on and celebration of his work in various media at Stanford University, January, 1992. Photo, Brigitte Carnochan.

vocated for performers and audiences alike belong to that new genre, the *Musicircus*, that he arranged to be staged at various celebrations of his work since the 1960s.[36] The *Musicircus*, together with its 1992 variant at Stanford University, what Cage named *House Full of Music*, encourages all forms of music, high and low, Western and non-Western, professional and amateur, indeed many forms of noise that might not ordinarily be called music, to be going on at once. (Figure 24 is a photo of Cage taken at the time of this performance.) The various spectators come and go at will and mingle easily with the performers; indeed, once a group is done performing, the members themselves turn into spectators. Cage liked to refer to the *Musicircus* not simply as a specific event at a specific time and place but as a principle—"a principle of a flexible relationship, of a flexibility of relationships"[37] as well as a "principle . . . of having many things going on at once" (*CC*, 84). To avoid turning into anarchy, the *Musicircus* needs an organizer or, better yet, from Cage's point of view, "several" organizers, with the result to be labeled "a practical, or practicable, anarchy"[38]—Cage would doubtless have found my own modifier "regulated" far too strong for his taste. Whether or not one calls the principles of the *Musicircus* embodiments of some peculiarly American aesthetic, they remain at a far extreme from that European aesthetic which has insisted on audience submission to one thing going on at a time. Seen from the point of view of these principles, Cage's achievement in the *Europeras* emerges as a celebration of familiar operatic sights and sounds which, liberated from their accustomed contexts, provoke our attention with constantly unexpected turns in this high-spirited, head-on collision he organized between his heterodox New World aesthetic and one of the most sanctified Old World cultural forms surviving into the present day.

Finale ✧ Opera Audiences

In July 1994, the night before the final competition for the soccer World Cup was to be held in the Los Angeles Coliseum, another much-publicized event took place several miles away at another sports site, Dodger Stadium, home of the local baseball team. This event, generally referred to as "The Three Tenors," brought together for the second time the three singers acknowledged by most opera fans to be the reigning representatives within their voice range during the last third of the twentieth century: José Carreras, Plácido Domingo, and Luciano Pavarotti. If Carreras was not fully acknowledged to be the equal of the other two, the remission of his cancer (the occasion for the first joint concert of the three singers four years before) served to compensate for whatever artistic inferiority audiences perceived between him and his somewhat more celebrated collaborators. Indeed, this recovery of one tenor's health had also provided a pretext for the public's decision to forget whatever rivalry had been thought to exist between Pavarotti and Domingo. The first concert, moreover, had been linked, though less overtly than the Los Angeles event, to the World Cup soccer competition held in Italy during the summer of 1990 (Figure 25). Unlike the later one, the Rome concert did not take place in a sports arena but in the Baths of Caracalla, which, however much this venue may have been devoted to recreational activities during antiquity, had become associated with opera during the preceding several decades by means of outdoor summer performances of grand-scale works, above all, of *Aida*.

Both the 1990 and 1994 events followed similar formats—a few not-so-well-known arias (by Meyerbeer, Massenet, Cilea), together with several quite

FIG. 25. The Three Tenors (*left to right*, Plácido Domingo, José Carreras, Luciano Pavarotti) singing the final note of their first joint concert, Rome, 1990. Photo, Robert Cahen © 1997.

familiar ones (from operas such as *Tosca, Turandot, Pagliacci*). Yet a good bit of each concert was taken up with numbers not from opera but from more "popular" musical forms such as Viennese operetta, zarzuela, American musical comedy. The concerts also included such chestnuts—marked by audience applause as soon as the orchestra poured out its introductory notes—as "O sole mio," "Granada," or "Torna a Surriento." There were also a number of pieces with Broadway-style orchestration in which all three tenors participated at once—among these some "medleys" for which an arranger put together a succession of popular pieces and, perhaps most memorable of all at these concerts, what one might dub a "relay race" among the three participants, in which each tenor sang a few lines of a famous aria ("Nessun dorma," "La donna è mobile," the drinking song from *La traviata*), then left the next few lines to one of the others, with one tenor sometimes introducing an unexpected improvisation and the others replying with their own embellishments.

The first concert was a distinctly more dignified affair than the next one, which, in accordance with its location in a sports stadium instead of an ancient ruin, featured three relay races and two medleys in place of the single relay and medley of the Roman performance. More telling even was the overt analogy that the Los Angeles event sustained throughout to the world of sports. To announce the various numbers the 1994 concert employed the distinguished violinist Itzhak Perlman, who was viewed sitting at the side of the TV screen in the pose of a sportscaster. "This is almost like a sport event here," he said at one point, and his commentary at various times sought to simulate the frenzy with which sportscasters like to whip up their TV spectators. "The audience is going rather wild. . . . Much more excitement is mounting and mounting," one could hear Perlman say. After pursuing the sports analogy with the remark, "We are scoring goals right and left," he remembered that he was speaking from a baseball stadium and added that the three tenors "were covering all their bases." And in an earlier interview with the tenors inserted into the 1994 broadcast, Pavarotti explicitly compared the act of performing "Nessun dorma" to winning a sports event.

In view of the popular success of these concerts (not to speak of the commercial success that the videos issuing from them have experienced), it is scarcely surprising that the three tenors, without even waiting for the World Cup scheduled for 1998, embarked on a worldwide tour in 1996–97 to deliver their wares in places such as New York, London, Stockholm, Tokyo, and Melbourne. To judge from the concert broadcast from Giants Stadium near New York in 1996, they made no attempt to change the formulas—the medleys, the "Nessun dorma's," the "La donna è mobile's," the "Granada's," the "Torna a Surriento's," the "O sole mio's"—that had prevailed in Rome and Los Angeles.

In a gender-conscious age such as ours it hardly seems accidental that a trio of sopranos should attempt to challenge the male hegemony established in these concerts. Thus, in 1996, the very year that the three tenors began their world tour, three not-yet-well-known sopranos, Kathleen Cassello, Kallen Esperian, and Cynthia Lawrence, gave a public concert in Los Angeles (not, however, in a sports arena) that imitated the format the tenors had established—including the mixture of classical and pop, the medleys, the mutual mugging. Although the appearance of "Granada" perhaps was inevitable, most selections were numbers designed for female singers, with the tenors' collective presentation of "La donna è mobile" replaced by a more gender-appropriate, collective "Sempre libera."

The three-tenor events, through their distinctly popular nature and their expressed affinity to sports, confirm that hierarchy of the arts within which opera has always occupied an uncertain status. On the one hand, as in the pronouncements of the great operatic reformers such as Gluck and Wagner, opera seeks the prestige accruing to "higher" forms of art while, on the other, as in the three-tenor concerts, it unashamedly foregrounds its semblance to a supposedly "lower" form of entertainment. Commentators on opera have in fact often noted the relation of certain aspects of operatic life to those of sports. For example, as the Handel specialist Winton Dean described the competition for the castrato Farinelli's services in London in 1733, "It is not inapposite to compare the practice of modern Association football clubs in their competitive buying of the best players."[1]

To be sure, the concerts by the three tenors do not belong precisely to the genre of opera but to that of the opera concert, in which a star singer performs a succession of high points from various operas with the intent of sustaining the crowd's excitement in a considerably more intense way than is possible within an operatic performance as such. One could say that the contemporary opera concert, often given in large arenas with the electronic enhancements frowned upon within the opera house, is closer in spirit to the rock concert than to other forms of entertainment. The popular nature of the opera concert becomes evident if one compares it to its high-art counterpart among vocal occasions, the lieder recital (or *Lieder-Abend*, as it is called in the German-speaking countries, in which its conventions were established). Whereas the opera concert exploits largeness—of sound, space, and audience response—the lieder recital cultivates an exquisite smallness. Its ideal venue is a small recital hall in which the audience can experience a degree of intimacy with the performer (though less intimacy than was possible in the household performances for which many of the great nineteenth-century lieder were intended). Whereas opera concerts are economically motivated, often selling out within minutes after tickets go on sale, lieder recitals rarely make their own way financially and are often dependent on a donor's subsidy or a singer's willingness to relinquish the usual operatic fee.

Although lieder singers are usually if not always opera singers as well, the genre demands a rigorous exclusion of the operatic—to the point that purists in the audience generally complain when an opera aria suddenly appears as an encore. Applause is kept within limits: whereas listeners at an opera concert sometimes interrupt an aria to cheer a particular vocal feat, those attending a lieder recital often hold back until a whole group of songs has been completed. The lied, in fact, rarely calls upon a singer's ability to show off high notes or to produce a florid run of notes; when the more dramatically conceived lieder such as "Der Erkönig" or "Die beiden Grenadicre" are done with more-than-usual bravura, lieder aficionados may, in fact, grumble that the singer was too "operatic." Some of the most respected lieder recitalists are performers whose vocal resources are considered limited; often, indeed, they are singers near the end of their operatic careers who can display a "maturity" of interpretive power that supposedly compensates for their lack of vocal freshness or agility. Praise is meted out at a lieder recital not for the vocal pyrotechnics expected at an opera concert but for the performer's ability to communicate the subtlety with which the composer supposedly interpreted the words of the poem being set to music. Indeed, the criteria by which a lieder singer, as well as a lieder composer, is judged are identical to those enunciated by Gluck and Wagner when they promulgated their operatic reforms, namely, the ability of music to provide an adequate expression to words.

A consciousness of the hierarchy descending from high art to the most popular forms remains present for those who buy videotapes of the three tenors or who struggle to get tickets for opera concerts. For the more pop-minded, watching the three tenors provides a way of participating in a world of art that had always seemed too difficult or foreign; it is as though one now discovered that art can be easy and fun much like sports or popular music. But this consciousness of the hierarchy also works in a strange way for many of those who think themselves committed to the hierarchy's "higher" reaches. Experiencing the three tenors—all of them, after all, skilled artists who also happen to possess extraordinary voices—the more snobbish feel they may temporarily let themselves go, grant their snobbery a brief respite, indulge in lower forms that they had deliberately left behind since adolescence—much as those who cultivate sophisticated tastes in food will occasionally return to Taco Bell or Burger King for a reminder of what they had once unself-consciously reveled in.

An understanding of the hierarchy of high and popular forms can go only partway to explaining the motives and the conduct of operagoers within urban culture today. Actually operagoers fall into a number of distinct and quite recognizable types, each with its own relation to the high and the popular. In his *Introduction to the Sociology of Music* Theodor Adorno proposed a range of eight types of music listener, including such figures as the "expert" listener, who seeks to analyze the technical, formal aspects of a score; the "emotional" listener, who lets himself be swept away; and the "entertainment" listener, a product of what Adorno had earlier dubbed the "culture industry" (*AGS*, 14: 178–98). Adorno's categories were conceived as ideal types in the Weberian manner without the transitions that a more empirical description would demand. Although these categories are to some degree applicable to the opera public, what Nietzsche disparagingly called the "culture of the opera" forms so distinctive a case among the arts that it demands a typology of its own.

I therefore propose the following five types to characterize operagoers in our own time:

> The AVID
> The PASSIVE
> The CONSCIENTIOUS
> The FAULTFINDING
> The UNCOMPROMISED

This particular configuration is peculiar to opera as it is to no other art or form of entertainment. The category I shall describe as the Avid, for instance, can rarely be found among audiences for nonvocal music, except for an occasional composer, like Mahler in our own time, whose admirers become addicted to his music much as operagoers do to opera in general. Although this category applies to some degree to the world of ballet, its most common manifestation is within film, rock music, and various sports. And although the other four types can be located within the music world in general, they rarely, with the exception of the Uncompromised, play as flagrant a role there as they do in opera.

Let us start with the AVID, that most conspicuous segment of the opera public who make their presence physically felt as they rush past one another (sometimes even knocking each other down) to get the most favorable standing-room spots or to cheer for additional curtain calls at the end of a performance while the rest of the audience is already heading home. The group interview of several young French Avids that opens Michel Poizat's *The Angel's Cry* reveals such characteristics of the Avid as the fetishizing of individual stars, the willingness to make inordinate financial sacrifices to attend a particular production in a faraway place, the ability of distinctive moments within a performance to initiate an unequivocal commitment to a singer, an opera, a composer, and even to a director.[2] For the Avid, in fact, opera is sometimes a surrogate for religion. Those moments in which the Avid become committed to a performer or composer mark turning points akin to religious conversion. For Avids there is usually some primordial such moment during which they acknowledged their commitment not simply to the singer or to the opera they were attending but to the idea of opera as a whole.

But religion is only one of several analogies to describe the Avids' operatic experience. One can also speak of an addiction to opera by means of which, like drink or dope, opera threatens to disrupt their lives—whether through the financial tolls it takes or through its ability to distract its victims from their obligations to their jobs, their studies, their family life. Avids expend an inordinate amount of their time in pursuit of opera, whether in attending performances (sometimes multiple, successive performances of a single production), searching for hard-to-find tickets (or the rigors of standing in line long in advance for standing room), listening for hours on end to discs (whether audio or video) of whole operas or of recitals by individual singers, or reading opera magazines to learn what is going on throughout the opera world. Avids share their addictive tendencies with persons addicted to specific sports, and, just as their corresponding fans in sport can cite famous home runs or touchdowns of the far past, Avids (whether through personal or reported experience) speak nostalgically of some famed Callas performance like the Mexico City *Aida* of 1951 or, to cite the title of a recent play on this topic, *The Lisbon Traviata*. Avids display a prodigious memory for their past operagoing experiences; though they may hold on to their programs throughout their lives, they rarely need to consult them to boast to fellow Avids of the now-legendary performances that they had the prescience, or simply the good fortune, to attend.

Although the ranks of the Avid include all forms of sexual orientation, the gay man, as Wayne Koestenbaum has chronicled in *The Queen's Throat*, has cultivated, indeed, even transformed, Avid practices with a special fervor. For gay Avids the diva is perhaps the most central element of opera—not, certainly, as an object of their own sexual desire but as an object with whom (whether in the diva's personal life or in the roles she plays, often both at once) they seek to identify. The divas fetishized by the gay among the Avid are those, like Callas above all, notable for their vulnerability, their fears of abandonment, their all-out commitment to love. Just as Avids in general share with sports fans a fascination for high points of the past, so gay Avids share their attraction to vulnerable divas with gay filmgoers who identify with a Garland or a Monroe. As Terry Castle has recently shown, lesbian Avids must be distinguished carefully from their male counterparts, for female singers, especially those with a deep chest register, provide alluring objects of desire distinct from those that attract gay males.[3] Regardless of sexual orientation, the Avid always sense a close connection between opera and sexuality. The moments of sublimity they experience as they go from one performance to another, or that are implanted in their operatic memories as peak moments for which they cultivate an inexhaustible nostalgia, do not seem to them altogether different from, indeed, sometimes even replace, sexual passion.

The Avid are at once both discriminating and undiscriminating about opera. They are highly judgmental of singers, conductors, directors, yet, however impatient they may be about operatic results in individual instances, they never allow their underlying commitment to opera to become threatened. Moreover, despite the vehemence with which they often express their judgments, the Avid are also catholic in their taste as far as works themselves are concerned, and, unlike the group I label the Uncompromised, they pursue their Puccini as avidly as their Mozart, their Strauss as avidly as their Schoenberg. The Avid simply love going to the opera, no matter what the style, the period, or the composer. This catholicity also encourages them to master a range of seemingly inconsequential detail—for instance, how many angels can be heard in opera singing offstage, or in what operas do characters mourn the loss of small objects such as pins? Without a sizable audience of Avids drawn to this sort of trivia, the Metropolitan Opera Quiz, broadcast weekly throughout that company's season, could not have survived for well over half a century.

Though the Avid are doubtless the most noticeable part of the opera audience, opera companies must depend largely on the PASSIVE to fill up their seats. The Passive are those for whom the initiative to attend the opera originates elsewhere—whether through a mate (more often than not a wife) who loves opera, or through the persuasive power of the marketing agent peddling subscriptions for the local company, or through the pressure exerted by other members of one's social subclass to be seen (often in formal attire) at the opera on particular subscription nights as well as to donate the funds that help subsidize the other types of operagoer. Although the Passive may complain at times that they'd rather be home watching a pro football game, they are generally willing to go along with the opinions of those around them—to the point that during the first intermission they are told that the soprano has a vibrato wide enough for an army to pass through, only to find that, when repeating this judgment elsewhere during the next intermission, they are chided for not appreciating the singer's greatness. In fact, they often learn simply to accept everybody's judgments since no two perceptions of what goes on in opera ever seem to be the same.

Tastes of the Passive, if they possess particular preferences at all, are guided less by aesthetic than by more practical concerns. They generally like operas with several intermissions, for the longer they have to sit without stretching out the more likely they are to fall asleep; *La Bohème*, with its four short acts (one of them only twenty minutes long) and its three opportunities to make it to the bar or the bathroom, is often their favorite opera. Passives attending the opera in cities whose last train to the suburbs leaves before midnight have rarely had the opportunity to witness famous operatic death scenes; as far as they are concerned, only the heroines of one-act operas such as *Salome* and *Elektra* actually die, while Violetta and Mimi can go on coughing forever. When traveling to famed opera capitals such as Vienna or Milan Passives generally feel the duty to go to the opera—just as they dutifully visit the local museum during the day—but on their return they often disappoint their friends among the Avid through their inability to remember who sang the Isolde, the Norma, or the Boris and sometimes even what precisely was the name of the opera they attended.

Ever since supertitles became part of the operagoing routine during the last decade or two, the Passive have displayed a greater contentment than before, for they now feel relieved of the need to read librettos and even plot summaries. The difficulties they noted earlier about following an operatic plot now seem less burdensome since they can concentrate on the dialogue from moment to moment. Though reluctant to express their opinions too openly for fear of antagonizing companions more pious about opera than they are, Passives easily feel frustrated by the fact that what they witness on the stage, whether the plot or the people cast to represent this plot, is never quite realistic enough. Passives would feel more comfortable with characters working out everyday problems than with the big emotional displays usual in opera (indeed, they would just as soon hear these problems *talked* rather than *sung* about), and they would prefer a narrow-waisted, pert soprano with a bland, small voice in an ingenue part to the clarion-voiced, obese grandmother who all too often graces the role.

Although the CONSCIENTIOUS share a certain lack of assertiveness with the Passive, their attitudes toward opera are wholly different. The Conscientious view themselves as opera-lovers, and they attend opera as regularly as they can. But they also feel they can never know enough about the complex world of opera to fully appreciate what they hear and see at the opera house. They envy the Avid for the confidence with which the latter express themselves on all matters operatic. To compensate for what they believe they lack, the Conscientious prepare themselves assiduously for every performance. They read the plot summary and the background materials in the many guidebooks they own; they study the libretto at least a week before, usually in conjunction with a listening session at home; when possible, they watch a videodisc or tape; they rush through dinner before the performance to hear some local expert analyze what they are about to hear; and they are relieved to know that whatever details they have forgotten about the intricate plot will come back as they watch the supertitles (even missing some important stage business while craning their necks to read). They also remind themselves and their friends not to allow the presence of supertitles to tempt them to cut corners on the considerable advance preparation necessary to understand an opera performance properly.

The dutifulness that the Conscientious display preparing themselves is mirrored in the sonic contribution they make to performances by means of the applause with which they reward the singers, who, after all, might withhold their best without constant shows of approval. Every aria—whether or not it has been satisfactorily sung—is deemed worth clapping one's hands for; if the conscientious hear an occasional "Boo!" from the Faultfinding, they voice their disapproval of such inconsiderateness with the most harshly sibilant "Shh!" The moment that the curtain rises on a new scene, the Conscientious applaud the scenery—no matter that they drown out whatever music is being played. And as soon as the curtain begins to fall, they clap at maximum volume—to the point that anybody in the audience unfamiliar with the opera will never know if the act ends on a cadence.

The opinions that the Conscientious express about operas, productions, and singers generally come from other, more knowing minds than their own, but they go to some effort to discern what authorities they can best rely on. When the local newspaper critic comes down too hard and too often on the productions of a particular season, they know better than to take these judgments at face value; indeed, they have little patience for those they deem hypercritical about opera. If the music of an opera is hard to grasp (even after repeated preparatory hearings at home), they blame their own limited listening proficiency. For the Conscientious, all opera—at least whatever gets performed or recorded by a reputable company—belongs to that mysterious realm labeled "high art." If acquaintances try to shame them for enjoying *Madama Butterfly* or *Porgy and Bess* too unself-consciously, the Conscientious feel genuinely disappointed, and they eagerly seek out some established authority who can reassure them that it is perfectly all right to love these works.

Unlike the Conscientious, the FAULTFINDING express their negative opinions at the slightest opportunity. Although the Avid also can be unsparing about what they dislike, they more often display a positive enthusiasm beyond the reach of the Faultfinding. Indeed, nothing ever seems to please the Faultfinding, yet still they continue going to the opera.

Although they claim to be upholding aesthetic standards, the Faultfinding actually care less about these standards than they care about finding fault. Nothing they hear today ever measures up to something that they (or the authorities they have read) heard in some distant past. When they first heard Elisabeth Schwarzkopf do the Marschallin, they let it be known during intermission that though she was clever enough in her own way, she wholly lacked the warmth of Lotte Lehmann; and when they later heard Kiri Te Kanawa, they insisted that despite her velvet-smooth voice she wholly lacked the striking presence of Schwarzkopf. After a brush or two in the lobby with the Faultfinding, operagoers learn to avoid greeting them during intermission. Still, the Faultfinding persist in whispering their feelings during the performance to those sitting next to them (the latter would choose to move if they could). Not only their immediate neighbors, but many others around them are forced to hear that the conductor is moving at a snail's pace, or (just as frequently) that the conductor is much more frenetic than he has any business being, or that the conductor is paying no regard to the soprano's needs, or that he is slowing down, despite very clear indications in the score, to indulge her wishes; or that the soprano entered too sharp and is taking forever to warm up, or that she's displaying a vibrato that will force her retirement within the year; or that the stage business is far too busy, or the lighting so dark you won't even notice (except for what the music tells you) that the soprano has dropped dead. The Faultfinding seek above all to be original, to observe phenomena that would not easily have occurred to others, but they also feel the urge to convince others that they too would perceive faults just as they themselves do if they were sufficiently knowing and attentive.

The Faultfinding represent a vast range of tastes and predilections. Some complain that a performance, or even the score itself, lacks the gutsiness and passion inherent within opera (these usually reject anything so unoperatic as *Pelléas et Mélisande*), while others complain that the performance, or the opera itself, lacks the finesse necessary for great art (these usually reject anything so hyper-operatic as *Il trovatore* or *Tosca*). Some clothe their arguments in the name of verisimilitude and remind you that the legitimate theater would never allow so gross a suspension of disbelief as Jessye Norman's telling her blond twin brother in *Die Walküre* how closely he resembles her. (A wise supertitler would of course know better than to include this line.) Others chide their friends among the Passive for demanding too naive a realism, and they remind them that opera is by its very nature distant and mythical.

To substantiate their arguments, the Faultfinding often find it convenient to cite what they call the "text," but even here they differ from one another (or even from their own earlier judgments). Some will object to the high C in "Di quella pira" because it is not in the original score but was added only later by tenors eager for applause; while others will object if Verdi's original version is done so literally as to undercut the audience's high expectations of that C: after all, the later, more spectacular version, they will remind you, has been done throughout most of the opera's performance history and thus has been legitimated by longstanding precedent; indeed, it was even reluctantly approved by the composer when he found he couldn't control his tenors.[4] In recent decades, with the rise of the star director, the Faultfinding have often aimed their guns at the concept behind a production. They will pull out the libretto of *Rigoletto*, for instance, to show how faithless Jean-Pierre Ponnelle was to the composer's intentions in placing the bed for Gilda's rape on stage (even if the bed's curtains were hiding her and her lover) at the very time her father was accusing her abductors only a foot or two away. By the same token, they will complain that an opera is being produced in the old and tired way as though nobody were directing it at all.

Though the Faultfinding come from all walks of life, their natural métier (if they are fortunate enough to land such a job) is that of newspaper music critic. Here they can exercise their pique at the foibles of directors, singers, conductors, impresarios, composers, and whole operatic styles and also receive a paycheck for their efforts. Readers who attend the same performance as Faultfinding critics often have cause to wonder if these critics were really in the same auditorium with them at the same time. Yet these critics are careful to balance their faultfinding with occasional if also grudging praise—else their jobs might be imperiled by those business executives on the opera board who threaten to withdraw their companies' advertising from the newspaper if the critics don't shape up.

Like the Faultfinding, the UNCOMPROMISED are prone to issue complaints, yet the motives for these complaints differ substantially from those of the former. Whereas the Faultfinding are little concerned with the consistency of their judgments or with justifying these judgments by means of a unifying aesthetic, the Uncompromised know precisely what they believe and why, and they let these beliefs be known to all who are willing to listen (as well as to some who do not care to listen). The primary commitment of the Uncompromised is not to opera as such (though they claim their devotion to the form when the right operas are properly performed), or even to music, but rather to an idea of art—of art as an elevated and disciplined activity that maintains its distance from the more mundane pleasures pursued by everyday people. They borrow this idea of art from the German philosophies of art that flourished during the late eighteenth and early nineteenth centuries—though the knowledge that the Uncompromised possess of these treatises is not necessarily at first hand.

Among all five types discussed here, the Uncompromised are doubtless the hardest for those belonging to the other types to tolerate. For one thing, they have few rivals in their ability to exercise an air of sureness and expertise. When Charles Rosen, in his single chapter on opera within his lengthy study of romantic music, describes the form (at least in its nineteenth-century embodiment) as "junk," "trash," and "cheap melodrama," he must surely give pain to opera lovers who admired his brilliant analyses of Schubert, Schumann, and Mendelssohn earlier in the book; this pain, moreover, is little mitigated by his ability to locate isolated passages of admirable music in Bellini and even Meyerbeer.[5] Whereas those who engage in conversation with the Fault-finding quickly learn to discount what they do not care to hear, the Uncompromised make it amply clear at every opportunity that it behooves you to change your tastes.

The central activity practiced by the Uncompromised is the making of discriminations—discriminations among operas, among composers, among periods, and also among performers and among theories of performance. Those who do not discriminate adequately, the Uncompromised firmly believe, are in constant danger (often unbeknownst to themselves) of finding their aesthetic standards eroded by the powerful, often insidiously persuasive, forces dominating the entertainment industry. Not that these dangers are new: Wagner's aesthetic theories, after all, were developed in reaction to the commercialization of opera (and much else) in the Paris of the 1830s and 1840s. When, nearly half a century ago, the then-director of the Metropolitan Opera fired his Wagnerian soprano Helen Traubel for taking a nightclub engagement, he was, in effect, issuing a public statement that the bastions of genuine art must hold the line against the encroachments of financially motivated amusements. One wonders what he might have done with the contracts of the three tenors if he were still in power.

But the particular aesthetic boundaries that the Uncompromised set may differ greatly in different times and places. As uncompromised an artist and theorist as we have known in our time, John Cage, as I indicate in Chapter 8, allowed these boundaries to spill over into the everyday world of street noises and audience coughs to which he sought to call our attention during the performer's long silence in *4'33"*. But Cage's critique of opera extended little beyond his attempt, in *Europeras 1 & 2*, to rethink the form within the framework of his larger aesthetic. Throughout much of the twentieth century the Uncompromised have generally embraced an operatic canon as it has been defined by German musicology. Within this mode of thought, opera as such is subordinate to the history of music as a whole. For the Uncompromised (at least until the upsurge of interest in early music during the last couple of decades) the great musical tradition begins vaguely with Palestrina, then moves through Monteverdi, Bach, and Handel (this last in his oratorios and instrumental music, not his operas) to Gluck, who, as I indicated in the first two chapters, became the foundation stone of opera as we know it (or at least *should* know it). Operatic greatness cannot be separated from musical greatness, above all as defined by the work of the great classical and romantic symphonists and thence by Wagner, who not only adapted the aesthetic of the symphony to opera but laid the groundwork for the canon-control traditional within musicology. Italian opera, in view of its presumptive links to popular culture, has little place within this scheme, though Verdi's final two operas have ordinarily been cited as proof that an ill-trained, popularly oriented composer could create real musical art when he set his mind to it. The post-Wagnerian canon allows places for Debussy, Stravinsky, Schoenberg, and Berg, with only limited room for the operas of Strauss, who after *Salome* and *Elektra*, according to this model, sold out to popular taste. The most impassioned defense of this approach to operatic history was, as I indicated earlier, Joseph Kerman's book of 1956, *Opera as Drama*, notable at once for the eloquence with which it argued the greatness of works such as *Le nozze di Figaro* and *Tristan und Isolde* and for its contemptuousness toward all but a handful of works in the operatic repertory at the time.

Central to the process of discrimination practiced by the Uncompromised is the principle of exclusion, by means of which musical greatness comes to be enshrined by excluding that which cannot measure up to it. The few works, indeed, the few moments within these works that make it into Kerman's canon impress us with their greatness through our knowledge of how much must of necessity be excluded. It is typical of the Uncompromised to remark that *Der Rosenkavalier* contains no more than twenty minutes of great music within its nearly four-hour span—parts of the Marschallin's monologue, a moment within the Silver Rose scene, and the trio near the end. A recent essay by Kerman, though acknowledging that "*Don Giovanni* is full of brilliant and beautiful music," also reminds us that the opera "contains passages that are less than brilliant or beautiful," after which he cites the catalogue aria as inferior to Bartolo's "La vendetta" in *Le nozze di Figaro*, Elvira's first aria as "puzzling and ineffective," Anna's second aria as "problematic," and then points out "dead spots" in each of the two finales.[6]

Although the Uncompromised are mainly concerned with discriminating among operatic texts, since the rise of the early-music movement much of their zeal to discriminate has been directed to performance practices. Those who once applauded Marilyn Horne for her revival of Handel operas have since been admonished by the Uncompromised to settle for nothing less than voices that have not been spoiled by singing nineteenth-century opera and that allow only period instruments to accompany them. Even if the Uncompromised may seem unpleasant to others, their passion to achieve historical authenticity (however problematic we now know this concept to be) has provided the world with a whole range of exciting new musical experiences—elegant old theaters restored and once again functioning; young voices trained to negotiate the rigors of what we take to be baroque style; long-forgotten, never-before-published operas testing the way we conceive the form's limits and possibilities.

Though the Uncompromised do not admit that there might be degrees to their uncompromisingness, in actual practice they differ in the allowances they make—much as religious Jews differ in their ways of observing dietary laws and sabbath restrictions. The very fact that opera is performed before audiences who laugh and cry and display the fact that they feel moved forces the Uncompromised to allow for a certain popular dimension even among those operas whose musical greatness is unchallenged. Yet the temptation to insist on maximum rigor in discriminating practices, especially when the Uncompromised deal with one another, can easily lead them to abandon opera-going, even to those operas and productions that meet their standards. They may come to feel that the unruliness and the musical naïveté of audiences renders opera-house attendance aesthetically inferior to listening to a good CD at home or even to just reading the score. They may also come to realize that even the greatest operas have their share of musical filler to keep the plot going and the audiences attentive. And they may also come to feel uncomfortable with the histrionics of virtuoso voices shamelessly seeking to thrill their listeners. Just as meat consumers convert to vegetarianism once they think too much about slaughterhouse life, the Uncompromised are always in danger of giving up altogether on vocal music and making do with the great instrumental repertoire that developed with the concept of "absolute music." They may also, as Schelling did in the disparaging statement about opera with which he ended his treatise on the philosophy of art, dream of some ideal future restoration of ancient theater more aesthetically gratifying than that caricature of Greek drama which is the opera we know.

Reference Matter

Notes

Prelude

1.   Tanner, "Multiperspectival Remarks."

Chapter 1

1.   For a photograph and description of the proscenium, see Merkling et al., eds., *Golden Horseshoe*, pp. 73, 79.

2.   For statistics on the operas performed during this period, see Kolodin, *Metropolitan Opera*, pp. 516–36. The preponderance of Wagnerian performances at the Metropolitan during these years owes to the fact that from 1884 to 1891 the house was under German management. For a detailed study of the Wagnerian impact on New York, see Horowitz, *Wagner*, especially pp. 89–156.

3.   If one compares the six composers immortalized on the Metropolitan's proscenium with the fourteen composers whose images grace the lobby of the Vienna State Opera (a building constructed a little over a decade before the old Metropolitan), one finds the German tradition even more dominant in Vienna, which includes only four non-Germanic figures—Cherubini, Boïeldieu, Rossini, and Spontini—none of whom was even represented in New York. The Vienna list, like the Met's, honors Gluck as the earliest composer, and it includes such prestigious composers as Haydn and Schubert, whose operas never played a significant role in establishing their reputations but who were central to the Viennese musical canon. The Vienna lobby includes as well such popular opera composers of the time as Mozart, Weber, Marschner, and Meyerbeer, and Beethoven of course is represented not only because of his much-performed single opera but because of his perceived centrality in music history. It also includes the late-eighteenth-century composer Carl Ditters von Dittersdorf and the early-

nineteenth-century Ludwig Spohr. If Wagner is still missing here, this may owe less to his status, which was still quite controversial when the house opened in 1869, than to the fact that the list included no living composers.

4. Curtis, "*Poppea Impasticciata.*"

5. See Jane Glover, "Solving the Musical Problems," in Whenham, ed., *Claudio Monteverdi*, pp. 138–55.

6. On the likely combinations of instruments and size of the instrumental group, see Rosand, *Opera*, pp. 24–25. On Venetian performing practice, see Denis Arnold, "Performing Practice," in Arnold and Fortune, eds., *New Monteverdi Companion*, pp. 329–32. For an earlier study of opera orchestras in the Venetian theaters, see Janet E. Beat, "Monteverdi and the Opera Orchestra of His Time," in Arnold and Fortune, eds., *Monteverdi Companion*, pp. 283–301. On the difference in the aesthetic principles between the early and late Monteverdi operas, see Jane Glover, "The Venetian Operas," in Arnold and Fortune, eds., *New Monteverdi Companion*, pp. 288–91.

7. According to William Weber, the word "classic" was first applied to music in England during the 1770s but did not come into general use until the second decade of the nineteenth century. See Weber, *Rise*, p. 194.

8. Key excerpts from Artusi's attack are printed in Strunk, ed., *Source Readings*, pp. 393–404, with Monteverdi's reply (in the supposed words of his brother) printed on pp. 405–12. On the background of the Artusi matter, see Claude V. Palisca's chapter "The Artusi-Monteverdi Controversy" in his *Studies*, pp. 54–87. See also Jerome Roche, "Monteverdi and the *prima prattica*," in Arnold and Fortune, eds., *New Monteverdi Companion*, pp. 159–82, and, in the same volume, Nigel Fortune, "Monteverdi and the *seconda prattica*," pp. 183–215. Dahlhaus argues intriguingly that, avant-gardist though he may sound to us, Monteverdi, to the extent that he was defending a form of monody that supposedly went back to antiquity, was actually on the "conservative" side of this ancient-modern debate, while the outdated style of the contrapuntalists represented the moderns (see Dahlhaus, *Idee*, p. 51). For an interpretation of the Artusi controversy as an expression of larger conflicts within Renaissance thought, see Tomlinson, *Monteverdi*, pp. 21–29.

9. See Rosand, "Descending Tetrachord."

10. Bianconi, *Music*, p. 210.

11. On the nature of Monteverdi's impact, see Rosand, *Opera*, pp. 3–4, 15–19, and Glover, "The Venetian Operas," in Arnold and Fortune, eds., *New Monteverdi Companion*, pp. 314–15.

12. Dryden, *Plays*, p. 5.

13. Algarotti, *Saggio*, p. 25.

14. Ibid., pp. 27, 13, respectively.

15. Martini, *Esemplare*, p. 194. On the Artusi controversy, see pp. 180–81.

16. Hawkins, *General History*, 2: 526.

17. Winterfeld, *Johannes Gabrieli*, 2: 37.

18. Fétis, *Biographie*, 6: 184–85. In his role as a conductor and entrepreneur of early music, Fétis presented excerpts from *Orfeo*, as well as pieces by composers from Peri through Gluck, at the first of his *concerts historiques* at the Paris Conservatory in 1832 (see Haskell, *Early Music Revival*, p. 131).

19. Vogel, "Claudio Monteverdi."

20. Ambros, *Geschichte*, 4: 365.

21. For his genealogy of opera before Handel, see Gervinus, *Händel*, pp. 25–27, 46–51. Monteverdi is not named here but is mentioned briefly in his role as madrigalist (p. 105) and in the early development of the aria (pp. 113–14). Nowhere is he given credit for his use of recitative; it seems evident that Gervinus was not acquainted with his music directly. By an interesting irony of history, Gervinus's depiction of early opera exercised an influence on a major operatic composer, Modest Musorgsky: Gervinus's description in this book of Peri's attempt to render speech in musical terms served to legitimize the Russian composer's experiment in setting the speaking voice for Gogol's *Marriage*. On Musorgsky's use of Gervinus, see Taruskin, *Musorgsky*, pp. 75–81.

22. Monteverdi, of course, composed for real theaters, but his expressive theory of music, applicable at once to opera and to nontheatrical music, was fundamentally dramatic in nature. On the affinities of Donne's lyric style with the drama of his time, see Helen Gardner, "The Metaphysical Poets," in Keast, ed., *Seventeenth Century English Poetry*, pp. 57–58. On Caravaggio's theatricality, see Moir, *Caravaggio*, pp. 43–44.

23. Donne, *Poems*, 1: 14.

24. Berenson, *Caravaggio*, p. 21.

25. For a detailed history of the lament from Monteverdi's *Arianna* through his own last lament, that of Ottavia in *Poppea* (with innumerable other composers coming in between), see Rosand, *Opera*, pp. 361–86. On the influence of this lament on later composers, see Denis Arnold, "Monteverdi: Some Colleagues and Pupils," in Arnold and Fortune, eds., *New Monteverdi Companion*, pp. 114–17, and Fortune, "Monteverdi and the *seconda prattica*," in this same volume, pp. 192–96. According to the latter essay, the fame of this lament was recorded as late as 1783 when the rest of Monteverdi's operatic writing seemed long forgotten (p. 194). For a recording of settings of Arianna laments by various seventeenth-century Italian composers, including Monteverdi's own three versions, see Monteverdi et al., *Lamento*.

26. For Monteverdi's description of the *stile concitato*, see "Madrigali guerrieri ed amorosi," in Strunk, ed., *Source Readings*, pp. 413–15. On the influence of the *stile concitato*, see Denis Arnold, "Monteverdi: Some Colleagues and Pupils," in Arnold and Fortune, eds., *New Monteverdi Companion*, pp. 120–22. In a larger sense one could say that Monteverdi's theorizing on the relation of a musical device to a particular emotion anticipates (even if his own statements were forgotten) the *Affektenlehre* of a century later.

27. For a detailed study of when and how his manuscripts were read, see Alan MacColl, "The Circulation of Donne's Poems in Manuscript," in Smith, ed., *John Donne: Essays*, pp. 28–46.

28. For quotations and echoes, see *DCH*, pp. 33–64.

29. For a brief survey of the spread of "Caravaggism," see Wittkower, *Art*, pp. 73–78. On artists' travels to Malta, see Bovi, *Caravaggio*, p. 278.

30. Well before Dryden's statement William Drummond of Hawthornden, who died in 1649, in an undated letter referred to poets with "Metaphysical *Ideas* and *Scholastical Quiddities*." See Gardner, "Metaphysical Poets," in Keast, ed., *Seventeenth Century English Poetry*, p. 32.

31. Bianconi, *Music*, pp. 76–80.

32. On the increasing domination of Venetian opera by singers in the years following Monteverdi's death, see Rosand, *Opera*, pp. 221–44.

33. Bianconi, *Music*, pp. 80–81.

34. On the earlier publication history, see A. J. Smith, "Donne's Reputation," in Smith, ed., *John Donne: Essays*, p. 1.

35. On Coleridge's remarks on Donne, see Granqvist, *Reputation*, pp.

77–87. For a detailed discussion of Donne's influence on Coleridge's theories about language as well as on several of his poems, including "The Flea," see Hodgson, "Coleridge." On Coleridge's fascination with Donne's irregular meters and conceits, see Shawcross, "Opulence."

36. On Donne selections in the various anthologies, see Granqvist, *Reputation*, pp. 47–52.

37. The monographs are Duncan, *Revival*, and Granqvist, *Reputation*. Articles and notes include, among others, Smith, "Donne's Reputation," in Smith, ed., *John Donne: Essays*, pp. 1–27; Campbell, *Retrospective Review*, pp. 50–56; and Singh, "Two Hitherto Unrecorded Imitations"; Winny, *Preface*, pp. 47–54. The special journal issue is Harrison, ed., *Metaphysical Poets*. The anthology is *DCH*.

38. On the history of Caravaggio's reputation, see Longhi, *Caravaggio*, pp. 53–58; Richard E. Spear, "La fortuna critica di un pittore realista," in *Caravaggio e il suo tempo*, pp. 22–27; and Bologna, *L'incredulità*, pp. 191–98. On Monteverdi's, see Nigel Fortune's essay on the editorial and performance history of *Orfeo*, "The Rediscovery of *Orfeo*," in Whenham, ed., *Claudio Monteverdi*, pp. 78–118.

39. Donne's relation to the progressive thought of his time has been studied beginning with Coffin, *John Donne*, in 1937.

40. Bologna, *L'incredulità*, especially pp. 56–57, 154–70, 207–8.

41. On his traditional humanism, see Tomlinson, *Monteverdi*, pp. 29–30. Tomlinson "blames" the poet Giambattista Marino for leading Monteverdi away from this humanism in his later madrigals (pp. 151–214, 257–60); he further blames the Marinism of the librettists of his Venetian operas for Monteverdi's turning away from the humanist ideals that Tomlinson sees embodied in *Orfeo* (pp. 215–39). On the involvement of his librettist for *Poppea*, Gian Francisco Busenello, with the neostoicism of the Venetian Accademia degl' Incogniti, see Fenlon and Miller, *Song*, pp. 5, 33, 41, 43, 45, 49.

42. See "Scientific Empiricism in Musical Thought," in Palisca, *Studies*, pp. 200–235. On Monteverdi's role, see pp. 210–11. For a brief statement linking "the Monteverdian subordination of the 'harmony' to the 'words'" with "the emerging modern science," see Berger, *Theories*, pp. 120–21.

43. For additional eighteenth-century comments on Donne, see Shawcross, "Opulence," pp. 203–5.

44. Donne, *Poems*, 1: 163 ("Satire IV," ll. 131–36).

45. Pope, *Imitations*, pp. 39, 41 (ll. 170–73).

46. On who copied or engraved Caravaggio's pictures and under what circumstances, see Moir, *Caravaggio and His Copyists*, pp. 1–29.

47. Agucchi's remarks are reproduced in Mahon, *Studies*, pp. 65–66. As Mahon points out, Agucchi was a partisan of the Carraccis.

48. Félibien, *Entretiens*, 2: 12.

49. Bellori, *Vite*, p. 230.

50. An engraving based on Fragonard's sketch, in which all the elements have a softness of focus that would not easily suggest their source in Caravaggio, is reproduced in Friedlander, *Caravaggio Studies*, p. 167. The Cézanne, full of swirling curves quite unlike the rigorous lines of the original, and with facial and bodily features only barely suggested, is described in Longhi, *'Me pinxit,'* p. 138. As with many copies of famous paintings, the later artist was working not from the original but from a meticulously detailed engraving. For a reproduction of the engraving juxtaposed with Cézanne's copy, see Rewald, *Cézanne*, p. 207.

51. Algarotti, *Essay on Painting*, pp. 168–69.

52. See Campbell, *Retrospective Review*, for a discussion of this essay (p. 50) and of the role that this journal played in reviving seventeenth-century poetry.

53. For a detailed study of the affinities between Donne and Browning, as well as of the impact of Donne on Browning's poetic style, see Maynard, "Browning."

54. Burckhardt, *Cicerone*, 2: 906, 922, respectively.

55. Ibid., 2: 900.

56. Lanzi, *History*, 2: 200.

57. Byron, *Poetical Works*, 5: 546 (canto 13, stanza 72).

58. Ruskin, *Works*, 3: 328, 56, respectively (*Modern Painters*, pt. 4, chaps. 16, 3). There are a number of similarly disparaging remarks about Caravaggio spread throughout Ruskin's writings.

59. Stendhal, *Écoles*, 1: 270.

60. Stendhal, *Voyages*, p. 985. For other uses of *énergie* and *énergique*, see pp. 875, 962.

61. Stendhal, *Voyages*, p. 727. For his reminders of Caravaggio's capital crime, see also pp. 459, 962. For more detailed discussions of Sten-

dhal's attitude toward Caravaggio's art, see Berthier, *Stendhal*, pp. 40–41, 85–86, 97–99, 101.

62. Longhi mentions a drama performed in France (1834), an Italian novella (1842), and an Italian drama (1848). See Longhi, *Caravaggio*, p. 57.

63. Stendhal, *Haydn*, pp. 65–66.

64. On Gesualdo's culminating place within the history of chromaticism in the late sixteenth century, see Lowinsky, *Tonality*, pp. 43–46. Lowinsky contrasts Gesualdo's "atonality" with that of twentieth-century composers (p. 46) and later uses the term "triadic atonality" to distinguish the earlier style (p. 75). On the controversy surrounding Lowinsky's use of the term "atonality," see Berger, *Theories*, pp. 111–16.

65. Stendhal, *Haydn*, pp. 141–42.

66. In *Haydn,* after comparing Caravaggio unfavorably with Correggio, Stendhal speaks of needing "a conscious resolution . . . [to] turn a second time in the direction of Caravaggio's *Christ laid in the Tomb*" (pp. 62–63); a few pages later he writes that "I cannot without discomfort sit through a complete opera by Gluck" (p. 75). The earnestness that characterizes both Caravaggio and Gluck doubtless did not fit Stendhal's bias toward ironic and pleasure-giving modes of presentation.

67. For reviews of the first performance of the *Orfeo*, see Laloy, "Schola"; Sauerwein, "Schola"; and Romain Rolland, "A Review of Vincent d'Indy's Performance (1904)," this last in Whenham, ed., *Claudio Monteverdi*, pp. 119–25.

68. For some pioneering art-historical examinations of the Caravaggio oeuvre, see, for example, Kallab, "Caravaggio," a posthumous, uncompleted study of 1906 by a young Austrian art historian who suggested some of the problems that art history would need to reckon with in studying Caravaggio; and Longhi, "Due opere," which, in 1913, at the beginning of Longhi's distinguished career, argued for attributing to Caravaggio two paintings that are no longer included in the canon.

69. Donne, *Poems*.

70. All quotations are from Parry, *Music*, p. 48.

71. Rolland devoted a chapter of his dissertation to Monteverdi (Rolland, *Les Origines*, pp. 83–106). Like Fétis before him, he spelled the composer's name "Monteverde."

72. Laloy, "Schola."

73. For an essay in which he not only defends Debussy but also mentions Monteverdi in passing, see Laloy, "Claude Debussy."

74. Reynolds, *Discourses*, p. 170.

75. Fry's enthusiasm for Caravaggio, based as it was on the affinities he located between the seventeenth-century painter and recent French painters, did not survive the development of new waves of modernism after 1905. In an essay of 1922, Fry publicly recanted his earlier praise by connecting Caravaggio with "the aspect of the Italian character which creates Futurism and Fascism." "Like the Futurists," Fry writes, Caravaggio "appealed to the love of violent sensations and uncontrolled passions. Like them he loved what was brutal and excessive." Fry goes so far as to blame Caravaggio and other Italian painters of the seventeenth century for "inventing the modern popular picture" as well as "the view of art which culminates in the drama of the cinematograph. In fact they may be said to have invented vulgarity" (Fry, "Settecentismo," p. 158). The claims of brutishness that classically-minded critics had long aimed at Caravaggio are now repeated by an influential modern critic whose adherence to the Bloomsbury distinction between "high" and "low" art easily overcame his early championing of a long-neglected painter.

76. Longhi recounts this episode over forty years later in his introduction to the catalogue of the Caravaggio retrospective in Milan in 1951 (*Mostra*, p. xxx). The particular Courbet painting that suggested the analogy with Caravaggio was *After Dinner in Ornans*. In a short history of Italian painting drafted in 1913–14 but not published until 1980, Longhi connected Caravaggio with both Courbet and Manet (Longhi, *Breve ma veridica storia*, pp. 179, 182). Michael Fried, in his recent book on Courbet, questions the validity of the analogy, which had become something of a commonplace. Comparing *After Dinner in Ornans* with the London version of Caravaggio's *Supper in Emmaus*, Fried contrasts the baroque illusionism of the earlier painter with the "*counter* illusionistic treatment of foreground objects" (Fried's italics) in the French artist, who like other artists of the preceding century whom Fried had previously analyzed, express a profound antitheatricality quite different from Caravaggio's conscious theatricalism (Fried, *Courbet's Realism*, pp. 129–32).

77. On late-nineteenth-century discussions of Donne that helped shape

Grierson's view of the poet, see Haskin, "Reading Donne's *Songs and Sonnets.*"

78. Eliot, *Selected Essays*, pp. 281, 287.

79. Ibid., pp. 281–91. These quotations are on p. 281, 287, 289–90, respectively. For a study of Donne's role in *fin-de-siècle* New England literary culture, see Granqvist, "A 'Fashionable Poet.'" Granqvist shows how some of Eliot's formulations on Donne's qualities were anticipated verbally by critics of the preceding two decades (pp. 345–46).

80. Reported to me in conversation by Selz, who accompanied Rothko to view the Caravaggio paintings in Rome at the time that the painter was working on the Rothko Chapel. The luminously dark paintings in the chapel come to seem distinctly Caravaggian once one becomes aware of Rothko's enthusiasm for a representational painter whose bias for narrative he could obviously not share.

81. Stella, *Working Space*, pp. 68, 104, respectively.

82. Eliot, *Selected Essays*, p. 15.

83. These statistics are drawn from Littlejohn, *Ultimate Art*, pp. 20–24. The high score reported for the Mozart operas may result from the fact that a large proportion of the opera companies included in Littlejohn's charts are located within the germanophone countries, in which Mozart enjoys particular popularity.

84. See Brooks, *Well Wrought Urn*, in which this poem is treated as a model for what all good poetry should be (pp. 10–21). The phrase occurs in line 33 of the poem.

85. On the problems of finding the proper non-castrato voices for productions of *Poppea* today, see Joke Dame, "Unveiled Voices: Sexual Difference and the Castrato," in Brett et al., eds., *Queering the Pitch*, pp. 148–51. Dame claims that Poppea herself, and not simply Nero and Ottone, was likely sung by a castrato (p. 149).

86. See Dreyfus, "Early Music" and "Mozart"; Taruskin, "On Letting the Music," "Tradition," and "The Pastness of the Present and the Presence of the Past," the last in Kenyon, ed., *Authenticity*, pp. 137–207.

87. The practice of reading one's present preoccupations into the art of the past has been questioned by historians of the various arts, who use the label "misreading" to castigate the more unhistorical consumers. See above for Michael Fried's skepticism about how viewers read their experience of Courbet into that of Caravaggio. For an early caveat

about reading Donne as an early-day modernist, see Tuve, *Elizabethan and Metaphysical Imagery.*

88.   See Rosselli, *Opera Industry*, p. 129.

89.   For a detailed discussion of the composer-librettist relationship over the centuries, see Lindenberger, *Opera*, pp. 108–44.

Chapter 2

1.   Elson, *History*, p. 34.

2.   Streatfeild, *Opera*, p. 17.

3.   On Wagner's role in the rewriting of Italian operatic history, see Surian, "Musical Historiography." Although his article does not go into much detail, Surian baldly accuses Wagner of "changing and misrepresenting history" to suit his own purposes (p. 168).

4.   Boileau, *Oeuvres*, p. 160 (chant I).

5.   Vasari, *Lives*, p. 15.

6.   Kerman, *Opera* (1956 ed.), p. 51. See my discussion of Kerman's view of operatic history in Lindenberger, *Opera*, pp. 57–59. In a later edition, published in 1988, Kerman qualified some of his more provocative earlier remarks.

7.   Grout, *Short History*, pp. 164, 167, respectively. The chapters devoted to *opera seria* comprise pp. 151–225.

8.   Dean and Knapp, *Handel's Operas*, p. 15.

9.   Ibid., pp. 490–94. These "unsuspected depths of suffering," which would doubtless have remained unsuspected in Handel's time, represent the imposition of a later aesthetic upon one that has become not only foreign to us but that we tend to resist—unless it is made palatable to our tastes as Dean seeks to do here. For a far more historically grounded analysis of *Giulio Cesare*, see Carl Dahlhaus, "Dramaturgie der italienischen Oper," in Bianconi and Pestelli, eds., *Geschichte*, 6: 116–19. Dahlhaus examines the disposition of arias in the opera's first act (p. 118) to show how they follow a pattern of contrasting *Affekte* regardless of the "character" who is supposedly singing them. In another passage of this seminal essay, Dahlhaus explains the abrupt "changes" in a *seria* character's mood with the words, "The soul is less the origin than the theater [*Schauplatz*] of *Affekte*" (p. 125). See also Dahlhaus's comparison of the way Gluck employs *Affekt* in his characterization of Oreste with that of Handel in the latter's treatment of Cesare: for Dahlhaus, Gluck's significant deviation from the *opera seria* tradition

lies in his linking Oreste's *Affekt*, which remains stable from aria to aria, with his character (see Dahlhaus, "Ethos," especially p. 295).

10. On Glass's questioning of this aesthetic, especially in his first opera, *Einstein on the Beach*, whose music is deliberately kept independent of the words and the visual drama enacted on the stage, see Lindenberger, *History*, pp. 180–88. On Cage's even more radical questioning, see Chapter 8 of the present volume.

11. Strohm, *Die italienische Oper*, p. 17. See also Strohm's essay "Towards an Understanding of the *Opera Seria*" in his book *Essays*, pp. 93–105.

12. Carl Dahlhaus sees the Italian operatic score functioning as essentially an outline (*Grundriß*) for the performer until the mid-nineteenth century (see Dahlhaus, "Dramaturgie der italienischen Oper," in Bianconi and Pestelli, eds., *Geschichte*, 6: 99). Examining the differing attitudes toward Shakespeare's *Othello* in Rossini's and Verdi's settings of the play, James Aldrich-Moodie demonstrates the change during the course of the nineteenth century from opera as a fluid "text" to a stable "work" (see Aldrich-Moodie, "False Fidelity").

13. Reinhold Kubik has shown how Handel designed castrato arias to suit the differing styles and talents of his various castrato stars. See Kubik, "' ... nach der verdorbenen Welschen Zwang-Art': Beobachtungen zum Stilwandel in Händels Londoner Opernschaffen," in Marx, ed., *Händel*, pp. 74–76.

14. Italians needed to carry their librettos to their boxes just as today's audiences often demand supertitles even when the opera is in their native language. Handel's London librettos present the text in both Italian and English, but, whereas the recitatives are fully translated, the arias are merely summarized in English.

15. See Franco Piperno, "Das Produktionssystem bis 1780," in Bianconi and Pestelli, eds., *Geschichte*, 4: 48. Piperno's essay (pp. 15–79) contains invaluable detail on the economics of the system.

16. On Handel as "borrower," see George J. Buelow, "The Case for Handel's Borrowings: the Judgment of Three Centuries," and John H. Roberts, "Why Did Handel Borrow?" in Sadie and Hicks, ed., *Handel Tercentenary Collection*, pp. 61–82 and 83–92, respectively. For a list of the borrowings for his earlier operas, see Dean and Knapp, *Handel's Operas*, pp. 647–65.

17. For a description of this pasticcio, see Dean and Knapp, *Handel's Operas*, pp. 320–23. For a detailed study of Handel's nine pasticci, includ-

ing lists of arias and their original composers, see Strohm, "Händels Pasticci," in Lippmann, ed., *Studien*, pp. 208–67; on *Elpidia*, see pp. 212–15, 241–43. For a general statement of the role of pasticci, see Strohm's article "Pasticcio" in Sadie, ed., *New Grove Dictionary*, 14: 288–89.

18. Addison and Steele, *Spectator*, 1: 23–24. Addison's hostility to the newly arrived Italian opera can be explained at least partially by the fact that an English opera for which he had written the libretto had failed miserably several years before. See Dean and Knapp, *Handel's Operas*, p. 182.

19. Marcello, "Il teatro," pp. 382–83, 384, respectively.

20. Algarotti, *Saggio*, p. 31.

21. For a genealogy of eighteenth-century comic opera, see Wolfgang Osthoff, "Die Opera buffa," in Arlt et al., *Gattungen*, pp. 678–743. On the role of the intermezzi, see pp. 704–6.

22. For a history of the increasing role of ballet in Italian opera during the eighteenth century, see Kathleen Kuzmick Hansell, "Das Ballett und die italienische Oper," especially the section entitled "Opera Seria, Dramma Giocoso and die Herausforderung durch die Ballett-pantomime (1720–1795)," in Bianconi and Pestelli, eds., *Geschichte*, 5: 248–89.

23. While reporting on the state of music in Italy, Burney at one point states that, as a composer of religious music, "Handel will, I believe, ever stand superior to all other writers; at least I have heard nothing yet on the continent of equal force and effect" (Burney, *Present State*, p. 164). On the development of the idea of a musical "classic" during the 1770s, see Weber, *Rise*, p. 194.

24. On Handel's relation to the system, see Piperno, "Das Produktions-system," in Bianconi and Pestelli, eds., *Geschichte*, 4: 38, and Dahlhaus, ed., *Die Musik*, pp. 89–97.

25. On Handel's incompatibility with Metastasian ideals, see Dean and Knapp, *Handel's Operas*, pp. 18–19; for a detailed treatment of what Metastasio meant to composers of his time and how Handel, in particular, used him in his opera *Ezio*, see Strohm, *Die italienische Oper*, pp. 177–81, 188–97.

26. See, for instance, some of his comments on the arias and duets of *Radamisto*, an opera that Burney much respected: "*Vanne sorella ingrata* is an admirable composition of the old school. . . . The duet

which ends the second act has no appearance of age, except in the plan" (*BGH*, 2:702). Of another aria he writes, "The vocal divisions [passagework] are now worn out, but the violin accompaniment to the second part is admirable" (p. 702). But of one aria, "Lascia pure," he writes, "There is a close for the first time to my knowledge, which at present is perfectly modern, elegant, and in good taste" (p. 703).

27. On changes in the form from the mid-eighteenth century until Mozart's *Idomeneo*, see Henze-Döhring, *Opera Seria*, pp. 18–68; on the relation of *La clemenza di Tito* to the changes the form underwent in Italy during the 1780s, see Heartz, "Mozart."

28. On the formal differences between Handel's operas and oratorios, see Dean, *Handel's Dramatic Oratorios*, pp. 67–70; on the differences between the audiences for the two forms, pp. 128–49; on the performance history of the oratorios during and after the composer's time, pp. 102–27.

29. For a fuller discussion of Gluck's and Wagner's statements on the primacy of words over music juxtaposed with similar statements by Monteverdi and Alban Berg, see Lindenberger, *Opera*, pp. 108–13.

30. For a discussion of how voice ranges were matched with character types, see Sergio Durante, "Der Sänger," in Bianconi and Pestelli, eds., *Geschichte*, 4: 385–86.

31. For general studies of the role of castrati in opera, see Heriot, *Castrati*, and Barbier, *The World*, the latter of which describes the physical effects of castration (pp. 13–18). For additional details from medical history, see Bergeron, "The Castrato," pp. 170-73; Bergeron describes the musical style of a castrato aria by showing how Handel recast "But Who May Abide," composed for a bass in the first performance of *Messiah*, to suit the range and the vocal flexibility of the castrato Gaetano Guadagni (pp. 175-78). As a transsexual construction the castrato is of particular interest to poststructuralist critics. See, for instance, Carolyn Abbate, "Opera; or, the Envoicing of Women," in Solie, ed., *Musicology*, pp. 231–34, and Frank, *Mechanical Song*, pp. 87–90, 98–105. Both Abbate and Frank, as well as Bergeron, build upon Roland Barthes's seminal treatment in *S/Z* of Balzac's depiction of a castrato in his story *Sarrasine*.

32. On Handel's interchanging roles for castrati and female singers, see Donald Burrows, "Die Kastratenrollen in Händels Londoner Opern: Probleme und Lösungsvorschläge," in Marx, ed., *Händel*, pp. 85–93.

33.   For some modern studies of the role of *Affekt* in *opera seria*, see
       Dahlhaus, "Zum Affektbegriff," on how *Affekt* is treated by the theo-
       rist Johann Mattheson as well as by German composers of *opera seria*;
       Dahlhaus, "Ethos," on how Gluck, in his portrayal of Oreste in
       Iphigénie en Tauride, turns his back on the earlier tradition; Dahlhaus,
       "Dramaturgie der italienischen Oper," in Bianconi and Pestelli, eds.,
       Geschichte, pp. 125–26, on how the earlier notion of *Affekt* is applicable
       even a century later to such operatic "characters" as Alfredo in *La
       traviata* and Siegfried in *Götterdämmerung*; and Buelow, "The *Loci
       Topici*," which, by examining the ideas of a particular theorist, Johann
       David Heinichen, shows how composers were urged to use the recita-
       tive preceding an aria, or simply a word or two in the aria itself, to
       suggest the emotion that the music should display. On how the con-
       cept of "expressiveness" shifted from something within the text or mu-
       sic to something within the composer himself in the course of the
       eighteenth century, see Dahlhaus's chapter, "Changing Phases of the
       Esthetics of Emotion," in *Esthetics*, pp. 16–24.

34.   Mattheson, *Die neueste Untersuchung*, p. 146.

35.   On the rivalry with Bononcini, see Hawkins, *General History*, 2: 863;
       on Handel's relationships with Senesino, Durastanti, Cuzzoni, and
       Faustina Bordoni, and the rivalries among them, see 2: 872–74.

36.   Dean and Knapp list 110 productions of *Giulio Cesare* between 1922
       and 1982, but their list includes only the first half of Handel's operatic
       oeuvre (see *Handel's Operas*, pp. 675–80). It is also the only Handel
       opera in Littlejohn's list of the 100 most frequently performed operas
       during 1988 and 1989; it occupies the 77th place, between *Die Frau
       ohne Schatten* and *West Side Story* (see Littlejohn, *Ultimate Art*, p. 23).

37.   On the "number-opera" as central to the Italian tradition, see Carl
       Dahlhaus, "Dramaturgie der italienischen Oper," in Bianconi and
       Pestelli, eds., *Geschichte*, 6: 113–16. Dahlhaus mentions *Simon Boccane-
       gra* briefly (p. 93) in relation to Bellini's *Norma* to show that, whereas
       the earlier opera still shares much of the method of eighteenth-cen-
       tury *opera seria*, the *Affekte* that Verdi's characters assume become part
       of a developing and integrated drama.

38.   For detailed studies of the differences between the two versions, see
       Wolfgang Osthoff, "Die Beiden 'Boccanegra'-Fassungen und der Be-
       ginn von Verdis Spätwerk," in Kost, *Studien*, pp. 70–89; Noske, *Signi-
       fier*, pp. 215–40; Budden, *Operas*, 2: 245–334; and Sopart, *Giuseppe Verdis*

'Simon Boccanegra.' For the Verdi-Boito correspondence during the process of revising *Boccanegra*, see Busch, ed., *Verdi's 'Otello,'* 1: 35–111.

39. For an excellent description of how, in the first act of *Giulio Cesare*, *opera seria* convention forces the plot to motivate a large variety of arias that alternate diverse *Affekte*, see Dahlhaus, "Dramaturgie der italienischen Oper," in Bianconi and Pestelli, eds. *Geschichte*, 6: 116–19.

40. For a detailed analysis of these two duets, see Sopart, *Giuseppe Verdis 'Simon Boccanegra,'* pp. 47–49, 183–85. Sopart aptly calls one of these sections "the duet as musical-dramatic dialogue" (p. 47).

41. On the history of the libretto see Dean and Knapp, *Handel's Operas*, pp. 486–87, and Strohm, *Essays*, p. 49.

42. Robinson, *Opera*, pp. 179–209.

43. On the various changes instituted by Hagen to make Handel "accessible," see Wolff, *Die Händel-Oper*, pp. 11–16.

44. For arguments on the relative merits of the countertenor and the female voice as substitutes for Handel's castrati in present-day performances, see Charles Farncombe, "Die Kastratenrollen und ihre Bedeutung," in Marx, ed., *Händel*, 103–9.

45. See Butler, *Gender Trouble*.

46. Carl Dahlhaus has warned against using too narrow a conception of drama—all too often derived from non-musical theater—to judge the dramatic quality of opera. "The teleological element is not very strong in opera, at least insofar as it consists of a configuration of affects, of extended lyrical elements—of arias, in short." Dahlhaus goes on to conclude that "the fact that in opera, especially number opera, the teleological element remains—in comparison with the spoken genre—less prominent than the structural one [by which Dahlhaus means 'the configuration of affects and characters'] is not a reason for denying the dramatic character of the former" (Dahlhaus, "What Is a Musical Drama?" p. 99).

Chapter 3

1. Reported by the travel writer and novelist Charles MacFarlane in *Reminiscences*, p. 6. I am grateful to Donald Reiman for calling my attention to this meeting, which I have not seen mentioned in any of the Shelley or Rossini biographies.

2. Rosselli, *Opera Industry*.

3. *MSL*, 1: 89. Rossini's habit of transferring passages from one opera to

another was much remarked upon in his time. Near the end of his life, when his publisher Tito Ricordi began publishing a complete edition, the composer expressed his dismay that an edition would make his repetitions evident to everyone. He excused his method by citing his need during his youth to earn money quickly to support his parents and relatives. For his letter to Ricordi, see Weinstock, *Rossini*, p. 333.

4.   Mary Shelley, *Journals*, 1: 243. Mary apparently attended a later production of this opera in Pisa, for in a letter of January 1822 she writes that the duet "Nati in ver noi siamo," from *Ricciardo*, "now singing at the Opera . . . is running in my head." *MSL*, 1: 215.

5.   Mary Shelley, *Journals*, 1: 197. According to her journals, Percy Shelley also attended a performance of *La Cenerentola* with Claire Clairmont in Pisa in February 1820 (*Journals*, 1: 308). During the years after her return to London, Mary attended several performances of Rossini operas. Quite in contrast to the reservations she expressed toward Rossini during her Italian years, she avidly sought tickets for these performances, though she balked at attending *Otello*. See *MSL*, 1: 482–83 and 2: 71, 73.

6.   Percy Shelley, *Letters*, 2: 69.

7.   Byron, *"The flesh,"* 6: 132.

8.   Whether or not Rossini and Stendhal actually met has long been a matter of dispute. Stendhal claims to have had several meetings with Rossini and mentions in a letter of December 21, 1819, that he had been spending evenings with Rossini and was about to dine with the composer that very day (Stendhal, *Correspondance*, 1: 1000). On the other hand, when Rossini, in the company of the singer Giuditta Pasta some years later, passed Stendhal, the composer asked his companion who this person was, only to be told it was Rossini's biographer Stendhal. "This is the first time I've seen him," said Rossini. The evidence for and against a meeting is presented in Matteini, *Stendhal*, pp. 167–73. Whatever the truth of the matter, it is clear that a personal relationship with the other was of considerably less consequence to the composer than to the writer, who cultivated a fascination with the famous past and present.

9.   Holmes, *Shelley*, p. 494.

10. Abrams, *Natural Supernaturalism*, pp. 299–307, 342–44, 460–62.

11. Stendhal, *Life*, p. 3.

12. Ibid., pp. 285–86.

13. Heine, *Sämtliche Werke*, 3: 249–52.

14. Stendhal, *Life*, p. 50.

15. Schopenhauer, *World*, 1: 262.

16. Hegel, *Briefe*, 3: 54–70 *passim.*

17. Browning, *On the Poet*, p. 18. This essay, originally written in 1851 as the introduction to what turned out to be some spurious Shelley letters, was reprinted here as one of the early Browning Society volumes. The marketability of forgeries three decades after Shelley's death gives some indication of his standing with the public at mid-century.

18. Elson, *History*, p. 153. It hardly seems accidental that this volume, intended as an introduction for the general musical public, sports on its cover an embossed portrait of Wagner, whose musical aesthetic, by then at its height, viewed Rossini as naïve.

19. Eliot, *Use*, p. 89.

20. Leavis, *Revaluation*, p. 232.

21. Elson, *History*, pp. 153, 167–68.

22. Leavis, *Revaluation*, p. 205. The four lines from "Ode to the West Wind" that Leavis cites may be seen in context in Shelley, *Poetry*, pp. 221–22.

23. Leavis, *Revaluation*, pp. 206, 213, 214.

24. Reported by Edmond Michotte, a Belgian musician who witnessed Richard Wagner's visit to Rossini in Paris in 1860. What we know of Rossini's visit to Beethoven 38 years before comes from what Michotte heard Rossini tell Wagner. See Michotte, *Richard Wagner's Visit*, pp. 45, 52.

25. Quoted in Osborne, *Rossini*, p. 58.

26. Arnold, *Poetry*, pp. 375, 380.

27. See Michotte, *Richard Wagner's Visit*, pp. 46–50.

28. See Philip Gossett's Rossini entry in Sadie, ed., *New Grove Dictionary*, 16: 236.

29. See Michotte, *Richard Wagner's Visit*, pp. 68–69.

30. See Osborne, *Rossini*, pp. 90, 104, 262, 268–69.

31. See Ludlam, "Meteorology," and the replies in the September 22 and 29 issues of the same journal.

32. See "Shelley's Urbanity," in Davie, *Purity*, pp. 133–59. When I once told Davie that this essay had helped me find a way back to Shelley after Eliot's and Leavis's strictures, that in fact I had now come to en-

joy such much-attacked poems as *Epipsychidion* and *Prometheus Unbound*, he replied, "*That* is not the Shelley we like."

33. See Frye, *Anatomy*, pp. 60, 65, 147, 150, 151, 157, 205, 302, 321, 322, and Bloom, *Shelley's Mythmaking*.

34. See Eliot's essay, "What Dante Means to Me," in *To Criticize the Critic*, pp. 130–32.

35. Bloom, ed., *Deconstruction*.

36. On the differences between poem and opera, see Mitchell, *The Walter Scott Operas*, pp. 19–28.

37. Shelley, "A Philosophical View of Reform," in *Shelley's Prose*, p. 240.

38. Intermission interview included in *Rossini Bicentennial Birthday Gala*. My citation of that evening as an "originary moment" derives not simply from the singer's and the editor's own testimony, but also from the fact that I happened to attend this now-historic performance. If this event had occurred exactly one month later, it would have coincided with one of Rossini's quadrennial birthdays.

39. Artaud's text is reproduced in Artaud, *Oeuvres*, 4: 147–210.

40. Artaud, *Artaud on Theatre*, pp. 147, 149.

41. Leavis, *Revaluation*, p. 223.

42. Curran, *Poetic Form*, p. 198. See also his list of other contemporary works designated by this term (p. 250).

43. For Shelley's attitudes toward opera and ballet, see Tetreault, *Poetry*, pp. 170–79. Tetreault analyzes passages from *Prometheus Unbound* as attempts to achieve operatic and ballet-like effects (pp. 176–79, 183–84, 190–91).

44. Percy Shelley, *Letters*, 2: 128.

45. On Shelley's knowledge of and attitude toward Mozart's operas, see Tetreault, *Poetry*, pp. 172–74, 176, 182–83, 185–86. Tetreault speculates that Shelley was motivated to attend Rossini's *Barbiere* the night before his departure for Italy because, after twice attending *Le nozze di Figaro*, he wanted "to learn more of the story of the wily servant Figaro" (p. 174).

46. See Schmidt, "Shelley's 'Spirit of the Age.'"

47. Artaud, *Artaud on Theatre*, p. 146.

48. Davidson, "Refiguring Shelley."

49. Palmer, "Some Notes," p. 275.

50. Vecchiarelli, *Canto*, p. 98.

Chapter 4

1. Schelling, *Philosophie*, p. 380. Although composed for lectures delivered between 1802 and 1805, this treatise was first published posthumously more than a half century later.

2. Aristotle, *Poetics*, in Russell and Winterbottom, eds., *Classical Literary Criticism*, p. 89.

3. Schelling, *Philosophie*, p. 163.

4. Sulzer, *Allgemeine Theorie*. The entry encompasses pp. 572–85, with an extensive bibliography following it; quotations here are drawn from pp. 573, 583, and 584.

5. Algarotti, *Saggio*, pp. 1, 2.

6. Kant, *Critique*, pp. 199, 198, and 200, respectively.

7. For a magisterial portrayal of the development of the concept of absolute music from these speculations, see Dahlhaus, *Idee*.

8. Schopenhauer, *World*, 1: 263. Subsequent quotations will be cited within the text.

9. Vischer, *Aesthetik*, p. 1112. Subsequent quotations will be cited within the text.

10. Thomas Grey's recent volume, *Wagner's Musical Prose*, is unique, among other things, for treating Wagner's theories within the history of aesthetic thought. Grey discusses Wagner's concept of melody, for example, in relation to earlier theories from Sulzer to Schopenhauer (pp. 267–68).

11. For the section on the role of the people, significantly entitled "The People as Generating Power for the Work of Art," see *WGS*, 10: 57–62. *The Artwork of the Future* encompasses pp. 47–185 of this volume.

12. For a discussion of how Wagner takes up and transforms the idea of absolute music for his own purposes, see Dahlhaus, *Idee*, pp. 24–33. For a far more detailed treatment building on, and also modifying, Dahlhaus's argument, see the chapter entitled "Questions of Autonomy" in Grey, *Wagner's Musical Prose*, pp. 1–50.

13. For an interesting argument that Wagner's turn to privileging music over text came less from his reading of Schopenhauer than from his practice as a composer, see Grey, *Wagner's Musical Prose*, pp. 4, 16–17.

14. This term appears in his 1872 essay "On the Term 'Music Drama'" (*WGS*, 13: 123), in which he explains his objections to the generic term that has remained attached to his later work up to the present day.

15. On Nietzsche's outdoing Wagner in his condemnation of the whole operatic tradition (the latter had, after all, praised Gluck's and Mozart's operas), see Silk and Stern, *Nietzsche*, pp. 239–42.

16. Nietzsche, *Birth*, p. 115. Subsequent quotations from this book will be cited within the text. On Nietzsche's view of opera as an extension of a larger bias he held against theatrical representation, see Barish, *Antitheatrical Prejudice*, pp. 400–417.

17. Saint-Évremond, *Letters*, pp. 207, 217.

18. Wagner's slogan, "Wirkung ohne Ursache," appears in *Opera and Drama*, in which Meyerbeer's supposed crassness is illustrated by a scene from *Le Prophète* (*WGS*, II: 91–95). On Wagner's early admiration for Meyerbeer and his debt to the composer in the development of larger musical structures to create "larger levels of scene and even act," see Grey, *Wagner's Musical Prose*, pp. 204–6.

19. Friedrich Nietzsche, *Unfashionable Observations*, p. 298.

20. Ibid., p. 262.

21. Nietzsche's laudatory essay "Richard Wagner in Bayreuth" was written just before the first festival, which Nietzsche left abruptly because of a migraine headache. The break between Wagner and Nietzsche came gradually during the succeeding two years. For the documents relevant to the Wagner-Nietzsche relationship, see Borchmeyer and Salaquarda, eds., *Nietzsche*. For a detailed analysis of the relationship, see the editors' essay "Legende und Wirklichkeit einer epochalen Begegnung" (2: 1273–1386).

22. Sadie, ed., *New Grove Dictionary of Opera*, 1: 695.

23. Not only is the musical style of Peking opera different from that of Western opera, but so are virtually all the conventions on which it is based. Characters in Peking opera are not distributed according to vocal range, as they are in the West, but according to the type of dramatic role they are playing: such conventional Peking-opera roles as the old man, the scholar-lover, and the warrior are comparable less to Western opera than to *commedia dell'arte*. Like Western opera, however, Peking opera can be described institutionally as a closed system. On the nature and early history of Peking opera, see Mackerras, *Rise*, and Mackerras's entry s.v. "China" in Sadie, ed., *New Grove Dictionary of Music*, 4: 254–60.

24. Rosen, *Romantic Generation*, pp. 539–40.

25. For a detailed and colorful description of this particular subsystem within opera, see Rosselli, *Opera Industry*.

Chapter 5

1. For an informed guess on how Wagner might have fared in histories of music if he had died after the completion of *Lohengrin*, see Arnold Whittall, "Musical Language," in Millington, ed., *Wagner Compendium*, p. 256. As Whittall puts it, "The triumphs of the three Romantic operas are not to be found in anticipations of later developments but in features more personal to them." Among these features he cites "the bold juxtapositions of Senta's Ballad" and "the magically sudden transformation from Venusberg to Wartburg."

2. A considerable amount of scholarly effort in recent years has gone into reconstructing Wagner's process of musical composition in the *Ring*. From the extant sketches made before 1853—all originally intended for what was then called *Siegfrieds Tod* and dating from 1850—individual musical themes are clearly evident, but the musical styles we associate with the *Ring* would have been hard to predict. As Curt von Westernhagen, analyzing a passage from an 1850 draft, puts it, "It is unlikely that at that date he envisaged an accompaniment richer than is found in comparable lyrical passages in *Lohengrin*" (Westernhagen, *Forging*, p. 187; for further discussions of the 1850 sketches, see pp. 13–15, 20–21, 82–84, 97, 185–88). Although Westernhagen's reproduction of Wagner's process of composition has been disputed, his view of the musical style of the earliest sketches has generally been accepted. Thus John Deathridge, while challenging Westernhagen's reading of later sketches, describes the 1850 setting of the Norn scene and the subsequent Siegfried-Brünnhilde dialogue as "a rather wan setting in the style of *Lohengrin*" (Deathridge, "Wagner's Sketches," p. 385). Similarly, in an earlier study, Robert Bailey describes "the vocal writing in 1850 . . . [as] representing a continuation of the ingratiating lyrical style of such a passage as the bridal chamber scene in *Lohengrin*" (Bailey, "The Musical Sketches for *Siegfrieds Tod*," in Powers, ed., *Studies*, p. 483). See also the discussion of Wagner's use of these early sketches in the *Rheingold* prelude in Darcy, "*Creatio*," pp. 81–84.

3. I quote the German from the 1853 edition—Wagner, *Ring des Nibelungen*, pp. 32–33. The translation, by Andrew Porter, comes from Wagner, *Ring of the Nibelung*, p. 70.

4. It is significant that Wagner did not attempt a simple metrical imita-

tion of his medieval models. As Carl Dahlhaus explains, "Wagner's lines of Stabreim [alliteration] differ from his old German models in that the number of strong accents is irregular: some lines have two, others three or even four. The consequence is nothing less than the dissolution of musical periodic structure, the syntax that had provided the framework of both instrumental and vocal melodic writing for the past hundred years and more" (Dahlhaus, *Richard Wagner's Music Dramas*, p. 105). In other words, Wagner was using the linguistic forms of what he saw as a lost past not simply to bring this past to life (though this was clearly part of his project), but he was reworking these forms as a means of creating a revolutionary new musical style.

5. Hopkins, *Poems*, p. 53. There is no evidence that Hopkins was aware of Wagner's experiments while he was writing these lines.

6. See the discussions in parts 2 and 3 of *Opera and Drama* in *WGS*, 11: 202–4, 238–40, 260–61. On Wagner's occasional use of alliteration in *Leubald*, a verse drama written when he was fifteen, see Peter Branscombe, "The Dramatic Texts," trans. Stewart Spencer, in Müller and Wapnewski, eds., *Wagner Handbook*, p. 270.

7. After citing the librettos of the *Ring, Tristan,* and *Meistersinger* as his greatest achievements in the form, Patrick J. Smith, in his history of opera librettos, states, "Richard Wagner, as librettist, is the greatest the form has produced, and if the libretto needs justification in terms of an artistic identity in its own right, Wagner will stand advocate of its strengths and its possibilities" (see Smith, *Tenth Muse*, p. 287).

8. A real test for the literary "independence" of a libretto would be its attractiveness to stage directors and audiences even without the music composed for it. Among famous librettos only one—Hofmannsthal's *Rosenkavalier*—has, as far as I know, a stage history independent of its music. There are of course librettos based on famous plays—for example, *Salome* and *Woyzeck*—whose stage history has continued at the same time that their musical embodiments remained in the operatic repertory.

9. For a detailed study of Wagner's reading during this period, see Magee, *Richard Wagner*, pp. 1–56, 213–15. For a survey of Wagner's relationship to the Middle Ages, see Volker Mertens, "Wagner's Middle Ages," trans. Stewart Spencer, in Müller and Wapnewski, eds., *Wagner Handbook*, pp. 236–68; the medieval background of the *Ring* is discussed on pp. 246–54.

10. Magee, *Richard Wagner*, pp. 185–86 and 204–5, respectively.

11. See Koch, *Richard Wagner's Bühnenfestspiel.* Koch's monograph sketches in not only some of the Old Norse sources, but cites many of the early-nineteenth-century lyrics and dramas on the Nibelungs that preceded Wagner's tetralogy, for example, the dramas of Friedrich de la Motte Fouqué (1810) and Ernst Raupach (1834). Scholarly (and often not-so-scholarly) treatments of Wagner's relation to his sources have continued to appear for over a century. Among the most distinguished one can cite Magee, *Richard Wagner*, as well as Cooke's unfinished *I Saw the World End.* Since the appearance of Magee's comprehensive book a new article by Stanley R. Hauer has demonstrated the centrality to the *Ring* of the *Völospá*, one of the texts from the *Poetic Edda* (Hauer, "Wagner").

12. On Wagner's relation to Rousseau's and Herder's theories on the origin of languages, see Grey, *Wagner's Musical Prose*, pp. 258–67; Grey also relates Wagner's concept of "endless melody" to Rousseau's concept of melody (pp. 276–78).

13. This prose draft, under the title *Der Nibelungen-Mythus: Als Entwurf zu einem Drama*, appears in *WGS*, 6: 139–50.

14. "Ich schreibe keine *Opern* mehr," in *Eine Mitteilung an meine Freunde* (*WGS*, 1: 173). At this point he chose to use the word *drama* as a generic label for what was to become the *Ring*. Two decades later, while working on *Götterdämmerung*, he rejected the term *Musikdrama* (which had not originated with him) and suggested instead the term *Bühnenfestspiel* to stress the festive, participatory form he was seeking (see "Über die Benennung 'Musikdrama,'" in *WGS*, 13: 124).

15. Note Marx's famous comment in the *Grundrisse* on the impossibility of a Homer in the modern world: "From another side, is Achilles possible with powder and lead? Or the *Iliad* with the printing press, not to mention the printing machine? Do not the song and the saga and the muse necessarily come to an end with the printer's bar, hence do not the necessary conditions of epic poetry vanish?" (Tucker, ed., *Marx-Engels Reader*, p. 246). At the very time that these lines were written (1857–58) Wagner had virtually finished setting the early, saga-influenced parts of the *Ring* to music. One might add that he was later to use modern stage technology, and to an extent that no previous composer had done, to renew the life of his seemingly antiquated materials.

16. On the relation of *The Prelude* to epic tradition, see Lindenberger, *On Wordsworth's 'Prelude,'* pp. 9–15, 99–129.

17. On the relation of *Don Juan* to epic tradition, see McGann, *Don Juan*, pp. 19–34, 79–99, 102–3.

18. See the section entitled "The General World-Situation of Epic," in *HA*, 2: 1051–62. For an argument that Hegel's other writings, above all the *Phenomenology of Mind*, left an imprint on the *Ring*, see Corse, *Wagner*.

19. See "Vorschlag zu einer Oper," in Vischer, *Kritische Gänge*, 2: 451–78. For the sake of dramatic economy, Vischer warns the prospective composer of his Nibelung opera to avoid the mythical events from the *Eddas* and the sagas that precede the story of the *Nibelungenlied* (2: 459–60); similarly, Wagner at first planned to concentrate on what was to become *Götterdämmerung* and to introduce the earlier events only in retrospect. As Vischer concludes his scenario, he notes that to accommodate all the material he has proposed (which, unlike Wagner's version, includes the whole of the *Nibelungenlied*) the composer who takes him up on his suggestion may well have to make a two-evening event out of it (2: 478); Wagner, of course, finally settled for four (or, more precisely, three and a half) evenings.

20. For the lure that *Faust* exercised for composers from Beethoven through Mahler, see Lindenberger, "Closing up *Faust*: The Final Lines According to Schumann, Liszt, and Mahler," in Brown et al., *Interpreting Goethe's 'Faust,'* pp. 123–32.

21. Liszt's term, which he also applied to Byron's *Cain* and *Manfred* and to Mickiewicz's *Dziady*, appears in his essay of 1855 on Berlioz's *Harold in Italy*, in Liszt, *Gesammelte Schriften*, 4: 53.

22. See Wagner's letter of April 7, 1858, to Mathilde Wesendonck on *Faust*, above all as this letter is placed within a larger biographical and intellectual context by Peter Wapnewski in his essay "Rivale Faust: Beobachtungen zu Wagners Goethe-Verständnis," in Perels, ed., *Jahrbuch*, pp. 128–56.

23. On the parallel between the endings of *Faust* and of the *Ring*, see Grey, *Wagner's Musical Prose*, p. 369. On the other hand, Hans Rudolf Vaget argues that the redemption at the end of the *Ring* actually represents a critique of the redemption with which Goethe brings his drama to its end (see Vaget, "Strategies for Redemption: *Der Ring des Nibelungen* and *Faust*," in Shaw et al., eds., *Wagner*, pp. 81–104).

24. On Wagner's fascination with and ambivalence toward Goethe's achievement in *Faust*, see the chapter on *Faust* in Borchmeyer, *Richard Wagner*, pp. 40–47. On Wagner's own idea of improvisation, or, more properly, "fixed improvisation," see the succeeding chapter, pp. 48–58.

25. See the section on panoramic drama in Lindenberger, *Historical Drama*, pp. 86–94.

26. See Ewans, *Wagner*. Ewans not only explains the importance of Aeschylus and Greek drama in general for Wagner's theory of musical theater, but he also devotes most of his book to a step-by-step comparison of the *Ring* and the *Oresteia*. Ewans's stress on the centrality of the *Oresteia* for Wagner has been challenged by Hugh Lloyd-Jones, who, though agreeing with Ewans on the significance of Aeschylus for Wagner's theory and practice, claims—as a number of earlier scholars had done—that the *Prometheus* exerted more influence on the *Ring* than the *Oresteia*. See the chapter on Wagner in Lloyd-Jones, *Blood*, pp. 126–42.

27. See the chapter on *Tristan und Isolde*, entitled "Opera as Symphonic Poem," in Kerman, *Opera*, pp. 192–216. On Wagner's appropriation at once of Beethoven's music and reputation, see Thomas S. Grey, "The Beethoven Legacy," in Millington, ed., *Wagner Compendium*, pp. 151–53.

28. On the difference between incest in the source and in the opera, see Cooke, *I Saw the World End*, pp. 297–98.

29. On the cultural significance of adultery, see Tanner, *Adultery*.

30. On the relationship between what I call the "higher" narrative of opera and the "lower" narrative of the novel, see the chapter "Opera in Novels" in my book *Opera*, pp. 145–96. Flaubert, as I point out (pp. 159–62), juxtaposes these two modes of narrative in the scene in which Emma Bovary attends a performance of *Lucia di Lammermoor*.

31. For a description and defense of the Chéreau *Ring* by its creators, see Boulez et al., eds., *Histoire*. For a sophisticated defense of what the author sees as Chéreau's underlying fidelity to Wagner in this production, see Nattiez, *Tétralogies*. For a summary of this book in English, together with some afterthoughts, see Nattiez, "'Fidelity' to Wagner: Reflections on the Centenary *Ring*," in Millington and Spencer, eds., *Wagner*, pp. 75–98.

32. For the endings that Wagner envisioned in the scenario and the early draft of *Siegfrieds Tod*, see *WGS*, 6: 149–50 and 192–93, respectively.

33. "Heuchelnder Sitte / hartes Gesetz," in Wagner, *Ring des Nibelungen*, p. 158.

34. This addition is printed in *WGS*, 4: 286. For a survey of the Wagner-Schopenhauer relationship, see Hartmut Reinhardt, "Wagner and Schopenhauer," trans. Erika and Martin Swales, in Müller and Wapnewski, eds., *Wagner Handbook*, pp. 287–96. For a detailed study of Schopenhauer's impact on the *Ring* and its relation to Wagner's anti-Semitism, see Rather, *Dream*, pp. 63–109.

35. For a description of how this ending was composed, see Westernhagen, *Forging*, pp. 235–40. For an interesting argument that, from a literary if not from a musical point of view, even this ending does not provide a full resolution, see Wapnewski, *Der traurige Gott*, pp. 185–97.

36. On the history of an opera's interpretation as an aspect of its historicity, see the chapter "The History in Opera: *La clemenza di Tito, Khovanshchina, Moses und Aron*" in Lindenberger, *History*, pp. 85–108.

37. Nietzsche, *Der Fall Wagner*, in Nietzsche, *Werke*, 2: 911. For an analysis of what Nietzsche meant by the term *décadence* in relation to Wagner, see Dieter Borchmeyer, "Wagner and Nietzsche," trans. Michael Tanner, in Müller and Wapnewski, eds., *Wagner Handbook*, pp. 340–42.

38. See *AGS*, 14: 18–25. See also Nattiez's connection of this reading with *Das Judentum in der Musik* (written the year before Wagner drafted the text for *Der junge Siegfried* and *Das Rheingold*), "Le Ring comme histoire métaphorique de la musique," in Shaw et al., eds., *Wagner*, especially pp. 46–48. For a strong indictment of Wagner's anti-Semitism, see Rose, *Wagner*. For a provocative argument that Wagner's early audiences would have seen a number of characters—not simply Alberich and Mime but also Beckmesser, Klingsor, and Kundry—as caricatures of Jews, see Weiner, *Richard Wagner*. (Weiner's findings, to be sure, have been seriously questioned in a searching review by Thomas Grey, "Bodies.") It may well be that, as a result of these writings, Wolfgang Wagner's 1996 Bayreuth production of *Die Meistersinger* presents a reconciliation at the end between Sachs and Beckmesser, the latter of whom, in the original text by the director's grandfather, is last seen angrily leaving the stage (see Levy, "Waiting for the Next Wagner").

39. Quoted from the notebooks by Joachim Fest, "Um einen Wagner von außen bittend," in Bermbach and Borchmeyer, eds., *Richard Wagner*, p. 186.

40. For a brief description of Wieland Wagner's *Ring* as deliberately "antifascist," see Barry Millington, "Staging," in Millington, ed., *Wagner Compendium*, pp. 376–77. For assessments of Wieland Wagner's various *Ring* productions within the history of Wagnerian stagings, see Mike Ashman, "Producing Wagner," in Millington and Spencer, eds., *Wagner*, pp. 40–41, and, in the same volume, Patrick Carnegy, "Designing Wagner: Deeds of Music Made Visible?" pp. 61–65.

41. See Wolf Siegfried Wagner, *Geschichte*, pp. 122–25.

Chapter 6

1. Melvin, "Puccini's Chinese Tale."
2. Ibid.
3. Turner, *Orientalism*, p. 44.
4. Byron, *Complete Poetical Works*, 4: 145 (ll. 405–8).
5. Said, *Orientalism*, p. 73.
6. Fonton's treatise, *Essai sur la musique orientale comparée à la musique européenne*, though sections had been published before, is printed in full for the first time in Betzwieser, *Exotismus*, pp. 371–419. The quotation cited here is on p. 381.
7. On Emma's orientalist reading, see Flaubert, *Madame Bovary*, p. 27 (pt. 1, sec. 6); on Djali, p. 32 (pt. 1, sec. 7); on the Algerian shawls, p. 74 (pt. 2, sec. 5); and on the incense, p. 210 (pt. 3, sec. 6). On Kuchuk Hanem, see Steegmuller, ed., *Flaubert*, pp. 113–19, 120n, 129–30. For a detailed analysis of Flaubert's orientalism, see Terdiman, *Discourse / Counter-Discourse*, pp. 227–57, and Lowe, *Critical Terrains*, pp. 75–101. From the point of view of this chapter it is significant that two major opera composers, Musorgsky and Massenet, attempted musical treatments of the two central orientalist texts by Flaubert, *Salammbô* and *Hérodias*, respectively (though Musorgsky's never went beyond the stage of fragment). I know of no major composers who turned to Flaubert's more realistic texts, such as *Madame Bovary* and *L'Éducation sentimentale*. For a detailed comparison of the story *Hérodias* and the once-popular opera made out of it, see Hollard, "Flaubert's *Hérodias*." In our present cultural climate one could well imagine a biographical opera about the author's adventures on the Nile.
8. See Kidwai, *Orientalism*, and Leask, *British Romantic Writers*.
9. See Qian, *Orientalism*.

10. See, for instance, Lew, "Lady Mary's Portable Seraglio," and Aravamudan, "Lady Mary Wortley Montagu."

11. Lowe, *Critical Terrains.*

12. See Nochlin, *Politics of Vision*, pp. 33–59. See such exhibition catalogues as Rosenthal, *Orientalism*, Thompson, *East*, and Martin and Koda, *Orientalism.*

13. See Said, *Culture*, pp. 111–32, and Locke, "Constructing the Oriental 'Other.'"

14. Said, *Orientalism*, pp. 56–57.

15. On the "Turkish" opera as a recognizable genre in the eighteenth century, see Wilson, *Humanität*, pp. 11–37.

16. On the precise rhythmic and harmonic devices, see Bauman, *W. A. Mozart*, pp. 62–65.

17. Quoted in Betzwieser, *Exotismus*, p. 195. On Gluck's use of Turkish music in other reform operas, see pp. 190–200. One might note that Gluck drew his Scythian music in *Iphigénie en Aulide* from *La Halte des Calmouckes* (1761), a ballet he had composed before any of the reform operas.

18. Ibid., p. 199.

19. Algarotti, *Saggio*, p. 21.

20. Ibid., pp. 62–63.

21. Ibid., pp. 63–65. Algarotti's recommendations of Egypt and China were not present in the original 1755 edition but were added for the edition of 1763.

22. On Puccini's use of Chinese musical style in *Turandot*, see Schatt, *Exotik*, pp. 44–51, and Ashbrook and Powers, *Puccini's 'Turandot,'* pp. 94–100; on his use of Japanese music in *Butterfly*, see Schatt, pp. 26–40, and Groos, "Return," pp. 168–77. In each instance, in his attempt to achieve the musical "realism" that other composers of his time strived for, he sought out traditional examples of the music of the country he was depicting. A listener unfamiliar with these two operas would likely associate both with the Far East but without being able to guess which had a Chinese and which a Japanese setting. Puccini's desire to achieve local color extends beyond the Orient; in *La fanciulla del west*, for example, the American setting is suggested by touches of ragtime (Schatt, p. 41).

23. On the musical complexities with which Mozart endowed Osmin's part, see Bauman, *W. A. Mozart*, pp. 66–71.

24. On Lully's music for Molière's play, see Betzwieser, *Exotismus*, pp. 125–28.
25. Ibid., p. 125.
26. On the musical advances achieved in this opera, see Dean, *Bizet*, pp. 195–99. For the negative contemporary reaction to Bizet's strange harmonies, see Hellmuth Christian Wolff, "Der Orient in der französischen Oper des 19. Jahrhunderts," in Becker, ed., *Die "Couleur locale,"* pp. 379–80.
27. Hanslick, *Am Ende*, p. 121.
28. Robinson, "Is *Aida*," pp. 139–40. However we evaluate the supposed orientalism of *Aida*, it has been noted that the Ethiopian world is suggested musically in a different way from the Egyptian; see Della Seta, "'O cieli azzurri,'" for a useful semiotic analysis of these two contrasting realms.
29. Hanslick, *Die moderne Oper*, pp. 249–50.
30. Ibid., p. 250.
31. On the *Turandot* overture, see Schatt, *Exotik*, p. 23; on *Oberon*, see Warrack, *Carl Maria von Weber*, pp. 332–33.
32. Said, *Culture*, pp. 120–21.
33. See the letters in Busch, *Verdi's 'Aida,'* pp. 31, 40, 409.
34. On the special *Aida* trumpet, see the letters in Busch, *Verdi's 'Aida,'* pp. 106–9, and the discussion in Budden, *Operas*, 3: 181.
35. Lindenberger, *Opera*, p. 271. Both the present chapter and Chapter 5 are essentially developments of an idea that I had not yet worked out in detail in my earlier study.
36. Said, *Culture*, pp. 18–19, 32, 43, 51, 66–67, 146, 194, 259, and, applied to *Aida*, 111, 114, 125.
37. Verdi's most recent and comprehensive biographer, Mary Jane Phillips-Matz has, with a 36-year interval between her reports of her findings, suggested two unrelated sources, both European, for Mariette's scenario: Metastasio's libretto *Nitteti*, which had been set by numerous composers during the eighteenth century, and the Hellenistic novel by Heliodorus, *Aethiopica*. See Matz, "An Ancestor," and Phillips-Matz, "Roots." The later article provides no indication whether she believes her earlier contention is still valid.
38. The depiction of local color in distant historical places central to French *grand opéra* since its heyday in the 1830s laid the groundwork for the orientalism of *L'Africaine*. On the connection between the

development of local color in music and in literary and pictorial realism in nineteenth-century France, see Gerhard, *Verstädterung*, pp. 57–60.

39. Said, "Uncertainties," p. 313.

40. For Glass's own commentary on the genesis, creation, and production of this opera, see Glass, *Music*, pp. 87–118.

41. For Glass's own account of his exposure to Indian music, see Glass, *Music*, pp. 16–18. The quotation cited here is on p. 17.

42. Ibid., p. 115.

43. Said, *Die tote Stadt*, p. 598.

44. See Rothstein, "'Klinghoffer' Sinks" and "Seeking Symmetry," and Sokolov, "Adamsweek." As Sokolov put it, "A truly even-handed treatment would have included a scene of wealthy robed Saudis in a gaudy palace in the desert."

45. Steinberg, *Death of Klinghoffer*, p. 18.

46. This very ceremoniousness is used by Edward Rothstein to question the appropriateness of the minimalist style to opera. Referring at once to Glass's and Adams's operas, Rothstein attacks both composers for distancing the audience from historical events instead of "engaging . . . in the lives of its subjects" (Rothstein, "'Klinghoffer' Sinks"). It is unclear from his review whether or not his critique of the music results from his evident distaste for the ideology he claims to see in *The Death of Klinghoffer*.

47. Steinberg, *Death of Klinghoffer*, p. 11.

48. Cott, *The Cave*, p. 16.

49. See Brett, "Eros and Orientalism," in Brett et al., eds., *Queering the Pitch*, p. 251.

50. See Taruskin, "'Entoiling the Falconet,'" pp. 269–79, and "Russian Musical Orientalism," p. 81.

51. Hugo, *Oeuvres poétiques*, 1: 580.

52. Nietzsche, *Werke*, 2: 906–7.

53. McClary, *Georges Bizet: 'Carmen,'* pp. 29–43, 51–58.

54. See Groos, "Madame Butterfly."

55. For an analysis of a prestigious ballet score, Ravel's *Daphnis and Chloë*, as a product of commodity culture, see Kramer, *Classical Music*, pp. 201–25.

56. See Robin Holloway's essay "'Salome': Art or Kitsch?" (in Puffett, ed., *Richard Strauss*, pp. 145–60) on the difficulty, in any analysis of

Strauss's opera, of separating the aesthetic categories named in the essay's title.

57. Gilman, "Strauss and the Pervert," in Groos and Parker, eds., *Reading Opera*, pp. 324–27.

58. Schoenberg, *Briefe*, p. 165. As Pamela C. White puts it in her detailed musical analysis of this opera, "Exotic rhythms are used to convey a vaguely Near Eastern sound." See White, *Schoenberg*, p. 158.

59. Lindenberger, *Opera*, pp. 267–69.

60. Said, "Orientalism Reconsidered," in Barker et al., *Literature*, p. 225.

61. These essays are, respectively, Said, "Orientalism Reconsidered," in Barker et al., *Literature*, pp. 210–29, and Said, "*Orientalism*, an Afterword."

62. Said, *Culture*, p. 18.

63. Anselm Gerhard, in his study of early nineteenth-century French opera, portrays the French audience of the 1830s as already considerably more passive than the Italian audiences of the preceding century (see Gerhard, *Verstädterung*, p. 27). Wagner, using the resources of a new technology and of his own musical invention, simply took this willingness of the audience to submit itself a crucial further step.

Chapter 7

1. Nono-Schoenberg, ed., p. 435.

2. Stuckenschmidt, "Mahagonny," *Die Scene* 20 (1930); rpt. in Lee et al., *Mahagonny*, p. 32.

3. Stuckenschmidt, *Arnold Schönberg*, p. 296.

4. In his treatise on the aesthetics of music, Carl Dahlhaus juxtaposed *Moses und Aron* and *Mahagonny* to show how both contain elements that can count as both progressive and retrograde, though in a distinctly different manner within each work. See Dahlhaus, *Esthetics*, pp. 68–69.

5. Schoenberg, *Style*, p. 296.

6. Weill's editor David Drew dates Adorno's cooling off toward Weill to before the two men went into exile. After *Mahagonny*, Weill's turn to a more "classical," less "explosive" style caused Adorno to lose faith in the composer's innovative powers. Drew also stresses the difficulty that Adorno must have felt championing a composer whom his idol Schoenberg despised. See Drew, ed., *Über Kurt Weill*, pp. viii–xi.

7. The nature and the extent of Hauptmann's role, as well as those of

other lover-collaborators, in the creation of Brecht's texts has been much in dispute. John Fuegi's *Brecht and Company*, a book dedicated to exposing what he claims to be a cover-up of the extent to which these collaborators were responsible for Brecht's oeuvre, discusses Hauptmann's role in these three works, as well as in *Happy End*, on pp. 143–44, 193–97, 215–17, 219–21. For an angry reply from other Brecht scholars, none of whom deny Hauptmann's role but assess it as smaller than Fuegi claims, see John Willett et al., "John Fuegi's *Brecht and Company*: A Summary of Problems and Errors," in Willett, ed., *Brecht damals und heute*, pp. 284, 292, 296–97.

8.   For a detailed study of the gap that developed during and after the work on *Mahagonny* in the artistic goals that each of the two collaborators was attempting to pursue, see Stephen Hinton, "The Concept of Epic Opera: Theoretical Anomalies in the Brecht-Weill Partnership," in Danuser et al., *Das musikalische Kunstwerk*, pp. 285–94.

9.   For a description of their conflict, see John Fuegi, "Most Unpleasant Things with *The Threepenny Opera*: Weill, Brecht, and Money," in Kowalke, ed., *New Orpheus*, p. 171. The financial dealings between the two are discussed throughout this article (pp. 157–82).

10. Lee et al., *Mahagonny*, p. 87.

11. See Taylor, *Kurt Weill*, pp. 279–80. For Weill's and Lenya's correspondence on the matter, see Symonette and Kowalke, eds., *Speak Low*, pp. 328–29, 331, 332, 334, and 336.

12. See Willett, *Brecht in Context*, pp. 180–82, for a description of Brecht's changing relationship to Marxism during this period.

13. For a history of the controversy and ultimate closing of the Kroll, see Curjel, *Experiment*, pp. 77–84; documents surrounding the Kroll crisis are reproduced on pp. 385–500. Although Weill had counted on the Kroll for *Mahagonny*'s premiere, Otto Klemperer, the musical director, despite his initial interest in the score, rejected the opera, presumably because he objected to the brothel scene (which, as it turns out, was later omitted at the opera's Leipzig premiere). For an account of Klemperer's rejection, see Heyworth, *Otto Klemperer*, 1: 294–98. Heyworth attributes the conductor's change of mind at the time to his having entered the depressive stage of his bipolar cycle. He also attributes Klemperer's decision the preceding year not to produce Schoenberg's *Von heute auf morgen* to a similar mental state (p. 292).

14. Schoenberg, *Style*, pp. 336–37.

15. "Building the City," p. 13.

16. Ibid., p. 14.

17. Lee et al., *Mahagonny*, p. 53.

18. See Jelavich, *Berlin Cabaret*, pp. 37–61.

19. On the impact of the cabaret and *commedia dell'arte* on *Pierrot lunaire*, see Dunsby, *Schoenberg: Pierrot*, pp. 4–9.

20. For Stravinsky on *Pierrot*, see Stravinsky and Craft, *Conversations*, pp. 68–71; for Weill on this piece, see *WM*, 225, 252.

21. Kowalke, *Kurt Weill*, pp. 296–98, and Hinton, "Vom Songspiel."

22. "Building the City," pp. 15–16, 18.

23. Schwarz, "Steve Reich," p. 13.

24. On Weill's "incorporating nascent features of what was to become epic opera" even before his collaboration with Brecht, see Susan C. Cook, "*Der Zar läßt sich photographieren*: Weill and Comic Opera," in Kowalke, ed., *New Orpheus*, p. 84.

25. See Hinton, "The Concept of Epic Opera: Theoretical Anomalies in the Brecht-Weill Partnership," in Danuser et al., *Das musikalische Kunstwerk*, pp. 285–94.

26. Ringer, *Arnold Schoenberg*, p. 98. Schoenberg's notes to Brecht's "Notes" are still unpublished. Ringer summarizes Schoenberg's comments (pp. 97–98), from which he quotes briefly.

27. Quoted in Smith, *Schoenberg*, p. 232.

28. Lee et al., *Mahagonny*, p. 36.

29. On the rejection of the oratorio proposal, see Stuckenschmidt, *Arnold Schönberg*, p. 305. On the original plans for the oratorio and their transformation into the opera, see White, *Schoenberg*, pp. 92–112.

30. On the history of Schoenberg's use of this discourse, see Stadlen, "Schoenberg's Speech-Song."

31. Lee et al., eds., *Mahagonny*, p. 39.

32. Ibid., p. 51.

33. Schwarz, "Steve Reich," p. 12.

34. "Building the City," p. 13.

35. See Kaes et al., eds., *Weimar Republic*.

36. From "A Four-Point Program for Jewry," in Ringer, *Arnold Schoenberg*, p. 235.

37. Schoenberg, *Style*, p. 180.

38. Ringer, pp. 234–36.

39. Although earlier published in Italian (see Schoenberg, *Testi poetici*, pp.

77–150), the play did not appear in its original German or in English translation until 1994. For more detailed discussions of the play, see Mäckelmann, pp. 70–138; Ringer, pp. 58–64 and, for a translation of one of Aruns's speeches in the play, pp. 227–29; and Lindenberger, "Arnold Schoenberg's *Der biblische Weg*," several passages of which have been adapted for the present discussion.

40.   Schoenberg, *Der biblische Weg*, p. 302.
41.   Ibid., p. 328.
42.   Yamaguchi, "Der Gedanke," pp. 11–12.
43.   Schoenberg, *Briefe*, p. 165.
44.   Ibid., p. 188.
45.   Wörner, *Gotteswort*, and Steck, *Moses*.
46.   Schoenberg, *Briefe*, p. 298.
47.   Abraham, "Schoenberg, Arnold," in Blom, ed., *Grove's Dictionary*, 7: 573.
48.   Schoenberg, *Briefe*, p. 298.
49.   Ibid., p. 153–54.
50.   Quoted in Reich, *Arnold Schönberg*, p. 129.
51.   Smith, *Schoenberg*, p. 171. An even bolder statement was reported by Schoenberg's brother-in-law, Rudolf Kolisch, to whom Schoenberg claimed "he had found something which would assure the hegemony of German music for centuries" (Smith, *Schoenberg*, p. 205).
52.   Quoted in E. Randol Schoenberg, "Arnold Schoenberg," p. 166.
53.   On his identification with Einstein, see Schoenberg, *Style*, pp. 51–52. For a history of his friendship and correspondence with Einstein, see E. Randol Schoenberg, "Arnold Schoenberg." For a further discussion of Schoenberg's correspondence with Wise, see Ringer, pp. 150–60.
54.   Ringer, *Arnold Schoenberg*, p. 243.
55.   Ibid. For a detailed discussion of "A Four-Point Program," see pp. 138–47; Ringer reproduces the whole document on pp. 230–44.
56.   This excerpt is printed in Ringer, *Arnold Schoenberg*, p. 147.
57.   Lee et al., eds., *Mahagonny*, p. 39.
58.   Ibid., p. 29.
59.   Benjamin, *Gesammelte Schriften*, vol. 2, pt. 2: 546.
60.   This version, produced in 1963, seven years after Brecht's death, was, according to David Drew, "a 60-minute play with incidental music" that "is faithful enough to the spirit of Brecht's famous 'Anmerkun-

gen'" but "bears no relation . . . to the art of musical composition as Weill understood it" (Drew, *Kurt Weill: A Handbook*, p. 174).

61. Pretzsch, "Cosima Wagner," in Pretzsch, ed., *Bayreuther Festspielführer*, pp. 6–10.

62. "Siegfried Wagner," in Pretzsch, ed., *Bayreuther Festspielführer*, p. 21.

63. Karl Alfons Meyer, "Hans von Bülow," in Pretzsch, ed., *Bayreuther Festspielführer*, p. 87.

64. Alfred Weidemann, "Verdi und Wagner," in Pretzsch, ed., *Bayreuther Festspielführer*, pp. 153–59.

65. Richard Reinhardt, "Durch Mitleid wissend . . . ," in Pretzsch, ed., *Bayreuther Festspielführer*, p. 106.

66. On the leitmotifs of *Moses und Aron* and their development in the course of the opera, see White, *Schoenberg*, pp. 160–225, 230, 248–56. Dahlhaus has cautioned against making too much of *Moses und Aron* as a Wagnerian music-drama; despite the larger structure that Schoenberg employs, the music of this opera, he reminds us, "is separated from Wagner by a historical rupture so profound that one more profound can hardly be imagined" (Dahlhaus, *Esthetics*, p. 69).

67. For some disparaging remarks about Bayreuth's tradition-boundedness made as early as 1912, see Schoenberg, *Style*, pp. 491–96.

68. Ibid., pp. 173–74.

69. Ibid., p. 503.

70. Busoni, *Entwurf*, p. 19.

71. On the development of this early version into the final opera, see Hinton, "Vom Songspiel." As Hinton puts it succinctly in another essay, the full-length opera "oscillates between two stylistic extremes: [Weill's] so-called 'song style' . . . at one extreme and a more austere 'neo-classical' idiom at the other" ("*Lehrstück*: An Aesthetics of Performance," in Gilliam, ed., *Music*, p. 71).

72. "Building the City," p. 15.

73. Ernst Latzko, "Weill-Brechts *Mahagonny*," in Drew, ed., *Über Kurt Weill*, p. 57.

74. Ibid., p. 56.

75. For a list of the various dance forms to be found in Weill's stage works composed in Germany, see Kowalke, *Kurt Weill*, pp. 120–22.

76. Berg, "The Problem of Opera," included in Reich, *Alban Berg*, pp. 63–66.

77. Drew, "Weill and Schoenberg," pp. 12–13. Drew also calls attention to the influence of Schoenberg on Weill's work (p. 11). See also Alan Chapman, "Crossing the Cusp: The Schoenberg Connection," in Kowalke, ed., *New Orpheus*, pp. 103–29.

78. On *Lulu*'s debt to *Mahagonny* as well as to other Weill compositions, see Douglas Jarman, "Weill and Berg: *Lulu* as Epic Opera," in Kowalke, ed., *New Orpheus*, pp. 147–56.

79. Thomson, *Virgil Thomson*, p. 227. Schoenberg's remark was evidently occasioned by Darius Milhaud's inviting him to the ballet, which Schoenberg refused to attend because of his distaste for Weill's music. The work in question was presumably *Die sieben Todsünden*.

80. Schoenberg's caustic annotations to Weill's piece are published in Ringer, *Arnold Schoenberg*, pp. 91–93.

81. Schoenberg, *Style*, pp. 476–77.

82. The notice is reprinted in *AGS*, 18: 544–47. For a discussion of this notice, see David Drew, "Reflections on the Last Years: *Der Kuhhandel* as a Key Work," in Kowalke, ed., *New Orpheus*, pp. 218–19; for further observations on the Weill-Adorno relationship, see pp. 248–49n and 252–53.

83. Quoted in Smith, *Schoenberg*, p. 151n.

84. From a letter that Weill wrote to Lotte Lenya. See Symonette and Kowalke, eds., *Speak Low*, p. 320.

85. Burckhardt, *Civilization*. See especially the section entitled "The Development of the Individual" (pp. 121–44). On the significance of Burckhardt's concept of individualism, see Watt, *Myths*, pp. 120–22.

86. Schorske, *Fin-de-Siècle Vienna*, pp. 322–66.

87. Willett, *Art*, pp. 227–28.

88. Gay, *Weimar Culture*, pp. 147–64.

89. Laqueur, *Weimar*, p. 40.

90. Besides the books by Willett, Gay, and Laqueur cited here, I mention such representative works as Barnouw, *Weimar Intellectuals*; Bullivant, ed., *Culture*; Hermand and Trommler, *Kultur*; Kaes et al., *Weimar Republic*; Phelan, ed., *Weimar Dilemma*; Raulet and Fürnkäs, *Weimar*; Schrader and Schebera, *"Golden" Twenties*; Willett, *Theatre*, and idem., *Weimar Years*.

91. On the influence of Herzl's writings on Schoenberg, above all on *Der biblische Weg*, see Mäckelmann, *Arnold Schönberg*, pp. 107–19.

92. For Jabotinsky's influence on the program of the Likud party when it came to power during the 1970s, see Erich and Rael Jean Isaac, "The Impact."
93. See Klatzkin, *Probleme*, p. 167.
94. Ibid., pp. 106–107.
95. See Hutcheon, *Theory*, pp. 62–63.

Chapter 8

1. "Ein teurer Spaß." Other statements claiming a parodistic intention can be found, for instance, in "Jeder für sich" and in "Komponierte Opern-Zerstörung."
2. Lindenberger, *Opera*, p. 15.
3. For discussions of such forms of parody, see Hunter, "Some Representations," and Lindenberger, *Opera*, pp. 44–45, 80, 102–3.
4. Quoted in Oestreich, "Empty Chairs." In fairness to the generally avant-garde-sympathetic Hunt, I should add that he went on to describe the work as creating "such a wonderfully theatrical laugh of the mind that by upsetting all our ideas of how things ought to be, it's affectionate."
5. Retallack, ed., *Musicage*, pp. 221–22.
6. Zuber, "Entrümpelung," pp. 106–7.
7. Hutcheon, *Theory*, p. 11.
8. My description of Cage's procedures is drawn from the detailed appendices in Kuhn, "John Cage's *Europeras 1 & 2*." I am grateful to Laura Kuhn for sending me not only her dissertation but also audiotapes of *Europeras 1 & 2* and *Europeras 3 & 4*. Her dissertation is invaluable both for the information in the appendices and for her depiction of Cage's intellectual traditions in the main body of her text. Kuhn's relation to the *Europeras* project is unique: as Cage's assistant before and during the Frankfurt production, she researched the costume designs used in the production, and as a research scholar she has presented the first detailed examination of the work in whose creation she participated.
9. For the "texts" surrounding *Europera 5*—lists of performances and props, directions for staging, time-brackets for performers and electronic instruments—see Retallack, ed., *Musicage*, pp. 333–40.
10. Ibid., p. 221.
11. On the meaning of chance operations in contexts as diverse as experi-

mental fiction, theories of time, and computer science, see the essay by N. Katherine Hayles, "Chance Operations: Cagean Paradox and Contemporary Science," in Perloff and Junkerman, eds., *John Cage*, pp. 226–41.

12. Communicated by Culver in a personal letter of March 10, 1995. Culver added that "John [Cage] took great pride in the lighting for the *Europeras*, and often cited lighting as the element most radically brought up-to-date by the work." I am grateful to Culver for explaining not only the lighting but many other details that I have incorporated into this chapter.

13. Quoted in Kuhn, "John Cage's *Europeras 1 & 2*," pp. 609–10.

14. For an analysis of the meaning of the monarch's box in Britain, see Orgel, *Illusion*, p. 16.

15. On some cultural meanings of the opera house, see Lindenberger, *Opera*, pp. 167, 236–39, 242–43, 272–73.

16. Tambling, *Opera*, p. 14.

17. Quoted by Gronemeyer, "Der Zufall." I have translated Gronemeyer's German translation of Cage's words in her interview with him.

18. Retallack, ed., *Musicage*, p. 223.

19. Ibid.

20. Quoted by Durner, "Past," p. 13. It is only fair to add that this comment was made in response to a question that Cage was asked about his attitude toward the presumed arsonist whose burning of the Frankfurt Opera House just before the premiere of *Europeras 1 & 2* had forced a month's postponement of the opening and also a change of venue to another theater. The report that the arsonist was an unemployed emigré from East Germany set off the contrast that Cage drew between the lot of the poor and the well-heeled audience that frequents the opera house.

21. For a longer discussion of the word-music debate in operatic history, see Lindenberger, *Opera*, pp. 108–44.

22. According to Kuhn, *your operas* might also suggest Cage's "populist leanings" (Kuhn, "John Cage's *Europeras 1 & 2*," p. 2). Thus, if I may extrapolate from Kuhn's observation, Cage might have been saying, "I am giving you *your own* operas, which, now that I have scrambled the contents of traditional European opera, you will find more suitable to your needs."

23. Whitman, *Leaves*, p. 732.

24. Although Schoenberg did not devote himself to literary endeavors to the degree that Cage did, his expressionist-style play, *Der biblische Weg*, described in Chapter 7 in relation to *Moses und Aron*, is substantial enough to allow him to be called a writer independent of his achievements in other arts.

25. Cage, *Year*, pp. 45–46.

26. The opera's music-drama form, as it turned out, did not bother John Cage, who called it "very beautiful to hear" at the same time that he said, "Wagner of course I find hopeless" (Retallack, ed., *Musicage*, p. 223).

27. Cage, *X*, pp. 53–101.

28. For assessments of Cage's role in the development of modern music, see Hermann Danuser, "Rationalität und Zufall—John Cage und die experimentelle Musik in Europa," in Welsch and Pries, eds., *Aesthetik*, pp. 91–105, and Robert P. Morgan, "Rethinking Musical Culture: Canonic Reformulations in a Post-Tonal Age," in Bergeron and Bohlman, eds., *Disciplining Music*, pp. 44–63. Danuser explains the cooling of the relationship between Cage and Pierre Boulez as resulting from the inability of Boulez, who sought to continue Schoenberg's serialism, to accept the radical form of experimentalism in which his senior American colleague engaged when he turned his back on rationality and authorial intentionality. For a striking inside view of this cooling off, see Nattiez, ed., *The Boulez-Cage Correspondence*. Morgan suggests that with another generation of hindsight the serialism represented by Boulez does not appear so opposed to Cage's anti-intentionality as it seemed at the time, for both approaches represent "an attempt to arrive at compositional decisions through an outside agent, in one case operations of a quasi-mathematical character, . . . in the other, operations of chance" (p.52).

29. The significance of Schoenberg's pronouncement—whether or not he actually uttered it—was confirmed by the fact that a number of the obituaries attempting to define Cage's achievement made note of this distinction between composer and inventor (see, for example, Kozinn, "John Cage," p. A17). The columnist John Rockwell, writing more than a week after the initial obituaries appeared, gave Schoenberg's remark an interesting twist by defending Cage's music (especially that of his early period) as "composition," not simply "invention." Rockwell's column bore the telling headline, "Cage Merely an Inventor? Not a Chance."

30. Although Duchamp's example is central to Cage's development, few Cage pieces are as thoroughly suffused with Duchamp's ideas as the *Europeras*, if only because, like Duchamp before him, Cage built this work out of ready-made materials. Many of the early reviews mention the influence of Duchamp. If my argument for Cage as "New World inventor" seems undercut because of the strong influence of that Old World inventor-artist Duchamp, I would reply that, as a long-term exile from France, Duchamp had himself established a distance from the aesthetic ambience of his European contemporaries. Note also Marjorie Perloff's demonstration of how Cage has distanced *himself* from such characteristically "European" aspects of Duchamp as his irony and his erotic quality; see Perloff, "'A duchamp unto my self': 'Writing through' Marcel," in Perloff and Junkerman, eds., *John Cage*, pp. 100–124. On Cage and Duchamp, see also Daniel Charles, "Cage et Duchamp," in Charles, *Gloses*, pp. 183–96, and Gottwald, "John Cage."

31. For a detailed discussion of contemporary iconoclastic stagings as attempts to introduce a postmodern sensibility into the opera house, see the discussion in my chapter entitled "From Opera to Postmodernity," in Lindenberger, *History*, pp. 163–88. See also Zuber's contrast of these stagings with Cage's different project in *Europeras 1 & 2* ("Entrümpelung," p. 102.)

32. For those who may not remember it, the *Hellzapoppin* to which Cage refers was a zany Broadway musical of the early 1940s full of absurd antics that often broke through the theatrical frame.

33. For a longer discussion of Glass's early operas, see Lindenberger, *History*, pp. 180–83, as well as Chapter 6 of this volume.

34. Schnebel, "'Wie ich das schaffe?'," p. 54.

35. Cage's German follower Dieter Schnebel has explained the composer's attempt to rid the audience of expectations in these terms: "If we find music boring, then it is only because we bring expectations to bear on it—if I listen without expectations, then I can't get bored because I am then open to every moment" (quoted in "Bunte Suche").

36. For a study of Cage's *Musicircuses*, see the essay by Charles Junkerman, "'nEw / foRms of living together'": The Model of the Musicircus," in Perloff and Junkerman, eds., *John Cage*, pp. 39–64.

37. Cage, *For the Birds*, p. 52.

38. Ibid., pp. 52–53.

Finale

1. Dean, *Handel's Dramatic Oratorios*, p. 267. Note also the comparison between athletes and opera singers in Mordden, *Demented*, pp. 11–12.

2. Poizat, *Angel's Cry*, pp. 12–28, 209–11.

3. See Castle, *Apparitional Lesbian*, p. 224. On the history of lesbian diva cults, see pp. 203–19.

4. On the history of the later addition of Manrico's high C, see Budden, *Operas*, 2: 98–99.

5. On the "popular" aspects of romantic opera, see Rosen, *Romantic Generation*, pp. 602–8; on Bellini and Meyerbeer, pp. 608–45.

6. Joseph Kerman, "Reading *Don Giovanni*," in Miller, ed., *Myths*, p, 116.

Works Cited

Abbate, Carolyn. *Unsung Voices: Opera and Musical Narrative in the Nineteenth Century.* Princeton, N.J.: Princeton University Press, 1991.

Abrams, M. H. *Natural Supernaturalism: Tradition and Revolution in Romantic Literature.* New York: Norton, 1971.

Adams, John. *The Death of Klinghoffer.* [New York]: Boosey and Hawkes, n.d. [ca. 1994].

Addison, Joseph, and Richard Steele. *The Spectator.* Ed. Donald F. Bond. 5 vols. Oxford: Clarendon Press, 1965.

Adorno, Theodor. *Gesammelte Schriften.* Ed. Rolf Tiedemann. 20 vols. Frankfurt: Suhrkamp, 1970–86.

Aldrich-Moodie, James. "False Fidelity: *Othello, Otello,* and Their Critics." *Comparative Drama* 28 (1994): 324–47.

Algarotti, Francesco. *Essay on Painting.* London: L. Davis and C. Reymers, 1764.

———. *Saggio sopra l'opera in musica.* 2d ed. Leghorn: Marco Coltellini, 1763.

Ambros, August Wilhelm. *Geschichte der Musik.* 2d ed. 5 vols. Leipzig: Leuckart, 1881–93.

Aravamudan, Srivinas. "Lady Mary Wortley Montagu in the *Hammam*: Masquerade, Womanliness, and Levantinization." *ELH* 62 (1995): 69–104.

Arlt, Wulf, Ernest Lichtenhahn, and Hans Oesch, eds. *Gattungen der Musik in Einzeldarstellungen: Gedenkschrift für Leo Schrade.* Bern: Francke, 1973.

Arnold, Denis, and Nigel Fortune, eds. *The Monteverdi Companion.* New York: Norton, 1968.

———. *The New Monteverdi Companion.* London: Faber and Faber, 1985.

Arnold, Matthew. *Poetry and Criticism of Matthew Arnold.* Ed. Dwight Culler. Boston: Houghton Mifflin, 1961.

Artaud, Antonin. *Artaud on Theatre*. Ed. Claude Schumacher. London: Methuen, 1989.

———. *Oeuvres complètes*. 26 vols. Paris: Gallimard, 1956–.

Ashbrook, William, and Harold Powers. *Puccini's 'Turandot': The End of the Great Tradition*. Princeton, N.J.: Princeton University Press, 1991.

Barbier, Patrick. *The World of the Castrati: The History of an Extraordinary Operatic Phenomenon*. Trans. Margaret Crosland. London: Souvenir Press, 1996.

Barish, Jonas. *The Antitheatrical Prejudice*. Berkeley: University of California Press, 1981.

Barker, Francis, Peter Hulme, Margaret Iversen, and Diana Loxley. *Literature, Politics and Theory: Papers from the Essex Conference 1976–84*. London: Methuen, 1986.

Barnouw, Dagmar. *Weimar Intellectuals and the Threat of Modernity*. Bloomington: Indiana University Press, 1988.

Barthes, Roland. *S/Z: An Essay*. Trans. Richard Howard. New York: Hill and Wang, 1974.

Bauman, Thomas. *W. A. Mozart: 'Die Entführung aus dem Serail.'* Cambridge, Eng.: Cambridge University Press, 1989.

Becker, Heinz, ed. *Die "Couleur locale" in der Oper des 19. Jahrhunderts*. Regensburg: Gustav Bosse, 1976.

Bellori, Giovan Pietro. *Le vite de' pittori, scultori e architetti moderni*. Ed. Evelina Borea. Turin: Einaudi, 1976.

Benjamin, Walter. *Gesammelte Schriften*. Ed. Rolf Tiedemann and Hermann Schweppenhäuser. 7 vols. Frankfurt: Suhrkamp, 1972–89.

Berenson, Bernard. *Caravaggio: His Incongruity and His Fame*. London: Chapman and Hall, 1953.

Berger, Karol. *Theories of Chromatic and Enharmonic Music in Late 16th Century Italy*. Ann Arbor: UMI Research Press, 1980.

Bergeron, Katherine. "The Castrato as History." *Cambridge Opera Journal* 8 (1996): 167–84.

Bergeron, Katherine, and Philip V. Bohlman, eds. *Disciplining Music: Musicology and Its Canons*. Chicago: University of Chicago Press, 1992.

Bermbach, Udo, and Dieter Borchmeyer. *Richard Wagner—'Der Ring des Nibelungen': Ansichten des Mythos*. Stuttgart: Metzler, 1995.

Berthier, Philippe. *Stendhal et ses peintres italiens*. Geneva: Droz, 1977.

Betzwieser, Thomas. *Exotismus und "Türkenoper" in der französischen Musik des Ancien Régime*. Laaber: Laaber-Verlag, 1993.

Bianconi, Lorenzo. *Music in the Seventeenth Century.* Trans. David Bryant. Cambridge, Eng.: Cambridge University Press, 1987.

Bianconi, Lorenzo, and Giorgio Pestelli, eds. *Geschichte der italienischen Oper.* Trans. Claudia Just and Paola Riesz. 6 vols. Laaber: Laaber-Verlag, 1990–92.

Blom, Eric, ed. *Grove's Dictionary of Music.* 5th ed. 10 vols. London: Macmillan, 1950.

Bloom, Harold. *Shelley's Mythmaking.* New Haven: Yale University Press, 1959.

Bloom, Harold, ed. *Deconstruction and Criticism.* New York: Seabury Press, 1979.

Boileau, Nicolas. *Oeuvres complètes.* Ed. Françoise Escal. Paris: Gallimard, 1966.

Bologna, Ferdinando. *L'incredulità di Caravaggio e l'esperienza delle "cose naturali."* Turin: Bollati Boringhieri, 1992.

Borchmeyer, Dieter. *Richard Wagner: Theory and Theatre.* Trans. Stewart Spencer. Oxford: Clarendon Press, 1991.

Borchmeyer, Dieter, and Jörg Salaquarda, eds. *Nietzsche und Wagner: Stationen einer epochalen Begegnung.* 2 vols. Frankfurt: Insel, 1994.

Boulez, Pierre, Patrice Chéreau, Richard Peduzzi, and Jacques Schmidt, eds. *Histoire d'un "Ring."* Paris: Robert Laffont, 1980.

Bovi, Arturo. *Caravaggio.* Florence: Edizioni d'arte il fiorino, 1974.

Brecht, Bertolt. *Stücke.* 14 vols. Frankfurt: Suhrkamp, 1953–67.

Brett, Philip, Elizabeth Wood, and Gary C. Thomas, eds. *Queering the Pitch: The New Gay and Lesbian Musicology.* New York: Routledge, 1994.

Brooks, Cleanth. *The Well Wrought Urn: Studies in the Structure of Poetry.* New York: Harcourt, Brace, 1947.

Brown, Jane K., Meredith Lee, and Thomas P. Saine, eds. *Interpreting Goethe's 'Faust' Today.* Columbia, S.C.: Camden House, 1994.

Browning, Robert. *On the Poet Objective and Subjective; on the Latter's Aim; on Shelley as Man and Poet.* 2d ed. London: Trübner, 1881.

Budden, Julian. *The Operas of Verdi.* 3 vols. New York: Oxford University Press, 1973–81.

Buelow, George J. "The *Loci Topici* and Affect in Late Baroque Music: Heinichen's Practical Demonstration." *Music Review* 27 (1966): 161–76.

"Building the City of . . . Mahagonny." *Kurt Weill Newsletter* 13 (fall 1995): 7–19.

Bullivant, Keith, ed. *Culture and Society in the Weimar Republic.* Manchester: Manchester University Press, 1977.

"Bunte Suche nach dem Nicht-Sinn: *Europeras 1 & 2* von John Cage in Frankfurt uraufgeführt." *Suddeutsche Zeitung*, December 14, 1987, 32.

Burckhardt, Jacob. *Der Cicerone: Eine Anleitung zum Genuß der Kunstwerke Italiens.* Ed. Wilhelm Bode. 8th ed. 4 vols. Leipzig: E. A. Seemann, 1900–1901.

———. *The Civilization of the Renaissance in Italy.* Trans. S. G. C. Middlemore. Rev. Irene Gordon. New York: New American Library, 1960.

Burney, Charles. *A General History of Music: From the Earliest Ages to the Present Period (1789).* 2 vols. New York: Dover, 1957.

———. *The Present State of Music in France and Italy.* 1773. New York: Broude Brothers, 1969.

Busch, Hans, ed. *Verdi's 'Aida': The History of an Opera in Letters and Documents.* Minneapolis: University of Minnesota Press, 1978.

———. *Verdi's 'Otello' and 'Simon Boccanegra' (Revised Version) in Letters and Documents.* 2 vols. Oxford: Clarendon Press, 1988.

Busoni, Ferruccio. *Entwurf einer neuen Ästhetik der Tonkunst.* 2d ed. 1916. Hamburg: Karl Dieter Wagner, 1973.

Butler, Judith P. *Gender Trouble: Feminism and the Subversion of Identity.* New York: Routledge, 1990.

Byron, George Gordon, Lord. *The Complete Poetical Works.* Ed. Jerome McGann. 7 vols. Oxford: Clarendon Press, 1980–93.

———. *"The flesh is frail": Byron's Letters and Journals.* Ed. Leslie A. Marchand. 12 vols. London: John Murray, 1973–82.

Cage, John. *For the Birds: In Conversation with Daniel Charles.* Boston: Marion Boyars, 1981.

———. *X: Writings '79–'82.* Middletown, Conn.: Wesleyan University Press, 1983.

———. *A Year from Monday: New Lectures and Writings.* Middletown, Conn.: Wesleyan University Press, 1969.

Campbell, Jane. *The Retrospective Review (1820–1828) and the Revival of Seventeenth-Century Poetry.* Waterloo, Ontario: Waterloo Lutheran University, [1972].

Caravaggio e il suo tempo. Naples: Electa, 1985.

Castle, Terry. *The Apparitional Lesbian: Female Homosexuality and Modern Culture.* New York: Columbia University Press, 1993.

Charles, Daniel. *Gloses sur John Cage.* Paris: Union Générale d'Editions, 1978.

Clément, Catherine. *L'Opéra, ou la défaite des femmes.* Paris: B. Grasset, 1979.

Trans. Betsy Wing as *Opera, or the Undoing of Women*. Minneapolis: University of Minnesota Press, 1988.

Coffin, Charles. *John Donne and the New Philosophy*. New York: Columbia University Press, 1937.

Cooke, Deryck. *I Saw the World End: A Study of Wagner's Ring*. London: Oxford University Press, 1979.

Corse, Sandra. *Wagner and the New Consciousness: Language and Love in the 'Ring.'* Rutherford, N.J.: Fairleigh Dickinson University Press, 1990.

Cott, Jonathan. Liner essay for Steve Reich, *The Cave*. Nonesuch compact disc 79327-2, 1995.

Curjel, Hans. *Experiment Krolloper: 1927–1931*. Ed. Eigel Kruttge. Munich: Prestel-Verlag, 1975.

Curran, Stuart. *Poetic Form and British Romanticism*. New York: Oxford University Press, 1986.

Curtis, Alan. "*La Poppea Impasticciata* or, Who Wrote the Music to *L'Incoronazione* (1643)?" *Journal of the American Musicological Society* 42 (1989): 23–54.

Dahlhaus, Carl. *Esthetics of Music*. Trans. William W. Austin. Cambridge, Eng.: Cambridge University Press, 1982.

———. "Ethos und Pathos in Glucks "Iphigenie auf Tauris." *Musikforschung* 27 (1974): 289–300.

———. *Die Idee der absoluten Musik*. Kassel: Bärenreiter, 1978.

———. *Richard Wagner's Music Dramas*. Trans. Mary Whittall. Cambridge, Eng.: Cambridge University Press, 1979.

———. "What Is a Musical Drama?" *Cambridge Opera Journal* 1 (1991): 95–111.

———. "Zum Affektbegriff der frühdeutschen Oper." *Hamburger Jahrbuch für Musikwissenschaft* 5 (1981): 107–11.

———, ed. *Die Musik des 18. Jahrhunderts*. Vol. 5 of Dahlhaus, ed., *Neues Handbuch der Musikwissenschaft*. Laaber: Laaber-Verlag, 1985.

Danuser, Hermann, Helga de la Motte, Silke Leopold, and N. Miller, eds. *Das musikalische Kunstwerk: Geschichte, Aesthetik, Theorie: Festschrift Carl Dahlhaus zum 60. Geburtstag*. Laaber: Laaber-Verlag, 1988.

Darcy, Warren. "*Creatio ex nihilo*: The Genesis, Structure and Meaning of the *Rheingold* Prelude." *19th-Century Music* 13 (1989): 79–100.

Davidson, Michael. "Refiguring Shelley: Postmodern Recuperations of Romanticism," paper presented at the annual meeting of the Modern Language Association, San Francisco, Dec. 1991.

Davie, Donald. *Purity of Diction in English Verse*. London: Chatto and Windus, 1952.

Dean, Winton. *Bizet*. Rev. ed. London: J. M. Dent, 1975.

———. *Handel's Dramatic Oratorios and Masques*. London: Oxford University Press, 1959.

Dean, Winton, and John Merrill Knapp. *Handel's Operas: 1704–1726*. Oxford: Clarendon Press, 1987.

Deathridge, John. "Wagner's Sketches for the 'Ring.'" *Musical Times* 118 (1977): 383–89.

Della Seta, Fabrizio. "'O cieli azzuri': Exoticism and Dramatic Discourse in *Aida*." *Cambridge Opera Journal* 3 (1991): 49–62.

Donne, John. *Poems of John Donne*. Ed. Herbert J. C. Grierson. 2 vols. Oxford: Oxford University Press, 1912.

Drew, David. *Kurt Weill: A Handbook*. London: Faber and Faber, 1987.

———. "Weill and Schoenberg." *Kurt Weill Newsletter* 12 (spring 1994): 10–13.

———, ed. *Über Kurt Weill*. Frankfurt: Suhrkamp, 1975.

Dreyfus, Laurence. "Early Music Defended Against Its Devotees: A Theory of Historical Performance in the Twentieth Century." *Musical Quarterly* 69 (1983): 297–322.

———. "Mozart as Early Music: A Romantic Antidote." *Early Music* 20 (1992): 297–309.

Dryden, John. *Plays: 'Albion and Albanus,' 'Don Sebastian,' 'Amphitrion.'* Ed. Earl Miner. Vol. 15 of Dryden, *Works*. Berkeley: University of California Press, 1976.

Duncan, Joseph. *The Revival of Metaphysical Poetry: The History of a Style, 1800 to the Present*. Minneapolis: University of Minnesota Press, 1959.

Dunsby, Jonathan. *Schoenberg: Pierrot lunaire*. Cambridge, Eng.: Cambridge University Press, 1992.

Durner, Leah. "Past and Future in John Cage's *Europeras 1 & 2*." *EAR Magazine* 13, no. 2 (Apr. 1988): 10–13.

"Ein teurer Spaß—oder mehr?" *Neue Zürcher Zeitung*, December 15, 1987.

Eliot, T. S. *Selected Essays*. 3d ed. London: Faber and Faber, 1951.

———. *To Criticize the Critic*. London: Faber and Faber, 1965.

———. *The Use of Poetry and the Use of Criticism*. London: Faber and Faber, 1933.

Elson, Arthur. *A History of Opera: Giving an Account of the Rise and Progress of the Different Schools, with a Description of the Master Works in Each*. Boston: L. C. Page, 1901.

Ewans, Michael. *Wagner and Aeschylus: The 'Ring' and the 'Oresteia.'* London: Faber and Faber, 1982.

Félibien, André. *Entretiens sur les vies et sur les ouvrages des plus excellens peintres anciens et modernes.* 2d ed. 2 vols. Paris: Denys Mariette, 1696.

Fenlon, Iain, and Peter N. Miller. *The Song of the Soul: Understanding 'Poppea.'* Royal Musical Association Monographs, no. 5. London: Royal Musical Association, 1992.

Fétis, F.-J. *Biographie universelle des musiciens.* 2d ed. 8 vols. Paris: Firmin-Didot, 1878–83.

Flaubert, Gustave. *Madame Bovary.* Ed. and trans. Paul de Man. New York: Norton, 1965.

Frank, Felicia Miller. *The Mechanical Song: Women, Voice, and the Artificial in Nineteenth-Century French Narrative.* Stanford, Calif.: Stanford University Press, 1995.

Fried, Michael. *Courbet's Realism.* Chicago: University of Chicago Press, 1990.

Friedlander, Walter. *Caravaggio Studies.* New York: Schocken, 1955.

Fry, Roger. "Settecentismo." *Burlington Magazine* 61 (Oct. 1922): 158–69.

Frye, Northrop. *Anatomy of Criticism: Four Essays.* Princeton, N.J.: Princeton University Press, 1957.

Fuegi, John. *Brecht and Company: Sex, Politics, and the Making of the Modern Drama.* New York: Grove, 1994.

Gay, Peter. *Weimar Culture: The Outsider as Insider.* New York: Harper, 1970.

Gerhard, Anselm. *Die Verstädterung der Oper: Paris und das Musiktheater des 19. Jahrhunderts.* Stuttgart: J. B. Metzler, 1992.

Gervinus, G. G. *Händel und Shakespeare: Zur Ästhetik der Tonkunst.* Leipzig: Wilhelm Engelmann, 1868.

Gilliam, Bryan, ed. *Music and Performance During the Weimar Republic.* Cambridge, Eng.: Cambridge University Press, 1994.

Glass, Philip. *The Music of Philip Glass.* Ed. Robert T. Jones. New York: Harper, 1987.

Goehr, Walter, conductor. *L'incoronazione di Poppea*, by Claudio Monteverdi. Concert Hall Society recording 1184, 1952.

Gottwald, Clytus, "John Cage und Marcel Duchamp." *Musik-Konzepte*, special issue on John Cage, vol. 1 (Apr. 1978): 132–46.

Gradenwitz, Peter. *Musik zwischen Orient und Okzident: Eine Kulturgeschichte der Wechselbeziehungen.* Wilhelmshaven: Heinrichshofen, 1977.

Granqvist, Raoul. "A 'Fashionable Poet' in New England in the 1890s: A

Study of the Reception of John Donne." *John Donne Journal* 4 (1985): 337–49.

———. *The Reputation of John Donne 1779–1873.* Dissertation, University of Uppsala, 1975.

Grey, Thomas. "Bodies of Evidence." *Cambridge Opera Journal* 8 (1996): 185–97.

———. *Wagner's Musical Prose: Texts and Contexts.* Cambridge, Eng.: Cambridge University Press, 1995.

Gronemeyer, Gisela. "Der Zufall regiert noch immer." *Kölner Stadt-Anzeiger*, Dec. 10, 1987.

Groos, Arthur. "Madame Butterfly: The Story." *Cambridge Opera Journal* 3 (1991): 125–58.

———. "Return of the Native: Japan in *Madame Butterfly / Madame Butterfly* in Japan." *Cambridge Opera Journal* 1 (1989): 167–94.

Groos, Arthur, and Roger Parker, eds. *Reading Opera.* Princeton, N.J.: Princeton University Press, 1988.

Grout, Donald Jay. *A Short History of Opera.* 2d ed. New York: Columbia University Press, 1965.

Hanslick, Eduard. *Am Ende des Jahrhunderts (1895–1899): Musikalische Kritiken und Schilderungen.* Berlin: Allgemeiner Verein für Deutsche Literatur, 1899.

———. *Die moderne Oper: Kritiken und Studien.* Berlin: A. Hofmann, 1875.

Harnoncourt, Nikolaus, conductor. *L'incoronazione di Poppea*, by Claudio Monteverdi. Teldec/Warner compact disc 2292-42547-2, 1986 (recorded 1974).

Harrison, Antony H., ed. *The Metaphysical Poets in the Nineteenth Century* (special issue). *John Donne Journal* 4 (1985).

Haskell, Harry. *The Early Music Revival: A History.* London: Thames and Hudson, 1988.

Haskin, Dayton. "Reading Donne's *Songs and Sonnets* in the Nineteenth Century." *John Donne Journal* 4 (1985): 225–52.

Hauer, Stanley R. "Wagner and the *Völospá*." *19th-Century Music* 15 (1991–92): 52–63.

Hawkins, Sir John. *A General History of the Science and Practice of Music.* 1776. 2 vols. London: Novello, Ewer & Co., 1875.

Heartz, Daniel. "Mozart and His Italian Contemporaries: 'La clemenza di Tito.'" In *Mozart-Jahrbuch 1978–79*, 275–93. Kassel: Bärenreiter, 1979.

Hegel, G. W. F. *Aesthetics: Lectures on Fine Art.* Trans. T. M. Knox. 2 vols. Oxford: Clarendon Press, 1975.

———. *Briefe von und an Hegel.* Ed. Johannes Hoffmeister. 4 vols. Hamburg: F. Meiner, 1969–81.

Heine, Heinrich. *Sämtliche Werke.* Ed. Ernst Elster. 7 vols. Leipzig: Bibliographisches Institut, n.d. [ca. 1890].

Henze-Döhring, Sabine. *Opera Seria, Opera Buffa und Mozarts 'Don Giovanni': Zur Gattungskonvergenz in der italienischen Oper des 18. Jahrhunderts.* Analecta Musicologica 24. Laaber: Laaber-Verlag, 1986.

Heriot, Angus. *The Castrati in Opera.* London: Calderbooks, 1960.

Hermand, Jost, and Frank Trommler. *Die Kultur der Weimarer Republik.* Munich: Nymphenburger-Verlag, 1978.

Heyworth, Peter. *Otto Klemperer: His Life and Times.* 2 vols. Cambridge, Eng.: Cambridge University Press, 1983–96.

Hickox, Richard, conductor. *L'incoronazione di Poppea,* by Claudio Monteverdi. Virgin Classics compact disc 90775-2, 1990.

Hinton, Stephen. *Kurt Weill: The Threepenny Opera.* Cambridge, Eng.: Cambridge University Press, 1990.

———. "Vom Songspiel zur Oper." Program for performance of *Aufstieg und Fall der Stadt Mahagonny,* by Kurt Weill, Frankfurt Opera, October 14, 1990, 45–56.

Hodgson, John A. "Coleridge, Puns, and 'Donne's First Poem': The Limbo of Rhetoric and the Conceptions of Wit." *John Donne Journal* 4 (1985): 181–200.

Hollard, T. L. "Flaubert's *Hérodias* and Massenet's *Hérodiade.*" *New Zealand Journal of French Studies* 13 (Nov. 1992): 15–31.

Holmes, Richard. *Shelley: The Pursuit.* New York: Dutton, 1975.

Hopkins, Gerard Manley. *Poems.* 4th ed. Ed. W. H. Gardner and N. H. Mackenzie. London: Oxford University Press, 1967.

Horowitz, Joseph. *Wagner Nights: An American History.* Berkeley: University of California Press, 1994.

Hugo, Victor. *Oeuvres poétiques.* Ed. Pierre Albouy. 3 vols. Paris: Gallimard, 1964–74.

Hunter, Mary. "Some Representations of *Opera Seria* in *Opera Buffa.*" *Cambridge Opera Journal* 3 (1991): 89–108.

Hutcheon, Linda. *A Theory of Parody: The Teachings of Twentieth-Century Art Forms.* New York: Methuen, 1985.

Hutcheon, Linda, and Michael Hutcheon. *Opera: Desire, Disease, Death.* Lincoln: University of Nebraska Press, 1996.

Isaac, Erich, and Rael Jean Isaac. "The Impact of Jabotinsky on Likud's Policies." *Middle East Review* 10 (Nov. 1977): 31–45.

"Jeder für sich—und alle durcheinander!" *NRZ*, December 15, 1987.

Jelavich, Peter. *Berlin Cabaret.* Cambridge, Mass.: Harvard University Press, 1993.

Kaes, Anton, Martin Jay, and Edward Dimendberg, eds. *The Weimar Republic: A Sourcebook.* Berkeley: University of California Press, 1994.

Kallab, Wolfgang. "Caravaggio." *Jahrbuch der Kunsthistorischen Sammlungen des allerhöchsten Kaiserhauses* 26 (1906–7): 272–92.

Kant, Immanuel. *Critique of Judgment.* Trans. Werner S. Pluhar. Indianapolis: Hackett, 1987.

Keast, William R., ed. *Seventeenth Century English Poetry: Modern Essays in Criticism.* 2d ed. Oxford: Oxford University Press, 1971.

Kenyon, Nicholas, ed. *Authenticity and Early Music: A Symposium.* Oxford: Oxford University Press, 1988.

Kerman, Joseph. *Opera as Drama.* New York: Vintage, 1956.

———. *Opera as Drama.* New and rev. ed. Berkeley: University of California Press, 1988.

———. "Wagner: Thoughts Out of Season." *Hudson Review* 13 (1960): 329–49.

Kidwai, Abdur Raheem. *Orientalism in Lord Byron's 'Turkish Tales.'* Lewiston, N.Y.: Mellen University Press, 1995.

Klatzkin, Jakob. *Probleme des modernen Judentums.* 3d ed. Berlin: Lambert Schneider, 1930.

Koch, Ernst. *Richard Wagner's Bühnenfestspiel 'Der Ring des Nibelungen' in seinem Verhältniss zur alten Sage wie zur modernen Nibelungendichtung betrachtet.* Leipzig: C. F. Kahnt, [1875].

Koestenbaum, Wayne. *The Queen's Throat: Opera, Homosexuality, and the Mystery of Desire.* New York: Poseidon Press, 1993.

Kolodin, Irving. *The Metropolitan Opera: 1883–1935.* New York: Oxford University Press, 1936.

"Komponierte Opern-Zerstörung." *Wiesbadener Tagblatt*, December 14, 1987.

Kost, Paul, ed. *Studien zur italienisch-deutschen Musikgeschichte I.* Analecta Musicologica 1. Cologne: Böhlau, 1963.

Kostelanetz, Richard. *Conversing with Cage.* New York: Limelight Editions, 1988.

Kowalke, Kim H. *Kurt Weill in Europe.* Ann Arbor: UMI Research Press, 1979.

———, ed. *A New Orpheus: Essays on Kurt Weill.* New Haven, Conn.: Yale University Press, 1986.

Kozinn, Allan. "John Cage, a Minimalist Enchanted with Sound, Dies." *New York Times,* Western edition, August 13, 1992, A1, A17.

Kramer, Lawrence. *Classical Music and Postmodern Knowledge.* Berkeley: University of California Press, 1995.

Kuhn, Laura Diane. "John Cage's *Europeras 1 & 2*: The Musical Means of Revolution." Dissertation, University of California, Los Angeles, 1992.

Laloy, Louis. "Claude Debussy: la simplicité en musique." *La Revue musicale* 6 (February 15, 1904): 106–11.

———. "Schola Cantorum—26 février." *La Revue musicale* 6 (March 15, 1904): 170.

Lanzi, Luigi. *The History of Painting in Italy.* Trans. Thomas Roscoe. 6 vols. London: W. Simpkin and R. Marshall, 1828.

Laqueur, Walter. *Weimar: A Cultural History, 1918–1933.* New York: Putnam, 1974.

Leask, Nigel. *British Romantic Writers and the East: Anxieties of Empire.* Cambridge, Eng.: Cambridge University Press, 1992.

Leavis, F. R. *Revaluation.* New York: Norton, 1963.

Lee, Joanna, Edward Harsh, and Kim Kowalke, eds. *Mahagonny: A Sourcebook.* New York: Kurt Weill Foundation for Music, 1995.

Leppard, Raymond, conductor. *L'incoronazione di Poppea,* by Claudio Monteverdi. Angel Records 3644, 1963.

Levy, Paul. "Waiting for the Next Wagner." *Wall Street Journal,* August 2, 1996, A12.

Lew, Joseph W. "Lady Mary's Portable Seraglio." *Eighteenth-Century Studies* 24 (1991): 432–50.

Lindenberger, Herbert. "Arnold Schoenberg's *Der biblische Weg* and *Moses und Aron*: On the Transactions of Aesthetics and Politics." *Modern Judaism* 9 (Feb. 1989): 55–70.

———. *Historical Drama: The Relation of Literature and Reality.* Chicago: University of Chicago Press, 1975.

———. *The History in Literature: On Value, Genre, Institutions.* New York: Columbia University Press, 1990.

———. *Opera: The Extravagant Art.* Ithaca, N.Y.: Cornell University Press, 1984.

————. *On Wordsworth's 'Prelude.'* Princeton, N.J.: Princeton University Press, 1963.

Lippmann, Friedrich, ed. *Studien zur italienisch-deutschen Musikgeschichte IX.* Analecta Musicologica 14. Cologne: Arno Verlag Hans Gerig, 1974.

Liszt, Franz. *Gesammelte Schriften.* Ed. L. Ramann. 6 vols. Leipzig: Breitkopf und Härtel, 1880–83.

Littlejohn, David. *The Ultimate Art: Essays Around and About Opera.* Berkeley: University of California Press, 1992.

Lloyd-Jones, Hugh. *Blood for the Ghosts: Classical Influences in the Nineteenth and Twentieth Centuries.* Baltimore: Johns Hopkins University Press, 1983.

Locke, Ralph P. "Constructing the Oriental 'Other': Saint-Saens's *Samson et Dalila. Cambridge Opera Journal* 3 (1991): 261–302.

Longhi, Roberto. *Breve ma veridica storia della pittura italiana.* Florence: Sansoni, 1980.

————. *Caravaggio.* Leipzig: Edition Leipzig, 1968.

————. "Due opere di Caravaggio." *L'Arte* 16 (1913): 161–64.

————. *'Me pinxit' e quesiti caravaggeschi: 1928–1934.* Florence: Sansoni, 1968.

Lowe, Lisa. *Critical Terrains: French and British Orientalisms.* Ithaca, N.Y.: Cornell University Press, 1991.

Lowinsky, Edward E. *Tonality and Atonality in Sixteenth-Century Music.* Berkeley: University of California Press, 1961.

Ludlam, F. H. "The Meteorology of Shelley's Ode." *Times Literary Supplement,* September 1, 1972, 1015–16. Replies: September 22, 1972, 1105, and September 29, 1972, 1157.

MacFarlane, Charles. *Reminiscences of a Literary Life.* New York: Charles Scribner's Sons, 1917.

Mäckelmann, Michael. *Arnold Schönberg und das Judentum: Der Komponist und sein religiöses, nationales und politisches Selbstverständnis nach 1921.* Hamburg: Karl Dieter Wagner, 1984.

Mackerras, Colin P. *The Rise of the Peking Opera, 1770–1830: Social Aspects of the Theatre in Manchu China.* Oxford: Clarendon Press, 1972.

Magee, Elizabeth. *Richard Wagner and the Nibelungs.* Oxford: Clarendon Press, 1990.

Mahon, Denis. *Studies in Seicento Art and Theory.* 1947. Westport, Conn.: Greenwood Press, 1971.

Marcello, Benedetto. "Il teatro alla moda," part 1. Trans. Reinhard G. Pauly. *Musical Quarterly* 34 (1948): 371–403.

Martin, Richard, and Harold Koda. *Orientalism: Visions of the East in Western Dress*. New York: Abrams, 1994.

Martini, F. Giambattista. *Esemplare o sia saggio fondamentale pratico di contrappunto fugato*. 2 vols. Bologna: Lelio dalla Volpe, 1774.

Marx, Hans Joachim. *Händel auf dem Theater: Bericht über die Symposien 1986 und 1987*. Laaber: Laaber-Verlag, 1988.

Matteini, Ottavio. *Stendhal e la musica*. [Turin]: Eda, 1981.

Mattheson, Johann. *Die neueste Untersuchung der Singspiele*. Hamburg, 1744. Facsimile ed., Kassel: Bärenreiter, 1975.

Matz, Mary Jane. "An Ancestor for *Aida*." *Opera News* 20 (December 26, 1955): 4–7, 26–28.

Maynard, John. "Browning, Donne, and the Triangulation of the Dramatic Monologue." *John Donne Journal* 4 (1985): 253–67.

McClary, Susan. *Georges Bizet: 'Carmen.'* Cambridge, Eng.: Cambridge University Press, 1992.

McGann, Jerome J. *Don Juan in Context*. Chicago: University of Chicago Press, 1976.

Melvin, Sheila. "Puccini's Chinese Tale in the Middle Kingdom." *Wall Street Journal*, February 13, 1996, A12.

Merkling, Frank, John W. Freeman, and Gerald Fitzgerald, eds. *The Golden Horseshoe: The Life and Times of the Met Opera House*. New York: Viking, 1965.

Michotte, Edmond. *Richard Wagner's Visit to Rossini*. Trans. Herbert Weinstock. Chicago: University of Chicago Press, 1968.

Miller, Jonathan, ed. *Myths of Don Giovanni: Seduction and Betrayal*. Baltimore: Johns Hopkins University Press, 1990.

Millington, Barry, ed. *The Wagner Compendium: A Guide to Wagner's Life and Music*. London: Thames and Hudson, 1992.

Millington, Barry, and Stewart Spencer, eds. *Wagner in Performance*. New Haven, Conn.: Yale University Press, 1992.

Mitchell, Jerome. *The Walter Scott Operas*. University: University of Alabama Press, 1977.

Moir, Alfred. *Caravaggio*. New York: Abrams, 1989.

———. *Caravaggio and His Copyists*. New York: New York University Press, 1976.

Monteverdi, Claudio. *Madrigali a 5 Voci, Libro Sesto*. Ed. Antonio Delfino. Vol. 10 of Monteverdi, *Opera Omnia*. Cremona: Fondazione Claudio Monteverdi, 1991.

Monteverdi, Claudio, Severo Bonini, Claudio Pari, Francesco Antonio
Costa, Antonio il Verso, and Francesco Maria Rascarini. *Lamento
d'Arianna*. Consort of Musicke. Anthony Rooley, dir. Deutsche Har-
monia Mundi compact disc 77115-2-RG, 1990.

Mordden, Ethan. *Demented: The World of the Opera Diva*. New York: Simon
and Schuster, 1984.

Mostra del Caravaggio e dei Caravaggeschi. Florence: Sansoni, [1951].

Müller, Ulrich, and Peter Wapnewski, eds. *Wagner Handbook*. Cambridge,
Mass.: Harvard University Press, 1992.

Nattiez, Jean-Jacques. *Tétralogies Wagner, Boulez, Chéreau: Essai sur l'infidé-
lité*. Paris: Christian Bourgeois, 1983.

———, ed. *The Boulez-Cage Correspondence*. Trans. Robert Samuels. Cambridge, Eng.: Cambridge University Press, 1993.

Nietzsche, Friedrich. *The Birth of Tragedy* and *The Case of Wagner*. Trans.
Walter Kaufmann. New York: Random House, 1967.

———. *Unfashionable Observations* [*Unzeitgemässe Betrachtungen*]. Trans.
Richard T. Gray. Stanford, Calif.: Stanford University Press, 1995.

———. *Werke*. Ed. Karl Schlechta. 3 vols. Darmstadt: Wissenschaftliche
Buchgesellschaft, 1966.

Nochlin, Linda. *The Politics of Vision: Essays on Nineteenth-Century Art and
Society*. New York: Harper and Row, 1989.

Nono-Schoenberg, Nuria, ed. *Arnold Schönberg 1874–1951: Lebensgeschichte in
Begegnungen*. Klagenfurt, Austria: Ritter, 1992.

Noske, Frits. *The Signifier and the Signified: Studies in the Operas of Mozart
and Verdi*. The Hague: Martinus Nijhoff, 1977.

Oestreich, James R. "Empty Chairs in Honor of Cage." *New York Times*,
August 17, 1992, B2.

Orgel, Stephen. *The Illusion of Power*. Berkeley: University of California
Press, 1975.

Osborne, Richard. *Rossini*. London: Dent, 1986.

Palisca, Claude V. *Studies in the History of Italian Music and Music Theory*.
Oxford: Clarendon Press, 1994.

Palmer, Michael. "Some Notes on Shelley, Poetics and the Present." *Sulfur*
33 (fall 1993): 273–81.

Parry, C. Hubert H. *The Music of the Seventeenth Century*. Oxford: Clarendon Press, 1902.

Perels, Christof, ed. *Jahrbuch des Freien Deutschen Hochstifts 1984*. Tübingen:
Niemeyer, 1984.

Perloff, Marjorie, and Charles Junkerman, eds. *John Cage: Composed in America*. Chicago: University of Chicago Press, 1994.

Phelan, Anthony, ed. *The Weimar Dilemma: Intellectuals in the Weimar Republic*. Manchester: Manchester University Press, 1985.

Phillips-Matz, Mary Jane. "Roots." *Opera News* 56 (December 21, 1991): 21–23.

Poizat, Michel. *The Angel's Cry: Beyond the Pleasure Principle in Opera*. Trans. Arthur Denner. Ithaca, N.Y.: Cornell University Press, 1992.

Pope, Alexander. *Imitations of Horace*. 2d ed. Ed. John Butt. London: Methuen, 1953.

Powers, Harold, ed. *Studies in Music History: Essays for Oliver Strunk*. Princeton, N.J.: Princeton University Press, 1968.

Pretzsch, Paul. *Bayreuther Festspielführer 1930*. Bayreuth: Georg Miehrenheim, 1930.

Puffett, Derrick, ed. *Richard Strauss: 'Salome.'* Cambridge, Eng.: Cambridge University Press, 1989.

Qian, Zhauming. *Orientalism and Modernism: The Legacy of China in Pound and Williams*. Durham, N.C.: Duke University Press, 1995.

Rather, L. J. *The Dream of Self-Destruction: Wagner's 'Ring' and the Modern World*. Baton Rouge: Louisiana State University Press, 1979.

Raulet, Gérard, and Josef Fürnkäs. *Weimar: Le tournant esthétique*. Paris: Anthropos, 1988.

Reich, Willi. *Alban Berg*. Trans. Cornelius Cardew. New York: Harcourt, Brace, 1965.

———. *Arnold Schönberg oder der konservative Revolutionär*. Vienna: Fritz Molden, 1968.

Retallack, Joan, ed. *Musicage: Cage Muses on Word Art Music*. Hanover, N.H.: University Press of New England, 1996.

Rewald, John. *Cézanne: The Watercolors, A Catalogue Raisonné*. Boston: Little, Brown, 1983.

Reynolds, Sir Joshua. *Discourses Delivered to the Students of the Royal Academy*. Ed. Roger Fry. London: Seeley, 1905.

Ringer, Alexander L. *Arnold Schoenberg: The Composer as Jew*. Oxford: Clarendon Press, 1990.

Robinson, Paul. "Is *Aida* an Orientalist Opera?" *Cambridge Opera Journal* 5 (1993): 133–40.

———. *Opera and Ideas: From Mozart to Strauss*. New York: Harper and Row, 1985.

Rockwell, John. "Cage Merely an Inventor? Not a Chance." *New York Times*, Western edition, August 23, 1992, B21.

Rolland, Romain. *Les Origines du théatre lyrique moderne: histoire de l'opéra en Europe avant Lully et Scarlatti*. Paris: Ernest Thorin, 1895.

Rosand, Ellen. "The Descending Tetrachord: An Emblem of Lament." *Musical Quarterly* 65 (1979): 346–59.

———. *Opera in Seventeenth-Century Venice: The Creation of a Genre*. Berkeley: University of California Press, 1991.

Rose, Paul Lawrence. *Wagner: Race and Revolution*. London: Faber and Faber, 1992.

Rosen, Charles. *The Romantic Generation*. Cambridge, Mass.: Harvard University Press, 1995.

Rosenthal, Donald. *Orientalism: the Near East in French Painting*. Rochester, N.Y.: Memorial Art Gallery, 1982.

Rosselli, John. *The Opera Industry in Italy from Cimarosa to Verdi: The Role of the Impresario*. Cambridge, Eng.: Cambridge University Press, 1984.

"Rossini Bicentennial Birthday Gala." "Live from Lincoln Center." PBS, February 29, 1992.

Rothstein, Edward. "'Klinghoffer' Sinks into Minimal Sea." *New York Times*, September 15, 1991, sec. 2, 25.

———. "Seeking Symmetry between Palestinians and Jews." *New York Times*, September 7, 1991, 15–16.

Ruskin, John. *Works*. Ed. E. T. Cook and Alexander Wedderburn. 39 vols. London: George Allen, 1903–12.

Russell, D. A., and M. Winterbottom, eds. *Classical Literary Criticism*. Oxford: Oxford University Press, 1989.

Sadie, Stanley, ed. *New Grove Dictionary of Music*. 20 vols. Washington, D.C.: Grove's Dictonaries of Music, 1980.

———, ed. *New Grove Dictionary of Opera*. 4 vols. London: Macmillan, 1992.

Sadie, Stanley, and Anthony Hicks, eds. *Handel Tercentenary Collection*. Houndmills: Macmillan, 1987.

Said, Edward W. *Culture and Imperialism*. New York: Knopf, 1991.

———. *Orientalism*. New York: Pantheon, 1978.

———. "Orientalism, an Afterword." *Raritan* 14 (winter, 1995): 32–59.

———. "*Die tote Stadt*; *Fidelio*; *The Death of Klinghoffer*." *The Nation*, November 11, 1991, 596–600.

―――. "Uncertainties of Style." *The Nation*, March 9, 1992, 312–15.

Saint-Évremond, Charles de Saint-Denis, Sieur de. *Letters of Saint Evremond.* Ed. John Hayward. Freeport, N.Y.: Books for Libraries Press, 1971.

Sanders, Ronald. *The Days Grow Short: The Life and Music of Kurt Weill.* New York: Holt, Rinehart and Winston, 1980.

Sauerwein, J. "Schola Cantorum." *Le Courrier musical* 7 (March 15, 1904): 193–94.

Schatt, Peter W. *Exotik in der Musik des 20. Jahrhunderts: Historisch-systematische Untersuchungen zur Metamorphose einer ästhetischen Fiktion.* Munich: Emil Katzbichler, 1986.

Schebera, Jürgen. *Kurt Weill: An Illustrated Life.* Trans. Caroline Murphy. New Haven, Conn.: Yale University Press, 1995.

Schelling, F. W. J. *Philosophie der Kunst.* Darmstadt: Wissenschaftliche Buchgesellschaft, 1960.

Schmidt, Claudia M. "Shelley's 'Spirit of the Age' Antedated in Hume." *Notes and Queries*, n.s., 38 (September 1991): 297–98.

Schnebel, Dieter. "'Wie ich das schaffe?'—Die Verwirklichung von Cages Werk." *Musik-Konzepte*, special issue on John Cage, vol. 1 (Apr. 1978): 51–55.

Schoenberg, Arnold. *Der biblische Weg.* German text with English translation. Trans. Moshe Lazar. *Journal of the Arnold Schoenberg Institute* 17 (1994): 162–329.

―――. *Briefe.* Ed. Erwin Stein. Mainz: B. Schott's Söhne, 1958.

―――. *Erwartung* and *Brettl-Lieder.* Jessye Norman, James Levine, Metropolitan Opera Orchestra. Philips compact disc 426 261-2, 1993.

―――. *Style and Idea: Selected Writings.* Ed. Leonard Stein. Trans. Leo Black. New York: St. Martin's Press, 1975.

―――. *Testi poetici e drammatici.* Ed. Luigi Rognoni. Trans. Emilio Castellani. Milan: Feltrinelli, 1967.

Schoenberg, E. Randol. "Arnold Schoenberg and Albert Einstein: Their Relationship and Views on Zionism." *Journal of the Arnold Schoenberg Institute* 10 (1987): 134–87.

Schopenhauer, Arthur. *The World as Will and Representation.* Trans. E. F. J. Payne. 2 vols. New York: Dover, 1958.

Schorske, Carl. *Fin-de-Siècle Vienna: Politics and Culture.* New York: Knopf, 1980.

Schrader, Bärbel, and Jürgen Schebera. *The "Golden" Twenties: Art and Liter-*

ature in the Weimar Republic. Trans. Katherine Vanovitch. New Haven, Conn.: Yale University Press, 1988.

Schwarz, K. Robert. "Steve Reich on Kurt Weill." *Kurt Weill Newsletter* 10 (fall 1992): 12–13.

Sellars, Peter, dir. *Giulio Cesare*, by George Frederick Handel. London videocassette 440 071 508-3, 1992.

Shawcross, John T. "Opulence and Iron Pokers: Coleridge and John Donne." *John Donne Journal* 4 (1985): 201–24.

Shaw, Leroy R., Nancy R. Cirillo, and Marion S. Miller, eds. *Wagner in Retrospect: A Centennial Reappraisal.* Amsterdam: Rodopi, 1987.

Shelley, Mary. *Letters of Mary Wollstonecraft Shelley.* Ed. Betty T. Bennett. 3 vols. Baltimore: Johns Hopkins University Press, 1980–88.

———. *The Journals of Mary Shelley: 1814–1844.* Ed. Paula R. Feldman and Diana Scott-Kilvert. 2 vols. Oxford: Clarendon Press, 1987.

Shelley, Percy Bysshe. *Letters of Percy Bysshe Shelley.* Ed. Frederick L. Jones. 2 vols. Oxford: Clarendon Press, 1964.

———. *Poetry and Prose.* Ed. Donald H. Reiman and Sharon B. Powers. New York: Norton, 1977.

———. *Shelley's Prose: or the Trumpet of a Prophecy.* Ed. David Lee Clark. Albuquerque: University of New Mexico Press, 1954.

Silk, M. S., and J. P. Stern. *Nietzsche on Tragedy.* Cambridge, Eng.: Cambridge University Press, 1981.

Singh, Brijraj, "Two Hitherto Unrecorded Imitations of Donne in the Eighteenth Century." *Notes and Queries* 18 (1971): 50.

Smith, A. J., ed. *John Donne: Essays in Celebration.* London: Methuen, 1972.

———, ed. *John Donne: The Critical Heritage.* London: Routledge & Kegan Paul, 1975.

Smith, Joan Allen. *Schoenberg and His Circle: A Viennese Portrait.* New York: Schirmer, 1986.

Smith, Patrick J. *The Tenth Muse: A Historical Study of the Opera Libretto.* New York: Knopf, 1970.

Sokolov, Raymond. "Adamsweek: Klinghoffer Dies Again." *Wall Street Journal,* September 18, 1991, A12.

Solie, Ruth A., ed. *Musicology and Difference: Gender and Sexuality in Music Scholarship.* Berkeley: University of California Press, 1993.

Sopart, Andreas. *Giuseppe Verdis 'Simon Boccanegra' (1857 und 1881): Eine musikalisch-dramaturgische Analyse.* Analecta Musicologica 26. Laaber: Laaber-Verlag, 1988.

Stadlen, Peter. "Schoenberg's Speech-Song." *Music and Letters* 62 (1980): 1–11.

Steck, Odil Hannes. *Moses und Aron: Die Oper Arnold Schönbergs und ihr biblischer Stoff.* Munich: Kaiser, 1981.

Steegmuller, Francis, ed. and trans. *Flaubert in Egypt.* New York: Penguin, 1996.

Steinberg, Michael. Liner essay for John Adams, *The Death of Klinghoffer.* Elektra/Nonesuch compact disc 7559 79281-2, 1992.

Stella, Frank. *Working Space.* Cambridge, Mass.: Harvard University Press, 1986.

Stendhal [Henri Beyle]. *Correspondance.* Ed. Henri Martineau. 3 vols. Paris: Gallimard, 1968.

———. *Écoles italiennes de peinture.* 3 vols. Paris: Le Divan, 1932.

———. *Haydn, Mozart and Metastasio.* Trans. Richard N. Coe. New York: Grossman, 1972.

———. *Life of Rossini.* Trans. Richard N. Coe. New York: Orion, 1970.

———. *Voyages en Italie.* Ed. V. del Litto. Paris: Gallimard, 1973.

Stravinsky, Igor, and Robert Craft. *Conversations with Igor Stravinsky.* Berkeley: University of California Press, 1980.

Streatfeild, R. A. *The Opera: A Sketch of the Development of Opera. With Full Descriptions of All Works in the Modern Repertory.* London: George Routledge, n.d. [ca. 1907].

Strohm, Reinhard. *Essays on Handel and Italian Opera.* Cambridge, Eng.: Cambridge University Press, 1985.

———. *Die italienische Oper im 18. Jahrhundert.* Wilhelmshaven: Heinrichshofen, 1979.

Strunk, Oliver, ed. *Source Readings in Music History.* New York: Norton, 1950.

Stuckenschmidt, H. H. *Schönberg: Leben, Umwelt, Werk.* Zurich: Atlantis, 1974.

Sulzer, Johann Georg. *Allgemeine Theorie der Schönen Künste.* 2d ed. Leipzig: Weidmannsche Buchhandlung, 1792.

Surian, Elvidio. "Musical Historiography and Histories of Italian Opera." *Current Musicology* 36 (1983): 167–75.

Symonette, Lys, and Kim Kowalke, eds. *Speak Low (When You Speak Love): The Letters of Kurt Weill and Lotte Lenya.* Berkeley: University of California Press, 1996.

Tambling, Jeremy. *Opera, Ideology and Film.* Manchester: Manchester University Press, 1987.

Tanner, Michael. "Multiperspectival Remarks." *Times Literary Supplement*, March 1, 1985, 229.

Tanner, Tony. *Adultery in the Novel: Contract and Transgression*. Baltimore: Johns Hopkins University Press, 1979.

Taruskin, Richard. "'Entoiling the Falconet': Russian Musical Orientalism in Context." *Cambridge Opera Journal* 4 (1992): 253–80.

———. "On Letting the Music Speak for Itself: Some Reflections on Musicology and Performance." *Journal of Musicology* 1 (1982): 338–49.

———. *Musorgsky: Eight Essays and an Epilogue*. Princeton, N.J.: Princeton University Press, 1993.

———. "Russian Musical Orientalism: A Postscript." *Cambridge Opera Journal* 6 (1994): 81–84.

———. "Tradition and Authority." *Early Music* 20 (1992): 311–25.

Taylor, Ronald. *Kurt Weill: Composer in a Divided World*. Boston: Northeastern University Press, 1991.

Terdiman, Richard. *Discourse/Counter-Discourse*. Ithaca, N.Y.: Cornell University Press, 1985.

Tetreault, Ronald. *The Poetry of Life: Shelley and Literary Form*. Toronto: University of Toronto Press, 1987.

Thomson, Virgil. *Virgil Thomson*. New York: Knopf, 1966.

Thompson, James. *The East: Imagined, Experienced, Remembered*. Dublin: National Gallery of Ireland, 1988.

"The Three Sopranos." Kathleen Cassello, Kallen Esperian, and Cynthia Lawrence. National television broadcast. Los Angeles, Oct. 1996.

"The Three Tenors." José Carreras, Plácido Domingo, and Luciano Pavarotti. Worldwide television broadcast. Rome, July 1990.

"The Three Tenors." José Carreras, Plácido Domingo, and Luciano Pavarotti. Worldwide television broadcast. Los Angeles, July 1994.

"The Three Tenors." José Carreras, Plácido Domingo, and Luciano Pavarotti. National television broadcast. New Jersey, Oct. 1996.

Tomlinson, Gary. *Monteverdi and the End of the Renaissance*. Berkeley: University of California Press, 1987.

Tucker, Robert C., ed. *The Marx-Engels Reader*. 2d ed. New York: Norton, 1978.

Turner, Bryan S. *Orientalism, Postmodernism and Globalism*. London: Routledge, 1994.

Tuve, Rosamond. *Elizabethan and Metaphysical Imagery*. Chicago: University of Chicago Press, 1947.

Vasari, Giorgio. *The Lives of the Artists.* Trans. Julia Conaway Bondanella and Peter Bondanella. Oxford: Oxford University Press, 1991.

Vecchiarelli, Enzo. *Il canto rossiniano e la critica.* Pesaro: Flaminia, 1988.

Vischer, Friedrich Theodor. *Aesthetik oder Wissenschaft des Schönen.* Stuttgart: Carl Mäcken, 1857.

———. *Kritische Gänge.* Ed. Robert Vischer. 2d ed. 2 vols. Leipzig: Verlag der Weissen Bücher, 1914.

Vogel, Emil. "Claudio Monteverdi." *Vierteljahrsschrift für Musikwissenschaft* 3 (1887): 315–450.

Wagner, Richard. *Gesammelte Schriften.* Ed. Julius Kapp. 14 vols. Leipzig: Hesse und Becker, n.d. [ca. 1914].

———. *Der Ring des Nibelungen: Ein Bühnenfestspiel für drei Tage und einen Vorabend.* [Zurich]: E. Kiesling, [1853].

———. *The Ring of the Nibelung.* Trans. Andrew Porter. New York: Norton, 1977.

Wagner, Wolf Siegfried. *Die Geschichte unserer Familie in Bildern: Bayreuth 1876–1976.* Munich: Rogner und Bernhard, 1976.

Wapnewski, Peter. *Der traurige Gott: Richard Wagner in seinen Helden.* Munich: C. H. Beck, 1978.

Warrack, John. *Carl Maria von Weber.* 2d ed. Cambridge, Eng.: Cambridge University Press, 1976.

Watt, Ian. *Myths of Modern Individualism: Faust, Don Quixote, Don Juan, Robinson Crusoe.* Cambridge, Eng.: Cambridge University Press, 1996.

Weber, William. *The Rise of Musical Classics in Eighteenth-Century England: A Study in Canon, Ritual, and Ideology.* Oxford: Clarendon Press, 1992.

Weill, Kurt. *Musik und Theater: Gesammelte Schriften.* Ed. Stephen Hinton and Jürgen Schebera. Berlin: Henschelverlag, 1990.

Weiner, Marc A. *Richard Wagner and the Anti-Semitic Imagination.* Lincoln: University of Nebraska Press, 1995.

Weinstock, Herbert. *Rossini: A Biography.* New York: Knopf, 1968.

Welsch, Wolfgang, and Christine Pries. *Aesthetik im Widerstreit.* Weinheim: VCH Acta Humaniora, 1991.

Westernhagen, Curt von. *The Forging of the "Ring": Richard Wagner's Composition Sketches for 'Der Ring des Nibelungen.'* Trans. Arnold and Mary Whittall. Cambridge, Eng.: Cambridge University Press, 1976.

Whenham, John, ed. *Claudio Monteverdi: 'Orfeo.'* Cambridge, Eng.: Cambridge University Press, 1986.

White, Pamela C. *Schoenberg and the God-Idea: The Opera 'Moses und Aron.'* Ann Arbor: UMI Research Press, 1985.

Whitman, Walt. *Leaves of Grass.* Ed. Sculley Bradley and Harold Blodgett. New York: Norton, 1973.

Willett, John. *Art and Politics in the Weimar Period: The New Sobriety, 1917–1933.* New York: Pantheon, 1978.

———. *Brecht in Context.* London: Methuen, 1984.

———. *The Theatre of the Weimar Republic.* New York: Holmes and Meier, 1988.

———. *The Weimar Years: A Culture Cut Short.* London: Thames and Hudson, 1984.

———, ed. *Brecht damals und heute: Das Brecht-Jahrbuch* 20. Madison: University of Wisconsin Press, 1995.

Wilson, W. Daniel. *Humanität und Kreuzungsideologie um 1800: Die "Türkenoper" im 18. Jahrhundert und das Rettungsmotiv in Wielands 'Oberon,' Lessings 'Nathan' und Goethes 'Iphigenie.'* New York: Peter Lang, 1984.

Winny, James. *A Preface to Donne.* 2d ed. London: Longman, 1981.

Winterfeld, Carl von. *Johannes Gabrieli und sein Zeitalter.* 2 vols. Berlin: Schlesinger, 1834.

Wittkower, Rudolf. *Art and Architecture in Italy 1600–1750.* 3d ed. Harmondsworth, England: Penguin, 1973.

Wolff, Hellmuth Christian. *Die Händel-Oper auf der modernen Bühne: Ein Beitrag zu Geschichte und Praxis der Opern-Bearbeitung und -Inszenierung in der Zeit von 1920 bis 1956.* Leipzig: Deutscher Verlag für Musik, 1957.

Wörner, Karl Heinrich. *Gotteswort und Magie: Die Oper 'Moses und Aron' von Arnold Schönberg.* Heidelberg: Schneider, 1959.

Yamaguchi, Koichi. "Der Gedanke Gottes und das Wort des Menschen: Zu Arnold Schönbergs 'Moses und Aron.'" *Neue Zeitschrift für Musik* 145, no. 7/8 (July-Aug. 1984): 8–13.

Zuber, Barbara. "Entrümpelung—Europeras *1 & 2.*" *Musik-Konzepte*, special issue on John Cage, 2 (May 1990): 100–112.

Index

In this index an "f" after a number indicates a separate reference on the next page, and an "ff" indicates separate references on the next two pages. A continuous discussion over two or more pages is indicated by a span of page numbers, e.g., "57–59." *Passim* is used for a cluster of references in close but not consecutive sequence. Titles of operas, literary works, and paintings are listed under the names of their creators. Operatic and literary characters are listed under their own names with cross-references to the composers and authors of the works in which they appear.

Library of Congress Cataloging-in-Publication Data
Lindenberger, Herbert Samuel
Opera in history: from Monteverdi to Cage / Herbert
Lindenberger.
  p. cm.
Includes bibliographical references and index.
ISBN 0-8047-3104-7 (cloth).—ISBN 0-8047-3105-5 (pbk.)
1. Opera I. Title.
ML1700.L54 1998
782.1—dc21   97-16405
                                                  CIP
                                                 MN

∞ This book is printed on acid-free, recycled paper.
Original printing 1998
Last figure below indicates year of this printing:
07 06 05 03 02 01 00 99 98